Instructor's Guide with Lecture Notes
to Accompany

AMERICAN GOVERNMENT

INSTITUTIONS AND POLICIES

Sixth Edition

James Q. Wilson

and

John J. DiIulio, Jr.

Prepared by

Brian M. Murphy
North Georgia College

D. C. HEATH AND COMPANY   Lexington, Massachusetts • Toronto

Address editorial correspondence to

D. C. Heath and Company
125 Spring Street
Lexington, MA 02173

Commissioned and developed for D. C. Heath and Company by P. S. Associates, Inc., Brookline, Massachusetts.
Copyright © 1995 by D. C. Heath and Company.
Previous editions copyright © 1992, 1989, 1986, 1983, 1980 by D. C. Heath and Company.

All rights reserved. Any materials in this instructor's guide may be reproduced or duplicated specifically to assist the teacher's efforts in conducting classes, including discussions and examinations. Reproducing these materials for commercial purposes is strictly prohibited.

Published simultaneously in Canada.
Printed in the United States of America.
International Standard Book Number: 0-669-35125-3

10 9 8 7 6 5 4 3 2

Contents

INTRODUCTION   vii

     Ways of Assigning the Text   vii
     Structuring the Course   xi
     Using Films and Videotapes in American Government   xi
     Using Chapter Resources with *American Government,* Sixth Edition   xi
     The *Test Item File*   xii
     The *Student Handbook*   xiii
     Other Supplements   xiii

RESOURCES AND REFERENCES IN AMERICAN GOVERNMENT   xv

     General References/Teaching American Government   xv
     History, Theory, and Additional Lecture Sources   xvii
     Readers   xvii
     Reprints   xviii
     Simulations and Games   xix
     Computerized Software   xx
     Careers in Political Science   xxi

FILM AND VIDEO GUIDE   xxi

     General Information and Film Sources   xxi
     Chapter-by-Chapter Film List   xxiii
     Addresses of Film Distributors   xxx
     Video Programs in American Government   xxxi

PART ONE • THE AMERICAN SYSTEM   1

     1   **The Study of American Government**   1

     2   **The Constitution**   11

     3   **Federalism**   25

     4   **American Political Culture**   36

PART TWO • OPINIONS, INTERESTS, AND ORGANIZATIONS — 47

- **5** Public Opinion — 47
- **6** Political Participation — 66
- **7** Political Parties — 79
- **8** Elections and Campaigns — 98
- **9** Interest Groups — 117
- **10** The Media — 137

PART THREE • INSTITUTIONS OF GOVERNMENT — 156

- **11** Congress — 156
- **12** The Presidency — 192
- **13** The Bureaucracy — 218
- **14** The Judiciary — 241

PART FOUR • THE POLITICS OF PUBLIC POLICY — 263

- **15** The Policy-Making Process — 263
- **16** Economic Policy — 285
- **17** Social Welfare — 301
- **18** Civil Liberties — 318
- **19** Civil Rights — 335
- **20** Foreign Policy — 358
- **21** Military Policy — 376
- **22** Environmental Policy — 388

PART FIVE • THE NATURE OF AMERICAN DEMOCRACY — 405

- **23** Who Governs? — 405
- **24** To What Ends? — 418

PART SIX • STATE AND LOCAL GOVERNMENT

25   **State and Local Government**   430

Introduction

The Sixth Edition of *American Government* by James Q. Wilson and John J. DiIulio, Jr., provides a thorough updating of material as well as new Critical Thinking features, a list of Key Terms with page references at the end of each chapter, and a new glossary providing definitions for the Key Terms in the text. Many chapters have been either rewritten or reorganized and several have entirely new sections. But in the end, continuity has been preserved.

This *Instructor's Guide* is designed to assist both in course preparation and in utilizing the text more fully. The essence of the *Instructor's Guide* is flexibility—allowing each instructor to decide how to use various teaching strategies and resources. Thus, more material is available than any teacher could incorporate in an introductory course.

The fundamental organization of the *Instructor's Guide* remains intact from the previous edition. However, the revision process devoted particular attention to the following features. First, the Lecture Outlines are somewhat expanded to supply a clearer presentation of the text's material. Second, about 40 percent of of the Themes are new or rewritten. And third, new information has been included under each subsection of a chapter: Abstracts, Data and Perspectives for Analysis, and Discussion Questions. Because much of the earlier material has been retained, prior users of the *Instructor's Guide* will not experience difficulty in switching to the Sixth Edition.

Ways of Assigning the Text

Most American government instructors face either a semester (fifteen-week) or quarter (ten-week) schedule. Regardless of your particular time constraints, you should give each student a clear idea of your class objectives and goals, a schedule of reading assignments, possible outside research assignments, methods of evaluation (types of tests, frequency, respective weighting, etc.), and so forth. A good course syllabus should cover these important considerations. The American Political Science Association is conducting a project on exemplary course syllabi. Information on the project can be obtained by writing to: P. S. Course Syllabi Project, APSA, 1527 New Hampshire Ave. NW, Washington, D.C. 20036.

In addition, the first day of class might be spent in telling the class what your teaching philosophy and methodology is, whether you favor lectures primarily or a variety of teaching techniques, your policy on absences (this is usually incorporated on your course syllabus), availability of outside assistance and office hours, and so forth. Some instructors also try to introduce the theme of the importance of American politics to the lives of students through a number of relevant, contemporary examples. A "precourse" inventory of political questions probing the extent of student knowledge of American government can be illuminating, especially because it can tell the professor where to pitch the instructional level. Finally, some attention might be paid to the text's approach and structure.

The following represent two "schedules" for teaching American government—ten and fifteen weeks. Each schedule contains periodic Part Examinations, a Midterm Examination, and a Final Examination so that students can have multiple opportunities to test their knowledge of content and concepts. Of course, instructors will vary in their preferences. Note that for some weeks (or for two consecutive weeks) both a Part Examination and a Midterm or Final Examination is indicated. These are presented as alternatives—you can choose either the shorter exam covering a single part of the text (Part Examination) or the longer exam covering approximately half of the text (Midterm or Final Examination). In addition, a "midcourse evaluation" is built into each schedule, so that the instructor can receive feedback from the class, resulting (in time) in possible instructional or substantive modifications.

Schedule 1: Fifteen Weeks (Three 45–60-minute classes per week)

NOTE: A fifteen-week course generally provides more time for student projects and for exploring institutions, personalities, etc., of American government than is possible in a ten-week course. Therefore, in the following syllabus, various student reports and activities have been suggested and possible outside speakers have been proposed. Again, each instructor's configuration will depend on individual preference and institutional variables. Naturally, an instructor who is on the quarter system can adopt some of the elements of the following semester syllabus.

Week	Coverage	Assignment
1	Introductory comments; course syllabus and administrative issues, including testing and grading. Stress key definitions in these early chapters and encourage students to think about political life. A precourse quiz on students' knowledge of government and politics may be administered. Outside readings on American politics might also be assigned for later classroom discussion or reports. Choose appropriate lecture themes and resources from Chapters 1 and 2 of the *Instructor's Guide*.	Chapters 1, 2: *The Study of American Government* *The Constitution*
2	Cover Chapters 3–4 with themes and resources from the *Instructor's Guide*. A few students' reports based on assignments in Week #1 might be presented to the class. PART EXAMINATION I (Chapters 1–4).	Chapters 3, 4: *Federalism* *American Political Culture*
3	Cover chapters 5–6 with appropriate themes and resources from the *Instructor's Guide*. Discuss exam results.	Chapters 5, 6: *Public Opinion* *Political Participation*
4	Cover Chapters 7–8 using themes and resources from the *Instructors Guide*. If time permits, invite a local party official to speak to the class for special insights.	Chapters 7, 8: *Political Parties* *Elections and Campaigns*
5	Cover Chapter 9 only. Use interest-group simulation, student reports on lobbying activities, and videotapes and films listed in the *Instructor's Guide*. This week can also be used to review key themes encountered in the course thus far.	Chapter 9: *Interest Groups*
6	Cover Chapters 10–11 with selected *Instructor's Guide* resources such as a congressional simulation, film, or videotape. Student reports on how media influence elections, present news, and impact on public opinion could be used. These activities could extend into Week #7. PART EXAMINATION II (Chapters 5–10). Discuss exam results.	Chapters 10, 11: *The Media* *Congress*

Week	Coverage	Assignment
7	Possible "spill-over" from Week #6. Cover Chapter 12 in depth and present appropriate *Instructor's Guide* films or videotapes and suggested resources and lectures. MIDTERM EXAMINATION (Chapters 1–10). Discuss exam results. Schedule midterm class evaluation and gauge student reactions so far.	Chapter 12: *The Presidency*
8	Cover Chapters 13–14 using appropriate *Instructor's Guide* resources. PART EXAMINATION III (Chapters 11–14). This exam also could be given in Week #9.	Chapters 13, 14: *The Bureaucracy* *The Judiciary*
9	Return and review exam results. Take this week to bring in contemporary issues in American government that reflect upon previous text chapters.	Instructor's discretion
10	Cover Chapters 15–16 with *Instructor's Guide* resources as appropriate.	Chapters 15, 16: *The Policy-Making Process* *Economic Policy*
11	Cover Chapters 17–18 with appropriate *Instructor's Guide* resources. Ask students to prepare position papers (individually or in groups) on possible political "solutions" to a policy problem facing American government, to be presented in class in Week #11 or 12.	Chapters 17, 18: *Social Welfare* *Civil Liberties*
12	Devote this week to Chapter 19 and use *Instructor's Guide* resources, such as a film on civil rights. Students can report on their "position papers" from Week #11. Ask two teams of students to research the "guns vs. butter" issue vis-a-vis defense spending for following week.	Chapter 19: *Civil Rights*
13	Cover Chapters 20–22 with relevant resources in the *Instructor's Guide*. PART EXAMINATION IV (Chapters 15–22).	Chapters 20, 21, 22: *Foreign Policy* *Military Policy* *Environmental Policy*
14	Cover Chapters 23–24 with *Instructor's Guide* resources. Return and review exams. Debate "guns vs. butter" issue in class.	Chapters 23, 24: *Who Governs?* *To What Ends?*
15	Cover Chapter 25 with appropriate *Instructor's Guide* resources. PART EXAM V (Chapters 23–25). Wrap-up of entire course. Review for Final Exam. FINAL EXAM (Chapters 11–25).	Chapter 25: *State and Local Government*

Schedule 2: Ten Weeks (Four or five 45-minute sessions per week)

Week	Coverage	Assignment
1	Introductory comments; course syllabus and administrative issues, including testing and grading; stress key definitions in these early chapters and encourage students to think about political life; select appropriate lecture themes in the *Instructor's Guide*.	Chapters 1, 2, 3: *The Study of American Government* *The Constitution* *Federalism*
2	Reading can be accelerated; move into Part II, covering Chapters 4–6 with themes and resources from the *Instructor's Guide*. PART EXAMINATION I (Chapters 1–4). Discuss exam results.	Chapters 4, 5, 6: *American Political Culture* *Public Opinion* *Political Participation*
3	Cover Chapters 7–10, using *Instructor's Guide* themes and resources. PART EXAMINATION II (Chapters 5–10). Discuss exam results.	Chapters 7, 8, 9, 10: *Political Parties* *Elections and Campaigns* *Interest Groups* *The Media*
4	Cover Chapters 11–12 with appropriate *Instructor's Guide* resources. MIDTERM EXAMINATION (Chapters 1–10). Go over exam results in class; schedule midterm class evaluation; gauge students' reactions so far.	Chapters 11, 12: *Congress* *The Presidency*
5	Cover Chapters 13–14 with selected *Instructor's Guide* resources. Use lighter week to involve students in discussion of contemporary political issues.	Chapters 13, 14: *The Bureaucracy* *The Judiciary*
6	Cover Chapters 15–17 with appropriate *Instructor's Guide* resources. PART EXAMINATION III (Chapters 11–14). Discuss exam results.	Chapters 15, 16, 17: *The Policy-Making Process* *Economic Policy* *Social Welfare*
7	Cover Chapters 18–20 with selected themes and resources from the *Instructor's Guide*.	Chapters 18, 19, 20: *Civil Liberties* *Civil Rights* *Foreign Policy*
8	Cover Chapters 21–22 with appropriate *Instructor's Guide* themes. PART EXAMINATION IV (Chapters 15–22). Discuss exam results.	Chapters 21, 22: *Military Policy* *Environmental Policy*
9	Cover Chapters 23–25; review for Final Exam or administer PART EXAMINATION V (Chapters 23–25).	Chapters 23, 24: *Who Governs? To What Ends?* *State and Local Government*
10	Review key themes of the course, i.e., a week of reflection and synthesis; schedule student reports, employ a capstone simulation or some other teaching summary device. FINAL EXAMINATION (Chapters 11–25).	Instructor's discretion

Structuring the Course

Resources and References in American Government, beginning on page xv, is a comprehensive bibliography containing a wealth of background information relevant to setting up and teaching a course in American government, including numerous supplements and resources that might be assigned along with the text. Contained in this section are references and sourcebooks, some with annotation, on teaching American government; books covering history, theory, and additional background materials; introductory government readers; sources of reprints; and compendia of games and simulations in the government field. The function of this section is to provide alternatives: from the many teaching approaches and ideas offered, you choose those that fit your style and interests. Although these lists are not all-inclusive, they should serve as a good starting point for organizing your course or as a supplement to your existing compilation of resources. Note that these materials are general in nature and are not tied to specific chapters.

Using Films and Videotapes in American Government

The Film and Video Guide, beginning on page xxi, provides suggestions for films to be used in conjunction with *American Government*, Sixth Edition. It includes general information about using films in government courses, as well as sources of pertinent films and a chapter-by-chapter listing of films that might be used with each chapter of the text. The annotations for these films include both the film distributor and the length of the film. Recent video presentations relevant to chapters in the text are also listed.

Using Chapter Resources with <u>American Government</u>, Sixth Edition

Beginning on page 1 of the *Instructor's Guide*, a variety of chapter-related summaries, outlines, lecture topics, projects and activities, book and article abstracts, and other resource items have been supplied for each chapter of the text. The components of each chapter are as follows.

Overview and Objectives. This section provides both a brief overview of the chapter and a list of specific learning objectives for the student reading the chapter. The objectives (which, along with the overview and chapter outline, also appear in the *Student Handbook*) constitute what the authors believe to be the key topics for students to master. They are phrased in the form "Describe . . . ," "Explain . . . ," "Give an example of . . . ," and so forth, thus encouraging students to develop their own abilities to summarize and apply what they have read.

Lecture Outline with Keyed-in Resources. This section contains a detailed outline of the text chapter, along with (1) references (in parentheses next to relevant outline entries) to lecture topics found in the *Instructor's Guide* that supplement or illustrate the topics covered in the text chapter, and (2) lecture inserts that expand on information in the text. The purpose of this section is to familiarize you with what is in the text and to suggest ways to elaborate on the text's treatment of certain key themes. The lecture outline has been created in the expectation that instructors will adapt it to suit their individual interests and perspectives, the amount of time available for teaching a given chapter, and the amount of supplementation desired. The outline covers more text material than you would probably want to cover in a single lecture. It is up to you, therefore, to decide what to omit. We suggest that you choose those themes that appeal to you most and then supplement them with ideas that reflect your own research, teaching style, and personal experiences.

Important Terms. This is a handy list of glossary items discussed in the chapter, with definitions. Those terms that are also listed at the end of each chapter of the text to help the student are marked with an asterisk (*).

Themes. The actual resource materials chosen for each chapter are organized around two or more general themes or topics (such as "Federal versus Unitary Systems"). Many of these themes correspond directly to a single major heading within a text chapter. Others cut across several headings in the chapter, helping the instructor to present broad relationships among major chapter topics. All themes contain a Summary and several Discussion Questions. Many include a book or article Abstract, a section of Data and Perspectives for Analysis, and Additional Lecture Topics focused on the theme. This thematic organization in each chapter of the *Instructor's Guide* helps address the questions "What's really important in the chapter? What should students come out of the chapter knowing?" The resources that follow then provide the necessary background for one or more lectures based on one of these central themes.

Summary. The summaries function in two ways: They *describe* what is in the text, and they *elaborate* on what is in the text. Although some of the descriptive information contained in the lecture outline is repeated in the summary, considerably more attention is given here to the theories and history behind political processes than you may want to cover in the lecture.

Discussion Questions. These are designed to be addressed to students in lecture or in small discussion groups. Discussion questions that accompany each theme include some fairly straightforward questions that merely require students to repeat what is in the text, as well as some broader, more demanding questions that can be used as the basis for an extended discussion or debate and that are intended to provoke student involvement. There are plenty of questions to choose from; you will want to select those that seem most appropriate to the level and interests of your class.

Data and Perspectives for Analysis. Here students are given the opportunity to analyze data, events, and theoretical perspectives drawn from the political arena and to follow through on simple projects that are focused on the chapter theme. Some of the research data (tables, graphs, and the like) are meant to be copied and distributed in class. Other exercises involve presenting scenarios or reading brief passages that call for assessment and interpretation by students. Most of the Data and Perspectives ideas call for some planning by the instructor.

Abstracts. Many chapter themes offer a synopsis of an article or book relevant to the theme. Sources of abstracts have been chosen for timeliness, interest, and appropriateness to the chapter and to the particular theme. Sufficient information has been provided in each abstract to allow you to use it as the basis for part of a lecture or discussion without having to go back to the original article or book, though you may find it desirable to spend some time with the resource if you plan to make it a major part of your presentation. Questions for Discussion follow all abstracts.

Additional Lecture Topics. Many themes also include a supplementary list of lecture ideas that might be expanded into part or all of a class presentation. A list of references is given for each suggested topic.

The Test Item File

A separate *Test Item File* of about 4,800 true/false, multiple-choice, and essay questions is available to users of *American Government*, Sixth Edition. (If you have not received your copy of the *Test Item File*, call the College Sales Division at 800-235-3565 or your local Heath sales representative.) A list of chapter topics (major chapter headings) and of questions pertaining to them appears on the first page of each *Test Item File* chapter. Within the chapter, questions are identified in the margin as either Factual or Conceptual, to assist you in making selections of items. In addition, text page references for all item answers are given in the marginal answer key. Quizzes and examinations can be constructed from the *Test Item File* or with D. C. Heath's computerized testing program. This program provides access to all questions in the *Test Item File* and allows instructors to tailor tests for their own classes. Instructors may also use the software to delete, add, or even change questions, as well as to print an answer key with page references for each question.

The Student Handbook

In addition to the *Instructor's Guide* and the *Test Item File*, a *Student Handbook* is available for purchase by students. This comprehensive workbook contains both summary and self-test materials designed to help students master factual information contained in the text, and a variety of applied exercises that test the students' ability to work with this factual information. Included in the *Student Handbook* are three major sections: "Reviewing the Chapter"—study objectives, chapter outline, key terms, list of possible misconceptions students may have, and a set of exercises based on text data; "Practicing for Exams"—a three-part exam offering true/false, multiple-choice, and essay questions; and "Applying What You Have Learned"—a detailed, interesting study activity that requires the student to gather, analyze, and interpret data. Also included in the *Student Handbook* are "Classic Statements" at the end of each part. These primary-source documents (by such authors as Weber and Tocqueville) are followed by discussion questions and give students historical perspective on the information and concepts presented in the part. A Practice Midterm Exam and a Practice Final Exam are also provided. The questions on these exams are selected from the True/False and Multiple Choice questions in the *Student Handbook*. Finally, answers are provided at the back of the *Student Handbook* along with text page references. We strongly recommend that you bring the *Student Handbook* to the attention of your class at the beginning of the term, even if you do not plan to make it a required part of the course.

Other Supplements

Video Study Guide (39124-7)
This new, one-of-a-kind aid allows students to review the main points of the text and to view relevant video footage that brings these points to life. Twenty units of approximately 6 minutes each provide a study and review resource both lively and convenient.

Transparencies (35127-X)
This package includes approximately fifty riveting, four-color transparencies, graphically illustrating key points and statistical data in the text.

Heath Guest Lectures in American Government series
The Supreme Court: Where Has it Been and Where is it Going?
William Lasser, Clemson University (35301-9)

Mexican-American Politics
Peter Skerry, University of California, Los Angeles (35302-7)

Showcasing the expertise of some of the leading scholars in political science, the *Guest Lectures* conveniently supplement classroom lectures and provide provocative insights on timely subjects.

Computerized Testing for MS-DOS, Macintosh, and Apple computers

Media Policy
D. C. Heath will offer to adopters of *American Government*, Sixth Edition, a variety of media supplements for classroom use. Choices include hands-on software simulating city management, political redistricting, passing legislation, the judicial process, polling, and political campaigning as well as a multitude of videos that are both current and popular.

Free with Every Student Copy:
Studying American Government: A Vade Mecum (28255-3)
Kenneth M. Holland
Memphis State University

Designed for the beginning student, this helpful guide to doing college-level work in political science covers reading and study strategies, library research, and writing assignments and is included free with every copy of the text ordered from D. C. Heath.

American Government, Interactive Edition
A Pathbreaking CD-ROM Resource
American Government, Sixth Edition, is also available in a CD ROM–based interactive edition, giving learners an integrated set of tools and resources for studying American politics.

The interactive edition of *American Government*, Sixth Edition, comprises the complete text of the book, including all the new Critical Thinking boxes; illustrations from the book as well as from other sources; video footage of campaign commercials, debates, and contemporary and historical events; on-screen video commentaries by James Q. Wilson and John DiIulio, authors of the *American Government* text; and self-tests including multiple-choice and true-false questions. Other features include suggested readings; glossary definitions of key terms; a customizable, on-line notebook; a Stick-on Notes feature; an index; primary sources; and a Feature Index that enables students to browse quickly the special media resources and boxed text features. The *Interactive Instructor's Edition*, available free to adopters, also offers a presentation tool for creating and saving lecture slideshows.

The interactive edition of *American Government* benefits students in all phases of the survey course. While reading a chapter, they can consult a glossary and index, access audio and video as well as supplementary text and graphics, write notes or annotate the text, and read relevant primary sources. After studying the chapter, learners can take a self-test and receive suggestions for further study. The *Instructor's Edition* makes all of these tools available to instructors and also allows them to arrange the full-screen graphics and illustrations into slideshows tailored to their lectures. In short, the interactive edition of *American Government* adds exciting new dimensions to the study of American politics for students and instructors.

Resources and References in American Government*

General References/Teaching American Government

The following sources contain a wide range of information on teaching ideas, philosophies, and approaches to teaching American government. They are also important sources of articles and book reviews.

The American Political Science Review. The profession's leading journal. Regional journals that are associated with the American Political Science Association include

  a. *The Journal of Politics.* Subscriptions include membership in the Southern Political Science Association. Editor, Department of Political Science, Texas A & M University, College Station, TX 77843.
  b. *American Journal of Political Science.* Subscriptions include membership in Midwest Political Science Association. 6525 N. Sheridan Rd. Chicago, IL 60626.
  c. *Political Research Quarterly* (formerly *Western Political Qusrterly*). Subscriptions include membership in the Western Political Science Association. Editor, Department of Political Science, University of Colorado, Boulder, CO 80309.
  d. *Polity.* Subscriptions include membership in the New England Political Science Association. Editor, Thompson Hall, University of Massachusetts, Amherst, MA 01002.
  e. *Social Science Quarterly.* The journal of the Southwestern Political Science Association and the Southwestern Social Science Association. Subscriptions include membership. Editor, University of Houston, Houston, TX 77204.

Atwater, Thomas. "Critical Thinking in Basic U.S. Government Classes," *PS: Political Science and Politics*, Vol. 24, No. 2 (June 1991), p. 209. Washington, DC: APSA.

Berch, Neil. "A Practical Project for Introductory American Politics Classes," *The Political Science Teacher*, Vol. 3, No. 2 (Spring 1990), p. 16. Washington, DC: APSA.

Biddle, Arthur W., et al., ed. *Writer's Guide: Political Science.* Lexington, MA: D. C. Heath and Company, 1987.

Cohen, Mel. "Making Class Participation a Reality," *PS: Political Science and Politics,* Vol. 24, No. 4 (December 1991), p. 699. Washington DC: APSA.

Congressional Quarterly, *Washington Information Directory, 1990–1991.* Washington, DC: Congressional Quarterly, 1990.

Cuba, Lee J. *A Short Guide to Writing about the Social Sciences.* Glenview, IL: Scott, Foresman/Little, Brown, 1988.

Cushman, Reid. "Textbooks, Technologies, and Tocqueville: Alternatives for Introductory American Government," *PS: Political Science and Politics,* Vol. 26, No. 2 (June 1993), pp. 223–227. Washington DC: APSA.

Educational Service Bureau. "List of Free Materials Available to Educators." Princeton, NJ: Dow Jones (published annually).

Education Index. New York: M. W. Wilson, since 1929.

Elliott, Jeffrey M., and Sheikh R. Ali. *The Presidential-Congressional Political Dictionary.* Santa Barbara, CA: ABC-CLIO, 1984.

———. *The State and Local Government Political Dictionary.* Santa Barbara, CA: ABC-CLIO, 1988.

---

*© 1995 by P. S. Associates, Inc. All rights reserved.

Evans, Graham, and Jeffrey Newnham, eds. *The Dictionary of World Politics: A Reference Guide to Concepts, Ideas, and Institutions.* New York: Simon and Schuster, 1991.

Green, Barbara. "Teaching American Government in a Comparative Context," *PS: Political Science and Politics,* Vol. 25, No. 1 (March 1992), p. 81. Washington, DC: APSA.

Guide to Current American Government. Congressional Quarterly, Inc., 1414 22nd St. N.W., Washington, DC 20037.

Kavelage, Carl, and Morley Segal. *Research Guide in Political Science,* 3rd ed. Morristown, NJ: General Learning Press, 1982.

Kruschke, Earl R., and Byron M. Jackson. *The Public Policy Dictionary.* Santa Barbara, CA: ABC-CLIO, 1987.

Levy, Leonard W. and Louis Fisher, eds. *Encyclopedia of the American Presidency.* New York: Simon and Schuster, 1993.

Londow, David Z. "Writing in Political Science: A Brief Guide to Resources," *PS: Political Science and Politics,* Vol. 26, No. 3 (September 1993), pp. 529–533. Washington, DC: APSA.

Luger, Stan, and William Scheuerman. "Teaching American Government," *PS: Political Science and Politics,* Vol. 26, No. 4 (December 1993), pp. 749–753. Washington, DC: APSA.

McKeachie, Wilbert J. *Teaching Tips,* 8th ed. Lexington, MA: D. C. Heath, 1990.

Peltason, J. W. *Corwin and Peltason's Understanding the Constitution,* 11th ed. New York: Harcourt-Brace, 1991.

Perspective. Published eight times a year by Heldref Publications, 4000 Albemarle Street, Washington, DC 20016. Editor, Jerome J. Hanus, School of Government, American University, Washington, DC 20016. A monthly review of new books on government, politics, and international affairs.

Plano, Jack C., and Milton Greenberg. *The American Political Dictionary,* 8th ed. New York: Holt, 1990.

The Political Science Teacher (Formerly DEA News: For Teachers of Political Science). Published by the American Political Science Association, 1527 New Hampshire Ave., NW, Washington, DC 20036. A quarterly that is distributed to all association members and focuses on instructional techniques and materials.

Political Science Thesaurus. Xerox University Microfilms, 300 North Zeeb Road, Ann Arbor, MI 48106. A major reference tool in political science. This volume represents a terminology-control device for a computer-based information-retrieval service.

The Presidential Documents Series (microfilm): *Franklin D. Roosevelt to Lyndon Johnson.* Frederick, MD: University Publications of America.

PS. Also published by the American Political Science Association. A quarterly that provides up-to-date information on research, training support, and professional conferences and notes on the profession.

Renstrom, Peter, and Chester Rogers. *The Electoral Politics Dictionary.* Santa Barbara, CA: ABC-CLIO, 1989.

Shafritz, Jay M., et al. *The Dorsey Dictionary of American Government and Politics.* Chicago, IL: Dorsey Press, 1988.

Smith, John, and John Klemanski. *The Urban Politics Dictionary.* Santa Barbara, CA: ABC-CLIO, 1990.

Taylor, Vernon L., and Juanita J. Taylor. *The Measuring Stick: A Guide to Self-Improvement in Teaching.* Chatham, IL: Key Productions, 1987.

Teaching Political Science: Politics in Perspective. Published quarterly by Heldref Publications, 4000 Albemarle Street, NW, Washington, DC 20016. Editor Jerome J. Hanus, School of Government, American University, Washington, DC 20016. The single best source of articles and reviews relevant to the teaching of the subject.

Washington Researchers, *A Researcher's Guide to Washington.* Washington, DC: Washington Researchers, Annual.

Weissberg, Robert. *Politics: A Handbook for Students.* New York: Harcourt-Brace, 1985.

Wellek, Alex (ed.). *The Encyclopedic Dictionary of American Government,* 4th ed. Guilford, CT: Dushkin, 1991.

Williams, C. Harvey. "Doing Critical Thinking Together: Applications to Government, Politics, and Public Policy," *PS: Political Science and Politics,* Vol. 24, No. 3 (September 1991), p. 510. Washington, DC: APSA.

History, Theory, and Additional Lecture Sources

Asher, Herbert. *Presidential Elections and American Politics—Voters, Candidates, and Campaigns since 1952,* 4th ed. New York: Penguin Books, 1988.
Baradat, Leon P. *Political Ideologies—Their Origins and Impact,* 3rd ed. Englewood Cliffs, NJ: Prentice-Hall, 1988.
Combs, J. E., and D. Nimmo. *A Primer of Politics.* New York: MacMillan Publishing Co., 1984.
Congressional Quarterly, Inc. *Guide to Current American Government—Spring 1991* (updated annually). Washington, DC: Congressional Quarterly Press, 1990.
Dolbeare, Kenneth M., and Linda J. Medcalf. *American Ideologies Today.* New York: Random House, 1988.
Fowler, R. B., and J. R. Orenstein. *Contemporary Issues in Political Theory.* New York: Praeger, 1985.
Glick, Henry R. *Courts, Politics and Justice,* 2nd ed. New York: McGraw Hill, 1988.
Hilsman, Roger. *The Politics of Policymaking in Defense and Foreign Affairs.* Englewood Cliffs, NJ: Prentice-Hall, 1987.
Holsworth, Robert D., and J. Harry Wray. *American Politics and Everyday Life,* 2nd ed. New York: MacMillan, 1987.
Hoover, K. R. *The Elements of Social Scientific Thinking,* 4th ed. New York: St. Martin's Press, 1987.
Kremyl, W. P. *A Model of Politics.* New York: MacMillan, 1985.
Markovich, Denise E., and Ronald E. Pynn, *American Political Economy.* Pacific Grove, CA: Brooks-Cole, 1988.
Roskin, Michael G., *et al. Political Science: An Introduction,* 3rd ed. Englewood Cliffs, NJ: Prentice-Hall, 1988.
Sargent, Lyman Tower. *Contemporary Political Ideologies: A Comparative Analysis,* 8th ed. Chicago: Dorsey Press, 1990.
Sherrill, Robert. *Why They Call It Politics,* 5th ed. New York: Harcourt-Brace, 1990.
Shively, W. Philips. *Power and Choice: Introduction to Politics,* 2nd ed. New York: Random House, 1991.
Spanier, John W. *American Foreign Policy Since WW II,* 12th ed. Washington, DC: Congressional Quarterly Press, 1990.
Strauss, Leo, and Joseph Cropsey, (eds.). *History of Political Philosophy,* 3rd ed. Chicago: University of Chicago Press, 1987.
Tinder, Glenn. *Political Thinking—The Perennial Questions,* 4th ed. Boston: Little, Brown, 1986.
White, Morton. *Philosophy, the Federalist and the Constitution.* New York: Oxford Press, 1987.
Wittkopf, E. R., and C. Kegley. *American Foreign Policy—Pattern and Process,* 3rd ed. New York: St. Martin's Press, 1987.

Readers

There are many good readers in political science. The choice depends largely on the area of interest of the instructor. A representative sampling of relevant readers follows.

Annual Editions, *Readings in American Government.* This volume is published annually by The Dushkin Publishing Group of Guilford, Connecticut.
Bressler, Robert, J., ed. *Contemporary Controversies: An American Government Reader.* New York: HarperCollins, 1993.

Bryan, Frank (ed.). *Readings in American Government*. St. Paul, MN: West, 1991.

Cigler, Allan, and Burdett Loomis. *American Politics: Classic and Contemporary Readings*. Boston: Houghton-Mifflin, 1989.

Davidson, Roger H., and Walter J. Oleszek, (eds.). *Governing: Readings and Cases in American Politics*, 2nd ed. Washington, DC: Congressional Quarterly Press, 1991.

DiClerico, R., and A. Hammock eds. *Points of View: Readings in American Government*, 5th ed., New York: Random House, 1992.

Dodd, Lawrence C., and Calvin Jillson, eds. *New Perspectives on American Politics*. Washington, DC: Congressional Quarterly Press, 1993.

Glover, William F., and Joseph G. Peshek, eds. *Voices of Dissent: Critical Readings in American Politics*. New York: HarperCollins, 1993.

Harmel, Robert, ed. *American Government—Readings on Continuity and Change*. New York: St. Martin's Press, 1988.

Harris, Fred R., ed. *Readings on the Body Politic*. Glenview, IL: Scott, Foresman/Little, Brown, 1987.

Krieger, Joel, ed. *The Oxford Companion to Politics of the World*. New York: Oxford University Press, 1993.

Krislov, Samuel, and Raymond Lee, eds. *The Clash of Issues: Readings and Problems in American Government*, 9th ed. Englewood Cliffs, NJ: Prentice Hall, 1989.

Levine, Herbert M., ed. *Point-Counterpoint: Readings in American Government*, 3rd ed. New York: St. Martin's Press, 1994.

———. *Political Issues Debated*, 3rd ed. Englewood Cliffs, NJ: Prentice Hall, 1990.

McKenna, George, and S. Feingold eds. *Taking Sides*, 7th ed. Guilford, CT: Dushkin, 1991.

Milkis, Sidney M., and Richard A. Harris, eds. *Remaking American Politics*. Boulder, CO: Westview, 1988.

Murphy, Bruce Allen. *Portraits of American Politics: A Reader*, 2nd ed. Boston: Houghton-Mifflin, 1994.

Nelson, Michael, ed. *The Presidency and the Political System*, 3rd ed. Washington, DC: Congressional Quarterly Press, 1990.

Nivola, Pietro S., and David H. Rosenbloom, eds. *Classic Readings in American Politics*, 2nd ed. New York: St. Martin's Press, 1990.

Opposing Viewpoints—Sources, 1987–1988. St. Paul, MN: Greenhaven Press, Inc.

Reichley, James A. ed. *Elections—American Style*. Washington, DC: Brookings, 1987.

Serow, Ann G. et al., eds. *The American Polity Reader*, 2nd ed. New York: W. W. Norton, 1993.

Woll, P., ed. *American Government: Readings and Cases*, 11th ed. Boston: Little, Brown, 1993.

———. *Behind the Scenes in American Government: Personalities and Politics*, 8th ed. Glenview, IL: Scott, Foresman/Little, Brown, 1991.

Reprints

1. Bobbs-Merrill Reprints in the Social Sciences
   4300 West 62nd Street
   Indianapolis, IN 46206

2. Eno River Press, American Politics I and II
   Box 4900, Duke Station
   Durham, NC 27706-4900

Selected Reading Lists

3. Ginn Press
   160 Gould Street
   Needham, MA 02194
   Phone: 617-455-7000

4. Irvington Publishing Co., Inc.
   740 Broadway, Suite 905
   New York, NY 10003

Simulations and Games

Alper, David. "Teaching the Federalist Papers by Simulating a Constitutional Convention," *The Political Science Teacher*, Vol. 2, No. 2 (Spring 1989), p. 6. Washington, DC: APSA.

American Political Science Association. *Supplementary Empirical Teaching Units in Political Science* (SETUPS). Washington, DC: APSA. A number of American politics games have been published.

Binford, Michael B. "Decision-Making and Participation." *NEWS for Teachers of Political Science*, No. 41 (Spring, 1984), p. 26. Washington, DC: APSA.

Claude, Richard and Paul E. Parker. "A Moot Court for Constitutional Issues." *NEWS for Teachers of Political Science*, No. 43 (Fall, 1984), p. 7. Washington, DC: APSA.

Coplin, William. *Simulation in the Study of Politics*. Chicago: Rand McNally, 1968.

Godek, Stephen. "Urban Revitalization Simulation," *The Political Science Teacher*, Vol. 3, No. 3 (Summer 1990), p. 11. Washington, DC: APSA.

Greenblat, Cathy. *Designing Games and Simulations: An Illustrated Handbook*. Beverley Hills, CA: Sage, 1987.

Greenblat, Cathy, and Richard Duke. *Gaming-Simulation*. New York: Halsted Press/John Wiley, 1975.

Gump, W. Robert, and James Woodworth. *Atlantis: Role-Playing Simulations for American Politics*. Chicago: Nelson Hall, 1986.

Hobbs, Heidi H., and Dario V. Moreno. "Bureaucratic Bargaining—An American Foreign Policy Simulation," *The Political Science Teacher*, Vol. 1, No. 1 (Winter, 1988), p. 5. Washington, DC: APSA.

Horn, Robert E., and A. Cleaves. *The Guide to Simulations/Games for Education and Training*, 4th ed. Beverly Hills, CA: Sage Publications, 1980.

Inbar, Michael. *Simulation and Gaming in Social Science*. New York: Free Press, 1972.

Maser, Steven, and John Orbell. "Two Games for Introducing Political Science," *NEWS for Teachers of Political Science*, No. 42 (Summer 1984), p. 1. Washington, DC: APSA.

McQuaid, Kathleen. "The Use of Guided Design Simulations in the Introductory Level American Politics and State and Local Politics Courses," *PS: Political Science and Politics*, Vol. 25, No. 3 (September 1992), p. 532. Washington, DC: APSA.

Mock, Carol. "Choice or Sequester? A Classroom Simulation in Budgetary Politics," *The Political Science Teacher*, Vol. 3, No. 4 (Fall 1990), p. 10. Washington, DC: APSA.

Moore, Malcolm J., and Jack Rubin. *Games Students Can Play*. Englewood Cliffs, NJ: Prentice-Hall, 1973.

Olsen, David M. *The Politics of Legislation: A Congressional Simulation*. New York: Praeger, 1976.

Olufs, Dick W. "Colonial Politics: A Game of Factions," *NEWS for Teachers of Political Science*, No. 52 (Winter, 1987), pp. 10–11. Washington, DC: APSA.

Pacelle, Richard. "Simulating Supreme Court Decision Making," *The Political Science Teacher*, Vol. 2, No. 2 (Spring 1989), p. 8. Washington, DC: APSA.

Roberts, Frederick J. "Play Games in This Department?" *Teaching Political Science* 2 (January 1975), pp. 123–143.

Simulation/Gaming. Simulation Gaming News, Box 303A, Moscow, ID 83843.

Woodworth, James, and W. Robert Gump. *Camelot: A Role-Playing Simulation for Political Decision Making*, 2nd ed. Pacific Grove, CA: Brooks/Cole, 1987.

NOTE: EMI (Box 4272, Madison, WI 53711) is a company that is especially strong in simulations, with specific items covering such diverse topics as the 1787 Constitutional Convention, science fiction "political games," public opinion role-playing, lobbying scenarios, campaigns and elections, plea bargaining, Supreme Court decision-making, and general simulations covering power and policy-making processes.

Also, the instructor may wish to write to the North American Simulation and Gaming Association's National Game Center, located at the University of North Carolina at Asheville, One University Heights, Asheville, NC 28804-3299.

Computer Software

NOTE: The following represents only a limited sample of the growing number of computerized resources and software available to the instructor of American government. Publishers of American government texts are also developing and promoting their own computerized packages, so you may wish to contact them for further information.

Crotty, Patricia McGee, "Introducing American Government Students to Data Analysis." *NEWS for Teachers of Political Science* (Winter, 1986), pp. 14–15.

Inter-University Consortium for Political and Social Research, P.O. Box 1248, Ann Arbor, MI 48106. Develops software and provides computer assistance. Also publishes a newsletter, MICRO NEWS, that reviews both hardware and software in the social science area.

Nagel, Stuart. "Updating Microcomputers and Public Policy Analysis," *The Political Science Teacher*, Vol. 2, No. 2 (Spring 1989), p. 20. Washington, DC: APSA.

Nagel, Stuart, "Using Microcomputers." *NEWS for Teachers of Political Science* (Fall, 1986), pp. 10–12. An APSA published article that reveals the ways computers can be applied to the analysis of public policy.

National Collegiate Software Clearinghouse, Box 8101, Raleigh, NC 27695. Phone: (919) 737-3067. Located on the North Carolina State University campus in the School of Humanities and Social Sciences, the Clearinghouse provides a catalog of latest software products. Software exists applicable to American military and foreign policy, campaigns and elections, interest groups, legislative behavior, and so forth.

National Director of Public Affairs, NAM, 1331 Pennsylvania Ave. NW, Suite 1500 North, Washington, DC 20004-1703. The National Association of Manufacturers provides a computerized simulation called *Congressional Insight*, which involves the decisions facing first-term members in the House of Representatives.

Poli-Ware Simulations, APSA, 1527 New Hampshire Ave. NW, Washington, DC 20036. Simulations are available in six areas: Political Redistricting, Political Campaigning, Legislative Coalition Building, Judicial Process, Public Opinion Polling, and Presidential Popularity. Computers must have 128K of memory and either two floppy disk drives or one floppy disk drive and a hard disk.

Ross, Robert S., "Microcomputer Simulations of Presidential Elections," *NEWS for Teachers of Political Science* (Summer, 1983), No. 38, p. 20.

SETUPS/APSA. The American Political Science Association publishes "Supplementary Empirical Teaching Units in Political Science" with appropriate data sets and code books. One notable example is Prysby, Charles and Carmine Scavo, *Voting Behavior—The 1988 Election*, which comes with a data set for microcomputer or mainframe computer users. For a complete listing of all computer-applicable SETUPS, write to the APSA, 1527 New Hampshire Ave. NW, Washington, DC 20036.

SPSS, Inc., 444 North Michigan Avenue, Suite 3000, Chicago, IL 60611. Phone: (312) 329-3326. Provides data analysis software for a variety of teaching, research, publishing, and presentation needs.

Syllabus, P.O. Box 2716, Sunnyvale, CA 94087-0716. Phone: (408) 773-0670. This invaluable newsletter, published bimonthly and available free to educators, serves as the link between Apple Computer and the higher education field. Included in each issue are descriptions of Macintosh-based software developed by teachers, text publishers, and software developers around the country, along with purchasing information about each program.

Careers in Political Science

Curzon, Mary H., ed. *Careers and the Study of Political Science: A Guide for Undergraduates*, 5th ed. Washington, DC: American Political Science Association, 1992. A monograph discussing the relationship between knowledge in political science and careers open in law, government, teaching, business, and journalism. Updated periodically and available in bulk orders from the APSA.

Reese, Laura, "The Role of the Political Science Department in Career Counseling." *The Political Science Teacher* (Spring, 1988), p. 19.

Film and Video Guide*

General Information and Film Sources

A detailed list of films and videotapes to use with each chapter of *American Government*, Sixth Edition, appears on the following pages. The films and tapes in these lists pertain to specific topics introduced and discussed in the text. As such, they are invaluable for highlighting important features of each chapter and for demonstrating concepts, research studies, and research methods covered in the text. It is standard educational practice to preview any film or tape before using it in class. Many films, although created several years ago, are still well suited for classroom use because they provide clear and informative illustrations of social settings and political processes. However, it would appear that the "video revolution" will replace many films, because tapes are less expensive, more durable, and easier to handle.

Plan your media schedule and place your orders well before the dates of intended use, because the best films or tapes are likely to be in great demand. If you are just starting to use films in your course, begin by familiarizing yourself with the audiovisual department at your school. Most colleges not only offer equipment and trained projectionists but run a film library as well. If this is the situation at your school, all you may have to do is tell people in the audiovisual department what you need. If they don't own the film, they will order it from the distributor. On the other hand, if your AV department is more modest (or nonexistent), you will have to take it upon yourself to order films, borrow a projector, and run the projector. Videotapes are now largely available on half-inch VHS machines, the most common format. Most colleges will have purchased VCRs for classroom use.

The film distributors listed below and following the chapter filmography fall into two general categories. The majority are the actual producers of the film (such as CRM/McGraw-Hill or Encyclopedia Britannica), whereas others simply purchase films from the producer and rent them out (such as Pennsylvania State University). Because companies in the first group act as direct distributors of their own films, they are usually happy to supply free copies of their catalogs and to send films out, on loan, for previewing by prospective users. Should you then decide to show one or more of their films, you (or your audio-visual department) may either rent or buy the film(s) you have chosen. The companies in the second group are in the rental business primarily, their margins are small, and most of them charge for their catalogs and do not allow free previewing of films. However, they also tend

---

*© 1995 by P. S. Associates, Inc. All rights reserved.

to charge less for their films than the firms in the first group. Similar procedures apply to the use of instructional videotapes. Consult each video distributor for details.

For additional information about films in government, consult the following sources (the most valuable sources are marked with an asterisk).

AAAS Science Books and Films, American Association for the Advancement of Science, Washington, DC 20005. Includes reviews of recent films.

ABC Merchandising, 330 W. 42nd Street, New York, N. Y. 10036.

Agency for Instructional Television, Box A, Bloomington, IN 47401. Catalog of films and videocassettes is available.

Audio Film Center, 2138 East 75th Street, Chicago, IL 60649.

Audiovisual Marketplace, R. R. Bowker Co., 1180 Avenue of the Americas, New York, NY 10036.

BFA Educational Media, P. O. Box 1795, Santa Monica, CA 90406.

*Blue Book of Audiovisual Materials, Educational Services and Audiovisual Guide, 434 Wabash Avenue, Chicago, IL 60605.

Coronet Films, 65 East South Water Street, Chicago, IL 60601.

*CRM/McGraw-Hill Films, 110 15th Street, Del Mar, CA 92014.

Educational Film Library, 43 West 61st Street, New York, NY 10023. Publishes updates of Bowker's *Feature Films on 8mm and 16mm*.

*Educational Film Locator of the Consortium of University Film Centers, 2nd ed., R. R. Bowker Co., 1180 Avenue of the Americas, New York, NY 10036.

*Educational Sound Film Directory, Dukane Corporation, Audio Visual Division, St. Charles, IL 60174.

*Educator's Guide to Free Films, J. D. Diffor and E. N. Diffor (eds.), Educators Progress Service, Inc., 214 Center Street, Randolph, WI 53956.

*Educator's Guide to Free Filmstrips, J. D. Diffor and E. N. Diffor (eds.), Educators Progress Service, Inc., 214 Center Street, Randolph, WI 53956.

Encyclopedia Britannica Films, Inc., 1822 Pickwick Avenue, Glenview, IL 60025.

Feature Films on 8mm and 16mm, and Videotape, R. R. Bowker Co., 1180 Avenue of the Americas, New York, NY 10036. Updated regularly through the Educational Film Library (address above).

*Film Programmers Guide to 16mm Rentals, Reel Research, Box 6037, Albany, CA 94706.

*Films Incorporated, P. O. Box 14127, Atlanta, GA 30324.

*Indiana University Audio-Visual Center, Division of University Extension, Bloomington, IN 47401.

Insight Media, 121 W. 85th St., New York, NY 10024.

International Film Bureau, Inc., 332 South Michigan Avenue, Chicago, IL 60604.

Kent State University, Audio Visual Services, Kent, OH 44242.

*Modern Talking Picture Service, 5000 Park Street North, St. Petersburg, FL 33709. Write: Attention Scheduling Center and ask for College Brochure. This is probably the best source of commercial films available for rental.

National Film Board of Canada, 1251 Avenue of the Americas, New York, NY 10020.

*The New Yorker Film Catalog, New Yorker Films, 43 West 61st Street, New York, NY 10023.

*NICEM Index to 16mm Educational Films, National Information Center for Educational Media (NICEM), University of Southern California, University Park, CA 90007.

*PBS Video, 1320 Braddock Place, Alexandria, VA 22314-1698.

*Pennsylvania State University, Audio-Visual Services, Special Services Building, University Park, PA 16802. Ask for business catalog.

Time-Life Video, Dept. 32-37, Time and Life Building, New York, NY 10020. (212) 556-4554.

Universal Education and Visual Arts, 425 North Michigan Avenue, Chicago, IL 60611.

*University of California Extension Media Center, 2223 Fulton Street, Berkeley, CA 94720.

University of Illinois, Visual Aids Center, Division of University Extension, Champaign, IL 61822.

University of Iowa, Audio-Visual Center, Iowa City, IA 52240.

University of Michigan, Audio-Visual Education Center, 416 Fourth Street, Ann Arbor, MI 48105.

University of Minnesota, Department of Audio-Visual Extension, General Education Division, 2037 University Avenue, Minneapolis, MN 55455.

*U. S. Government Films: A Catalog of Motion Pictures and Filmstrips for Sale by the National Audiovisual Center, National Archives, GSA, Washington, DC 20409.

Chapter-by-Chapter Film List

Chapter 1 The Study of American Government

Alexander Hamilton and Thomas Jefferson on Democracy (BFA, 26 min.). A good philosophical contrast between two alternative "views" of democracy.

Future Shock (CRM, 42 min.). Examines the problems of rapid social change and the people affected by it.

Social Class in America (CRM, 16 min.). The nature and consequences of social class are revealed through the lives of three people, each from a different class, and their opportunities for social mobility are examined.

The Secret Government: The Constitution in Crisis (PBS, 90 min.). Bill Moyers explores the Iran-Contra affair to discover whether democratic government is threatened by the need for secrecy in covert activities.

Political Systems (Insight, 30 min.). Compares how different political systems (autocracy, totalitarianism, and democracy) view power and resolve conflicts.

Chapter 2 The Constitution

American Revolution: The Background Period (Coronet, 10 min.). The background of the American Revolution is explored fully.

The Constitution: One Nation (1781–1791) (T-L, 30 min.). Another good historical overview.

Inventing a Nation: The Making of the Constitution (T-L, 52 min.). An examination of the spirit of compromise in which our Constitution was created and our nation born.

Origins of the Constitution—The Struggle for Consensus, Parts 1, 2, 3 (PHM, 25 min. each). A thorough historical recounting of how the U.S. Constitution was eventually created.

The Constitution at 200: Why Does It Still Work? (T-L, 60 min.). The evolution of the Constitution is explored through case studies.

In Search of the Constitution (FLINC, 156 min.). Bill Moyers conducts a series of interviews on the origins, meaning, and relevance of the Constitution (set of two videos).

Chapter 3 Federalism

Federalism: The National Government vs. the States (NET, 60 min.). "Marble-cake" Federalism is explored.

Gibbons vs. Ogden (1824) (IU, 35 min.). Re-enacts the case that decided whether the authority to regulate commerce lay with the states or with Congress.

Government: A Plus . . . or a Minus? (NBC, 27 min.). A 1978 NBC production highlighting national political figures and their views pertaining to "big government." Interesting as a precursor to the Reagan years.

McCulloch vs. Maryland (1819) (IU, 35 min.). Re-enacts the case that decided whether states could tax operations of the federal government.

Our Federal Constitution (IU, 21 min.). An analysis comparing and contrasting unitary versus federal systems, democracy versus dictatorship, and parliamentary versus presidential systems.

The Role of the States in the American Federal System (BRIT, 26 min.). A good overview of the state-federal relationship with special emphasis given to the "marble-cake" thesis.

Federalism: The National Government vs. the States (FLINC, 56 min.). Part of "That Delicate Balance" series focusing on the use of federal grants to school boards.

Federalism (Insight, 30 min.). Examines the "garbage barge" incident of the 1980s to illustrate the distribution of power between national and state governments.

Chapter 4 The American Political Culture

The Right to Believe (Xerox, 20 min.). In a 1975 ABC production, historian Henry S. Commager discusses the progress of Americans toward greater tolerance.

USA: A Time for Decision (NET, 60 min.). A description of population trends in the United States over the past 200 years.

The Heart of the Nation (Humanities, 58 min.). Hedrick Smith explores the values of Japan, Germany, and the United States and focuses on what drives each society.

Chapter 5 Public Opinion

Media Politics: The Big Hype (CAF, 16 min.). Depicts how candidates and campaigns in general are "packaged" for the media and the effect of this "selling" on public opinion. Can also be used with Chapter 7 or 9 of the Wilson text.

Pollsters and Politics (ASOCF, 26 min.). The pros and cons of polling are explored.

The Selling of the Pentagon (CBS, 52 min.). An exploration of the public-opinion tools used by the Pentagon to gain favor with the American public.

The Conservatives (Humanities, 88 min.). Examines the rise of the conservative involvement in America from the 1940s to the Reagan era.

Chapter 6 Political Participation

The Young Vote (BFA, 15 min.). A discussion of voting attitudes of the 18-to-21-year-old sector of the electorate.

Latino Voting Behavior (Humanities, 26 min.). Explores the changes in Hispanic voting trends and the traditionally low turnout problem.

The Betrayal of Democracy (PBS, 120 min.). A *Frontline* episode examining why fewer Americans are voting.

Chapter 7 Political Parties

If Elected (WEF, 50 min.). Involves a party's role in a state election.

The Last Hurrah (MTPS, 120 min.). Concerns the last days of an old-style boss and his big-city political machine.

Mayor Daley: A Study in Power (CBS, 49 min.). A 1972 study of the mayor's "political machine."

Political Parties in America: Getting the People Together (IU, 19 min.). Defines and explores the changing roles of American parties from their beginnings to the 1976 election.

Prime Time in the Old Town Tonight (DMM, 66 min.). Internal party factions, the national convention, and party-media relationships are all covered.

Chapter 8 Elections and Campaigns

Campaign (CH, 20 min.). Describes day-to-day campaign activities in a California State Senate race.

Campaign: American Style (CBS, 60 min.). Explores modern "political technology."

The Candidate (Ideal, 110 min.). An idealistic young lawyer finds his ideals eroded as he runs for the U. S. Senate.

Diary of a Dark Horse (WEF, 28 min.). Bill Moyers follows Rep. John B. Anderson's campaign for the presidency in 1980.

Early Return (WEF, 50 min.). Discusses the impact of the New Hampshire primary.

Edge of the Arena—Portrait of a Black Candidate (STER, 28 min.). Covers the 1970 campaign of Andrew Young, a black candidate, for a congressional seat from the state of Georgia. Stresses the ultimate victory of the "coalition" over the strictly black and the stictly white campaign.

The First Tuesday After the First Monday—Election of a President (HEARST, 15 min.). An informative and entertaining look at the history of presidential elections in America.

The True Story of an Election (CH, 30 min.). Good on dynamics of process.

Vote Power (H2M, 18 min.). Stresses the importance of the individual vote. Documents the history of voting with an emphasis on the involvement of the new "youth" vote.

The Young Vote (BFA, 15 min.). A discussion of voting attitudes of 18- to 21-year-olds.

Congressional Elections (Insight, 30 min.). Looks at the similarities and differences in conducting campaigns for the House and Senate.

Chapter 9 Interest Groups

Battleground Washington: The Politics of Pressure (ABC, 52 min.). Washington lobbyists in action.

A Continuing Responsibility (NFBC, 43 min.). Documents the techniques of Saul Alinsky in organizing politically powerful community organizations.

Inside Government—Lobbying (CH, 25 min.). The activities, responsibilities, and influence found within the ranks of lobbyists in a typical state legislature are defined. Using California as an example, the film follows two lobbyists as they go about their jobs.

Lobbying: A Case History (IU, 17 min.). Illustrates how lobbying can influence national policy by showing a controversy in Alton, Illinois, over the replacement of a dam.

Lovejoy's Nuclear War (GMP, 60 min.). The battle of an antinuclear activist to prevent a nuclear power plant from being built in Montague, Massachusetts.

Protest—Anti-War (INT, 15 min.). Approaches the problem of waging politics without parties by examining the protests against the war in Vietnam.

The Role of the Interest Group Leader (Xerox, 23 min.). How a Sierra Club lobbyist operates as he attempts to influence legislators on a bill opposed to strip mining.

Interest Groups (Insight, 30 min.). A general overview on how interest groups influence policy making.

Who Owns Our Government? (PBS, 60 min.). Bill Moyers explores how political contributions made by lobbyists co-opt the policy process.

The Power of PACs (Insight, 30 min.). Experts are interviewed on the purpose and functions of PACs.

Chapter 10 The Media

Politics in the Television Age (FLINC, 20 min.). How TV has affected presidential campaigning.

Television: A Political Machine (UCAL, 14 min.). Looks at how the mass media have affected politics by examining how candidates used TV in the 1968 Indiana primary.

Television and Politics (IU, 25 min.). Outlines the influence the media have had on elections from 1948 to 1968.

Network News: That's the Way It Is (PBS, 30 min.). Hodding Carter examines how news coverage of issues has suffered to create network media stars.

The Press Open to Question (PBS, 29 min.). Reporters discuss how they use self-regulation to prevent bias.

Government and the Media (Insight, 30 min.). Uses an international situation and a local controvertsy to illustrate how the media both influences public opinion and reflects it.

Chapter 11 Congress

An Act of Congress (IU, 59 min.). Follows the Clean Air Act from debate in subcommittees through the vote on the House floor.

Congress: We the People (APSR, 26-30 min., videocassettes). A comprehensive series that depicts the daily activites of Congress and the legislative process and offers an accompanying political analysis by congressional scholars.

How a Bill Becomes a Law (TSK, 18 min.). Step-by-step procedures (animated) that illustrate the full scope of the legislative process.

Inside Government—Legislator (CH, 25 min.). A behind-the-scenes look at a state legislator's attempts to maneuver a bill through the legislature.

Mr. Speaker (FLINC, 58 min.). Former speaker Tip O'Neill in action.

The Legislative Branch (NATG, 22 min.). A congressman's effort to prevent a budget cut is portrayed.

The Role of a Congressman (ASOCF, 23 min.). Film depicting the several legislative roles that Richard Bolling played during a workday in Congress.

Congress: What It Is, How It Works, and How It Affects You (T-L, 60 min.). An examination of Congress, including its powers, committee system, and leadership.

The U.S. Congress (T-L, 60 min.). A general overview that investigates changes in congressional power.

The Congress (Insight, 30 min.). Interviews on the organization and structure of the House and Senate.

The Legislative Process (Insight, 30 min.). Focuses on the Japanese-American Reparation Bill of 1988 to demonstrate how a bill becomes a law.

Chapter 12 The Presidency

The American Parade: Power and the Presidency (BFA, 30 min.). A historical view of how eighteenth- and nineteenth-century presidents used the powers of their office.

Every Four Years: An Examination of the American Presidency (PBS, three 60-min. videocassettes). Howard K. Smith has a series of conversations with presidents, presidential scholars, and presidential advisors.

F. D. R.: The Man Who Changed America (CH, 60 min.). Examines the presidency of F. D. R. from the Great Depression through World War II.

Five Presidents on the Presidency (CBS, 50 min.). Presents edited statements of Presidents Truman, Eisenhower, Kennedy, Johnson, and Nixon relative to the following: presidential power, presidential choice, the president and Congress, the president and the press, the presidency and foreign policy, the president as a politician, and the president in retrospect.

The Making of the President, 1960 (NBC, 120 min.). Based on Theodore White's Pulitzer-Prize winning volume of the same title.

President of the U.S.—Too Much Power? (BRIT, 25 min.). An examination of the powers and duties of the president with commentary by the late Senator Hubert Humphrey.

Stroke of the Pen—Dimensions of a Presidential Decision (ENV, 16 min.). A recreation of John F. Kennedy's executive order banning discrimination in housing.

The Presidency in Perspective (T-L, 60 min.). A recent video that considers the degree to which the president influences the political system.

The Challenge of the Presidency (PBS, 60 min.). A discussion of how the person shapes the office.

The Presidency (Insight, 30 min.). Presents the organization and power of the executive branch in general.

Chapter 13 The Bureaucracy

Bureaucracy (CRM, 16 min.). Examines the conflict between reducing government bureaucracy and increasing housing for the elderly.

The Bureaucracy (CFM, 10 min.). An animated film of a "fantasy trip" through the bureaucratic maze.

Federal Civil Service (IU, 20 min.). Discusses the system's operation and overall significance.

The Invisible Government (PHM, filmstrip). Bureaucratic procedures and problems are covered; narration is provided by Rep. Morris Udall.

Rise and Fall of the CIA (NET, 60 min.). A documentary study of the CIA, beginning with its charter in 1947. Focuses on the CIA's relationship to foreign security and domestic liberty. Also applicable to Chapter 20 on foreign policy.

The Role of the Government (GRP, 25 min.). Bureaucratic implementation of anti-pollution laws is covered.

The Tenth Level (NBC, 90 min.). Dramatization of the Yale experiment in shock treatment. Demonstrates how bureaucratization leads to ethical dilemmas.

Assault on Big Brother: Regulating the Regulators (NBC, 52 min.). NBC special that follows the regulatory process from the formulation of a rule to its implementation.

The Bureaucracy (Insight, 30 min.). Discusses the relationship between the bureaucracy and the needs of citizens and the degree of bureaucratic accountability that exists.

Chapter 14 The Judiciary

Congress and the Courts (APSA, 30 min.). The interaction between the two branches is discussed.

Equal Justice Under the Law (NET, 180 min.). Examines landmark Supreme Court cases (set of three films).

Justice on Trial (CRM, 49 min.). Focuses on inequities in sentencing that affect both criminals and victims.

Marbury vs. Madison (1803) (IU, 33 min.). Re-enacts the case that established the Supreme Court's power to review the constitutionality of acts of Congress.

Nature and Scope of Judicial Power (NBC, 30 min.). The title is self-explanatory.

The U. S. Supreme Court: Guardian of the Constitution (BRIT, 24 min.). Factual treatment of the history and operating procedures of the Court.

Interpreting the Law: The Role of the Supreme Court (T-L, 60 min.). A general overview of the Supreme Court, from selecting justices to its organization.

An Introduction to the Federal Courts (Insight, 29 min.). A general introduction to the organization, jurisdiction and administration of the federal judicial system.

The Judiciary (Insight, 30 min.). Interviews with experts on the role of the judiciary, including the jurisdiction of courts in the United States.

Chapter 15 The Policy-Making Process

Policy Negotiation (ALA, 25 min.). How a local school board developed educational policies amidst a welter of cross-cutting pressures.

Chapter 16 Economic Policy

Anatomy of Inflation (CRM, 23 min.). Examines political and economic forces that lead to inflation.

The Business of America (HEARST, 21 min.). An examination of the free-enterprise system and how it has contributed to economic growth.

Economic Choices (BROOK, 40 min.). Proposals for a balanced budget in 1989 are discussed.

Government—How Much Is Enough? (EMI, 120 min.). A series of filmstrips and cassettes on government-economic relationships as well as the effect of those relationships on the individual.

The Culture of Commerce (Humanities, 58 min.). Hedrick Smith explores the systematic differences between the individualistic capitalism of America and Britain and the communitarian capitalism of Japan and Germany.

Curing the Economy (PBS, 60 min.). Bill Moyers hosts an examination of the economic problems of the American economy along with proposed solutions.

Chapter 17 Social Welfare

America's Aged—The Forgotten Many (CAF, 18 min.). The plight of the elderly in American society is covered.

Appalachia: Rich Land, Poor People (NET, 59 min.). A look at the people of eastern Kentucky and the unemployment that has followed mechanization of the mines.

Harvest of Shame (UCAL, 54 min.). A vivid account of the conditions of life and work of migrant workers in America.

Reforming Entitlements: Medicare and Health Costs (Brook). A 1984 study on how the entitlement programs can remain solvent.

Growing Up Poor (PBS, 58 min.). A "Frontline" episode that follows children through the social welfare services in Chester, Penn.

Living Below the Line (PBS, 60 min.). A "Frontline" episode that examines the welfare system.

Workfare, Welfare: What's Fair? (Humanities, 26 min.). Focuses on a welfare program involving workfare, an effort to get people off welfare rolls and into jobs.

Condition Critical: The American Health Care Forum (Humanities, 116 min.). A guide to understanding health care in America and an explanation of the alternatives for reform.

Chapter 18 Civil Liberties

American Government: Civil Liberty, The Means/Primary End of Government (NBC, 30 min.). The historical importance of civil liberties is examined.

The Bill of Rights—Due Process of Law (BFA, 23 min.). Features a legal debate involving the reinstatement of a student who has been summarily suspended after an act of violence during a campus demonstration. Explains that the due process of law is, by its very nature, time-consuming, whereas the need to avoid violence and anarchy is often immediate. Questions whether there are times when due process should give way to summary punishment in violation of the Fifth Amendment.

Censored—The Story of Book Censorship in the U. S. (KRSK, 30 min.). The title is self-explanatory.

Fear on Trial (CBS, 120 min.). Examines the libel case of John Henry Faulk when he was blacklisted by CBS.

The First and Essential Freedom (Xerox, 52 min.). Covers the First Amendment and its implications for the media and American society.

Freedom and Security: The Uncertain Balance (WLC, 50 min.). The basic conflict is examined through an analysis of court cases and disputes.

Justice Under Law: The Gideon Case (BRIT, 23 min.). The study of the classic case involving the right to have counsel.

Police Power (NET, 60 min.). A debate on the role of police power in a modern democratic society and police methods and the effects of Supreme Court decisions.

The Trial of the Catonsville Nine (CIN, 85 min.). Courtroom drama of Rev. Daniel Berrigan and others on trial for napalming draft board files.

God and the Constitution (PBS, 60 min.). Bill Moyers interviews Martin Marty on topics such as the legality of school prayer and the tax-exempt status of churches.

Books Under Fire (FLINC, 56 min.). Explores the effort to ban Ronald Glasser's book *365 Days*.

School Prayer, Gun Control and the Right to Assemble (FLINC, 60 min.). Part of "That Delicate Balance" series in which Arthur Miller moderates a debate.

Individual Rights (Insight, 30 min.). Focuses on the right of privacy but also examines the due process and equal protection clauses.

First Amendment Freedoms (insight, 30 min.). Interviews are used to present the current status of First Amendment rights.

Rights of the Accused (insight, 30 min.). A discussion of the Fourth, Fifth, Sixth, and Eighth Amendments.

Search and Seizure: The Supreme Court and the Police (PBS, 60 min.). Roger Mudd explores questions of privacy and the Fourth Amendment.

Chapter 19 Civil Rights

Black History: Lost, Stolen, or Strayed? (UCAL, 54 min.). The contributions of black Americans to the development of the United States are examined. Narrated by Bill Cosby.

Busing: Constructive or Destructive? (AEI, 60 min.). Good debate is offered on the issue.

Civil Disorder: The Kerner Report (IU, 80 min.). Investigates the ghetto riots of the 1960s.

Daddy, Don't Be Silly—A Case for Equal Rights (IU, 27 min.). The origins of ERA are explored and cases of sex discrimination are also presented. "Pro" and "con" arguments surrounding the ERA are also featured.

Guilty by Reason of Race (FLINC, 51 min.). The story of the illegal detention of over 20,000 Japanese-Americans during World War II.

Martin Luther King, Jr.—From Montgomery to Memphis (BFA, 27 min.). Examines the efforts of Dr. King to bring about civil rights legislation.

Women's Liberation (ABC, 23 min.). An early analysis of factionalism within the women's movement.

Affirmative Action Versus Reverse Discrimination (FLINC, 60 min.). Part of "That Delicate Balance" series of a moderated discussion.

Racism in America (Humanities, 26 min.). An examination of the resurgence of bigotry and racially motivated acts of violence.

Chapter 20 Foreign Policy

America Gets Involved (T-L, 20 min.). Good historical overview of U. S. foreign policy from Wilson to the post–World War II era.

Beyond War: A New Way of Thinking (UCAL, 22 min.). Discusses the question of war's obsolescence.

Focus on Foreign Policy: The Public and the Experts (PIN, 58 min.). The role of public opinion and Congress in the formulation of foreign policy.

The Missiles of October (NBC, 210 min.). A dramatization of the decision-making process in the United States and the Soviet Union during the Cuban missile crisis of 1962.

The Powers of the Presidency—Armed Intervention (BFA, 23 min.). Presents a crisis scenario wherein the president must decide on a course of action.

State of Siege (CIN, 119 min.). Controversial film on the kidnapping of an American "advisor" in Latin America.

War Without Winners (CDI, 20 min.). Depicts the possible results of nuclear warfare.

The Media and Human Rights (PBS, 60 min.). Ted Koppel moderates a discussion on the role of the media in publicizing human rights.

Chapter 21 Military Policy

American Military Strength: Second to None? (ABC, 51 min.). Ted Koppel explores the dynamics of the arms race.

Armaments: The War Game (UCAL, 22 min.). How military spending and the economy are linked in a variety of ways.

Defense and Domestic Needs: A Contest for Tomorrow (IU, 77 min.). A film that raises questions about the size of the defense budget and the guns-versus-butter dilemma.

Mr. Aspin and the Pentagon (WEF, 55 min.). Documentary on Rep. Les Aspin's fight to cut military spending.

A Trillion Dollars for Defense (AEI, 60 min.). Explores what the defense dollar "buys."

The Peace Dividend with Seymour Melman (PBS, 30 min.). Bill Moyers interviews Seymour Melman, author of *Profits without Production*, on how military spending has drained resources from the U.S. economy.

Chapter 22 The Environment

Acid Rain (PBS, 57 min.). An episode of "Nova" that presents a general overview on the topic.

Toxic Trials (PBS, 120 min.). An episode of "Nova" about a cluster of leukemia cases and its causes.

Air Pollution: A First Film (Revised) (BFA, 12 min.). An overview that explores the problem and presents suggestions.

The State of the World (PBS, 30 min.). Bill Moyers interviews Lester Brown, founder of Worldwatch Institute, who argues that the degradation of the planet is the principal threat to world security.

After the Warming (PBS, 90 min.). A computer simulation of the environmental consequences of global warming in the year 2050 at various global locations.

The Endangered Earth: The Politics of Acid Rain (Humanities, 58 min.). An analysis of the acid rain controversy with representatives from both sides of the debate.

Radioactive Waste Disposal: The 10,000 Year Test (Humanities, 50 min.). Investigates a nuclear dump in Nevada.

Politics, People and Pollution (PBS, 60 min.). Bill Moyers explores the balance between corporate productivity and environmental resonsibility.

Chapters 23 and 24 Who Governs? To What Ends?

We Hold These Truths (OX, 15 min.). The ideals of the Declaration of Independence are reconsidered.

Chapter 25 State and Local Government

Beseiged Majority (FLINC, 53 min.). Examines urban crime from the victim's perspective.
Challenge of Urban Renewal (NBC, 60 min.). Explores the problems involved in urban change.
Inside Government: Legislator (CH, 25 min.). A state legislator maneuvers to have his legislation passed.
Law and Order (ZIP, 81 min.). The role of the police in a large U. S. city.
Local Governments in the United States (BFA, 30 min.). Discusses the evolution of the city manager, mayor-council forms.
Making Government Work (PBS, 60 min.). A visit to Chicago with Bill Moyers to investigate solutions to inner city problems.

Addresses of Film Distributors

ABC	American Broadcasting Company, 1330 Ave. of the Americas, New York, NY 10019
AEI	American Enterprise Institute, 4720–A Boston Way, Lanham, MD 20706
ALA	Institute of Higher Education Research & Services, P. O. Box 6293, University, AL 35486
APSR	American Political Science Association, 1527 New Hampshire Ave., N.W., Washington, DC 20036
ASOCF	Associate Films, 600 Madison Ave., New York, NY 10022
BFA	BFA Educational Media, 2211 Michigan Avenue, Santa Monica, CA 90404
BRIT	Encyclopedia Britannica Educational Corp., Dept. 10-A, 425 North Michigan Avenue, Chicago, IL 60611
BROOK	Brookings Institute, 1775 Mass. Ave., N.W., Washington, DC 20036
CAF	Current Affairs Films, 24 Danbury Rd., Wilton, CT 06897
CBS	CBS-TV, Columbia Broadcasting System, 383 Madison Ave., New York, NY 10017
CDI	Center for Defense Information, 122 Maryland Ave., N.E., Washington, DC 20002
CFM	Canadian Film-Makers Distribution Center, Toronto, Canada
CH	Churchill Films, 12210 Nebraska Avenue, Los Angeles, CA 90025
CIN	Cinema 5–16mm, 595 Madison Ave., New York, NY 10022
COLP	Columbia Pictures Corp., 711 5th Ave., New York, NY 10022
COR	Coronet/MTI Films and Videos, 108 Wilmot Road, Deerfield, IL 60015
CRM	CRM Productions, 2999 Overland Ave., Suite 211, Los Angeles, CA 90064
DMM	Doubleday Multimedia, 1371 Reynolds Ave., Santa Ana, CA 92705
EMI	EMI, Box 4272, Madison, WI 53711
ENV	Envision Corporation, 323 Newbury Street, Boston, MA 02115
FLINC	Films, Inc., 733 Green Bay Road, Wilmette, IL 60091
GMP	Green Mountain Post Films, P.O. Box 229, Turners Falls, MA 01376
GRP	Great Plains National ITV Library, P.O. Box 80669, Lincoln, NE 68501

HEARST	Hearst Metronome News, 450 W. 56th Street, New York, NY 10019
H2M	H2M Productions, American Educational Films, 9879 Santa Monica Blvd., Beverly Hills, CA 90212
Humanities	Films for the Humanities, P.O. Box 2053, Princeton, NJ 08543-2053
Ideal	Ideal Pictures, 1712 Illinois St., Indianapolis, IN 46202
Insight	Insight Media, 121 W. 85th Street, New York, NY 10024
INT	IEP, Dun-Donnelley Publishing Corporation, 666 Fifth Ave., New York, NY 10019
IU	Indiana University, Audio-Visual Center, Bloomington, IN 47401
KRSK	Krusek Films, 1045 Prairie St., Beloit, WI 53511
MLKP	Martin Luther King Productions, 309 East 90th St., New York, NY 10028
NATG	National Geographic Educational Services, 17th and M Streets, NW, Washington, DC 20010
NBC	NBC-TV, National Broadcasting Co., 30 Rockefeller Plaza, New York, NY 10020
NET	Address inquiries to IU.
NFBC	National Film Board of Canada, 1251 Avenue of the Americas, 16th Floor, New York, NY 10019
OX	Oxford Films, 1136 North Las Palmas Ave., Hollywood, CA 90038
PBS	PBS Video, 1320 Braddock Place, Alexandria, VA 22314-1698
PHM	Prentice-Hall Media, 150 White Plains Road, Tarrytown, NY 10591
PIN	Public Issues Network, Ninth Floor, 11 Dupont Circle, N.W., Washington, DC 20036
RB	Red Ball Films, Inc., Box 298 Village Station, New York, NY 10014
STER	Sterling Educational Films, 241 E. 34th Street, New York, NY 10016
T-L	Ambrose Video Publishing, 381 Park Avenue South, Suite 1001, New York, NY 10016
TSK	Thomas Klise Productions, P.O. Box 3418 Peoria, IL 61614
UCAL	University of California Extension Media Center, 2223 Fulton Street, Berkeley, CA 94720
WEF	Wayne Ewing Films, P.O. Box 32269, Washington, DC 20007
WLC	Washington Learning Center, 100 Park Ave., New York, NY 10017
Xerox	Xerox Films, P.O. Box 1540, Rochester, NY 14600
ZIP	Zipporah Films, 54 Lewis Wharf, Boston, MA 02110

Video Programs in American Government

Many media firms are emphasizing videotape programs relevant to the study of American government. The following list is a representative sampling of (relevant and recent) video materials now available to the instructor. (Most of the titles were produced in the 1980s. The media-oriented instructor may wish to contact the companies listed below in order to obtain catalogs or related information so that he or she can correlate chapters in the Wilson text with the appropriate video presentations. Addresses and telephone numbers are provided in most cases.

1. CORONET FEATURE VIDEO
   Simon and Schuster School Group
   108 Wilmot Rd.
   Deerfield, IL 60015

   Toll-Free: 1-800-621-2131
   In Illinois and Alaska: Call Collect, 312-940-1260

Sampling of Video Programs from Coronet

America and the World Since World War II, 1945–1985, four volumes, each 52–54 minutes. An ABC News presentation that chronicles the changes in America's international relations during the Cold War era. Narrated by Peter Jennings and Ted Koppel. An excellent historical narrative.

How We Got the Vote, 52 min. Jean Stapleton narrates the history of women's suffrage in America. Relevant to the Wilson chapter on Civil Rights.

Vietnam: Chronicle of War, 89 min. A documentary covering the origin, progress, and impact of the Vietnam War as well as the war's impact upon American society.

The 21-Inch World, 28 min. Explores the effects of television upon society. Would fit in well with Wilson's media chapter.

The Many Modes of Media, 28 min. Strong on the history of the mass media.

A Case of Libel, 92 min. A courtroom drama that makes some telling points about freedom of the press. Relevant to the text's chapter on civil liberties.

Government and Its Influences, 28 min. Explores the role that government plays in its regulation of the economy. This 1985 production can be related to the text's policy chapters.

Independence, 30 min. This video traces the events that precipitated the signing of the Declaration of Independence. A good review for students who may need to have their historical perspectives strengthened.

The Missiles of October, 150 min. A recreation of the history of the Cuban Missile Crisis. Relevant to the chapters on the presidency, bureaucracy, and foreign policy.

Roots of Democracy, 60 min. A study of the beliefs of the Founding Fathers and how those beliefs were reflected in the U. S. Constitution and the Bill of Rights.

NOTE: All Coronet titles are available only in the one-half inch videocassette format.

2. CLOSE-UP FOUNDATION
   Educational Media
   Department G-1
   1235 Jefferson Davis Highway
   Arlington, Virginia 22202

   Toll-Free: 1-800-336-5479

Sampling of Video Programs from Close-Up

A Look at U. S. Foreign Policy, 60 min. Former Secretary of State Alexander Haig talks to educators about a variety of U. S. foreign policy initiatives. Drawn from the C-SPAN cable network.

The Intelligence Community and Foreign Policy, 60 min. Former CIA director Stansfield Turner answers questions from students on the CIA's role in the policy process and the difficulties of covert operations. (C-SPAN)

NOTE: A number of other topics are drawn from the C-SPAN series, including 30-60 min. programs on defense, civil rights, Congress, the arms race, crime, and so forth. The instructor should contact the Close-Up Foundation for further details.

The Constitution: A Framework to Govern a Nation, 30 minutes. Explores the relevance of the Constitution to contemporary America.

The Changing American Presidency, 30 min. Former special assistant to LBJ, Jack Valenti, analyzes recent trends that have influenced the conduct and operation of the presidency.

Congress: Representing the Will of the People, 30 min. The powers of Congress are clarified.

The Supreme Court: Guardian of the Constitution, 30 min. CBS correspondent Fred Graham discusses Supreme Court rulings in the areas of capital punishment, search and seizure, and abortion.

Lobbying and Political Action Committees, 60 min. Good analysis of PACs and their impact upon the integrity of the political process.

Voting: A Right or a Responsibility? 30 min. Spirited debate over the issue.

The Media and the Election Process, 30 min. Self-explanatory.

Political Imagemaking, 60 min. Some interesting thoughts are expressed by political consultants on how to "sell" candidates to the voters.

The Media and the Presidency, 60 minutes. Tape reveals why some presidents are more effective in "using" the media than other chief executives.

The U. S. Constitution and a Balanced Budget, 60 minutes. The issue is debated in a clear and spirited fashion.

3. CATTICUS CORPORATION
   2600 10th Street
   Berkeley, CA 94710

   Phone: 415-548-0854

   The First 50 Years: Reflections on U.S.—Soviet Relations, 58 min. This is an outstanding program, comprehensively describing the relationship between the two superpowers from 1933 to the present. (It was considered the best independent televison production of 1984.) The superpowers' interactions are described by such foreign policy luminaries as Averell Harriman, Thomas J. Watson, Jr., Walter Stoessel, George Kennan, Richard Nixon, and Marshall Shulman. The tape is hosted by former *New York Times* Moscow correspondent Harrison Salisbury. An instructor who wishes to supplement the Wilson text's chapter on foreign policy with effective visual reinforcement would do well to consider this video.

4. FILMS INCORPORATED
   5547 N. Ravenswood Avenue
   Chicago, Illinois 60640-1199

   Toll-Free: 1-800-323-4222, Ext. 43
   In Illinois: 312-878-2600

Sampling of Video Programs from Films Incorporated

The Constitution: That Delicate Balance—13 one-hour programs. The series covers such controversial constitutionally-related issues as capital punishment, abortion, executive privilege and national security, etc.

Congress: We the People—26 programs, 30 min. each. The entire series represents "an inside view of the United States Congress and the complex range of individuals, organizations and processes it embodies" (quoted from catalog). All of the programs are hosted by NBC correspondent Edwin Newman and were taped at the United States Congress. While the instructor of American government will not be able to use all 26 tapes due to time constraints, he or she can perhaps select those programs most relevant to instructional or methodological needs.

The Decision to Drop the Bomb—Truman and Hiroshima, 82 min. A good "case study" tape on presidential decision-making. Applicable to text chapters on the presidency and foreign policy.

The War Game, 49 minutes. Simulates the after-effects of a nuclear attack.

Beyond Deterrence, 50 min. Discusses Reagan and SDI. Good for military policy chapter in the Wilson text.

Books Under Fire, 56 min. Deals with book banning. Relevant to the theme of civil liberties.

The Economics, USA series, 28 programs, each 28 min. Program 6 on Fiscal Policy, 9 on the Federal Reserve, 12 on Federal Deficits, 13 on Monetary Policy, and 28 on International Trade may be especially valuable.

America's Embattled Economy, Parts I and II, two tapes, each 60 min. Both tapes trace the role of the American government in managing the national economy from FDR to the present. Good for the economic policy sections of the Wilson text.

The Speaker from Texas, 58 min. Speaker Jim Wright of Texas discusses his job.

A Trillion for Defense: What Have We Bought? 50 min. A Tom Brokaw–NBC news special on the need to prioritize defense expenditures.

Moyers—In Search of the Constitution, eleven 58-min. programs. Includes interviews and conversations with Supreme Court justices, historians, scholars, and citizens whose lives have been directly involved with constitutional issues.

NOTE: Most Films Inc. tapes are available in one-half inch or three-quarter inch sizes.

5. FILMS FOR THE HUMANITIES, INC.
Box 2053
Princeton, N. J. 08543

Sampling of Video Programs from Films for the Humanities, Inc.

We the People—four tapes, each one 56 min. A series designed to celebrate the 200th anniversary of the Constitution and produced by KQED-TV, the San Francisco Public Broadcasting station, and the American Bar Association. Hosted by Peter Jennings, the programs cover first-amendment freedoms, the issue of equality, the rights of the accused vs. the power of the police, and the dispersion of powers in a constitutional system.

6. WQED/Pittsburgh
4802 Fifth Avenue
Pittsburgh, PA 15213

Equal Justice Under Law, six 30-min. tapes. Produced by WQED and presented on Public Television with funding from the Judicial Conference of the United States. Four landmark cases are recreated—*Marbury vs. Madison, Gibbons vs. Ogden, McCulloch vs. Maryland*, and The Trial of Aaron Burr. E. G. Marshall is the narrator. Relevant to a number of chapters in the Wilson text.

7. E. C. GRACE AND ASSOCIATES
207 Calle Serena
San Clemente, CA 92672

Toll-Free: 800-624-3074
In California: 714-492-2462

Sampling of Video Programs from E. C. Grace and Associates

Korea: The Forgotten War, 92 min. Robert Stack is the narrator, describing the conduct, operations, and lessons of the Korean War. Excellent for American government instructors who wish to discuss American foreign policy and the impact of a limited war upon the domestic political system.

Vietnam—The Ten Thousand Day War, six taped volumes, ranging from 98 to 147 minutes each. Complete history, covering both the domestic and global implications of the war. Particularly good is Volume 4, covering the political effects of Tet. Relevant for text chapters on foreign and military policies, public opinion, and the presidency.

Television's Vietnam, 120 min. Narrated by Charlton Heston. Involves a probing look at the errors of journalists recorded during the Vietnam War and the impact of those errors on public opinion at home.

King, 254 min. Tapes cover Martin Luther King's life and his leadership of the civil rights revolution in America.

8. GUIDANCE ASSOCIATES
Communications Park, Box 3000
Mount Kisco, New York 10549-0900

Toll-Free: 800-431-2266

Sampling of Video Programs from Guidance Associates

The Aging of America, 30 min. A CNN special report that raises the social welfare problems posed by the growing over-65 segment of the U. S. population.

Target America, 30 min. CNN report on terrorism, with special emphasis upon how the American government is trying to handle the problem.

UN: Divided it Stands, 30 min. CNN report on the 40th anniversary of U. N. founding and the role of the United States in the world organization.

NOTE: Guidance Associates has a large number of politically-relevant motion pictures on tape, including *All the President's Men, Animal Farm, Inherit the Wind, Independence*, etc.

Capitalism and Communism, four 60-min. tapes. Effective comparison between the two economic systems, but also has a strong emphasis upon the political economy as well.

9. AUDIO-VISUAL CENTER, INDIANA U.
   Bloomington, Indiana 47401-5901

   Toll-Free: 800-552-8620 (except Indiana)

Sampling of Video Programs from IU

Last Reflections on a War, 44 min. An examination of the war through the experiences of journalist Bernard B. Fall. While produced in 1967, some of Fall's doubts about whether the war could be won were remarkably prophetic.

Essay on Watergate, 59 min. Bill Moyers reviews the impact of the scandal and includes some of the taped testimony. Certainly relevant to chapters on Congress and the presidency in the Wilson text.

You've Come a Long Way, Maybe? 55 min. Covers some of the major cases involving the controversial concept of "comparable worth." Clearly applicable to text chapter on Civil Rights.

10. PBS VIDEO
    Public Broadcasting Service
    1320 Braddock Place
    Alexandria, VA 22314-1698

    Toll-Free: 800-424-7963, Ext. 4101

    Eyes on the Prize—America's Civil Rights Years, six tapes, 60 minutes each. An award-winning, public television series that covers the civil rights period from 1954-1965. The series was awarded the 1987 Best Program of the Year, Best Documentary of the Year, by the Television Critics Association. Invaluable for the instructor who wishes to bring depth to his/her presentation of civil rights in the American government classroom.

11. PENNSYLVANIA STATE UNIVERSITY
    Audio-Visual Services
    Special Services Building
    University Park, PA 16802

    Telephone: 814-865-6314

NOTE: Pennsylvania State University has well over 1300 films and videos in its catalog, with about 250 programs acquired since 1980 in the fields of politics and political history. The instructor may wish to obtain the current catalog.

Sampling of Video Programs from Pennsylvania State University

The Constitution: That Delicate Balance—see Films Incorporated for description. The 13 one-hour programs can also be ordered from Penn State.

Labor-Management Relations in Steel: Conflict or Cooperation, 26 min. Labor-management relationships are tied to changes in the political environment. Good for Wilson chapters on interest groups and the economy.

Old Folks at Home, 29 min. Outlines some of the problems of growing old in the 1980s and includes interviews with elderly citizens, government officials, etc. Good for Wilson's social welfare chapter or possibly interest group material.

The Real War in Space, 87 min. Examines the research and development of space-based weapons for both the U. S. and the Soviet Union. Would be applicable to the Wilson chapter on national defense and military spending.

TV Democracy, 29 min. This production argues that political campaigns and the daily activities of government have undergone radical changes due to televison. Newsman Dan Rather is a participant.

NOTE: The instructor should consider three other important video sources:

12. UNIVERSITY OF CALIFORNIA EXTENSION MEDIA CENTER
    2223 Fulton Street
    Berkeley, CA 94720

13. CRM/McGRAW HILL FILMS
    110 15th Street
    Del Mar, CA 92014

14. ENCYCLOPEDIA BRITANNICA FILMS, INC.
    1822 Pickwick Avenue
    Glenview, Illinois 60025

PART ONE

The American System

1

The Study of American Government

Overview and Objectives

The purpose of this chapter is to give the student a preview of the major questions to be asked throughout the textbook, as well as to introduce some of the key terms in the basic vocabulary of American politics. After reading and reviewing the material in this chapter the student should be able to do each of the following:

1. List the two basic questions to be asked about American (or any other) government and show that they are distinct questions.

2. Explain what is meant by power in general human terms, and by political power in particular, relating the latter to authority, legitimacy, and democracy in the context of American government.

3. Distinguish among the three concepts of democracy mentioned in the chapter, explaining in which of three senses the textbook refers to American government as "democratic."

4. Differentiate between majoritarian politics and elitist politics, explaining the four major theories on the latter.

5. Explain how the phenomenon of political change tends to make political scientists cautious in stating how politics works, or what values dominate it.

Chapter Outline with Keyed-in Resources

I. What is political power? (THEME A: POLITICAL POWER AND AUTHORITY)
   A. Two great questions about politics
      1. Who governs: those who govern will affect us
      2. To what ends: tells how government affects our lives
      3. The text focuses on who governs and, in answering this question, looks at how the government makes decisions on a variety of issues
   B. Power
      1. Definition: the ability of one person to cause another person to act in accordance with the first person's intentions
      2. Text's concern: power as it is used to affect who will hold government office and how government will behave
      3. Authority: the right to use power; not all who exercise political power have it
      4. Legitimacy: what makes a law or constitution a source of right

A belief in the legitimacy of the political system should not be confused with trust in those running the government. In a 1989 Gallup poll, only 16 percent of Americans believed members of Congress have a "very high" degree of honesty, ranking behind lawyers at 18 percent.

   5. Struggles over what makes authority legitimate
   6. Necessity to be in some sense "democratic" in the United States today

II. What is democracy? (THEME B: DEMOCRACY AND INDIVIDUAL CHOICE)
   A. Where the "true interests" of the people are served, whether or not those people affect the decision making (democratic centralism)
      1. China
      2. Cuba
      3. European, Asian, Latin American dictatorships

Jeane Kirkpatrick, former U.S. ambassador to the United Nations, caused a controversy when she argued that a distinction should be made between authoritarian and totalitarian regimes. Authoritarian regimes are paternalistic in nature and serve as a transition for countries not prepared for democracy. Totalitarian regimes are simply dictatorships. Thus the United States should not condemn governments by rulers like Marcos and Noriega.

   B. Aristotelian "rule of the many" (participatory democracy)
      1. Fifth-century B.C. Greek city-state
      2. New England town meeting
      3. Community control in self-governing neighborhood
      4. Citizen participation in formulating programs

Switzerland is a rare example of a country that in certain instances is governed by a form of direct democracy. The country permits a national referendum on a law of parliament if a hundred thousand citizens petition the government. This system is not wholly satisfactory. Each referendum costs the government about $3 million; over thirty such votes occur annually, with turnouts of as low as one-third of voters.

   C. Acquisition of power by leaders via competitive elections (representative democracy)
      1. Sometimes disapprovingly referred to as the elitist theory
      2. Justifications of representative democracy
         a. Direct democracy is impractical
         b. The people make unwise decisions based on fleeting emotions

III. Direct v. representative democracy
   A. Text uses the term "democracy" to refer to representative democracy
      1. Constitution does not contain word "democracy" but "republican form of government"
      2. Representative democracy requires leadership competition if system is to work

B. Push-button democracy
    1. Many Americans dissatisfied with representative democracy
        a. Responds too slowly
        b. Serves special interests
        c. Is unresponsive to majority opinion
    2. Push-button democracy an alternative: experts debate on TV and people vote by phone
    3. Push-button democracy may not be better
        a. Quick decisions can be bad
        b. Special interests can spend heavily to influence voters in direct democracy
        c. Basic liberties should not hinge on majority vote
IV. How is power distributed in a democracy? (THEME C: POWER DISTRIBUTION IN AMERICAN GOVERNMENT)
    A. Majoritarian politics
        1. Leaders constrained to follow wishes of the people very closely
        2. Applies when issues are simple, clear, and feasible
    B. Elitism
        1. Rule by identifiable group of persons who possess a disproportionate share of political power
        2. Theories on political elites
            a. Marxism: government merely a reflection of underlying economic forces
            b. C. Wright Mills: power elite composed of corporate leaders, generals, politicians
            c. Max Weber: bureaucracies based on expertise, specialized competence
            d. Pluralist view: no single elite has monopoly on power; hence must bargain and compromise

It is interesting to note that a person like Henry Kissinger does not fit any of the descriptions of a member of the political elite prepounded by the four major theories on the topic.

    C. Cynical view that politics is self-seeking
        1. Good policies possible from bad motives
        2. Self-interest an incomplete guide to actions
            a. AFL-CIO and civil rights
        3. Alexis de Tocqueville on America
V. Political change (THEME D: POLITICAL CHANGE IN THE 1990s)
    A. Necessary to refer to history frequently since no single theory adequate
        1. Government today influenced by yesterday
        2. Government today still evolving and responds to changing beliefs
    B. Politics about "the public interest," not just "who gets what"

Discussions of political change point out the dangers in not responding to changes in society. However, theories of political violence also underscore the dangers in making changes. James Davis notes that political violence is most common when periods of rapid development are followed by sharp reversals; Bernard Gorfman and Edward Muller discovered that any change, even a positive one, is correlated with political violence.

VI. Finding out who governs
    A. Often we give partial or contingent answers
    B. Preferences vary, and so does politics
    C. Politics cannot be equated with laws on the books
    D. Sweeping claims are to be avoided

Important Terms

*authority The right to use power.

*bureaucrats Appointed officials who operate government agencies and large corporations.

bureaucratic theory A theory that appointed civil servants make the key governing decisions

*democracy A word used to describe at least three different political systems that each embody the principle of popular rule, if only in the interests of the people.

*democratic centralism A form of democracy in which the true interests of the masses were discovered through discussion within the Communist party, and then decisions were made under central leadership to serve those interests.

*direct (participatory) democracy A form of democracy in which all, or most, of the citizenry participate directly by either holding office or making policy.

*elite An identifiable group of persons who possess a disproportionate share of some valued resource.

elitist theory A theory that a few top leaders make the key decisions without reference to popular desires.

*legitimacy What makes a law or constitution a source of right.

*majoritarian politics A political system in which leaders are constrained to follow closely the wishes of the people.

Marxist theory The ideology espoused by Karl Marx which holds that government is a reflection of economic forces, primarily based on the pattern of ownership of the means of production.

*pluralist theory A theory that holds that political resources are sufficiently divided among different kinds of elites, giving each relevant interest the chance to influence the outcome of decisions.

political power Power used to determine who will hold government office and how the government will behave.

*power The ability of one person to cause another person to act in accordance with the first person's intentions.

power elite A political theory espoused by C. Wright Mills which holds that a nongovernment elite makes most political decisions. This elite is composed of three groups—corporate leaders, top military officers, and key political leaders.

*representative democracy A political system in which political power is conferred on those selected by voters in competitive elections.

Max Weber A German historian and sociologist who criticized the theories of Karl Marx, arguing that all institutions have fallen under the control of large bureaucracies whose expertise is essential to the management of contemporary affairs.

Theme A Political Power and Authority

Summary

The two great questions about politics are, "Who governs?" and "To what ends?" The question of who governs is the question of who has *power*, which is defined as the ability of one person to cause another person to act in accordance with the first person's intentions. Power is found in all human relationships; however, this text is primarily concerned with its exercise in the American federal government.

People who exercise power may also have *authority*—the right to use power. Some authority is *formal authority*—the right to use power vested in a governmental office.

Power and authority must be based on *legitimacy*—what makes a law or constitution a source of right. Power, authority, and legitimacy can become divorced from one another, resulting in a government that rules by the force of brutality. The developments in Eastern Europe provide a relevant illustration of how such dysfunctional governments can survive despite the absence of support. Thus legitimacy does not automatically flow from power and authority.

Discussion Questions

1. The text notes that representative democracy requires that certain conditions be satisfied: freedom of speech and press, freedom to organize, fair access to political resources, respect for others, and a belief in the legitimacy of the political system. These conditions have one thing in common—they are all political in nature. Seymour Martin Lipset, by contrast, argues that democracy cannot survive without economic prosperity. Consider how the economic dimension fits into notions of how democracy works. Do any genuine democracies exist in economically deprived countries today? Was America's democratic form of government threatened during the Great Depression of the 1930s?

2. Representative democracies are considered "legitimate" governments because their policies are based on the will of the people. Is this statement true or merely a myth? Consider the following. First, the American public is less involved in elections than are voters in European nations. Only 59 percent of Americans on average vote in presidential elections. Participation is far higher in European countries: Holland (95 percent), Germany (87 percent), Norway (81 percent), France (79 percent), and Britain (77 percent). The text concludes that representative democracy requires competitive elections. Is American government then somehow less legitimate? Second, the American public has poor knowledge of its government. For example, 81 percent cannot indicate how their representative in Congress voted on any bill in the last two years; 46 percent cannot name their district representative in the House; 21 percent cannot even name the vice president correctly. Does this level of ignorance suggest that the American people are satisfied with the government's policies or that the government's "authority" is meaningless?

Data and Perspectives for Analysis

Read the questions in the table below to your class and ask students to write their answers on a separate sheet of paper. Tabulate the results.

Which Governmental Powers Are Legitimate?

Some people say that the federal government has to have certain powers to protect the interests of the country as a whole, while others say that the rights of the individual always come first. Which of the following do you think the government in Washington should be able to do, and which do you think it should not do?

Governmental Power	Should Be Able to Do	Should Not Be Able to Do	Don't Know
Limit the amount of gas you can use during a crisis	63%	33%	4%
Require everyone to carry national identification cards	36	56	8
Regulate local business to meet job safety standards	68	25	7
Look into your background if you apply for unemployment benefits, welfare, or a passport	71	24	5
Require pollution equipment on new cars even if it increases the price	58	32	10
Wiretap phones for national security reasons	44	49	7

SOURCE: 1976 American National Election Study, Center for Political Studies, University of Michigan.

1. Is the class more or less likely than the American public in general to accord legitimacy to various sorts of government activity? Why?

2. This poll was taken more than fifteen years ago. Would the American public today feel differently on any of these issues? Does the concept of legitimacy vary over time? If so, does this mean the Constitution is outdated?

Theme B Democracy and Individual Choice

Summary

Democracy is a word used in at least three ways in the discussion of government. Authoritarian governments define democracy as a system that represents the "true interests" of the people, whether or not they directly affect those interests. Another interpretation approximates Aristotle's definition of the "rule of the many." This system, also called *direct* or *participatory democracy*, was most practical in the Greek polis, and survives in the modern *New England town meeting*. But some have argued that *community control* and the *referendum* allow a substantial measure of direct democracy in modern political systems.

Finally, *representative democracy* involves leaders acquiring power by means of a competitive struggle for the people's vote. Sometimes called disparagingly the *elitist* theory of democracy, this sort of government is supported by those who feel that it is impractical for the public to make policy across a vast array of issues and that people often decide large issues on the basis of fleeting passions. For this sort of government to function, it is necessary that there be competing elites and free communication.

Discussion Questions

1. Why shouldn't democratic decision making be extended to all spheres of life—for example, to the workplace, to the government of colleges and universities, and to the marketplace through consumer cooperatives?

2. Mikhail Gorbachev, when president of the former Soviet Union, argued that American democracy defines human rights in terms of political liberties, such as freedom of speech and religion. These liberties, according to Gorbachev, mean nothing in the absence of adequate housing, medical care, and employment. Is Gorbachev's criticism of American democracy valid? Is it more important to survive or to live happily?

3. Democracy, Winston Churchill once said, is the worst form of government, except for all the others. Americans tend to think of democracy as the only legitimate form of government. Yet two questions on individual choice must be asked. First, how democratic is the United States? For example, over 70 percent of the American people favor allowing prayer in the public schools and over 65 percent favor handgun control, yet Congress has failed to respond to this overwhelming public sentiment. Second, should the majority always rule? Tocqueville feared that majority rule could culminate in tyranny: "if ever the free institutions of America are destroyed, that event may be attributed to the omnipotence of the majority, which may at some future time urge the minorities to desperation and oblige them to recourse to physical force." How should minority rights be balanced against majority rule?

Data and Perspectives for Analysis

Americans tend to consider the former Soviet system oppressive and not committed to the protection of human rights. We assume that the absence of democracy leads the Soviet people to despise their government. Surprisingly, the attitudes of Soviet citizens toward their government are similar to those of American citizens. Present the following survey results to your students:

	New York	Moscow
How much of the time do you think you can trust the national government . . . to do what is right . . . ?		
Always	6%	37%
Most of the time	34	38
Sometimes	51	15
Never	7	2
Other/not sure	2	8
Average people don't have much say about what the government does.		
Agree	52	43
Disagree	46	46
Other/not sure	2	11
Public officials don't care much what average people think.		
Agree	55	46
Disagree	40	41
Other/not sure	4	13

Source: *The Polling Report*, April 24, 1989.

1. What reasons can your class give for the responses of Soviet citizens? Do the results support the text's assertion that communist democracies aim to satisfy the "true interests" of the people?

2. Here are some questions to prod your students with:

   Were the Soviet citizens who participated in this poll afraid to answer truthfully? If so, were American citizens also afraid to answer truthfully since their answers are similar?
   Were Soviet citizens unaware of what their government was doing?
   Was President Gorbachev's program of *glasnost* (openness) an admission that the Soviet system was not open to the people?
   Why aren't the American citizens surveyed more proud of their system if it is so open?

Theme C   Power "Distribution" in American Government

Instructor References

Thomas R. Dye, *Who's Running America?* 5th ed. Englewood Cliffs, NJ: Prentice-Hall, 1990. A comprehensive treatment that incisively describes the structure of institutional elites and how those elites wield power in American society.

Richard Gillam, ed., *Power in Postwar America*. Boston: Little, Brown, 1971. Highly useful collection of articles and excerpts from the debate between elitists and pluralists. Features Dahl, Mills, Domhoff, Rose.

Fred H. Willhoite, *Power and Government: An Introduction to Politics*. Pacific Grove, CA: Brooks-Cole, 1988. Chapters 1–3 cover the relationship of power to political ideas and competition strategies.

Summary

In *majoritarian* politics leaders are forced to follow the preferences of citizens very closely. On the vast majority of issues, however, political elites determine the outcome. An *elite* is an identifiable group that possesses a disproportionate share of some valued resource—in this case, political power.

There are four major theories that purport to explain the actions of political elites. The *Marxist* theory holds that government is merely a reflection of underlying economic forces. Whichever class dominates the economy controls the government; therefore, the interests of large corporations are particularly powerful in American government. A second, related view holds that elites outside government, in addition to corporate leaders, have power. C. Wright Mills expressed this view in his book *The Power Elite*. A third theory holds that appointed officials who operate government and large corporations—*bureaucrats*—have come to dominate. Max Weber, the foremost exponent of this view, felt the power of bureaucrats would become "overtowering." The fourth, *pluralist* view, holds that political resources are so widely scattered that no single group can dominate most, or even much, of the political process.

It should not be assumed that any political outcome is merely the result of the self-interest of some group or other. The support of the AFL-CIO for civil rights legislation, for example, cannot be explained by organizational self-interest. Overly simplistic thinking cannot explain political changes such as the unprecedented growth of federal power after 1932 and the attempt to cut back on that power starting in 1981. Also, any particular outcome (for example, consumer-protection laws) may result from any of several different processes. In short, policy shifts reflect responses to changing beliefs about government's role as well as the evolution of political institutions and elites over time.

For these reasons, no single theory of political power is capable of adequately explaining the decision-making process. Even the factors that identify the political elite change over time. Land ownership, once so critical to the exercise of influence, is largely irrelevant today. Thus no stable pattern of decision making will survive as valid for long.

Discussion Questions

1. The text implies that majoritarian politics cannot apply to more than a handful of political issues. Is this not equivalent to saying that only a few issues can be decided in a genuinely democratic way?

2. Assign the material in the *Student Handbook* from the "Applying What You've Learned" exercise. Under what theory of political elites (Marx, Weber, Mills, or pluralist) does the model of Thomas Dye fit?

3. If political elites influence the preferences of public opinion, can't majoritarian politics and elite theories of political power coexist without contradicting one another?

Data and Perspectives for Analysis

The power of the "military-industrial complex" is a much debated topic. The term originated in 1961 in the farewell address of President Eisenhower, who warned that in the councils of government, we must guard against the acquisition of unwarranted influence, whether sought or unsought, by the military-industrial complex. The potential for the disastrous rise of misplaced power exists and will persist. We must never let the weight of this combination endanger our liberties or democratic processes.

Since Eisenhower's assertion, critics have pointed to the MIC as a conspiratorial alliance of the military, defense contractors, members of Congress with military bases in their districts, labor unions (whose members find employment and paychecks in defense industries), universities engaged in military research, and diverse state and local economic interests that generally benefit from the money spent on defense. To radicals, these elements are all engaged in a "conspiracy" to increase defense budgets to the detriment of social programs, to promote the war threat, and to acquire a stranglehold on the national economy.

Does the MIC truly exist? Does the MIC dominate in the areas of both political and economic power? Arguments surrounding the MIC can be gleaned from John Spanier's *Games Nations Play* (New York: Congressional Quarterly Press, 1987, pp. 505–510) as well as from some other sources, such as Thomas R. Dye's *Who's Running America? The Bush Era*

(Englewood Cliffs, NJ: Prentice-Hall, 1990, pp. 101–103). You can present the following pros and cons to your students.

Assertions Supporting Dominance of the MIC

1. Defense spending is beneficial for the entire economy. It supports valuable research and also boosts employment and profits.
2. The Defense Department is the primary employer, contractor, purchaser, owner, and spender in the nation. The enormous economic bulk of the Pentagon and its allies translates into equally effective political power.
3. There is strong evidence of personnel "crossover" among the discrete elements of the MIC; considerable numbers of retired military personnel find jobs on defense corporation payrolls, and ex-congressmen serve as lobbyists for these very same defense firms. Similarly, industrialists are frequently recruited to serve in the DOD and other related MIC agencies in the federal government. (Robert McNamara is one example.)
4. It is logical that members of Congress will vote to support the development of new weapons systems and the building of defense bases in their district (or state, in the case of a U.S. senator), because the jobs and profits that are generated translate into good constituent relationships and enhance the prospect of reelection.

Assertions Rejecting Dominance of the MIC

1. As Dye points out, the largest industrial corporations in the country do not depend heavily on defense contracts. Also, if the MIC is so powerful, why does the stock market seemingly rise with increased prospects for peace and fall when war clouds loom?
2. The percentage of GNP spent on defense declined through much of the 1970s. Also, as Spanier asserts, defense-related employment (until Reagan) was "about half" the 10 percent it had reached during the 1950s.
3. Spanier asserts that "despite the widely accepted radical wisdom that war production is necessary for a capitalist economy to maintain high employment, a war economy in fact slows economic growth and reduces the capacity to generate prosperity and jobs." In addition, defense spending creates fewer jobs than similar amounts of money spent in civilian fields. Thus $1 billion spent on defense created 51,000 jobs, whereas the same $1 billion spent in the civilian sector would have created "61,000 jobs in public housing, 88,000 jobs in Veterans Administration health care, and 136,000 jobs if spent on manpower training." (Spanier, p. 507)
4. As Dye points out, Brookings Institute studies show that crossover personnel account for a relatively small percentage of top executives in the DOD or the large defense corporations.
5. If the MIC is so powerful, how does one explain cancellation of key military programs (the ABM, B-1 Bomber) or the creation of some arms-control agreements (SALT 1)?

Discussion Questions

1. The MIC has two components, the military and industry. Of the two components, which is the more influential on military purchases? What resources does the military possess to influence public policy?
2. Can the MIC influence policy outside the area of national defense? If so, what areas? If not, what does this suggest about the power of the MIC?
3. President Bush announced in 1990 a 25 percent reduction in military personnel by 1995. Could the MIC have intervened to alter this policy? Are there any reasons why the MIC wouldn't act?

Theme D   Political Change in the 1990s

Summary

Political changes are brought on by changing beliefs about what the government is supposed to do. This question involves identifying the dominant political problem of the time because, in the end, it is the government's responsibility to provide a remedy. To identify a problem, however, is not to solve it. When change is deemed necessary, a direction still needs to be determined. The only appropriate solution is one that serves the pubic interest. This task is the object of politics.

Discussion Questions

1. The dominant political problem of the 1960s was probably the inequities in civil rights. Did the civil rights movement change people's attitudes, or did changing attitudes about race relations produce the movement? In other words, what came first—the movement or a change in attitude?

2. President Reagan attempted to curtail the power of the federal government. Did this cutback in governmental power stall changes in the 1980s? Must the government always be the agent of political change? For example, could the civil rights movement have been successful without the help of key Supreme Court decisions?

Data and Perspectives for Analysis

Newsweek magazine's last issue of 1990 (December 31) attempted to identify the major problems of the 1990s and to forecast probable outcomes. "To survive these troubled times," the magazine concluded, "we first have to understand them."

First, ask your class to identify the dominant political problems of our time. Second, read the problems isolated in the *Newsweek* article and have students explain why their selection of issues differed from those of the magazine.

Problem	*Prediction*
Force	There will be an army coup in a slimmed-down Soviet Union. And Europe will see more bloodshed than it has seen since World War II.
Leadership	President Bush will face a revolt within the GOP that won't derail his renomination but could weaken him.
Quotas	With a recession deepening the resentments of white swing voters, quotas will be the hot-button issue of the 1992 presidential race.
Survival	More and more American cities will mandate separation of trash for recycling.
Education	A growing movement to extend the 180-day school year will set off bruising battles at the local level.
Censorship	Hollywood will trade in more of its megabuck violence for hugely profitable heartwarmers like *Ghost*.

2

The Constitution

Overview and Objectives

The purpose of this chapter is to introduce students to the historical context within which the United States Constitution was written, and in particular to the colonists' quest for liberties they felt had been denied under British rule. After reading and reviewing the material in this chapter the student should be able to do each of the following:

1. Compare the American and French revolutions of the same era with respect to the ideals that motivated each.

2. Explain the notion of "higher law" by which the colonists felt they were entitled to certain "natural rights." List these rights.

3. Discuss the Declaration of Independence as a lawyer's brief prepared for court argument of a case.

4. Compare the basis on which the colonists felt a government could be legitimate with the basis of legitimacy as assumed in monarchies like that in Great Britain at the time.

5. List and discuss the shortcomings of government under the Articles of Confederation.

6. Discuss the backgrounds of the writers of the Constitution and explain why these men tended to be rather mistrustful of the notion of democracy.

7. Compare and contrast the Virginia and New Jersey plans, and show how they led to the "Great Compromise."

8. Explain why separation of powers and federalism became key parts of the Constitution. Hint: not to make the system more democratic. Another hint: not to make it more efficient either!

9. Show how James Madison's notions of human nature played an important role in the framing of the Constitution.

10. Explain why a bill of rights was not included in the Constitution. Then explain why one was added.

11. Explain why the Founding Fathers failed to address the question of slavery in any definitive way.

12. Discuss the question of whether "women were left out of the Constitution."

13. Summarize Charles Beard's analysis of the economic motivations of the Framers, as well as counteranalyses of those who disagree with Beard.

14. List and explain the two major types of constitutional reform advocated today, along with specific reform measures.

Chapter Outline with Keyed-in Resources

I. The problem of liberty (THEME A: THE POLITICAL PHILOSOPHY OF THE FOUNDERS)
   A. The colonial mind
      1. Belief that British politicians were corrupt and thus English constitution inadequate
      2. Belief in higher law of natural rights
         a. Life
         b. Liberty
         c. Property (Jefferson notwithstanding)

In *Inventing America*, Garry Wills challenges conventional wisdom in arguing that the Declaration of Independence was not inspired by the philosophy of John Locke. Wills doubts whether Thomas Jefferson even read Locke's *Second Treatise*, noting that Jefferson's only copy was purchased in 1769 but was destroyed in a fire one year later.

      3. A war of ideology, not economics
      4. Specific complaints against George III for violating inalienable rights

Voting was not widespread in England itself at this time. Only about one in twenty-five Englishmen had the suffrage in 1776.

   B. The real revolution (ADDITIONAL LECTURE TOPIC A-1)
      1. The "real" revolution was the radical change in belief about what made authority legitimate and liberties secure.
      2. Government by consent, not by prerogative
      3. Direct grant of power: written constitution
      4. Human liberty prior to government
      5. Legislative superior to executive branch
   C. Weaknesses of the confederation
      1. Could not levy taxes or regulate commerce
      2. Sovereignty, independence retained by states
      3. One vote in Congress for each state
      4. Nine of thirteen votes in Congress required for any measure
      5. Delegates picked, paid for by legislatures
      6. Little money coined by Congress
      7. Army small; dependent on state militias

The weakness of the national government under the Articles is illustrated by the following story. In 1784, eighty drunken soldiers in Philadelphia raided the arsenal, stole a cannon, and aimed it at where Congress was meeting. The membership of Congress was forced to flee to New Jersey since the government was incapable of intervening.

      8. Territorial disputes between states
      9. No national judicial system
     10. All thirteen states' consent necessary for any amendments

The newly created government almost succumbed to a military coup in an incident in 1783 called the Newburgh Mutiny. When the military was ordered to disband after the war, about two thousand officers refused to obey since they had not been paid in two years. The government, lacking the power to tax, was broke. Why was there no coup? George Washington, in addressing the officers, had to put on eyeglasses to read and said, "Gentlemen, you will permit me to put on my spectacles, for I have not only grown gray but almost blind in the service of my country." Rather than carrying forward their revolt, the soldiers wept.

II. The Constitutional Convention (THEME B: THE CONSTITUTIONAL CONVENTION)
   A. The lessons of experience
      1. State constitutions
         a. Pennsylvania: too strong, too democratic
         b. Massachusetts: too weak, less democratic

        2. Shays's Rebellion brought fear that states about to collapse
- B. The Framers
  1. Who came: men of practical affairs

The Founding Fathers were a different breed of politician from the architects of the revolution. To illustrate, William Livingston of New Jersey wrote, "The people have been and ever will be unfit to retain the exercise of power in their own hands." Gouverneur Morris, who wrote a draft of the Constitution, referred to the common people as "reptiles."

        2. Who did not come

Rhode Island was the sole state that refused to send any delegates to the convention.

        3. Intent to write a whole new constitution
        4. Lockean influence
        5. Doubts that popular consent could guarantee liberty
        6. Results: "a delicate problem"; need strong government for order but not threaten liberty
           a. Democracy of that day not the solution
           b. Aristocracy not a solution either
           c. Government with constitutional limits no guarantee against tyranny
- III. The challenge
  - A. The Virginia Plan
    1. Design for a true national government
    2. Two houses in legislature
    3. Executive chosen by legislature
    4. Council of revision with veto power
    5. Two key features of the plan
       a. National legislature with supreme powers
       b. One house elected directly by the people
  - B. The New Jersey Plan
    1. Sought to amend rather than replace Articles
    2. Proposed one vote per state
    3. Protected small states' interests
  - C. The compromise
    1. House of Representatives based on population
    2. Senate of two members per state
    3. Reconciled interests of large and small states
    4. Committee of Detail
- IV. The Constitution and democracy
  - A. Founders did not intend to create "pure democracy"

The term "founding fathers" was coined by Warren G. Harding.

        1. Physical impossibility in a vast country
        2. Mistrust of popular passions
        3. Intent instead to create a republic with system of representation
- B. Popular rule only one element of new government
  1. State legislators to elect senators
  2. Electors to choose president

It has happened three times in American history that the candidate receiving the most votes did not become president: in 1824 Andrew Jackson received 43.1 percent of the vote to John Q. Adams's 30.5 percent, but Adams became president; in 1876 Samuel Tilden received 51 percent of the vote to Rutherford Hayes's 47.9 percent, but Hayes became president; and in 1888 Grover Cleveland received 48.6 percent of the vote to Benjamin Harrison's 47.8 percent, but Harrison became president.

        3. Two kinds of majorities: voters and states
        4. Judicial review another limitation
        5. Amendment process

- C. Key principles
  1. Separation of powers
  2. Federalism
- D. Government and human nature
  1. Aristotelian view: government should improve human nature by cultivating virtue
  2. Madisonian view: cultivation of virtue would require a government too strong, too dangerous; self-interest should be freely pursued
  3. Federalism enables one level of government to act as a check on the other

V. The Constitution and liberty
- A. Whether constitutional government was to respect personal liberties is a difficult question
  1. Ratification by conventions in at least nine states a democratic feature
  2. But a technically illegal one
- B. The Antifederalist view
  1. Liberty could be secure only in small republics
     a. Otherwise national government would be distant from people
     b. Strong national government would use powers to annihilate state functions
  2. There should be many more restrictions on government
  3. Madison's response: personal liberty safest in large ("extended") republics
     a. Coalitions likely more moderate there
     b. Government *should* be somewhat distant to be insulated from passions
  4. Reasons for absence of bill of rights
     a. Several guarantees in Constitution
        (1) *Habeas corpus*
        (2) No bill of attainder
        (3) No *ex post facto* law
        (4) Trial by jury
        (5) Privileges and immunities
        (6) No religious tests
        (7) Obligation of contracts
     b. Most states had bills of rights
     c. Intent to limit federal government to specific powers

James Madison had another reason for opposing the inclusion of a bill of rights. He feared that no list of rights could ever be complete, and that the government would thus be invited to abridge the "forgotten" rights. To deal with this problem, Madison proposed what became the Ninth Amendment, which declares that citizens have additional rights beyond those enumerated. When introducing the amendment, Madison told Congress: "This is one of the most plausible arguments that I have ever heard urged against the admission of a bill of rights into this system; but, I conceive, that it may be guarded against. I have attempted it, as the gentlemen may see."

- C. Need for a bill of rights
  1. Ratification impossible without one
  2. Promise by key leaders to obtain one

The Bill of Rights did not require the approval of all states for ratification, and it did not initially receive such approval. For example, Georgia did not ratify the Bill of Rights until 1939.

  3. Bitter ratification narrowly successful

VI. The Constitution and slavery
- A. Slavery virtually unmentioned
- B. Apparent hypocrisy of Declaration signers

Rhode Island was the first colony to make slavery illegal in 1652.

- C. Necessity of compromise: otherwise no ratification
  1. Sixty percent of slaves counted for representation
  2. No slavery legislation possible before 1808

            3. Escaped slaves to be returned to masters
        D. Legacy: civil war, continuing problems
VII. The motives of the framers
    A. Acted out of mixture of motives: economic interests played modest role
    B. Economic interests at the convention
        1. Economic interests of framers varied widely
        2. Beard: those who owned government debt supported Constitution
        3. But no clear division along class lines found
        4. Recent research: state considerations outweighed personal considerations
            a. Exception: slaveholders
    C. Economic interests and ratification
        1. Played larger role in state-ratifying conventions
        2. In favor: merchants, urban, owned western land, held government IOUs, no slaves
        3. Opposed: farmers, held no IOUs, owned slaves
        4. But remarkably democratic process since most could vote for **delegates**
        5. Federalists versus Antifederalists on ideas of liberty
    D. The Constitution and equality
        1. Critics: government today is too weak
            a. Bows to special interests
            b. Fosters economic inequality
            c. Liberty and equality are therefore in conflict
        2. Framers more concerned with political inequality
            a. Weak government reduces political privilege
VIII. Constitutional reform—modern views (THEME C: CONSTITUTIONAL REFORM—MODERN VIEWS)
    A. Reducing the separation of powers to enhance national leadership
        1. Urgent problems unable to be solved
        2. President should be more powerful, accountable to produce better **policies**
        3. Government agencies exposed to undue interference
        4. Proposals
            a. Choose cabinet members from Congress
            b. Allow president to dissolve Congress
            c. Empower Congress to require special presidential election
            d. Require presidential/congressional teams
            e. Establish single six-year term for president

Lyndon Johnson himself publicly endorsed a single, six-year term for the president.

            f. Lengthen terms in House to four years
        5. Contrary arguments: results uncertain, worse
    B. Making the system less democratic
        1. Government does too much, not too little
        2. Attention to individual wants over general preferences
        3. Proposals
            a. Limit amount of taxes collectible
            b. Require a balanced budget

In opposing a balanced budget amendment in 1994, President Clinton pointed to a government study which concluded that such an amendment would produce the reverse consequence of its goal, culminating in higher taxes.

            c. Grant president a line-item veto
            d. Narrow authority of federal courts
        4. Contrary arguments: unworkable or open to evasion
    C. Who is right?
        1. Decide nothing now

2. Crucial questions
   a. How well has it worked in history?
   b. How well has it worked in comparison with others?

Important Terms

amendment (constitutional) A change in, or addition to, a constitution. Amendments are proposed by a two-thirds vote of both houses of Congress or by a convention called by Congress at the request of two-thirds of the state legislatures and ratified by approval of three-fourths of the states.

*Antifederalists Opponents to the ratification of the Constitution who valued liberty above all else and believed it could be protected only in a small republic. They emphasized states' rights and worried that the new central government was too strong.

Articles of Confederation The document establishing a "league of friendship" among the American states in 1781. The government proved too weak to rule effectively and was replaced by the current Constitution.

Charles Beard A historian who argued that the Constitution was designed to protect the economic self-interest of its framers. Beard's view is largely rejected by contemporary scholars.

*bill of attainder A law that declares a person, without trial, to be guilty of a crime. The state legislatures and Congress are forbidden to pass such acts Article I, Sections 9 and 10, of the Constitution.

Bill of Rights The first ten amendments of the U.S. Constitution, containing a list of individual rights and liberties, such as freedom of speech, religion, and the press.

checks and balances The power of the legislative, executive, and judicial branches of government to block some acts by the other two branches.

*coalition Part of a theory espoused by James Madison that hypothesized that different interests must come together to form an alliance in order for a republican government to work. He believed that alliances formed in a large republic, unlike in small ones, would be moderate due to the greater variety of interests that must be accommodated.

Constitutional Convention A meeting of delegates in 1878 to revise the Articles of Confederation, which produced a totally new constitution still in use today.

*ex post facto law A law which makes criminal an act that was legal when it was committed, or that increases the penalty for a crime after it has been committed, or that changes the rules of evidence to make conviction easier. The state legislatures and Congress are forbidden to pass such laws by Article I, Sections 9 and 10, of the Constitution.

*faction A term employed by James Madison to refer to interests that exist in society, such as farmers and merchants, northerners and southerners, debtors and creditors. Madison postulated that each interest would seek its own advantage and that the pulling and hauling among them would promote political stability on a national basis.

Federalist **No. 10** An essay composed by James Madison which argues that liberty is safest in a large republic because many interests (factions) exist. Such diversity makes tyranny by the majority more difficult since ruling coalitions will always be unstable.

Federalist **papers** A series of eighty-five essays written by Alexander Hamilton, James Madison, and John Jay that were published in New York newspapers to convince New Yorkers to adopt the newly proposed Constitution.

*Federalists A term used to describe supporters of the Constitution during ratification debates in state legislatures.

*Great Compromise The agreement that prevented the collapse of the Constitutional Convention because of friction between large and small states. It reconciled their interests by awarding states representation in the Senate on a basis of equality and in the House of Representatives in proportion to each state's population.

*inalienable rights Rights thought to be based on nature and Providence rather than on the preferences of people.

*judicial review The power of courts to declare an act of Congress unconstitutional. It is also a way of limiting the power of popular majorities.

*line-item veto The power of an executive to veto some provisions in an appropriations bill while approving others. The President does not have the right to exercise a line-item veto and must approve or reject an entire appropriations bill.

natural rights A philosophical belief expressed in the Declaration of Independence that certain rights are ordained by God, are discoverable in nature and history, and are essential to human progress. The perception that these rights were violated by Great Britain contributed to the American Revolution.

New Jersey Plan A plan of government proposed by William Patterson as a substitute for the Virginia Plan in an effort to provide greater protection for the interests of small states. It recommended that the Articles of Confederation should be amended, not replaced, with a unicameral Congress, in which each state would have an equal vote.

*republic The form of government intended by the Framers that operates through a system of representation.

*separation of powers An element of the Constitution in which political power is shared between the branches of government to allow self-interest to check self-interest.

Shays's Rebellion A rebellion in 1787 by ex–Revolutionary War soldiers who feared losing their property over indebtedness. The former soldiers prevented courts in western Massachusetts from sitting. The inability of the government to deal effectively with the rebellion showed the weakness of the political system at the time and led to support for revision of the Articles of Confederation.

Virginia Plan A plan submitted to the Constitutional Convention which proposed a new form of government, not a mere revision of the Articles of Confederation. The plan envisioned a much stronger national government structured around three branches. James Madison prepared the initial draft.

*writ of habeas corpus A court order directing a police officer, sheriff, or warden who has a person in custody to bring the prisoner before a judge to show sufficient cause for his or her detention. The purpose of the order is to prevent illegal arrests and unlawful imprisonment. Under the Constitution, the writ cannot be suspended, except during invasion or rebellion.

Theme A	The Political Philosophy of the Founders

Summary

The goal of the American Revolution was liberty. The colonists sought to protect the traditional liberties due British subjects—liberties embodied in the (unwritten) *British constitution*. Initially colonists believed these liberties were best protected by remaining part of the British empire, but opinion slowly shifted to favor independence. John Adams estimated that one-third of Americans supported the Revolution, one-third remained loyalists, and one-third were indifferent.

The liberties the colonists fought to protect were based on *natural rights* ordained by God and discoverable in nature and history. These rights included life, liberty, and property. The Founders were heavily influenced by Englishman John Locke and his theory of a *state of nature*. In a state of nature, without government, people cherish life, liberty, and property, but these things are not secure because the strong can deprive the weak of their rights. Government is instituted to prevent this exploitation but must be based on the *consent of the governed*. *Limited government* is therefore required, because people will not consent to be ruled by a government that threatens their liberty.

The Founders' pessimistic view of human nature also influenced them in favor of limited government. A natural human lust for domination meant that a too-powerful government could easily become an engine of exploitation.

The Founders clearly distrusted *aristocracy*, the rule of the few, but they also distrusted *democracy*, the rule of the many, which for many of the Founders meant mob rule. They feared that a democracy would be excessively subject to temporary popular passions and that minority rights would be insecure. The highly democratic *Pennsylvania constitution*, adopted in 1776, demonstrated this danger.

Yet the ineffectiveness of the national government under the *Articles of Confederation* and the inability of government to deal with *Shays's Rebellion* convinced many of the need for a stronger central government. Thus arose a difficult problem: how to devise a government strong enough to keep order yet not strong enough to threaten liberty.

Faced with conflicting claims of aristocracy and democracy, the Founders devised a *republic* with a system of representation. The direct election of the House of Representatives by the people was an important democratic provision. On the other hand, the election of senators by state legislatures, the practice of *judicial review*, and the difficulty of amending the constitution were substantial limitations on popular rule.

The *separation of powers* and *federalism* are the key means by which the Founders protected liberty. In a system in which political power is divided among three separate branches of government, a usurpation by one branch will be fought by officials of the other two. It is not necessary that these officials be public-spirited; their own ambition and desire for power will lead them to maintain the balance. Federalism likewise provides for state and federal governments to check each other.

It should be noted that these principles reflect the Founders' distrust of the people to govern themselves. According to William Livingston, a delegate from New Jersey, "The people have been and ever will be unfit to retain the exercise of power in their own hands." Thus the separation of powers ensures that the national government controls itself and, if this check fails, federalism enables the states to protect the people from abuse by the central government. The people were given little opportunity to influence public policy. The only "voice of the people" was in the election of members to the House of Representatives; the people were denied selection of any other national officials. Moreover, any action taken by the House could be blocked by the Senate. The Constitution clearly watered down the concept of democracy after the experience under the Articles of Confederation.

The stress the Founders placed on liberty was consistent with equality as they understood it. They favored political equality or equal rights before the law: government should not create unnatural and undesirable inequalities. To many people today, the proper role of government is to promote a greater degree of equality than when society is left alone.

Discussion Questions

1. Why, if one is concerned with protecting human liberty, would one want to make the legislative branch of government dominant (rather than the executive or judicial)? Could not the courts be a better protector of individuals' liberties than the legislature? Could not the president? Are there good reasons why someone concerned with liberty would distrust a strong executive? A powerful judiciary? Is liberty most often threatened by (a) powerful political elites who escape public control or (b) a majority intent on imposing its will on a minority? Which of these cases would lead one to favor a strong legislative branch?

2. What features of the Constitution make it difficult for government to do or achieve anything? Why were they included? Suppose you wanted to make government more capable of acting to solve the pressing problems of the country. Which of the following changes would you favor?

Having a unicameral (one-house) rather than a bicameral (two-house) Congress
Eliminating the president's veto power
Having binding national referenda on important issues
Abolishing the Supreme Court's power of "judicial review," the power to overrule an act of Congress
Giving more power to state governments

3. Historian Arthur Ekirch contends that the Constitution is a complete repudiation of the American Revolution. Does any evidence support Ekirch's allegation? Is Ekirch correct? Point out that the spiritual leaders of the revolution (Thomas Jefferson, John Adams, Samuel Adams, Patrick Henry, Thomas Paine) were absent from the convention. Henry refused to attend, saying he "smelled a rat."

4. The fragmentation of power under the Constitution—the separation of powers, checks and balances—makes the enactment of public policy a slow process. Can the United States survive in the nuclear age when the government cannot respond quickly? Do events in which the president has acted independently, such as in Vietnam and Kuwait, indicate that the system of checks and balances has broken down? If not, how can these events be explained consistent with a functioning system of checks and balances?

5. James Madison argued that a democratic government was safest in an "extended republic" because no single faction could dominate. However, public opinion polls show that despite the fact that about two-thirds of Americans favor restrictions on handguns, such restrictions have clearly been blocked by the National Rifle Association (NRA). Was Madison wrong?

Data and Perspectives for Analysis

Instructor: The following questionnaire should be given to your students before they read Chapter 2 of the text and before you have discussed the Founding. After you have distributed the questionnaire, you might want to use simple marginal tabulations of your class's responses as a basis for discussion. See the references and the comment in the Additional Lecture Topic below.

Designing a Political System

Suppose you had a chance to design a political system. What sort would you design? First, you would need to decide what you value in a political system. Look at the following pairs of statements and circle (a) or (b) in each case to indicate which tribute you would value more highly in your political institutions.

Which would you rather have?

a. A political system with the greatest possible political democracy—that is, one that translates popular demands into laws and policies as effectively as possible

or

b. A political system that gives elected officials considerable latitude to do what they want to or feel is best without having to worry too much about public opinion

a. A political system that can make major policy changes quickly

or

b. A political system where major changes in policy are very hard to effect and happen only rarely

a. A political system that allows minority groups to block governmental actions that they feel are unfair or unjust to them

or

b. A political system in which the majority always prevails even in the face of minority opposition

a. A political system that seeks to make its citizens virtuous and good

or

b. A political system that leaves its citizens alone to live as they wish

a. A political system with power centralized in one place, to allow coherent and consistent policy across an entire nation

or

b. A political system with power decentralized to represent the needs and wants of various localities

a. A political system that assumes that people are generally self-seeking and attempts to make the best of that fact

or

b. A political system that seeks to make its citizens unselfish and concerned with the common good

1. Are the preferences of the majority of this class the same as those of the Founders, or would the class prefer a very different sort of political system?
2. How would you have to change the Constitution to produce a political system closer to what members of the class say they want?

Additional Lecture Topic A-1

Evaluating the Work of the Founders

Martin Diamond, "The Declaration and the Constitution: Liberty, Democracy, and the Founders," *The Public Interest*, Fall 1975.

Martin Diamond, "Ethics and Politics: The American Way." In Robert H. Horwitz, ed., *The Moral Foundations of the American Republic*. Charlottesville: University Press of Virginia, 1977.

Edward Handler, *The American Political Experience*. Lexington, MA.: Heath, 1968. Essays by Dahl, Huntington, Fischer, and Current.

Richard Hofstadter, "The Founding Fathers: An Age of Realism." In Horwitz, op. cit.

Alpheus Thomas Mason, "America's Political Heritage: Revolution and Free Government—A Bicentennial Tribute," *Political Science Quarterly*, Summer 1976; and Robert A. Dahl, "On Removing Certain Impediments to Democracy in the United States," *Political Science Quarterly*, Spring 1977. Both are reprinted in Demetrios Caraley and Mary Ann Epstein, eds., *The Making of American Foreign and Domestic Policy*. Farmingtondale, NY: Dabor, 1978.

S. M. Lipset, *The First New Nation*. New York: Basic Books, 1963. A classic examination of the sociocultural patterns that played a major role in developing the American experience.

V. L. Parrington, *The Colonial Mind, 1620–1800*. New York: Harvest Books, 1927. An old but classic study of the colonial "ideology" and its evolution.

J. W. Peltason, *Understanding the Constitution*. 13th ed. New York: Holt, Rinehart & Winston, 1994. A reliable, incisive look at the main features of the Constitution.

Jack N. Rakove, *The Beginnings of National Politics*. New York: Knopf, 1979.

Suggested Student Reading

1. *Federalist*, Nos. 10 and 51. The classic exposition of the philosophy of the American Founding. Unless you are teaching very sophisticated students, you will find that many of them have difficulty with the eighteenth-century prose style. Spending class time to discuss the text, paragraph by paragraph and sentence by sentence, may well be worthwhile.

2. Gary Wills, *Explaining America: The Federalist*. Garden City, NJ: Doubleday, 1981. An effective analysis of the core ideas contained in the *Federalist* papers.

Theme B   The Constitutional Convention

Summary

The Constitutional Convention assembled in Philadelphia in 1787 with the delegates in general agreement that defects in the Articles of Confederation ought to be remedied. Immediately the delegates were presented with the *Virginia Plan*, a comprehensive scheme for a wholly new national government with strongly centralized power. The *New Jersey Plan*, supported by opponents of strong national government, merely revised the existing Articles of Confederation. A committee was appointed to meet during the Fourth of July holidays to work out a compromise. The Great Compromise produced by this committee balanced the interests of the small and the large states by establishing a House of Representatives apportioned according to population and a Senate consisting of two senators from each state. A host of other issues remained, but acceptable compromises were reached on all of them (including the slavery issue), and the new Constitution was approved on September 17.

However, ratification of the Constitution could not take place until the Federalist view of a strong central government prevailed over Antifederalist assertions of state privileges and power (in favor of a small, loose confederation). Accordingly, Madison, a staunch Federalist, effectively argued that liberty would best be preserved in a large republic that would allow greater diversity of thought. Still, the Federalists had to compromise on a "bill of rights" in order to attain ratification.

Ironically, Madison would later adopt a states' rights position in composing the Virginia Resolutions while his opponent at the ratifying convention in Virginia, Patrick Henry, would become a Federalist. Ideology is a slippery thing.

Discussion Questions

1. How did the original concept of the electoral college reflect the Founders' distrust of democracy? What other constitutional features limited the role of popular majorities?

2. Did the Philadelphia convention itself exemplify the principles that Madison set forth in *Federalist* 10? Were there factions? Could any faction dominate? Were justice and the general good reflected in the outcomes of the convention?

3. Explain what Jefferson meant when he asserted that "the tree of liberty must be refreshed from time to time with the blood of patriots and tyrants?" What is the meaning of this statement for the current generation of Americans?

Data and Perspectives for Analysis

Although the specific provisions of the Bill of Rights may be scrutinized at a later time in the course, you may wish to generate some discussion in keeping with the themes of Chapter 2. Here are some questions you might ask.

1. Assume that the United States had established an "official" national religion—that is, that the "freedom of religion" and church/state separation provisions of the First Amendment did not exist. How would American democracy have been changed in your opinion, and why?

2. What is the rationale behind the idea of "no double jeopardy" in the Fifth Amendment? Similarly, why do you think the Founders also placed a prohibition against "self-incrimination" in the Fifth Amendment? You may also wish to link this query with the "right to remain silent," established by the *Miranda v. Arizona* Supreme Court decision.

3. Research the *Gideon v. Wainwright* Supreme Court decision and explain how it was related to the Sixth Amendment's "right to a speedy, public, impartial trial with defense counsel." (Have students report their findings in class the next day if possible.)

4. Explain how opponents of capital punishment could construe the practice as a violation of the Eighth Amendment's provision against "cruel and unusual punishment." Then have a few students argue that the death penalty does *not* violate the Eighth Amendment. (A debate in class could be arranged later in the course.)

Theme C Constitutional Reform—Modern Views

Summary

Modern criticisms involving constitutional reform focus on whether the federal government should be stronger or weaker. Critics of the former view attack the separation-of-powers concept, arguing for increased presidential authority with fewer "checks" from the bureaucracy and members of Congress. Elements of the British model, such as a fusion of the legislative and executive processes and functions, are also suggested. Defenders of the current system argue that congressional "interference" improves policies and ensures citizen "protection" against powerful interest groups and agencies.

The "weaker-government" adherents believe that government is currently too big and thus promotes an "adding-machine" mentality (that is, government officials promise more for everyone). Proposed remedies include a balanced-budget amendment, a line-item veto, and restriction of the authority of the federal courts. These proposals, of course, draw criticism as well. Clearly, the entire debate symbolizes the essential fact that, although the U.S. Constitution is nearly two centuries old, it is not "out of date."

Discussion Questions

1. Would the American political system be improved if various features of the British system were "transplanted" to this country? Why or why not?

2. Why was the philosophy of President Reagan that "government is too big" so popular with the voters in the 1980 and 1984 presidential elections? Do Americans still accept this philosophy now that Reagan is out of office?

Abstract for Theme C

Constitutionally "Reforming" the Presidency

In his book *The Imperial Presidency*, Arthur Schlesinger, Jr., argues that the president's powers have grown at a faster rate than those of the other branches of government. This process began more than fifty years ago with the administration of Franklin D. Roosevelt. It was strengthened by the Great Depression, World War II, Korea, the cold war, Vietnam, and fears of nuclear war. According to Schlesinger, the president had been an "absolute monarch" on the issues of war and peace. Consequently, Schlesinger argues for change in the constitutional role and structure of the presidency and, in particular, for the adoption of the British style of executive decision making. Schlesinger offers the following proposals, among others.

1. Change the current four-year term of the president to one six-year term. Under this plan, a president could not run for reelection. In other words, a president's maximum number of years in office would be reduced from eight to six, but no president would have more than six years to lead the nation.

2. Give the president a "council of state," a body that the president would be bound by law to consult. Half of the Council's members would come from Congress, and some would have to be chosen from the opposite political party.

3. Adopt a version of the British parliamentary system. In other words, a president would be compelled at regular intervals to explain and defend his policies to key members of the political opposition. If the Congress, by a two-thirds or three-fourths vote, issued a vote of "no

confidence," a new national election would have to be called within six weeks. (Assume that this vote of no confidence could not occur before three years of the president's term had passed—be it the one six-year term or the traditional four-year term.)

In reference to the three proposals, the six-year term would remove the pressures of reelection from the president, but might it not make him less responsive to public and congressional wishes, particularly in the last few years of his one term? The "council of state" concept sounds fine in theory, but the mechanics of implementation might prove troublesome. How many members would there be? Would the council have veto power over presidential decisions or not? Would members of the opposition attempt to "sabotage" presidential initiatives, or would they cooperate fully? Finally, "no-confidence" elections could remove an unpopular president from office, but would Congress be tempted to abuse this power? And would the American electorate be willing to confront the prospect of multiple elections? Also, the no-confidence feature presupposes a majority for the president's party in both houses of Congress. It would therefore require an election system that guaranteed the congressional victory of a victorious president's party. Thus implementation of these three constitutional reforms would have a dramatic and extensive impact on the entire American political system.

Would any of these proposals strengthen or weaken the American system of government? What impact would such constitutional changes have on American society and on the entire system of checks and balances?

Questions for Discussion

1. Do you think Schlesinger's proposals for constitutionally reforming the presidency had a less receptive audience in the 1980s than in the 1960s and 1970s? Why or why not?

2. Obviously, the Schlesinger proposals strengthen the hand of Congress in the policy-making process. Conversely, the president would have to be more responsive to congressional wishes and ideas. Under what political circumstances would this be good for the country? Under what political circumstances might this harm the country?

Data and Perspectives for Analysis

The text discusses proposed constitutional amendments in the context of the separation of powers. Changes in the Constitution are intended to make the government operate more efficiently. Yet public complaints and proposed constitutional amendments have recently dealt with other issues. Proposed constitutional amendments have been forwarded on the following:

Amendment	*Public Support*	
	In favor	*Opposed*
Equal rights shall not be denied on account of sex (1984)	63%	31%
Abortions shall be permissible at any time in the first three months of pregnancy (1986)	45	45
The federal government's budget shall be balanced annually (1987)	53	45

Source: Harold Stanley and Richard Niemi, *Vital Statistics on American Politics*, 2nd ed. (Washington, DC: Congressional Quarterly, 1990), pp. 20–21. Reprinted by permission of CQ Press.

Discussion Questions

1. Austin Ranney argues that the public's concerns about constitutional amendments reflect a desire "to limit the reach and power of the national government." Does this mean that the public is less concerned about efficient government than about abusive government?

2. Does the American public agree with the concerns of the Antifederalists that the Constitution created too powerful a central government? Surely the data can be interpreted to support this suggestion.

3. Why hasn't Congress acted in any of these areas, despite massive public anxiety? Should the amendment process be simplified?

3

Federalism

Overview and Objectives

The central purpose of the chapter is to introduce the student to some of the complexities of government in the United States caused by the adoption of a federal system—that is, one where both the national and state governments have powers independent of one another. The student should also note how the nature and the effects of American federalism have changed throughout American history, and continue to change to this day. After reading and reviewing the material in this chapter the student should be able to do each of the following:

1. Explain the difference between federal and centralized systems of government, and give examples of each.

2. Show how competing political interests at the Constitutional Convention led to the adoption of a federal system, but one that was not clearly defined.

3. Outline the ways in which national and state powers were interpreted by the courts, and how the doctrine of "dual federalism" came to be a dead letter of the law.

4. State the reasons why federal grants-in-aid to the states have been politically popular, and cite what have proved to be the pitfalls of such grants.

5. Distinguish between categorical grants and block grants or general revenue sharing.

6. Explain why, despite repeated attempts to reverse the trend, categorical grants have continued to grow more rapidly than block grants.

7. Distinguish between mandates and conditions of aid with respect to federal grant programs to states and localities.

8. Discuss whether or to what extent federal grants to the states have succeeded in creating uniform national policies comparable to those of centralized governments.

Chapter Outline with Keyed-in Resources

I. Governmental structure (THEME A: FEDERAL VERSUS UNITARY STRUCTURE)
   A. Federalism: good or bad?
      1. Definition: political system with local government units, besides national one that can make final decisions (ADDITIONAL LECTURE TOPIC A-1)
      2. Examples of federal governments: Canada, India, Germany
      3. Examples of unitary governments: France, Britain, Italy

Some unitary governments are confronting pressures to relinquish a degree of control. In Great Britain, both Scotland and Wales have agitated for a "devolution" of certain powers to their control, such as health, land use, and tourism. The movement was propelled by the desire to protect the native language in Wales and receive a greater return of profits from North Sea oil in Scotland. When put to the vote in 1979, the devolution proposal failed in both countries. However, the movement has picked up support recently in Scotland, with 47 percent favoring devolution and 33 percent outright independence.

        4. Special protection of subnational governments in federal system due to:
           a. Constitution of country
           b. Habits, preferences, and dispositions of citizens
           c. Distribution of political power in society
        5. National government largely does not govern individuals directly, but gets states to do so in keeping with national policy
        6. Negative views: blocks progress and protects powerful local interests
           a. Laski: states "poisonous and parasitic"
           b. Riker: perpetuation of racism
        7. Positive view
           a. Elazar: strength, flexibility, liberty
        8. Federalism makes good and bad effects possible
           a. Different political groups with different political purposes come to power in different places
           b. *Federalist* No. 10: small political units dominated by single political faction

It is necessary to convince students that state governments today retain power independently of Washington. A good example concerns the destruction of a Korean passenger jet (KAL 007) in 1983 by the Soviet air force when it drifted into USSR territory. Shortly afterward the Soviet foreign minister was to come to New York City to address the United Nations. The governor of New York refused permission for the Soviet minister to land. Despite a personal appeal by President Reagan, the governor refused to yield, and the address was never delivered.

     B. Increased political activity
        1. Most obvious effect of federalism facilitate mobilization of political activity
        2. Federalism lowers the cost of political organization at the local level
  II. The Founding
     A. A bold, new plan to protect personal liberty
        1. Founders believed that neither national nor state government would have authority over the other since power comes from people who shift support
        2. New plan had no historical precedent
        3. Tenth Amendment was added as an afterthought, to define power-of-states

The Tenth Amendment is poorly worded. It prohibits Congress from exercising any power not specifically conferred by the Constitution. In other words, Congress could not create an air force, since this power is not listed. It follows that each state must have its own air force.

     B. Elastic language in Article I: necessary and proper
        1. Precise definitions of powers politically impossible due to competing interests, e.g., commerce
        2. Hence vague language—"necessary and proper"
        3. Hamilton's view: national supremacy since Constitution supreme law
        4. Jefferson's view: states' rights with the people as ultimate sovereign
  III. The debate on the meaning of federalism (THEME B: FEDERALISM AND CONSTITUTIONAL LAW)
     A. The Supreme Court speaks
        1. Hamiltonian position espoused by Marshall
        2. *McCulloch* v. *Maryland* settled two questions
           a. Could Congress charter a national bank? (yes, because "necessary and proper")

            b. Could states tax such a bank? (no, because national powers supreme)
        3. Later battles
            a. Federal government cannot tax state bank
            b. "Nullification" doctrine led to Civil War: states void federal laws they deem conflicting with Constitution

The importance of the doctrine of nullification in the discontent that led to the Civil War cannot be minimized. According to Richard Hofstadter, "It was tariffs, not slavery, that first made the South militant."

    B. Dual federalism
        1. Both national and state governments supreme in their own spheres
        2. Hence interstate vs. intrastate commerce
            a. Early product-based distinction difficult
            b. "Original package" also unsatisfactory
            c. Today dual federalism virtually extinct
IV. Federal-state relations (THEME C: THE POLITICS OF FEDERALISM)
    A. Grants-in-aid

The public has greater trust in the fiscal management of state and local governments. According to the Advisory Commission on Intergovernmental Relations in 1991, 41 percent said they got the least for their money from the federal government compared to 26 percent who felt this way about their state government and 12 percent about their local government.

        1. Grants show how political realities modify legal authority
        2. Began before Constitution with "land-grant colleges," various cash grants to states
        3. Dramatically increased in scope in twentieth century
        4. Were attractive for various reasons
            a. Federal budget surpluses (nineteenth century)
            b. Federal income tax became flexible tool
            c. Federal control of money supply and authority to print more money
            d. "Free money" for state officials
        5. Required broad congressional coalitions
    B. Meeting national needs
        1. 1960s shift in grants-in-aid
            a. From what states demanded . . .
            b. . . . To what federal officials found important as national needs
    C. The intergovernmental lobby
        1. Hundreds of state, local officials lobby in Washington
        2. Purpose: to get more federal money with fewer strings
    D. Categorical grants versus revenue sharing
        1. Categorical grants for specific purposes; often require local matching funds
        2. Block grants devoted to general purpose with few restrictions
        3. Revenue sharing requires no matching funds and freedom on how to spend
            a. Distributed by statistical formula
            b. Ended in 1986
        4. Neither block grants nor revenue sharing achieved goal of giving states more freedom in spending
V. The slowdown in "free" money
    A. Block grants grow more slowly than categorical grants
        1. No single interest group has a vital stake in multipurpose block grants, revenue sharing
        2. Categorical grants are matters of life or death for various agencies
        3. Revenue sharing was wasteful and lacked a "constituency"
    B. Rivalry among the states
        1. Increased competition a result of increased dependency
        2. Snowbelt (Frostbelt) versus Sunbelt states
        3. Actual difficulty telling *where* funds spent

            4. Census takes on monumental importance
    VI. Federal aid and federal control
        A. Mandates
            1. Federal rules states or localities must obey, whether or not receiving aid
                a. Antidiscrimination rules
                b. Pollution control laws
            2. Administrative and financial problems often result
            3. Most controversial mandates result from court decisions
                a. Easier now for citizens to sue localities
        B. Conditions of aid
            1. Attached to grants states receive "voluntarily"
            2. Conditions range from specific to general

States have attempted subtle means of eluding federal conditions of aid. Massachusetts, for example, was opposed to the federal requirement that states permit automobiles to turn right at red lights except where safety dictates otherwise. (The condition was attached to grants of highway funds and was intended to save gasoline during the oil crisis.) Massachusetts placed signs prohibiting turns under almost each light in the state. The federal government threatened a cutoff of aid for this act of defiance.

            3. Divergent views of states and federal government on costs, benefits
                a. Example: Rehabilitation Act of 1973
            4. Failed presidential attempts to reverse trend
                a. Example: Nixon's "New Federalism" creating revenue sharing
            5. Reagan's attempt to consolidate categorical grants; Congress's cooperation in name only

Categorical grants constitute by far the largest proportion of federal grants-in-aid. In 1991, there were 478 separate "categories," which amounted to nearly 90 percent of all federal aid to state and local authorities.

        C. The states respond
            1. Experiments with new ways of delivering services
                a. Encouraged by federal laws like Federal Support Act
                b. Discouraged by federal rules but still some innovation
                c. Examples: child care, welfare, education (Minnesota, Rhode Island, Maryland)
        D. Sorting things out
            1. One view
                a. Federal government pays for national programs
                b. States pay for local programs
            2. Eisenhower's attempt (1957)
            3. Reagan's "swap" (1981)
                a. Failed because Constitution purposely left responsibilities vague
    VII. Federalism and public policy
        A. Nation still far from wholly centralized
            1. Members of Congress still *local* representatives
            2. But represent different constituencies from the same localities

Some local governments, frustrated by federal requirements, have taken steps to escape blame for the escalating costs associated with certain services. For example, the city of Toccoa, Georgia, enclosed the following insert with its property tax bill: "State and Federal Costs are beyond the control of your Mayor and Council. To discuss these costs, please call your Senator and Representative, and your U.S. Senators and Representative."

            3. Line to local political groups eroded
            4. No single national policy in most policy areas
                a. Example: welfare

5. Increasing difficulty of managing programs
   a. Example: Oakland aircraft hangar
6. Differences of opinion over which level of government works best

Important Terms

Article VI A provision of the Constitution that makes the laws and treaties of the federal government the "supreme law of the land."

*block grants Grants given by the federal government to state and local authorities for a general purpose and with few restrictions imposed.

*categorical grants Grants given by the federal government to state and local authorities for a specific purpose defined in federal law. State and local governments must usually provide matching funds to receive the grant.

*confederation A form of government in which sovereignty is wholly in the hands of the national government, so that the states and localities are dependent on its will.

conditions of aid A condition which a state government must fulfill for taking federal funds.

*dual federalism An interpretation of the Constitution which holds that states are as supreme within their sphere of power as is the federal government within its sphere of power. The Supreme Court no longer supports this interpretation.

*federal system A form of government in which sovereignty is shared, so that on some matters the national government is supreme and on others the states are supreme.

*federalism The division of power between a national government and regional (state) governments.

*grants-in-aid Federal Funds provided to states and localities. Grants-in-aid are typically provided for airports, highways, education, and major welfare services.

intergovernmental lobby Lobbying activities by state and local officials who establish offices in Washington, D.C., to compete for federal funds.

*mandates Requirements imposed against state and local governments to perform. The requirements usually have nothing to do with the receipt of federal funds and often originate from court orders.

McCulloch v. Maryland A Supreme Court decision that settled two issues. First, Congress can exercise powers not specifically mentioned in the Constitution if the power can be implied from an enumerated one. This authority is conferred by the "necessary and proper" clause. Second, the federal government is immune from taxation by the states.

necessary-and-proper clause The final paragraph of Article I, section 8, of the Constitution, which authorizes Congress to pass all laws "necessary and proper" to carry out the enumerated powers.

*nullification A doctrine espoused on behalf of the states' rights position which holds that states are empowered to void federal laws considered in violation of the Constitution. The Civil War made the doctrine moot.

*revenue sharing A grant-in-aid program that allowed states maximum discretion in the spending of federal funds. States were not required to supply matching funds, and they received money according to a statistical formula. The program was terminated in 1986.

*sovereignty The supreme or ultimate political authority. A sovereign government is one that is legally and politically independent of any other government.

Tenth Amendment An amendment to the Constitution which defines the powers of the states, stipulating that the states (or the people) retain all powers not specifically delegated to the national government by the Constitution. The amendment has been stripped of its significance by decisions of the Supreme Court.

unitary system A system in which sovereignty is wholly in the hands of the national government, so that subnational units are dependent on its will.

Theme A   Federal Versus Unitary Structure

Summary

Most countries have adopted a unitary form of government over a federal one. The United States could hardly make such a change. The reason is not simply that the Constitution mandates a federal political system. More important, the values of the American public remain committed to local government. However, local control has been weakened by two developments. First, federal courts have invaded local institutions like schools to impose national standards. Second, the advent of "fiscal" federalism has enabled Congress to manipulate powers constitutionally denied to it. Under fiscal federalism, Congress invites states to seek federal grants in exchange for the states enacting legislation in areas outside the zone of federal authority. Thus it was not Congress that lowered the speed limit on highways to fifty-five miles per hour, but rather each state acting independently in order to receive highway funds from the national government.

These developments have not gone unchallenged. The new conservative majority on the Supreme Court has restrained the federal judicial authority to some extent, while presidents Nixon, Reagan and Bush worked to lessen the impact of federalism. Still, the overall balance of power has been slipping in the direction of the national government since the Civil War. The process is somewhat inevitable as numerous problems have become national in scope and beyond the capacity of local governments to resolve in isolation.

While the United States has relaxed certain elements of federalism, unitary governments—like those in France and Great Britain—have been moving in the opposite direction. These countries have come to appreciate the benefit of relinquishing national authority as a means of preserving internal harmony. Too much central management ignores local differences and, as a result, provokes resistance. Conflict arose in both countries over minority languages—Welsh in Britain and Corsican in France. What makes the case of France interesting is that the shift toward decreased central control occurred under a socialist government.

The end result is that the distinction between federal and unitary forms of government is becoming blurred in practice. Theory is being overtaken by the pressures of changing priorities.

Discussion Questions

1. The effects of federalism are not entirely positive. Didn't federalism contribute to the perpetuation of racial discrimination? Isn't federalism enabling the crisis in environmental pollution to worsen? In other words, doesn't a federal form of government inhibit quick responses to serious problems?

2. Have the American states become outmoded? Why should Delaware possess as much power constitutionally as California? Should state lines be redrawn to reflect natural boundaries—perhaps, for example, merging industrial centers in the northern sections of Ohio, Michigan, and Pennsylvania? Aren't most problems today national in scope, or at least regional?

Data and Perspectives for Analysis

The Founding Fathers created in the federal form of government an additional barrier between the people and the central government—the states. Federalism, in effect, is intended to protect individual rights from being trampled by national sovereignty. Yet the nature of modern society has cast the public's eyes to Washington, D.C., whenever a problem emerges. To what degree does the American public endorse federalism as a practical matter? Present the following data to your students:

Public Attitudes Toward Federalism

Which of these statements comes closest to your view about government power?

The federal government has too much power.	28%
The federal government is using about the right amount of power.	24
The federal government should use its power more vigorously.	41

Should there be one national policy set by the federal government, or should the fifty states make their own rules . . .

	Federal	State
in controlling pollution?	49%	46%
in setting penalties for murder?	62	34
in setting safety standards in factories?	65	31

Source: Thomas R. Dye, *Politics in States and Communities*, 6th ed. (Englewood Cliffs, NJ: Prentice-Hall, 1988) p. 79. Reprinted by permission of Prentice-Hall, Englewood Cliffs, New Jersey.

Discussion Questions

1. On balance, the data seem to suggest a preference for federal authority over public policy. Is the public exhibiting a distrust of state governments or admitting that problems are beyond the capacity of a single state?

2. Are there any areas in which the public might prefer state authority over federal? Are there any areas in which the states might do a better job regulating than the federal government?

Abstract for Theme A

The Merits and Demerits of Federalism

As a political system, federalism has had both its supporters and its detractors. In a famous political science treatise, James Bryce argued that the merits of federalism far outweighed its demerits (*The American Commonwealth*, 3rd ed., New York: Macmillan, 1897). He listed the following arguments on behalf of federalism.

1. Federalism promotes national unity while permitting local "diversities" to continue.

2. Federalism prevents the rise of a despotic central government and does not threaten "the private liberties of the citizen." The states are "bulwarks" against the encroachment of the federal government.

3. Federalism "stimulates" the interest of citizens in local affairs, thereby sensitizing the people to their civic duties.

4. Federalism encourages local "experimentation" and reforms in political life that might not be tried initially at the federal level. In short, new policies can filter up from the state to the federal level.

Detractors, on the other hand, argue that federalism has a number of disadvantages.

1. Federalism encourages wasteful duplication of services between the levels of government and at times slows the political process to a snail's pace (as in the lengthy appeals of the court system).

2. Diversity of state laws and procedures creates inequities from a national perspective. (For example, the average felony conviction leads to thirteen months in jail in South Dakota as opposed to fifty-eight months in Massachusetts.)

3. There is ample proof that dispensing more powers to the states may be an unwise decision because states run their respective governments no more efficiently than federal bureaucrats run the national government in Washington, D.C.

4. Federalism can result in unequal opportunities, because the wealthier states can provide better schools, more advanced medical care, and more effective services than the poorer states.

5. The fragmentation of authority under federalism permits unscrupulous interest groups concentrated in specific states to acquire undue influence and political power in those states.

Questions for Discussion

1. Which arguments, pro or con, seem most plausible? Why?

2. Assume that the federal government took over many of the traditional powers of the states. Or suppose the states were abolished in favor of dividing the country into "administrative zones," as some political scientists have urged. What are the respective advantages and disadvantages of such actions?

Answer Guidelines

Focus on the importance of limiting political power at any specific governmental level.

Additional Lecture Topic

A-1. Understanding Contemporary Federalism

Ann O'M Bowman and Richard Kearney, *The Resurgence of the States*. Englewood Cliffs, NJ: Prentice-Hall, 1986.

Christopher Hamilton and Donald T. Wells, *Federalism, Power, and Political Economy: A New Theory of Federalism's Impact on American Life*. Englewood Cliffs, NJ: Prentice-Hall, 1990.

Richard H. Leach and Timothy G. O'Rourke, *State and Local Government: The Third Century of Federalism*. Englewood Cliffs, NJ: Prentice-Hall, 1988. An excellent overall work on the subject.

David B. Walker, *Toward a Functioning Federalism*. Cambridge, MA: Winthrop Press, 1981. A long-time Assistant Director of the Advisory Commission on Intergovernmental Relations explains how the federal system is organized and operates.

Deil S. Wright, *Understanding Intergovernmental Relations*. 2nd ed. Monterey, CA: Brooks-Cole, 1982. A good general treatise of the dynamics of federalism.

Theme B	Federalism and Constitutional Law

Summary

The Founders disagreed over the exact division of powers in a federal system. Hamilton argued for national supremacy, Jefferson for states' rights. The *Tenth Amendment* spelled out what was assumed from the outset: that the federal government would have only those powers given to it by the Constitution. On the other hand the *elastic language* of Article I—the "necessary and proper" clause—provided a basis for holding that the federal government had broad powers.

The Supreme Court became the arbiter of this dispute. Chief Justice John Marshall supported the Hamiltonian position, and in *McCulloch* v. *Maryland* the court held not only that the Congress had the right to set up a bank, but also that such an enterprise was immune to state taxation. After the Civil War, conflict focused on the commerce clause and the power of the federal government to regulate commerce. At first the Court distinguished between *interstate commerce*, which the federal government could regulate, and *intrastate commerce*, which it could not. Practical difficulties in distinguishing one from the other led the Court, by the 1940s, to hold that the federal government could regulate virtually any economic transaction it wanted to regulate.

The Supreme Court's struggles with defining the scope of federal power were influenced largely by economic theory. Under the *laissez-faire* beliefs that dominated nineteenth-century American politics, the government was to remain neutral toward the economy and not become involved in its management. The court infused this concept into its decisions on federalism by striking down most government efforts to intervene in the economy. The Great Depression of 1929 compelled the federal government under President Franklin Roosevelt's New Deal to take steps to alleviate the people's misery, but the justices consistently voided most such legislation as exceeding federal authority. An exasperated President Roosevelt, upon reelection in 1936, sought to increase the membership on the Supreme Court by "packing" it with justices who favored his perspective on federalism. While the court-packing plan failed, a majority of justices suddenly altered their view and began to uphold an expanded federal role in the economy. This "switch in time that saved nine" has prevailed to the present time. Since 1937, the Supreme Court has only once declared a federal law void for invading the power of the states under the Tenth Amendment and this decision was later reversed. The Tenth Amendment, in the words of Justice Harlan Stone, is nothing more than a "truism" and lacks much relevance as an impediment to Congressional power.

Where federalism has been revived, however, is in the area of civil liberties. With the Supreme Court adopting a more conservative stance on constitutional liberties since 1969, when Warren Burger became chief justice, state supreme courts have become more active in expanding individual rights at the local level. The Supreme Court's rulings in this area represent the *minimal* rights that must be guaranteed; states can always provide their citizens more freedom under a state's constitution so long as no federal interest is impeded. This trend is most pronounced in the context of criminal rights and has been encouraged by members of the Supreme Court, most notably by retired Justice William Brennan. Clearly, federalism remains vibrant in constitutional law.

Discussion Questions

1. Historically, power has flowed to the central government. What reasons exist for the states to continue exercising independent power? Given the Supreme Court's decision in *McCulloch*, what prevents the central government from assuming legal authority over any area of public policy?

2. Why doesn't the federal government always intervene when states defy its authority? For example, Hall County, Georgia, forbids the sale of *Playboy* magazine in violation of the First Amendment.

3. Certain areas in Nevada permit prostitution; Alaska until recently allowed the private possession of small amounts of marijuana. Could the federal government legally intervene to forbid such practices in these states? Explain why or why not.

Theme C The Politics of Federalism

Summary

The political dynamics of federalism have changed over the years. The balance between state and federal power has clearly slipped in favor of the national government. As early as the 1960s, Senator Everett Dirksen of Illinois warned that soon "the only people interested in state boundaries will be Rand-McNally." This concern exaggerated the extent to which the federal government is capable of invading local prerogatives. The reason is that the constitutional structure forces members of Congress to remain focused on local issues—if only to achieve reelection.

The shift to national control began in the late nineteenth century, but it was not until the growth of grant-in-aid programs during the 1960s that the symmetry of authority—the key to federalism—became one-sided. As state and local governmental budgets became increasingly dependent on federal resources, the "intergovernmental lobby," in which local officials set up offices in Washington to compete for federal money, developed. The rivalry between states intensified when Congress began to loosen the strings of categorical grants and replace them with block grants based on distributional formulas.

The absence of federal "strings" and the greater leeway in spending federal funds did not produce a corresponding increase in the freedom of local officials. First, "creeping cateogrization" occurred in which the federal government began to disapprove of the way block grants were utilized. Its response was to impose more restrictions on block grants. Second, categorical grants spawned interest groups that relied on such grants for their survival. Since these groups were frequently successful in convincing congressional committees to preserve a particular grant from being merged into a larger block grant program, the result was to limit the overall number of block grants. And third, the ideological dimension of federalism became more prominent. Liberals, Democrats, and minority groups preferred to continue the practice of prescribing national standards as an antidote to the prejudices of local officials. Conservatives, Republicans, and business leaders preferred to transfer decision-making to the local level to avoid the inflexibility of national regulations. Thus the 1980s and early 1990s were locked in stalemate as a Democratic Congress pushed in one direction while Republican administrations pushed in the other.

The Clinton administration holds the promise of untangling the politics of federalism. Two new trends are forcing a change. First, many states are becoming frustrated by federal meddling in local affairs. In 1993, for example, the state of Hawaii refused to fly the American flag for an entire weekend as a sign of protest, and an active movement on behalf of secession has emerged. Second, local governments are not what they were. The level of professionalism has improved and states are again serving as experimental grounds for new programs. Policy innovation is no longer a federal monopoly. In short, the politics of federalism could be entering a new era.

Discussion Questions

1. Doesn't the system of grants-in-aid upset the balance of federalism? Consider the speed limit requirement of fifty-five miles per hour and the drinking age requirement of twenty-one. Don't the grant programs enable Congress to do what it pleases by bribing states into compliance? What would be the consequence if a state refused federal grant money?

2. To what extent have interest groups produced grants-in-aid, and to what extent have grants-in-aid produced interest groups? Who constitutes the "intergovernmental lobby"?

3. Why can't federal agencies attack complex problems by producing and implementing a coherent systematic policy? Why don't (can't) federal bureaucrats issue orders where necessary?

4. How and why do conservatives and liberals differ over giving aid to the states "without strings"?

5. Why does the text assert that "there remains more political and policy diversity in the United States than one is likely to find in any other large industrialized nation"?

Data and Perspectives for Analysis

"Fiscal federalism" results from the federal government's superior capacity to raise revenues. Income taxes constitute the federal government's primary source of revenue. Additional funds can be obtained by a simple majority vote of Congress. By contrast, state and local governments depend largely on sales and property taxes for their budgets. Such taxes usually require voter approval to increase. Even when essential services (like schools, hospitals, and police) are at stake, voters frequently reject revenue-enhancement measures.

The problems of fiscal federalism can be looked at from several perspectives. Present the following data to the class:

Table 1. Composition of Tax Revenues

Source	State	Local
Individual income	21.4%	5.5%
Corporation income	7.5	5.5
Sales and excises	38.5	13.3
Property	2.9	72.2
Payroll	22.2	5.0
Death and gift	1.1	—
Other	6.3	4.8

Source: Harold Stanley and Richard Niemi, *Vital Statistics on American Politics*, 2nd ed. (Washington, DC: Congressional Quarterly, 1990), p. 296. Reprinted by permission of CQ Press.

Table 2. Tax Attitudes: Which Is the Worst Tax?

Tax Type	1972	1985
Federal income tax	19%	36%
State income tax	13	10
State sales tax	13	15
Local property tax	45	29
Don't know	11	10

Source: Thomas Dye, *Politics in States and Communities*, 6th ed., © 1988, p. 491. Reprinted by permission of Prentice-Hall, Englewood Cliffs, NJ.

Discussion Questions

1. The federal government relies most heavily on income taxes for revenue, state governments on sales taxes, and local governments on property taxes. Which of these taxes is the fairest to the poor? Does the public agree that the most oppressive tax method is also the worst? What accounts for this discrepancy?

2. Given the inability of states to raise revenue, what has been the effect of the cutback in federal grants-in-aid?

3. The American public is concerned about the decline in educational quality. Since education is a state responsibility under the Tenth Amendment, can the federal government intervene somehow to assist? If not, why does the federal government have a Department of Education? Does the existence of this department violate the Tenth Amendment?

4

American Political Culture

Overview and Objectives

This chapter departs rather sharply from the previous ones, which focused on the legal and historical aspects of American government, and concentrates instead on the somewhat less concrete notion of "political culture," or the inherited set of beliefs, attitudes, and opinions people (in this case, Americans) have about how their government ought to operate. After reading and reviewing the material in this chapter the student should be able to do each of the following:

1. Define what scholars mean by political culture, and list some of the dominant aspects of political culture in the United States.

2. Discuss how American citizens compare with those of other countries in their political attitudes.

3. List the contributions to American political culture made by the Revolution, by the nation's religious heritages, and by the family. Explain the apparent absence of class consciousness in this country.

5. Explain why some observers are quite concerned about the growth of mistrust in government and why others regard this mistrust as normal and healthy.

6. Define internal and external feelings of *political efficacy*, and explain how the level of each of these has varied over the past generation.

7. Explain why a certain level of political tolerance is necessary to the conduct of democratic politics, and review the evidence that indicates just how much political tolerance exists in this country. Agree or disagree with the text's conclusion that no group is truly free of political intolerance.

Chapter Outline with Keyed-in Resources

I. Political culture (THEME A: THE MEANING AND UNIQUE QUALITIES OF THE AMERICAN POLITICAL CULTURE)
   A. Tocqueville on American democracy
      1. Abundant and fertile soil for democracy to grow
      2. No feudal aristocracy; minimal taxes; few legal restraints
      3. Westward movement; vast territory provided opportunities
      4. Nation of small, independent farmers
      5. "Moral and intellectual characteristics"—today called "political culture"

B. Definition of political culture (ADDITIONAL LECTURE TOPIC A-1)
   1. Distinctive and patterned way of thinking about how political and economic life ought to be carried out.
   2. For example, stronger American belief in political than in economic equality
C. Elements of the American political system
   1. Liberty
   2. Democracy
   3. Equality
   4. Civic duty
D. Some questions about the U.S. political culture
   1. How do we know people share these beliefs?
      —before polls, beliefs inferred from books, speeches, etc.
   2. How do we explain behavior inconsistent with beliefs?
      —beliefs still important, source of change
   3. Why so much political conflict in U.S. history?
      —conflict occurs even with beliefs in common

Historians have debated the degree to which basic political values are shared in the United States. "Consensus" historians (like Louis Hartz) contend that Americans agree on political values based on the principles articulated by John Locke. "Conflict" historians (like Vernon Parrington) discern a liberal-conservative dimension to American values and dispute the existence of a unified culture.

   4. Most consistent evidence of political culture
      —use of terms "Americanism," "un-American"
E. The Economic System

The Constitution is a political document, not an economic one. As such, it is not an authority on the economic values shaping American culture. To quote Justice Oliver Wendell Holmes: "But a Constitution is not intended to embody a particular economic theory. . . . It is made for fundamentally differing views." Thus the capitalist system is not itself protected in the Constitution.

   1. Americans support free enterprise, but see limits on marketplace freedom
   2. Americans prefer "equality of opportunity" over "equality of result"; individualist view
   3. Americans have a shared commitment to economic individualism/self-reliance (see 1924 and 1977 polls)

II. Comparing America with other nations
   A. Political system
      1. Swedes: more deferential than participatory
         a. Defer to government experts and specialists
         b. Rarely challenge governmental decisions
         c. Believe in "what is best" more than "what people want"
         d. Value equality over liberty
         e. Value harmony and observe obligations

The degree of harmony in Sweden is reflected in the nation's relations between employers and workers. In the 1970s, the number of strikes annually averaged 87 in Sweden compared to 2,604 in Britain, 3,258 in France, and 5,249 in the United States.

      2. Japanese
         a. Value good relations with colleagues
         b. Emphasize group decisions and social harmony
         c. Respect authority
      3. Americans
         a. Tend to assert rights
         b. Emphasize individualism, competition, equality, following rules, treating others fairly (in contrast with the Japanese)
      4. Cultural differences affect political and economic systems

          5. Danger of overgeneralizing: many diverse groups within a culture
          6. Almond and Verba: U.S. and British citizens
              a. Stronger sense of civic duty/competence
              b. Institutional confidence
              c. Pride in country and fight for it
              d. Action to rectify "unjust laws"
      B. Economic system
          1. Swedes (contrasted with Americans): Verba and Orren
              a. Equal pay and top limit on incomes
              b. Less income inequality
          2. Cultural differences make a difference in politics
              a. Private ownership in United States versus public in Europe
      C. Religious belief
          1. Americans highly religious compared to Europeans

The United States, according to British writer G. K. Chesterton, is a "nation with the soul of a church."

          2. Religious beliefs have played an important role in American politics
          3. Both liberals and conservatives use the pulpit to promote political change
   III. The sources of political culture (THEME B: POLITICAL CULTURE: SOURCES, EFFICACY, TOLERANCE)
      A. Historical roots
          1. Revolution essentially over liberty; preoccupied with asserting rights
          2. Adversarial culture due to distrust of authority and a belief that human nature is depraved
          3. Federalist-Jeffersonian transition in 1800
              a. Legitimated role of opposition party; liberty and political change can coexist
      B. Legal-sociological factors
          1. Widespread participation permitted by Constitution
          2. Absence of an established national religion
              a. Religious diversity a source of cleavage

The diversity of religious denominations at the time of the American Revolution should not be exaggerated. Historian Sidney Ahlstrom estimates that 80 percent of the population grew up in families espousing Puritanism.

              b. Absence of established religion has facilitated the absence of political orthodoxy

England is an example of a nation with an established church, the Church of England. Since the monarch is the formal head of the religion, Prince Charles is caught in a marital dilemma: he cannot divorce Princess Diana without relinquishing a claim to the throne because a divorced person cannot serve as head of the faith. However, the Church of England is not the established religion of the entire United Kingdom; Scotland recognizes the Presbyterian church as the official state religion.

              c. Puritan heritage (dominant one) stress on personal achievement:
                  (1) Work
                  (2) Save money
                  (3) Obey secular law
                  (4) Do good
                  (5) Embrace "Protestant ethic"
              d. Miniature political systems produced by churches' congregational organization
          3. Family instills the ways we think about world and politics
              a. Great freedom of children
              b. Equality among family members

    c. Rights accorded each person
    d. Varied interests considered
   4. Class consciousness absent
    a. Most people consider themselves "middle class"
    b. Even unemployed do not oppose management
    c. Message of Horatio Alger stories is still popular
  C. The culture war
   1. Two cultural classes in America battle over values
   2. Culture war differs from political disputes in three ways:
    a. Money is not at stake
    b. Compromises are almost impossible
    c. Conflict is more profound
   3. Culture conflict animated by deep differences in people's beliefs about private and public morality
   4. Culture war about what kind of country we ought to live in
   5. Two camps
    a. Orthodox: morality more important than self-expression with rules from God
    b. Progressive: personal freedom more important than tradition with rules based on circumstances
   6. Orthodox associated with fundamentalist Protestants and progressives with mainline Protestants and those with no strong religious beliefs
   7. Culture war occurring within religious denominations

The degree of intrafaith tension is revealed by an interesting development among Episcopalians. Split over liberalizing tendencies in the faith such as the ordination of women, over a hundred Episcopalian priests in the United States have switched ministries to the more conservative Catholic church, producing numerous instances of Catholic priests who are married with children!

   8. Current culture war has special historical importance due to two changes:
    a. More people consider themselves progressives than previously
    b. Rise of technology makes it easier to wage culture war
 IV. Mistrust of government
  A. Evidence of increase since mid-1960s
   1. Jimmy Carter speech in 1979 on American malaise
   2. Perceived number of crooks in government
   3. Government run for a "few big interests"
   4. "Lots" of tax money wasted
   5. Government does right only "some of the time"
  B. Causes
   1. Watergate
   2. Vietnam
   3. But same trend before and after these events
  C. Necessary to view in context
   1. Mistrust of leaders, not of system mainly
   2. Present view closer to historical norm—unusually high confidence in 1950s
   3. Mistrust shared with most other institutions
   4. Mistrust possibly static since 1980
  D. In summary
   1. No loss of confidence in Americans themselves or in their system
   2. But people less ready to support leaders than in 1950s
 V. Political efficacy
  A. Definition: citizen's capacity to understand and influence political events
  B. Parts
   1. Internal efficacy
    a. Ability to understand and influence events
    b. About the same as in 1950s

2. External efficacy
      a. Belief that system will respond to citizens
      b. Not shaped by particular events
      c. Declined steadily through 1960s and 1970s
   C. Comparison: still much higher than Europeans'
   D. Conclusion
      1. Americans today may not be more "alienated"...
      2. ...but simply more realistic
VI. Political tolerance
   A. Crucial to democratic politics
      1. Citizens must be reasonably tolerant...
      2. ...but not necessarily perfectly tolerant
   B. Levels of American political tolerance
      1. Most Americans assent in abstract...
      2. ...but would deny rights in concrete cases
         a. Liberals intolerant of extreme right
         b. Conservatives intolerant of extreme left
      3. Most are willing to allow expression by others

Americans have become more tolerant over the past few decades according to survey data.

   C. Question: How do very unpopular groups survive?
      1. Most people do not act on beliefs
      2. Usually no consensus exists on whom to persecute
      3. Courts are sufficiently insulated from public opinion to enforce protection

The courts are not, of course, immune to public opinion. In a study on the sentences received by draft resisters during the Vietnam War, it was discovered that the lengths of jail terms varied with public opinion on the war.

   D. Conclusions
      1. Political liberty cannot be taken for granted
      2. No group should pretend it is always tolerant
         a. Conservatives once targeted professors
         b. Later professors targeted conservatives

Important Terms

*Americanism A belief that Americans consider themselves bound by common values and common hopes.

*civic competence A belief that one can affect government policies.

*civic duty The belief that citizens have an obligation to participate in civic and political affairs. This belief is part of the American political tradition.

*class consciousness The tendency to think of oneself as a worker whose interests are in opposition to those of management and vice versa. This belief is not part of the American political tradition.

culture war A split in the United States on people's beliefs about private and public morality and what standards ought to govern individual behavior and social arrangements.

*democracy An element of the American view of the political system, in which Americans believe that government officials should be accountable to the people.

*equality An element of the American view of the political system, in which Americans believe that everybody should have an equal vote and an equal chance.

equality of opportunity An economic value in American culture which maintains that all people should have the same opportunity to get ahead but that people should be paid on the basis of ability rather than on that of need.

*****external efficacy** The belief that the political system will respond to what citizens do. This belief has declined in recent years because of public sentiment that the government has become too big to be responsive.

*****internal efficacy** Confidence in one's own ability to understand and to take part in political affairs. This confidence has remained stable over the past few decades.

*****liberty** An element of the American view of the political system, in which Americans believe that people should be free to do what they please as long as they don't hurt other people.

*****orthodox (social)** One of two camps in the culture war that believes morality is as important or even more so than self-expression and that moral rules are derived from God.

*****political ideology** A comprehensive set of political, economic, and social views or ideas, concerned with the form and role of government.

*****political culture** A patterned way of thinking about how political and economic life ought to be carried out.

*****political efficacy** The sense that citizens have the capacity to understand and influence political events.

*****progressive (social)** One of two camps in the culture war that believes personal freedom is more important than traditional rules and that rules depend on the circumstances.

*****rights** A preoccupation of the American political culture that has imbued the daily conduct of politics with a kind of adversarial spirit quite foreign to the political life of countries that did not undergo a libertarian revolution or were formed from an interest in other goals.

*****secular humanism** The belief that moral standards do not require religious justification.

*****work ethic** A tradition of Protestant churches that required a life of personal achievement as well as religious conviction; a believer had an obligation to work, save money, obey the secular law, and do good works. Max Weber attributed the rise of capitalism in part to this ethic.

Theme A	The Meaning and Unique Qualities of the American Political Culture

Summary

The American constitutional machinery has not been directly applicable or exportable to many other nations. As the noted French observer Alexis de Tocqueville pointed out, the special conditions prevailing in America—vastness of territory, opportunity, the lack of a feudal aristocracy, minimal taxes, and so on—help to explain American political uniqueness. Still, it appears that the "moral and intellectual characteristics" of Americans (the political culture) are equally important.

The *political culture* is a "distinctive and patterned way of thinking about how political life ought to be carried out." The key elements of American political culture are (1) *liberty*—freedom from government restraints and protection of rights; (2) *individualism*—based on personal achievement; (3) *equality of opportunity*—the idea that each American should have an equal chance to succeed, but some will do better than others; (4) *civic duty*—the obligation to take part in community affairs. It is interesting to note how these elements of the American political culture almost mirror the principles articulated by John Locke, making the United States a "liberal" nation in a philosophical sense. Although one cannot prove that these elements exist, they can be inferred from the books that Americans read, the speeches they hear, the slogans to which they respond, the political choices they make, and the observations of insightful foreign visitors. Inconsistent behavior and political conflict in American history can also be logically correlated with the political culture.

Daniel Elazar has identified the existence of a unique political culture within each state derived largely from the values of the dominant religious denomination. Subsequent research has generally supported Elazar. Kenneth Wald, after reviewing this body of research, found evidence of "a strong link between religious affiliation and government 'morality' politics." If true, it would seem to follow that the elements of American political culture should take on a slightly different character regionally across the nation.

A five-nation study by Gabriel Almond and Sidney Verba in 1959–1960 showed Americans to have an especially high sense of *civic duty* and *political efficacy* (a belief that one can affect government policies). Although Americans may have less trust in government today, they still exhibit pride in their nation—particularly when compared to Germans, Italians, or Mexicans. One may also compare and contrast political cultures by analyzing American participatory attitudes versus Sweden's deferential style or Japan's emphasis on social harmony/hierarchy versus America's competitiveness and impersonality.

Discussion Questions

1. Since Tocqueville, the United States has experienced waves of immigration from cultures alien to the ethnic identities existing at the country's founding: Russians, Poles, Chinese, and so on. Wouldn't the influence of these groups change the "moral and intellectual characteristics" of the nation? For example, the number of Catholics increased from three million in 1860 to 20 million in 1930 (one-sixth of the nation's population). Wouldn't this religious change alter the nation's moral character? Or is the reverse true—that recent immigrants are eager to assimilate and adopt the values of their new country?

2. Japan has almost 125 million people—about half the population of the United States. Although the total land mass of the country is equivalent to the size of California, the habitable area is only about the size of Ohio. Could geography shape culture, such as Japan's emphasis on harmony? Since America's "vast territory" is now largely populated, is a change in political values imminent?

3. Argue for or against the proposition that the elements of American political culture or those "special conditions" that created it still exist today.

Data and Perspectives for Analysis

Ethnic Composition of the United States

German/Austrian	19%
English/Scotch/Welch	17
African	12
Irish	11
Hispanic	7
Italian	6
Scandinavian	6
Polish	3
Russian/Czech	3
Other	16

Source: U.S. Census Bureau, 1985.

Questions for Discussion

1. Almond and Verba's study of political cultures discovered marked differences between the values of the United States and those of Germany. But wouldn't the two cultures actually be very similar since Germans constitute the largest ethnic group in the United States?

2. Political values in the United States have not remained static. The enactment of Franklin Roosevelt's New Deal, for example, made the government increasingly responsible for the social welfare of its citizens. This change clearly bends some of the core values of American culture, like individualism and equality of opportunity. Could the influx of immigrants with socialist orientations (including Germans, Russians, Swedes) have influenced this cultural change?

Abstract for Theme A

The American and Russian Political Cultures

Tocqueville, in *Democracy in America* (1835), a classic commentary on the political cultures of the United States and Russia, wrote as follows:

> There are at the present time two great nations in the world, which started from different points, but seem to tend toward the same end. *I allude to the Russian and the American*. Both of them have grown up unnoticed; and while the attention of mankind was directed elsewhere, they have suddenly placed themselves in the front rank among the nations, and the world learned their existence and their greatness at almost the same time.
> All other nations seem to have nearly reached their natural limits, and they have only to maintain their power; but these are still in the act of growth. All other nations have stopped, or continue to advance with extreme difficulty; these two nations alone are proceeding with ease and speed along a path to which no limit can be perceived. *The American struggle against the obstacles that nature opposes to him; the adversaries of the Russian are men.* The former combats the wilderness and savage life; the latter combats civilization with all its arms. *The conquests of the American are therefore gained by the plowshare; those of the Russian by the sword. The American relies on personal interest to accomplish his ends and gives free scope to the unguided strength and common sense of the people; the Russian centers all the authority of society in a single arm. The principal instrument of the American is freedom; of the Russian, servitude.* Their starting point is different and their courses are not the same; yet each of them seems marked out by the will of heaven to sway the destinies of half the globe. (Emphasis added.)

Questions for Discussion

1. According to your reading of the excerpt, what appear to be the major differences in political culture between the Russian and the American as viewed by Tocqueville?
2. In this excerpt from Tocqueville, what appears to be the relationship between the political culture and national greatness or power?

Answer Guidelines

In Question 1, a key difference lies in the relationship of the individual to state authority. The Russian political culture is more force-oriented rather than relying on legal protections. In addition, you might also stress that the Russian political culture was a "natural" foundation for the imposition of Marxist-Leninist thought, given the supremacy of the centralized party and the principle of democratic centralism. Conversely, the strain of liberalism and the idea of the social contract in American democracy seemed to "fit" the value of state accountability to the individual. For Question 2, the answer may boil down to whether the values in a nation's political culture are conducive to full realization of the human spirit. To put it another way, can a nation's power or international status be based on two fundamental value configurations: coercion and suppression of freedom by an omnipotent state or the limitation of power and leadership responsibility to the governed? Finally, it is certainly true that historical conditioning plays a role in changing or reinforcing a nation's political culture. Students may wish to discuss events in either American or Russian history that have retarded or advanced national power and prestige (examples: the role of the American frontier, Russia and its periodic invasions).

Additional Lecture Topic

A-1. Understanding and Comparing the American Political Culture

Donald Devine, *The Political Culture of the United States*. Boston: Little, Brown, 1972.

Louis Hartz, *The Liberal Tradition in America*. New York: Harcourt Brace, 1955.

Walter A. Rosenbaum, *Political Culture*. New York: Praeger, 1975. Pp. 75–89.

Hedrick Smith, *The Russians*. New York: New York Times, 1976. Chapter 4.

Theme B Political Culture: Sources, Efficacy, and Tolerance

Summary

The sources of the American political culture include the following four elements. (1) The American Revolution had liberty as its object, and the founding experience created a preoccupation with the assertion and maintenance of rights. (2) The absence of an official religion encouraged religious pluralism and, ultimately, political pluralism. (3) The dominance of Protestantism promoted an especially participant culture. (4) Child-rearing practices stressing equality among family members and freedom for children produced corresponding political values. All of these influences shaped a political culture in which "class consciousness" is relatively unimportant.

However, the values of the American political culture are not immune to change. For example, the trust that Americans have in their government has varied considerably, dropping substantially during the days of Vietnam and Watergate and apparently rising again since 1980. Americans no longer support their political leaders to the degree that they did in the 1950s, however, and the decline is perhaps attributable to unrealized governmental policies and social turmoil. A similar drop has occurred in the public's sense of external efficacy (system responsiveness); Americans are twice as likely as they were in 1950 to say that public officials care little about what the people think or want. (Still, American political efficacy remains higher than in many other countries.) Finally, Americans remain more tolerant of unpopular ideas, individuals, and groups in the abstract than in reality. Yet because Americans often do not act on their beliefs, cannot agree on which group, individual, or idea should be suppressed, and permit the courts to enforce constitutional protections, personal liberties and constitutional freedoms endure.

Discussion Questions

1. How do we know that the sources of political culture listed in the text are really important? Did the Revolution really make a difference? Or would the attitudes attributed to the Revolution have grown up anyway in response to another aspect of the American experience (the frontier, for example)?

2. Americans turned more cynical about the government after Vietnam and Watergate, but levels of trust began rising again in the 1980s. Why didn't cynicism return after the Oliver North episode revealed misdeeds even by President Reagan?

3. If Americans possess higher degrees of both internal and external efficacy than do other peoples, why are participation rates for elections lower in the United States than in Europe? Since Americans believe they can influence the government and the government will respond, isn't it logical that they should participate in elections at a higher rate?

4. What policies could public officials adopt to increase the sense of political efficacy among citizens? Cite some possible examples.

5. Shouldn't both Vietnam and Watergate have increased the sense of political efficacy in the United States, since the system did respond?

Data and Perspectives for Analysis

Political efficacy involves a sense that citizens have the capacity to understand and influence political events. Compared to Europeans, Americans possess a greater sense of political efficacy. As defined, political efficacy focuses on the "capacity" to understand and influence politics. It does not necessarily mean that citizens have these capacities. While it is difficult to evaluate whether citizens influence political events, it is easily possible to ascertain whether citizens have knowledge of such events. To provide a comparative perspective, a recent survey queries citizens of eight nations on current political topics. First, have your students answer the questions to discover their knowledge base. Second, have your students explain why Americans score so poorly on the questions. Is it because the questions focus on foreign affairs? Point out that this same low level of information is reflected on domestic issues as well (a topic discussed later in the text). Why is it that countries with low levels of political efficacy, like Germany, have superior knowledge of political events? What does the survey reveal about the relationship between political knowledge and political influence?

Correct Responses by Country

Question	Canada	Britain	France	Germany	Italy	Mexico	Spain	USA
Do you know the name of the ethnic group that has conquered much of Bosnia?	42%	46%	55%	77%	51%	12%	24%	28%
Do you know the name of the ethnic group with which the Israelis reached a peace accord?	51%	59%	60%	79%	56%	21%	29%	40%
Who is President of Russia?	59%	63%	61%	94%	76%	42%	65%	50%
Who is Boutros Boutros-Ghali?	26%	22%	32%	58%	43%	14%	15%	13%

Adapted from a poll by Times Mirror Center for the People and the Press, 1994.

Abstract for Theme B

Crisis in the American Spirit

In Theodore White's *America in Search of Itself: The Making of the President, 1956–80* (New York: Harper & Row, 1982), some attention is paid to the circumstances that led up to the "malaise" speech referred to in the text chapter. President Carter was facing severe economic problems. His pollster, Pat Caddell, sent him a memo in late April 1979 that started out as follows:

> America is a nation deep in crisis. Unlike civil war or depression, this crisis, nearly invisible, is unique.... *Psychological more than material, it is a crisis of confidence marked by a dwindling faith in the future.*... This crisis is not your fault as President. It is the *natural result of historical forces and events which have been in motion for twenty years.* This crisis threatens the political and social fabric of the nation.... The pessimism has extended to the elites; the young, the college-educated, and the higher-income groups.... *1 out of every 3 Americans see their own lives going downhill.* (p. 258, emphasis added)

White describes how the president wrestled with this "loss of trust, this failure of will." The situation was further complicated by the gasoline panic of 1979, a result of the cutoff of oil from Iran. Starting in California, the gas crisis spread across the country. By June motorists were fighting for a tank of gas, and deaths even resulted from these quarrels. Although the crisis eventually subsided by Labor Day, public support for Carter dropped as the president inevitably received blame for the panic.

In July the president gathered his advisers together at Camp David and sought some answers about the crisis of the American spirit. President Carter wanted to

> speak to the nation about his driving concern; somewhere, though never voiced, the problem was that the American nation could *not* be governed without *a common faith* of Americans in one another, and a readiness to sacrifice for *a common cause*. (p. 267, emphasis added)

After ten days of consultation with prominent leaders at Camp David, the president delivered his speech (July 15). The core of the speech was inspirational.

> The crisis . . . strikes at the very heart and soul and spirit of our national will. . . . The symptoms of this crisis . . . are all around us . . . Washington, D.C., has become an island. The gap between our citizens and our government has never been so wide. . . . We simply must have faith in each other. . . . Let us commit ourselves together to a rebirth of the American spirit. Working together with our common faith, we cannot fail. (p. 268)

Though it was delivered exceptionally well, the speech had a negligible impact—it did little to arrest Carter's drop in popularity. This "malaise" speech would later contrast sharply with challenger Ronald Reagan's optimism about American "greatness" and the fundamental "worth" of the American people.

Questions for Discussion

1. What do you believe a "crisis of confidence" involves? Did Americans lack confidence in themselves, in the country, in its leadership, or in all three?

2. Do you think President Carter violated a cardinal tenet of the American political culture when he intimated that the nation and its people were losing the way toward progress and a better lifestyle? In short, are optimism and belief in the future values that should not be attacked by a president so openly, because the president is the very symbol of the nation to most citizens?

3. Can a president, through national speeches of a highly dramatic nature, restore trust and renew the spirit of political efficacy among the population?

Answer Guidelines

Although President Carter may have believed that all three components were involved, it seems apparent that many Americans blamed the "crisis" on their leaders—and more specifically on the president. In other words, internal efficacy may have been less important than external efficacy. What Question 2 boils down to is whether national pride—a key component of the political culture—can be punctured so directly. Invariably citizens may feel that the crisis is something they have not caused and that the roots of the problem are to be found elsewhere. For Question 3 obviously much depends on the individual president—his style, his ability to communicate, and whether his promises lead to improvements that are clearly noticeable by the public. The differences in presidential effectiveness between Carter and Reagan can be readily observed.

The theme of how a president enhances or detracts from the prevailing consensus within the general political culture could serve as an additional lecture topic. The sources are plentiful and need not be itemized here.

PART TWO

Opinions, Interests, and Organizations

5

Public Opinion

Overview and Objectives

The purpose of this chapter is to explore what we mean by "public opinion" and to ask what sorts of effects public opinion has on our supposedly democratic form of government. After reading and reviewing the material in this chapter the student should be able to do each of the following:

1. List the sources of our political attitudes, and indicate which are the most important. Assess the influence of various religious traditions on political attitudes.

2. Explain why there is no single cleavage between liberals and conservatives in this country and why there are crosscutting cleavages. Explain the significance of these facts. Assess the significance of race in explaining political attitudes.

3. Define "political ideology" and give reasons why most Americans do not think ideologically. Summarize the "liberal" positions on the economy, civil rights, and political conduct. Describe the major "policy packages" in the Democratic party and indicate which groups in the Democratic coalition can be identified with each package.

4. Identify which "elite groups" have become liberal, and compare their present attitudes with the past political preferences of these groups. Discuss the "new class" theory as an explanation for changes in attitudes. Analyze why these changes are causing strain in the political party system.

Chapter Outline with Keyed-in Resources

I. What is public opinion? (THEME A: PUBLIC OPINION AND AMERICAN DEMOCRACY)
   A. Government does not always do what people want
      1. Unbalanced budget
      2. Opposition to busing
      3. Support for ERA
      4. Aid to Nicaragua
   B. Reasons public policy and public opinion may differ
      1. Many constitutional checks on public opinion, many "publics"
      2. Limits on effectiveness of opinion polling; difficult to know public opinion
      3. Government listens more to elite views
   C. Influences and limitations (ADDITIONAL LECTURE TOPIC A-1)
      1. Public ignorance: Monetary Control Bill ruse, poor name recognition of leaders

While public ignorance of political issues is well documented, the same is not true of members of Congress. *Spy* magazine in 1993 called twenty first-term members of the House and asked, "Do you approve of what we're doing to stop what's going on in Fredonia?" (The country, of course, is a fictitious creation from the Marx Brothers' movie *Duck Soup*). Some of the responses were the following: From Rep. Corrine Brown (D-Fla): "I think all of those situations are very, very sad, and I think we need to take action to assist the people." And from Rep. Steve Buyer (R-Ind.): "Yeah. It's a different situation than the Middle East."

      2. Importance of wording of questions: affects answer
      3. Instability of public opinion
      4. Public has more important things to think about—need clear-cut political choices
      5. Specific attitudes less important than political culture
II. The origins of political attitudes
   A. The role of the family
      1. Party identification of family absorbed, but more independent as child grows

Since party affiliation is largely handed down from parents, what happens when the parents have different party identifications? According to research, the children of such marriages are more likely to adopt the affiliation of their mother.

      2. Much continuity between generations
      3. Declining ability to pass on identification
      4. Younger voters exhibit less partisanship; more likely to be independent
      5. Meaning of partisanship unclear in most families; less influence on policy preferences
      6. Clear ideologies passed on in a few families
   B. Religion
      1. Religious traditions affect families
         a. Catholic families somewhat more liberal

The liberal orientation of Catholics is not necessarily a product of their theology. Indeed, Catholicism has been historically suspect for harboring antidemocratic tendencies. According to George Marsden, "by the late nineteenth century Catholic communities were conspicuous . . . in their emphasis on authority." And even liberal Protestants were "fearful that Catholic influences in politicals would lead to authoritarianism."

         b. Protestant families more conservative

            c. Jewish families decidedly more liberal
        2. Two theories on differences
            a. Social status of religious group
            b. Content of religion's tradition
    C. The "gender gap"
        1. Has existed as long as voting records exist
        2. Changing: partisan advantage
            a. Women were likely to be Republicans in 1950s
            b. Women were likely to be Democrats in 1980s
            c. Change due to shift in party positions on "gender" issues

Not all "gender" issues divide along logical sexual lines. For example, men are actually less likely to be opposed to abortion than women. In a poll taken in 1989, 11 percent of men (but 17 percent of women) believed abortion should be illegal under all circumstances.

            d. Woman give more votes to female candidates but may be due to more women candidates being Democrats
    D. Schooling and information
        1. College education has liberalizing effect; longer in college, more liberal
        2. Effect extends beyond end of college
        3. Cause of this liberalization?
            a. Personal traits: temperament, family, intelligence
            b. Exposure to information on policies
            c. Liberalism of professors
        4. Effect growing as more go to college
        5. Increasing conservatism since 1960s?
            a. Yes (legalizing marijuana) and . . .
            b. . . . No (school busing)
III. Cleavages in public opinion (THEME B: GROUP CLEAVAGES, POLITICAL ATTITUDES, AND POLITICAL IDEOLOGY)
    A. Social class: less important in U.S. than in Europe
        1. More important in 1950s on unemployment, education, housing programs
        2. Less important in 1960s on poverty, health insurance, Vietnam, jobs

While the influence of social class on political ideology diminished, the proportion of the population classified as middle class shrank in the 1980s. Could social class revive as a factor shaping political ideology?

        3. Why the change?
            a. Education: occupation depends more on schooling
            b. Noneconomic issues now define liberal and conservative
    B. Race and ethnicity
        1. Becoming more important even on nonracial matters

The persistence of a difference in the attitudes of African-Americans in relation to whites is at least partially due to a perception that discrimination lingers. In 1992, 51 percent of blacks said that the quality of life for blacks has worsened, with only 24 percent saying it has improved.

        2. Blacks most consistently liberal group; little cleavage
        3. Other minorities less liberal
    C. Region
        1. Southerners more conservative than northerners: military and civil rights issues, but difference fading overall

The change in southern views is illustrated by the following polling data. In 1972, 52 percent of whites in the South said they would vote for a qualified black running for president. By 1989, that figure had risen to 72 percent!

        2. Southern lifestyle different
        3. Lessening attachment to Democratic party

IV. Political ideology (ADDITIONAL LECTURE TOPIC B-1)
   A. Consistent attitudes
      1. Ideology: patterned set of political beliefs about who ought to rule, and their principles and policies
      2. Most citizens display little ideology; moderates dominate
      3. Yet many have strong political predispositions
      4. "Consistency" criterion somewhat arbitrary
      5. Some believe ideology increased in 1960s
      6. Others argue that poll questions were merely worded differently
   B. What do "liberalism" and "conservatism" mean?
      1. "Liberal" and "conservative" labels have complex history
         a. Europe during French Revolution: conservative = church, state, aristocracy
         b. Roosevelt and New Deal: activism = liberalism
         c. Conservative reaction to activism (Goldwater): free market, states' rights, economic choice
         d. Today's imprecise and changing meanings
   C. Various categories (THEME C: PUBLIC-OPINION POLLING)
      1. Three useful categories emerge from studies
         a. Economic policy: liberals favor jobs for all, subsidized medical care and education, taxation of rich
         b. Civil rights: liberals prefer desegregation, equal opportunity, etc.
         c. Public and political conduct: liberals tolerant of demonstrations, use of marijuana, etc.
   D. Analyzing consistency: people can "mix" categories
      1. Pure liberals: liberal on both economic and personal conduct issues
      2. Pure conservatives: conservative on both economic and personal conduct issues
      3. Libertarians: conservative on economic issues, liberal on personal conduct issues
      4. Populists: liberal on economic issues, conservative on personal conduct issues
   E. Political elites
      1. Definition: those who have a disproportionate amount of some valued resource
      2. Elites, or activists, display greater ideological consistency
         a. They have more information than most people
         b. Their peers reinforce consistency
   F. Is there a "new class"?
      1. Definition: those who are advantaged by the power, resources, and growth of government (not business)

Linda Medcalf and Kenneth Dolbeare contend that the "new class" has evolved a distinctive ideology, one they call neoliberalism. Instead of assigning priority to equality and freedom, as in classical liberalism, this ideology focuses on producing new wealth through high technology. Neoliberalism uses public needs as a guide and relies on government incentives to encourage industrial development. Gary Hart and Paul Tsongas are politicians endorsing neoliberal values.

      2. Two explanations of well-off individuals who are liberals
         a. Their direct benefits from government
         b. Liberal ideology infusing postgraduate education
      3. Traditional middle class: four years of college, suburban, church-affiliated, probusiness, conservative on social issues, Republican
      4. Liberal middle class: postgraduate education, urban, critical of business, liberal on social issues, Democrat
      5. Emergence of new class creates strain in Democratic party
V. Political elites, public opinion, and public policy (THEME D: DO ELITES CONTROL OPINION AND PUBLIC POLICY?)
   A. Elites influence public opinion in two ways
      1. Raise and form political issues
      2. State norms by which to settle issues, defining policy options

    3. Elite views shape mass views
  B. Limits to elite influence on the public (ADDITIONAL LECTURE TOPIC D-1)
    1. Elites do not define problems
    2. Many elites exist, hence many elite opinions

Important Terms

*conservative A political ideology that, although changing in meaning, adheres to the following principles and practices: on economic matters, it does not favor government efforts to ensure that everyone has a job; on civil rights, does not favor strong federal action to desegregate schools and increase hiring opportunities for minorities; and on political conduct, does not favor tolerance toward protest demonstrations, legalizing marijuana, and protecting the rights of criminals.

*elite People with a disproportionate amount of a valued resource.

*gender gap Differences between the political views of men and women.

*John Q. Public The average man or woman on the street, often portrayed by cartoonists as bespectacled and befuddled.

*liberal A political ideology that, although changing in meaning, adheres to the following principles and practices: on economic matters, it favors government efforts to ensure that everyone has a job; on civil rights, it favors strong federal action to desegregate schools and increase hiring opportunities for minorities; and on political conduct, it favors tolerance toward protest demonstrations, legalizing marijuana, and protecting the rights of criminals.

*libertarianism A political ideology that is conservative on economic matters and liberal on social ones. The ideology's goal is the creation of a small, weak government.

*Middle America A phrase coined by Joseph Kraft in a 1968 newspaper column to refer to Americans who have moved out of poverty but who are not yet affluent and who cherish the traditional middle-class values.

new class People whose advantages stem not so much from their connections with business but from the growth of government.

*norm A standard of right and proper conduct. Elites tend to state the norms by which issues should be settled.

partisanship Identification with a political party.

*political ideology A coherent and consistent set of beliefs about who ought to rule, what principles rulers ought to obey, and what policies rulers ought to pursue.

poll A survey of public opinion.

*populism A political ideology that is liberal on economic matters and conservative on social ones. It believes the government should reduce economic inequality but regulate personal conduct.

*pure conservatism A political ideology that is conservative on both economic and personal conduct.

*pure liberalism A political ideology that is liberal on both economic and personal conduct.

random sample A sample selected in such a way that any member of the population being surveyed (e.g., all adults or voters) has an equal chance of being interviewed.

*religious tradition The values associated with the major religious denominations in America: Protestant, Catholic, and Jewish. In general, Catholic families are somewhat more liberal on economic issues than white Protestant ones, while Jewish families are much more liberal on both economic and social issues than families of either Christian religion.

*sampling error The difference between the results from two different samples of the same population. This difference in answers is not significant and its likely size can be computed mathematically. In general, the bigger the sample and the bigger the differences between the percentage of people giving one answer and the percentage giving another, the smaller the error.

*silent majority A term referring to people, whatever their economic status, who uphold traditional values, especially against the counterculture of the 1960s.

Theme A	Public Opinion and American Democracy

Summary

The Greeks invented the term "idiot" to refer to a person who cares nothing about politics. They could not understand why anyone would be unconcerned about matters affecting war and peace, poverty and wealth, or the standards of right and wrong. It is for this reason that Aristotle called politics the "queen of sciences." Yet polling data seem to suggest that the average American citizen fits the Greek definition of *idiot*. People manifest a high degree of ignorance about political issues. The explanation, according to Wilson, is that most people do not feel it is worthwhile to invest much time analyzing public affairs. This justification, however, does little to remove the label of "idiot" from the average citizen.

The situation is not entirely as bleak as it might appear. To begin with, polls are not always able to tap public opinion accurately. The wording of questions influences public responses; a question can conceal as much as it reveals. Thus it is almost impossible to uncover the depth of public knowledge with a high level of certainty. In the second place, opinions on public issues are not stable over time. They may not even be truthful. Soon after the assassination of President Kennedy, for example, more people reported having voted for him in 1960 than the actual votes he received. Pollsters can be deceived. Despite these qualifications, the picture of American democracy is still not a flattering one. If democracy is based on the "will of the people," how does the political system endure?

The answer, of course, is that the Constitution did not design a form of government intended to reflect public opinion. It established goals independent of the moody fluctuations of public preferences. In this sense, politicians should regard public opinion more as a barometer than as a compass.

Discussion Questions

1. If the American public is so ignorant about political issues, should politicians seek to abide by opinion polls? Are there certain instances when politicians should be more or less likely to follow the "will of the people"? If not, why have a democracy at all? How has the United States survived as democracy given the apathy and ignorance of the public?

2. The Founding Fathers worried about the ability of the "average" citizen to make wise decisions on political issues. This concern seems to remain valid. Why hasn't the situation changed given the increase in number of Americans receiving education? Shouldn't such ignorance decrease with education?

Data and Perspectives for Analysis

A. Democratic Beliefs and the Public

Studies have consistently revealed that public opinion does not reflect much commitment to the values of democratic government in concrete situations. Indeed, the people display a lack of confidence even in themselves to govern. As the text points out, the system endures because the Constitution was designed not to rely on public opinion for political guidance. In analyzing opinion data, Herbert McCloskey concluded that American democracy owes its existence to political elites who have kept the system going "as the carriers of the Creed." Elites alone, according to McCloskey, manifest an allegiance to the fundamental principles of democratic government.

Have your class discuss and interpret the data below. McCloskey identifies "political influentials" as delegates to national party nominating conventions.

Issue	Percent Agree	
	Political Influentials	General Electorate
The majority has the right to abolish minorities if it wants to.	6.8%	28.4%
People ought to be allowed to vote even if they can't do so intelligently.	65.6%	47.6%
The true American way of life is disappearing so fast that we may have to use force to save it.	12.8%	34.6%
The main trouble with democracy is that most people don't really know what's best for them.	40.8%	58.0%
Few people really know what is in their own best interest in the long run.	42.6%	61.1%
"Issues" and "arguments" are beyond the understanding of most voters.	37.5%	62.3%
Most people don't have enough sense to pick their own leaders wisely.	28.0%	47.8%
It will always be necessary to have a few strong, able people actually running everything.	42.5%	56.2%

Adapted from Herbert McCloskey, "Consensus and Ideology in American Politics," *The American Political Science Review* 58 (June 1964): pp. 361–382.

It is interesting to note that this trend has persisted to the present day. Moreover, the same difference between elite and mass opinion is shared in the United Kingdom. Have your students examine the following data for differences from the above table and for differences between nations. The authors define "political elites" in the United States as members of the House of Representatives and in the United Kingdom as members of Parliament. The authors' conclusion supports the argument of the text: "We are led to the tentative conclusion that two of the key factors protecting political freedom in Britain and the United States are elite tolerance and constitutional organization. The political elites . . . are substantially more likely to be tolerant . . . than are members of the public. In addition, constitutional arrangements buttress the policy-making autonomy of such elites and guarantee competition among governmental institutions" (734).

Least Liked Group Should	Percent Tolerant			
	General Public		Political Elites	
	USA	UK	USA	UK
Be banned from running for office	18%	14%	46%	36%
Be allowed to hold a political rally	33%	34%	93%	64%
Be allowed to make a public speech	50%	51%	81%	78%
Have phones tapped by government	63%	62%	78%	49%

Adapted from David G. Barnum and John L. Sullivan, "The Elusive Foundations of Political Freedom in Britain and the United States," *Journal of Politics* 52 (August 1990): p. 729.

B. College and Political Ideology

Ideological Self-Identification of College Freshmen, 1970–1988

How would you characterize your political views? Mark one: Far left, liberal, middle-of-the-road, conservative, far right.

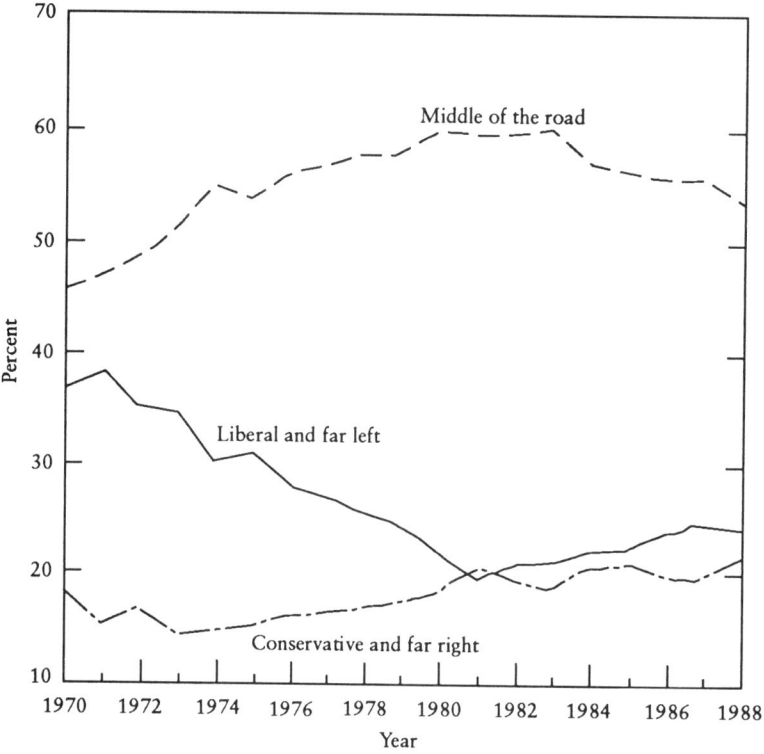

Source: Alexander W. Astin et al., *The American Freshmen: Twenty-Year Trends, 1966–1985* (Los Angeles. Higher Education Research Institute, 1986–1988), 64 (1986), 61 (1987), 61 (1988).

1. The trends in ideological self-identification reveal several shifts, especially in the percentage of liberal college freshmen. To what degree is a person's ideology a reflection of national mood? Why weren't more college freshmen conservative during the Reagan era of the 1980s?

2. The text asserts that the liberal attitudes of college students could be due, in part, to the fact that college attracts a particular type of person. Do the data suggest that college freshmen are somehow different from the population as a whole?

3. The text asserts that the liberal attitudes of college students could be due, in part, to the fact that college professors are more liberal than the population in general. Since many of the radical students of the early 1970s are now college professors, shouldn't college students today become an extremely liberal generation? Is this actually the case?

C. Freedom of Speech

The percentages in the following table indicate the number of respondents who would allow each of the three speakers to speak.

Education and Support for Freedom of Speech

Type of speaker	General Public	College Graduate	High School Graduate	Grade School Graduate
An advocate of government ownership of industry	77%	95%	83%	55%
An opponent of churches and religion	65	90	74	33
An admitted communist	52	84	56	22

Source: National Opinion Research Center, General Social Survey, 1972.

1. What meanings can be derived from this table relating opinions and level of education?
2. What is the relationship between an individual's level of education and his or her support of freedom of speech for the three types of speakers listed in the table?

Additional Lecture Topic A-1

Influences and Nature of Public Beliefs

Robert S. Erikson, Norman R. Luttbeg, and Kent L. Tedin, *American Public Opinion: Its Origin, Content, and Impact,* 3rd ed. New York: John Wiley, 1988.

Benjamin Ginsberg, *The Captive Public: How Mass Opinion Promotes State Power.* New York: Basic Books, 1986.

Harry Holloway and John George, *Public Opinion: Coalitions, Elites and Masses.* New York: St. Martin's Press, 1986.

Michael Margolis and Gary A. Mauser, *Manipulating Public Opinion.* Pacific Grove, CA: Brooks-Cole, 1989.

Russell W. Neuman, *The Paradox of Mass Politics: Knowledge and Opinion in the American Electorate.* Cambridge, MA: Harvard University Press, 1986.

Benjamin I. Page and Robert Y. Shapiro, *The Rational Public: Fifty Years of Americans' Policy Preferences.* Chicago: University of Chicago Press, 1992.

Abstract for Theme A

Socialization and Political Integration

In his book *Public Opinion in American Politics* (Harcourt Brace Jovanovich, 1980), W. Lance Bennett argues (pp. 141–142) that young people acquire the important political attitudes or core values of *individualism and equality*. Despite the fact that these values are in competition with each other, they are ultimately responsible for creating "broad support" for the institutions and principles that comprise the heart of the American political system. Furthermore, these core values explain "a good deal about the development of individual political orientations and the patterns of change in public opinion." As Bennett goes on to explain:

> Most people, during socialization, probably become attached in varying degrees to both core values. The presence of two competing values at the base of a system of political belief lets people develop different, but personally coherent and sensible, political orientations as their social experiences and immediate value concerns change.
>
> This hypothesis . . . also argues that most individuals are not simply political chameleons who change political colors in perfect response to their surroundings. Changes are to some degree limited and predictable responses based on the relations between the core values in an individual's belief system. If most individuals have some commitment to equality and individualism . . . it also becomes possible to explain broad patterns of political realignment and policy change in society.

Bennett argues that this "value cycle," or alternation between equality and individualism in the mass public (a byproduct of the early socialization process), is linked to the concomitant rise of conservative political coalitions (emphasizing individualism) subsequently followed by liberal coalitions, "which shift the policy emphasis in the direction of economic regulation and social redistribution (equality)." In short, a "so-called pendulum effect both in individual thinking and in patterns of public opinion may also explain the limits of political change in America and the role of public opinion as a moderating influence during periods of change."

Questions for Discussion

1. Do students agree that the two most important political values they learned during the political socialization process were those of individualism and equality? Why or why not?

2. Why do these "core values" conflict with each other? How can they be reconciled in actual political practice or policies? Have student cite some examples, if possible.

3. What "cycle" of American politics is operative now? Is the evidence conclusive regarding such an assertion?

Answer Guidelines

Answers will naturally vary, but students should cite some actual examples or attitudes that exemplify the core values that Bennett suggests. One central question that you might consider is whether individual "equality" should be managed or created by government or whether the value of equality is an ideal rather than a practical reality. Students might also be asked whether their family lifestyle when they were growing up emphasized competitiveness (among family members or between parents) or stressed fairness and equal allocation of resources (love, attention by parents, playing "favorites"). Some link between socialization experiences and current political attitudes might be discovered.

Theme B — Group Cleavages, Political Attitudes, and Political Ideology

Summary

Cleavages in opinion in the United States are numerous and crosscutting. No single feature of an individual's life (such as social class) explains all (or even most) of that individual's attitudes. Among the important cleavages are:

1. *Occupation.* Today occupation has a weaker association with political opinions than it did in the 1950s. The traditional gap—manual workers were more liberal than business or professional persons in their attitudes toward the economy and social welfare legislation—has narrowed. This is not necessarily because class no longer matters but rather because a new elite whose status is based on education and technical skills, the "new class," has arisen over the past generation.

    This new class is situated not in traditional, capitalist business enterprise but in government, academia, "think tanks," and the media. This class has strained the Democratic party; it is younger, urban, and more liberal on economic and social issues than the traditional middle class, which is conservative and blue-collar. Gary Hart appealed to this new class in the primary campaigns of 1984, as did Paul Tsongas in 1992.

2. *Race.* Blacks are generally far more liberal than whites, not only on racial issues (busing, housing discrimination) but also on issues such as the death penalty, national defense, and national health insurance. Blacks believe they are better off today than ten years ago, but it is well-off blacks who hold the most negative attitudes toward American society.

3. *Region*. The South is the least liberal of the four regions, with the Midwest somewhat more liberal and the East and West most liberal. The South became, and long remained, part of the Democratic coalition because southerners were fairly liberal on economic issues. However, the rise of racial and "social" issues (on which the South is quite conservative) ended southern attachment to the Democratic party.

An *ideology* is a coherent and consistent set of beliefs about who ought to rule, what principles rulers ought to obey, and what policies rulers ought to pursue. Whether people have a political ideology can be measured in two ways: (1) by seeing how frequently people speak in terms of broad political *categories*—"liberal," "conservative," or "radical"—when they discuss politics; and (2) by measuring *constraint*, the extent to which we can predict a person's view on one issue by knowing his view on another issue.

Most studies show relatively little ideological thinking among Americans. However, several qualifications should be kept in mind. Ideological "consistency" is defined somewhat arbitrarily. It is assumed that "consistent" liberalism involves favoring social welfare policies at home and opposing a strong stand against communism abroad. Some evidence (controversial among political scientists) suggests that the events of the 1960s produced more ideological thinking among Americans. Also, voters may think more ideologically when one or both presidential candidates take sharply ideological positions (as in 1964, 1972, 1980, and 1984). It is clear, however, that political activists are much more likely than the average citizen to think in ideological terms and to take "consistent" positions on issues.

Discussion Questions

1. How is religion related to political attitudes? Why? The text suggests that the theologies of various religions have an important effect. Can you think of other explanations for the correlation between religion and political attitudes? For example, does it matter that, historically, Catholics tended to be blue-collar workers in northern cities? That Jews were disproportionately intellectuals? To what extent would self-interest explain why religious groups differ in the ways they do?

2. The text contends that public opinion in the United States is split by many cleavages. Yet historian Louis Hartz argues that Americans embrace the same fundamental values. Alexis de Tocqueville concurs; he found that "Americans were agreed upon the most essential points." Donald Devine examined polling data and derived the same conclusion: "In the United States, consensus support for the liberal tradition has provided the framework within which serious conflict has been resolved." Does the text exaggerate the degree of cleavage in public opinion? What major disagreements exist in the United States today?

3. What is a political elite? Do we have one unified elite, or are there different elites with radically different views on policy? How have the political attitudes of well-off Americans changed in recent years?

4. Who constitutes the "new class"? How does the new class differ from more traditional elites in its political attitudes? How do you explain the attitudes of the new class? Are its members "enlightened" by higher education? Do they have class interests different from more traditional elites? Consider the two occupational categories mentioned in the text—bankers, doctors, corporation presidents, and Wall Street lawyers (the traditional elite) versus government officials, research scientists, professors, and the mass media. Which group would benefit most from each of the following developments?

   - large-scale nationalization of industry
   - a reduction of income taxes on high incomes
   - an increase in the number of social welfare programs
   - increased government control over the economy
   - more political democracy through, for example, referenda

5. How is race related to political attitudes? To what extent are the distinctive political beliefs of blacks "obvious"? Which liberal beliefs among blacks are not "obvious"? Can you explain them? Can any be explained by the socioeconomic position of individual blacks? Can they be explained by the historical experience of blacks as a group?

6. Long ago, James Prothro and Charles Grigg discovered a problem with the views of Americans on democratic values. The general public manifests opinions that are often contrary to basic values essential to sustain a democratic government. Political elites are both more aware of and more committed to constitutional liberties. How has the United States managed to endure with such low levels of public tolerance? Does this indicate that the general public has little input into governmental policy?

Data and Perspectives for Analysis

A. Lifestyle and Politics

Mother Jones is a left-wing magazine of considerable importance. Like most periodicals, it surveys the consumption habits of its subscribers to help advertisers target their audiences appropriately. Unlike most periodicals, *Mother Jones* discussed the results in a column.

> For readers of a magazine of the Left, most of you are surprisingly well off. You buy ten hardback books a year, 47.4 percent of you own 35 mm cameras, 91 percent own stereo equipment, and 41 percent drink Perrier or some other bottled water, for God's sake. Don't try to get off the hook by claiming that you only enjoy simple pleasures like herb tea (70.2 percent), yoghurt (83 percent) and camping out (47 percent); your average household income is $23,300....
>
> Actually, you shouldn't feel guilty about your relative affluence. Drink that champagne (46.8 percent) and enjoy life; if there's anything we all should have learned from the '60s, it's that poverty itself is no virtue—and no gauge of how much good one does.... The day when MJ readers who are imported-wine drinkers (64 percent) are outnumbered by camper-truck owners (13 percent) is probably as far off as the day when hard-hats start marching in affirmative action demonstrations.
>
> Adam Hochschild, "Yoghurt, Perrier and Politics," *Mother Jones*, April 1979.

1. Do these number suggest that there is a distinctive lifestyle associated with the left-wing politics of *Mother Jones* readers?

2. Can you think of cultural artifacts other than automobiles and the items mentioned that have *political* significance?

B. Religion and Political Values

The text suggests that different religious orientations produce people with different political attitudes. Charles Dunn has devised a format to make comparisons between conservative (evangelical) and liberal (mainline Protestant and Catholic) theologies. Does this comparison illustrate why evangelicals adopt conservative political values and Catholics do not? (Mainline Protestant denominations include Episcopalians, Presbyterians, Lutherans, Congregationalists, and most Methodists.)

Comparison of Conservative and Liberal Theology[a]
Tendency of Belief

Liberal		Conservative
Nature, reason	Ultimate source of knowledge	Bible
Fallible	Bible	Infallible
More symbolic	Biblical interpretation	More literal
Relative/situational	Moral standards	Absolute
Man	Relative emphasis	God
Remote/impersonal	Conception of God	Sovereign/personal
Evolution	Creation of man	God's direct act
Good	Human nature	Evil
Social	Moral emphasis	Personal
Rights	Relative importance to man	Responsibilities
Unjust social systems	Origin of evil	Satan and fall of man
Good works	Basis of salvation	Grace/faith
Earth	Relative focus	Heaven
Man	Locus of government power	God
To man	Accountability of government	To God
More unlimited	Role of government	More limited
Equality	Relative importance	Liberty
Make society just	Primary citizen duty	Seek salvation of souls
Governmental reform	Justice achieved by	Spiritual regeneration
National	Preferred government	State/local
Internationalist	Direction of sentiment	Nationalist
Direct	Primary method of government influence	Indirect
More socialist	Economic tendency	More capitalist
Faster, within or outside existing institutions	Preferred rate/type of change	Slower, within existing institutions

[a] Developed from content analysis of major theological and political documents from the late 1700s to early 1980s.

Source: Reprinted by permission of Greenwood Publishing Group, Inc., Westport, CT, from *American Political Theology*, by Charles W. Dunn, p. 5. Copyright © 1984 by Praeger Publishers.

C. The Gender Gap

The "gender gap" refers to differences in political views between men and women. Since the late 1960s, women have largely shifted political allegiance to the Democratic party. According to Wilson, "the biggest male-female differences are over the use of force and confidence in the future." Otherwise, the difference between the sexes on "gender sensitive" policies are not great except when an issue is in the limelight. Subject this conclusion to analysis by presenting the following data to your class from the 1992 presidential election.

Issue	Women	Men
Believe poverty and homelessness should be an "extremely important" government priority	44%	29%
Favor increased child-care funding so that parents on welfare can work or attend school	91%	91%
Believe in the death penalty for murderers	46%	54%
Think that the criminal justice system should be tougher on drunk drivers	76%	58%
Want stricter gun control	70%	50%
Would not vote for a candidate who is gay	30%	43%

Source: Gallup Poll (April 1992).

Additional Lecture Topic B-1

Political Ideologies in America

Donald Devine, *The Political Culture of the United States*. Boston: Little, Brown, 1972.

Kenneth M. Dolbeare and Linda J. Medcalf, *American Ideologies Today: From Neopolitics to New Ideas*. New York: Random House, 1988. An excellent overview text.

Robert D. Holsworth and J. Harry Wray, *American Politics and Everyday Life*. 2nd ed. New York: Macmillan, 1987. See Chapters 7 and 8 on conservatism and liberalism, respectively.

Robert E. Lane, *Political Ideology: Why the American Common Man Believes What He Does*. New York: Free Press, 1962. See also Lane's *Political Thinking and Consciousness: The Private Life of the Political Mind*. Chicago: Markham, 1969.

Sandford Levinson, *Constitutional Faith*. Princeton: Princeton University Press, 1988.

H. Mark Roelofs, *Ideology and Myth in American Politics*. Boston: Little, Brown, 1976.

John L. Sullivan, James Peterson, and George E. Marcus, *Political Tolerance and American Democracy*. Chicago: University of Chicago Press, 1982.

Abstract for Theme B

Public Opinion and Political Behavior

Public opinion may conceal much about how people really react toward an issue. One such area is the difference between opinion and behavior. Take the example of court-ordered busing to integrate public schools. Research has consistently shown that the views of white parents whose children are affected by a desegregation plan are not dissimilar in their attitude toward busing than parents whose children are not so affected. However, Donald Philip Green and Jonathan A. Cowden ("Who Protests: Self-Interest and White Opposition to Busing," *Journal of Politics* 54 [May 1992], pp. 471–496) have discerned a substantial difference in the context of behavior. They discovered that "those adversely affected by busing are much more likely to engage in collective political action to oppose court-ordered school desegregation, despite the fact that parents and nonparents express similar *opinions* about busing. In essence, while self-interest does not influence how white citizens feel about busing, it does determine whether they act on their convictions."

The problem is to explain what accounts for the activation of behavior. According to the authors, "the most persuasive explanation for why self-interest influences antibusing action but not antibusing sentiment seems to be that the question 'Shall I act?' leads people to reflect on their personal stake in the issue. Apparently, the more costly the action in question, the more likely people are to reflect on their personal interests." In short, it is important to keep in mind that public opinion on an issue is deceptive since it conceals the number of people who are willing to do something to implement that opinion.

Theme C   Public-Opinion Polling

Summary

To survey public opinion properly, several conditions must be met. First, a *random sample* must be drawn. Second, questions must be comprehensible, because people will make up answers when they do not understand or actually have no opinion. Third, the questions must be asked fairly, without the use of loaded language. Fourth, answer categories matter, as a comparison between Gallup and Harris questions on presidential popularity demonstrates. Finally, differences so small that they could easily be attributed to *sampling error* should not be overinterpreted. In a close call, sampling error could be quite significant (a three-point sampling-error range would mean a spread of 6 percent).

Discussion Questions

1. Why must a public-opinion sample be a random sample? Why not simply stop a "random" group of citizens on the street downtown?
2. Why is the sampling-error margin so important to the accurate prediction required by modern polling methods?

Data and Perspectives for Analysis

A question seldom discussed about polls is their morality. Numerous ethical issues surround the use of polls:

1. Polls can interfere with the political process by creating a bandwagon effect. When the public hears that a particular candidate is ahead, some undecided voters jump on the bandwagon and support the candidate.
2. A candidate who looks good in the polls has an easier time getting people to contribute to the campaign and receives more media attention.
3. Polls showing that one candidate is far ahead may deter other potential candidates from running.
4. When a race is projected as decided before election day, some citizens may not vote at all.
5. People change their attitudes on political issues because they want to agree with the majority.
6. A bad poll could affect the outcome of an election.
7. Release of exit-poll results during voting hours discourages some people from voting.
8. Media reports of poll results are often misleading.
9. Polls weaken the role of public opinion rather than strengthen it. Polls now dominate other means of expressing opinions, such as protests.

Adapted from: Herbert Weisberg, Jon Krosnick, and Bruce Bowen, *Introduction to Survey Research and Data Analysis*, 2nd ed. (Glenview, IL: Scott, Foresman, 1989), pp. 294–297.

Additional Lecture Topic C-1

Problems with the Polls

Herbert Asher, *Polling and the Public*. Washington, DC: Congressional Quarterly Press, 1988.

Leo Bogart, *Silent Politics: Polls and the Awareness of Public Opinion*. New York: Wiley, 1972.

Irving Crespi, *Public Opinion, Polls and Democracy*. Boulder, CO: Westview Press, 1989.

Robert S. Erikson, Norman R. Luttbeg, and Kent L. Tedin, *American Public Opinion*. 4th ed. New York: Wiley, 1991. Chapter 2.

Elizabeth Noelle-Neumann, *The Spiral of Silence*. Chicago: University of Chicago Press, 1984.

George F. Bishop et al., "Pseudo-Opinions on Public Affairs." *Public Opinion Quarterly*, Summer 1980, pp. 198–209.

Donald J. Devine, "The Problem of Question Form in Describing Public Opinion." *Polity*, Spring 1980, pp. 522–534.

C. W. Roll, Jr., and A. H. Cantril, *Polls: Their Use and Misuse in Politics*. New York: Basic Books, 1972.

Barry Orton, "Phoney Polls: The Pollster's Nemesis." *Public Opinion*, June/July 1982, p. 60.

Abstract 1 for Theme C

The 1936 Literary Digest "Biased Sample"

Modern polling is a costly process in terms of resources, time, and personnel. Yet when the process is conducted in a proper fashion, the results are noteworthy indeed. However, the accuracy of the polling process is not a sure thing. In the prescientific polling days, there were some notable mistakes. A classic example of how *not* to handle survey research was the *Literary Digest* poll of 1936.

As described in *Public Opinion* by Bernard Hennessy (Monterey, CA: Brooks-Cole, 1981, pp. 42–44), *Literary Digest* was a popular magazine during the first third of this century. The magazine had conducted nationwide polls on prohibition (1922, 1930, and 1932) and had accurately predicted the outcome of the presidential elections of 1924, 1928, and 1932. The principal method that the magazine used to obtain poll data was to mail a ballot card with a subscription blank to each voter. But in the 1936 presidential election year, the *Digest* predicted that Alf Landon, the Republican nominee, would win decisively over Franklin D. Roosevelt, the presidential Democratic incumbent. Just the reverse happened, and soon thereafter (1938) the *Digest* went out of business. What went wrong?

The *Digest* had mailed out poll cards to persons whose names it had obtained from telephone books and lists of automobile owners. Individuals who were so inclined mailed them back with the name of the presidential candidate they preferred. Unwittingly, the *Digest* had vastly overestimated the potential Republican vote. In short, a "biased sample"—a miniature replica of the voting population—wrongly reflected the voting universe in 1936. The true Democratic vote had not shown up in the *Digest* poll.

Questions for Discussion

1. What specific sampling mistakes did the *Digest* make?
2. If the *Digest* had been correct in predicting presidential winners in previous elections with the same procedure, why was the *Digest* suddenly wrong in 1936?

Answer Guidelines

Because of the severity of the Depression, individuals who owned cars and had telephones were much more likely than ever before to be upper-middle-class or upper-class voters (Republicans) in 1936. By mailing out ballots to these voters, the *Digest* largely ignored the Democratic groundswell—hence the "biased sample." Also, in this type of straw poll, those who felt strongly about the election outcome were more likely to return the cards. Thus probably more rabid Landon (or anti-FDR) voters returned the cards than did enthusiastic FDR supporters, who were less likely to receive a card from the *Digest* in the first place. This slanted the results even more. Earlier, during the 1920s, the majority of voters were still Republican (prior to the stock market crash), so sampling errors by the *Digest* were not so crucial during this time period.

Abstract 2 for Theme C

Early Polls and the 1988 Election

According to Burns W. Roper in an article entitled "Political Polls" (*Society*, May/June 1985, pp. 28–31) there are a number of problems with polls. One is with "early polls," particularly in a presidential election year before the conventions have begun. In Roper's words:

> I do not think that polling prior to the start of an election does either the candidates for office or the public at large a service. Early polling does not reflect real preferences. It tends to reflect two things only: candidate name recognition and the public's whim of the moment. The question that is normally asked begins with the phrase "if the election were being held today." In fact the election is not being held today and people do not answer such a question from the same thoughtful perspective that they use to decide their vote on election day.

Keeping Roper's statement in mind, one could have noted a *New York Times/CBS News Poll* (published in the *New York Times*, May 17, 1988, pp. 1, 12), which revealed that Michael Dukakis, the Democratic nominee, was preferred by voters over George Bush, the GOP nominee, by a margin of 49 percent to 39 percent among 1,056 registered voters.

Questions for Discussion

1. Was the May 1988 poll a clear guide to the eventual winner in the November 1988 presidential election? Have students check how the polls changed (if they did) from May to November, thus confirming or denying Roper's assertion.

2. What conclusions can be reached from this exercise?

Theme D Do Elites Control Opinion and Public Policy?

Summary

Elite theorists argue that mass public opinion is largely inconsequential in the ultimate shaping of public policy. Rather, it is the thin strata of the politically informed and active through which policy agendas and norms are established. Dye and Zeigler's *Irony of Democracy*, 7th ed. (Monterey, CA: Brooks-Cole, 1987), makes a strong case for the power of elite opinion:

> Opinions flow downward from elites to masses. Public opinion rarely affects elite behavior, but elite behavior shapes public opinion. Elites are relatively unconstrained by public opinion for several reasons. First, few people among the masses have opinions on most policy questions confronting the nation's decision makers. Second, public opinion is very unstable; it can change in a matter of weeks in response to "news" events precipitated by elites. Third, elites do not have a clear perception of mass opinion. Most communications decision makers receive are from other elites—newsmakers, interest-group leaders, influential community leaders—not from ordinary citizens. (p. 164)

Dye and Zeigler elaborate on the above points, noting that polls elicit "doorstep opinions" (poorly thought out responses by citizens who feel they *should* have some opinion on an issue, even if they really know little about the topic). Second, public opinion's "instability" characteristic means that consistent opinions are rare among the mass public, accounting for less than 20 percent of the general population. Finally, the concept of *intra-elite communications* means that elites receive opinion messages that have an "upper-class" bias, that is, friends, wealthy contributors, educated opinion leaders, and so on, most of whom have congruent public attitudes. As Dye and Zeigler put it, "people who initiate communication with decision makers, by writing or calling or visiting their representatives, are decidedly more educated or affluent than the average citizen." (p. 165)

In reference to the central issue of elite response to mass opinion, the authors reinforce their argument of elite determinism:

> When government policy and public opinion are in agreement, is it because the policy adapted to prevailing opinion or because decision makers molded opinion to accept predetermined policy? These questions are difficult to answer, yet so often are policies enacted in the face of widespread public opposition, which eventually melts away into acquiescence, that public opinion seems to follow elite decisions rather than the other way around. (p. 165)

Dye and Zeigler offer national policy on civil rights, as formulated by decisions from the courts, Congress, and the executive branch, as proof of elite preferences dominating contrary mass attitudes. Accordingly, the 1954 *Brown* decision on school integration, the Civil Rights Act of 1968 banning discrimination in the sale or rental of housing, and judicial support for busing to achieve racial balances (voters have consistently rejected busing in several state referenda) were all initiated against the backdrop of a hostile mass opinion framework. As the authors argue, "elite support for civil rights at the national level is not a response to mass opinion." (p. 166)

Discussion Questions

1. Could you conclude from the Dye and Zeigler account that elites are more committed to democracy than members of the mass public? Why or why not?
2. Can you think of any national policies that were changed or created as a result of a massive public protest or outcry?

Data and Perspectives for Analysis

A. The Power of the President to Shape Public Opinion

Despite being a "lame-duck" president in 1988, Ronald Reagan remained popular with the American people. As the 1988 presidential campaign started to take shape, president Reagan began to use communication skills to create an "image" of the Democratic nominee, Michael Dukakis, as a free-spending "liberal." George Bush could clearly profit from Reagan's rhetoric. The first real attack on Dukakis occurred on June 29, 1988, in a presidential speech given in Miami. The *Wall Street Journal* gave the following description:

> President Reagan launched his first detailed attack on Massachusetts Gov. Michael Dukakis, labeling him a "true liberal" who would be sure to raise taxes and imperil economic recovery if elected president....
> The president charged that Mr. Dukakis has raised state taxes, increased spending at twice the federal government's rate and squandered "every dime and more" of revenue generated by the Reagan-Bush economic recovery." (p. 62)

The Dukakis campaign team struck back, arguing that the governor had run a disciplined fiscal policy in Massachusetts, unlike the president. Susan Estrich, Mr. Dukakis's campaign manager, asserted that "since Ronald Reagan has raised taxes many more times than Dukakis has in the past six years, then by the president's definition, Ronald Reagan is the liberal—the most liberal guy around." Other supporters of Dukakis noted that Massachusetts state law requires balanced budgets, so the governor had not run up a huge state deficit.

What was significant about Reagan's attack was its desire to resurrect voters' fears of a tax increase (Walter Mondale's promise in 1984) and to contrast Democratic spending with Republican conservative economic policies, which had promoted prosperity. Interestingly enough, the president did not make a detailed pitch on behalf of Vice President Bush, but the themes of the speech did seem to be a forerunner of the strategy Bush would use against Dukakis in the fall presidential campaign. Whether President Reagan's charges could shape the opinion of voters to back Bush remained an open question.

B. Research Assignment

Have students review the Bush campaign themes used in 1988 against Dukakis. Did the "liberal–big-spender–tax-raiser" ideas play prominent roles in the Bush campaign or not? Did Dukakis effectively refute those charges or not (assuming they were used)? Finally, ask the class whether a lame-duck president can change the minds of voters on a significant scale. Was there any evidence that Reagan's campaigning for Bush helped the vice president to a considerable extent in 1988? Have students report some of their findings in class.

Additional Lecture Topic D-1

Political Elites in America

Allen Barton, "Consensus and Conflict Among American Leaders." *Public Opinion Quarterly*, Winter 1974.

Thomas R. Dye, *Who's Running America? The Bush Era*. Englewood Cliffs, NJ: Prentice-Hall, 1990.

John S. Jackson III et al., "Herbert McCloskey and Friends Revisited: 1980 Democratic and Republican Party Elites Compared to the Mass Public." *American Politics Quarterly* (April 1982): 158–190.

S. Robert Lichter and Stanley Rothman, "Media and Business Elites." *Public Opinion*, (October/November 1981): 42–60.

Michael Parenti, *Land of Idols: Political Mythology in America*. New York: St. Martin's Press, 1994.

Leonard Silk and Mark Silk, *The American Establishment*. New York: Basic Books, 1980.

Barry Sussman, "Elites in America," a series of five articles in the *Washington Post*, September 26–30, 1976.

6

Political Participation

Overview and Objectives

This chapter reviews the much-discussed lack of voter turnout and of other forms of political participation in the United States and comes to the conclusion that individual Americans may not be at fault for their seeming nonparticipation, but that other factors may be at work. After reading and reviewing the material in this chapter the student should be able to do each of the following:

1. Explain why the text believes that the description, the analysis, and the proposed remedy for low voter turnout rates in this country are off base.

2. Compare the way turnout statistics are tabulated for this country and for other countries, and explain the significance of these differences.

3. Describe how control of elections has shifted from the states to the federal government, and explain what effects this shift has had on blacks, women, and youth.

4. State both sides of the debate over whether voter turnout has declined over the past century, and describe those factors that tend to hold down voter turnout in this country.

5. List and explain Nie and Verba's four categories of political participation.

6. Discuss those factors that appear to be associated with high or low political participation.

7. Compare participation rates in various forms of political activity here and in other countries.

Chapter Outline with Keyed-in Resources

 I. A closer look at nonvoting (ADDITIONAL LECTURE TOPIC A-1)
   A. Alleged problem: low turnout compared to Europeans
     1. But this compares registered voters to eligible adult population
   B. Common explanation: voter apathy on election day

It is not only voters who have become dismayed by the number of elections but candidates as well. In 1992, the city of Dutton, Alabama, faced the problem of having no candidates at all in the elections for mayor and the four city council seats. The governor of the state had to appoint individuals to fill the vacancies to enable the city to conduct business.

     1. But the real problem is low registration rates
   C. Proposed solution: get-out-the-vote drives

                1. But this will not help those who are not registered
            D. Apathy not the only cause of nonregistration
                1. Costs here versus no costs in European countries where registration automatic
                2. Motor-voter law of 1993 takes effect in 1995
            E. Voting is not the only way of participating
        II. The rise of the American electorate (THEME A: POPULAR PARTICIPATION IN ELECTIONS)

The highly exclusive requirements for voting at the country's founding reduced the number of eligible adults in the first presidential election to an estimated 8 percent of the population. The excluded groups included women, slaves, and men without property.

            A. From state to federal control
                1. Initially, states decided nearly everything
                2. This led to wide variation in federal elections
                3. Congress has since reduced state prerogatives
                    a. 1842 law: House members elected by district
                    b. Suffrage to women
                    c. Suffrage to blacks
                    d. Suffrage to eighteen- to twenty-year-olds
                    e. Direct popular election of U.S. senators
                4. Black voting rights
                    a. Fifteenth Amendment gutted by Supreme Court as not conferring a right to vote
                    b. Southern states then use evasive stratagems
                        (1) Literacy test

Great Britain rewarded the highly literate with additional voting power. Until 1948, college graduates were entitled to two votes in elections!

                        (2) Poll tax
                        (3) White primaries
                        (4) Grandfather clauses
                        (5) Intimidation of black voters
                    c. Most of these stratagems ruled out by Supreme Court
                    d. Major change with 1965 Voting Rights Act; black vote increases
                5. Women's voting rights
                    a. Western states permit women to vote
                    b. Nineteenth Amendment ratified 1920

Women do not have full voting privileges in all western nations. For example, although women have been allowed to vote in all national elections in Switzerland since 1971, 2 half-cantons and 29 communes still do not permit women to vote in local elections.

                    c. No dramatic changes in outcomes
                6. Youth vote
                    a. Voting Rights Act of 1970
                    b. Twenty-sixth Amendment ratified 1971
                    c. Lower turnout; no particular party
                7. National standards now govern most aspects
            B. Voting turnout
                1. Debate over declining percentages: two theories
                    a. Real decline as popular interest and party competition decrease
                    b. Apparent decline, induced in part by more honest ballot counts of today
                        (1) Parties once printed ballots
                        (2) Ballots cast in public
                        (3) Parties controlled counting
                    c. Most scholars see some real decline due to several causes:
                        (1) Registration more difficult; longer residency; educational qualifications; discrimination

(2) Continuing drop after 1960 cannot be explained
III. Who participates in politics? (THEME B: POLITICAL PARTICIPATION AND VOTING)
   A. Forms of participation
      1. Voting the commonest, but 8 to 10 percent misreport it
      2. Verba and Nie's six forms of participation
         a. Inactives
         b. Voting specialists
         c. Campaigners
         d. Communalists
         e. Parochial participants
         f. Complete activists
   B. The causes of participation (ADDITIONAL LECTURE TOPIC B-1)
      1. Those with schooling, or political information, more likely to vote
      2. Church-goers vote more
      3. Men and women vote same rate
      4. Race
         a. Black participation lower than that of whites overall
         b. But controlling for SES, higher than whites
      5. Level of trust in government?
         a. Studies show no correlation
      6. Difficulty of registering?

In a 1990 poll, 40 percent of the unregistered voters said that their excuse for not registering was that they were too busy to do so.

         a. As turnout declines, registration gets easier
      7. Several small factors decrease turnout
         a. More youths, blacks, and other minorities
         b. Decreasing effectiveness of parties
         c. Remaining impediments to registration
         d. Voting compulsory in other nations

The lengthiness of election campaigns is another factor that depletes interest in elections. In 1984, 69 percent of the American public believed that the campaign season was too long in the presidential race. In contrast, campaigns are limited to three weeks in Great Britain.

         e. Ethnic minorities encounter language barriers, while blacks are involved in nonpolitical institutions
         f. Possible feeling that elections do not matter
      8. Democrats, Republicans fight over solutions
         a. No one really knows who would be helped
         b. Nonvoters tend to be poor, black, etc.
         c. But an increasing percentage of college graduates are also not voting
         d. Hard to be sure that turnout efforts produce gains for either party: Jesse Jackson in 1984
   C. The meaning of participation rates
      1. Americans vote less, but participate more

Americans participate unevenly in even the easiest forms of political activity. While 15 percent of the population have written letters to their representative in the House of Representatives, just 3 percent of the population account for two-thirds of all letters received by members of Congress.

         a. Other forms of activity becoming more common
         b. Some forms commoner here than in other countries
      2. Americans elect more officials than Europeans do and have more elections
      3. U.S. turnout rates heavily skewed to higher status
         a. Meaning of this is unclear

Important Terms

activist An individual, usually outside of government, who actively promotes a political party, philosophy, or issue he or she cares personally about.

*****Australian ballot** An election ballot of uniform size printed by the government and cast in secret.

*****campaigners** According to Sidney Verba and Norman Nie, people who not only vote but like to get involved in campaign activities as well. They are better educated than the average voter, but what distinguishes them most is their interest in the conflicts of politics, their clear party identification, and their willingness to take strong positions.

*****communalists** According to Sidney Verba and Norman Nie, people who tend to reserve their energies for community activities of a nonpartisan kind. Their education and income are similar to those of campaigners.

*****complete activists** According to Sidney Verba and Norman Nie, people who are highly educated, have high incomes, and tend to be middle-aged rather than young or old. These people participate in all forms of politics and account for 11 percent of the population.

Fifteenth Amendment The constitutional amendment that guaranteed the right to vote regardless of race, color, or previous condition of slavery.

*****grandfather clause** A state law allowing people to vote, even if they did not meet legal requirements, if an ancestor had voted before 1867. The clause was used as a vehicle to enable poor and illiterate whites to vote while excluding blacks (who had no ancestor voting prior to 1867). Such clauses were ruled unconstitutional by the Supreme Court.

*****inactives** According to Sidney Verba and Norman Nie, people who rarely vote, do not get involved in organizations, and do not even talk much about politics. They account for about 22 percent of the population.

*****literacy test** A state law requiring potential voters to demonstrate basic reading skills. The laws were frequently implemented in a discriminatory fashion to prevent otherwise qualified blacks from voting. These tests were suspended by the Voting Rights Act.

*****motor-voter bill** A law passed by Congress in 1993 that requires states to allow people to register to vote when applying for a driver's license and to provide registration through the mail and at some state offices that serve the disabled and provide public assistance. The law takes effect in 1995.

Nineteenth Amendment An amendment to the Constitution allowing women the right to vote.

*****parochial participants** According to Sidney Verba and Norman Nie, people who do not vote and stay out of election campaigns and civic associations, but who are willing to contact local officials about specific, often personal, problems.

*****poll tax** A state tax paid prior to voting. The tax was designed to prevent blacks from voting since poor whites were usually exempted through a grandfather clause. Poll taxes have been made illegal.

*****registered voters** People who are eligible to vote in an election and who have signed up with the government to vote.

Twenty-sixth Amendment The constitutional amendment that lowered the voting age in both state and federal elections to eighteen. Congress had attempted to achieve this goal through legislation, but the Supreme Court ruled that the federal government had no authority to do so with respect to state elections.

Twenty-third Amendment A constitutional amendment permitting residents of Washington, D.C., to vote in presidential elections.

Voting Rights Act of 1965 The federal law that suspended the use of literacy tests in elections and authorized federal examiners to order the registration of blacks in states and counties where fewer than 50 percent of the voting-age population were registered or had voted in the last presidential election.

*voting-age population The percentage of people in a country who are eligible to vote because they satisfy the minimum age requirement.

*voting specialists According to Sidney Verba and Norman Nie, people who vote but participate in little else politically. They tend not to have much schooling or income, and to be substantially older than the average person.

*white primary The exclusion of blacks from voting in the primary elections of political parties. Such primaries were employed largely in the South where the Democratic party won almost all general elections. In effect, winning the Democratic primary meant winning the election. The Supreme Court voided the use of white primaries.

Theme A	Popular Participation in Elections

Summary

Americans are less likely to vote than are Europeans. The reasons for this difference are complex. First, the United States has an almost bewildering number of elective offices, an estimated 521,000 positions. Voters' enthusiasm for elections is surely deflated by the sheer volume of names with which they must familiarize themselves. A study in New York City discovered that about half the voters simply skip over the judicial races on the ballot; few know these people and, thus, few care. In Europe, in contrast, each voter generally is confronted with only one or two offices to fill per election, so that electoral decisions do not impose a burden upon the voter. Even in Europe, however, voter apathy increases with the number of elections. Switzerland has a lower level of voter participation than the United States, due to the demands placed on its citizens by an average of thirty referendums and initiatives annually. Too much democracy, in terms of either selecting government officers or making policy, is exhausting.

A second explanation for the poor turnout rate involves the mechanics of voting procedures. It is common in other countries for voting to be compulsory by law and for registration to be carried out automatically by the government. Mandatory voting would probably fail to survive a constitutional challenge in this country on First Amendment grounds; just as people have a right *not* to speak (like refusing to salute the flag), it would seem to follow that they have a right to refrain from voting—a form of speech—as well. Simplifying registration is a different matter. Proposals of this kind have been opposed on the ground that they enhance the possibility of fraud in the electoral system. Republicans in particular have tended to resist any easing of registration standards. President Bush, for example, vetoed legislation designed to enable voters to register when obtaining a driver's license, legislation that President Clinton favors. In states where such "motor-voter" registration is available, registration jumped 2.8 percent and actual turnout 6 percent between 1988 and 1992; states without such legislation experienced almost negligible gains of 0.5 percent in registration and only 3.3 percent in voter turnout during the same period. The reluctance of Republicans to encourage efforts to relax registration requirements is understandable; they have the most to lose from a political standpoint, since the citizens who are not registered fit the profile of potential Democratic supporters.

Attempts at the state level to facilitate the registration process have ranged from allowing registration by mail to allowing registration on election day. These efforts have produced only marginal improvements in the turnout rate, with one study calculating that turnout would increase only 9 percent if same-day registration occurred nationwide. Thus the mechanics of voting constitute a partial explanation for low voter participation in the United States. But the weakness of political parties must also be considered. Unlike in the past, parties today lack the ability to mobilize voter blocs on their behalf without patronage and welfare incentives to offer. Moreover, the impact of progressive reforms—such as the Australian ballot and stricter registration requirements for voting—have contributed to the loss of party influence over the electorate.

All these factors combine to explain why people do not vote in large numbers in the United States. Yet it is equally important to comprehend the other side of the issue, namely, the factors that do make people vote. Research underscores the significance of personal characteristics in motivating a person's decision to participate on election day. Education is the most critical variable. As their educational level increases, individuals develop a stronger sense of civic duty and a greater interest in, and knowledge of, politics. But education alone is not a sufficient explanation, since voting rates have continued to decline—by at least 10 percent in presidential elections—despite the proliferation of college degrees in the past twenty-five years. Another characteristic that correlates with voting is age; older voters are more likely to participate. But here again, overall voting rates have diminished while the population has aged. Something other than personal characteristics plays a role in election turnout: the characteristics of the election itself. Most recent elections have presented voters with uninspiring candidates who failed to stimulate interest or excitement. The lack of a "realigning" issue has made politics boring. However, turnout reaches notable peaks in certain elections, as in 1964 (a sharp ideological choice between candidates) and 1992 (an economy in recession and the charismatic H. Ross Perot). Voters participate when aroused to do so.

Discussion Questions

1. Why is voter participation lower in the United States than in European countries? Would one not expect voter participation to be *higher* here, because more offices are up for election and therefore the election "means more"? Is there any reason to suppose that more people might turn out where *fewer* offices are elective?

2. What have been the *policy* consequences of a broader electorate? Which extensions of the suffrage have changed policy outcomes, and which have mattered little?

3. Why do so few Americans vote? What could be done to increase voter turnout? Look at the list of costs and benefits. Would a program of reforms to increase voting turnout need to focus on the costs of voting, the benefits, or both? Which do current reform proposals do?

4. Why not simply do as Australia and Italy do and make voting compulsory? If you do not want to use coercion to induce voting, why not pay people to vote? If elections are a "public good" in which all citizens have a stake, why should we depend on unpaid voluntary action? We don't depend on volunteers to put out fires, to police the city, or to repair the streets. Why are elections less important? Are they different?

5. Does it matter if so many people don't care enough to come out and vote? Why is a large turnout a good thing? We say, rightly, that we have free speech in this country, even though most people have nothing particularly controversial or interesting to say. Why is our country less "democratic" if people simply choose not to vote? Why should members of Congress worry about public opinion, given its ignorance about them?

Additional Lecture Topic A-1

Who Votes, Why, and What Does It Matter?

Herbert Asher, *Presidential Elections and American Politics*. 5th ed. Pacific Grove, CA: Brooks-Cole, 1992.

M. Margaret Conway, *Political Participation in the United States*. 2nd ed. Washington, DC: Congressional Quarterly Press, 1990.

William H. Flanigan and Nancy H. Zingale, *Political Behavior of the American Electorate*. 6th ed. Boston: Allyn & Bacon, 1987. Chapter 1.

Frances Fox Piven and Richard Cloward, *Why Americans Don't Vote*. New York: Pantheon, 1988.

Gerald Pomper, *Voter's Choice: Varieties of American Electoral Behavior*. New York: Harper & Row, 1975.

James A. Reichley, ed., *Elections American Style*. Washington, DC: The Brookings Institution, 1987.

Ruy A. Teixeira, *Why Americans Don't Vote: Turnout Decline in the United States, 1960–84*. Westport, CT: Greenwood Press, 1987.

Sidney Verba, et al., "Citizen Activity: Who Participates? What Do They Say?" *American Political Science Review* 87 (June 1993): 303–318.

Raymond E. Wolfinger and Steven J. Rosenstone, *Who Votes?* New Haven, CT: Yale University Press, 1980.

Data and Perspectives for Analysis

A. Voter Perspectives

The following are "eight American perspectives" of voters as described by Alan L. Clem in *American Electoral Politics: Strategies for Renewal* (New York: Van Nostrand, 1981, pp. 49-51). In each voter profile, the student should explain the probable party affiliation (or lack of one), what kinds of issues would be important to the individual in a campaign, and whether the individual is likely to be a voter or a nonvoter. Reasons for each analysis should be given.

1. A union member who works in an automobile plant in one of the large factories located in the industrial belt encompassing Buffalo, Cleveland, Toledo, Detroit, Chicago, and Milwaukee. He is a college graduate.

2. A retired elementary school teacher in a small New Jersey city who is dependent, in part, on Social Security. She has a liberal orientation on most national issues.

3. A university student in Georgia who is studying architecture and will be ready to enter the work force within the next six months.

4. A corn-belt farmer in western Illinois who is concerned with raising corn, sorghum, and other feed grains to sell on the grain market.

5. A young woman in California whose husband is completing a tour in the armed services. She is a high school graduate and is expecting her first child.

6. A bank executive in a small county seat in Colorado whose main concern is her career. She is unmarried and is about to buy her own home.

7. A retail clerk working in a shopping center in eastern Texas. He is black, attends a local junior college, and has a wife and two small children.

8. A dentist in an older New England city whose office is in a deteriorating downtown business district. He is thinking about moving his family to the South—probably Florida—even if it means having to be relicensed in that state. His annual income is over $100,000 a year.

B. Registration and Voting

Citizens Registered and Voting, 1972–1988

| | *Percentage Reporting They Registered* | | | | | | | | | *Percentage Reporting They Voted* | | | | | | | | |
| | Presidential Election Years | | | | | Congressional Election Years | | | | Presidential Election Years | | | | | Congressional Election Years | | | |
	1972	1976	1980	1984	1988	1974	1978	1982	1986	1972	1976	1980	1984	1988	1974	1978	1982	1986
Race/Ethnicity																		
White	73	68	68	70	68	64	64	66	65	65	61	61	61	59	46	47	50	47
Black	44	59	60	66	65	55	57	59	64	52	49	51	56	52	34	37	43	43
Hispanic origin[a]	44	38	36	40	36	35	33	35	36	38	32	30	33	29	23	24	25	24
Sex																		
Male	73	67	67	67	65	63	63	64	63	64	60	59	59	56	46	47	49	46
Female	72	66	67	69	68	62	63	64	65	62	59	59	61	58	43	45	48	46
Region																		
Northeast	—	66	65	67	65	62	62	63	62	—	60	59	60	57	49	48	50	44
Midwest	—	72	74	75	73	67	68	71	71	—	65	66	66	63	49	51	55	50
South	—	68	64	64	67	66	60	62	63	55	55	56	57	55	36	40	42	43
West	—	63	63	65	63	60	59	61	61	—	58	57	59	56	48	48	51	48
Age																		
18–20	58	47	45	47	45	36	35	35	35	48	38	36	37	33	21	20	20	19
21–24	60	55	53	54	51	45	45	48	47	51	46	43	44	38	26	26	28	24
25–34	68	62	62	63	58	55	56	57	56	60	55	55	55	48	37	38	40	35
35–44	75	70	71	71	69	67	67	68	68	66	63	64	64	61	49	50	52	49
45–64	80	76	76	77	76	74	74	76	75	71	69	69	70	68	57	59	62	59
65 and older	76	71	75	77	78	70	73	75	77	64	62	65	68	69	51	56	60	61
Employment																		
Employed	74	69	69	69	67	64	63	66	64	66	62	62	62	58	47	47	50	46
Unemployed	59	52	50	54	50	44	44	50	51	50	44	41	44	39	29	27	34	31
Not in labor force	70	65	66	68	67	61	63	64	65	59	57	57	59	57	43	46	49	48
Education																		
8 years or less	62	54	53	53	48	54	53	52	51	47	44	43	43	37	34	35	36	33
1–3 years high school	63	56	55	55	53	54	53	53	52	52	47	46	44	41	36	35	38	34
4 years high school	74	67	66	67	65	62	62	63	63	65	59	59	59	55	45	45	47	44
1–3 years college	82	75	74	76	74	67	69	70	70	75	68	67	68	65	50	52	53	50
4 or more years college	88	84	84	84	83	76	77	79	78	84	80	80	79	78	61	64	67	63
Total	72	67	67	68	67	62	62	64	64	63	59	59	60	57	45	46	49	46

[a] Persons of Hispanic origin may be of any race.

Source: Harold Stanley and Richard Niemi. *Vital Statistics on American Politics*, 2d ed. (Washington: Congressional Quarterly Press, 1990), pp. 80–81. Reprinted by permission of CQ Press.

Discussion Questions

1. The text asserts that both registration and voting rates have declined. From the data, note that certain gaps in registration are widening. For example, the percentage of people between the ages of eighteen and twenty who are registered to vote has dropped much more compared to that of people aged sixty-five and over. Does this indicate that voting turnout will continue to decline in the future?

2. The unemployed are much less likely to vote. Isn't this fact detrimental to their well-being? Doesn't it in effect allow politicians to ignore the plight of the jobless? What factors account for the lack of involvement by the unemployed in an activity that could benefit them?

3. Why do fewer people participate in congressional than in presidential elections? Note that even fewer people report being registered in congressional election years. In most states, however, people remain on the election rolls for three years before being deleted for nonparticipation. In other words, about the same number of people should be registered for both types of elections. What accounts for this discrepancy? Do people lie about their registration status? Why would they lie more frequently in presidential election years?

Abstract for Theme A

The "Problem" of Voter Turnout

Many political observers decry the declining voter turnout in American elections, particularly presidential contests. However, some scholars assert that the situation is not as bad as it might seem. Thus Martin Plissner and Warren Mitofsky, in "What If They Held an Election and Nobody Came?" *Public Opinion* (February/March, 1981, pp. 50–51), assert that the 53.9 percent turnout in 1980 reflects not the percentage of eligible Americans who voted but rather "the ratio of the recorded vote for president to the voting-age population." The "recorded vote" excludes people who go to the polls but do not vote for the president or who accidentally cast invalid ballots; the voting-age population includes ineligible people such as prisoners and mental patients. In short, "if all those who went to the polls were counted as voters and only the genuinely eligible were counted as 'eligible Americans,' the turnout for 1980 would approach 60 percent."

Furthermore, the authors argue that failure to vote was not due to a huge reservoir of alienation, as "only one nonvoter in four gave something disparaging about the candidates or about voting itself as a reason for not casting a ballot." Even more surprising, polls showed that two-thirds of the nonvoters said they "cared a lot" about the presidential election.

Finally, the authors argue that the growth in southern voting will probably continue and thus "offset the voting decline in the Northeast." They conclude by stating that registration remains the chief impediment to voting, particularly for our highly mobile population. (One person in five moves each year.)

Questions for Discussion

1. Ask students to research the voting trends exhibited in the 1984 and 1988 presidential elections. Do these trends reinforce Plissner and Mitofsky's assertions?

2. How could registration requirements be changed to eliminate the current nonvoting problem?

3. Do your students think a "60 percent" voter turnout in presidential elections is satisfactory for a democracy? Why or why not?

Answer Guidelines

Replies to these questions are very open-ended. You might wish to mention the idea of "election-day registration" as a means of increasing voter turnout (including pros and cons).

Theme B   Political Participation and Voting

Summary

There are many ways in which Americans can participate in politics—ranging from voting, which a majority do with some regularity, to belonging to a political club or organization, which only a few do. In an elaborate analysis of the ways people participate, Verba and Nie discovered six different kinds of citizens and quantified them as a percentage of the population:

1. *Inactives* participate little if at all (22 percent).
2. *Complete activists* participate in all forms of political activity (1 percent).
3. *Voting specialists* regularly vote but do little else (21 percent).
4. *Campaigners* vote and also participate in conflictual political activities, such as campaigns (15 percent).
5. *Communalists* engage in community activities of a nonpartisan nature (20 percent).
6. *Parochial participants* neither vote nor engage in campaigns or community activity, but they do contact officials about specific, often personal, problems (4 percent).

Considering how few tangible rewards participation produces, it is not surprising that over 40 percent of Americans either do not participate at all or limit their participation to voting. Compared to citizens of other democracies, Americans vote less but engage more in communal activity.

Who participates in politics is an important issue, because those who participate are likely to have more political influence than those who do not. Higher education is the single most important factor in producing a high degree of participation. Older persons and men are also likely to be active. Blacks participate more than whites of equal socioeconomic status.

Although voter turnout has decreased over the past twenty years, it seems that other forms of participation, such as writing letters to public officials and engaging in demonstrations, have increased.

The absence of citizen involvement in other countries carries a cost in that governments have a freer hand to operate without much public scrutiny. As levels of participation escalate, governments come under greater pressure to exchange responsible behavior for openness. B. Guy Peters has found this pattern to exist in contemporary Great Britain: "The increasingly participative nature of British citizens . . . is making them increasingly resentful of their lack of involvement in government, and there is now a need to reexamine the secrecy and limited democracy of British government." Thus the participative character of Americans has compelled the government to address public concerns despite the weakness of political parties.

Political scientists have failed to reach a consensus on the questions of how and why people cast their votes in elections. (Some voters explain their decisions as based on the "clothespin" approach.) Some, like the authors of *The American Voter*, stress the importance of party identification and downplay the importance of issues. Others, like V. O. Key, have shown issues to be important in determining how votes are cast. To Key, voters "are not fools." Probably the nature of the times determines the fundamental basis of people's votes. In the 1950s (when the data for *The American Voter* were collected), there were few contentious issues on the public agenda. In the 1930s (which supplied the most convincing of Key's data), the opposite was true. In short, voters change with the times and the kinds of elections involved. (Voters may also vacillate between retrospective and prospective voting decisions.)

Discussion Questions

1. What sorts of people are overrepresented among those who participate a great deal? What political implications does this fact have? Does this bias in participation suggest a bias in the policies that the government will adopt? If so, what sort?

2. Do Americans participate more or less than citizens of other nations? Why does the American pattern of participation differ from that in other nations?

   Instructor: You might wish to review the argument in Chapter 3 that the decentralized nature of our political system encourages participation.

3. What forms of political participation have become more common in recent years? Which are less common now? Why do you think this is the case?

Additional Lecture Topic B-1

Political Participation: Its Social and Cultural Bases

M. Margaret Conway, *Political Participation in the United States*. 2nd ed. Washington, DC: Congressional Quarterly Press, 1990. Good survey data on social and cultural roots of participation.

William H. Flanigan and Nancy H. Zingale, *Political Behavior of the American Electorate*. Washington, DC: Congressional Quarterly Press, 1991.

Richard M. Merelman, "Racial Conflict and Cultural Politics in the United States," *Journal of Politics*, 56 (February 1994): 1–20.

Michael B. Preston, Lenneal J. Henderson, Jr., and Paul Puryear, eds., *The New Black Politics: The Search for Political Power*. New York: Longman, 1982.

Sidney Verba and Norman H. Nie, *Participation in America: Political Democracy and Social Equality*. New York: Harper & Row, 1972.

Raymond E. Wolfinger and Steven J. Rosenstone, *Who Votes?* New Haven: Yale University Press, 1980. A good overview of nonvoting in American society.

Data and Perspectives for Analysis

Explore the other side of the coin. The text examines the political activity of the American public. Does such involvement affect members of Congress? One way to analyze this issue is to consider the work preformed by the typical staff of a member of Congress. One study produced the following results:

Time Allocation: Congressional Staff

Activity	Percentage of Work Activity
Constituency service	25%
Answering mail	41
Education and publicity	10
Legislative support	14

Source: Randall Ripley, *Congress: Process and Policy*, 4th ed. (New York: Norton, 1988), p. 291. Reprinted by permission of Brooks-Cole Publishing Company.

Given the data, does citizen involvement have an effect on Congress?

Abstract 1 for Theme B

How to Increase Political Participation in America

In an article entitled "Voting Is Not Enough: A Plan for Strengthening Democracy" (*Atlantic Monthly*, June 1984, pp. 45–52) Benjamin Barber proposed the following ten measures for promoting a strong democratic program aimed at participatory self-government:

1. *A national system of neighborhood assemblies* would instill civic competence, serve as a forum for public discussion on local, national, and international issues, and might eventually become "legislative bodies for local laws and even for national referenda." In short, "strong democracy rescues the neighborhood from nostalgia and restores it to a central position in the democratic body politic."

2. *A civic communications cooperative* would embrace the latest satellite transmission, video-computer interactions, and information retrieval systems, loosely modeled on the British Broadcasting Corporation. The cooperative would experiment with innovative civic broadcasting, develop standards for regional and national video town meetings and oversee electronic polling and voting, among other functions.

3. *A civic videotex service and civic education postal act* would collectively enrich the flow of information to Americans. The former would be "a standard, nationwide, interactive service providing viewers with regular news, discussions of issues, and technical, political, and economic data. . . . As a free channel offered by every cable company, the service would equalize access to information." The latter postal act "would offer a heavily subsidized rate to all legitimate publishers of newspapers, journals, magazines, and books."

4. *Selective experiments in decriminalization and informal justice* would allow local communities to handle minor disputes (petty misdemeanors, traffic violations, etc.) through surrogate civic judges and juries.

5. *A national initiative and referendum process* would enhance public political consciousness and probably participation as well.

6. *Selective experiments in electronic balloting* would allow it first to "be exploited as an instrument of deliberation and discussion—a medium for polling rather than for final voting."

7. *Selective use of a lottery system of election* would "neutralize the skewing effect of wealth on public service, spread public responsibilities more equitably across the entire population, and involve a great many more citizens than is usual in representative systems in making and administering policy."

8. *Selective experiments with voucher systems* would help to mobilize citizens to exercise choice in the development of public services such as schools and housing.

9. *A program of universal citizen service* "would enlist every young American—male and female—in a service corps for one to two years of either military or nonmilitary training and service. Service in the corps would thus become a concomitant of citizenship." Areas of service would include the military, urban or rural projects, the international arena, and the logistics and administrative services corps. Rigorous training would precede service in any of the five corps.

10. *Common work and common action programs* would involve volunteers primarily at the neighborhood level.

Questions for Discussion

1. Which of these ten measures seems to have the greatest appeal to your students? Why? Which proposal seems to arouse the most opposition?

2. Would an increase in voting in local, state, and federal elections be a logical consequence of the adoption of Barber's proposals? Why or why not?

Abstract 2 for Theme B

Political Participation: A Comparative Perspective

The text contends that political participation is much different in European democracies. While Americans tend to vote less often, they tend to engage in other forms of political activity at a higher rate. Jurg Steiner (*European Democracies*, 2nd ed. New York: Longman, 1991) examines political participation in Europe and derives some interesting conclusions based on empirical research. To begin with, he concurs with the text's assessment of European political behavior in general: "The conventional way in which European citizens participate in politics is to vote in elections and to become a member of a political party." However, Steiner points to research that provides an unusual interpretation of the type of individuals who do engage in collective action in Europe. As in the United States, they are highly educated and frequently young, but that is where the similarity ends. Steiner turns to the research of political scientist Hanspeter Kriesi. Kriesi focused on the younger citizens of the Netherlands and derived the following results:

> He could identify an interesting subcategory, which he calls "the young specialists in social and cultural services." By this he means mainly "medical services, teaching, social work, arts and journalism." What these professionals have in common is that their jobs do not directly depend on profit maximization. This contrasts with other young, highly educated people whose jobs depend on efficiency and profits, such as managers in private enterprises and computer experts. Kriesi also included in this latter category managers of public bureaucracies. Although they do not have to look out for profit maximization, efficiency is at the core of their job description . . . . [In short,] (he) sees a split that "separates the social and cultural specialists from the technocrats."

Steiner investigates one other question with respect to political participation in Europe—what motivates someone to engage in collective action? Research by Steven Finkel, Edward Muller, and Karl-Dieter Opp in Germany provides an insight into the psychology of participants.

They discovered one important thing: The group had to be seen as having a good likelihood of success. It is difficult to motivate people to fight for a losing cause. They found also that many people actually think that their personal participation will make a difference and that everyone has to take part if the group is to succeed. Such a belief clearly contrasts with the assumptions of the conventional rational-choice model.

Collective action has a long history both in the United States and in Europe. Yet it seems that important differences exist in terms of both who participates and why.

Questions for Discussion

1. Do American youth differ from European youth with respect to political participation? Do the more technocratic youth participate less frequently here? Does the difference between "social and cultural specialists" and "technocrats" have any relevance in the United States?

2. The text had previously concluded that Americans possess a higher sense of political efficacy than Europeans. Given that European youth who engage in collective action "feel that their personal participation will make a difference," what does this suggest in terms of political efficacy among Europeans?

7

Political Parties

Overview and Objectives

This chapter provides a fairly detailed exploration of one of the unique aspects of American politics: political parties, with emphasis on the two-party system that has evolved in the United States. After reading and reviewing the material in this chapter the student should be able to do each of the following:

1. Define the term *political party* and contrast the structure of the European and American parties, paying particular attention to the federal structure of the American system and the concept of party identification.

2. Trace the development of the party system through its four periods, and offer reasons why parties have been in decline since the New Deal period.

3. Describe the structure of a major party and distinguish powerful from powerless party organs.

4. Define *intraparty democracy* and indicate its effect on the Democratic nominating conventions in the last few contests. Evaluate the relative strengths of state party bosses in recent years, and discuss the increasing importance of primaries in relation to the "boss" system at conventions.

5. Describe the machine, discuss its functions, and trace its decline. Contrast its structure with that of ideological and reform parties.

6. Offer two explanations for the persistence of the two-party system. Explain why minor parties form and discuss different kinds of parties. Analyze why they are so rarely successful.

7. Describe some of the issue differences between delegates at Democratic and Republican conventions, and indicate whether there are major differences between the parties. Compare these differences with those of the party rank and file.

Chapter Outline with Keyed-in Resources

I. Parties—here and abroad (THEME A: PARTY STRENGTH)
   A. Decentralization
      1. A party is a group that seeks to elect candidates to public office by supplying them with a label
      2. Arenas
         a. In minds of the voters as label
         b. Organization recruiting and campaigning

            c. Set of leaders in government
        3. American parties have become weaker in all three arenas
            a. As label, more independents
            b. As set of leaders, organization of Congress less under their control
            c. As organization, much weaker since 1960s
    B. Reasons for differences with European parties
        1. Federal system decentralizes power
            a. Early on, most people with political jobs worked for state and local government
            b. National parties were coalitions of local parties
            c. As political power becomes more centralized, parties have become weaker still
        2. Parties closely regulated by state and federal laws
        3. Candidates chosen through primaries, not by party leaders

The United Kingdom exercises little control on access to the ballot. A candidate needs only the signatures of ten qualified voters and a deposit of 500 pounds (about $825) to be placed on the ballot. However, the deposit is lost if the candidate fails to receive 12.5 percent of the vote.

        4. President elected separately from Congress
        5. Political culture
            a. Parties unimportant in life; Americans do not join or pay dues
            b. Parties separate from other aspects of life
II. The rise and decline of the political party
    A. The Founding (to 1820s)
        1. Founders' dislike of "factions"
        2. Emergence of Republicans, Federalists: Jefferson vs. Hamilton

Although considered the founder of America's first political party, Thomas Jefferson wrote in 1801, "The greatest good we can do our country is to heal its party divisions and make them one people."

            a. Loose caucuses of political notables
            b. Republicans' success and Federalists' demise
        3. No representation of clear economic interests
    B. The Jacksonians (to Civil War)

While Andrew Jackson made the "common man" a political force in the United States, Thomas Jefferson—the champion of equality—despised him: "I feel much alarmed at the prospect of seeing General Jackson President. He is one of the most unfit men I know for such a place. . . . He is a dangerous man."

        1. Political participation a mass phenomenon
            a. More voters to reach
            b. Party built from bottom up
            c. Abandonment of presidential caucuses
            d. Beginning of national conventions to allow local control
    C. The Civil War and sectionalism
        1. Jacksonian system unable to survive slavery issue
        2. New Republicans become dominant because of
            a. Civil War and Republicans rely on Union pride
            b. Bryan's alienation of northern Democrats in 1896
        3. Most states one-party
            a. Party professionals, or "stalwarts," one faction in GOP
            b. "Mugwumps," "Progressives," or "reformers" other faction
                (1) Balance of power at first
                (2) Diminished role later
    D. The era of reform

The politician most identified with implementing progressive policies at the national level is Theodore Roosevelt. Much of this reputation is falsely inflated. In seven years as president, Roosevelt brought fifty-four antitrust proceedings, compared to ninety such suits brought by William Howard Taft in the latter's four years as president.

1. Progressive push measures to curtail parties
    a. Primary elections
    b. Nonpartisan elections
    c. No party-business alliances
    d. Strict voter registration requirements
    e. Civil service reform

Civil service reform was achieved at the national level much earlier than at the state level. The Pendleton Act, which required merit-based appointments for many federal jobs, was enacted in 1883. Such quick action was in response to the assassination of President James Garfield. Garfield (the country's first left-handed president) was shot by Charles Guiteau, who was denied appointment as U.S. counsel to Paris.

    f. Initiative and referendum elections
2. Effects
    a. Reduction in worst form of political corruption
    b. Weakening of all political parties
III. The national party structure today (THEME B: PARTY STRUCTURE TODAY)
    A. Parties similar on paper
        1. National convention ultimate power; nominate presidential candidate
        2. National committee composed of delegates from states
        3. Congressional campaign committees
        4. National chair manages daily work
    B. Party structure diverges in late 1960s
        1. RNC moves to bureaucratic structure; a well-financed party devoted to electing its candidates
        2. Democrats move to factionalized structure to distribute power
        3. RNC uses computerized mailing lists to raise money
            a. Money used to run political consulting firm
            b. Democrats still manage to outspend
            c. Public opinion polls used to find issues and to get voter response to issues and candidates
        4. RNC now tries to help state and local organizations
        5. Democrats remain a collection of feuding factions
    C. National conventions
        1. National committee sets time and place; issues call setting number of delegates for each state
        2. Formulas used to allocate delegates
            a. Democrats shift formula away from South, to North and West
            b. Republicans shift formula from East to South and Southwest
            c. Result: Democrats move left, Republicans right
        3. Democrat formula rewards large states; and Republican rewards loyal states
        4. Democrats set new rules
            a. In 1970s, rules changed to weaken party leaders and increase influence of special interests
            b. Hunt Commission in 1981 increases influence of elected officials and makes convention more deliberative
        5. Consequence of reforms: parties represent different sets of upper-middle-class voters
            a. Republicans represent traditional middle class
            b. Democrats represent "new" class
            c. Democrats hurt since traditional middle class closer in opinions to most citizens

6. To become more competitive, Democrats adopt rule changes
   a. In 1988, number of superdelegates increased while special interests decreased
   b. In 1992, three rules: winner-reward system, proportional representation, and states penalized that violate rules
7. Conventions today only ratify choices made in primaries (ADDITIONAL LECTURE TOPIC B-1)

IV. State and local parties (THEME C: AMERICAN PARTIES AS BROAD COALITIONS)
   A. The machine
      1. Recruitment via tangible incentives

Mayor Richard Daley of Chicago maintained control of about 35,000 patronage jobs and could deliver an estimated 350,000 votes in any election.

      2. High degree of leadership control
      3. Abuses
         a. Gradually controlled by reforms
         b. But machines continued
      4. Both self-serving and public-regarding
      5. Winning above all else
   B. Ideological parties
      1. Principle above all else
      2. Usually outside Democrats and Republicans
      3. But some local reform clubs
      4. Reform clubs replaced by social movements
   C. Solidary groups
      1. Most common form of party organization
      2. Members motivated by solidary incentives
      3. Advantage: neither corrupt nor inflexible
      4. Disadvantage: not very hard working
   D. Sponsored parties
      1. Created or sustained by another organization
      2. Example: Detroit Democrats controlled by UAW
      3. Not very common
   E. Personal following
      1. Examples: Kennedys, Curley, Talmadges, Longs
      2. Viability today affected by radio and television
      3. Advantage: vote for the person
      4. Disadvantage: takes time to know the person

V. The two-party system
   A. Rarity among nations today

The United Kingdom, for practical purposes, has a two-party system. Since 1970, two parties (Labour and Conservative) have averaged 73 percent of the total popular vote in parliamentary elections.

   B. Evenly balanced nationally, not locally
   C. Why such a permanent feature?
      1. Electoral system—winner-take-all and plurality system
      2. Opinions of voters—two broad coalitions work

VI. Minor parties (ADDITIONAL LECTURE TOPIC C-1)
   A. Ideological parties—comprehensive, radical view; most enduring
      Examples: Socialist, Communist, Libertarian
   B. One-issue parties—address one concern, avoid others
      Examples: Free Soil, Know-Nothing, Prohibition
   C. Economic Protest Parties—regional, oppose depressions
      Examples: Greenback, Populist
   D. Factional parties—from split in a major party
      Examples: Bull Moose, Henry Wallace, American Independent

  E. Movements *not* producing parties; either slim chance of success or parties accommodate
    Examples: civil rights, antiwar, labor
  F. Factional parties have had greatest influence
VII. Nominating a president

By tradition, the party "out of power"—the one not holding the presidency—holds its convention first.

  A. Two contrary forces: party's desire to win motivates it to seek an appealing candidate, but its desire to keep dissidents in party forces a compromise with more extreme views
  B. Are the delegates representative of the voters?
    1. Democratic delegates much more liberal
    2. Republican delegates much more conservative
    3. Explanation of this disparity?
      a. Not quota rules: quota groups have greater diversity of opinion than do the delegates
  C. Who votes in primaries?
    1. Primaries now more numerous and more decisive
      a. Truman and Stevenson never entered a primary

As late as 1968, Hubert Humphrey won the Democratic nomination for president without entering a single primary.

      b. By 1988: thirty-seven primaries and twenty-two caucuses
    2. Little ideological difference between primary voters and rank-and-file party voters
    3. Caucus: meeting of party followers at which delegates are picked
      a. Only most dedicated partisans attend
      b. Often choose most ideological candidate: Jackson, Robertson in 1988
  D. Who are the new delegates?
    1. However chosen, today's delegates a new breed—unlikely to resemble average citizen: issue-oriented activists
    2. Advantages of new system
      a. Increased chance for activists within party
      b. Decreased probability of their bolting the party
    3. Disadvantage: may nominate presidential candidates unacceptable to voters or rank and file
VIII. Parties versus voters (THEME D: ARE THERE SIGNIFICANT DIFFERENCES BETWEEN DEMOCRATS AND REPUBLICANS?)
  A. Democrats: win congressional elections but lose presidential contests
    1. Candidates are out of step with average voters on social and taxation issues
    2. So are delegates . . . and there's a connection
  B. Republicans had same problem with Goldwater (1964)
  C. Rank-and-file Democrats and Republicans differ on many political issues
    1. But differences are usually small

Representative Craig Hosmer (R-Cal) inserted the following differences between the two parties into the *Congressional Record:* Democrats buy most of the books that have been banned somewhere, while Republicans form committees to read them as a group; Republicans tend to keep their shades drawn, although there is seldom any reason why they should, while Democrats ought to, but don't; Democrats make up plans and then do something else, while Republicans follows the plans their grandfathers made.

  D. Delegates from two parties differ widely on these same issues
    1. Especially Democrats: 1988 convention
    2. This means convention was filled with delegates who disagreed with voters
    3. True since 1972
    4. Democratic delegates (and candidates) need to "get in touch"

5. But candidates must often play to the ideological extremes to win delegate support.

Important Terms

*caucus (nominating) An alternative to a state primary in which party followers meet, often for many hours, to select party candidates.

*congressional campaign committees Separate committees in Congress for each political party to help members who are running for reelection or would-be members running for an open seat or challenging a candidate from the opposition party.

direct primary A proposal originated by progressive reformers to open up political parties to their membership. It permits a vote of party members to select the party's nominee in the general election.

economic-protest parties Parties, usually based in a particular region, especially involving farmers, that protest against depressed economic conditions. These tend to disappear as conditions improve. An example would be the Greenback party.

factional parties Parties that are created by a split in a major party, usually over the identity and philosophy of the major party's presidential candidate. An example would be the "Bull Moose" Progressive party.

first party system The original party structure in which political parties were loose caucuses of political notables in various locations. It was replaced around 1824.

*ideological party A political party organization that values principle above all else and spurns money incentives for members to participate.

initiative A proposal favored by progressive reformers to curtail corruption. It allows a law to be enacted directly by vote of the people without approval of a legislative body.

*mugwumps One of two major factions largely within the Republican party who opposed the heavy emphasis on patronage and disliked the party machinery because it only permitted bland candidates to rise to the top, was fearful of immigrants, and wanted to see the party take unpopular stances on certain issues. They challenged the Old Guard from around 1896 to the 1930s.

*national chairman The person responsible for managing the day-to-day work of a national political party. The person is given a full-time, paid position and is elected by the national committee.

*national committee Delegates from each state and territory who manage party affairs between national conventions. These exist at the national level for both major political parties.

*national party convention The ultimate authority in both major political parties in the United States. The conventions are held every four years to nominate each party's candidate for the presidency.

Old Guard One of two major factions largely within the Republican party, composed of the party regulars and professional politicians. They were preoccupied with building up the party machinery, developing party loyalty, and acquiring and dispensing patronage. They were challenged by progressives from around 1896 to the 1930s.

one-issue parties Parties seeking a single policy, usually revealed by their names, and avoiding other issues. An example would be the Free Soil party.

*personal following A type of local party organization in which a candidate gets people to work for him or her for a campaign and then the organization disbands until the next election. To run this type of campaign, a candidate needs an appealing personality, a lot of friends, or a large bank account.

plurality system An electoral system in which the winner is that person who gets the most votes, even if they do not constitute a majority of the votes.

political machine A political party organization that recruits its members by the use of tangible incentives and is characterized by a high degree of leadership control over members' activities. This form of party organization is largely extinct today.

political party A group that seeks to elect candidates to public office by supplying them with a label by which they are known to the electorate.

second party system The second party structure in the nation's history that emerged when Andrew Jackson first ran for the presidency in 1824. The system was built from the bottom-up as political participation became a mass phenomenon.

solidary group A political party organization based on gregarious or game-loving instincts. It survives on the basis of a friendship network.

solidary incentive An inducement that attracts people out of gregarious or game-loving instincts. It is one reason why people become involved in a state or local party organization.

special-interest caucus A group within a political party united by a concern over a specific cause. The Democratic party has attempted to assure many special-interest groups representation at its national convention, although lately the party has moved away from this commitment.

sponsored party A political party organization created or sponsored by another organization. This form of local party organization is rare in the United States.

superdelegates Elected officials and party leaders represented at the national convention of the Democratic party. Such representation was provided for by a recent party reform to ensure that an electable presidential candidate is selected.

two-party system An electoral system with two dominant parties that compete in state or national elections. Third parties have little chance of winning.

unit rule A requirement that all delegates representing a state at a national party convention vote with the majority of their state delegation.

winner-take-all system An element of the electoral system used in the United States which requires that only one member of the House of Representatives can be elected from each congressional district.

Theme A Party Strength

Summary

A *political party* is a group that seeks to elect candidates to public office by supplying them with labels by which they are known to the electorate. A party thus exists in three arenas:

1. A label in the mind of the voters. A powerful party is one whose label has strong appeal.

2. An organization that recruits and campaigns for candidates. A powerful party's organization can decide who will be candidates and how their campaigns will be managed.

3. A set of leaders who try to organize and control the legislative and executive branches of government. A powerful party's leaders can dominate one or all branches of government.

American parties are much weaker than European parties. In Europe, the only way to run for office is to obtain a party nomination, campaigns are run by the party using party funds and workers, and candidates who gain office are expected to vote and act together with other members of their party. Party label, not personal attractiveness, is the chief guide used by voters.

American parties are weak for several reasons. Federalism has produced a highly decentralized party system, because parties traditionally have acquired money and jobs from local sources and fought local contests. The recent centralization of political authority in Washington has failed to produce a stronger party system because of laws—particularly laws requiring *primary elections*—that have weakened the parties. The separation of powers makes it more difficult for any party to take over the government decisively, and it gives executive and legislative members of a party a separate, independent electoral base. Finally, the American political culture separates political activity from social, business, working, and cultural activity. In contrast to the situation in Europe, parties play a segmental, rather than a comprehensive, role in our lives.

American political parties have passed through four broad historical periods:

1. The first, from the Founding until the 1820s, saw the creation of parties in spite of the fact that the Founders saw parties as "factions" motivated by ambition and self-interest, and in spite of the unwillingness of early partisans to concede the legitimacy of party competition. The "Republicans," under Jefferson's leadership, opposed the "Federalists," who followed Hamilton. Each doubted the commitment of the other to the basic principles of the new government; however, when Jefferson won the presidency in 1800 and adopted a conciliatory posture upon taking office, the legitimacy of parties was established. The Federalist party withered quickly after 1800 because of its limited sectional and class base.

    The first party system was quite weak: no one had an ancestral party loyalty, parties consisted of local notables rather than political professionals, and there was little mass participation. The first parties were, like parties since, heterogeneous coalitions.

2. Andrew Jackson's run for the presidency in 1824 marked the beginning of the "second party system," which lasted until the Civil War became inevitable. This era saw a vast increase in political participation on the part of a vastly more numerous electorate. Popular election of members of the electoral college became almost universal, and the *party convention* replaced the congressional *caucus* as a means of selecting presidential candidates.

3. The Whigs and the Democrats were competitive national parties, but they proved unable to straddle the emerging crisis between the North and South over slavery. The modern Republican party, which began as a third party, displaced the Whigs and, on the strength of loyalties gained by its support of the Union side in the Civil War, came to dominate American politics until the New Deal. The Democrats were further harmed by the 1896 presidential candidacy of populist William Jennings Bryan. Bryan alienated voters in the Northeast while attracting voters in the South and West—thus deepening the regional split between the parties. The result was that competition between parties virtually ceased in many states, so one-sided were party loyalties.

4. Within the dominant Republican party, two major factions emerged. The *stalwarts* or *Old Guard* consisted of party professionals concerned with building up party loyalty and the party machinery through patronage. By contrast, the *mugwumps*, *Progressives* or *reformers*, opposed patronage, disliked party machinery, and were fearful of the influx of immigrants into the cities. At first the mugwumps tried to play a balance-of-power role between parties, but as many states became one-sidedly Republican, they increasingly attacked the very concept of partisanship.

    The agenda of the Progressives included (a) primary elections; (b) nonpartisan elections at the local level; (c) strict voter registration; (d) civil service reform to eliminate patronage; and (e) measures such as the *initiative* and *referendum* to allow citizens to vote directly on proposed legislation. These reforms succeeded in substantially reducing political corruption and "boss rule," but they also weakened parties, making them less able to hold officeholders accountable and to assemble the power necessary for governing.

Discussion Questions

1. Since political parties are so weak in the United States, what purpose do they continue to serve? Since candidates raise most of their own campaign funds, do they even need party affiliation? Would the nation be unable to run itself without political parties?

2. Primary elections were instituted to make the selection of candidates more democratic. They have, however, contributed to the decline of political parties. Since few people vote in primaries, is their purpose not being achieved as a practical matter? In the 1984 presidential election, many states abandoned the use of primaries. Does this trend indicate that a problem exists with primaries? If so, why did many states revive the primary system in the 1988 presidential election?

3. Doesn't a strong party system, as exists in most European countries, make government more accountable since voters know whom to blame for failed policies? For that reason, in place of the current method of state control, why shouldn't Congress regulate political parties?

Date and Perspective for Analysis

The degree of party competition within states varies according to how it is measured. Consider the following ranking of the states based on two different measures. The first ranking is derived from district-level competition in state legislative elections from 1982 to 1986. The "Folded Ranney" ranking is based on party control of the state legislature and the governorship from 1981 to 1988. Replicate the table for your class and have them analyze it. Do the data support the book's contention on regional competition, such as in the South and Northeast? How can the differences in the rankings be explained? Which is more accurate?

Measures of Political Competition in the States

STATE	DISTRICT-LEVEL COMPETITION	RANK	FOLDED RANNEY	RANK
North Dakota	56.58	1	1.000	1
Oregon	54.25	2	.900	14
Nebraska	54.06	3	.980	7
Washington	53.94	4	.830	26
Alaska	53.46	5	.970	9
Connecticut	52.81	6	.920	13
Minnesota	52.44	7	.860	18
New Jersey	51.81	8	.990	3
Ohio	49.61	9	.960	12
Nevada	49.60	10	.990	3
Michigan	49.58	11	.980	7
Vermont	49.16	12	.970	9
Wisconsin	49.13	13	.820	29
Iowa	48.55	14	.860	18
New York	47.68	15	.990	3
California	47.29	16	.840	23
Maine	45.90	17	.800	30
Utah	45.29	18	.750	39
West Virginia	44.97	19	.730	43
Indiana	44.59	20	.860	18
Montana	43.34	21	.990	3
Illinois	41.61	22	.860	18
Virginia	40.71	23	.760	34
Pennsylvania	40.19	24	.970	9
Colorado	40.18	25	.830	26
Delaware	39.66	26	1.000	1
Rhode Island	39.49	27	.780	33
South Dakota	39.19	28	.760	34
New Mexico	37.10	29	.830	26
Kansas	35.81	30	.890	15
Idaho	35.60	31	.800	30
Arizona	33.90	32	.890	15
North Carolina	33.42	33	.800	30
Hawaii	33.40	34	.730	43
Florida	31.13	35	.760	34
Maryland	31.00	36	.740	41
Wyoming	30.46	37	.840	23
Massachusetts	30.39	38	.760	34
New Hampshire	29.01	39	.840	23
South Carolina	28.32	40	.710	46
Kentucky	27.81	41	.730	43
Alabama	27.27	42	.660	49
Missouri	27.12	43	.880	17
Tennessee	26.72	44	.860	18
Oklahoma	25.49	45	.760	34
Texas	21.96	46	.750	39
Mississippi	16.48	47	.640	50
Georgia	16.19	48	.740	41
Arkansas	9.26	49	.700	47
Louisiana	—	—	.690	48

Source: Thomas M. Holbrook and Emily Van Dunk, "Electoral Competition in the States," *American Political Science Review* 87 (December 1993): 957.

Abstract for Theme A

Party Strength and the Democratic Party

The Democrats have managed to win only two presidential elections in the last seven contests. In other words, the Republicans have controlled the White House for twenty of the last twenty-eight years. The Democratic party is in disarray. Are Democrats out of touch with the voters? A struggle is currently taking place within the party to define a new image. Two factions have emerged with competing agendas: the Democratic Leadership Council and the Coalition for Democratic Values.

The Democratic Leadership Council (DLC) was created in 1985 to lead Democrats "back to the mainstream." Its roots are in the South, but an effort is being made to expand its base of support nationally. The DLC aspires to move the Democratic party toward a moderate direction. Its 1991 "convention" in Cleveland, for example, refused both Jesse Jackson and George McGovern invitations to speak. At present, the DLC has about two thousand members, with chapters in twenty-two states. The power of the organization has grown as it acquires substantial corporate support. Bill Clinton, while chairman of the DLC, said the group will soon exceed the Democratic National Committee in importance.

The Coalition for Democratic Values (CDV) was established by party liberals in response to the emergence of the DLC as a political force. Senator Howard Metzenbaum of Ohio used funds from his own campaign treasury to inaugurate the CDV in 1990. The basic tenet of the CDV is that "the nation does not need two Republican parties." Membership has grown to eight hundred, including seventy-five members of Congress. "It is not a fight for control of the party," according to Metzenbaum, "but it may be a fight for the hearts of the Democrats in this country." The soul of the Democratic party is up for grabs.

Source: Adapted from Tom Baxter and A. L. May, "Democratic Factions Battling for Soul of Party," *Atlanta Journal and Constitution*, May 5, 1991.

Theme B   Party Structure Today

Summary

Although very similar on paper, the structure of the national Democratic party differs substantially from that of the Republican party in practice. The Democrats, torn by ideological conflicts, have evolved into a *factional* party emphasizing the mobilization and conciliation of party activists. As the minority, the Republican party has become a *bureaucratic* party devoted to winning elections by focusing on raising money and providing consulting services to its candidates. The result is that the Democrats have selected presidential candidates with a decidedly liberal orientation, while Republicans have fielded more moderate nominees capable of attracting middle-class voters. Thus the numerical advantage of the Democratic party has been offset by the electoral appeal of Republican candidates.

These generalizations, however, apply to national—largely presidential—elections. The parity of the two parties breaks down at the state and local levels where party strength varies by region. Moreover, the key organizational unit of the party structure is located at the city, county, and state levels. The national parties are little more than an affiliation of these regional entities and lack any real control over them. Five distinct types of local party organizations have developed.

1. *The machine* is a party organization that recruits its members by the use of tangible incentives and is characterized by a high degree of leadership control over member activity. Machines, in their heyday, were dependent on federal patronage jobs (such as in the Post Office), kickbacks on contracts, payments extracted from officeholders, and funds raised from businessmen. With the influx of poor immigrants the machine adopted a social welfare function. The abuses of the machine were curtailed through stricter voter registration laws, civil service reforms, competitive bidding laws, and the *Hatch Act*, which made it illegal for federal civil servants to take part in most political

activities. More important, increased income and sophistication made voters less dependent on what the machines could offer; so did the growth of the federal welfare system. It is easy to scorn the machine as venal and self-serving; however, machines mobilized a very high level of participation. Furthermore, their interest in winning elections meant that machines supported popular candidates, regardless of ideology.

2. *Ideological parties* value principle above all else. Because of their unwillingness to compromise, ideological parties are typically "third" parties such as the Socialist, Prohibition, or Libertarian parties. However, some local organizations within the two major parties fit into this category. Ideological parties are marked by intense internal conflict over issues, and leaders have little room for maneuvering and bargaining.

3. *Solidary groups* are composed of people who find politics fun. Such groups have the advantage of being neither corrupt nor inflexible; however, often they will not work very hard.

4. *Sponsored parties* can be created without patronage, or ideology, or members who find the work fun if some other organization provides money and workers for a local party. These instances are rare, the UAW's role in the Detroit Democratic party being the best example.

5. *Personal followings* attracted by the personality of the candidate have become much more important as other forms of party organization have declined. Such a following can allow a candidate to be "independent," but the politics of personality (as opposed to machine or ideological politics) deprives the average voter of any reasonable basis for judging most candidates.

The various types of local parties are all important. But increasingly, political activists who become nationally known enter that scene from interest groups such as NOW, NEA, and the AFL-CIO.

Despite the concentration of power at the local level, most Americans define the parties on the basis of their national identities. Yet an odd role reversal seems to be taking place, as each national party has begun to assimilate characteristics of the other. The electoral fortunes of the parties have much to do with this process. The string of presidential victories from 1980 through 1988 lulled Republicans into equating their success with the conservative ideology of Ronald Reagan. This assumption proved fatal in 1992. The genial personality of Reagan had concealed the rough edges of his conservative principles; voters were attracted more to the person than to the value system. In the 1984 election, for example, pollster Louis Harris discovered that Americans preferred the position of Democrat Walter Mondale to that of Reagan on twelve of sixteen issues surveyed. George Bush, pushed by a special-interest group (the religious right), moved to an ideological extreme in 1992 and succumbed to the same fate as previous Democratic candidates.

On the other hand, the Democratic party has been embracing aspects of the Republican party structure, adopting techniques like direct mail and the use of *superdelegates* to ensure a more "electable" candidate. Bill Clinton revealed himself to be an untraditional Democratic nominee, purposely alienating himself from certain African-American leaders (like Jesse Jackson) and attacking liberal policy icons (like the welfare system and the ban against prayer in the public schools). As the Democrats have moved to the center, the Republicans have become more isolated on the ideological extreme. Neither party is especially pleased by these developments, with Democrats complaining about "selling out" and Republicans complaining about the influence of the Christian Coalition. The very soul of each party is up for grabs. Is it better to win or to be ideologically pure? The two goals are seldom compatible.

Discussion Questions

1. Consider the five types of local political party organizations that the text lists. What advantages and disadvantages does each type have? Rank the five types according to whether they can:

    - Introduce needed political reforms
    - Successfully assemble enough power to govern effectively

- Induce active political participation
- Induce a broad cross section of society to participate
- Avoid corruption
- Give the voters a reasonable choice of policies
- Allow the voters to hold politicians responsible for the success or failure of their policies
- Rejuvenate the political process by allowing "outsiders" in

Are all your rankings similar? That is, are some types of parties better than others? Or do all types have both their virtues and their disadvantages?

2. Political parties have little control over the behavior of their members or of the candidates representing them. For example, David Duke—a former grand wizard of the Ku Klux Klan—entered the Louisiana legislature as a Republican despite radio broadcasts by President Reagan calling for his defeat. How is the political system hurt by the loose organization of political parties? Voter loyalty to a particular party is diminishing; 40 percent of voters could tell no difference between the parties. Would a strengthened party structure prevent defections? Would this be a positive development? For example, wouldn't the power of the states be restricted? Wouldn't candidates be less responsive to local interests?

3. Suppose you wanted more powerful parties in the United States today. Which alternative from each item listed below would be more likely to achieve your goal?

- Public financing of campaigns or private contributions
- More primaries or more caucuses
- More openness to outside political forces or more control by established political figures
- More power in Washington or more power in state and local governments
- More people in politics because of ideology or "principle" or more in it for jobs and money

Data and Perspectives for Analysis

The text notes that the Democratic and Republican parties have different structures. The Democratic party has adopted a "factionalized" structure to embrace all relevant social groups. The Republican party, on the other hand, is constructed around a "bureaucratic" structure for purposes of efficiency. As a result, the minority Republican party has achieved a high degree of electoral success at the national level despite the paucity of its membership numbers. In the process, the Republican party has developed a competent campaign-financing operation. Thus structure has an influence on party behavior. The Democratic party has belatedly attempted to emulate some of these Republican practices. Is it more important for a party to represent its membership interests or to win elections? Both parties have arrived at the same conclusion: ideals are secondary to winning.

With this change in focus, will Democrats become more competitive in presidential elections? The data reveal the comparative disadvantage of the Democratic party in fund raising.

Financial Activity of the National Political Parties (in millions)

Party	1979–1980	1983–1984	1987–1988
Democrat			
Raised	$37.2	$98.5	$127.9
Spent	35.0	97.4	121.9
Republican			
Raised	169.5	297.9	263.3
Spent	161.8	300.8	257.0

Source: Federal Election Commission, "FEC Summaries 1988 Political Party Activity," March 27, 1989.

Additional Lecture Topic B-1

Do We Need a Stronger Party System?

David Broder, *The Party's Over*. New York: Harper & Row, 1972.

Committee on Political Parties of the American Political Science Association, *Toward a More Responsible Two-Party System*. New York: Rinehart, 1950.

Evron Kirkpatrick, "Toward a More Responsible Two-Party System: Political Science, Policy Science, or Pseudo-Science?" *American Political Science Review*, December 1971.

Sandy L. Maisel, ed., *The Parties Respond*. Boulder, CO: Westview Press, 1990.

J. Roland Pennock, "Responsiveness, Responsibility, and Majority Rule." *American Political Science Review*, September 1952, pp. 790–807. Also in Munger and Price, op. cit.

Frank J. Sorauf and Paul Allen Beck, *Party Politics in America*. 6th ed. Glenview, IL: Scott, Foresman, 1988. See Chapter 17, "The Future of the American Parties."

Abstract 1 for Theme B

The Republican Party's "Conversion" of Democrats, 1985–1991

Although American political parties are decentralized, the national party level can at times exercise leadership or initiate policy vis-a-vis lower party levels. One example of such an action occurred in 1985 when Republican party leaders (the Republican National Committee and White House political officials) launched a drive to change the registration and/or party affiliation of disenchanted Democratic officeholders and voters. Two articles in the *New York Times* discussed this attempt. According to Gerald M. Boyd in "G.O.P. Pressing Efforts to Convert Officeholders" (March 19, 1985, p. 1), the Republican National Committee launched a campaign to convince state legislators (particularly in the South) to switch to the Republican party. The Republican aim was to build the party's strength in state legislatures in order "to influence the redrawing of congressional district lines after the 1990 census." The Democratic National Committee chairman, Paul G. Kirk, Jr., countered that this effort would be "short-lived and unsuccessful." Democratic leaders also noted that a similar Republican effort in 1981 had netted few conversions. Still, the overall aim of the Republicans was to strengthen the party at all levels of governing.

Phil Gailey's article, "G.O.P. Is Trying to Persuade Democrats to Change Parties" (May 8, 1985, p. 13), revealed the Republican plan to persuade one hundred thousand registered Democrats to switch to the Republican party (these Democratic voters were concentrated in Florida, Louisiana, and Pennsylvania). Frank Fahrenkopf, Chairman of the Republican National Committee, asserted that "political realignment" was taking place between the parties (this was especially true in the South). Other Republican officials explained that they had registered twice as many new voters as the Democrats in the last four years in Florida and that the trend was similar elsewhere in the nation. Would the Republicans eventually become the new majority party in the country?

Questions for Discussion

1. Party identification, while noticeably weaker in recent years, is still a powerful political force for many voters and officeholders. Speculate on some of the specific reasons a Democrat would convert to the Republican party.

2. Speculate on how the Democrats could counter the various Republican "converting" efforts described in the Abstract. Did they succeed or fail, as measured by national registration figures during 1985–1991?

Answer Guidelines

You may wish to present up-to-date registration figures (nationally) for the two respective parties and then note what the trends are. Democrats could counter most effectively if national and international trends begin to deteriorate to the point where they could be used as political "ammunition" in future electoral contests. Finally, Democratic conversions, particularly for officeholders, will depend on the particular races in question and on the profile of voter registration applicable to an electoral contest.

Abstract 2 for Theme B

"Superdelegates" and the 1988 Democratic Convention

Until the political juggernaut of Governor Michael Dukakis smashed his primary opposition in the latter stages of the 1988 primary campaign, it appeared that the Democratic Convention might be a "brokered" affair, that is, that no presidential contender would go to the convention in Atlanta with the necessary 2,082 delegates' votes needed to secure the party's presidential nomination. In late March of 1988, press speculation centered on the increasing importance of the 645 *superdelegates*. These professional politicians and party leaders (senators, representatives, governors, national committee members, and honorary members such as ex-president Jimmy Carter) were created as a group after 1980 to dilute the role of amateurs in the nomination process and consequently to allocate greater nominating power to active politicians.

Not everyone felt that the "superdelegates" concept was fair or appropriate. Jesse Jackson's campaign manager argued that his candidate could win the greatest number of popular votes and delegates but still be denied the nomination through a "smoke-filled room" agreement by the superdelegates. After all, the voters in the primaries had not selected the superdelegates.

Fortunately for party harmony, the Jackson scenario was not realized. Conversely, if superdelegates were retained by the Democratic party, could not the unjust aspects of the idea be manifested in future presidential election years?

Question for Discussion

Should superdelegates be retained by the Democratic party? What are the strengths and weaknesses of this concept? Debate the issue in class.

Theme C   American Parties as Broad Coalitions

Summary

It is remarkable that we have had only two major parties for most of our history; most European democracies are multiparty systems. Two factors account for this. First, our elections are based on the *plurality, winner-take-all* system. (The most dramatic example of the winner-take-all principle is the U.S. electoral college.) This means that to win anything, one must be part of a coalition broad enough to get a plurality of votes. A vote for a minor party will be as "wasted vote." Under *proportional representation*, which is common in Europe, even very small parties have a chance of winning something, and therefore an incentive to organize. Second, in spite of occasional bitter dissent, Americans have not faced divisive and longstanding controversies over the organization of the economy, the prerogatives of the monarchy, and the role of the church. Thus they have agreed on enough issues to make broad coalitions possible. Finally, state laws make it exceedingly difficult for third parties to get on the ballot, as third-party candidates George Wallace and John Anderson quickly discovered in 1968 an 1980, respectively. Matters were only somewhat better for Ross Perot in 1992.

Minor parties have formed, however. They have included *ideological parties* such as the Socialist, Communist, and Libertarian parties; *one-issue parties* such as the Free Soil or Prohibition parties; *economic protest parties* such as the Greenback and Populist parties; and *factional parties* such as the Progressive party in 1924 and the American Independent party in 1968. Of these, factional parties probably have had the greatest influence on public policy.

This is due to the impact of a factional split on the unity of a major political party and the subsequent possibility of an electoral defeat.

The major parties face two contrary forces: the desire to win the presidency pushes them toward the middle of the road, whereas the need to accommodate ideologically extreme elements within the party requires concessions of which voters may disapprove. This problem has become particularly acute of late because reforms of the parties have shifted power from professionals to *amateur* or *purist* activists. It may be that voters in the increasingly prevalent primaries are more extreme and ideological than the general electorate; both parties' convention delegates are certainly more ideological and extreme than the population as a whole. Between rank-and-file Democrats and rank-and-file Republicans, there are some modest differences in policy preferences. But among party activists, leaders, and officeholders, the differences between the two parties are very large, with Democratic activists leaning very far to the left and Republicans very far to the right. Thus, at least from this perspective, there is a great deal more than merely "a dime's worth of difference" between the two major parties.

Discussion Questions

1. Democratic politics always require a majority coalition in order to win. In the United States the coalition is formed before an election, in the makeup of political parties. In European multiparty systems the coalition is formed after the election, when a political leader bargains for the support of other parties in order to form a majority of seats in parliament. What difference might it make whether the coalition is put together before or after the election? Which system allows the most meaningful elections? Which allows citizens to express their attitudes best in the polling booth? Which most effectively allows citizens to hold politicians accountable for what they do?

2. Why is it almost always irrational for a voter to vote for a party other than one of the two major ones? What would a voter who found the Democrats insufficiently liberal have gained by voting for a candidate such as McCarthy in 1976? What would a voter who found the Republicans insufficiently conservative have accomplished by voting for the American Independent party in 1972? Can you conceive of circumstances where it would be rational to vote for a minor-party candidate? What would a Republican voter have gained by voting for John Anderson in 1980? Use the 1980 and 1984 elections as examples in your answer.

3. Are the two major political parties different? If not, why do voters as different as blacks and Jews consistently vote Democratic? If so, how do the parties differ? A 1988 *New York Times* poll revealed that 51 percent of the public believes the Democrats are better able to handle unemployment (versus 31 percent for Republicans) but that 53 percent feels the Republicans are more likely to keep American defense strong (versus 24 percent for Democrats). Are these evaluations rooted in genuine policy differences between the parties?

Additional Lecture Topic C-1

The Role of Third or Minor Political Parties

Marshall Frady, *Wallace*. New York: World, 1968.

Daniel A. Mazamian, *Third Parties in Presidential Elections*. Washington, DC: Brookings Institute, 1974.

Howard R. Penniman, "Presidential Third Parties and the Modern American Two-Party System." In William Crotty, ed., *The Party Symbol*. San Francisco: Freeman, 1980.

Stephen J. Rosenstone, Roy L. Behr, and Edward H. Lazarus, *Third Parties in America*. Princeton, NJ: Princeton University Press, 1984.

David A. Shannon, *The Socialist Party of America*. New York: Macmillan, 1955.

Frank Smallwood, *The Other Candidates: Third Parties in Presidential Elections*. Boston: University Press of New England, 1983.

George Thayer, *The Farther Shores of Politics*. New York: Simon & Schuster, 1967.

Abstract 1 for Theme C

The Two-Party System and the Electoral College

The existence of the American two-party system is linked to the "winner-take-all" character of the electoral system. Unlike many European nations, the United States does not have a proportional representation system (which encourages multiparty systems) but rather a single-member district system whereby only one candidate can win the public office being contested. Given the additional middle-class/centrist nature of the American electorate, preferring candidates from either one of the two major political parties becomes a natural choice for most voters. Why waste a vote on a third-party candidate who cannot possibly win (assuming that the great bulk of registered voters belong to the two major parties)?

Indeed, those who support the two-party system are not keen on drastically altering the electoral college, a system of electing presidents that deters the proliferation of parties. Thus Robert Weissberg's "In Defense of the Electoral College" (in Robert DiClerico and Allan S. Jammock's *Points of View* [Reading, MA: Addison-Wesley, 1983,] pp. 116–121) points out that the college's most "important" virtue is that it *preserves a moderate two-party system*. Weissberg explains this in the following paragraphs:

> Under the existing system, winning the presidency means winning numerous electoral votes. Since to win electoral votes you must win pluralities in many states, it takes a formidable political organization to win these big prizes. A group that won, say, 5 or 10 percent of the vote in a few states would be doomed.... In contemporary politics, the only organizations capable of such a massive electoral undertaking are large, diverse compromise-oriented political parties such as the Democratic and Republican parties.
>
> To appreciate this contribution of the existing electoral-college system, imagine presidential candidates *without* the two major parties. Instead of two major candidates and a dozen or two inconsequential candidates, there would be numerous hopefuls with some reasonable chance of success. These candidates would likely draw most of their support from relatively small segments of the population. There might be an anti-abortion candidate, a strong civil-rights candidate.... The incentive to create broad-based coalitions ... would be considerably reduced and *thus the two major parties would virtually disappear*.

Weissberg goes on to assert that any candidate who managed to be elected would have a narrow base of support and would also have to deal with a Congress "composed of people with no party attachment whose primary purpose was to advance a particular group or regional interest." In short, the perpetuation of the electoral college strengthens the two-party system and reduces conflict while promoting postelection governance.

Questions for Discussion

1. Assume that the electoral college was eliminated in favor of *direct popular election* of the president. That is, whichever candidate got the greatest number of popular votes (at least 40 percent of the total vote) would be elected. How would such a plan affect the two-party system?

2. Despite the handicap imposed on them by the mechanics of the electoral college, should third or minor political parties be encouraged to offer candidates for public office and the presidency? Why or why not?

Answer Guidelines

It is possible that direct popular election might result in runoff presidential elections, precisely because a coalition of minor parties might draw off enough popular votes to deny a major-party presidential candidate the necessary 40 percent requirement (particularly in a close election). Also, the prospects of a runoff could galvanize the future development of a major third party, one that could at least leap past an old declining major party into the runoff. Regarding the value of minor parties, the standard argument is that such parties publicize issues or ideas that, though they may be popular only among a vocal minority, nevertheless must then be considered by either or both of the two major political parties.

Abstract 2 for Theme C

Are Political Parties Meaningless in Today's Political System?

In Peter Woll's *Debating American Government*, 2nd ed. (Glenview, IL; Scott-Foresman, 1988), political scientist Samuel J. Eldersveld argues that parties have significant roles to play in the political system and that the "decline" of American political parties is probably more one of "image" than reality ("Party Decline: Fact or Fiction," pp. 79-92). Eldersveld asserts the following:

1. Party organization activism at the local level has increased, despite the rise of the direct primary and the new campaign technology. Thus the proportion of the public contacted by party campaign workers has increased. As Eldersveld argues, "whereas in 1952 only 12 percent of the public reported contacts, by 1976 it was close to 30 percent; in 1980 it was 24 percent."

2. In addition, these party contacts "are reaching out to a larger proportion of blacks and less well-educated people than ever before, and this seems to be going on throughout the country."

3. Local party organizations have not necessarily been superseded by the mass media or the personal campaign staffs of the incumbent congressperson or state legislator.

4. The evidence that state and national party organizations have lost their power is "not conclusive." The national committees of each party have expanded their control over delegate selection to the national conventions. In addition, the national conventions continue to play an important role in writing a platform and in serving as a "major forum for consensus-building party unity."

5. The public's indifference or "neutralism" toward party efficacy may result from the media's portrayal of party images. Inaccurate communication masks the continuing relevance of political parties to American government.

Conversely, Martin P. Wattenberg ("The Decline of American Political Parties," pp. 94–98 of the Woll reader) argues the following:

1. The public now views candidates, not parties, as the "problem-solvers" for the political and social ills of the nation.

2. If political leaders would again act as partisans and be presented by the media as such, then public perceptions of parties might change and the decline of partisanship might be arrested.

3. Policy compromises in American politics are becoming more difficult and the tone of politics more bitter owing to the ability of the parties to aggregate diverse interests.

4. Voter volatility is linked to weakening party identification. Party ineffectiveness leads to an emphasis on short-term issues and a candidate's personality.

Questions for Discussion

1. Which arguments seem to have greater weight with the students in your class? Have them defend their opinions by presenting data or evidence which can be linked to either Eldersveld or Wattenberg's arguments.

2. Both authors stress the "image" of parties as communicated by the media to the public. If you were a party leader at the national level, what strategies could you devise to heighten the consciousness of party importance to both the media and the general public?

Theme D   Are There Significant Differences Between Democrats and Republicans?

Summary

America's two main parties are both centrist, democratic institutions. Nevertheless, as the text asserts, policy preferences and philosophical assumptions relating to the most effective way of governing *do exist* between rank-and-file members and activist leaders, that is, strong ideologues. Furthermore, most Democrats remain more liberal on a majority of issues than their Republican counterparts. Also, the proportion of the electorate believing that there are "important differences" between the two parties has increased from 46 percent in 1972 to some 62 percent in 1984 (see Sabato, *The Party's Just Begun*, p. 142). Citizens see the two parties as having major policy differences on defense, handling the economy, welfare, drug enforcement, busing, gun control, nuclear arms, and so forth.

In reference to each party's ability to win national office, differences *within each* party may be the most significant of all. The Republican party under the leadership of Ronald Reagan was able to form a more cohesive conservative orientation, thus overriding the traditional split between centrist and rightist Republican factions. The result has been a more coherent policy agenda than the Democrats have been capable of offering. Democratic internal factionalism is far more extensive, ranging from the solid liberal wing to conservatives to populists to a vast panoply of minority interests. Surmounting this internal divisiveness was one of the main challenges for Michael Dukakis in the 1988 election year. He failed. Bill Clinton, on the other hand, moved to the political center and took the support of party extremist factions for granted. It worked.

Questions for Discussion (open-ended replies are expected)

1. Would the national deficit increase at an even faster rate under a Democratic administration than under a Republican one? Why or why not?

2. Which major political party do you think is better for the country and why?

Data and Perspectives for Analysis

Does the public perceive differences between the Democratic and Republican parties? The data reveal some interesting differences in how the parties are viewed with respect to potential policy performance.

Question: Which political party, Democrat or Republican, do you trust to do a better job?

	Democrats	*Republicans*
helping the poor?	66%	24%
providing affordable health care?	60%	25%
helping the middle class?	55%	34%
improving education and the schools?	55%	29%
holding taxes down?	41%	45%
reducing the federal deficit?	40%	39%
handling the crime problem?	39%	35%
handling foreign affairs?	33%	56%
maintaining a strong national defense?	29%	60%

Source: ABC News/Washington Post Poll (January 1992).

8

Elections and Campaigns

Overview and Objectives

This chapter conducts the student on a "Cook's Tour" of some of the scholarly examinations, the common folklore, and the amazing intricacies of America's most enduring and exciting political institution, the election. Major topics include, but are not limited to, the debate over just how democratic they really are (given a very low voter turnout), the new personalistic nature of campaigning in the latter part of the twentieth century, the role that money plays in determining outcomes, the role of special-interest groups, so-called realigning elections, and the elements of successful coalition building by Democrats and Republicans. After reading and reviewing the material in this chapter the student should be able to do each of the following:

1. Explain why elections in the United States are both more democratic and less democratic than those of other countries.

2. Demonstrate the differences between the party-oriented campaigns of the nineteenth century and the candidate-oriented ones of today, explaining the major elements of a successful campaign for office today.

3. Discuss how important campaign funding is to election outcomes, what the major sources of such funding are under current law, and how successful reform legislation has been in purifying United States elections of improper monetary influences.

4. Discuss the partisan effects of campaigns, or why the party with the most registered voters does not always win the election.

5. Define the term *realigning election* and discuss the major examples of such elections in the past as well as recent debates over whether realignment is again underway.

6. Describe what the Democrats and the Republicans respectively must do to put together a successful national coalition to achieve political power in any election.

7. Outline the major arguments on either side of the question of whether elections do or do not result in major changes in public policy in the United States.

Chapter Outline with Keyed-in Resources

I. Presidential versus congressional campaigns
   A. Introduction
      1. Two phases: getting nominated and getting elected
      2. Getting nominated

               a. Getting your name on the ballot
               b. An individual effort (versus organizational effort in Europe)
               c. Parties play a minor role (compared to Europe)
               d. Parties used to play a major role
        B. Major differences
            1. Presidential races are more competitive
               a. House races have lately been one-sided for Democrats
               b. Presidential winner rarely gets more than 55 percent of vote

The most lopsided presidential election occurred in 1964, when Lyndon Johnson received 61.1 percent of the popular vote.

               c. Most House incumbents are reelected (over 90 percent)
            2. Fewer people vote in congressional elections
               a. Unless it coincides with a presidential election
               b. Gives greater importance to partisan voters (party regulars, etc.)
            3. Congressional incumbents can serve their constituents
               a. Credit for government grants, programs, etc.
               b. President can't: power is not local

Presidents are not utterly without power in local matters; they have a certain amount of influence in establishing program priorities. When Senator Frank Church opposed President Johnson on Vietnam, Johnson vowed never to authorize another dam for Church's state of Idaho.

            4. Congressional candidates can duck responsibility
               a. "I didn't do it—the people in Washington did"
               b. President is stuck with blame
               c. But local candidates also suffer when their "leader's" economic policies fail
            5. Power of presidential coattails has declined
               a. Congressional elections have become largely independent
               b. Reduces meaning (and importance) of party
        C. Running for president
            1. Getting "mentioned"
               a. Using reporters, trips, speeches, famous name
               b. Sponsoring legislation, governor of large state
            2. Setting aside time to run
               a. Reagan: six years
               b. May have to resign from office first
            3. Money
               a. Individuals can give $1,000, PACs $5,000
               b. Candidates must raise $5,000 in twenty states to qualify for matching grants to pay for primary
            4. Organization
               a. Need a large (paid) staff
               b. Need volunteers
               c. Need advisers on issues: position papers
            5. Strategy and themes
               a. Incumbent versus challenger: defend or attack?
               b. Setting the tone (positive or negative)
               c. Developing a theme: "trust," "confidence," etc.
               d. Judging the timing
               e. Choosing a target voter: who's the audience?
    II. Primary versus general campaigns (THEME A: HOW CAMPAIGNS ARE CONDUCTED)
        A. Kinds of elections and primaries
            1. General versus primary elections

Theodore Roosevelt was the first candidate to use primaries to seek a party's nomination in 1912. He lost the Republican nomination to William Howard Taft despite winning nine out of ten primaries.

    B. Differences between primary and general campaigns
        1. What works in a general election may not work in a primary
            a. Different voters, workers, media attention
            b. Must mobilize activists with money and motivation to win nomination
            c. Must play to the politics of activists
        2. Iowa caucuses

Participation is a more serious problem in caucuses than in primaries. For example, participation dropped from 595,000 to 3,200 when Michigan Republicans switched from a primary system in 1980 to a caucus in 1984.

            a. Held in February of presidential election year
            b. Candidates must do well
            c. Winners tend to be "ideologically correct"
            d. Most liberal Democrat, most conservative Republican
            e. The caucus system: "musical chairs and fraternity pledge week"
        3. The balancing act
            a. Being conservative (or liberal) enough to get nominated
            b. Move to center to get elected
            c. True nationwide in states where activists are more polarized than average voters
            d. The "clothespin vote": neither candidate appealing
        4. Even primary voters can be more extreme ideologically than average voters
            a. McGovern in 1972
    C. Television, debates, and direct mail

Television time is closely guarded in elections elsewhere. In France, parties and candidates are barred from buying television time; broadcast time is allocated to parties on the basis of their strength in the national legislature, with no charge for such official time. Britain follows a similar practice. In 1987, the total television time allotted to *all* political parties was two-and-a-half hours.

        1. Paid advertising ("spots")
            a. Seems to have little (or a very subtle) effect on outcome: tend to balance each other out
            b. Most voters rely on many sources for information
        2. News broadcasts ("visuals")
            a. Cost little
            b. May have greater credibility with voters
            c. Rely on having television camera crew around
            d. May actually be less informative than spots
        3. Debates

The type of media plays an important role in evaluating performance. In the first debate between Richard Nixon and John Kennedy in 1960, radio listeners actually gave a slight advantage to Nixon.

            a. Usually an advantage only to the challenger
            b. Reagan in 1980: reassured voters
            c. Primary debates: the "dating game" in 1988
        4. Risk of slips of the tongue on visuals and debates
            a. Ford and Poland, Carter and lust, Reagan and trees
            b. Forces candidates to rely on stock speeches
            c. Sell yourself, not your ideas
        5. The computer
            a. Makes possible direct-mail campaigns

    b. Allows candidates to address specific voters
    c. Importance of mailing lists
  6. The gap between running a campaign and running the government
    a. Party leaders had to worry about reelection
    b. Today's political consultants don't
III. Money (THEME B: MONEY IN ELECTORAL CAMPAIGNS)
 A. How important is it? (ADDITIONAL LECTURE TOPIC B-1)
  1. "Money is the mother's milk of politics."
  2. Presidential candidates spent $500 million in 1988
    a. Up from $325 million in 1984
  3. Are candidates being "sold" like soap?

John Kennedy was the first candidate to retain his own pollster, Louis Harris.

    a. Answer is not so obvious
 B. The sources of campaign money
  1. Presidential primaries: part private, part public money
    a. Federal matching funds

Candidates are not required to take matching funds in presidential primaries. In 1980, John Connally sought the Republican nomination solely on the basis of private financing, which allowed him to avoid the spending ceiling imposed on candidates receiving federal funds. He lost.

    b. Only match contributions of small donors: less than $250; $5,000 in 20 states
    c. Gives incentive to raise money from small donors
    d. Government also gives lump-sum grants to parties to cover conventions
  2. Presidential general elections: all public money
  3. Congressional elections: all private money
    a. From individuals, PACs, and parties
    b. Most from individual small donors ($100–$200 a person)
    c. $1,000 maximum for individual donors
    d. Benefit performances by rock stars, etc.
    e. $5,000 limit from PACs . . .
    f. . . . but most give only a few hundred dollars
    g. Tremendous PAC advantage to incumbents: backing the winner
    h. Challengers have to pay their own way; only one-sixth from PACs
 C. Campaign finance rules
  1. Watergate and illegal donations
    a. From corporations and unions
    b. Brought about the 1974 federal campaign reform law and FEC
  2. Reform law
    a. Set limit on individual donations ($1,000 per election)
    b. Reaffirmed ban on corporate and union donations . . .
    c. . . . but allowed them to raise money through PACs
    d. PACs in turn raised money from members or employees
    e. Set limit on PAC donations ($5,000 per election)
    f. Primary and general election counted separately
  3. Supreme Court ruled that limits could not be set on campaign spending

The majority opinion of the Supreme Court held that campaign spending limits where no federal funds are received violated the free speech provision of the First Amendment.

    a. But set limit of $50,000 on out-of-pocket spending by a presidential candidate
  4. Law did not limit "independent" political advertising
    a. Typically done by ideologically oriented PACs
    b. Usually attack a candidate on particular positions (guns, etc.)

5. Loopholes of law
   a. Allows "soft money"—money for local party activities, e.g., getting out the vote
   b. Allows money for general voter registration campaigns: Alan Cranston and and Charles Keating
   c. Allows individual donations to be bundled together
D. Effects of reform
   1. Goal was to get "fat cats" out of elections
      a. Has succeeded, but . . .
   2. . . . has greatly increased power of PACs
   3. . . . has shifted control of money away from parties to candidates
      a. Limits influence of parties
   4. . . . has given advantage to wealthy challengers
      a. Can just write out a check for campaign expenses
   5. . . . has given advantage to ideological candidates
      a. Direct mail appeals to special interest groups on issues like abortion, gun control, school prayer, etc.
   6. . . . has penalized candidates who start campaigning late
      a. No war chest to start with
   7. . . . has helped incumbents and hurt challengers
      a. PACs more likely to support an incumbent
E. Money and winning
   1. Money makes a difference in congressional races
      a. Challenger must spend to be recognized
      b. Jacobson: big-spending challengers do better
      c. Big-spending incumbents also do better
   2. But it doesn't make the only difference
      a. Party, incumbency, and issues also have a role
   3. Advantages of incumbency

One estimate calculates incumbency as providing an automatic 9 percent vote advantage.

      a. Easier to raise money
      b. Can provide services to constituency
      c. Can use "franked" mailings
      d. Can get free publicity through legislation, etc.
   4. Ideas for reform
      a. Chances are unlikely: Congress won't agree since incumbent has advantage
      b. The "constitutional right to campaign" involved
      c. Public financing of congressional races would give incumbents even more of an advantage
      d. Abolishing PAC money might allow fat cats to reemerge as major force
      e. Shorter campaigns might help incumbents
IV. What decides elections?
   A. Party identification, but why don't Democrats always win?
      1. Democrats less wedded to their party
      2. GOP does better among independents
      3. Republicans have higher turnout
   B. Issues
      1. V. O. Key: most voters who switch parties do so in their own interests
         a. They know what issues affect them personally
         b. They care strongly about emotional issues (abortion, etc.)
         c. System can function without well-informed citizens
      2. Prospective voting
         a. Know the issues and vote for the best candidate
         b. Most common among activists and special interest groups
         c. A minority of voters use since requires information

3. Retrospective voting
    a. Judge the incumbent's performance and vote accordingly
    b. Have things gotten better or worse, especially economically?
    c. Examples: presidential campaigns of 1980, 1984, 1988
    d. Usually helps incumbent . . . unless economy has gotten worse
    e. Most elections decided by retrospective voters
    f. Midterm elections: voters turn against president's party
C. The campaign
    1. Campaigns do make a difference
        a. They reawaken voters' partisan loyalties
        b. They let voters see how candidates handle pressure
        c. They let voters judge candidates' characters
    2. Campaigns tend to emphasize themes over details
        a. True throughout American history
        b. What has changed is importance of primary elections and tone of campaigns
        c. Gives more influence to single-issue groups

Jay Mathews of the *Washington Post* has isolated another variable that contributes to a candidate's electoral success: height. He calculates that the taller candidate has won nine of eleven presidential elections in the television era (1972 and 1976 are the exceptions). In 1992, Clinton stood at 6' 2 1/2" to Bush's 6' 2". The shortest president in history was James Madison at 5' 4", while the tallest was Abraham Lincoln at 6' 4".

D. Finding a winning coalition
    1. Ways of looking at various groups
        a. How *loyal*, or percentage voting for party
        b. How *important*, or number voting for party
    2. Democratic coalition
        a. Blacks most loyal

Complaints have been voiced that Democratic candidates take the black vote for granted while they ignore black concerns. For example, former Atlanta mayor Andrew Young criticized the "smart-assed white boys" running Walter Mondale's unsuccessful 1984 presidential campaign.

        b. Jews slipping somewhat
        c. Hispanics somewhat mixed
        d. Catholics, southerners, unionists departing the coalition lately
    3. Republican coalition
        a. Party of business and professional people
        b. Very loyal, defecting only in 1964
        c. Usually wins vote of poor due to retired, elderly voters
    4. Contribution to Democratic coalition
        a. Blacks loyal but small proportion
        b. Catholics, union, and southerners largest part but least **dependable**
V. Election outcomes (THEME C: ELECTIONS AND PARTISAN ALIGNMENTS)
    A. Party realignments (ADDITIONAL LECTURE TOPIC C-1)
        1. Definition: sharp, lasting shift in the popular coalition supporting one or both parties
        2. Occurrences: change in issues
            a. 1800: Jeffersonians defeated Federalists
            b. 1828: Jacksonian Democrats came to power
            c. 1860: Whigs collapsed; Republicans won

The last Whig president was Millard Fillmore (1850–1853). Intraparty tension was reflected in the Whigs' not renominating Fillmore in 1852. Fillmore eventually deserted the party and ran in the 1856 presidential election as the candidate of the Know-Nothing party.

            d. 1896: Republicans defeated Bryan

    e. 1932: FDR Democrats came to power
  3. Kinds of realignments
    a. Major party disappears and is replaced (1800, 1860)
    b. Voters shift from one party to another (1896, 1932)
  4. Clearest cases
    a. 1860: slavery
    b. 1896: economics
    c. 1932: depression

The depression and Hoover's failure to respond to economic disruption were the issues in 1932; FDR had no clearly articulated program for dealing with the depression. An exasperated Hoover complained that FDR was like a "chameleon on plaid."

  5. 1980 not a realignment
    a. Expressed dissatisfaction with Carter
    b. Also left Congress Democratic
  6. 1972–1988: shift in presidential voting patterns in the South
    a. Fewer Democrats, more Republicans, more independents
    b. Independents vote Republican
    c. Now close to fifty-fifty Democratic, Republican
    d. Party "de-alignment," not realignment
 B. Party decline
  1. Evidence for it

Party commitments were so strong in the 1950s that Harry Truman refused to ride Dumbo when visiting Disneyland because the elephant is the symbol of the Republican party.

    a. Fewer people identify with either party
    b. Increase in ticket splitting
VI. The effects of elections on policy
 A. Argument: public policy remains more or less the same no matter which official or party is in office
 B. Comparison: Great Britain, with parliamentary system and strong parties, often sees marked changes, as in 1945
 C. Reply: evidence indicates that many American elections do make great differences in policy
 D. Why, then, the perception elections do not matter? Because change alternates with consolidation; most elections are only retrospective judgments

Important Terms

*blanket primary A variant of the open primary in which the voter receives a ballot that lists the candidates for nomination of all the parties, enabling the voter to vote for candidates of different parties.

*closed primary A type of primary in which the voter must be a registered member of a political party to vote in that party's primary.

*coattails (political) The tendency of lesser-known or weaker candidates to profit in an election by the presence of a more popular candidate on the ticket.

*critical or realigning periods Periods during which a sharp, lasting shift occurs in the popular coalition supporting one or both parties. The issues that separate the two parties change, so the kinds of voters supporting each party change.

electoral coalition A base of committed partisans supporting an electoral candidate who also attracts swing votes.

electoral realignment The situation when a new issue of utmost importance to voters cuts across existing party divisions and replaces old issues that formerly formed the basis of party identification.

*general election The second election in a campaign that determines which party's nominee will win office.

*incumbent The person currently in office.

negative ad Media advertising meant to cast an unfavorable light on an opponent.

*office-bloc ballot A ballot, sometimes called the Massachusetts ballot, that lists all candidates by office to minimize a straight party ticket vote. It was an innovation championed by the Progressives.

*open primary A type of primary in which the voter can decide upon entering the voting booth in which party's primary to participate.

*party-column ballot A ballot, sometimes called the Indiana ballot, that was government-printed and contained a list in columns of all candidates of each party. A voter could simply mark the top of one column to vote for every candidate in that column. It was replaced by the office-bloc ballot.

*political action committee A committee set up by a special-interest group representing a corporation, labor union, or other special interest.

*position issue A campaign issue on which the rival parties or candidates take different positions in order to reach out for electoral support. It tends to divide the electorate.

*presidential primary A special kind of primary used to pick delegates to the presidential nominating conventions of the major parties.

*primary election The first election in a campaign that determines a party's nominee for an office.

*prospective voting Voting on the basis of a person's views of rival candidates' positions on the issues.

public finance law A federal law providing funds to candidates seeking the presidency. In primaries, only matching funds are available after eligibility requirements are fulfilled. In the general election, the federal government gives candidates of major parties the option of complete financing. The section of the law imposing spending limits on congressional candidates was voided by the Supreme Court.

*retrospective voting Voting on the basis of how things have gone in the recent past and then voting for the party that controls the White House, if the voter approves of the current administration's performance, or voting against that party if the voter disapproves.

*runoff primary A type of primary used in some southern states if no candidate gets a majority of the votes in the first primary vote. In this second primary election, the two candidates with the most votes in the first primary vie.

*split-ticket voting An election result in which a congressional district votes for the presidential candidate of one party and the congressional candidate of the other party.

spots Short ads on behalf of a candidate on television. Such ads convey a substantial amount of information.

*straight-ticket voting Voting for candidates who are all of the same party; for example, voting for the Republican candidates for senator, representative, and president.

*target An element of campaign strategy that involves selecting when to enter an electoral race.

theme An element of campaign strategy that is a simple, appealing idea that can be repeated over and over again.

tone An element of campaign strategy that involves either a positive (build-me-up) or negative (attack-the-opponent) approach.

*valance issue A campaign issue that is linked in the voters' mind with conditions, goals, or symbols that are almost universally approved or disapproved by the electorate, e.g., corruption.

visual A campaign appearance that is covered in a news broadcast.

Theme A   How Campaigns Are Conducted

Summary

Several developments have led to the rise of the *personalistic campaign*. The decline of parties is the most important. The primary election has taken from party leaders the power to select the party's nominee for office; they therefore have little reason to work hard to help that person win the general election. Political funds and political jobs are increasingly under the control of candidates and officeholders, not party leaders. Public financing funds go to the individual candidate, not the party. And the decline in party identification among voters means that candidates have less incentive to stress party ties. In addition, the increased use of mass media for campaigning encourages the building of an image based on personal qualities.

Any campaign tends to be composed of four distinct types of workers. First, the *paid professionals* may be either members of the incumbent's office staff or outside "hired-gun" specialists. Second, unpaid *senior advisers* are usually old and trusted acquaintances of the candidate who have no personal political ambition. Third, *citizen volunteers* are a diverse lot who are given routine and boring tasks. Finally, *issue consultants* define issues and write position papers, which lack practical importance but are "expected." Other professional consultants include media personnel, organizers of computerized direct-mail campaigns, and pollsters. It should also be noted that modern political consultants, unlike their counterparts in the old-style campaigning of the past, usually take no responsibility for governing.

After assembling a campaign staff, the candidate must make a series of important decisions about campaign strategy. The primaries present the first problem. One may take strong, ideological positions on the issues and attract the support of ideological activists who loom large in the primary electorate. This, as George McGovern found out in 1972, makes it difficult to appeal to independents and members of the other party. The candidate must also decide whether to run a "positive" or a "negative" campaign, how to time the campaign (peaking early or late), what groups to appeal to, and how money should be spent. Sometimes choices are restricted: an incumbent will necessarily be judged on his record, and a member of the president's party will be saddled with the record of the incumbent president. Finally, a candidate must guard against making a blunder—such as Carter's *Playboy* interview, Reagan's claim that trees are a major source of pollution, or Clinton's claim not to have inhaled marijuana—that could cost the election.

Television is an important factor in modern campaigns. Paid advertisements, called *spots*, can be useful, especially in primary elections in which voters do not have the cues of party and ideology and large amounts of information from other sources. *Visuals*, on the other hand, are segments on television newscasts. To get this exposure a candidate must contrive to do something visually interesting, and at a time and place convenient for TV camera crews. Ironically, television newscasts are not very informative, focusing as they do on campaign hoopla. Paid spots, on the other hand, contain a good deal of issue information that the public sees, remembers, and intelligently evaluates. Conversely, television "debates" between presidential candidates can sometimes sway an election outcome (such as the 1960 Kennedy-Nixon debate). However, their total effect on an election may frequently appear uncertain or mixed (as the Clinton-Bush-Perot 1992 debates illustrate).

The computer is increasingly an important part of campaigns. It allows for the targeting of various groups in the population—whether persons interested in particular issues or proven campaign contributors—and communicating with them via direct mail.

Public opinion polls are part of any large-scale campaign. Occasionally they suggest a particular stance to the candidate: in 1952 they helped Eisenhower turn the Korean War issue to his advantage, and in 1966 they informed Edward Brooke that he should not endorse black riots. More often, they will suggest an image the candidate should convey: in 1980 the Reagan campaign learned that it needed to counteract an image of Reagan as careless and aggressive.

Single-issue, ideological groups have received much attention lately. It is not clear how much effect they have in general elections. Their touted "successes" in defeating liberal senators in 1980 came mostly in traditionally Republicans states. However, they may have particular influence in primary elections, in which money and the ability to mobilize a small, dedicated following are especially important. The success of Jerry Brown in the 1992 Colorado primary as a result of the support of environmentalists is a good example.

One undisputed effect of campaigns is to allow the passage of time so that partisan loyalties can reassert themselves. People who identify themselves as Democrats substantially outnumber people who call themselves Republicans. This does not prevent presidential races from being highly competitive, however, because (1) independents historically have leaned toward the Republicans, (2) Republicans have been less likely to defect to the opposite party than have Democrats, and (3) a higher percentage of Republicans than Democrats vote in elections.

Discussion Questions

1. Is it *fair* to hold a member of the incumbent party—such as Nixon in 1960, or Humphrey in 1968—responsible for the policies of the president, even though the individual may have had no role in formulating them? Are voters better off if it is fair? Is there any way in which the voters' willingness to do this (fair or not) might make our political system work better?

2. Recent scholarship indicates that issues do influence voters. In the 1960 presidential debate between Kennedy and Nixon, however, television viewers overwhelmingly considered Kennedy the victor while radio listeners considered Nixon a narrow victor. What does this evidence suggest about the impact of issues on elections? Does issue interpretation vary by media source? If so, how should a candidate devise an electoral strategy?

3. Why would a candidate rarely wish to run a campaign focused solely on issues with his or her stands on those issues clearly explained?

Data and Perspectives for Analysis

Incumbent Power

Campaign strategy varies depending on whether the candidate is an incumbent or a challenger. Moreover, the incumbent possesses numerous advantages that the challenger must overcome. Present the data in the table on the following page to your students to illustrate the different strategies of candidates as well as the advantages of incumbency. How can the advantages of the incumbent be overcome? What strategies must a challenger adopt?

The Importance of Being an Incumbent: Voters' Reports
of Familiarity, Contacts, and Evaluations of House Incumbents and Their Challengers in 1978

Voters' Reports	Incumbents	Challengers
Familiarity with the candidates		
Recalled candidate's name	49.9%	16.6%
Recognized name and could rate candidate	93.7	45.9
Neither	6.3	54.1
Contact with the candidates		
Any	90.3	44.6
Met personally	23.6	4.3
Attended meeting where candidate spoke	20.6	3.5
Talked with staff member	12.4	2.3
Received mail from candidate	71.8	16.7
Read about candidate in newspaper or magazine	71.7	32.6
Heard candidate on radio	34.4	15.1
Saw candidate on television	50.2	23.9
Family or friends had contact with candidate	40.1	11.1
Evaluations of the candidates		
Mean "thermometer" rating[a]	74.4	52.8
Like something about candidate	64.0	11.6
Dislike something about candidate	18.5	12.8

Source: Gary C. Jacobson, "Incumbents' Advantages in the 1978 Congressional Elections," *Legislative Studies Quarterly*, 6 (May 1981): 186 (as modified by Comparative Legislative Research Center).

[a]Rating of candidate on scale of 0 to 100, with 50 designated as neutral; the higher the percentage, the more favorable the rating.

Source: William Keefe, *Congress and the American People*, 2nd ed. (Englewood Cliffs, NJ: Prentice-Hall, 1984), p. 77.

Abstract 1 for Theme A

Television Campaign Costs and Voting

The tremendous power of television in modern campaigns has had an impact not only upon candidates' costs but apparently also upon voter participation. In an interesting *New York Times* article by Curtis B. Gans, entitled "Is TV Turning Off the American Voter?" (July 3, 1988, p. 25), the relationship between increasing campaign costs and declining voter turnout is explored. Gans, the director of the Washington-based Committee for the Study of the American Electorate, notes that turnout over the last twenty years has declined by 20 percent (i.e., more than twenty million former voters) while "during the last decade and a half, spending in congressional campaigns has increased by 482 percent." To Gans, the answer behind the inverse turnout-spending relationship may lie partly with television's "central place in both the conduct of American politics and in the lives of most Americans."

Gans first delineates the awesome cost of television political advertising:

> While overall campaign spending has increased nearly fivefold since 1972, the amount spent on television advertising in campaigns has increased tenfold. Whereas in 1974 the average competitive campaign that used television advertising spent 30 percent of its budget on TV commercials, the same type of campaign today spends 55 percent of its budget on television. In 1974, the overall average cost of the five most expensive U.S. Senatorial campaigns was 67 cents a vote; in 1984, the overall average cost was $7.74. In 1974, the average amount spent on television advertising in these campaigns was 12 cents a vote; in 1984, it was $3.54.

As Gans puts it, the "demand of political campaigns to compete dollar for dollar, commercial for commercial, attack for attack in the arena of television advertising" has affected turnout negatively for the following reasons:

1. Television as an institution "atomizes the citizenry" by creating passive watchers of politics rather than "participants and stockholders."
2. The six hours a day that the average American spends viewing television shows is no longer available for reading and discussing political issues.
3. There has been a "30 percent reduction in prime-time public-affairs programming on network television during the past decade." This reduction, coupled with the plethora of mindless soap operas, game shows, and evening escapism on the networks, erodes the development of serious political thinking amongst the citizenry.
4. Reportorial cynicism, early projection by the networks of winners while citizens are still voting on election day, hurried television journalism, overemphasis on the Iowa caucuses and New Hampshire primary, the bias of the medium "toward the visually interesting at the expense of the substantively serious," the magnification of both good and bad qualities in a candidate, which in turn produces voter cynicism, and the media perpetuation of the myth that political problems can be solved quickly through "aspirinlike" remedies all produce negative effects for democratic political participation.

Gans suggests some remedies to counter the deleterious influence of television. Among them (a) a uniform format law for political advertising on television that would require an "identified spokesperson talking to the camera," thus eliminating demagogic appeals, reducing the power of political consultants, and eliminating excessive campaign costs; (b) a refusal by the network to predict electoral winners while the polls remain open *and* expansion of their political coverage—candidates, issues, policies, events (the national conventions), etc.; (c) a renewed commitment by the networks to the presentation of public programming in a more creative, historically accurate, and socially responsible fashion; and finally, (d) a congressional review of former decisions deregulating broadcast programming, in light of "the diminution of public-affairs programming during prime time and the failure the networks to carry debates this year" (1988 primary debates). Gans concludes that in the absence of these steps, "it is likely the turnout will continue to decline and that American government will be increasingly one of, for and by the few."

Abstract 2 for Theme A

The 1988 Presidential Primaries: "Lessons" from Two Unsuccessful Candidates

Senator Paul Simon of Illinois and ex-governor Bruce Babbitt of Arizona were contenders for the Democratic presidential nomination in 1988. Neither man was able to muster the necessary support required for the nomination. However, both men imparted some valuable lessons from their primary experiences, revealing the unfortunate "reality" of contemporary campaigning. Bruce Babbitt, who dropped out of the presidential race in early February, 1988, offered the following observations in a *Wall Street Journal* article of February 18, 1988, entitled "Campaign Isn't the Place for New Ideas, Babbitt Says as He Drops Out of Race," written by staff reporter David Shribman. Babbitt had finished in fifth place in the Iowa caucuses and sixth place in the New Hampshire primary. His reflections on issues in the campaign were reported as follows:

> Mr. Babbitt . . . talked about the twin difficulties of campaigning on behalf of an unpopular idea—a consumption tax to help balance the budget—and of introducing new policy ideas in the middle of the campaign.
> "A political campaign is the wrong place to raise new ideas . . . I now understand . . . that a campaign is an outreach process that has to start with ideas that are already in the dialogue."
> So all-but-ignored in the 1988 campaign were his notions of instituting tax changes to encourage performance pay for all employees, providing universal child-care vouchers, making the Social Security benefits of the wealthy subject to taxation, and requiring that companies receiving government financial assistance give partial ownership and control to employees.
> "These were simply too broad and too new to get in the course of the campaign," he says. "I now know that you can't walk into a presidential race and spring these kinds of things on people."

Babbitt's idea of a consumption tax to eliminate the deficit did receive attention, but Democratic rivals vigorously attacked the concept, labeling it "regressive" and "Republican" in philosophy. The public also rejected the idea, as they usually reject tax increases of any kind suggested by a candidate. Babbitt left the race, discouraged by a presidential campaign (on both party sides) which eschewed the realities of the economic system and discouraged risk taking on the part of the contenders.

Paul Simon's "lessons" were contained in his *New York Times Magazine* article of July 3, 1988, pp. 18–20, entitled "What I Learned—Reflections on My Run." Simon finished a close second in Iowa, and third in the New Hampshire primary. He left the race after the Wisconsin primary in April, 1988. Simon made the following points about his campaign:

1. Primary "debates" were numerous, but these debates were "as different from the Lincoln-Douglas debates as a Beethoven symphony is from a radio jingle." The required brief replies were great for television news but did not provide any depth on candidates or the issues. As Simon puts it, "these exchanges were designed to provide fireworks while not testing the viewers' attention span." (p. 18)

2. As usual, the press emphasized the "horse-race" aspects of the primaries instead of issues. Admittedly, part of the problem involved the reluctance of most of the candidates to spell out their stands on the issues of the day. Simon parallels Babbitt on this point when he describes his own creative policy proposals for creating new jobs and educational opportunities:

   > It is no accident that the two men who have emerged from the Democratic and Republican primary campaigns are precisely the two candidates who were the least specific on the issues. ... I outlined an approach ... that would combine a jobs program and a creative educational uplift effort. My proposal was criticized by at least three of the Democratic Presidential candidates and a variety of columnists, none of whom—all too obviously—had taken the trouble to look seriously at either the proposal or the problem. If I had simply talked vaguely about providing opportunities for people, I probably would have received applause and no criticism.
   >
   > *The lesson for candidates is clear: Be vague. Sound knowledgeable but don't get too specific.* (Italics mine) (p. 20)

Simon also had the following proposals for improving the campaign process: (a) debates should focus on one issue; (b) instead of concentrating on trivia, the media should concentrate on analyzing issue positions, thus giving voters a chance to think about the implication of those positions; (c) money is a key factor, so public financing for all primaries or caucuses should be set at the same level for every candidate.

Questions for Discussion

1. Do you think the average voter in this country is really interested in hearing a presidential contender talk about issues during a primary campaign? Why or why not?

2. If you had the power to pass one campaign-reform law, which one would it be and why?

Theme B   Money in Electoral Campaigns

Summary

Political campaigns cost a lot. This has been particularly true in recent years, because political machines cannot supply battalions of precinct workers, and expensive media (such as television and direct mail) have become more important. But can money buy elections? In twenty-nine presidential elections between 1860 and 1972, the winner outspent the loser twenty-one times. This does not necessarily mean that money can buy votes, because popular candidates who look like winners can raise more money than others. Nixon outspent George McGovern in 1972 but almost certainly would have won even if he had spent less. The best studies on the effect of money in elections have been done on congressional races. It seems that how much an incumbent spends is of little importance, whereas higher spending by the *challenger* produces more votes. Such spending can overcome the natural advantages enjoyed by incumbents.

Campaign money comes from several sources:

1. *The candidates themselves.* The Supreme Court has held that spending one's own money in campaign activity is a form of free speech protected by the First Amendment.

2. *Other well-to-do people.* Usually they give for ideological reasons, or out of ambition for prestige or power. Traditionally, however, some high federal appointments, especially ambassadorships, went to campaign contributors. In 1972 President Nixon appointed thirteen noncareer ambassadors to Western European countries; eight of them had contributed at least $50,000 to his reelection campaign. The 1974 campaign-finance reform law limited to $1,000 the amount any individual could contribute to any single candidate in any given federal election.

3. *Organizations and interest groups.* These may be motivated by either a material interest in a policy area (for example, milk producers or schoolteachers) or by a liberal or conservative ideology. *Political action committees* can be set up to solicit contributions from donors and contribute sums of up to $5,000 to a candidate. PACs have produced a great increase in the total amount of business and labor spending on elections; business now spends much more than labor. This does not necessarily give Republicans an advantage, because business tends to contribute heavily to incumbents (including Democratic incumbents). In 1982, 2,665 political action committees gave money to candidates.

4. *Small individual donors.* Barry Goldwater made a television appeal in 1964 and received 300,000 checks. George Wallace in 1968 and George McGovern in 1972 followed the same strategy. Recent campaign-finance reform laws have given candidates a strong incentive to solicit small contributions.

5. *The federal government.* In presidential primaries, the federal government will match the money a candidate raises from individuals in amounts of $250 or less, up to a limit of $5 million. In the presidential general election, candidates of "major parties" get full federal support (amounting to $55 million in 1992). A candidate who accepts federal funding cannot accept private donations. Minor parties, if they obtain at least 5 percent of the vote, also get federal money. (However, there remain ways for candidates to spend money outside the limits imposed by the law.)

Campaign-finance reform laws have effects that are not yet entirely clear. But the following seem likely: First, candidates who are personally wealthy have an advantage, as do candidates who can successfully appeal to many small donors. Second, candidates have to spend much more time on fund raising in order to appeal to a large group of small donors. Third, incumbents will continue to enjoy a substantial advantage in fund raising. Fourth, late starters will be at a disadvantage, because the raising of money from many small donors must begin long in advance of an election. Fifth, the political parties are weakened. Federal funding goes to the presidential candidate and not to the party. (However, laws have recently been amended to allow the party congressional committees to spend more money on congressional candidates.) Sixth, the role of celebrities in politics will increase because they can stage benefit concerts to raise money for the candidates.

Campaign-finance reforms cannot be credited with a wholesale cleaning up of American politics, because relatively few things were "for sale" before they were passed. Their best justification is the conviction that elections must not only be fair but must also *appear* to be fair.

Discussion Questions

1. Suppose we consider campaign-finance reform an attempt to *redistribute political influence*. That is, "fat cats" are thought to have excessive influence and campaign finance

reform attempts to take away that influence and give it to more deserving people—for example, small contributors. Consider the groups listed below. Judge whether each has *gained* or *lost* influence as the result of campaign-finance reform, or whether reform has made no difference. Then judge whether each group *should have* more influence in American politics.

- Labor unions
- Large corporations
- Incumbent politicians
- Poor people
- Issue-oriented members of the middle class
- Media managers
- Average workers
- Rich individuals
- Popular entertainers
- Political party officials

2. Have campaign finance reforms produced more harm than good? Can't large contributors still evade the laws? Consider the scandal involving the so-called Keating Five in Congress and what it reveals about deficiencies in the law.

3. One of the conditions of campaign finance laws is that contributions to PACs must be voluntary. Yet coercion can take subtle forms. In 1986, the president of NBC distributed a memo suggesting that network employees who refused to contribute to a proposed corporate PAC should "question their own dedication to the company." Was this memo legal under the rules regulating PACs?

Data and Perspectives for Analysis

The perception in the United States is that election campaigns are too long and too costly. Surely the issue of length cannot be debated. However, the cost factor is another issue. Television viewing is flooded with election ads; telephone posts are plastered with campaign posters; and mailboxes are teeming with leaflets on behalf of candidates. These activities cost money and lots of it. Yet a nagging question persists: are we different than other countries? Have your students examine and discuss the data below. The data do not include free time allocated by governments. Is the United States that bad off?

Election Costs Compared

Country	Amount Spent Per Voter In National Election Dollars
United States	$3.25
Venezuela	$26.35
Great Britain	.50
Ireland	$3.93
Canada	$1.43
West Germany	$3.20
Israel	$4.34

Source: Howard Penniman, "U.S. Elections: Really a Bargain?" *Public Opinion* (June/July, 1984): 51

Additional Lecture Topic B-1

Political Money and How We Can Reform Its Use

Frank Sorauf, *Money in American Elections*. Glenview IL: Scott, Foresman, 1988.

Elizabeth Drew, *Politics and Money: The New Road to Corruption*. New York: Macmillan, 1983.

Marc F. Plattner, "Campaign Financing: The Dilemmas of Reform." *Public Interest*, Fall 1974.

David Adamany, "Political Finance in Transition." *Polity*, Winter 1981, pp. 314–331.

Gary C. Jacobson, "The Effects of Campaign Spending in Congressional Elections." *American Political Science Review*, June 1978.

Michael J. Malbin, "Campaign Financing and the 'Special Interests.'" *Public Interest*, Summer 1979.

Herbert E. Alexander, *Financing Politics: Money, Elections, and Political Reform*. 3rd ed. Washington, DC: Congressional Quarterly Press, 1984.

Gary Jacobson, *Money in Congressional Elections*, New Haven: Yale University Press, 1980.

Marjorie Randon Hershey, *Running for Office: The Political Education of Campaigners*. Chatham, NJ: Chatham House, 1984. Chapter 1.

Larry Sabato, *PAC Power*. New York: Norton Press, 1985.

Fred Wertheimer, "Campaign Finance Reform: The Unfinished Agenda." *Annals of the American Academy*, July 1986.

The problem here is how to produce genuine reform without producing the sort of "unintended consequences" that often accompany reform. These readings contain both worthwhile suggestions and warnings of pitfalls.

Abstract For Theme B

PAC Money and Campaigns

Political action committees (PACs) have become important sources of funds for candidates since the passage of campaign finance reform laws in the mid-1970s. Business and labor PACs have accounted for most of the spending over the years. Surprisingly, though, a neat correlation of party and specific occupational PAC rarely exists.

An example of the foregoing is a *Wall Street Journal* article by Brooks Jackson entitled "Republicans in House Are Pressuring Business PACs to Donate More Money" (June 27, 1985, p. 64). According to the article, Congressman Richard Cheney, chairman of the House Republican Policy Committee, revealed that "business PACs gave more to Democrats than to Republicans in the 25 most closely contested House races" in 1984. Due to this allegation, "some unidentified GOP congressmen were threatening to support legislation to put new limits on PACs because so much money had gone to the other side."

Congressman Cheney asserted that Republicans were determined to become the new majority party in the House and that they did "not look kindly on organizations that help the Democrats perpetuate their majority." In terms of total PAC donations, Democrats got twice the PAC donations of Republicans—roughly $5.5 million against $2.4 million in twenty-five close House races. (PACs gave $75.6 million to all House candidates in 1984.) Cheney concluded that the Republican party had to convince the PAC community "that the political tides are running in the GOP's favor."

Questions for Discussion

1. How can one explain the fact that more business PAC contributions go to Democrats than to Republicans?

2. If the GOP made additional gains in the House of Representatives during the next few years, would the pattern of PAC spending change dramatically?

3. Have students research the patterns of PAC spending in the 1988 and 1992 elections. Have reports presented in class.

Answer Guidelines

You can point out that past "independent spending" by PACs has gone overwhelmingly to the GOP. Regarding the House, the business preference for Democrats (in twenty-five key races) may obscure the fact that many of these members of Congress may either be politically conservative or have built up strong relationships with key business groups in their districts. Also, many PACs frequently support both incumbent and challenger in order to hedge their bets. Finally, new House gains by the GOP would probably result in an acceleration of PAC spending on that party.

Theme C   Elections and Partisan Alignments

Summary

When political scientists look at election outcomes, they are interested in broad trends in winning and losing and in what these imply about the attitudes of voters, the operation of the electoral system, and the fate of the political parties. Looking at the historical record, we note several eras in American elections divided by *critical*, or *realigning*, *periods*. During such periods there occurs a sharp, lasting shift in the popular coalition supporting one or both parties. This may occur at the time of the election as voters choose sides in new patterns, or just after an election, when the new administration creates, by its policies, a new supporting coalition. The five realigning periods in American history have been:

1. 1800—when the Jeffersonian Republicans defeated the Federalists, who then disappeared as an organized party.

2. 1828—when the Jacksonian Democrats came to power.

3. 1860—when the Whig party collapsed and the Republicans (a "minor" or "third" party) rose to replace them.

4. 1896—when, reacting to economic discontent in the country, the Democrats nominated populist William Jennings Bryan and adopted a Populist party platform. This alienated urban Catholic workers in the Northeast, leaving the Republicans in control of the industrial states and the Democrats strong in the farm states of the South and Midwest.

5. 1932—when, in the midst of an economic depression, Roosevelt gained office on the basis of popular dissatisfaction and proceeded to implement policies that drew urban workers, blacks, and Jews away from the Republicans to form a new majority coalition.

Thus alignments occur when a highly salient new issue (slavery, the economy) appears and cuts across existing party divisions. A party may try to *straddle* the issue, as the Whigs did with slavery in 1860. Or it may take a distinct position, as the Republicans did in 1860 and as both parties did in 1896 and 1932. Either way, the salient new issue creates a new alignment, both by converting existing voters and by recruiting new voters into the dominant party.

Some people feel that the nation is overdue for another realigning period. Indeed, some think the 1980 election signaled the breakup of the New Deal coalition and its replacement with an alignment by which the Republicans will benefit from a new conservative coalition. Neither the 1980 nor the 1984 elections per se signaled a realigning shift among voters. Apparently, economic issues and personalities affected the voters more than any fundamental repudiation of the entire New Deal political philosophy.

Perhaps, however, the party system has lost so much of its meaning for voters that parties will decay rather then realign. Evidence of this is found in the decreasing proportion of voters who identify themselves with one or another party and in the consequent increase in *ticket splitting*.

Even at the peak of the New Deal alignment, the Democratic party never had a dependable winning coalition in each election. The groups most loyal to the Democratic party—blacks and Jews—are small and have given the party only a small fraction of the votes it needs to win an election. The nation's blacks have been the most loyal (two-thirds or more of all black voters have voted Democratic since 1952). The groups that make up the largest part of the Democratic vote—Catholics, union members, and southerners—are also the least dependable parts of the coalition. Defections in these categories of the coalition have occurred often in past elections.

Realigning periods often bring substantial changes in public policy. The election of 1860 resulted in a chain of events that ended slavery; that of 1896 produced Republican dominance and high tariffs, a strong currency, urban growth, and business prosperity; the 1932 election produced a vast enlargement of federal authority. The election of 1964 allowed the Democrats to implement the Great Society programs; and the 1980 election brought into office a Republican administration committed to reversing the growth of government over the preceding half-century. Between such elections are periods of consolidation and continuity.

Discussion Questions

1. Who constitutes the Democratic coalition? Which groups are the most *loyal* members of the Democratic coalition? Which contribute the largest proportion of the Democratic vote? How does it matter that the most *loyal* groups are not among the largest contributors of votes? Conversely, what does the fact that the Democrats must rely on groups like Catholics and southerners for a winning vote total say about the positions the party can take? Can you imagine a realignment that would allow the Democrats to take more liberal positions on issues?

2. Do elections in the United States matter? Why is a crisis often required to produce major policy changes? Does the fact that a crisis is required to produce major policy changes suggest that our system is excessively biased against change? Or does our system produce changes only when clear majorities *want* a change, which is likely to occur during a crisis?

3. How should the 1992 election be classified?

Additional Lecture Topic C-1

Party Realignments in Elections

David W. Brady and Patricia A. Hurley, "The Prospects for Contemporary Partisan Realignment." *PS* (Winter 1985): 62–70.

Jerome M. Clubb, William H. Flanigan, and Nancy H. Zingale, *Partisan Realignment: Voters, Parties and Government in American History*. Beverly Hills, CA: Sage, 1980. Good data on voting-bloc realignments from 1840 to 1978.

Everett C. Ladd, Jr., "On Mandates, Realignments, and the 1984 Presidential Election." *Political Science Quarterly*, Spring 1985.

Nelson Polsby, "Did the 1984 Election Signal Major Party Realignment?" *Key Reporter*, 50 (Spring 1985): 2.

James L. Sundquist, *Dynamics of the Party System: Alignment and Realignment of Political Parties in the United States*. Rev. ed. Washington, DC: Brookings Institute, 1983. Good historical review of key party alignments that have occurred in certain elections.

Data and Perspectives for Analysis

A candidate seeking office must make serious decisions about which groups to target, and campaign themes must then be devised to lure the support of the targeted groups. The concerns of nontarget groups can be ignored, either because their support is assured or their opposition is unconquerable.

Have your students analyze the data presented on the following page and determine what groups a Democratic and a Republican candidate should target to win an election.

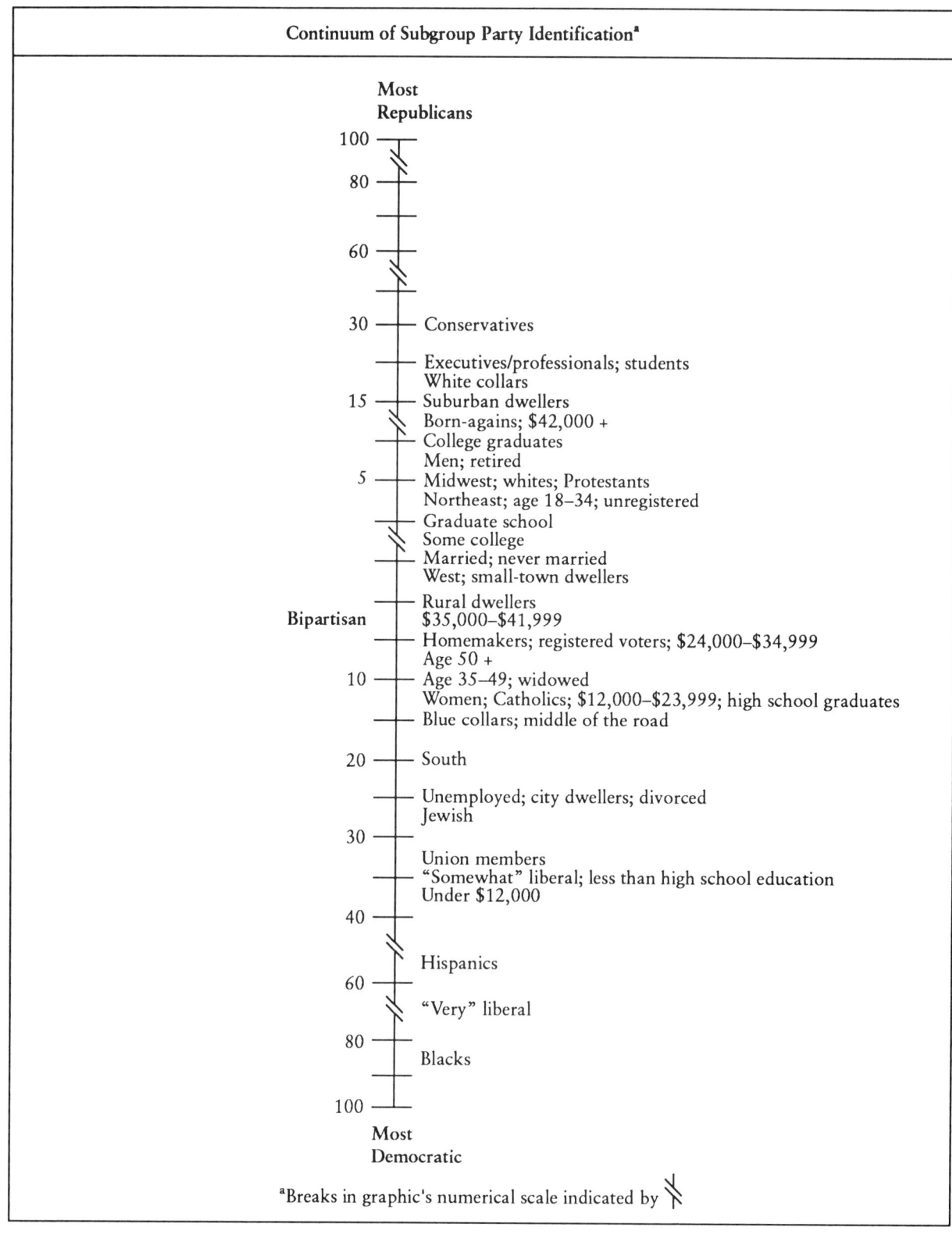

Source: *The Party's Just Begun: Shaping Political Parties for America's Future* by Larry J. Sabato, p. 125. Copyright © 1988 by Larry J. Sabato. Reprinted by permission of HarperCollins Publishers.

9

Interest Groups

Overview and Objectives

The purpose of this chapter is to survey the wide variety of interest groups or lobbies that operate in the United States and to assess the impact they have on the political system of the country. After reading and reviewing the material in this chapter the student should be able to do each of the following:

1. Explain why the characteristics of American society and government encourage a multiplicity of interest groups, and compare the American and British experiences in this regard.

2. Indicate the historical conditions under which interest groups are likely to form and specify the kinds of organizations Americans are most likely to join.

3. Describe relations between leaders and rank-and-file members of groups, including why the sentiments of members may not determine the actions of leaders.

4. Describe several methods that interest groups use to formulate and carry out their political objectives, especially the lobbying techniques used to gain public support. Explain why courts have become an important forum for "public interest" groups.

5. List the laws regulating conflict of interest and describe the problems involved with "revolving door" government employment. Describe the provisions of the 1978 conflict-of-interest law. Explain the suggestions that have been made for stricter laws. Describe the balance between the First Amendment's freedom of expression and the need to prevent corruption in the political system.

Chapter Outline with Keyed-in Resources

I. Explaining proliferation (THEME A: AMERICAN INTEREST GROUPS IN COMPARATIVE PERSPECTIVE)
   A. Why interest groups are common in America
      1. Many kinds of cleavages in the country
      2. Constitution makes for many access points
      3. Political parties are weak
II. The birth of interest groups (THEME B: HISTORY AND INTEREST-GROUP FORMATION)
   A. Periods of rapid growth
      1. Since 1960, 70 percent established their D.C. office
      2. 1770s—independence groups
      3. 1830s, 1840s—religious, antislavery groups

        4. 1860s—craft unions
        5. 1880s, 1890s—business associations
        6. 1900–1920—most major lobbies of today
    B. Factors explaining rise of interest groups
        1. Broad economic developments create new interests
            a. Farmers produce cash crops
            b. Mass-production industries begin

The rapid transformation of American society associated with industrialization cannot be exaggerated. Manufacturing output increased 1,200 percent in the half century following the Civil War.

        2. Government policy itself
            a. Created veterans' groups—wars
            b. Encouraged formation of Farm Bureau
            c. Launched Chamber of Commerce
            d. Favored growth of unions
        3. Emergence of strong leaders, usually at certain times
        4. Expanding role of government

Despite the expanding role of the government, Americans are still reluctant to assign the government a large role in economic matters. Only 33 percent believe it is the government's responsibility to ensure full employment, a low rate compared to 69 percent in Britain and 88 percent in Italy.

III. Kinds of organizations (THEME C: BIAS IN THE GROUP PROCESS AND KINDS OF ORGANIZATIONS)
    A. Institutional interests
        1. Defined: individuals or organizations representing other organizations
        2. Types
            a. Business firms: example, General Motors
            b. Trade or governmental associations
        3. Concerns—bread-and-butter issues of concern to their clients
            a. Clearly defined, with homogeneous groups
            b. Diffuse, with diversified groups
        4. Other interests—governments, foundations, universities
    B. Membership interests
        1. Americans join some groups more frequently than in other nations
            a. Social, business, etc.—same rate as elsewhere
            b. Unions—less likely to join
            c. Religious/civic groups—more likely to join
            d. Greater sense of efficacy, duty explain tendency to join civil groups
        2. Most sympathizers do not join because:
            a. Individuals not that significant
            b. Benefits flow to nonmembers too
    C. Incentives to join (ADDITIONAL LECTURE TOPICS C-1, C-2)
        1. Solidary incentives—pleasure, companionship (League of Women Voters, AARP, NAACP, Rotary, etc.)
        2. Material incentives—money, things, services (farm organizations, retired persons, etc.)
        3. Purpose of the organization itself—public interest organizations

Public interest groups frequently get locked in futile causes. In 1993, Ralph Nader was able to persuade only twenty-two members of the House of Representatives to sign a pledge supporting a congressional pay cut. Nader received even less support in 1994 with a proposal to rollback pay from the current $133,600 to $89,500, the salary in 1990.

            a. Ideological interest groups appeal of controversial principles
            b. Engage in research and bring lawsuits

- D. The influence of the staff
    1. Staff must influence if solidarity or material benefits
    2. National Council of Churches and unions are examples
- IV. Interest groups and social movements
    - A. Social movement is a widely shared demand for change
    - B. The environmental movement
    - C. The feminist movement; three kinds
        1. Solidary—LWV, etc. (widest support)
        2. Purposive—NOW, NARAL (strong position on divisive issues)
        3. Caucus—WEAL (material benefits)
    - D. Union movement; left over after social movement dies
- V. Funds for interest groups
    - A. Foundation grants

Foundation assets are both massive and concentrated. Foundations possess an estimated $47.5 billion in assets, but the fifty largest foundations control 40 percent of total foundation assets.

    1. Ford Foundation and public interest groups
    2. Scaife foundations and conservative groups
    - B. Federal grants and contracts
        1. National Alliance for Business and summer youth job programs
        2. Jesse Jackson's PUSH
    - C. Direct mail
        1. Unique to modern interest groups through use of computers
        2. Common Cause a classic example
        3. Techniques
            a. Teaser
            b. Emotional arousal
            c. Celebrity endorsement
            d. Personalization of letter
- VI. The problem of bias
    - A. Reasons for belief in upper-class bias
        1. More affluent more likely to join
        2. Business/professional groups more numerous; better financed
    - B. Why these facts do not decide the issue
        1. Describe inputs but not outputs
        2. Business groups often divided among themselves
    - C. Important to ask what the bias is
        1. Many conflicts are within upper middle class
        2. Resource differentials are clues, not conclusions
- VII. The activities of interest groups (THEME D: INTEREST GROUPS IN ACTION)
    - A. Information
        1. Single most important tactic
            a. Nonpolitical sources insufficient; provide detailed, current information
        2. Most effective on narrow, technical issues
        3. Officials also need "cues"; ratings systems
    - B. Public support
        1. Politicians dislike controversy
        2. Key targets: the undecided
        3. Some groups attack their likely allies to embarrass them

Rating systems evaluating the voting behavior of members of Congress sometimes produce anomalous results. In 1986, the Christian Voice devised a Candidates Biblical Scorecard rating members on their degree of support for Judeo-Christian values as reflected in their voting record. The results: three ordained ministers (Baptist, Methodist, and Episcopalian) failed to qualify as Christians!

        4. Legislators sometimes buck public opinion, unless issue important

           5. Some groups try for grassroots support
               a. Saccharin issue
               b. "Dirty Dozen" environmental polluters
       C. Money and PACs
           1. Money is least effective way to influence politicians
           2. Campaign finance reform law of 1973 had two effects
               a. Restricted amount interest groups can give to candidates
               b. Made it legal for corporations and unions to create PACs
           3. Rapid growth in PACs has not led to vote buying
               a. More money is available on all sides
               b. Members of Congress take money but still can decide how to vote
           4. Almost any organization can create a PAC
               a. Over half of PACs sponsored by corporations
               b. Recent increase in ideological PACs; one-third liberal, two-thirds conservative
           5. Ideological PACs raise more but spend less due to cost of raising money

The differential between the amount of money raised by a PAC and the amount allocated to candidates can reach absurd proportions. In 1982, for example, Senator Jesse Helms's PAC, the National Congressional Committee, obtained $8,356,865 in donations and spent a mere $58,762 on behalf of congressional candidates.

           6. In 1992, unions and business organizations gave the most
           7. Incumbents get most PAC money
               a. Business PACs split money between Democrats and Republicans
               b. Democrats get most PAC money
           8. PAC contributions small
           9. No evidence PAC money influences votes in Congress
               a. Most members vote their ideology
               b. When issue of little concern to voters, slight correlation but may be misleading
               c. PAC money may influence in other ways, like access
               d. PAC money most likely to influence client politics
       D. The "revolving door"
           1. Promise of future jobs to officials
           2. Few conspicuous examples of abuse
       E. Trouble
           1. Disruption always part of American politics
           2. Used by groups of varying ideologies, etc.
           3. Better accepted since 1960s
           4. History of "proper" persons using disruption—suffrage, civil rights, antiwar movements
           5. Officials dread "no-win" situations
VIII. Regulating interest groups (ADDITIONAL LECTURE TOPIC E-1) (THEME E: CONTROLLING INTEREST GROUPS AND LOBBYISTS)
       A. Protection by First Amendment
           1. 1946 law accomplished little in requiring registration
               a. Supreme Court restricted application to direct contact
               b. Grassroots activity not restricted
               c. No staff to enforce law

In 1990, slightly over six thousand interest groups were registered with the Senate in compliance with the Federal Regulation of Lobbying Act.

       B. Recent suggestions
           1. Disclosure of contributors
               a. Likely to dry up contributions
           2. Complex reporting requirements
               a. Disadvantage to small groups

C. Significant restraints
1. Tax code; lose tax-exempt status
2. Campaign-finance laws

Federal regulations are extremely lax on what constitutes a legitimate campaign expense. A report by the Federal Election Commission listed the following expenditures from campaign funds: babysitters' fees, lawyer's fee for defending against a DUI, donation to the Miss Georgia Teen contest, auto tags, and football tickets.

Important Terms

direct mail A mailing from an interest group focused at a specialized audience whose purpose is both to raise money and to mobilize supporters.

Federal Regulation of Lobbying Act A law passed in 1946 which requires groups and individuals seeking to influence legislation to register with the secretary of the Senate and the clerk of the House of Representatives. Quarterly financial reports on expenses must also be filed.

*ideological interest group An organization that attracts members by appealing to their interests on a coherent set of controversial principles.

*incentive Something of value offered by mass-membership organizations to get people to join that they cannot get without joining.

institutional interests Bread-and-butter issues of concern to the clients of individuals or organizations representing other organizations.

*interest group Any organization that seeks to influence public policy.

*lobbies Groups that attempt to influence legislation through direct contact with members of Congress.

*material incentive Something of value, such as money or services, which attracts people to join mass-membership organizations.

membership interests A type of interest group that represents the interest of its members. Americans, unlike Europeans, have a much higher tendency to join religious and civic associations.

pluralistic political system A description of the American political system, once used by scholars, contending that the system reflects effective competition of interest groups. This account is generally considered wrong, or at least incomplete.

political action committee An organization frequently created by a corporation or labor union which supports candidates and legislation in the group's interest. Such organizations were legalized under the campaign finance reform law of 1974 and can contribute no more than $5,000 to a federal candidate in any election.

*political cue A signal, frequently provided by interest groups, that tells a politician what values are at stake in an issue—who is for and who is against a proposal—and how that issue fits into his or her own set of political beliefs.

*public-interest lobby An interest group whose principal purpose is to benefit nonmembers. Such groups are common in environmental and consumer protection matters.

*purposive incentive An incentive to join a mass-membership organization based on the appeal of the group's goal.

*ratings A type of cue supplied by some interest groups that ranks legislators on their degree of support for a particular cause, such as unions or the environment. These can be helpful sources of information, but are sometimes biased.

*social movement A widely shared demand for change in some aspect of the social or political order.

*solidary incentive An inducement to join a mass membership organization to derive a sense of pleasure, status, or companionship.

Theme A — American Interest Groups in Comparative Perspective

Summary

An interest group is any organization that seeks to influence public policy. Interest groups are found in any society, but there is an unusually large number of them in America. This proliferation is a result of

1. The great number of social cleavages along income, occupational, religious, racial, and cultural lines.

2. The American constitutional system, which stimulates political activity, including interest group activity. Because of federalism and the separation of powers, there exist many different centers in which important decisions are made. Therefore many different interest groups can exercise some power. In Britain, on the other hand, groups are fewer in number and larger in scale (to match the centralized governmental structure).

3. The decline of political parties, which has made the wielding of power by interest groups more practical (because the system is more fragmented in the absence of parties) and seemingly more needed (if parties cannot take action on a policy, perhaps groups can). In European countries with strong parties, interest groups—such as labor unions and professional societies—tend to be closely allied to parties.

There are two kinds of interest groups: "institutional" and "membership." The former are individuals or organizations representing other groups and intensely interested in "bread-and-butter issues of vital concern to clients." Typical of institutional interests are business, governments, foundations, and universities. Membership groups are "supported by the activities and contributions of individual citizens."

Both institutional and membership interest groups play roles in other countries that would be considered improper in the United States. In Britain, for example, political candidates can be sponsored by organized interests. Over 60 percent of Labour party's members of Parliament are financially supported by trade unions. Even active involvement of interest groups in the formulation of legislation occurs in many European democracies. According to William Safran, "One of the most important features of French interest-group politics is the fact that most groups have a fairly institutionalized relationship to government authorities. Several hundred advisory councils are attached to ministries; these councils, composed largely of representatives of interest groups, furnish data that may influence policy suggestions and regulations that emanate from ministries." It would seem that what constitutes the legitimate function of interest groups in democratic government varies widely. Interest groups must fit into the prevailing cultural norms of each country. There is no standard model of interest-group behavior.

Additional Lecture Topic A-1

Interest Groups in Other Countries

Instructor: You may wish to explain briefly the role and function of interest groups in other comparable political systems. The following texts give a capsule summary for three countries.

David Conradt, *The German Polity*. 4th ed. White Plains, NY: Longman, 1989. Chapter 4.

Philip Norton, *The British Polity*. 2nd ed. White Plains, NY: Longman, 1991. Chapter 7.

William Safran, *The French Polity*. 3rd ed. White Plains, NY: Longman, 1991. Chapter 5.

See also Jurg Steiner, *European Democracies*. 2nd ed. White Plains, NY: Longman, 1991. Chapters 9 and 11.

Theme B — History and Interest-Group Formation

Summary

Since 1960 the number of interest groups has increased rapidly. There have been other historical eras of interest group proliferation. These include the 1770s (proindependence groups), the 1830s and 1840s (religious and antislavery groups), the 1860s (trade unions, the Grange, and fraternal organizations), the 1880s and 1890s (business organizations), the 1900s and 1910s (a vast array of organizations), and the 1960s (environmental, consumer, and political-reform organizations). Interest group do not, therefore, arise "spontaneously" or automatically out of natural social processes. At least four factors help explain the rise of interest groups.

1. *Broad economic developments.* For example, the rise of mass-production industry allowed the rise of mass-membership labor unions.

2. *Government policy.* Public programs create constituencies with an incentive to organize to maintain their benefits. Veterans' benefits create veterans' groups; the licensing of professionals by state governments gives societies of doctors and lawyers a strong reason to exist. Sometimes the government supports the formation of organizations (the American Farm Bureau Federation is an example) by providing benefits to their members. Sometimes government policies are designed to make private interest-group formation easier, as was the case with the passage of laws in the 1930s to aid labor organization.

3. *Religious and moralistic movements.* These produce people, frequently young people, who are willing to form organizations, often at large personal cost. The religious revivals of the 1830s and 1840s thus fed the antislavery crusade, and the civil rights and antiwar movements of the 1960s likewise produced an organizational explosion.

4. The more activities government undertakes, the more interest groups form as a response to those activities. Accordingly, public interest lobbies have increased since 1970, when government became active in civil rights, social welfare, and consumer rights.

Discussion Questions

1. Which have been more important in the formation of interest groups: changes in the economic structure of society or changes in people's ideas and beliefs? What evidence does the text give on this point? Can you think of other examples?

2. The text contends that governmental policy encourages the growth and activity of interest groups; programs create constituencies. What about the reverse—do interest groups "create" governmental programs? Could interest-group activity be responsible for the expansion of government itself? In *The End of Liberalism*, Theodore Lowi presents the theory that public policy is formulated by government bureaucrats in conjunction with interest groups. Has the complexity of contemporary society shifted the advantage to interest groups?

3. The proportion of the labor force engaged in manufacturing dropped from 26.4 percent in 1977 to 18.5 percent in 1988. The labor force is increasingly focused in the service sector. According to the text, shouldn't this change in economic focus spawn many new interest groups? Is this happening? Labor union membership is diminishing as well, from 31.8 percent of the labor force in 1955 to 19.4 percent in 1984. Who now represents the interests of workers to the government?

Data and Perspectives for Analysis

Frequently one interest group makes demands that conflict with another interest group's wishes. For example, suppose a federal highway is proposed through a picturesque site. The building of this highway will be favored by construction firms and related labor unions, but it may be opposed by groups dedicated to preserving the environment.

In a similar fashion, suppose the government agency responsible for promoting highway safety announces that it is considering the adoption of a new regulation. The proposed regulation would compel automobile manufacturers to include air bags (an expensive safety device that inflates to protect front-seat passengers in a collision) as a *mandatory* feature in all new cars and trucks. Which of the following interest groups do you think would be for and which against the regulation? Explain your reasoning below.

> Automobile manufacturers
> United Auto Workers Union
> Consumer rights groups
> An association of safety engineers
> An association of independent truck drivers

Abstract for Theme B

"Wave Patterns" of Interest-Group Formation

Do interest groups form according to the particular historical era and social conditions? In *Interest-Group Politics in America* by Ronald J. Hrebenar and Ruth K. Scott (Englewood Cliffs, NJ: Prentice-Hall, 1982, pp. 9–12), this question is considered via the examination of various theories of group formation. In an earlier work, James Q. Wilson argued that there had been three great waves of association between 1800 and 1940. The great explosion between 1900 and 1920 had been due to a communications revolution, the government's attempt to regulate business activity, the increased division of labor, and immigration, which had added to the growing diversity of the American population. In short this era, like those that preceded it, was related to important social movements and unrest, which collectively produced new interest groups in the United States.

In a related theory, dubbed the "disturbance theory" by David Truman and Robert Salisbury, it was argued "that interest groups arise as a result of two interrelated societal processes. One process involves the increased complexity of society, while the second is the natural tendency to seek a condition of equilibrium" (pp. 10–11). The "complexity" axiom asserts that specialized groups will form associations by which they can articulate their needs. The "equilibrium theory" argues that disadvantaged groups that have lost political ground because of societal disturbances try to renew that balance by fresh efforts at reorganizing.

Salisbury suggests another theory, the "entrepreneurial theory," which "sees as the key element in group formation the organizer or entrepreneur of the new group . . . the desire of the organizer to establish a viable organization." In the final analysis, "it may be that the disturbance theory better fits economic groups, while ideological or cause groups are better explained by the entrepreneurial theory."

Questions for Discussion

1. If one assumes that American society will become more complex in the future, can one rightfully assume that new "waves" of interest-group formation are also likely to occur?

2. What *specific* social trends and changes in contemporary America have the distinct ability to trigger interest-group formation?

Answer Guidelines

This is a totally open-ended discussion. You can use your discretion in shaping the direction and scope of that discussion.

Theme C   Bias in the Group Process and Kinds of Organizations

Summary

If it is true that America has more interest groups than other nations, does it follow that more Americans belong to groups? The answer is no for unions and for business, professional, and charitable organizations. It is yes for civil or political organizations and religious associations. Americans' willingness to join civic or political organizations probably reflects a greater sense of civic duty and political efficacy here.

Interest-group joiners tend to be high-status individuals: they have the income, the free time, and the wide range of interests necessary for group activity. Some believe that interest-group activity therefore has an "upper-class bias." However, this bias must be considered in light of political outputs (who wins and who loses in particular issues at particular times) and internal divisions within groups (farmers, for example). Accordingly, there are major opinion cleavages among elites. In fact, there is a great deal of disagreement among groups composed of better-off persons: a business association will be opposed by an environmentalist organization, and pro- and anti-ERA groups will both consist of well-off individuals. Furthermore, some organizations of better-off persons have considerable political influence (the NAACP or consumer groups, for example), whereas others (taxpayer associations or pro-gun control groups) are relatively poorly organized and ineffective. Also, interest groups representing business and the professions seem more influential and better financed than groups representing the poor, consumers, and minorities. In Washington, more than three-quarters of the seven thousand groups represented are corporations or professional groups, and less than 2 percent are civil rights or minority groups.

Furthermore, we cannot assume that what an interest group does in the political arena is simply the expression of the interests of its members. Every political organization has an *external* political strategy and an *internal* recruitment strategy. These may be different or even in conflict. The active support of labor unions for civil rights legislation in spite of the opposition or skepticism of union members, and the consistently leftist positions of the National Council of Churches, which represents fairly conservative Protestants (many of them southerners), are examples. Whether an organization's political positions will represent its members' interests will depend on at least four factors.

1. *The homogeneity of the group.* The southern textile mills represented by the American Cotton Manufacturers Institute are few and homogeneous in outlook; therefore the organization takes clear positions in opposition to foreign-made textiles. The United States Chamber of Commerce consists of many different types of businesses and thus can say little or nothing about tariffs.

2. *People's motives for joining.* As long as union members are satisfied with the union's performance on bread-and-butter issues, and as long as Protestant churchgoers receive spiritual or social satisfaction in local congregations, the national AFL-CIO and the National Council of Churches can do pretty much as they please. Thus members motivated by solidary or material incentives will give great discretion to the staff to pursue their own goals.

3. *The size of the staff.* Organizations with large staffs are more likely to take political positions in accordance with staff beliefs. Furthermore, staffs will tend to have distinct views, either liberal/left (National Council of Churches) or conservative/right (American Farm Bureau Federation).

4. *The level of militance and activity of the membership.* Members of some organizations, such as the John Birch Society or the Sierra Club, tend to be passionately convinced of the rightness of particular policies. Leaders of these organizations will not find members indifferent or easily satisfied, and they will be forced to take strong stands— perhaps even stands they would prefer to avoid. *Social movements* also create dedicated interest groups, as exemplified by civil rights, feminism, and the environment.

Not only do groups not necessarily represent the views of their members, but also large constituencies (consumers, or women, or taxpayers) are particularly hard to organize. This is not because such people are "apathetic" but because of the "free-rider" problem. No single individual's membership perceptibly affects the likelihood that the group will succeed in achieving its goals, yet if it does achieve its goals, every person in the class represented will share in the benefits, regardless of whether he or she was actually a member. The average individual has virtually no incentive to join.

Organizations may overcome this problem by supplying services to individual members, in addition to engaging in political activity. The Illinois Farm Bureau and the American Association of Retired Persons follow this strategy. On the other hand, *sponsored organizations* find some other organization willing to recruit members or pay the bills. The AFL-CIO supports the National Council of Senior Citizens, and foundations (particularly the Ford Foundation) were very important in the rise of "public interest" organizations in the 1960s and 1970s. Such sponsored groups either have no members or offer no way for members to influence the organization's policies. They therefore reflect the goals of the elites that dominate them, and they increasingly fight their battles in court, where lack of voting membership is not a serious disadvantage. Finally, groups such as Common Cause or Ralph Nader's Public Citizen may raise large amounts of money through direct mail. (Organizations that make their appeals to broad, controversial principles are termed *ideological interest groups*.)

Discussion Questions

1. According to a 1981 Gallup survey, the type of interest group Americans would "most like to join" (by a two-to-one margin) involves protection of wildlife, followed by conservation and environmental groups. Why isn't protection of wildlife a major political issue, on the level of gun control, say? How do the two issues differ from an interest-group perspective?

2. Former President Carter opined that politics has done more to alleviate the condition of the poor than has religion. Yet the text concludes that membership in a charitable organization does not promote a sense of civic duty, whereas membership in a religious association does. How can Carter's assertion be justified?

3. In what sense can Ralph Nader be said to "represent" consumers? In the same sense in which a congressman represents a constituency? In the sense that he works for what is good for consumers? Has Nader ever taken positions opposed to consumer interests?

Instructor: There should be plenty of discussion of this. Try discussing Nader's opposition to nuclear power and his support of air bags, as well as his support of the saccharin ban. You may agree with all the Nader positions, but not all your students will. The important point is that Nader represents consumers only to the extent that his views actually reflect their views or interests—and while this may happen to be the case, no process holds Nader accountable to the people he claims to represent.

4. As a consumer, how is your interest in lower sugar prices represented in the group process? Following is a list of interests that you as a consumer probably share. Which of them are likely to be represented by an existing business or trade association?

    Low sugar prices
    An extensive network of good highways
    A clean environment
    Good public schools
    Low tax rates
    Low interest rates for loans

Data and Perspectives for Analysis

A. Representatives of Interest Groups

A major controversy surrounding interest groups is the degree to which they represent the concerns of the American public. To paraphrase a famous quotation, does the interest group chorus sing with an upper-class accent? The danger posed by interest groups is that they challenge the democratic process by failing to present all sides of a controversy to government leaders. Is this popular belief true? Present the following data to your students and have them analyze the information to answer the question of whether interest groups adequately reflect American society.

Organizational Focus of Groups in Comparison with Characteristics of U.S. Adults

Organizational focus	Percentage of organizations	Percentage of U.S. adults	Occupation or other characteristic
Trade, business, commercial chambers of commerce, tourism	25	36	Managerial, professional, sales, supervisors
Agriculture	6	3	Farming, forestry, fishing
Legal, governmental, military	4	15–17	Governmental employees, military personnel
Science, engineering technical	9	5	Scientists, engineers, technicians
Education	8	5	Teachers, counselors, librarians
Social welfare	11	16	Social insurance recipients
Health and medical	13	5	Health and medical
Public affairs	14	a	
Religious	7	40–60	Churchgoers, members
Veterans, hereditary, patriotic	2	11	Veterans
Unions	1	16	Union member

Note: Percentages of organizations sum to 100 percent. Categories for adults are overlapping and do not include all types of workers; therefore they do not sum to 100 percent. Categories used for organizations are those of the first source. Excluded were approximately 5,800 (of about 23,000) groups; those excluded were cultural, ethnic, athletic, hobby, and Greek-letter organizations and fan clubs.

[a] This category of groups includes political parties and numerous special-interest groups. Partly because of overlapping memberships, there is no clearly comparable set of individuals.

Source: Harold Stanley and Richard Niemi, *Vital Statistics on American Politics*, 2nd ed. (Washington: Congressional Quarterly Press, 1990), p. 174.

B. Pac Money and Bias

The political system operates fairly when each group has an equal chance to influence the outcome of policies. In contemporary politics, the competition has become skewed with the introduction of PACs in the mid-1970s. While small contributors still constitute the largest source of financial support for candidates, the power of PACs is clearly increasing in the area of campaign money. This generalization is especially true of incumbents who receive a disproportionate share of PAC money. Are organized interests at a disadvantage if they don't create a PAC? What do the data below reveal that respect to bias in the political process?

Election Year	PAC Money as Percentage of the Totals Raised by Incumbent Candidates
1975–1976	25%
1977–1978	25%
1979–1980	30%
1981–1982	33%
1983–1984	37%
1985–1986	37%
1987–1988	40%

Source: *The New York Times*, June 12, 1988.

Discussion Questions

1. The text downplays the influence of money as a tactic in the arsenal of interest groups. Instead, the text points to the importance of supplying information and political cues. In addition, it suggests that the multiplicity of groups giving money acts to counteract the role of any single interest group. If true, how can your students explain why PACs have increased the amount of money they contribute?

2. Wouldn't the influence of staff be especially heightened when it comes to deciding what members of Congress seeking election actually receive money from a PAC? Can a contributor have any power in this decision?

3. Does a group's level of militancy have anything to do with the amount of financial support it receives from its members?

Additional Lecture Topics

C-1. Economists and the Group Process

James M. Buchanan and Gordon Tullock, *The Calculus of Consent*. Ann Arbor: University of Michigan Press, 1962. Chapter 10.

Anthony Downs, *An Economic Theory of Democracy*. New York: Harper & Row, 1957. Chapter 13. (Those not familiar with Downs's theories should also review Part I of the book.) It is often blandly assumed that a good citizen will become well informed in all relevant areas of public policy and that most of the evils of government could be cured by an "informed" citizenry. Downs demonstrates that a rational individual is necessarily ill informed in most policy areas. Who is informed? Interest groups.

Anthony Downs, "Why the Government Budget Is Too Small in a Democracy." *World Politics*, July 1960.

David Knoke, *Organizing for Collective Action: The Political Economies of Associations*. Hawthorne, NY: A. DeGruyter, 1990.

Mancur Olson, *The Logic of Collective Action*. Cambridge: Harvard University Press, 1971. Chapters 1–2. It is often assumed that individuals will "spontaneously" join groups that represent their interests. Olson asks what rational individuals will do and concludes they usually will not join even a group that is, in fact, promoting their interests.

These last three readings address the following question: Does the group process lead to a government that is too big and spends too much money or to one that fails to do those things it should do?

C-2. How Can Hard-to-Organize Interests Be Represented?

Jeffrey M. Berry, *Lobbying for the People*, Chapters 1–3. Princeton: Princeton University Press, 1977.

Mark Nadel, *The Politics of Consumer Protection*. Indianapolis: Bobbs-Merrill, 1971.

Mancur Olson, *The Logic of Collective Action*. Cambridge: Harvard University Press, 1971. Chapter 6.

Nadel's volume deals with the process of "policy entrepreneurship." Olson deals with the "surplus value" theory of representation, whereby an organization with a secure base of support can direct some of its extra resources into political action on behalf of hard-to-organize groups. Berry deals with sources of support for public interest groups.

Abstract for Theme C

When Interest Groups Clash

Frequently, coalitions of interest groups will clash over a controversial policy issue, particularly when each coalition feels strongly about the issue in question. In an article entitled "Military and Preservationists Clash over Mojave's Future" (*New York Times*, June 25, 1988, pp. 1, 8), Robert Reinhold fully delineated the ongoing battle among environmentalists, the military, the Bureau of Land Management, dune-buggy enthusiasts, motorcyclists, and politicians over control of the vast Mojave Desert. Reinhold explained the basic outlines of the battle over the California desert as follows:

> Preservationists want to protect it from further human depredations by creating a new 1.5 million-acre national park and millions of acres of new "wilderness" areas in which vehicles and commercial activity would be banned. They are being stoutly resisted by the Army, which wants another 200,000 acres of desert for tank maneuvers, and by the Air Force and Navy, seeking to protect the remote expanses they use to train jet pilots and test new weapons; by mining companies fearful of losing access to valuable minerals on public lands; by off-the-road enthusiasts who come each weekend to drive Jeeps, dirt bikes, dune buggies and motorcycles over dunes and valleys, and by a handful of remote ranchers who fear losing access to their ancestral grazing lands. (p. 1)

The then Secretary of Interior, Donald P. Hodel, argued that his Bureau of Land Management had not permitted destruction of the desert terrain from mining and off-road vehicles, but the Wilderness Society and Sierra Club together charged that the land was "crumbling" and that wildlife in the desert had suffered:

> Preservationists assert that vehicles are hastening erosion of the fragile desert, killing plants and animals, and even deafening small mammals. They also contend that mining companies have illegally bulldozed roads and would pollute the environment with waste chemicals if allowed to. (p. 8)

At the crux of the matter was legislation dating from 1976, which planned for 1.9 million acres of the desert to be set aside as wilderness, accessible only by foot. Senator Alan Cranston's more ambitious bill of 1988 proposed saving 8.8 million acres of wilderness, prompting protests from the California Association of Four Wheel Drive Clubs and the American Motorcyclists Association that their members would be "locked out" of the protected area. It was, however, military leaders who were most vehement about the Cranston bill:

> The remote California desert is one of the main training and testing grounds for new weapons. Above it is an 18,000-square-mile expanse of airspace known as R-2058, "the most important military airspace in the world." . . . The commanders of four bases here . . . say 90,000 training sorties a year are flown over the desert, a fifth of them at very low levels to avoid radar. While the Cranston proposal, called Senate Bill 7, does not prohibit such flights, the Department of Defense has voluntarily agreed to avoid flying below 3,000 feet over the wilderness areas and officers say that expanding them might impinge on training. (p. 8)

Another issue was mining, according to the Bureau of Land Management; its spokesman stressed that there were vital strategic minerals and gold in the area, especially "rare-earth metals, elements essential in superconductor and other technologies." Would it be wise to deny the nation these resources by excessive conservation policies?

The outlook for the Cranston bill was uncertain and so was the exact nature of the final solution to the Mojave problem. But it was likely that the clash of interest-group coalitions would intensify. As Reinhold put it, "a century and a half after early settlers traded shots with the desert Indians, the new battle for the Wild West has only begun."

Questions for Discussion

1. On which side of the issue would students align? Are the sympathies of the class mainly with the environmentalists, the military, etc.?

2. What eventually happened to the Cranston bill? Was a compromise worked out that satisfied the two opposing coalitions? Have students research the issue and then report their findings in class.

Answer Guidelines

Discussion should be left open-ended and flexible.

Theme D   Interest Groups in Action

Summary

Interest groups attempt to influence policy by supplying public officials with things they want. Government agencies are themselves interest groups and will supply the same sorts of things private-sector groups do. These things include:

1. *Credible information.* This may include valuable policy information to allow a legislator to take a position on an issue. Legislators cannot be experts on every issue, so they often need help. It may include the technical information needed to implement a policy. When the Federal Energy Administration was trying to allocate scarce oil and gasoline supplies, it discovered that the information it needed was possessed only by the oil companies. An interest group is most powerful when the issue is narrow and technical and there are no competing interest groups to supply competing information, as in the traditional CAB regulation of the airlines. Finally, it may involve *political cues* that will allow a public official to line up on the "liberal" or "conservative" or "proenvironment" side of an issue.

2. *Public support.* An interest group may commission public opinion polls, stimulate local citizens to write letters or send telegrams, have constituents visit the legislator, or get newspapers to run editorials supporting its position. It is unlikely that these tactics are effective for more than a handful of visible issues with great emotional significance (abortion, the Panama Canal treaties). Although there has been a recent rise in *single-issue politics*, which often generates *grass-roots lobbying*, members of Congress generally hear what they want to hear and deal with interest groups that agree with them. However, interest groups can mobilize support for and against legislators, as was the case with Environmental Action and the "Dirty Dozen."

3. *Money.* Interest groups can legally supply money to political campaigns, they can lobby Congress to reduce or increase the appropriations for government agencies, they can provide jobs for former government officials (revolving door), and on occasion they may offer a cash bribe. In order to obtain money beyond mere dues, interest groups have turned to foundation grants (Ford Foundation, Environmental Defense Fund), federal grants and contracts, and direct-mail solicitation. (Common Cause is an interest group created by direct-mail contributions.) Letters must be effective in raising money through "teasers," arousal of emotions, endorsements, and "personalization."

Business/labor PACs have become influential since 1975, but ideological PACs have increased at an even faster rate and raised more money than the other two. However, they actually spend less on campaigns and candidates due to direct-mail costs. Basically, PAC contributions tend to be small, and their influence on congressional voting seems to be marginal.

4. *The absence of "trouble."* Tactics such as protest marches, sit-ins, picketing, and violence have always been part of American politics, used by both the left and the right. They have been used by "have-not" groups (civil rights demonstrations) and very middle-class citizens (feminists around the turn of the century). The object is to disrupt the workings of some institution to force it to negotiate with you, to enlist the support of third parties (for example, the media), or to provoke attacks and arrests so that martyrs are created.

Many policies have been enacted or proposed to regulate interest groups; all must deal with the fact that interest-group activity is a form of political speech protected by the First Amendment. For example, the Federal Regulation of Lobbying Act of 1946 requires interest groups to register with the secretary of the Senate and clerk of the House of Representatives, as well as to file quarterly financial reports. The Supreme Court upheld the law but limited its impact to groups whose "principal purpose" is to influence legislation. This ruling provides two loopholes for interest groups to exploit. First, it applies to the groups least likely to manipulate the political system to their advantage, such as consumer protection and environmental organizations. Labor unions, in contrast, hardly qualify as organizations with a "principal purpose" to lobby the government. Second, grass-roots activity that does not involve direct contact with government officials is exempt from the law. Various proposals for reform encounter similar legal problems. Disclosure rules raise concerns over the invasion of privacy, while the Clinton administration's regulation forbidding former officials from contacting their agency (for a set period of time) infringes upon the freedom of association.

The most effective restraints on interest-group activity result from the tax code (which threatens to revoke a group's tax-exempt status if it engages in substantial amounts of lobbying) and campaign finance laws. Yet interest groups have discovered ways to evade even these restraints. Consider the restriction on campaign contributions. According to Hedrick Smith, these spending limits can be circumvented by "bundling." "Bundling is the practice by which a central PAC in some industry will appeal to individual executives in its field for contributions to individual senators or congressmen. The PAC acts as the collection point for private checks, but since these funds are not its own, these contributions do not count against its $5,000 legal limit. The PAC puts these checks together in a 'bundle,' delivers them to the politician, and reaps the political credit for raising the money." Thus, even the best regulations are ineffective barriers against the power of interest groups.

It is probably not possible to regulate interest groups in any way that would limit their influence without impairing important constitutional rights. Moreover, members of Congress lack an incentive to design effective laws since incumbents are the primary beneficiaries of PAC money. Ultimately, it is necessary to have a political system that gives each citizen an opportunity to be heard. Democracy has negative consequences that must be endured.

Discussion Questions

1. Information is the primary tactic employed by interest groups. For example, a study by John Deakin revealed that 40 percent of the legislation introduced into Congress was written either entirely or in part by interest groups. Why would members of Congress introduce such legislation? Do members of Congress have so little information available to them? Is the public vulnerable to exploitation by powerful groups due to their monopoly over information?

2. PACs have been called "collection agencies" for interest groups. They were created to evade laws that forbid corporations and labor unions from giving money "directly" to federal candidates. These laws still exist. Aren't the laws now a farce? Why does Congress permit the law to be trampled by allowing the existence of PACs? In 1982,

Time Magazine concluded that PACs threaten "to undermine America's system of representative democracy." Is this statement accurate given the information provided in the text?

3. Interest groups attempt to stimulate "public support" for their causes. One tactic is to manipulate public opinion through use of the media. To illustrate, Elizabeth Whelan, executive director of the American Council on Science and Health, reports that from 1964 to 1984 there was "no major story on the health impact of cigarette smoking in any major U.S. popular publication. . . . Some 10%–40% of advertising revenues for U.S. magazines comes from tobacco advertisements." Is there a correlation between these two facts? Can't interest groups achieve their objectives without even contacting the government? What can be done to prevent such exploitation of public information?

4. Since passage of the Federal Regulation of Lobbying Act in 1946, only four persons have been prosecuted under its provisions—with only one conviction. Why is the law so ineffective? Why doesn't Congress enact a stronger law? Why would the First Amendment constitute a major impediment to any attempt to curtail the activities of interest groups?

Data and Perspectives for Analysis, 2

Interest-group activity is cyclical. Because they are energized by issues, the interest groups that are most involved in Washington politics change almost yearly. Unless the federal government is deciding an issue of concern to it, an interest group has little to gain by applying pressure. Few organizations, even major ones like oil companies and labor unions, want to be constantly at the door of a members of Congress. Political capital can be depleted by too active a presence.

The correlation between issues and interest-group activity is illustrated by the levels of contributions by political action committees. Based on the data below, have students discuss the political factors accounting for the differences in PAC contributions for 1989 and 1990. This is a relationship much neglected by political scientists. Why did any one group's contribution increase or decrease from one year to the next?

PAC Contributions, 1989 and 1990

Category A: Contribution Increases of over $500,000

Insurance: $8.7 million, up $939,127
Tobacco products: $2 million, up $653,779
Railroads: $1.6 million, up $564,048
Construction unions: $6.2 million, up $525,429
Electric utilities: $3.5 million, up $521,516
Cable and broadcasters: $1.2 million, up $509,000

Category B: Contribution Decreases of over $500,000

Securities: $1.7 million, down $1,065,887
Savings and loans: $971,000, down $999,292
Sea transport unions: $2.4 million, down $696,710
Nondefense aircraft: $254,000, down $591,000
Government unions: $3.8 million, down $510,421

Source: Andrew Mollison, "Deep Pockets," *Atlanta Journal-Constitution*, May 8, 1991.

Abstract 1 for Theme D

The Activities of Interest Groups and Lobbyists

Interest groups play important roles in influencing the course of public policy. In a similar vein, salaried representatives of interest groups, or lobbyists, try to gain access both to the lawmaker's office and mind! Accordingly, many lobbyists are themselves former officeholders who already "know the ropes" politically.

Three newspaper articles published in 1985 reflect the foregoing assertions. The first, by Philip Shabecoff (*New York Times*, June 26, 1985, p. 1), was entitled "Atomic Shift by U.S. Proposed in Agenda of Conservationists." Shabecoff reported that the leaders of ten conservationist groups had compiled a policy "agenda" urging the U.S. government to consider over one hundred proposals dealing with a "broad range of environmental threats and problems." Some of the recommendations included (a) stabilizing the U.S. population at a level that would permit a high quality of life to be maintained; (b) adopting a fuel efficiency standard of sixty miles per gallon for cars by 1995; (c) requiring a 50 percent reduction in sulfur emissions by industry in order to fight the problem of acid rain; (d) formulating a $12 billion program for cleaning up toxic waste dumps; (e) developing a policy to combat indoor air pollution; and (f) tightening controls on diesel emissions and other forms of air pollution. Russell W. Peterson, president of the National Audubon Society, suggested that the environmentalists had "a fighting chance" to attain these goals and that the agenda was directed toward the long term. In short, Congress was confronted with a systematic, exhaustive environmental policy agenda.

Congress is also sensitive to financial contributions from PACs. Robert Pear's article, "$8.2 Million in Farm Gifts to Congress" (*New York Times*, March 4, 1985, p. 11), briefly explores the influence of agricultural money on members of Congress. The PACs formed by farmers, ranchers, farm bureaus, and companies that produce fertilizer and pesticides had given $4.4 million to House members and $3.8 million to senators. The aim had been to influence the general thrust of congressional farm policy and in particular emergency credit relief for debt-ridden farmers. (The credit plan had been approved despite a veto threat by the president.) Members of Congress admitted that contributions did open up access to the farmers' point of view, although they denied that the money "had played a major role in the votes to approve the farm credit legislation." Still, some key members had received substantial contributions over a two-year period, ranging anywhere from $13,000 to over $215,000 (Senator Wilson, R-Calif.). Farm lobbyists had obviously made some impact on the policy decision-making process.

The Washington lobbyists were active in another key policy area: President Reagan's tax-overhaul proposal of 1985. As detailed in a *Wall Street Journal* report of June 19, 1985 (p. 62), by Brooks Jackson and Monica Langley ("Washington's Lobbyists Enjoy Added Prosperity as Special Interests Gear Up for Tax Overhaul"), the proposed tax bill had resulted in the hiring of lobbyists by a plethora of corporations, trade associations, and other special interest groups to protect their vital economic concerns. The authors of the report described it this way:

> The Tobacco Institute wants cigarette excise taxes cut by half, back to eight cents a pack. Brewers fear taxes on beer may be raised. Drug and software companies want to retain tax benefits from their operations in Puerto Rico. Professional sports teams worry that ticket sales will drop if they aren't deductible. Country clubs want to keep their dues as write-offs, too. They've all hired lobbyists, and few of them come cheap.

The fees charged by the more prominent lobbyists ranged from $250 to $400 an hour of consulting time. Some lobbyists even insisted that their clients pay a "success premium" if they won a reduction in taxes. In short, the report went on to state, nearly a hundred tax clients had been added by lobbying firms since the previous year. Lobbyists expected their business to increase as the tax bill made its way through various congressional hearings and committee discussions. It should be noted that many of the top lobbying firms were composed of individuals who had previously had extensive experience in or contacts with Congress or the executive branch. Examples included a former Democratic party chairman (Robert Strauss), a former undersecretary of the treasury (Charles E. Walker), the son of Speaker Tip O'Neill, and the son of Representative Lindy Boggs, an ex-IRS commissioner (Donald C. Alexander), and a former aide to the current House Ways and Means Chairman Dan Rostenkowski (James Healey). To put it simply, an effective Washington lobbyist was certainly *not* a political novice.

Questions for Discussion

1. Does any of the policy proposals put forth by the environmentalists seem more politically feasible than any of the others? If so, why?
2. If you were an environmentalist lobbyist, how would you try to "persuade" a key member of Congress of the worth of the policy agenda described here?
3. Do you think the sizable farm contributions to key legislators had some impact on the way they voted despite their denials? Why or why not?
4. After considering these three newspaper reports, would you agree that money is the "milk of politics"? Why or why not?
5. The Reagan tax proposal did become law in 1986. Have students research how effective the lobbyists were in creating "loopholes" in the new law.

Answer Guidelines

Discussion should be left open-ended and flexible.

Abstract 2 for Theme D

Interest-Group Effectiveness in Influencing Policy

Interest groups vary in their ability to influence policy outcomes in the American political system. A variety of factors can erode or enhance interest group "policy effectiveness." For example, even normally powerful interest groups can encounter setbacks due to ineffective internal leadership, new rivals, and a poor image. Thus, in an article entitled "Mighty Gun Lobby Loses Its Invincibility by Taking Hard Line," by Jeffrey H. Birnbaum (*Wall Street Journal*, May 21, 1988, pp. 1, 24), it was revealed how the National Rifle Association (NRA) was beginning to lose its "aura of invincibility" and its hold over even pro-NRA congressional backers. The NRA was losing its credibility by championing armor-piercing bullets and undetectable handguns. The NRA's "strong-arm tactics and inflammatory statements" had not helped either. Birnbaum pointed out that the NRA's tactics could be linked to

> internal divisions and management turmoil that have racked it (NRA) for several years. While the NRA has always vehemently opposed gun registration and similar curbs, a large faction in the membership takes an even harder line. In 1986, for example, dissidents at its annual meeting unsuccessfully fought the decision to change course and back a ban on armor-piercing ammo.

Furthermore, the NRA's attitudes had attracted some unwelcome adversaries, that is, the nation's police.

> It is the police . . . who have emerged as the association's most dangerous foes. For years police organizations did only occasional lobbying themselves, generally deferring to the NRA to represent them on law-and-order issues. But the NRA's recent stances have strained relations to the breaking point, as have its attacks on local police chiefs who it says oppose efforts to protect gun ownership.
>
> In late 1985, several law-enforcement groups, including the Fraternal Order of Police and the International Association of Chiefs of Police, banded together as the Law Enforcement Steering Committee. The committee now lobbies strenuously for law-enforcement issues, often against the NRA. Legislators who once dreaded the thought of voting against the NRA have become more willing to do so, as long as they are backed by the police.

Finally, highly respected individuals can be important in determining interest-group effectiveness. In the case of the NRA, one such individual was

> Sarah Brady, the wife of James Brady, the White House spokesman severely wounded along with President Reagan by a handgun wielded by John Hinckley in 1981. . . . Mrs. Brady has assumed a highly visible role for Handgun Control Inc. which favors restrictions. "The leadership of the NRA

is out of touch and out of step with the mainstream," she says. "They don't espouse any common-sense solutions anymore."

Mrs. Brady's political ties and willingness to discuss her family's suffering guarantee her a respectful hearing in Congress. "She's been a very powerful spokesman," says GOP Sen. John McCain of Arizona, an NRA enthusiast. One sign of the association's concern: It has dispatched a letter to its members criticizing Mrs. Brady's activities and labeling her a "misdirected woman."

Conversely, Birnbaum asserted that the NRA was by no means "finished as a legislative powerhouse." Its 2.8 million members, $71 million in annual revenue, and its sponsorship of the seventh-largest PAC in the nation could not be discounted. Nevertheless, the NRA could not automatically assume that it would be able either to veto gun-control legislation through its lobbying activities or to defeat anti-NRA congressmen seeking reelection in the future.

Questions for Discussion

1. If the NRA were to soften its hard-line policy views in the future, would it lose support from its membership—why or why not?

2. What does the article reveal about interest-group pluralism in the United States?

3. Have students research current NRA stands on prospective gun-control legislation. What do those stands reveal about the NRA's traditional desire to protect the right of Americans to bear arms?

Answer Guidelines

Once again, discussion should be left open-ended and flexible. Have students compare the above result with the failure of the NRA on the Brady Bill in 1991.

Theme E   Controlling Interest Groups and Lobbyists

Summary

Many policies have been enacted or proposed to regulate interest groups; all must deal with the fact that interest-group activity is a form of political speech protected by the First Amendment. Congress has, at least in theory, been concerned with the possible corrupting influence of pervasive lobbying activities. As far back as 1852, the House of Representatives tried to halt lobbyists posing as journalists from occupying newsmen's seats in the legislative chamber. The first few decades of the twentieth century saw a large number of congressional investigations into lobbying excesses. One result was legislation requiring the registration of lobbyists who represented holding companies before Congress, the Federal Power Commission, or the Securities and Exchange Commission (1935). In 1936 and 1938, similar restrictions were placed upon lobbyists for maritime interests and foreign governments. All of these attempts eventually led to the Federal Regulation of Lobbying Act of 1946, a law which unfortunately contained some serious flaws.

The 1946 Act did not directly restrict lobbying activities—it merely required disclosure and registration standards (quarterly financial reports, which disclosed the money received and spent for lobbying, had to be filed). The Supreme Court upheld this law but said that grass-roots lobbying involving direct contacts between citizens and officials could not be restricted. Disclosure rules have also posed problems for privacy: suppose you are a covert homosexual who gives money to a gay rights group, only to have your name published. Even where questions of individual rights are not involved, disclosure requirements may become so burdensome as to discourage smaller, less affluent groups.

The 1946 Act had a number of other weaknesses: (a) it applied only to lobbyists' efforts to influence Congress (not to the executive branch); (b) it covered only efforts to influence, not efforts to provide information, and (c) it did not apply to contracts between lobbyists and congressional staff members. Perhaps even more vital was the absence of enforcement mechanisms in the law. There was no agency monitoring compliance, and Congress appropriated no funds for oversight. Even the Justice Department has not been active in prosecuting violators of the law, having only five prosecutions from 1946 to 1979 to its credit (see *The Washington Lobby*, 3rd ed. Washington, DC: Congressional Quarterly Press, 1979, p. 20).

Since the 1946 law, congressional efforts to pass a stronger lobbying law have literally gone nowhere, although Congress did make a concerted effort to pass a new law in 1976. Lobbyists representing a diverse number of interest groups will likely voice a strong unified protest if similar legislation is proposed in the future.

Discussion Questions

1. Imagine you were going to write a new lobbying law. What elements or controls would you incorporate into the bill and why?
2. Should all lobbyists be banned from Capitol Hill—why or why not?

Additional Lecture Topic E-1

Can We Reform the Lobbying Process?

Hope Eastman, *Lobbying: A Constitutionally Protected Right*. Washington, DC: American Enterprise Institute, 1977. The author, a former ACLU official, argues that many of the current proposals to regulate lobbying run afoul of the Constitution. Pamphlet length.

Ronald J. Hrebenar and Ruth K. Scott, *Interest-Group Politics in America*. 2nd ed. Englewood Cliffs, NJ: Prentice-Hall, 1989. Chapter 8.

H. A. Malrood, *Group Politics in America: A New Approach*. Englewood Cliffs, NJ: Prentice-Hall, 1990.

Norman J. Ornstein and Shirley Elder, *Interest Groups, Lobbying and Policymaking*. Washington, DC: Congressional Quarterly Press, 1978. Chapter 4. A brief and useful history of lobby regulation, with a review of reform proposals.

Kay L. Schlozman and John T. Tierney, "More of the Same: Washington Pressure-Group Activity in a Decade of Change." *Journal of Politics*, May 1983.

Kay L. Schlozman and John T. Tierney, *Organized Interests and American Democracy*. New York: Harper & Row, 1986.

Philip Stern, *The Best Congress Money Can Buy*. New York: Pantheon, 1988.

The Washington Lobby. 5th ed. Washington, D.C.: Congressional Quarterly Press, 1987.

Graham Wooton. *Interest Groups: Policy and Politics in America*. Englewood Cliffs, NJ: Prentice-Hall, 1985. Chapter 8.

10

The Media

Overview and Objectives

In this chapter students will examine the historical evolution and present status of relations between the government and the news media—how the media affect government and politics and how government seeks to affect the media. After reading and reviewing the material in this chapter the student should be able to do each of the following:

1. Describe the evolution of journalism in American political history and indicate the differences between the party press and the mass media of today.

2. Demonstrate how the characteristics of the electronic media have affected the actions of public officials and candidates for national office.

3. Describe the impact of the pattern of ownership and control of the media on the dissemination of news and show how wire services and TV networks have affected national news coverage. Discuss the impact of the "national press."

4. Describe the rules that govern the media and contrast the regulation of electronic and print media. Indicate the impact of libel laws on freedom of the press and of government rules on broadcasters.

5. Assess the impact of the media on politics and indicate why it is so difficult to find evidence that can be used to make a meaningful and accurate assessment. Explain why the executive branch probably benefits at the expense of Congress.

6. Describe the "adversarial press" and the way in which reporters use their sources. Indicate how an administration may develop tactics to use against the adversarial press.

Chapter Outline with Keyed-in Resources

I. Journalism in American political history (THEME A: THE HISTORY AND STRUCTURE OF THE AMERICAN NEWS MEDIA)
   A. The party press
      1. Parties created and subsidized various newspapers
      2. Possible because circulation small, newspapers expensive, few advertisers
      3. Newspapers circulated among political and commercial elites
   B. The popular press
      1. Changes in society and technology made press self-supporting and mass readership
         a. High-speed press
         b. Telegraph

             c. Associated Press, 1848; objective reporting
             d. Urbanization allowed large numbers to support paper
             e. Government Printing Office—end of subsidies in 1860
          2. Influence of publishers, editors created partisan bias
             a. "Yellow journalism" to attract readers
             b. Hearst foments war against Spain
          3. Emergence of a common national culture
       C. Magazines of opinion
          1. Middle class favors new, progressive periodicals
             a. *Nation, Atlantic, Harper's* in 1850s and 1860s on behalf of certain issues
             b. *McClure's, Scribner's, Cosmopolitan* later on
          2. Individual writers gain national followings through investigative reporting
          3. Number of competing newspapers declines, as does sensationalism
          4. Today, national magazines focusing on politics account for a small and declining fraction of magazines
       D. Electronic journalism (ADDITIONAL LECTURE TOPIC A-1)
          1. Radio arrives in 1920s, television in 1940s
          2. Politicians could address voters directly but people could easily ignore
          3. But fewer politicians could be covered
             a. President routinely covered
             b. Others must use bold tactics
          4. Recent rise in talk show as political forum has increased politicians' access to electronic media
             a. "Big three" networks have made it harder for candidates by shortening sound-bites
             b. But politicians have more sources: cable, early-morning news, news magazine shows
             c. These new sources feature lengthy interviews
          5. No research on consequences of two changes:
             a. Recent access of politicians to electronic media
             b. Narrowcasting, where segmented audience targeted
          6. Politicians continue to seek visuals even after they are elected
          7. New era of electronic journalism emerging
   II. The structure of the media (THEME B: MEDIA OWNERSHIP AND ITS IMPACT ON THE NEWS) (ADDITIONAL LECTURE TOPIC B-1)
       A. Degree of competition
          1. Newspapers
             a. Number of newspapers has not declined

The number of Americans with subscriptions to newspapers has dropped from 35.7 percent in 1927 to 25 percent in 1990.

             b. Number of cities with multiple papers *has* declined
                (1) Sixty percent of cities had competing newspapers in 1900
                (2) Four percent in 1972
          2. Radio and television
             a. Intensely competitive, becoming more so

Proliferation of television stations exploded in the 1980s, but with a twist: the increase occurred in the number of "independent" television stations, those not affiliated with any of the three major networks. Between 1983 and 1989, independent stations almost doubled in number.

             b. Composed mostly of locally owned and managed enterprises unlike in Europe

Ownership of network television is monopolized by one institutional source—banks; Of the major stockholders of the three networks (NBC, ABC, and CBS), 75 percent are banks.

             c. Orientation to local market

            d. Limitations by FCC—widespread ownership created
      B. The national media
         1. Existence somewhat offsets local orientation
         2. Consists of
            a. Wire services
            b. National magazines
            c. Television networks
            d. Newspapers with national readerships
         3. Significance
            a. Washington officials follow it closely
            b. Reporters and editors a distinctive group from local press
               (1) Better paid
               (2) From more prestigious universities
               (3) More liberal outlook

In 1984, 55 percent of journalists classified themselves as liberal, compared to only 17 percent as conservative.

               (4) Do investigative or interpretive stories
         4. Roles played (THEME C: MEDIA SELECTION OF, AND BIAS IN, THE NEWS)
            a. Gatekeeper: what is news, for how long
               (1) Auto safety
               (2) Water pollution
               (3) Prescription drugs
               (4) Crime rates
            b. Scorekeeper: who is winning, losing
               (1) Attention to Iowa, New Hampshire
               (2) Gary Hart in 1984
            c. Watchdog: investigate personalities and expose scandals
               (1) Hart's name, birthdate, in 1984; Donna Rice in 1987
               (2) Watergate (Woodward and Bernstein)
III. Rules governing the media (THEME D: GOVERNMENT INFLUENCE ON THE MEDIA)
      A. Newspapers versus electronic media
         1. Newspapers almost entirely free from government regulation
            a. Prosecutions only after the fact and limited: libel, obscenity, incitement
         2. Radio and television licensed, regulated

The Supreme Court justifies tighter restrictions on the broadcast media than on the press because of the "scarcity" of airwave frequencies. Since only a finite number of frequencies is available, the government must allocate them in the public interest. The sinking of the *Titanic* brought this situation to the government's attention; the ship could not transmit an SOS for some time because no open frequency existed.

      B. Confidentiality of sources
         1. Reporters want right to keep sources confidential
         2. Most states and federal government disagree

By 1991, twenty-six states had enacted "shield laws" providing journalists with varying degrees of protection to withhold the identity of confidential sources from courts.

         3. Supreme Court allows government to compel reporters to divulge information in court if it bears on a crime
         4. Myron Farber jailed for contempt
         5. Police search of newspaper office upheld
      C. Regulation and deregulation
         1. FCC licensing
            a. Seven years for radio
            b. Five years for television
            c. Stations must serve "community needs"

In the presidential elections of both 1980 and 1984, the FCC prohibited the airing of movies in which Ronald Reagan appeared on television as being in the public interest.

        d. Public service, other aspects can be regulated
- 2. Recent movement to deregulate
  - a. License renewal by postcard
  - b. No hearing unless opposed
  - c. Relaxation of rule enforcement
- 3. Other radio and television regulations
  - a. Equal-time rule
  - b. Right of reply rule
  - c. Political editorializing rule
- 4. Fairness doctrine was abolished in 1987

In announcing the abandonment of the fairness doctrine, the chair of the FCC commented: "The First Amendment does not guarantee a fair press, only a free one." An effort by Congress to restore the doctrine was vetoed by President Reagan.

- D. Campaigning
  1. Equal-time rule applies
     - a. Equal access for all candidates
     - b. Rates no higher than cheapest commercial rate
     - c. Debates formerly had to include all candidates
       - (1) Reagan-Carter debate sponsored by LWV as "news event"
       - (2) Now stations and networks can sponsor
  2. Efficiency in reaching voters
     - a. Works well when market and district overlap
     - b. Fails when they are not aligned
     - c. More Senate than House candidates buy television time

IV. The effects of the media on politics
- A. Studies on media impact on elections
  1. Generally inconclusive, because of citizens'...
     - a. Selective attention

According to Doris Graber, newspaper readers are highly selective. The average person reads only about 20 percent of newspaper stories in full.

        b. Mental tune-out
  2. Products can be sold more easily than candidates
  3. Newspaper endorsements of candidates
     - a. Often for Republicans locally, while Democrats won nationally

During the 1988 election, 31.4 percent of U.S. newspapers surveyed endorsed George Bush for president and only 13.3 percent Michael Dukakis. Most newspapers, however, made no endorsement at all in the election.

        b. But worth 5 percent of vote to endorsed Democrats
- B. Major effect: on how politics is conducted not how people vote
  1. Conventions scheduled to accommodate television
  2. Candidates win party nomination via media exposure
     - a. Estes Kefauver
  3. Issues established by media attention
     - a. Environment
     - b. Consumer issues
  4. Issues that are important to citizens similar to those in media
     - a. TV influences political agenda
     - b. But people less likely to take media cues on matters that affect them personally
  5. Newspaper readers see bigger candidate differences than do TV viewers
  6. TV news affects popularity of presidents; commentaries have short-run impact

V. Government and the news
   A. Prominence of the president
      1. Theodore Roosevelt: systematic cultivation of the press
      2. Franklin Roosevelt: press secretary a major instrument for cultivating press

The relationship between the media and the president has changed to a more adversarial one. To illustrate, the media largely abided FDR's request not to publish photos of him in his wheelchair. FDR was concerned about weakening confidence in the government at a time of national emergency.

      3. Press secretary today: large staff, many functions
      4. White House press corps focus of press secretary
      5. Unparalleled personalization of government
   B. Coverage of Congress
      1. Never equal to that of president; members resentful
      2. House quite restrictive
         a. No cameras on floor until 1978
         b. Sometimes refused to permit coverage of committees
         c. Gavel-to-gavel coverage of proceedings since 1979
      3. Senate more open
         a. Hearings since Kefauver; TV coverage of sessions in 1986
         b. Incubator for presidential contenders through committee hearings
VI. Interpreting political news (ADDITIONAL LECTURE TOPICS D-1, D-2)
   A. Are news stories slanted?
      1. Most people believe media, especially television where they get most news

Television has clearly eclipsed all other media in the area of news. Leo Bogart estimates that 45 percent of a person's information on issues is derived from television, only 30 percent from newspapers.

         a. But percentage increasing among those who think media biased
         b. Press itself thinks it is unbiased
      2. Liberal bias of national media elite, especially national media

Austin Ranney's analysis of the media concludes that cynicism pervades reporting, not liberalism. The loss of public confidence in the government may be the consequence.

      3. Various factors influence how stories are written
         a. Deadlines
         b. Audience attraction
         c. Fairness, truth imposed by professional norms
         d. Reporters', editors' beliefs
      4. Types of stories
         a. Routine stories: public events, regularly covered
            (1) Reported similarly by all media; opinions of journalists have least effect
            (2) Can be misreported: Tet offensive
         b. Selected stories: public but not routinely covered
            (1) Selection involves perception of what is important
            (2) Liberal and conservative papers do different stories
            (3) Increasing in number; reflect views of press more than experts or public
         c. Insider stories: not usually made public; motive problem
      5. Studies on effects of journalistic opinions
         a. Nuclear power: antinuclear slant
         b. School busing: probusing
         c. Media "spin" almost inevitable
      6. Insider stories raise questions of informant's motives
         a. From official background briefings of the past . . .
         b. . . . To critical inside stories of post-Watergate era

B. Why are there so many news leaks?
      1. Constitution: separation of powers
          a. Power is decentralized
          b. Branches of government compete
          c. Not illegal to print most secrets

Sometimes, however, even nonclassified material can be banned. In an unusual case, a C+ student at Princeton wrote a senior thesis on how to build a hydrogen bomb. Although the information was obtained from nonclassified documents, the thesis itself was classified top secret by the government. The student received an A for the course.

      2. Adversarial press since Watergate
          a. Press and politicians distrust each other
          b. Media are eager to embarrass officials
          c. Competition for awards, etc.
          d. Spurred by Irangate: arms for hostages
      3. Cynicism created era of attack journalism
          a. Most people do not like this kind of news
          b. Cynicism of media mirrors public's increasing cynicism of media
          c. People believe media slant coverage
      4. Public confidence in big business down, and now media are big business
      5. Drive for market share forces media to use theme of corruption
  C. Government constraints on journalists
      1. Reporters must strike a balance between . . .
          a. Expression of views
          b. Retaining sources
      2. Abundance of congressional staffers makes it easier
      3. Governmental tools to fight back
          a. Numerous press officers
          b. Press releases—"canned news"
          c. Leaks and background stories to favorites
          d. Bypass national press to local
          e. Presidential rewards and punishments for reporters based on their stories

Important Terms

adversarial press The suspicious nature of the national press toward public officials in seeking to break an embarrassing story that will win for its author honor, prestige, and sometimes money.

*attack journalism The current era of media coverage that seizes upon any bit of information or rumor that might call into question the qualifications or character of a public official. It is based on the cynicism and distrust of government and elected officials.

*background story A tactic by government officials to win journalistic friends. The official purportedly explains current policy on condition that the source of the information not be identified by name.

confidentiality Reporters' keeping sources of their stories secret. Most states and the federal government allow courts to decide whether the need of a journalist to protect sources outweighs the interests of the government in gathering evidence in a criminal investigation.

*equal-time rule An FCC regulation requiring that if a station sells time to one candidate seeking an office, it must sell time to the opposing candidate as well.

*fairness doctrine An FCC rule abolished in 1987 which required broadcasters to give time to opposing views if they broadcast a program giving one side of a controversial issue.

*feature stories A type of news story that involves a public event not routinely covered by reporters and that requires a reporter to take initiative to select the story and persuade an editor to run it.

Federal Communications Commission An agency of the federal government with authority to develop regulations for the broadcast media.

gatekeeper The role played by the media in influencing what subjects become national political issues and for how long.

*insider stories A type of news story that involves information not usually made public which requires investigative work on the part of a reporter or a "leak" by some public official. These stories frequently raise the issue of a reporter's motive.

*loaded language The use of words to persuade people of something without actually making a clear argument for it.

*market An area easily reached by a television signal.

mental tune-out The attitude of a person who ignores or is irritated by messages from radio or television which do not agree with his or her existing beliefs.

*muckraker A journalist who investigates the activities of public officials and organizations, especially business firms, seeking to expose and publicize misconduct or corruption.

party press Newspapers created, sponsored, and controlled by political parties to further their interests. This form of press existed in the early years of the American republic. Circulation was chiefly among political and commercial elites.

*political editorializing rule A regulation of the FCC providing a candidate the right to respond if a broadcaster endorses the opposing candidate.

popular press Self-supporting daily newspapers aimed at a mass readership. This form of press was made possible by technological advances that enabled cheap printing of massive numbers of issues.

prior restraint Government censorship of the press. The First Amendment makes such censorship difficult except under narrowly defined circumstances.

*right of reply rule A regulation by the FCC permitting a person the right to respond if attacked on a broadcast other than in a regular news program.

routine stories A type of news story that involves a public event regularly covered by reporters. These stories are related in almost exactly the same way by all the media. The political opinions of journalists have the least effect on these stories.

scorekeeper The role played by the national media in keeping track of and helping make political reputations.

*selective attention The perception of only what one wants to perceive from television or radio reporting.

*sound-bite A video clip used on nightly newscasts of a presidential contender speaking. The average length of such clips has decreased, making it harder for candidates to get their message across.

*trial balloon A tactic by an anonymous source to "float" a policy that the source supports to ascertain public reaction to it before the policy is actually proposed.

watchdog The role played by the national media in investigating political personalities and exposing scandals.

yellow journalism The use of sensationalism to attract a large readership for a newspaper.

Theme A The History and Structure of the American News Media

Summary

Changes in the organization and technology of the press have brought major changes in the organization of American politics. In the era of the *party press* in the early years of the Republic, parties and factions established newspapers and supported them by giving journalists government jobs. The press was relentlessly partisan and reached only the commercial and political elites. Changes in society and technology made the *popular press* possible. Urbanization created large cities that could support mass circulations, and the invention of the rotary press made producing papers cheaply and quickly possible. In order to create mass circulation, newspapers—under the leadership of men like Joseph Pulitzer and William Randolph Hearst—stressed violence, romance, patriotism, and exposes of wrongdoing in business and government. The mass circulation newspaper facilitated the emergence of mass politics, the mobilization of voters, and the development of strong party loyalties. The rising middle class was repelled by the *yellow journalism* of the popular press and provided the market for *magazines of opinion*. During their peak around the turn of the century, these magazines promoted the causes of the Progressive movement: business regulation, the purification of municipal politics, and civil service reform. *Muckrakers* such as Lincoln Steffens set the pattern for today's "investigative reporting." *Electronic journalism*, which began with the emergence of radio in the 1920s and continued with the spread of television in the late 1940s, places great stress on the personal characteristics of politicians—whether they are attractive, speak well, or behave in a manner sufficiently colorful to justify inclusion in newscasts that must hold audience attention.

In the contemporary media era, the media's structure is characterized by (a) a decline in the number of cities in which there are competing newspapers; (b) an orientation to the local market; (c) the decentralized nature of the broadcasting industry; (d) three national television networks, over seven hundred television stations, six thousand cable systems, and nearly seven thousand radio stations; (e) national media consisting of the news magazines, television networks, and newspapers such as the *New York Times*, the *Washington Post*, and the *Wall Street Journal*.

Discussion Questions

1. In the United States, the concept of a "party press" has a negative connotation by imputing bias to a newspaper. Yet many major newspapers in Western Europe are subsidized by political parties and retain a reputation of quality. Consider some of the benefits of a party press. Doesn't the desire of American newspapers to be "fair" prevent hard questions from being asked? Is political debate in the United States less informed for this reason?

2. Doesn't a "popular" press hurt quality by pandering to the lowest common denominator of interest and taste? If so, what has prevented American newspapers from emulating the British press by featuring sensational stories?

3. Explain how the localism and decentralized qualities of the American news media contribute to the promotion of democracy.

Additional Lecture Topic A-1

Media Structure and the Policy Process

Dean Alger, *The Media and Politics*. Englewood Cliffs, NJ: Prentice-Hall, 1989.

David Broder, *Behind the Front Page*, New York: Simon & Schuster, 1987.

Doris A. Graber, ed. *Media Power in Politics*, 2nd ed. Washington, DC: Congressional Quarterly Press, 1989. An excellent collection of essays that emphasize the effects of the mass media on the political system in general and on subsystems such as Congress, parties, and lobbies.

David Halberstam, *The Powers That Be*. New York: Knopf, 1979. An excellent treatise on how the media (*Time*, CBS, and the *Los Angeles Times*) have shaped the course of American politics.

Michael Parenti, *Inventing Reality: The Politics of the Mass Media*. New York: St. Martin's Press, 1986. See Chapters 2 and 3.

Theme B	Media Ownership and Its Impact on the News

The mass media in the United States have undergone a transformation in terms of ownership—from party-sponsored newspapers to ownership by powerful individuals to corporate control today. To what degree does the content of the news hinge on the source of ownership? The Federal Communications Commission (FCC) has stepped in to encourage wide ownership of the broadcast media. No one individual may own more than one AM radio station, one FM radio station, or one television station in any given market; nationally, no one may own more than twelve television stations and twelve AM and twelve FM radio stations; and the networks may not compel a local affiliate to accept any particular broadcast. The Supreme Court has condoned such attempts to create diversity on the grounds that broadcasting is different from the press. As Justice Frankfurter wrote in 1943, "Unlike other modes of expression, radio inherently is not available to all. That is its unique characteristic, and that is why, unlike other modes of expression, it is subject to governmental regulation."

Yet this attempt at producing diversity in information by limiting ownership is undercut by at least two factors. First, the FCC is hardly equipped to deal with its supervisory role over the broadcast industry. In 1993, the FCC was responsible for regulating 1,505 television stations, 11,275 radio stations and 11,385 cable systems with a staff of only 1,783 personnel. The resources clearly do not correspond to the task. Second, the power of the three major television networks over the content of national news is not as easily displaced. In the 1970s, according to Lewis Lapham, 90 percent of the national news reaching Americans via television was from the three major networks. The emergence of cable networks has diminished, but certainly not replaced, the network monopoly of television news. Thus while ownership of broadcasting is dispersed, information on national politics remains concentrated in the hands of the major networks.

Newspaper ownership is somewhat deceptive. On the one hand, the number of newspapers in circulation has not declined in this century. On the other hand, Thomas Dye reports that nine chains account for one-third of total newspaper circulation in the country. It seems that the large volume of newspapers being published is partially offset by the concentration of ownership in a few hands. Michael Parenti, a neo-Marxist analyst, concludes that the "objectivity" in news reporting really means presenting opinions "that support existing arrangements of economic and political power." This interpretation can surely be supported by the facts just presented, but it ignorers much as well. The national media are intensely competitive and it is they, not the local stations, that officials in Washington follow. More important, it does not take into consideration what people believe and how much of that is derived from the media.

Discussion Questions

1. Is it legal in the United States for the owner of a radio or television station to tell newscasters what to report, or is this a violation of the First Amendment? Should the FCC be empowered to prevent an owner from spewing racist beliefs on radio? Would the government's authority to ban such speech be any different with regard to newspapers?

2. How can the FCC constitutionally deny ownership of a radio or television station (which it does do) without violating the First Amendment? When should such denials occur? For example, the FCC threatened to block the purchase of additional radio stations by the company that employed "shock jock" Howard Stern for its history of airing "indecent" language. Is this appropriate since indecent language regularly appears in magazines?

Additional Lecture Topic B-1

Media Ownership and Controlling the News

Elie Abel, ed., *What's News*. San Francisco: Institute for Contemporary Studies, 1981.

Ben Bagdikian, *The Media Monopoly*. Boston: Beacon Press, 1983.

Benjamin Compaine, ed., *Who Owns the Media? Concentration of Ownership in the Mass Communication Industry*. New York: Harmony Books, 1979.

Herbert J. Gans. *Deciding What's News*. New York: Vintage, 1980.

Edward Herman and Noam Chomsky, *Manufacturing Consent: The Political Economy of the Mass Media*. New York: Pantheon, 1988.

Jarol Manheim, *All of the People All of the Time: Strategic Communications and American Politics*. Armonk, NY: M. E. Sharpe, 1991.

William Rusher, *The Coming Battle for the Media: Curbing the Power of the Media Elite*. New York: William Morrow, 1988.

Theme C Media Selection of, and Bias in, the News

Summary

The mass media do not simply mirror reality. The process of selection, editing, and emphasis provides an opportunity for slanting the news, further enhanced by the general absence of "fast-breaking" stories. Thomas Dye estimates that 70 percent of television news stories are preplanned (selected or insider), with only 30 percent involving spontaneous events. This potential to bias the news is important to recognize given that the national press is staffed by people who are more liberal than the public as a whole. A 1984 poll by the *Los Angeles Times* discovered that 55% of journalists identified themselves as liberal and 17 percent as conservative. The complaint of media bias even reached Congress in 1992 when Senator Jesse Helms attempted to curtail the budget of the Public Broadcasting System (PBS) for perceived liberal prejudice.

The national press not only reports the news but also fulfills three additional roles for the public: gatekeeper—determining what will be on the political agenda; scorekeeper—passing judgment on who is winning and who is losing; and watchdog—exposing scandals and intrigues. These multiple functions suggest that the media have a profound impact on politics. But social scientists have been unable to detect any great ability of the media to swing votes toward one or another candidate. From a logical standpoint, an influential press would have converted the American public to liberalism long ago. Michael Parenti, a critic of the national press, challenges even the common assumption of media distortion in the liberal direction. He contends that the objective of the news media "is not to produce an alert, critical, and informed citizenry but the kind of people who will accept an opinion universe dominated by corporate and governmental elites, almost all of whom share the same ideological perspective about political and economic reality."

It is less likely that the media mold public opinion than arrange the political agenda by determining what issues become prominent. This constitutes an entirely different sort of influence. In this capacity, the national press does exhibit a kind of bias. Its stories focus on activities in Washington D.C. Ronald Berkman and Laura Kitch report that twelve of fifteen lead stories on the network evening news come from the nation's capital. What makes this fact significant is that reporters at the national level have greater occasion to distort the news, since they have freedom to write investigative or interpretive stories rather than merely factual accounts of events. FCC rules, however, have achieved a degree of balance by forbidding monopoly control of the media, forcing a local orientation outside the network news programs.

Discussion Questions

1. The television series "All in the Family" broke new ground in programming. However, much of the American public initially misunderstood the show's message: to demonstrate the foolishness of Archie Bunker's bigotry. In 1972, 41 percent believed that Archie won his argument at show's end, 64 percent "admired" Archie, and bigoted individuals actually liked the show more than nonbigoted ones. What do these data indicate about the influence of television over public opinion? Why were people misinterpreting the show's message? What factors are preventing the media from molding public opinion? (Note to instructor: The answer is "selective perception.")

2. The media have much freedom in the selection and publication of material in the United States. In 1979, *The Progressive* magazine announced its intention to publish the blueprint to a hydrogen bomb. Why would the magazine do such a thing? Should the government intervene? The blueprint *was* published.

3. If most reporters hold liberal views, why hasn't the American public become more liberal over the years? Could reporters alter public opinion if they tried? Have students consider the text's analysis of the influence of the media on public opinion in answering this question.

4. What are the some recent examples of the media's role as *watchdog*? Is the watchdog function ever exercised in a biased way? How?

5. Does it matter that reporters of the national media tend to be more liberal than the public at large, as well as more liberal than reporters in the local media? What factors might offset the liberalism of reporters in determining the ideological balance of media output?

6. What is the philosophical justification for tighter regulation of the broadcast media than of newspapers? (*Note*: In theory, the airwaves are publicly owned and merely held in trust by broadcast stations.) If the government is largely required to keep its hands off newspapers, why should a similar policy not be required for broadcasting?

7. Studies show that the issues the public considers important are substantially the same issues featured by the media. Does this prove that the media set the agenda? What other interpretation of this piece of information is possible?

8. On what *sorts* of issues would we expect the media to have the most impact—whether in setting the agenda, shaping attitudes, or determining how politics is conducted? Would we expect the media to have greater influence on:

    a. Domestic issues or foreign-policy issues?

    b. Issues where the parties have traditional positions, or issues that cut across party lines?

    c. New issues or old issues?

    d. National issues or local issues?

    e. Socially divisive issues, where deeply committed segments of the population are lined up against each other, or "salience" issues (such as corruption or the economy), where almost all Americans share similar notions of what is right but are not sure which policy or candidate can achieve it?

f. Young people or old people?

g. People much exposed to the media or people who are little exposed to the media?

Data and Perspectives for Analysis

A. Public Evaluation of Various Media

All media are not equal in the eyes of the public. Some are more reliable, both in terms of accuracy and neutrality. Present the data below to your students and have them determine whether it corresponds to the text's assertions on the media and whether it reflects their own opinions. What accounts for the differences in perception about the various media?

	Newspapers	News Magazines	Radio	Local TV News	National TV News
Accurate	73%	78%	77%	81%	81%
Arrogant	28%	37%	24%	25%	39%
Biased	62%	60%	52%	54%	61%
Intelligent	83%	87%	85%	85%	90%

Source: Adapted from Gallup Poll, October 1984.

B. Media Bias and Word Choice

Compare the following terms used by the *Chicago Tribune* and the *New York Times* to describe the same persons, policies, and programs. (The list was compiled in the 1930s, but it still serves as a good tool for studying the media.)

Various Chicago Tribune *Terms and Other Terms Used in the Same Connection by the* New York Times

CT—Radical NYT—Progressive	CT—Farm dictatorship NYT—Crop control
CT—Government witch hunting NYT—Senate investigation	CT—Loyal workers NYT—Nonstrikers
CT—Regimentation NYT—Regulation	CT—Inquisitor NYT—Investigator
CT—Communist CIO leader NYT—Maritime leader	CT—CIO dictator NYT—CIO chieftain
CT—Labor agitator NYT—Labor organizer	CT—Alien NYT—Foreign
CT—The dole NYT—Home relief	CT—Mass picketing NYT—Picketing

Source: S. S. Sargent, "Emotional Stereotypes in the *Chicago Tribune,*" *Sociometry,* No. 2, 1939, p. 74.

1. What can one infer about the editorial policies of the *Tribune* from the terms it used?

2. Pick a current issue and analyze the sorts of words partisans and the media on each side of the issue use. Example: proabortion can be "prochoice" or "killing babies." Antiabortion can be "prolife" or "imposing religious views on others." Think of other examples, and make a list on the board.

C. News Headlines

Newspaper headlines represent a *capsule interpretation* of a news event. Like any interpretation, the headline may be fair or unfair, accurate or inaccurate.

1. Some precisely opposite interpretations of the same event are possible.

    JAPAN INDICATES IT WOULD NOT JOIN IN TRADE CURBS ON IRAN AND SOVIET (*New York Times*, Jan. 17, 1980)

    JAPAN TO JOIN DRIVE FOR CURBS ON IRAN DESPITE OIL THREAT (*Washington Post*, Jan. 17, 1980)

    ALCOHOLIC STUDY SUPPORTS FINDING THAT SOME CAN RESUME DRINKING (*New York Times*, Jan. 24, 1980)

    EARLIER STUDY ON ALCOHOLICS REFUTED; MOST CAN'T LEARN TO DRINK MODERATELY (*Washington Post*, Jan. 24, 1980)

2. Sometimes the same newspaper will run contrary headlines in different editions.

    PLAN FLAWS BLAMED FOR ABORTIVE RESCUE (*Milwaukee Journal*, Aug. 24, 1980. Sunrise ed.)

    SECRECY HANGUPS DOOMED IRAN RESCUE (*Milwaukee Journal*, Aug. 24, 1980. Late 2nd ed.)

3. The tone of a headline can be either soothing or terrifying. These headlines appeared in various morning papers on March 31, 1979, during the Three Mile Island nuclear accident.

    RACE WITH NUCLEAR DISASTER (*New York Post*)

    1,200 FLEE AS U.S. WARNS OF ATOMIC FUEL MELTDOWN (*Chicago Tribune*)

    U.S. AIDES SEE A RISK OF MELTDOWN AT PENNSYLVANIA NUCLEAR PLANT (*New York Times*)

    "MELT" CALLED REMOTE; MANY EVACUATE AREA (*Washington Star*)

    PLANT STABLE; NO EVACUATION, MELTDOWN POSSIBILITY "REMOTE" (*Miami Herald*)

    CHANCES OF MELTDOWN TERMED "VERY REMOTE" (*Columbia [S.C.] Record*)

    A-PLANT MELTDOWN FEARED (*Milwaukee Sentinel*)

4. Sometimes headlines clearly reflect the ideology of the newspaper. During Watergate, the following headlines appeared over identical wire-service stories.

    PROSECUTOR FAILS TO PROVE NIXON INVOLVEMENT (*Phoenix Republic*)

    NIXON INVOLVEMENT SUSPECTED, NOT YET PROVEN (*Boston Globe*)

Additional Lecture Topics

C-1. A Media Bias? Left- and Right-Wing Views

Robert Cirino, *Don't Blame the People*. New York: Vintage, 1971. Representing the left, Cirino presents a large number of cases where some information he feels the public needed to know was not covered by the press. See also Ben Bagdikian, *The Media Monopoly*. Boston: Beacon Press, 1983.

The *Columbia Journalism Review, Washington Journalism Review*, and the *AIM Report*, all periodicals. See a selection of the latest issues. The *AIM Report* criticizes the media from the hard right, whereas the two journalism reviews are more centrist. The *Columbia Journalism Review* publishes the reports of the National News Council.

Edith Efron, *The News Twisters*. Los Angeles: Nash, 1971. Representing the political right, Efron does an extensive content analysis of the network news treatment of the 1968 presidential election, as well as a more general analysis. See also S. Robert Lichter et al., *The Media Elite*. Bethesda, MD: Adler & Adler, 1986.

C-2. How Has the Media Affected the Political Process?

Dean Alger, *The Media and Politics*. Englewood Cliffs, NJ: Prentice-Hall, 1989.

W. Lance Bennett, *The Politics of Illusion*. New York: Longman, 1988.

George Comstock, "The Impact of Television on American Institutions." *Journal of Communications*, Spring 1978, pp. 12–18.

Edwin Diamond, *The Tin Kazoo: Television, Politics, and the News*. Cambridge: MIT Press, 1975.

Shanto Iyengar and Donald R. Kinder, *News That Matters*. Chicago: University of Chicago Press, 1987.

Richard Joslyn, *Mass Media and Elections*. Reading, MA: Addison-Wesley, 1984.

Thomas E. Patterson, *The Mass Media Election*. New York: Praeger, 1980.

Charles Press and Kenneth Verburg, *American Politicians and Journalists*. Glenview: IL: Scott, Foresman/Little, Brown, 1988.

Austin Ranney, *Channels of Power: The Impact of Television on American Politics*. New York: Basic Books, 1983.

Michael J. Robinson and Margaret A. Sheehan, *Over the Wire and on TV: CBS and UPI in Campaign 80*. New York: Russell Sage Foundation, 1983.

Michael J. Robinson, "Public Affairs Television and the Growth of Political Malaise: The Case of 'The Selling of the Pentagon.'" *American Political Science Review*, June 1976, pp. 409–432.

Michael J. Robinson, "Television and American Politics: 1956-1976." *Public Interest*, Summer 1977.

Latty Sabato, *Feeding Frenzy: How Attack Journalism Has Transformed American Politics*. New York: Macmillan, 1991.

Robert Rutherford Smith, "Mythic Elements in Television News." *Journal of Communication*, Winter 1979, pp. 78–82.

Where the previous lecture topic deals with the supposed ability of the media to bias public opinion to the left or right through straightforward manipulation, this literature suggests many more subtle and complicated possibilities of how mass media may have changed our political process. Note that, though *provocative suggestions* are plentiful here, hard evidence is scarce.

Abstract 1 for Theme C

Do Television Media Distort the News? A Pro/Con Discussion

In Herbert Levine's *Point-Counterpoint* (Glenview, IL: Scott-Foresman, 1983), an edited collection of readings in American government, authors Marvin Maurer and Herbert Schlosser (former president of NBC) debate the connection of television media to news distortion. Maurer, a political scientist, argues that television news "is helping to undermine traditional values and beliefs necessary for any established order to function" (p. 148). In other words, television's "scandal-minded" approach threatens those ideals of national pride, family concern, and respect for the law and authority. In short, too little time is given to positive news about the nation and its leaders.

This negative reporting is due in large measure to television's need to hold the interest of a large audience and attain large ratings. According to Maurer, the television networks will "fictionalize" events, cooperate with extremist groups, and ignore issues that do not seem to be attracting viewers. (As an example, television ignored the slaughters in communist-controlled Cambodia because of audience lack of interest.) Maurer concludes with the following observation:

> Television, then, is by no means a neutral reporting instrument.... Television is able to alter once positively held views about American institutions and, perhaps even more important, reduce the viewer's belief in his own ability to cope with and solve political problems.... It is clear ... that ... there is no effective force capable of countering television's undermining of America's leaders and institutions. (p. 151)

Conversely, Herbert Schlosser refutes the bad image of TV by asserting that "charges of bias can usually be attributed to any news report that does not coincide with the complainer's own point of view." Overriding all considerations, according to Schlosser, is the fact that the "independent news judgments formed by professional journalists hold greater promise of contributing to an informed public than any official truth dictated by government." Also, Schlosser quotes some public-opinion polls that reveal a strong pattern of support for television as a medium of information.

Schlosser cautions that there is an (illogical) temptation to blame TV for American society's problems. Television, as a free broadcasting medium, is a bulwark against public or private tyranny, "a vital communications force and a means for informing the public of its fears, its hopes, its needs and controversies.... If it were to be dispersed, the government and other self-serving interests—for whatever their purpose—could dominate the resulting fragments to the damage of the public at large." In essence, Schlosser sees TV as a "conveyor of reality and an instrument of democracy" (p. 155).

Questions for Discussion

1. Which argument—Maurer's or Schlosser's—is more compelling, and why?
2. Would federal regulation of the national mass media improve the media's overall performance, or would this be a dangerous idea? Discuss the merits and demerits of the suggestion.

Answer Guidelines

You can expect a variety of ideas from your students. Certainly, the idea of protection under the First Amendment and the fact that television is a profit-seeking medium should be included in the discussion.

Theme D Government Influence on the Media

Summary

A free press is a rarity in the world: one study of ninety-four nations found that only sixteen had a high degree of press freedom. Even among democracies that do have a high degree of press freedom, many have restrictions not found here. Britain has an Official Secrets Act that can be used to punish any "leak" of confidential governmental information. In France, broadcasting is controlled by a government agency that acts to protect the image of the government in power.

There are significant governmental restraints on what the American media can print or broadcast, however.

1. *Libel*. To sue a news organization for libel successfully, one must show that what was published was not merely untrue but was printed maliciously—that is, with "reckless disregard" for its truth or falsity. This is very difficult to do.
2. *Obscenity*. Governments in the United States may outlaw obscenity; however, the definition of obscenity has been steadily narrowed by the federal courts. Laws against obscenity have no effect on newspapers and magazines primarily interested in reporting political news.

3. *Incitement.* Media may not directly incite someone to commit an illegal act. However, the mere advocacy of, say, the violent overthrow of the government, is protected under the First Amendment.

A newspaper may, in theory, be punished for any of the foregoing, but none of them may be used as a basis for *prior restraint*: government action to prevent the publication of the material.

Radio and television face further controls.

1. *Licensing.* To stay in business, every broadcaster must have a license from the Federal Communications Commission (FCC), and the license must be renewed every seven years for a radio station and every five years for a television station. This makes broadcasters quite sensitive to the FCC's view of what constitutes the "informational needs" of the community. Recently, a move to deregulate broadcasting that would allow each station to define and serve community needs has gained prominence.

2. *The equal-time provision.* If a broadcaster allows time for one candidate for public office, it must allow equal time for all other candidates. (Newscasts are exempt.) Because "all other candidates" include minor party candidates to whom few people really want to listen, in order to stage a presidential debate it is necessary either for Congress to suspend the rule (as it did in 1960) or for a private organization like the League of Women Voters to sponsor the debate (as in 1976 and 1980). Though laws guarantee that candidates can buy time at favorable rates on television, television may not always be the most efficient way of reaching the voters.

Given the weakness of government controls on the media, it is not surprising that officials devise other strategies to manipulate the media. These may include the gift of *background stories* with much inside information to favored reporters, private tongue-lashings administered to reporters who publish embarrassing stories (a technique used by Kennedy and Johnson), and public attacks on the press (used by Nixon). In the long run, the press wins.

Discussion Questions

1. The media have much freedom in the selection and publication of material in the United States. In 1979, for example, the *Progressive* magazine announced its intention to publish the blueprint to a hydrogen bomb in its next issue. Should the government have intervened to prevent publication? What standards should be used in determining when information could be kept from publication? It should be noted that the blueprint was eventually published. Should a government agency like the FCC be established to regulate the press?

2. Freedom of press has greater First Amendment protection than freedom of broadcasting. To illustrate, cigarette advertisements are forbidden on radio and television but not in newspapers and magazines. Are the two forms of media so different to justify this disparity in treatment? How so? Doesn't the decentralization of the broadcast media make enforcement more difficult?

Data and Perspectives for Analysis

The Broadcast Policy-Making System

The Federal Communications Commission is hardly in a position to make regulatory policy on its own. It is enmeshed in a complicated web of political forces, with its regulations reflecting the outcomes of compromises. Students rarely comprehend the intricate process by which broadcasting policy is formulated in this country. Replicate and distribute the following diagram to your students and have them attempt to untangle the logic of the regulatory process. Ask them to explain how the FCC is capable of establishing quality policy given the cross-pressures it must endure.

The Regulatory Process

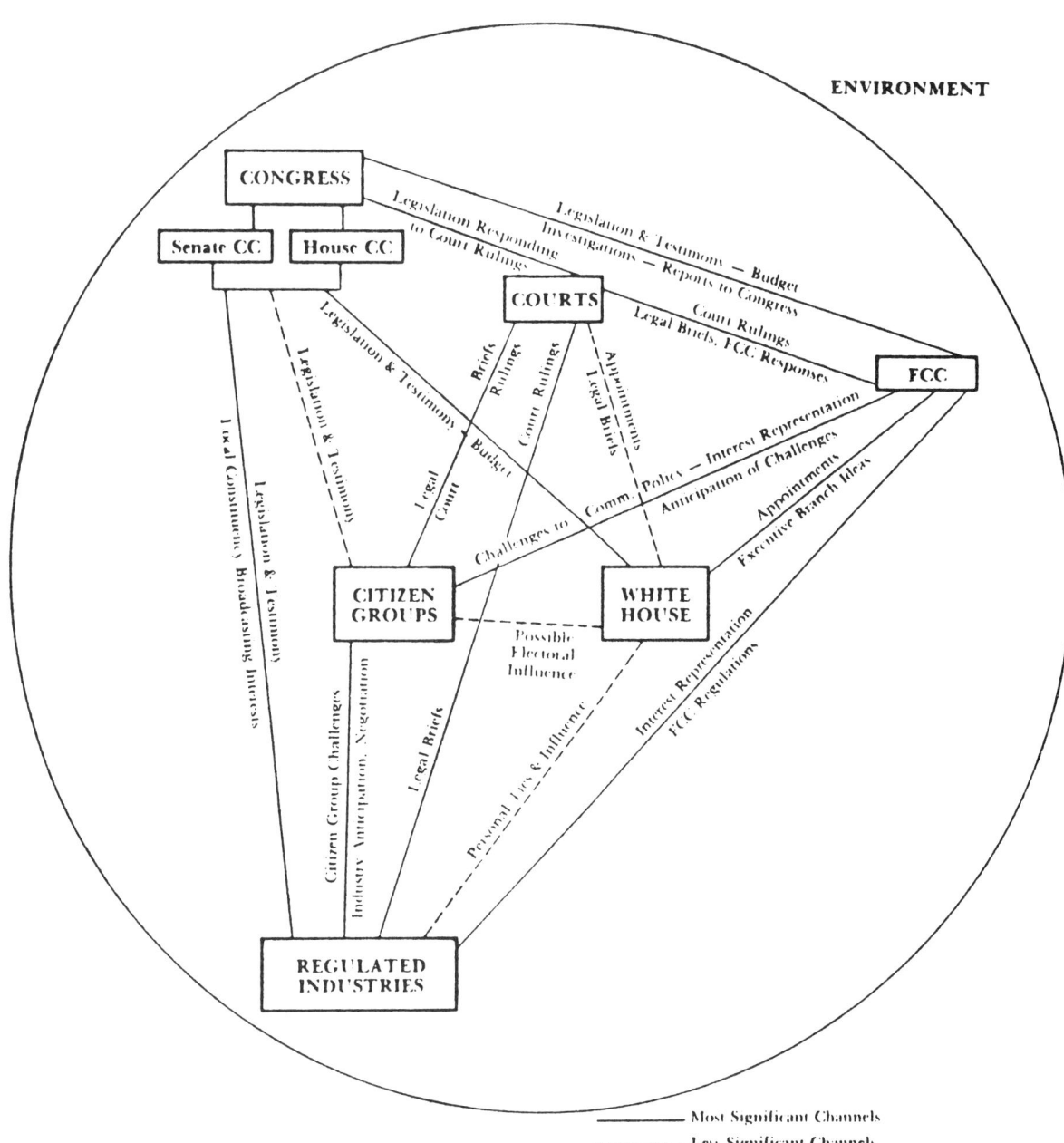

Source: Erwin G. Krasnow, Lawrence D. Longley, and Herbert A. Terry, *The Politics of Broadcast Regulation*, 3rd ed. New York: St. Martin's Press, 1982, p. 136.

Abstract 1 for Theme D

The Presidential Press Conference—Manipulation of the News?

Presidential press conferences, particularly in the hands of an effective communicator/image-maker, can be effective vehicles of distortion rather than realistic channels of information for the public. Why is this so?

In a publication entitled *Presidential Leadership*, by George C. Edwards III and Stephen J. Wayne (New York: St. Martin's Press, 1985), the reasons for the deficiencies of the modern presidential press conference become abundantly clear. Edwards and Wayne argue as follows:

1. Presidential press conferences do not occur frequently enough (averaging once or twice a month), so when they do occur, the wide range of questions that have accumulated guarantees the superficiality of coverage by the press.

2. Presidents' press conferences are too big, inhibiting the "likelihood of follow-up questions to cover a subject in depth." Also, the size of the press conference creates too formal an atmosphere.

3. Presidential "rehearsal" before the press conference and total control over which reporter is allowed to ask a question prevent true spontaneity.

4. Televised press conferences prevent the informality and candid nature of presidential answers that once existed before the days of television (those of FDR, for example). Presidents must choose their words carefully, so "responses to questions are often not terribly enlightening."

5. Because presidents are in control, they can evade tough questions or, conversely, call on a friendly reporter for a "soft" question. The authors quote a scholarly study of press conferences between 1961 and 1975, which found that there were "only two occasions in fifteen years when the number of hostile questions asked by reporters at any press conference exceeded three."

The authors offer the following conclusions:

> The advent of television has further increased the potential for distortion, since a president's physical attractiveness, delivery, and flair for the dramatic may leave more of an impression on the public's mind than the substance of his answers.
> In sum, presidential press conferences are not very informative . . . we cannot depend upon them for revealing the real president, and the nature of television may distort more than it reveals. (p. 145)

Questions for Discussion/Answer Guidelines

For this abstract, you might show a videotape of a recent press conference to illustrate the points made by Edwards and Wayne. Questions will occur spontaneously as the tape is viewed by the members of the class. Particular stress can be placed on how well the president "controls" the pace and content of the press conference and on whether any reporters try to "pressure" the president with a tough question.

Abstract 2 for Theme D

The Government and the Media—Conflict or Cooperation?

A case can be made either that the government-media relationship is one of nearly total enmity or that both institutions are mutually supportive. The former view is expressed in a July 12, 1986, *National Journal* article by Dom Bonafede, pp. 1716–1720, entitled "Muzzling the Media." Bonafede attacks the Reagan administration "that from all appearances is intent on stemming the free flow of information and muzzling the national news media." The article focuses on the threats of then CIA Director William J. Casey (now deceased) to prosecute news organizations that revealed intelligence secrets and jeopardized national security. Furthermore, Bonafede itemized other administration measures that impeded the ability of the press to have a free flow of information:

1. The administering of lie detector tests to all high-security risk government employees and political appointees as a way of tracing leaks of information to the press.

2. The expansion of federal agencies' discretion to classify information and thus withhold that information indefinitely, and their authority to reclassify information "already in the public domain."

3. The exclusion of the press from military operations such as the Grenada intervention.

4. The broadening of existing exemptions in the Freedom of Information Act.

In short, as Defense Secretary Weinberger put it, "the role of the news media in U.S. society had to be weighed against competing national security requirements—that depending on national priorities, one constitutional right sometimes *superseded* (italics mine) another constitutional right."

Walter Guzzardi's "The Secret Love Affair Between the Press and Government" (originally published in *Public Opinion*, August/September 1985, pp. 2–5) argues that the adversarial relationship between the press and government has been exaggerated. To Guzzardi, "the exchange of insults obscures the ties and common interests that bind the institutions together." For example, "government officials must have the media to get across their message, and the media must have the officials, for they are irreplaceable sources." Furthermore, the media is supportive of American institutional life, including the presidency, private ownership, individual entrepreneurship, and "benevolent capitalism." In particular, the big businessman may be depicted as a hero or villain, but "his power and perquisites are still envied" in media reporting. The author concludes his argument by stating the following:

> In the end, the media have to make their way in the world of commerce. That may lead to many kinds of reporting that we don't like, but it remains the best system. The media so often support the machinery of power because we, their audience, would not have them do otherwise. The press can be much improved despite the conclusion, but still the conclusion stands: We get the kind of press we deserve.

Questions for Discussion

1. Is the conflict between the demands of national security and the freedom of the media to report the news a continuing problem, whichever presidential administration is in power?

2. Should a newspaper or television network be charged with treason for revealing important government secrets? Why or why not?

3. Is your own attitude toward the media-government relationship closer to Bonafede's or to Guzzardi's, and why?

Answer Guidelines

The discussion will probably be open-ended, but the theme of whether the public's right to know must be limited at times for the good of the nation could profitably be pursued.

PART THREE

Institutions of Government

11

Congress

Overview and Objectives

The central purpose of this chapter is to describe the Framers' understanding of the role of Congress and to describe the roles and organization of Congress today. The student should pay particular attention to the effects of organizational characteristics on the behavior of members of Congress and on the way that the House and the Senate perform their functions. After reading and reviewing the material in this chapter the student should be able to do each of the following:

1. Explain the differences between Congress and Parliament.
2. Delineate the role that the Framers expected Congress to play.
3. Pinpoint the significant eras in the evolution of Congress.
4. Describe the characteristics of members of Congress.
5. Outline the process for electing members of Congress.
6. Identify the functions that party affiliation plays in the organization of Congress.
7. Explain the impact of committee reform on the organization of Congress.
8. Describe the formal process by which a bill becomes a law.

9. Identify the factors that help to explain why a member of Congress votes as he or she does.
10. Explain the ethical problems confronting Congress.

Chapter Outline with Keyed-in Resources

I. Uniqueness of the U.S. Congress
   A. Only democratic government with a legislative branch
   B. Comparison with British Parliament
      1. Parliamentary candidates are selected by party
         a. Members of Parliament select prime minister and other leaders
         b. Party members vote together on most issues

The role of "no confidence" votes has been watered down in the British Parliament. Traditionally, the defeat of any government bill was automatically considered a vote of no confidence. This practice has been abandoned, with numerous prime ministers losing on a vote but remaining in office (Edward Heath lost six times, Harold Wilson and James Callaghan lost twenty-three times from 1974–1979, and Margaret Thatcher lost twice). Now, the government must specifically designate an important bill for such a vote.

         c. Renomination depends on remaining loyal to party
         d. Principal work is debate over national issues
         e. Very little actual power, very little pay
      2. Congressional candidates run in a primary election, with little party control
         a. Vote is "for the man" (or woman), not the party
         b. Result is a body of independent representatives
         c. Members do not choose president
         d. Principal work is representation and action
         e. Great deal of power, high pay; parties cannot discipline members
II. The evolution of Congress (THEME A: THE POWER OF CONGRESS IN THE AMERICAN SYSTEM)
   A. Intent of the Framers (ADDITIONAL LECTURE TOPIC A-1)
      1. To oppose concentration of power in a single institution

An often neglected justification for the creation of a separate upper house was to ensure representation of the wealthy, enabling them to protect their interests. At the constitutional Convention, Charles Pickney twice moved to forbid a salary to members of the Senate. As he explained: "As this branch was meant to represent the wealthy of the country, it ought to be composed of persons of wealth."

      2. To balance large and small states: bicameralism
      3. To have Congress be the dominant institution
   B. General characteristics of subsequent evolution
      1. Congress generally dominant over presidency for more than 140 years
         a. Exceptions: brief periods of presidential activism
      2. Major political struggles were *within* Congress
         a. Generally over issues of national significance, e.g., slavery, new states, internal improvements, tariffs, business regulation
         b. Overriding political question: distribution of power within Congress
            (1) Centralization—if the need is for quick and decisive action
            (2) Decentralization—if congressional constituency interests are to be dominant
            (3) General trend toward decentralization
   C. The period of the Founding
      1. Congressional leadership supplied by the president in first three administrations

2. Preeminence of House of Representatives; originated legislation and nominated presidential candidates

The early dominance of the House was owing, in part, to the initial secrecy of the Senate's proceedings. Reputations could be made only in the House. "The rising and vigorous intellects of the country," Harry Ammon has written, "sought the arena of the House of Representatives as the appropriate theater for the display of their powers." The Senate, in contrast, Ammon describes as the "graveyard of talent."

D. Decline of the House in 1820s
1. Assertiveness of Andrew Jackson who vetoed bills if he opposed policy
2. Caucus system disappears
3. Issue of slavery and Civil War shatter party unity
E. The importance of the Senate
1. Increasing importance of issues that Senate alone could deal with
2. Opportunity for unlimited debate
3. Close association with local parties and use of patronage
F. The rise of party control in the House (1889–1910)
1. Powerful leaders produced central leadership

The autocratic control of the Speaker is illustrated by a statement made by Speaker Thomas Reed (1889–1891 and 1895–1899) on introducing a new rule into the House: "Gentlemen," Reed asserted, "we have decided to perpetrate the following outrage." According to Reed, the Speaker had but one superior and no peer.

2. Party caucus control and speaker selects committees and chairs
3. Rules Committee decides what legislation to come up
G. The decentralization of the House
1. House Speaker has power taken away (1910–1911)

The limitations placed on the power of the Speaker should not be construed as meaning that the office lost all prestige. Carl Chelf quotes Speaker Sam Rayburn as saying that "he never served *under* any President, but had served *with* eight."

a. Party caucus increases in power
b. Rules Committee increases in power; decides what bills voted on and defeated
c. Committee chairmen's powers increase; decides what bills taken up and sent out
H. Recent changes in House: 1960s and 1970s
1. Chairmanships become elective
2. Subcommittees strengthened

The strengthening of subcommittees also contributed to their proliferation, which has slowed the legislative process and made the enactment of laws more difficult. For example, eighty-three subcommittees in the House had jurisdiction over President Carter's energy legislation.

3. Congressional staff increased
III. The "democratization" of the Senate
A. Popular election of senators in 1913—Seventeenth Amendment
B. Filibuster restricted by Rule 22
IV. Who is in Congress? (THEME B: WHO GETS TO CONGRESS)
A. The beliefs and interests of members of Congress can affect policy
B. Sex and race
1. House has become less male and less white
2. Senate has been slower to change
a. But several blacks and Hispanics hold powerful positions
C. Incumbency (ADDITIONAL LECTURE TOPIC B-1)
1. Membership in Congress now a career: low turnover
2. Marginal districts are decreasing, especially in House
a. Name recognition of incumbents

The importance of name recognition should not be underestimated. During the congressional campaign of 1982, a newspaper in Bloomsburg, Pennsylvania, offered $5 to anyone who could name the two candidates running for the House of Representatives in the district. After asking 120 people in three shopping centers, only $30 was distributed.

           b. Emphasis on constituency service
- D. Party
  1. Democrats are beneficiaries of incumbency
  2. Gap between votes and seats: Republican vote higher than number of seats won
     a. One explanation: Democratic legislatures redraw district lines to favor Democratic candidates
     b. But research does not support; Republicans run best in high-turnout districts, Democrats in low-turnout ones
     c. Another explanation: incumbent advantage increasing
     d. But not the reason; Democrats field better candidates whose positions are closer to those of voters
  3. Electoral convulsions alter membership
     a. Important since members not always vote party line
     b. Size of majority is significant
     c. Conservative coalition sometimes prevents majority party from passing legislation
- V. Getting elected to Congress: each state has two senators, but House representation based on population
  - A. Determining fair representation
    1. Now elected from single-member districts
    2. Problem of drawing district boundaries
       a. Malapportionment: deliberately creating disparity in number of people in each district
       b. Gerrymandering: drawing boundaries to ensure party victory
    3. Congress decides size of House

In 1910, when the size of the House was limited to 435 members, each member represented 212,000 people. Today, each member represents about 575,000 people. To achieve the same ratio as in 1910, the House would require a membership of almost 1,200.

    4. Congress reapportions representatives every ten years
    5. 1964 Supreme Court decision requires districts to be drawn to assure "one man, one vote"
    6. Majority-minority districts remain vexing question
       a. Districts drawn to make it easier to elect minority representatives
       b. *Shaw* v. *Reno*: Supreme Court allows constitutionality of majority-minority district to be raised and rules permissible if narrowly tailored to further compelling interest
       c. Pitkin: descriptive versus substantive representation
       d. Research reveals liberal white members of Congress represent black interests
- B. Winning the primary
  1. Candidate needs to win the party primary in order to appear on the ballot in the general election
  2. Reduces influence of political party
  3. Incumbents almost always win: "sophomore surge" due to use of office to run personal campaign
  4. Candidates run personalized campaigns—offers them independence from party in Congress
  5. Way people get elected has two consequences
     a. Legislators closely tied to local concerns

        b. Effects how policy is made: office geared to help people, committee pork for district
- VI. The organization of Congress: parties and caucuses (THEME C: CONGRESSIONAL ORGANIZATION AND PROCEDURES)
  - A. Party organization of the Senate
    1. President pro tempore presides; member with most seniority in majority party
    2. Leaders are the majority leader and the minority leader—elected by their respective party members
    3. Party whips—keep leaders informed, round up votes, count noses
    4. Policy Committee—schedule Senate business
    5. Committee assignments
       a. Democratic Steering Committee
       b. Republican Committee on Committees
       c. Emphasizes ideological and regional balance
       d. Other factors: popularity, effectiveness on television, favors owed
  - B. Party structure in the House
    1. Speaker of the House is leader of majority party; presides over House
       a. Decides whom to recognize to speak on the floor

The power of the Speaker to recognize members and to rule on points of order has even altered American history. In 1941, the House passed the Draft Extension Bill by a single vote (203 to 202). Speaker Rayburn was afraid that following the usual parliamentary motion in such a case, a motion to reconsider, might be approved as members left the floor or changed their minds. He avoided the trap by declaring, "Without objection, a motion to reconsider is laid on the table." When Rayburn was challenged on this move, since no such motion had been made, he retorted, "The chair does not intend to have his word questioned." The legislation was enacted only months before Pearl Harbor.

        b. Rules on germaneness of motions
        c. Decides to which committee bills go

A bill is sent to a committee on the basis of its subject matter. However, the definition of what constitutes a bill's subject matter is sometimes quite arbitrary, thus enabling the Speaker to forward a bill to the committee which will produce the desired outcome. For example, a civil rights bill based on the commerce clause was sent to the Judiciary Committee in 1963 rather than the Commerce Committee because the latter's chairman was unsympathetic to civil rights.

        d. Appoints members of special and select committees
        e. Has some patronage power
    2. Majority leader and minority leader
    3. Party whip organizations
    4. Democratic Steering and Policy Committee, chaired by Speaker
        a. Makes committee assignments
        b. Schedules legislation
    5. Republican Committee on Committees; makes committee assignments
    6. Republican Policy Committee; discusses policy
    7. Democratic and Republican congressional campaign committees
- C. The strength of party structure
  1. Loose measure of strength of party structure is ability of leaders to determine party rules and organization
  2. Tested in 103rd Congress: 103 freshmen
     a. Ran as outsiders
     b. Yet reelected entire leadership and committee chairs
  3. Senate different since transformed by changes in norms, not rules
     a. Now less party-centered, less leader-oriented, more hospitable to freshmen
- D. Party voting
  1. Problems in measuring party votes
  2. Party voting quite low today but increasing.

3. Ideology an important variable explaining party voting as advice from fellow party members and rewards from party leaders
   E. Caucuses: rivals to parties in policy formulation
      1. Examples: Democratic Study Group (DSG), staff delegations, Congressional Black Caucus, and other specialized caucuses
VII. The organization of Congress: committees
   A. Legislative committees—most important organizational feature of Congress
      1. Consider bills or legislative proposals

Most bills sent to committees are never heard of again. One estimate calculates that only 6 percent of the bills introduced in Congress are ever reported by a committee for floor action. Committees are the graveyards of legislative proposals.

      2. Maintain oversight of executive agencies
      3. Conduct investigations

The major frailty of committee investigations is that no legal mechanism requires any action to be taken in response to a committee report. Thus many investigations amount to little. For example, a select committee in the House of Representatives investigated the assassination of President Kennedy and concluded in 1979 that he "was probably assassinated as a result of a conspiracy." Nothing has been done, even though the death of a president is involved.

   B. Types of committees
      1. Select committees—groups appointed for a limited purpose and limited duration
      2. Joint committees—those on which both representatives and senators serve
      3. Conference committee—a joint committee appointed to resolve differences in Senate and House versions of the same piece of legislation before final passage

In conference committee, both houses are extremely jealous about their version of proposed legislation. One room in the Capitol, EF 100, is the only meeting room in the building without a prefix of "H" or "S." The reason is that at the turn of the century the chairmen of the House and Senate appropriations committees refused to allow a conference committee from convening on the other's turf. According to Albert Mikva and Patti Saris, EF 100 was established as neutral ground.

      4. Standing committees—most important type of committee
         a. Majority party has majority of seats on the committees
         b. Each member usually serves on two standing committees
         c. Chairmen are elected, but usually the most senior member of the committee is elected by the majority party
         d. Subcommittee "bill of rights" of 1970s changed several traditions

The subcommittee bill of rights was prompted by abuses of power by committee chairs. A classic example was "Judge" Howard Smith, chairman of the Rules Committee for two decades. Smith opposed civil rights and prevented action on such bills by simply "going fishing" whenever civil rights legislation was to be considered. The committee could not convene in the absence of its chair.

            (1) Opened more meetings to the public
            (2) Allowed television coverage of meetings, etc.
   C. Committee styles
      1. Decentralization has increased influence of individual members
         a. Less control by chairmen
         b. More amendments proposed and adopted
      2. Ideological orientations of committees vary, depending on attitudes of members
      3. Certain committees tend to attract particular types of legislators
         a. Policy-oriented members
         b. Constituency-oriented members

VIII. The organization of Congress: staffs and specialized offices
  A. Tasks of staff members (ADDITIONAL LECTURE TOPIC C-1)
    1. Constituency service—major task of staff
    2. Legislative functions—monitoring hearings, devising proposals, drafting reports, meeting with lobbyists
    3. Staff members consider themselves advocates of their employers
  B. Growth and impact of staff
    1. Rapid growth: a large staff itself requires a large staff
    2. Larger staff generates more legislative work

The Legislative Reorganization Act of 1946 mandated that standing committees are empowered to hire professional staffs. Within two years, the number of bills introduced into Congress doubled.

    3. Members of Congress can no longer keep up with increased legislative work and so must rely on staff
    4. Results in a more individualistic Congress

The growth of the number of staff members has caused concern. In 1979, Senator William Proxmire gave a Golden Fleece award to Congress for allowing the number of congressional staffers to reach unwarranted size. According to Proxmire, "Senators and staff are stumbling over themselves." The cost had escalated from $150 million in 1968 to $550 million in 1979.

  C. Staff agencies—offer specialized information
    1. Congressional Research Service (CRS)
    2. General Accounting Office (GAO)
    3. Office of Technology Assessment (OTA)
    4. Congressional Budget Office (CBO)
IX. How a bill becomes law (ADDITIONAL LECTURE TOPIC C-2)
  A. Bills travel through Congress at different speeds
    1. Bills to spend money or to tax or regulate businesses move slowly
    2. Bills with a clear, appealing idea move fast
      a. "Stop drugs," "End scandal"
  B. Introducing a bill
    1. Introduced by a member of Congress: hopper in House, recognized in Senate
    2. Most legislation has been initiated in Congress
    3. Presidentially drafted legislation is shaped by Congress
    4. Resolutions
      a. Simple—passed by one house affecting that house
      b. Concurrent—passed by both houses affecting both
      c. Joint—passed by both houses, signed by president (except for a constitutional amendment)
  C. Study by committees
    1. Bill is referred to a committee for consideration by either Speaker or presiding officer
    2. Revenue bills must originate in the House

By tradition, appropriations bills as well as revenue bills originate in the House of Representatives. An attempt in the 1960s by the Senate to initiate an appropriations bill met with House resistance.

    3. Most bills die in committee
    4. Hearings are often conducted by several subcommittees: multiple referrals
    5. "Mark-up" of bills—bills are revised by committees
    6. Committee reports a bill out to the House or Senate

What happens in committee is usually the final product of Congress. According to one study, 70 percent of the bills reported from committees in the House are passed unchanged by the full membership on the floor; the comparable figure in the Senate is 65 percent.

      a. If bill is not reported out, the House can use the "discharge petition"
      b. If bill is not reported out, the Senate can pass a discharge motion

7. House Rules Committee sets the rules for consideration
   a. "Closed rule": sets time limit on debate and restricts amendments
   b. "Open rule": permits amendments from the floor
   c. "Restrictive rule": permits only some amendments
   d. Use of closed and restrictive rules growing
   e. Rules can be bypassed in the House
   f. No direct equivalent in Senate
D. Floor debate—the House
   1. Committee of the Whole—procedural device for expediting House consideration of bills but cannot pass bills
   2. Committee sponsor of bill organizes the discussion
E. Floor debate—the Senate
   1. No rule limiting debate or germaneness
   2. Entire committee hearing process can be bypassed by a senator
   3. Cloture—three-fifths of Senate must vote for a cloture petition
      a. Cloture sets time limit on debate
   4. Both filibusters and cloture votes becoming more common
      a. Easier now to stage filibuster
      b. Roll calls are replacing long speeches
      c. But can be curtailed by "double-tracking": disputed bill is shelved temporarily—makes filibuster less costly
F. Methods of voting
   1. To investigate voting behavior, one must know how a legislator voted on amendments as well as on the bill itself
   2. Procedures for voting in the House

William Natcher (D-Ky), who died in 1994, compiled a record 18,401 consecutive floor votes in twenty-one terms in the House.

      a. Voice vote
      b. Division vote
      c. Teller vote
      d. Roll-call vote
   3. Senate voting is the same except no teller vote
   4. Differences in Senate and House versions of a bill
      a. If minor, last house to act merely sends bill to the other house, which accepts the changes
      b. If major, a conference committee is appointed
         (1) Decisions are by a majority of each delegation; Senate version favored

About 10 to 15 percent of bills end up in a conference committee. Which house's version is most likely to prevail in the dispute? Successive studies by Richard Fenno, Stephen Horn, and David Vogler indicate that the Senate is the most likely victor about 60 percent of the time, the House in only about a third of the cases.

         (2) Conference reports back to each house for acceptance or rejection
   5. Bill, in final form, goes to the president
      a. President may sign it
      b. If president vetoes it, it returns to house of origin
         (1) Either house may override president by vote of two-thirds of those present
         (2) If both override, bill becomes law without president's signature

The president's veto is typically sustained. Historically, presidents' vetoes have prevailed 96 percent of the time. A veto threat has teeth.

X. How members of Congress vote (THEME D: DOES CONGRESS REPRESENT CONSTITUENTS' OPINIONS?) (ADDITIONAL LECTURE TOPIC D-1)
   A. Representational view
      1. Assumes that members vote to please their constituents

Does public opinion sway members of Congress in voting? Senator Ashurst once commented, "You must learn that there are times when a man in public life is compelled to rise above his principles."

      2. Constituents must have a clear opinion of the issue
         a. Very strong correlation on civil rights and social welfare bills
         b. Very weak correlation on foreign policy
      3. May be conflict between legislator and constituency on certain measures: gun control, Panama Canal treaty, abortion
      4. Constituency influence more important in Senate votes
      5. Members in marginal districts as independent as those in safe districts
      6. Weakness of representational explanation: no clear opinion in the constituency

Does a member's vote matter to constituents? One survey discovered that only 15 percent of Americans could correctly identify how their representative in the House had voted on any issue in the last two years.

    B. Organizational view
      1. Assumes members of Congress vote to please colleagues
      2. Organizational cues
         a. Party
         b. Ideology
      3. Problem is that party and other organizations do not have clear position on all issues
      4. On minor votes, most members influenced by party members on sponsoring committees
    C. Attitudinal view
      1. Assumes that ideology affects a legislator's vote
      2. House members tend more than senators to have opinions similar to those of the public
         a. 1970s—senators more liberal
         b. 1980s—senators more conservative
      3. Southern Democrats often align with Republicans to form a conservative coalition

XI. Reforming Congress
    A. Numerous proposals to reform Congress
    B. Representative or direct democracy?
      1. Framers: representatives refine, not reflect, public opinion
      2. Today: representatives should mirror public opinion
      3. Move toward direct democracy would have consequences
    C. Proper guardians of the public weal?
      1. Madison: national laws guarantee public interest that transcend local prejudices
      2. Madison: Legislator should make compromises and not be captive of special interests
      3. Problem is that many special-interest groups represent professions and public-interest groups
    D. A decisive Congress or a deliberative one?
      1. Framers designed Congress to balance competing views and thus act slowly
      2. Today, complaints of policy gridlock
      3. But if Congress moves too quickly it may not move wisely
      4. Benefits to acting slowly, like weighing all sides
    E. Imposing term limits
      1. Anti-Federalists distrusted strong national government; favored annual elections and term limits
      2. Today, 95 percent of House incumbents reelected, but 80 percent of public supports term limits
      3. Fourteen states in 1992 had term-limit proposals pass

4. Effects of term limits vary depending on type of proposal
   a. Lifetime limits produce amateur legislators who are less prone to compromise
   b. Limiting continuous sequence leads to office-hopping and outrageous behavior
   c. Constitutionality of term limits questionable
F. Reducing power and perks
   1. Ban legal bribes such as gifts
   2. Fence in the frank as taxpayer subsidy supporting members' campaigns
   3. Place Congress under law and not exempt itself from laws
   4. Trim pork to avoid wasteful projects
      a. Main cause of deficit is entitlement programs, not pork
      b. Some spending in districts is for needed projects
      c. Members supposed to advocate interests of district
      d. Price of citizen-oriented Congress is pork
   5. Cut number of committees and assignments to slow pace and allow reasoned consideration of bills
      a. Downsize staff as well
      b. But staff size same as 1980s
      c. Cutting staff makes Congress more dependent on executive

XII. Ethics and Congress (THEME E: ETHICS AND CONGRESS)

On congressional ethics, Mark Twain opined, "There is no distinctly American criminal class except Congress."

A. Separation of powers and corruption
   1. Fragmentation of power increases number of officials with opportunity to sell influence
      a. Example: "senatorial courtesy" offers opportunity for office seeker to influence a senator
   2. Forms of influence
      a. Money
      b. Exchange of favors
B. Problem of defining unethical conduct
   1. Violation of criminal law is obviously unethical
      a. Since 1941, almost a hundred charges of misconduct
      b. Most led to convictions
      c. Most infamous: Abscam (1980–1981) and Jim Wright (1989)
      d. Fewer crimes since Abscam
   2. Other issues are more difficult (e.g., how can campaigns be paid for in ways that are both fair and honest?)
C. New ethics rules (1989)
   1. Disclosures: annual financial statement
   2. Honoraria: House bans, Senators up to 27 percent
   3. Campaign funds: ban retaining of surplus
   4. Lobbying: former members ban for one year
   5. Gifts: $200 House limit, $300 Senate
   6. Free travel limited
D. Problems with ethics rules
   1. Rules assume money is the only source of corruption
   2. Neglect political alliances and personal friendships
   3. The Framers were more concerned to ensure liberty (through checks and balances) than morality

XIII. Summary: The old and the new Congress (THEME F: CONGRESS AND REFORMS)
   A. House has evolved through three stages
      1. Mid-1940s to early 1960s
         a. Powerful committee chairmen, mostly from the South

            b. Long apprenticeships for new members
            c. Small congressional staffs
        2. Early 1970s to early 1980s
            a. Spurred by civil rights efforts of younger, mostly northern members
            b. Growth in size of staffs
            c. Committees became more democratic
            d. More independence for members
            e. Focus on reelection
            f. More amendments and filibusters
        3. Early 1980s to present
            a. Strengthening and centralizing party leadership
            b. Became apparent under Jim Wright
            c. Return to more accommodating style under Tom Foley
        4. Senate meanwhile remained decentralized throughout this period
    B. Reassertion of congressional power in 1970s
        1. Reaction to Vietnam and Watergate
        2. War Powers Act of 1973
        3. Congressional Budget and Impoundment Act of 1974

Congress has a difficult time containing expenditures even on itself. According to *Money* magazine, the annual cost of running Congress has increased from $343 million in 1970 to $2.8 billion in 1992. This works out to an estimated $5.2 million per legislator.

        4. Increased requirement for legislative veto
    C. Congressional power never as weak as critics have alleged

Important Terms

attitudinal view of representation The theory of congressional voting behavior which assumes that members vote on the basis of their own beliefs because the array of conflicting pressures on members cancel out one another.

***bicameral legislature** A legislative assembly composed of two separate houses, such as the U.S. Congress, which consists of the House of Representatives and the Senate.

***caucus** An association of members of Congress created to advocate a political ideology, a constituency, or regional or economic interests. Almost a hundred of these groups now exist, and they rival political parties as a source of policy leadership.

***Christmas tree bill** A bill that has lots of riders.

Committee of the Whole A device used in the House of Representatives to expedite the passage of legislation. The quorum is reduced from 218 members to 100, and the Speaker appoints a member of the majority party as chairman. Time allotted for debating the bill in question is split equally between its proponents and opponents. The committee cannot itself pass legislation but may debate and propose amendments.

***closed rule** Limitation imposed by the Rules Committee of the House of Representatives on the amount of debate time allotted to a bill and on the introduction of amendments from the floor (or of any amendments other than those from the sponsoring committee).

***cloture** Rule 22 of the Senate, providing for the end of debate on a bill if three-fifths of the members agree. A cloture motion is brought to the floor if sixteen senators sign a petition. The purpose is typically to terminate a filibuster and to force a vote on a bill.

***concurrent resolution** A resolution used to settle housekeeping and procedural matters that affect both houses. Such resolutions are not signed by the president and do not have the force of law.

***conference committee** A special type of joint committee appointed to resolve differences in House and Senate versions on a piece of legislation.

Congress A meeting place of representatives of local constituencies who can initiate, modify, approve, or reject laws. It also shares supervision of government agencies with the executive.

Congressional Budget Office Created in 1974 to advise Congress on the economic effects of spending programs and to provide information on the cost of proposed policies.

Congressional Research Service Created in 1914 to respond to congressional requests for information. It also keeps track of every major bill and produces summaries of legislation for members of Congress.

*conservative coalition A vote in Congress in which conservative Democrats join with Republicans. Such votes occur on about 20 to 25 percent of legislation. On issues on which both conservative Democrats and Republicans vote together, the coalition prevails about two-thirds of the time.

*descriptive representation A term coined by Hannah Pitkin to refer to the statistical correspondence of the demographic characteristics of representatives with those of their constituents.

*discharge petition A procedure for removing legislation from the control of a committee and bringing it to the floor for immediate consideration. In the House, the petition must contain the names of 218 members to succeed. In the Senate, any member may move to discharge a bill from committee, but the petition requires a majority vote to succeed.

*division vote A method of voting used in both houses in which members stand and are counted.

*double tracking A method to keep the Senate going during a filibuster, whereby a disputed bill is shelved temporarily so that the Senate can go on with other business.

*filibuster A prolonged speech or series of speeches made to delay action on legislation in the Senate. The purpose is to kill the measure by talking it to death.

*franking privilege The ability of members of Congress to mail letters to their constituents free of charge of substituting their facsimile signature (frank) for postage.

General Accounting Office Created in 1921 to perform routine audits of the money spent by executive departments. It also investigates agencies and makes recommendations on every aspect of government.

*gerrymandering Drawing congressional district lines in a bizarre or unusual shape to make it easy for a candidate of one party to win elections in that district. The practice remains legal.

honoraria Speaking fees accepted by members of Congress. In 1991, the House forbade members to accept honoraria, while the Senate limited such income to 27 percent of a senator's salary.

*joint committee Committee on which both representatives and senators serve.

*joint resolution A resolution requiring approval of both houses and the signature of the president and having the same legal status as a law.

*majority leader The legislative leader elected by party members holding the majority of seats in the House of Representatives or the Senate.

*majority-minority districts Congressional districts designed to make it easier for minority citizens to elect minority representatives.

*malapportionment The creation of congressional districts in a state which are of unequal size. The Supreme Court in 1964 eliminated the practice by requiring that all districts in a state contain about the same number of people.

*marginal districts A congressional district in which the winner of the general election gets less than 55 percent of the vote. Such districts could easily switch to the other party in the next election. The number of these districts has sharply decreased.

mark-up Revisions and additions to legislation made by committees and subcommittees. These changes are not part of a bill unless approved by the house of which the committee is a part.

***minority leader** The head of the minority party in each house of Congress chosen by the caucus of the minority party. This person formulates the minority party's strategy and program.

***multiple referral** The recently introduced practice of referring a bill to several committees simultaneously. Each committee is empowered to consider the bill either in part or as a whole. About 20 to 25 percent of House bills are now referred in this manner.

***open rule** Consent from the Rules Committee of the House of Representatives which permits amendments from the floor on a particular piece of legislation.

organizational view of representation The theory of congressional voting behavior which assumes that members make voting decisions in order to please fellow members and obtain their goodwill. Such behavior is possible since constituents seldom know how their representatives vote. Members vote by following cues provided by colleagues.

parliament An assembly of party representatives which chooses a government and discusses major national issues. Tight party discipline usually regulates the voting behavior of members.

***party vote** The extent to which members of a party vote together in the House and Senate. By any measure, the extent of such voting has fluctuated and is lower now than at the turn of the century, although a slow but steady increase has developed since 1972.

***pork-barrel legislation** A bill introduced by a member of Congress that gives tangible benefits, like a highway or bridge, to constituents in the hopes of winning votes in return.

president pro tempore A position created in the Constitution to serve as presiding officer of the Senate in the absence of the vice president.

***private bill** Legislation that pertains to a particular individual, such as a person pressing a financial claim against the government or seeking special permission to become a naturalized citizen.

***public bill** Legislation that pertains to affairs generally.

***quorum call** A calling of the roll in either house of Congress to see whether the number of representatives in attendance meets the minimum number required to conduct official business.

representational view of representation The theory of congressional voting behavior that assumes that members make voting decisions based on their perception of constituents' wishes to ensure their own reelection. A correlation between district attitudes and members' votes has been found on issues of importance to constituents (e.g., civil rights and social welfare) but not on issues of remote concern to constituents (foreign policy).

***restrictive rule** Consent from the Rules Committee of the House of Representatives which permits certain amendments to a piece of legislation but not others.

***riders** Amendments on matters unrelated to a bill that are added to an important bill so that they will "ride" to passage through the Congress. When a bill has lots of riders, it is called a Christmas tree bill.

***roll-call vote** A method of voting used in both houses in which members answer yea or nay when their names are called. These votes are recorded and occur in the House at the request of 20 percent of its members.

rules committee In the House of Representatives, the committee that decides which bills come up for a vote, in what order, and under what restrictions on length of debate and on the right to offer amendments. The Senate Rules Committee, by contrast, possesses few powers.

***select committee** Congressional committee appointed for a limited time period and purpose.

senatorial courtesy The tradition observed in the Senate in which that body refuses to confirm an appointment to a federal office when the candidate is personally obnoxious to either senator from the candidate's state.

Seventeenth Amendment A constitutional amendment ratified in 1913 requiring the popular election of U.S. senators. Senators were previously chosen by state legislatures.

*****simple resolution** A resolution passed by either house to establish internal chamber rules. It is not signed by the president and has no legal force.

*****sophomore surge** An increase in the number of votes candidates receive between the first time elected and their reelection.

Speaker of the House The constitutionally mandated presiding officer of the House of Representatives. The Speaker is chosen in the caucus of the majority party and is empowered to recognize members to speak on the floor, to rule whether a motion is germane, to assign bills to committee, to appoint House members to select and joint committees, and to appoint the majority members of the Rules Committee.

*****standing committees** The permanent committees of each house with the power to report bills.

*****substantive representation** A term coined by Hannah Pitkin to refer to the correspondence between representatives' opinions and those of their constituents.

*****teller vote** A method of voting used only in the House. Members' votes are counted by having them pass between two tellers, first the yeas and then the nays. Since 1971, teller votes are recorded at the request of twenty members.

*****voice vote** A method of voting used in both houses in which members vote by shouting yea or nay. Votes are not recorded.

*****whip** A member of the party leadership in each house who helps the party leader stay informed about what party members are thinking, rounds up members when important votes are to be taken, and attempts to keep a nose count of how the voting on a controversial issue is likely to go.

Theme A	The Power of Congress in the American System

Summary

There are essentially two kinds of legislative bodies—congresses and parliaments. We in the United States have a congress; most Western European nations have parliaments. A person gets to be in a parliament by persuading a political party to put his or her name on the ballot. Upon taking office, the member of parliament can make only one important decision: to support or not to support the party in power. If a member of the majority fails to support his or her party, this may bring down the government, and the individual may be denied renomination in the next election. Thus party discipline is tight. In the U.S. Congress, on the other hand, nomination is gotten by winning a primary election, in which voting is based on personality or issues, not party. Congress has constitutionally defined powers independent of the executive, little party discipline, and vast perquisites, such as staff and expense money, for each member. Thus Congress functions as the meeting place of representatives of local constituencies, and in the minute details of policy making and oversight.

The Framers intentionally created a *bicameral* legislature with powers independent of the executive. They did this for philosophical reasons (to create a separation of powers within the legislative branch as well as between branches) and out of practical necessity (small states demanded that they not be overwhelmed in the legislature). They expected Congress to be the dominant institution in the national government, which it was (except during a few isolated periods of strong presidencies) for a century and a half. As Congress has developed, there has been a recurrent struggle over *centralization* versus *decentralization*. If Congress is to act as a body quickly and decisively there must be strong central leadership, restrictions on debate, few opportunities for stalling tactics, and minimal committee interference. On the other hand, weak leadership, great latitude for committee action, and rules that allow extended debate serve the interests of the individual member and of varied local constituencies.

The power of the leadership and the power of each house have waxed and waned during American history. In the early 1800s House Speaker Henry Clay dominated the *party caucus* of Democratic-Republicans in the House. This caucus selected the party's candidate for the presidency and was influential on policy matters. Between 1889 an 1910 the House saw another era of strong, partisan, central leadership. Speaker Thomas B. Reed selected all committee members and chairmen, would not permit dilatory tactics on the part of members, and chaired the Rules Committee, which decided what business would come up for a vote and what the limitations on debate would be. Speaker Joseph Cannon followed Reed, but in 1910–1911 the House revolted and stripped Cannon of his position on the Rules Committee and of his right to appoint committee members and chairmen.

The power Reed had held flowed to the party caucus, to the Rules Committee, and to the chairmen of the standing committees. However, the caucus lacked any real sanctions over members, and its influence waned. In the 1960s and 1970s, chairmen of standing committees lost much of their power as the number and power of subcommittees were increased and the *seniority* system was breached. Thus the general trend has been toward decentralizing decision making and enhancing the power of the individual member at the expense of the congressional leadership.

The two chief controversies regarding the Senate have concerned the selection of its members and the filibuster. For more than a century after the Founding, senators were chosen by state legislators. This created intense factional fights in state legislatures, and the dominance of rich party leaders and businessmen in the Senate led to its being known as the "Millionaires' Club." Intense popular pressure, including the threat of a constitutional convention, led the Senate to acquiesce and pass the Seventeenth Amendment, approved in 1913, which required popular elections for Senate seats. The *filibuster*, a prolonged speech or series of speeches made to delay action, is a longstanding tradition in the Senate, used by liberals and conservatives alike. In 1917, after a filibuster had defeated one of President Wilson's foreign policy measures, *Rule 22* provided that a two-thirds majority (now a three-fifths majority) could cut off debate.

Discussion Questions

1. The trend has been to decentralize power in Congress to achieve greater democracy in decision making. As a result, over half of all Democrats in Congress in 1989–1991 chaired either a committee or a subcommittee. Has democracy been purchased at the expense of efficiency? Is anyone in charge if everyone is in charge?

2. Before World War I, party caucuses made members accountable for their voting behavior. Several members were expelled from their parties for the way they voted on key legislation. Wouldn't Congress be more accountable if party caucuses could do the same today since the public would know whom to blame for bad policies? Would binding caucus decisions make democratic government more vibrant or less so since individual members would no longer be responsible for their votes?

Data and Perspectives for Analysis

The evolution of Congress reflects the changes that have occurred in American society. As society became more complex, Congress responded by developing increased professionalism and establishing centralized leadership positions coupled with structures to facilitate efficiency (committee system and party organizations). Note how Congress marched in step with social progress:

Party Development and Related Events in House and Senate

Event	House	Senate
Centralization of power	1875–1895	1885–1895
Professionalization of career	1890–1910	1875–1895
Hardening of seniority as criterion for advancement on committees	1911–1925	1885–1895
Creation of central leadership positions	1897–1900	1911–1915
Creation of party committees and organizations	1919–present	1885–1895

Source: Randall Ripley, *Congress: Process and Policy*, 4th ed. (New York: Norton, 1988), p. 65. Reprinted by permission of Brooks-Cole Publishing Company.

Additional Lecture Topic A-1

Congress As An Institution

Roger H. Davidson and Walter J. Oleszek, *Congress and Its Members*. 2nd ed. Washington, DC: Congressional Quarterly Press, 1985.

Barbara Hinckley, *Stability and Change in Congress*. New York: Harper & Row, 1988.

Bruce Oppenheimer and Lawrence Dodd, *Congress Reconsidered*. 3rd ed. Washington, DC: Congressional Quarterly Press, 1985.

Randall B. Ripley, *Congress: Process and Policy*. 4th ed. New York: Norton, 1988.

Edward V. Schneier and Bertram Gross, *Congress Today*. New York: St. Martin's Press, 1993.

David J. Vogler, *The Politics of Congress*. 5th ed. Boston: Allyn & Bacon, 1988.

Abstract for Theme A

Congress as a "Citizen Legislature"

The Founders originally conceived of Congress as the institution that would be closest to the people—the essence of the public will (at least in the House initially; popular election of Senators would take some time). However, some critics today charge that Congress has become distant from its true political "roots."

One critic is certainly qualified to comment on this problem—former senate majority leader Howard Baker of Tennessee. Baker presented his point of view in an insightful article in the *New York Times Magazine* (April 1, 1984, pp. 68–69):

> I have been waging a one-man crusade to restore the Congress to its original and intended character as a "citizen legislature" and not an assemblage of elected bureaucrats. To this end, I propose a greatly reduced Congressional session, so Congress can stay in closer touch with the people we represent.... Not so long ago, members of Congress were real people with real jobs in real communities throughout the country. They were truly representative of the people who elected them because they played an integral and active part in the civic and economic and social affairs of their constituencies. They went to Washington temporarily and they came home.

Baker considers the current crop of Congress members to "tourists" in their own constituencies because they must devote their full time to law making and passing "thousand-page" bills. The problem thus becomes one of faithful representation.

> We in Congress are trustees of the ultimate sovereignty in this country—the full expression of the desires and demands of the American people. But in our self-imposed isolation, we grow more and more susceptible to the loudest voice or the largest mailing on any given issue. We surrender the power of independent judgment when we have no personal experience or insight to guide us—when we lose contact with the real world and the practical consequences of our political actions.

Baker argues that Congress gets unnecessarily involved with "everything," such as interfering with public education (a local concern) with the result that educational quality has declined over time. Thus, in his view Congress should be in session only six months of the year and should spend the other half staying in touch with real life in America and seeing firsthand the impact of laws on the citizenry. As he points out, "no law states that every Congressional hearing must be in Washington." Holding more oversight hearings around the country would encourage both greater citizen participation and broader understanding of local problems on the part of Congress members. Other side benefits of a congressional return to popular roots would be improved presidential-congressional relations, the implementing of more effective "sunset" provisions into outmoded laws, and a greater awareness of whether specific policies are relevant.

Questions for Discussion

1. Do you think that a large number of congressional hearings throughout the country (for half a year) would attract greater voter attention? Or would these hearings go largely unattended by the public?

2. Do you agree with Senator Baker that Congress has become a "remote" political institution vis-a-vis the American people? Why or why not?

Answer Guidelines

Answers here are open-ended. No particular responses are expected.

Theme B   Who Gets to Congress

Summary

Members of the House and Senate are predominantly middle-aged, white, Protestant, male lawyers. If people with these characteristics all held similar opinions, Congress would be radically unrepresentative on policy matters, but they do not. Of late, the number of blacks and women in the House has been slowly increasing.

More important is the fact that larger proportions of representatives have served several terms and occupy "safe" rather than *marginal* seats. In 1869 the average representative had served only one term in Congress; by the 1950s over half the representatives had served four or more terms. In the nineteenth century the federal government was not very important, Washington was not a pleasant place in which to live, and being a member of Congress did not pay well. Because the job is more attractive today, one would expect more serious challenges; by 1970 over three-fourths of running incumbents won with 60 percent or more of the vote. (Senators are somewhat less secure; in fewer than half of their races does the winner get 60 percent or more of the vote.) Why this is the case is a subject of controversy among scholars. One theory stresses that voters are voting their party identification less and less and may therefore be voting for the candidate whose name they recognize. Incumbents have extensive means of getting their names known. Also, incumbents can use their powers to get (or may simply take credit for) federal grants, projects, and protection for local interest groups. Accordingly, the typical representative today has served in the House just under five terms.

Representatives are more likely to be not merely white, male, and senior in terms of years of service, but also Democrats. This is because more voters consider themselves Democrats than Republicans (though this is changing) and because the advantages of incumbency (whatever they are) began to take effect after the Democrats gained control of Congress. In only five Congresses since the New Deal have the Democrats failed to control both houses (1947-1948, 1953-1954, 1981-1982, 1983-1984, and 1985-1986). However, the existence of the conservative coalition of Republicans and conservative Democrats means that Democrats are far from being guaranteed that they can get their programs through.

Malapportionment (gross disparity in the size of congressional districts) and *gerrymandering* (the drawing of district boundaries solely for partisan advantage) have been conspicuous features of American politics. In 1964 the Supreme Court adopted the principle of "one-man, one vote," requiring all congressional districts to be of approximately equal size.

Discussion Questions

1. Should the number of terms served by members of Congress be limited (as they are for the president)? If not, what justification exists for imposing a term requirement on the president but not on Congress? Wouldn't corruption be less likely if members of Congress were regularly rotated in office?

2. Should congressional districts be purposely gerrymandered to ensure the election of minority members? Would such gerrymandering support or violate the principle of "one man, one vote"?

Data and Perspectives for Analysis

A. Citizen Contact with Members of Congress

The public can know its members of Congress only by coming into contact with them. How does that contact occur? The table below reflects the ways in which constituents gain insight into their elected representatives. Clearly, most people report having some contact, and yet polls reveal that few in the public can even name their district's representative in the House. What does this suggest about attempts by members of Congress in acquiring name recognition? Note that the data disclose differences between senators and representatives in the ways in which they interact with constituents. How can these differences be explained? Why is it that members of the House have much higher rates of direct contact with constituents (personal and group meetings), but remain less well known than senators?

Citizen Contact with Members of the House and Senate

Type of Contact	Percentage in House	Percentage in Senate
Personal meeting	14	7
Group meeting	12	8
Staff	8	5
Mailing	52	41
Radio	27	40
Television	43	72
Newspaper	52	60
Indirect[a]	28	b
Total reporting any contact	77	84

[a] Those persons who knew of someone else who had contact with the representative
[b] Not asked about Senate candidates.

Source: Alan J. Abramowitz, "A Comparison of Voting for U.S. Senator and Representative in 1978," *American Political Science Review* (September 1980), LXXIV: 635.

B. Public Perceptions of Campaign Promises

Do candidates running for Congress say anything to get elected? This seems to be the impression of the general public. No great deal of public confidence exists in the campaign statements of congressional candidates. Have your students analyze the following data:

Most members of Congress...

Will tell lies if they feel the truth will hurt them politically—76% agree
Care more about special interests than they care about people like you—75% agree
Care more about keeping power than they do about the best interests of the nation—66% agree
Make a lot of money by using public office improperly—57% agree
Care deeply about the problems of ordinary citizens—52% disagree
Have a high personal moral code—47% disagree

Source: Survey by ABC News, *Washington Post*, May 19–23, 1989.

C. "Does Franked Mail Have an Effect on Voters?"

If members of Congress think that franked mail will help them with their constituents, they might be right or wrong. We can use the 1980 Election Study of the Center for Political Studies at the University of Michigan to determine whether people who have gotten such mail are actually more likely to vote for the incumbent.

Percentage Vote for the Incumbent by Party Identification and Receipt of Mail from the Incumbent, 1980

	Party Identification		
	Opposite to Incumbent	Independent	Same as Incumbent
Has gotten mail	54.6% (130)	79.3% (164)	94.6% (221)
Has not gotten mail	42.5% (80)	61.8% (76)	90.7% (118)

Note: Number of respondents is shown in parentheses.
Source: Author's calculations for 1980 CPS survey.

1. Does sending mail to constituents pay off in votes? What sorts of people are most subject to being influenced by mail from an incumbent? What sorts are least influenced?

2. How does the effect of getting mail compare to the effect of ideological or policy agreement (see "The Voter in Congressional Elections" in Theme C following)? Why might incumbents favor sending out more mail (as opposed to voting more in line with the preferences of constituents) when faced with electoral challenge?

3. Does the ability to use the "franking privilege" constitute an unfair advantage for incumbents? If so, what can be done about this?

Additional Lecture Topic B-1

Why Are Congressmen So Secure in Their Seats?

Richard Fenno, Jr., *Home Style: House Members in Their Districts*. Boston: Little, Brown, 1978.

John A. Ferejohn, "On the Decline of Competition in Congressional Elections," and Morris Fiorina, "The Case of the Vanishing Marginals: The Bureaucracy Did It." Both in the *American Political Science Review*, March 1977. Taking issue with Tufte, these two authors argue two alternative hypotheses. Fiorina stresses the superior ability of incumbents to win votes by handling "casework"—taking care of constituents' problems with the bureaucracy. Ferejohn stresses differences in the way *voters* behave; for example, they seem more likely to vote according to name recognition.

John R. Johannes and John C. McAdams, "The Congressional Incumbency Effect." *American Journal of Political Science*, August 1981, pp. 512–542. Challenges the view that incumbents can convert the perquisites of office into electoral security.

John R. Johannes, *To Serve the People: Congress and Constituency Service*. Lincoln: University of Nebraska Press, 1984.

Edward Tufte, "The Relationship Between Seats and Votes." *American Political Science Review*, June 1973. Documents a decline in the "swing ratio"—the percentage of seats that change hands in a House race relative to the percentage change in the national vote. Blames the power of incumbents to gerrymander congressional districts for this decline.

Abstract 1 for Theme B

Why Congressional Incumbents Win

Congressional incumbents do have certain advantages over their challengers. In Marjorie Randon Hershey's *Running for Office* (Chatham, NJ: Chatham House, 1984, pp. 103–107, 166), these advantages are explored is some depth. First, the experience of winning elections gives an incumbent a set of developed "strategies that seemed to work at least once, in the sense of having ended in victory. They may not know exactly why; indeed, they may have won *in spite of* the choices they made. But they do know that the whole package of strategies apparently brought voter approval" (p. 104). In short, in future electoral contests, "tradition" serves as an important guide for the incumbent. Alas, for the challenger, that reservoir of experience is simply not there.

Second, incumbents "also have the great advantage of more time to learn, since they receive campaign-related stimuli between elections as well as during campaigns" (p. 104). In other words, incumbents are constantly contacting their constituents and powerful groups, whereas the challenger has only limited contact prior to the campaign. (Casework also builds good relationships for the incumbent.) Hershey summarizes these advantages as follows:

> Incumbency, then, is a resource for learning—for gaining information, for developing more finely tuned expectations about the links between actions and consequences. Thus it is not only the lack of money or name recognition that puts so many challengers at a disadvantage in campaigns; it is their relative inexperience with the difficult learning situation that campaigns provide. Without an already successful strategy, and with fewer opportunities to learn from experience and assess the usefulness of possible models, challengers start out with a learning deficit compared with most incumbents. It is a deficit from which most challengers never recover. (p. 105)

Does this mean that the challenger's quest is hopeless? Far from it. Incumbent members of Congress can be defeated. Hershey asserts that incumbency can lead to stagnation; existing strategies may become so fixed that the incumbent fails to adapt in time to a changing political environment. In short, "incumbents can become victims of victory" (p. 105). An innovative challenger who senses shifts in the district's mood, population, and policy preferences before the "ossified" incumbent does can emerge victorious.

Regarding the patterns of incumbency and victory in the House versus the Senate, Hershey specifies that senators "have been more electorally vulnerable than House members..." (p. 166). The reason rests with the greater media exposure given to Senate races. Just as U.S. senators gain a great deal of media attention, "so do their challengers—and that gives challengers a boost in gaining name recognition among voters." By contrast, reporters "frequently treat House challengers like surprise packages at rummage sales: potentially interesting, but not worth the effort or the cost to investigate" (p. 166).

Questions for Discussion

1. If you were a challenger for the House seat in your district, what strategy could you devise to unseat the incumbent?

2. Assume you are an incumbent member of Congress running for reelection. What mistakes would you most like to avoid?

Answer Guidelines

As a challenger, you must get your name known before the voters. An ample campaign fund would also help. If the incumbent has been in office for some time, an early start in the campaign would be imperative (this would also permit sufficient time to assemble a capable staff and plot a strategy). The incumbent must not misjudge the mood of the district nor take an extreme stand on issues that would seem inconsistent with his or her traditional "home style."

Abstract 2 for Theme B

Should House Members Be Elected for Four-Year Terms?

In Herbert Levine's *Point-Counterpoint, Readings in American Government*. 2nd ed. (Glenview, IL: Scott, Foresman, 1983), Senator J. Bennett Johnston (D-La.) and political scientist Charles O. Jones debate the issue of the four-year term for members of the House (pp. 298–307). In congressional testimony recorded in 1979, Senator Johnston gave four reasons for a "four-year amendment" to be passed (pp. 299–300):

1. By lengthening the term to 4 years, [a] congressman could at least have 2 years to be a legislator and 2 years to be a candidate, or perhaps generously 3 years to be a legislator and 1 year to be a candidate. It would give the Congress that kind of time which it needs to do the people's business.

2. ... In the present system where House members must run every 2 years, congressmen are spending most of their time either campaigning or raising money. To lengthen those terms to 4 years would cut in half the need to spend the time for, and the need to have the influence of, campaign funds. There are many congressmen ... who, every time they have a tough race, go into debt for the whole 2-year period of their term. That should not be.

3. The third reason ... is the quality of people. ... I know from personal experience candidate after candidate in my state who will refuse to run, having an excellent chance to get elected, because the term is simply too short.

4. Finally ... this constitutional amendment, if passed, will strengthen the two-party system. ... To have congressmen run at the same time a president does would tend to give to the people an ability through an election to carry out a program on which the president is running.

Senator Bennett also mentions that public opinion polls reveal support for a four-year amendment.

Conversely, Charles O. Jones argues that the two-year term enhances frequent communication with the district, whereas a four-year tenure could possible weaken this vital legislator-citizen link. To Jones, "a longer term will (not) somehow solve one of the oldest problems of an elected legislature: ... how to campaign, represent, and still make law." Also, if the four-year term will attract more candidates to public office, then the total cost of campaigns may increase, since primary challenges will multiply accordingly for the incumbent. Furthermore, Jones dismisses the idea that the cost of living in Washington and the uncertainty of being reelected under the two-year pattern prevent "quality people" from running for Congress. Finally, "having representatives run every four years with the president, and not at midterm, will not solve the problems of split party control ... nor will it solve the Carter phenomenon" (a presidential candidate running "against Washington").

Theme C Congressional Organization and Procedures

Summary

Congress is not a single organization but a vast collection of organizations.

1. *Party organization.* In the Senate, real leadership is in the hands of a *majority leader*, chosen from among the majority party, and a minority leader, chosen from the other

party. The *whip* takes a nose count of how votes are lining up on controversial issues, keeps the party leader informed, and rounds up members for important votes. The Democratic *Steering Committee* and the Republican *Committee on Committees* assign senators to standing committees. Such assignments are extremely important to a senator's career prospects, as Senator Moynihan's campaign to get on the Finance Committee illustrates.

The party structure is essentially the same in the House as in the Senate, with two important exceptions. The leadership in general has more power in the House, because the House is a very large body that must restrict debate and schedule its business with great care. In the House, the position of *Speaker* carries considerable power. The Speaker may decide whom to recognize in debate, whether a motion is relevant and germane, and to which committees new bills are assigned. The Speaker also influences which bills are brought up for a vote, appoints members of special and select committees, and nominates majority-party members of the Rules Committee.

The effect of this party machinery can be seen in the *party vote* in Congress. Party is a very important determinant of a member's vote—more important than any other single thing. However, party voting in Congress does not approach the levels that prevail in a parliamentary system. As parties in Congress have weakened over the last century, party voting has been declining. And much party voting is probably actually ideological voting: Republicans in both houses are predominantly conservative and Democrats liberal (although there is a significant minority of conservative Democrats). However, even the average southern Democrat is more liberal than the average northern liberal Republican.

2. *Opinion and interest groupings*. These include ideological groupings, such as the Democratic Study Group or the Conservative Democratic Forum; state delegations from large states, such as California, New York, and Texas; and groupings representing various interests such as the Black Caucus, Environmental Policy Committee, and the Roller and Ball-Bearing Coalition. Specifically, caucuses (associations of Congress members created to advocate an ideology or regional economic interest) have become rivals to parties, numbering more than seventy by the early 1980s.

3. *Committees*. Here is where the real work of Congress is done and where most of the power is found. *Standing committees* are the most important, because they are (with a few exceptions) the only ones that can propose legislation by reporting a bill out to the full House or Senate. *Select committees* last for only a few Congresses and have a limited purpose. Joint committees are those on which both senators and representatives serve. A *conference committee*, which tries to resolve differences between House and Senate versions of the same legislation, is an especially important kind of joint committee.

Traditionally, committees have been dominated by their chairmen, who (throughout most of this century) were chosen by seniority. In the early 1970s a series of reforms, voted by the Democratic Caucus, decentralized and democratized committee operations. The election of committee chairmen by secret ballot allowed the seniority system to be breached, meetings were opened to the public, and the prerogatives of subcommittees and individual members were enhanced at the expense of committee chairmen. It is too early to tell whether these changes will be for good or ill.

Different committees attract different kinds of Congress members. Some, such as the House Ways and Means Committee and the Senate Foreign Relations Committee, attract policy-oriented members; others, such as the House Post Office and Civil Service Committees, provide means of servicing a constituency and bolstering reelection prospects.

4. *Staff*. Congress has produced the most rapidly growing bureaucracy in Washington. In 1935 the typical representative had two aides; by 1979 the average had increased to sixteen but has held fairly steady since then, with the average standing at seventeen in 1994. Some staff members (increasingly located in district offices) service requests from constituents. Other staff members do legislative work, helping the Congress mem-

bers keep abreast of a vast workload (over 15,000 bills are introduced in a typical Congress). The vast increase in staff has reduced contact among members of Congress, making the institution less collegial, more individualistic, and less of a deliberative body.

5. *Staff agencies.* These provide specialized knowledge and expertise and are an important congressional counter to the resources the president can muster as chief of the executive branch. Examples include the CRS, GAO, OTA, and CBO.

Crucial to the process of how a bill becomes a law is the number of points at which it may be blocked. A majority coalition must be assembled slowly and painstakingly.

1. *Introduction.* In the House, a bill is introduced by dropping it into the "hopper" or handing it to a clerk; in the Senate, by announcing the bill's introduction on the floor. Bills may be *public* (pertaining to affairs generally) or *private* (pertaining to a particular individual). It is often said that legislation is initiated by the president and enacted by Congress. Actually Congress often initiates legislation; the consumer and environmental legislation of the 1960s and 1970s are good examples.

2. *Study by committee.* The bill is referred to a committee by either the Speaker of the House or the presiding officer of the Senate. There are rules that govern which bills go to which committees, but sometimes a choice is possible and the bill can be sent to a receptive (or unreceptive) committee. Most bills die in committee. Important bills are generally referred to a subcommittee for hearings. Then the subcommittee (or committee) will *mark up* the bill—make revisions and additions. If a majority of the committee votes to *report out* the bill, it goes to the full House or Senate. Otherwise the bill dies, unless a *discharge petition* (a maneuver that is rarely successful) brings it to the full House. In the Senate any bill can be proposed on the floor as an amendment to another measure, so discharge petitions are not needed.

    At this point the bill goes on a *calendar*, a fact that still does not guarantee consideration. In the Senate the majority leader, in consultation with the minority leader, schedules bills for consideration. In the House, the *Rules Committee* reviews major bills and may block action or send them to the floor under a *closed rule*, which limits debate and forbids amendments, or under a less favorable *open rule*, which permits amendments from the floor.

3. *Floor debate.* In the House, major bills are discussed by the *Committee of the Whole* under rather tight restrictions. The committee sponsoring the bill guides the debate, amendments (if they are allowed at all) must be germane, and the time allowed for debate is limited. The sponsoring committee usually gets its version passed by the House. Four voting procedures in the House are the voice, division, teller, and roll-call votes.

    In the Senate, there is no limit on debate (except for *cloture*). Nongermane amendments may be offered, producing a "Christmas tree" (with "goodies" for lots of groups) or forcing the Senate to deal with an important policy issue in connection with a trivial bill.

4. *Conference committee.* If a bill passes the House and Senate in different forms, the differences must be reconciled before the bill can become law. If the differences are minor, one house may simply accede to the changes made by the other. If differences are major, a *conference committee* must iron them out. In most cases, conference votes tend to favor, slightly, the Senate version of the bill.

5. *The president's signature.* If both houses accept the conference report, the bill goes to the president for signature or veto. If the president vetoes the bill, the veto can be overridden by a two-thirds vote of those present in each of the two houses.

Discussion Questions

1. *Instructor: Draw a track on the board and then start to draw hurdles on the track.* Look at the chart "How a Bill Becomes Law" in the text, and count the "hurdles" a bill must surmount if it is to become law. List them all.

2. Consider each of the following features of Congress (including some that no longer apply), and discuss the *policy implications* of each. Does each (a) lead to more or less logical and coherent policies? (b) lead to more or less representation of various local and parochial interests? (c) make it easier or harder to pass legislation?

   Party voting in Congress
   A strong Speaker of the House
   A highly specialized committee structure
   Committee reforms that have taken power away from chairmen
   Ideological caucuses
   Open meetings of committees
   Large staffs, including those of congressional members, those of committees, and staff agencies
   Powerful support for the president in Congress
   The filibuster
   The "closed rule"

3. Students should be aware of two significant facts about the legislative process. First, almost all legislation is considered in subcommittees composed of from six to ten members. Second, most legislation enacted into law passes without any changes in the way the bill is reported from committee (70 percent of House and 65 percent of Senate). To be successful, therefore, wouldn't interest groups have to influence only a few members of Congress? Why does Congress rubber-stamp the work of its committees?

Data and Perspectives for Analysis

A. The Legislative Process and Public Policy

The formulation of public policy is much more complicated than following the formal rules of the legislative process. The role of Congress, even though it is the actual decision maker, varies by the type of policy under consideration. Six different types of public policy issues have been identified:

   Distributive: policies that promote private activities beneficial to society (farm subsidies, tax benefits for home owners)
   Protective/regulatory: policies that protect the public from private activities (unfair labor laws, food inspection regulations)
   Redistributive: policies that shift wealth from the privileged to the unprivileged (welfare programs, progressive income tax)
   Structural: policies that deal with the procurement of military materiel and the organization of the military
   Strategic: policies that establish foreign and defense positions of the nation
   Crisis: policies that involve short-term responses to immediate national problems

The table on the following page conveys a more accurate understanding of lawmaking. A simplified version of the table is found in the *Student Handbook*.

Policy type	Primary actors	Relationship among actors	Stability of relationship	Visibility of decision	Influence of President Presidency & Centralized Bureaucracy	Influence of Bureaus	Influence of Congress as a whole	Influence of Congressional subcommittees	Influence of Private sector
Distributive	Congressional subcommittees and committees; executive bureaus; small interest groups	Logrolling (everyone gains)	Stable	Low	Low	High	Low (supports subcommittees)	High	High (subsidized groups)
Protective regulatory	Congressional subcommittees and committees; full House and Senate; executive agencies; trade associations	Bargaining; compromise	Unstable	Moderate	Moderately high	Moderate	Moderately high	Moderate	Moderately high (regulated interests)
Redistributive	President and his appointees; committees and/or Congress; largest interest groups (peak associations); "liberals, conservatives"	Ideological and class conflict	Stable	High	High	Moderately low	High	Moderately low	High ("peak associations" representing clusters of interest groups)
Structural	Congressional subcommittees and committees; executive bureaus; small interest groups	Logrolling (everyone gains)	Stable	Low	Low	High	Low (supports subcommittees)	High	High (subsidized groups and corporations)
Strategic	Executive agencies; president	Bargaining; compromise	Unstable	Low until publicized; then low to high	High	Low	High (often responsive to executive)	Low	Moderate (interest groups, corporations)
Crisis	President and advisers	Cooperation	Unstable	Low until publicized; then generally high	High	Low	Low	Low	Low

Source: Randall Ripley, and Grace Franklin, *Congress, the Bureaucracy, and Public Policy*. 4th ed. (Chicago: Dorsey Press, 1987), p. 22–23.

B. Congressional Committees and Interest Groups

Political scientists have long been interested in the *committee structure* in Congress and its relationship to interest groups in the political system. Bruce A. Ray has done a study of the Armed Services Committees of the House and the Senate and of their support of military spending. Look at Table 1 and determine whether committee members are more or less likely to support the military in House votes.

1. If committee members are more supportive of the military than are nonmembers, why might this be the case? What sorts of processes could account for the difference?

Instructor: Discourage your students from making comparisons between houses and across congresses. The index is based on different votes in different houses and different congresses.

Look at Table 2 and try to infer *what process* makes committee members more supportive of the military in each house.

TABLE 1 Support for the "Military-Industrial Complex," Comparing Armed Services Committee Members and Nonmembers

	Congress	Mean NSI Scores[a]	
		Committee Members	Committee Nonmembers
House	91st	86.4%	73.9%
	92nd	82.4	66.6
	93rd	80.4	62.3
	94th	75.6	58.6
	95th	78.2	59.9
Senate	91st	68.7%	53.6%
	92nd	74.0	54.2
	93rd	77.1	48.2
	94th	70.3	49.5
	95th	65.4	42.2

[a] Percentage of time each member voted "correctly" on selected national security issues according to the American Security Council (ASC).

Table 2 Support for the "Military-Industrial Complex": Average NSI Index Scores, 91st Through 95th Congresses

	All Freshmen	Armed Services Committee Freshmen	All Nonfreshmen	Armed Services Committee Nonfreshmen
House	59.45%	82.51%	67.00%	80.17%
Senate	51.97	53.99	53.17	75.80

1. Look first at the House. How do freshmen on the Armed Services Committee compare to other freshmen? How do Armed Services Committee freshmen compare to nonfreshmen on that committee?

2. Look now at the Senate. How do Armed Services Committee freshmen compare to all freshmen? How do Armed Services Committee freshmen compare to nonfreshmen on that committee? What processes serve to make the committees more supportive of the military than the Congress as a whole is? How does the process differ between the House and the Senate?

Instructor: See Bruce A. Ray, "The Responsiveness of the U.S. Congressional Armed Services Committees to Their Parent Bodies," Legislative Studies Quarterly, November 1980, pp. 501–515.

C. The Role of the Conference Committee in Legislation

Frequently, different versions of the same bill will be passed by both the House and the Senate. A conference committee, composed of key leaders and representatives from both chambers, must work out those differences so that the same bill will be sent back to each house for approval.

An example of this process occurred in May, 1988, when the U.S. Senate followed the House's example in approving a bill to prohibit the manufacture, sale, or possession of undetectable plastic firearms and other similar weapons (see "Senate, Following House Move, Votes Ban on Plastic Firearms" by Susan F. Rasky, *New York Times*, May 26, 1988, p. 10). The purpose of the legislation was described in this manner:

> The goal of both the House and Senate legislation is to bar firearms made of plastic or other substances that elude detection by security devices at airports and in many public buildings. Supporters of the legislation have said their primary concern is the possibility that a terrorist could smuggle such a weapon onto an airplane or into a courthouse because its plastic components are not clearly detectable by an X-ray machine.
>
> The Senate legislation is also partly aimed at halting the production of toy guns so closely resembling real ones that they can be used in the commission of crimes.

The Senate legislation had the following features: (a) All firearms manufactured or sold nationally would be "as detectable as a stainless steel revolver weighing 3.7 ounces." (b) Improved security would be required at all federally regulated airports, courthouses, and security checkpoints (not in the House version). (c) All toy or similarly constructed firearms would have an orange plug permanently inserted into the gun barrel (not in the House version). (d) Penalties of up to five years in prison would be imposed for violations of the law (same as House). (e) Maximum fines and/or imprisonment would be imposed for violations of the law associated with drug trafficking or violent crimes (not in House version).

1. Ask selected students to research the final form of this bill. What provisions were eventually placed into the legislation by the conference committee?

2. Since the Reagan administration favored the Senate version of the bill over the House form, did the conference committee retain most of the Senate features? If so, why? If not, speculate on the reasons.

3. Did this bill eventually become law? If so, when?

Additional Lecture Topic C-1

The Institutionalization of Congress

Harrison W. Fox and Susan Webb Hammond, *Congressional Staffs: The Invisible Force in American Lawmaking*. New York: Free Press, 1977.

Richard Hall, "Participation and Purpose in Committee Decision Making." *American Political Science Review*, March 1987.

Susan Hammond, Arthur G. Stevens, Jr., and Daniel P. Mulhollan, "Congressional Caucuses: Legislators as Lobbyists." In Allan J. Cigler and Burdett A. Loomis, eds. *Interest Group Politics*. Washington, DC: Congressional Quarterly Press, 1983. pp. 275–297.

Michael J. Malbin, "Congressional Committee Staffs: Who's in Charge Here?" *Public Interest*, Spring 1977.

Michael Malbin, *Unelected Representatives: Congressional Staffs and the Future of Representative Government*. New York: Basic Books, 1980.

Randall B. Ripley, *Congress: Process and Policy*. 4th ed. New York: Norton, 1988. Chapter 2.

Steven S. Smith and Christopher J. Deering, *Committees in Congress*. 2nd ed. Washington, DC: Congressional Quarterly Press, 1990.

Randall Strahan, *New Ways and Means: Reform and Change in Congressional Committees.* Chapel Hill, NC: University of North Carolina Press, 1990.

Joseph Unekis and Leroy Rieselbach, *Congressional Committee Politics.* New York: Praeger, 1984.

Among the long-term changes in Congress are (a) increasing professionalization; (b) an increasingly elaborate committee structure; and (3) vastly increased staffs and support services. These changes have doubtless allowed Congress to deal with its vastly expanded work load. But they may be of little help in allowing Congress to deal with important national problems.

Additional Lecture Topic C-2

The Legislative Process

Matthew D. McCubbins and Terry Sullivan, eds. *Congress: Structure and Policy.* Boston: Cambridge University Press, 1987.

Walter J. Oleszek, *Congressional Procedures and the Policy Process.* 3rd ed. Washington, DC: Congressional Quarterly Press, 1989.

Instructor: Congressional procedures can seem deadly dull to students, but a few anecdotes can arouse interest. You will need to show students how important matters of national policy turn on questions of congressional organization and procedures. Oleszek is invaluable for this purpose.

Howard E. Schuman, *Politics and the Budget: The Struggle Between the President and Congress.* 2nd ed. Englewood Cliffs, NJ: Prentice-Hall, 1988.

Stephen Smith, *Call to Order: Floor Politics in the House and Senate.* Washington: Brookings Institution, 1989.

Abstract for Theme C

The Role of Congressional Hearings

Congressional committees get a great deal of information about possible legislation by holding hearings. A good example of this process was reported in a *New York Times* article entitled "Senate Hears of Abuse in States' Mental Care" (April 2, 1985, p. 11). The legislative issue involved the allegation that residents of state mental institutions has been abused and exploited. Senator Lowell P. Weicker, Jr. (R-Conn.), presided over the hearing, reacting to expert testimony on subhuman conditions with the statement, "This is the shame of America."

Hospital officials disputed this damaging testimony, but Senate investigators who had visited thirty-one institutions in twelve states insisted that residents face "abuse and serious physical injury, sexual advances and rape, as well as verbal threats of injury and other forms of intimidation." Senator Weicker had called the hearings as chairman of the Senate Labor and Human Resources Subcommittee on the Handicapped, a unit of the Committee on Labor and Human Resources, and as chairman of the Appropriations Subcommittee on Health and Human Services. The article went on to state that Senators Weicker, Robert T. Stafford (R-Vt.), and Paul Simon (D-Ill.)

> wanted to pass legislation to correct the problems described today. Thus, *the hearing appeared to mark the start of a new phase of Congressional concern about problems that have been sporadically reported in the last few years.* (emphasis added)

In final testimony from David Ferleger, a Philadelphia lawyer who had represented people in state institutions, it was proposed that

Congress authorize courts to award "treble damages against state officials who violate the civil rights of people in institutions."

In addition, he testified, Congress should pass a criminal law prohibiting such abuse, and the Justice Department should establish a special "appointed counsel to inmates of mental institutions who bring habeas corpus proceedings in Federal Court."

Questions for Discussion

1. Did these hearings in April 1985 ever lead to passage of any laws to help residents of state mental institutions? (You can assign a group of students to check this.)

2. The issue of state mental care had been one of concern for several years, according to the article. Why had Congress not previously acted to correct the problem?

Answer Guidelines

The first query will require appropriate library research by students. Regarding the slowness of Congress to act on this problem, you could cite such matters as the crowded congressional agenda, the competition among social problems and their perceived priority, and the institutional roadblocks within Congress itself.

Theme D   Does Congress Represent Constituents' Opinions?

Summary

There are at least three theories on why members of Congress vote the way they do:

1. *Representational.* This view holds that members want to get reelected and therefore vote to please their constituents. It seems to be true when the issue is highly visible and the constituency is fairly united in its stance, as was the case on civil-rights bills in the 1950s and 1960s.

2. *Organizational.* This view holds that members of Congress respond to cues provided by their fellow members. Party is the single most important of these cues, but ideological organizations, such as the Democratic Study Group, may also be important. Members also tend to go along with their party's representatives on the sponsoring committee and with their state delegations.

3. *Attitudinal.* Members of Congress, like other political elites, are more ideological in their thinking than the public at large. Democratic members tend to be strongly liberal, and Republicans conservative. One 1970 study showed the House to be quite close to the opinions of the public as a whole and the Senate to be far more liberal. The results of this survey would probably have been different had it been done in the 1950s (an era of conservative dominance in the Senate) or after the 1980 election (when many liberal senators were defeated).

Discussion Questions

1. Suppose you are a rational voter and want your representative in Congress to vote for the policies you prefer. How could you make this come about? What do you have to *know* to do anything about the matter?

2. What is "party voting"? Has it been increasing or declining in the House? If representatives vote "party," does that mean they are less likely to be representing constituents' attitudes?

Data and Perspectives for Analysis

Members Respond to Constituent Opinions

The extent to which members of Congress should reflect constituent opinion on political issues is a much debated topic. As discussed in the text, democratic theorists are divided over whether elected representatives should mirror public attitudes or do what is best even if in conflict with constituent desires. Moreover, the text discusses how difficult it is for members of Congress to discover constituent opinion on most issues. What about the other side of the coin? How difficult is it for constituents to know the position of their member of Congress on a vital issue? Consider the following exchange of letters between Senator John Kerry and one of his constituents concerning the Gulf War. The letters were presented in a series of articles in the *Boston Globe*.

Letter faxed to Senator Kerry from Walter Carter on January 9, 1991:

> Dear Senator Kerry,
> I urge you to support President Bush's request that Congress approve the "use of all necessary means" to get Iraqi forces out of Kuwait.
> To deny the president's request would encourage further aggression, and to support the request is the most appropriate and effective means to preserve a liberal democratic world order with minimum human suffering in the long run.

Response of Senator Kerry to Mr. Carter dated January 22, 1991:

> Dear Mr. Carter,
> Thank you for contacting me to express your opposition to the Bush administration's additional deployment of US military forces in Saudi Arabia and the Persian Gulf, and to the early use of military force by the US against Iraq. I share your concerns.
> On Jan. 11, I voted in favor of a resolution that would have insisted that economic sanctions be given more time to work and against a resolution giving the president immediate authority to go to war against Iraq to force it out of Kuwait, warning that a decision to go to war was "rolling the dice" with our future.

Response of Senator Kerry to Mr. Carter dated January 31, 1991:

> Dear Mr. Carter,
> Thank you very much for contacting me to express your support for the actions of President Bush in response to the Iraqi invasion of Kuwait.
> From the outset of the invasion, I have strongly and unequivocally supported President Bush's response to the crisis and the policy goals he has established with our military deployment in the Persian Gulf.
> The bottom line for the administration and the international community, in which I concur completely, is the total unconditional withdrawal of all Iraqi forces from Kuwait. Two of the most critical elements in our ability to accomplish this goal have been the administration's skillful use of the United Nations and the new relationship with the Soviet Union to bring almost universal condemnation and isolation of the brutal regime of Saddam Hussein.
> ... Again thank you for contacting me to express your strong support for our government's actions in standing up to this shocking aggression in the Persian Gulf.

Letter by Senator Kerry to the Boston Globe explaining the contradictory responses to Mr. Carter:

Sen. Kerry responds to contradictory letters

> Yesterday's Globe inaccurately—and, I think, unfairly—reflected my position on the gulf war.
> Part of the reason for the misrepresentation is my fault and I take the responsibility. By accident our computer mailing system sent out two letters. We should not have done so but considering that we respond to approximately 6,000 letters a week such mistakes happen rarely. During the period of debate on the war we received 6,000 letters a day.
> Unfortunately, the second letter appeared to contradict the first. In fact it does not. The second letter was an old letter I mailed immediately after the August invasion of Kuwait.

In was totally supportive of the president because I was supportive of Desert Shield in its original defensive mission, together with the policy of involving the United Nations and the development of international economic sanctions against Iraq. I was one of 97 votes supporting the president at that time and the letter reflected that. Subsequently, when we debated the war resolution I mailed a different letter, which is the one Walter Carter should have received. In the letter he should have received, which has been mailed to thousands of others, I squarely state my position. I quote:

"The debate in the Senate was not about *whether* we should or should not have used force, but *when* force should be used. I supported the resolution which would have given the sanctions more time to deteriorate further Saddam Hassein's capacity to wage war . . . Now that the war has begun, Congress has overwhelmingly affirmed its support for our men and women risking their lives in the conflict against Iraq. We must not allow the nation to turn its back on the soldiers as we did in Vietnam. I will work to assure that this does not occur."

This position was expressed in detail by me during the mid-January floor debate on the war.

Unfortunately, the Globe, by playing on a computer error without contacting me to see if there was a possible explanation for the apparent inconsistency of the two letters, created a mistaken impression, which I hope this letter will put to rest.

JOHN F. KERRY
US Senate

Additional Lecture Topic D-1

Do Representatives in Congress Represent?

Robert Bernstein, *Elections, Representation, and Congressional Voting Behavior*. Englewood Cliffs, NJ: Prentice-Hall, 1989.

John Kingdon, *Congressional Voting Decisions*. 3rd ed. Ann Arbor: University of Michigan Press, 1989.

David Mayhew, *Congress: The Electoral Connection*. New Haven: Yale University Press, 1974.

In a very broad sense, these studies show that, on highly visible issues, Congress is a highly representative institution. They do not deal with client politics, which is Congress's favored way of handling low-visibility issues.

Abstract 1 for Theme D

Constituent Needs and the Congressional Staff's Importance

Members of Congress face a fundamental dilemma—they must represent their constituents while at the same time considering innumerable pieces of legislation during each congressional term. Hence the importance of the congressional staff. In Robert Sherrill's *Why They Call It Politics* (Orlando, FL: Harcourt Brace Jovanovich, 1984) the problem is spelled out clearly:

> So great are the demands on their time that members have increasingly turned over more and more duties to their staffs and have themselves become more and more remote from the public. This is especially true in the Senate, where a member's constituency can be well into the millions. Senate members receive more than 50 million pieces of mail in a typical year. Senators from a large state may receive 20,000 letters a week. (p. 150)

In short, the staffs must shield the representative from the impossible demands of constituents who wish either to meet or talk to the legislator.

The Congress member's staff also plays another key role in the legislative process—researching bills, drafting policy statements and speeches, recruiting witnesses for hearings in subcommittees and committees, and even monitoring the executive branch's implementation of a law. (See "The Shadow Government," *U.S. News and World Report*, June 27, 1983, pp. 63–65.) Even a Congress member's vote will be based on the counsel of his or her staff. So long as members are caught in the constituency-lawmaking dilemma, they will continue to rely on their key congressional aides.

Questions for Discussion

1. Some observers argue that a Congress member's reliance on staff could be lessened somewhat if each representative were awarded an *ombudsman*—a salaried federal employee who could function as an "action-line" official for constituents who need help or favors from the government. The ombudsman approach is used in a number of Scandinavian countries and in a few cities across the nation. Is this idea a good or bad one? Why?

2. Would allowing each representative and each senator even more staff members than the current allocation help or hinder the legislative process? Explain your reasons for holding either opinion.

Answer Guidelines

Some critics think the ombudsman approach would not work well in a large, complex nation such as the United States, where the number of constituent demands are overwhelming. An ombudsman could be overloaded as well. Also, adding another layer to the federal bureaucracy is distasteful to many. Adding to the staff payroll might actually create more legislative work, because new staffers could research supplementary legislative subjects in order to justify their existence!

Abstract 2 for Theme D

Members of Congress and Their Districts

Reelection prospects for members of Congress are often directly linked to how well they serve the needs of their districts. While House members may choose to exercise their independent judgment on an important issue, votes or positions that contradict the prevailing social and economic interests of the district are taken at great political risk. "Voting one's district" is a strong congressional norm.

An example of this principle was found in an article (*New York Times*, February 11, 1988, by Richard Halloran entitled "Budget Cuts? Not in My District" p. 10). The issue that affected certain select congressmen was a defense cut in the Air Force Logistics Command of some $1.6 billion. Civilian workers would necessarily be fired, affecting employment in a number of congressional districts. Predictably, seventeen House members sent a letter to Edward C. Aldridge, secretary of the air force, expressing concern over the "crippling budget cuts assigned to this command." The eleven Democrats and six Republicans argued in the letter that the readiness of the nation's combat forces would be impaired.

A perusal of the members of congress involved and of their districts revealed the following: Representatives Albert G. Bustmante (D), Henry B. Gonzalez (D), and Lamar S. Smith (R) were all from San Antonio—Kelly Air Force Base, where the Logistics Command employed 20,600 civilians, was five miles away; Representatives Dave McGurdy, Glenn English, and Wes Watkins (all Democrats) and Mickey Edwards (R) were from Oklahoma—Tinker Air Force Base in Oklahoma City has 19,800 civilian employees; three members of Congress from Ohio (Wright-Patterson Air Force Base—17,500 employees), two members of Congress from Georgia (Robins Air Force Base—16,700 employees), two from California (McClellan Air Force Base—15,000 civilian employees), and two from Utah (Hill Air Force Base—16,200 workers) also signed the letter.

Questions for Discussion

1. What general observations can be deduced about the congressman-district relationship from the excerpted *New York Times* article?

2. Would you vote for a congressman who had urged that a key military base be closed in your home town—why or why not?

Answer Guidelines

Clearly, open-minded discussion is favored here. You may wish to raise the importance of economic prosperity in the district as a link to reelection for a congressman.

Theme E   Ethics and Congress

Summary

The system of checks and balances is designed to fragment political power to prevent any single branch from becoming tyrannical. The problem is that this system also provides multiple points of access to influence government officials and in the process enhances the potential for corruption. Congress has been especially prone to instances of corruption and the abuse of power in recent years. This fact has contributed to the public's low opinion of Congress, with only 17 percent approving of its performance in 1992. The series of scandals can be lumped into three categories: financial, sexual, and political.

The financial improprieties of members of Congress generally involve use of their political office to obtain some monetary benefit they would ordinarily not receive. Representative Tony Coehlo, for example, took a loan from a political fund-raiser and resigned over the apparent conflict of interest; Senator David Durenburger was "denounced" by the Senate for requiring groups to purchase numerous copies of his book as payment for speaking. In 1989, even the powerful Speaker of the House, Jim Wright of Texas, was compelled to resign over a book deal. Perhaps the most controversial scandal pertained to the House bank, which allowed members of Congress to cash checks with insufficient funds.

The sexual escapades of members of Congress have resulted in much media coverage. The problems have ranged from Representative Barney Frank's homosexual relationship with a male prostitute to Representative Donald Luken's 1989 conviction for a sexual encounter with a sixteen-year-old female. Recently attention has focused on sexual harassment on Capitol Hill; Senator Robert Packwood has been accused by twenty-three women of making unwanted sexual advances over a twenty-year period. The incidence of such harassment is probably more widespread than this isolated case. A 1993 poll by the *Washington Post* discovered that one of every nine female staffers reports having been a victim of sexual harassment by a member of Congress.

The political abuse of power is usually difficult to prove. The "Keating Five" illustrates the complexity of this issue. Charles Keating, head of Lincoln Savings and Loan (S&L), contributed an estimated $1.3 million to the campaigns of five senators. These senators in turn intervened on Keating's behalf during a government investigation into the mismanagement of his S&L, an intervention that delayed government action and eventually cost taxpayers $2 billion to bail out the institution when it failed. The senators responded that they were acting only to represent a constituent, a key function of their job. Only one senator, Alan Cranston (who was about to retire), received a formal censure for his activities in this episode. In other words the line between "politics as usual" and the "abuse of political power" is sometimes blurred.

Both houses have enacted codes of ethics to clean up the image of Congress. The codes suffer from the same defect—they assume that corruption is mainly a monetary concern. But money is only one way in which an official can be improperly influenced. Even the monetary controls imposed by the codes are problematic in that they inherently favor wealthy members of Congress who have no need to supplement their incomes. Moveover, the executive branch has used these scandals (such as Abscam) to unleash investigations into Congress, which act as a form of harassment and weaken the separation of powers. It is quite clear that political corruption in Congress has no easy resolution.

Abstract for Theme E

Congressional Ethics and the House Leader

A well-publicized question of congressional ethics occurred in June, 1988, when the House Ethics Committee voted to launch an inquiry into Speaker Jim Wright's political conduct, that is, alleged violations of House rules. Speaker Wright, a Democrat from Texas, was accused by a Republican, Newt Gingrich of Georgia, of improper lobbying on behalf of a constituent with whom he had an interest in a private gas well venture, assisting two Texas oil ventures through unethical influence upon American and Egyptian government officials, illegally using a member of his staff to help him write a book, and possibly converting campaign funds for personal use. A fifth charge, brought by Common Cause, involved the "possible exercise of undue influence in dealings with officials of the Federal Home Loan Bank board" to help two Texas banking executives (who had strong ties to the Democratic party). The Ethics Committee wrote a sixth charge involving the Speaker's possible improper use of a condominium in Fort Worth, his home town (see the *New York Times,* June 10, 1988, p. 1 and June 11, 1988, p. 1).

Questions for Discussion

1. Have students research how the various charges leveled against Speaker Wright related to possible violations of House ethics. Also, did the House Ethics Committee fully investigate the charges enumerated above? What did the investigation eventually prove about the validity of those charges?

2. Why and how can it be argued that whenever a congressman helps a constituent, a charge of unethical behavior can result?

Answer Guidelines

In helping a constituent, a congressman is open to accusations by critics that the very act of assistance is subtly linked to an expectation that the constituent will "pay off" the representative in some manner. Of course, this is hyperbole, but students in the class may wish to explore why this image persists among many citizens.

Data and Perspectives for Analysis

How to Punish Members of Congress

Members of Congress are not subject to the impeachment process because the Constitution limits impeachable officials to the president, vice president, and "all civil officers." In 1797, the Senate refused to apply the impeachment procedure to William Blount on the ground that members of Congress are "legislative" officers rather than "civil" ones.

> For offenses of sufficient gravity, each house of Congress may punish its members by expulsion or censure [the words *condemn* and *denounce* have been used as synonyms for censure]. Of the two degrees of punishment, censure is milder and requires a two-thirds majority. Censure also has the advantage of not depriving constituents of their elected senators or representatives. Grounds for disciplining members usually consist of a member's action during service in Congress. Both houses have seldom used their power to punish a member for their offenses committed prior to an election and have been shy about punishing misdeeds committed during a previous Congress....
>
> Conspiracy against a foreign country (the 1797 case in the Senate) and support of a rebellion (the Civil War cases of 14 senators and 3 representatives) were the only grounds on which a member of Congress was expelled until the Abscam corruption scandal in 1980....
>
> In the Senate, censure proceedings are carried out with a degree of moderation typical of that chamber's proceedings. The alleged offender, for example, is granted the privilege of speaking on his own behalf.
>
> In the House, the treatment of an offender is more harsh. The house often has denied the privilege of speaking to a representative accused of wrongdoing. In most cases in the House, a cen-

sured member is treated like a felon; the Speaker calls the person to the bar of the House and makes a solemn pronouncement of censure.

How Congress Works (Washington, DC: Congressional Quarterly Press, 1983), pp. 180–183. Reprinted by permission of CQ Press.

Theme F   Congress and Reforms

Summary

There can be little doubt that Congress has usually been perceived by the public as ineffective, particularly when citizens contrast the apparent slow pace of legislation with the apparent speed and drama of presidential action. (This feeling is not germane only to our modern era; Woodrow Wilson once termed the nineteenth-century House of Representatives "a disintegrated mass of jarring elements" in his famed *Congressional Government*, p. 210.) Yet it seems ironic that while Congress as an institution is criticized, individual voters seem content with their own representatives, since incumbents are reelected at an incredibly high rate. Apparently, congressmen do make a maximum effort to implement their representative function, so it is safe to say that "constituency relationships" are a strong feature of the national legislature. Furthermore, can one realistically expect Congress to work quickly, given the innumerable structural and procedural roadblocks deliberately ingrained into the institution? Since Congress is a microcosm of the nation's great diversity, it must seek a legislative consensus, and consensus is often slow and at times downright impossible to realize. Still, Congress can be responsible for momentous change in the nation's history.

In "What's Wrong with Congress?" (*Atlantic Monthly*, December, 1984), Greg Easterbrook poses the question whether structural changes in U.S. politics and Congress have "pushed Congress across the fine line separating creative friction from chaos." Easterbrook cites the end of seniority, the transfer of party loyalty to PACs, the stress on media campaigning, the approach of running against the Washington establishment and yet paradoxically being a member of it, ideological "anti" campaigns, the rise of congressional subcommittee power and staff size, and the increase in the number of lobbyists and the intensity of the lobbying process.

Easterbrook explains that the breaking of the seniority system and subcommittee expansion have limited congressional cohesion and increased the congressional work load. "Multiple referral" allows several subcommittees to consider the same legislation, slowing the legislative process even further. Testimony at these subcommittee hearings may become redundant as well. Furthermore, "the velocity at which campaign spending has increased over the past ten years has engendered a permanent state of anxiety in which members of Congress can never stop worrying about fund raising and the compromises it entails." Finally, Easterbrook lambastes the entire system of lobbying in Congress, particularly deploring the fact "that it is not uncommon to see them (lobbyists) outside the main chamber doors in the House and Senate giving thumbs-up or thumbs-down signals to congressmen rushing in for roll-call votes."

Easterbrook recommends the following changes in Congress: the "reeling back" of seniority system reforms; substantial raises for congressmen, who would then be required to forsake all outside income; a two-year budget cycle; a cap on total campaign expenditures for each congressional candidate (for example, $100,000 for the House and $500,000 for the Senate); and the denial of "access" to the Capitol for lobbyists. As Easterbrook concludes, "before Congress can lead the nation, it must lead itself."

A rejoinder to Easterbrook's views is put forth by *Wall Street Journal* correspondent Albert Hunt in his article "In Defense of a Messy Congress" (*Washingtonian*, September, 1982). Hunt acknowledges the public's impression of Congress as inept, bulky, bureaucratic, shallow, greedy, cowardly, and even lacking the "legislative giants of yesteryear." But Hunt notes that society expects more of Congress today than in past eras and that there are more talented people in Congress in a general sense. He notes that most criticisms are "exaggerated":

The simple fact is that Congress isn't *supposed* to operate neatly, efficiently, or expeditiously. Any system of checks and balances has built-in tensions and rough edges. Bismarck said the two things one never should watch being made are sausage and legislation. And he was talking about a legislative process much tidier than ours.

Hunt also has some suggestions for improving Congress. He proposes public finance for congressional campaigns and curbs on PACs; a reduction in overlapping committee jurisdictions; a reduction of one-fifth in congressional staff (oversized staffs generate work overloads and impede direct communication among and between congressmen); enlargement of oversight and a decrease in the amount of legislation; the use of sunset legislation on all entitlement and tax provisions; and "new ways" to set congressional pay (thus avoiding public passion over congressional pay raises).

Discussion Questions

1. Which suggested congressional reforms seem to make the most sense and why? Have any of these reforms been implemented?

2. If major structural reforms were implemented in Congress and the legislative process thus speeded up, would this be desirable or not? Explain fully.

Additional Lecture Topic F-1

Congressional Reform

William J. Keefe, *Congress and the American People.* Englewood Cliffs, NJ: Prentice-Hall, 1988. See Chapter 5, "Change and Constancy."

Ralph K. Huitt, "Congress: Retrospect and Prospect." *Journal of Politics*, 38 (August 1976).

Leroy N. Rieselbach, *Congressional Reform.* Washington, DC: Congressional Quarterly Press, 1986.

Bruce I. Oppenheimer, "Policy Effects of U.S. House Reform: Decentralization and the Capacity to Resolve Energy Issues." *Legislative Studies Quarterly*, February, 1980, pp. 5–30.

Mark Green, *Who Runs Congress?* 4th ed. New York: Dell, 1984.

12

The Presidency

Overview and Objectives

This chapter introduces the student to the institution that has become the hub of American government over its two centuries of history: the presidency. The chapter will demonstrate that this institution is unique, or at least significantly different from other positions of government leadership. It will also survey the changes that have occurred in the office—from the original, limited position intended by the Founders, through historical evolution, and down to the office of the president as we know it today. After reading and reviewing the material in this chapter the student should be able to do each of the following:

1. Explain the differences between the positions of president and prime minister.
2. Discuss the approach of the Founders toward executive power.
3. Sketch the evolution of the presidency from 1789 to the present.
4. List and describe the various offices that go to make up the office of the president.
5. Review discussions of presidential "character," and how these relate to the achievements in office of various presidents.
6. Enumerate and discuss the various facets—formal and informal—of presidential power.

Chapter Outline with Keyed-in Resources

I. Presidents and prime ministers (THEME A: THE POWER OF THE PRESIDENT VERSUS OTHER INSTITUTIONS)
   A. Characteristics of parliaments
      1. Parliamentary system twice as common
      2. Chief executive chosen by legislature
      3. Cabinet ministers chosen from among members of parliament
      4. Prime minister remains in power as long as his/her party or coalition maintains a majority in the legislature

   The stability of parliamentary government varies greatly. In Italy, for example, a succession of almost four dozen governments has come to power since World War II, with the average government enduring only seven months.

   B. Differences
      1. Presidents are often outsiders; prime ministers are always insiders, chosen by party members in parliament

        2. Presidents choose cabinet from outside Congress; prime ministers choose members of parliament
        3. Presidents have no guaranteed majority in the legislature; prime ministers always have a majority
        4. Presidents and legislature often work at cross-purposes
            a. Even when one party controls both branches
            b. A consequence of separation of powers
            c. Only Roosevelt and Johnson had much luck with Congress
    C. Divided government common in U.S. but Americans dislike it for creating gridlock
        1. But divided government passes as many important laws as a unified government
        2. Unclear whether gridlock is always bad; it is a necessary consequence of representative democracy
        3. Divided governments are occurring more frequently

In one unusual case, a split government existed within the presidency itself when John Tyler became president on the death of William Henry Harrison. Although elected as a Whig, Tyler had troubles with his own party and began appointing Democrats to the cabinet. Thus a Whig president presided over a Democratic cabinet.

II. The evolution of the presidency
    A. Delegates feared both anarchy and monarchy
        1. Idea of a plural executive
        2. Idea of an executive checked by a council
    B. Concerns of the Founders
        1. Fear of military power of president who could overpower states

George Washington was the only president who took active control of the military. During the Whiskey Rebellion of 1794, Washington requested state governors to provide a force of 12,900 militia troops—and ended up with a volunteer force larger than the one he had commanded during the Revolutionary War.

        2. Fear of presidential corruption of Senate
        3. Fear of presidential bribery to ensure reelection
    C. The electoral college
        1. Each state to choose own method of selecting electors
        2. Electors to meet in own capital to vote for president and vice president

The actual election of the president and vice president does not occur until January 6, when the sitting vice president, in the presence of both houses of Congress, opens the ballots of the electors. Although usually a formality, numerous electors have deviated from the way they were supposed to vote.

        3. If no majority, House would decide
    D. The president's term of office
        1. Precedent of George Washington and two terms
        2. Twenty-second Amendment in 1951 limits to two terms
        3. Problem of establishing the legitimacy of the office

The legitimacy of the office depended to a large degree on demonstrating that it would not culminate in a monarchy. This was not easy to do. A Senate committee even proposed the following title: "His Highness the President of the United States and Protector of the Rights of the Same."

        4. Provision for orderly transfer of power
    E. The first presidents
        1. Prominent men helped provide legitimacy
        2. Minimal activism of early government contributed to lessening fear of the presidency
        3. Appointed people of stature in the community (rule of fitness)
        4. Relations with Congress were reserved; few vetoes; no advise

    F. The Jacksonians
       1. Jackson sought to maximize powers of presidency
       2. Vigorous use of veto for policy reasons
       3. Challenged Congress
    G. The reemergence of Congress
       1. With brief exceptions the next hundred years was a period of congressional ascendancy
       2. Intensely divided public opinion
       3. Only Lincoln expanded presidential power
         a. Asserted "implied powers" and commander in chief
         b. Justified by emergency conditions

The Supreme Court rejected Lincoln's emergency powers rationale for exercising power beyond the president's constitutional authority. In *Ex Parte Milligan* (1866), the Court declared that "the Constitution of the United States is a law for rulers and people, equally in war and in peace."

       4. President mostly a negative force to Congress until New Deal
       5. Since 1930s, power has been institutionalized in the presidency
       6. Popular conception of president as center of government contradicts reality; Congress often policy leader
  III. The powers of the president (ADDITIONAL LECTURE TOPIC A-1)
    A. Formal powers found in Article II
       1. Not a large number of explicit powers
       2. Potential for power found in ambiguous clauses of the Constitution—e.g., power as commander in chief, duty to "take care that laws be faithfully executed"
    B. Greatest source of power lies in politics and public opinion
       1. Increase in broad statutory authority
       2. Expectation of presidential leadership from the public

The public's perception that presidential power is vast should not be exaggerated. In a 1990 survey, 31 percent believed that the Supreme Court was more powerful than the president (21 percent endorsed the opposite position).

  IV. The office of the president (THEME B: THE INSTITUTIONALIZATION OF THE PRESIDENCY)
    A. The White House Office
       1. Contains the president's closest assistants
       2. Three types of organization
         a. Circular
         b. Pyramid
         c. Ad hoc
       3. Staff typically worked on the campaign: a few are experts
       4. Relative influence of staff depends on how close one's office is to the president's
    B. Executive Office of the President (ADDITIONAL LECTURE TOPICS B-1, B-2, B-3)
       1. Composed of agencies that report directly to the president
       2. Appointments must receive Senate confirmation
       3. Office of Management and Budget most important
         a. Assembles the budget
         b. Develops reorganization plans
         c. Reviews legislative proposals of agencies
    C. The cabinet
       1. Largely a fiction, not mentioned in Constitution

The term "cabinet" was coined by a journalist during the administration of George Washington.

       2. President can appoint fewer than 1 percent of departmental employees

3. Secretaries become preoccupied and defensive about their own departments
    D. Independent agencies, commissions, and judgeships
        1. President appoints members of agencies that have a quasi-independent status
        2. Agency heads can be removed only "for cause" and serve fixed term
        3. Judges can be removed only by impeachment
V. Who gets appointed
    A. President knows few appointees personally

A story published in *Time* magazine recounts how President Reagan, at a conference of mayors, shook the hand of his own secretary of housing and urban development, Samuel Franklin Pierce, and greeted him as "Mr. Mayor."

    B. Most appointees have had federal experience
        1. "In-and-outers"—alternate federal and private sector jobs
        2. No longer have political followings but picked for expertise
    C. Need to consider important interest groups when making appointments
    D. Rivalry between department heads and White House staff
VI. Presidential character
    A. Eisenhower—orderly

President Eisenhower wanted his options clearly spelled out in simple terms. Thus decision memos were reduced to a one-page synopsis.

    B. Kennedy—improviser
    C. Johnson—deal maker
    D. Nixon—mistrustful
    E. Ford—genial

Ford, whose original name was Leslie King, Jr., had the reputation of being an amiable bumbler. According to Barbara Holland, Ford attended his own wedding wearing one brown shoe and one black one.

    F. Carter—outsider
    G. Reagan—communicator
    H. Bush—hands-on manager
    I. Clinton—focus on details
VII. The power to persuade
    A. Formal opportunities for persuasion
    B. The three audiences
        1. Fellow politicians and leaders in Washington, D.C.—reputation very important
        2. Party activists and officials outside Washington
        3. The various publics
    C. Popularity and influence

Presidents usually enjoy a temporary surge in popularity following a national crisis, even disasters like the Bay of Pigs (President Kennedy) and the hostage rescue mission in Iran (President Carter). This phenomenon is known as the "rally round the flag" syndrome. However, recent scholarship has identified numerous exceptions to this rule.

        1. Presidents try to transform popularity into support in Congress
        2. Little effect of "presidential coattails"
        3. Members of Congress believe it is politically risky to challenge a popular president
    D. The decline in popularity
        1. Popularity highest immediately after an election
        2. Declines by midterm after honeymoon
VIII. The power to say no
    A. Veto
        1. Veto message
        2. Pocket veto (only before end of Congress)
        3. Congress rarely overrides vetoes; no line-item veto

B. Executive privilege

Wide variations exist in the use of executive privilege. President Eisenhower asserted the claim forty-four times, whereas Kennedy and Johnson did so only twice each.

    1. Confidential communications between president and advisers
    2. Justification
        a. Separation of powers
        b. Need for candid advice
    3. *U.S.* v. *Nixon* (1973) rejected claim of absolute executive privilege
  C. Impoundment of funds
    1. Defined: presidential refusal to spend funds appropriated by Congress
    2. Countered by Budget Reform Act of 1974
        a. Requires president to notify Congress of funds he does not intend to spend
        b. Congress must agree in 45 days

IX. The president's program
  A. Putting together a program

The preparation of a presidential program was not institutionalized until the administration of Franklin Roosevelt. When Eisenhower assumed office, he failed to submit a program in the belief that initiating legislation was a congressional responsibility. Congress finally requested the president to forward his policies for action.

    1. President can try to have a policy on everything (Carter)
    2. President can concentrate on a small number of initiatives (Reagan)
    3. Constraints
        a. Public reaction may be adverse
        b. Limited time and attention span
        c. Unexpected crises
        d. Programs can be changed only marginally
    4. Need for president to be selective about what he wants
  B. Measuring success
    1. "Box score"—proportion of president's measures approved by Congress (wins half)
    2. Proportion of votes in Congress on which president's position prevails (wins three-fourths)
  C. Attempts to reorganize

When Congress rebuffed President Nixon's proposal to streamline executive departments, Nixon attempted to institute the reorganization by establishing a few "superdepartments" and having certain secretaries assume supervision over several departments. Watergate intervened.

    1. Reasons for reorganizing
        a. Large number of agencies
        b. Easier to change policy through reorganization
    2. Reorganization outside the White House staff must be by law

X. Presidential transition (ADDITIONAL LECTURE TOPICS C-1, C-2) (THEME C: HOW THE PRESIDENT IS SELECTED)
  A. Few presidents serve two terms

The House of Representatives passed a resolution in 1875 declaring that an attempt by Ulysses Grant to pursue a third term would be "unwise, unpatriotic and fraught with peril to our free institutions."

  B. The vice president
    1. May succeed on death of president
        a. Has happened eight times

The last words of the man who assassinated President McKinley were: "I am an anarchist. I don't believe in marriage. I believe in free love."

        b. John Tyler defined status of ascending vice president: president in title and in powers

The odds of both the president and the vice president dying in the same term are 1 in 840. To avoid a succession calamity, the Secret Service insists that one member of the cabinet should be absent when the president delivers the State of the Union message. Since all high-ranking members of the administration attend, the possibility exists that the entire line of presidential succession could be wiped out by an act of terrorism. In 1993, Secretary of Interior Bruce Babbitt—eighth in order of succession—did not attend President Clinton's speech.

    2. Rarely are vice presidents elected president
        a. Unless they first took over for a president who died
        b. Only five instances otherwise: Adams, Jefferson, Van Buren, Nixon, Bush

Both John Adams and Thomas Jefferson were vice presidents prior to the adoption of the Twelfth Amendment, which provided for the election of a single ticket to the top executive offices (president and vice president). Adams and Jefferson, therefore, had no official party connection to the president.

    3. "A rather empty job"
        a. Candidates still pursue it
        b. Vice president presides over Senate and votes in case of tie
        c. Leadership powers in Senate are weak
  C. Problems of succession
    1. What if president falls ill?
        a. Examples: Garfield, Wilson

President Garfield had the rather unusual talent of being able to write in Greek with one hand while writing in Latin with the other hand—at the same time.

    2. If vice president steps up, who becomes new vice president?
        a. Succession Act (1886): designated secretary of state as next in line
        b. Amended in 1947 to designate Speaker of the House
    3. Twenty-fifth Amendment resolved both issues
        a. Allows vice president to serve as acting president if president is disabled
            (1) Decided by president, by vice president and cabinet, or by two-thirds vote of Congress

President Reagan was the first president to use the incapacity provision of the Twenty-fifth Amendment. While in the hospital to have an intestinal tumor removed, Reagan signed a statement allowing the then vice president, George Bush, to exercise power "in my stead commencing with the administration of anesthesia to me in this instance." However, Reagan never formally mentioned compliance with the Twenty-fifth Amendment.

        b. Requires vice president who ascends to office on death or resignation of president to name a vice president
            (1) Must be confirmed by both houses
            (2) Examples: Agnew's and Nixon's resignations
  C. Impeachment
    1. Judges most frequent objects of impeachment
    2. Indictment by the House, conviction by the Senate

Although the impeachment process has been successfully used against federal judges, it has never succeeded against a member of the Supreme Court. Only Samuel Chase was impeached by the House while serving as a justice of the Supreme Court in 1804, but, as in the case of President Andrew Johnson, the Senate failed to convict.

  XI. How powerful is the president? (THEME D: PRESIDENTIAL POWER AND FUTURE REFORMS)
    A. Both president and Congress are more constrained
    B. Reasons for constraints
        1. Complexity of issues

2. Scrutiny of the media
3. Power of interest groups

Important Terms

*ad hoc structure A method in which the president organizes his personal staff that employs task forces, committees, and informal groups of friends dealing directly with him.

Budget Reform Act of 1974 A congressional effort to control presidential impoundments. It requires, among other things, that the president spend all appropriated funds unless he first tells Congress which funds he wishes not to spend and Congress, within forty-five days, agrees to delete the items. If he wishes simply to delay spending money, he need only inform Congress, but Congress in turn can refuse the delay by passing a resolution requiring immediate release of the funds.

*cabinet By custom, the heads of the thirteen major executive departments who meet to discuss matters with the President. These "secretaries" receive their positions by presidential nomination and confirmation by the Senate. They can be removed at the will of the president.

*circular structure A method in which the president organizes his personal staff that has cabinet secretaries and assistants reporting directly to the president.

*direct democracy A form of democracy in which the people legislate for themselves.

*divided government A government in which one party controls the White House and a different party controls one or both houses of Congress.

electoral college The body that formally selects the president. Each state is allotted electoral votes equal to the number of its representatives in Congress. It can decide how its electors are to be chosen and under what method they cast their votes for president. The candidate for the presidency who receives a majority of these votes wins. If no candidate obtains a majority, the House of Representatives chooses from the top three in electoral votes.

Executive Office of the President Executive agencies that report directly to the president and whose purpose is to perform staff services for the president. Top positions are filled by presidential nomination with Senate confirmation.

executive privilege A claim by the president entitling him to withhold information from the courts or Congress. In 1973, the Supreme Court ruled that such a claim is valid when sensitive military or diplomatic matters are involved, but it refused to recognize an "absolute unqualified" presidential privilege of immunity.

*impeachment A form of indictment voted on by the House of Representatives. It can be brought against the president, the vice president, and all "civil officers" of the federal government. To be removed from his or her position, the impeached officer must be convicted by a two-thirds vote of the Senate.

impoundment The refusal of the president to spend money appropriated by Congress. The Constitution is silent on this power, but the Budget Reform Act of 1974 limits the president's ability to impound funds.

independent agencies Federal agencies that are part of the executive branch but outside the structure of cabinet departments. Their heads typically serve fixed terms of office and can be removed only for cause.

inherent powers Powers not specified in the Constitution which the president claims. These powers are asserted by virtue of office.

*lame duck A politician whose power has been diminished because he or she is about to leave office as a result of electoral defeat or statutory limitation.

*legislative veto A method by which Congress in a law allows either one or both houses to block a proposed executive action. It is frequently used for presidential reorganization plans of the executive branch. These vetoes were declared unconstitutional in 1981.

line-item veto A power possessed by most state governors, but not the president, to approve some provisions in a law and to disapprove of others. The president must accept or reject an entire bill.

Office of Management and Budget Created as the Bureau of the Budget in 1921, the OMB was reorganized in 1970. It assembles and analyzes the national budget submitted to Congress by the president. Additional duties include studying the organization and operation of the executive branch, devising plans for reorganizing departments and agencies, developing ways of getting better information about government programs, and reviewing proposals that cabinet departments want included in the president's legislative program.

perks A short form of the term "perquisites," meaning the fringe benefits of office.

pocket veto One of two ways for a president to disapprove a bill sent to him by Congress. If the president does not sign the bill within ten days of receiving it, and Congress has adjourned within that time, the bill does not become law.

presidential coattails The charismatic power of a president which enables congressional candidates of the same party to ride into office on the strength of his popularity. This influence has declined in recent elections.

prime minister The head of government in a parliamentary system. Chosen by the legislature, this official selects the other ministers of government from among the members of parliament and remains in power as long as his or her party has a majority of seats in the legislature, as long as the assembled coalition holds together, or until the next scheduled election.

pyramid structure A method in which the president organizes his personal staff that has most assistants reporting through a hierarchy to a chief of staff.

representative democracy A form of government in which the people elect representatives to act on their behalf.

rule of propinquity A dictum that applies to the behavior of presidential assistants. The rule holds that power is wielded by people who are in the room when a decision is made. Thus members of the White House Office jockey for offices close to that of the president.

Twenty-fifth Amendment A constitutional amendment ratified in 1967 which deals with presidential disability. It provides that the vice president is to serve as acting president whenever the president declares he is unable to discharge the duties of office or whenever the vice president and a majority of the cabinet declare the president incapacitated. If the president disagrees, a two-thirds vote of Congress is needed to confirm that the president is unable to execute his duties. The amendment also deals with a vacancy in the vice presidency by allowing the president to nominate a new vice president subject to confirmation by a majority vote of both houses.

Twenty-second Amendment A constitutional amendment ratified in 1951 which limits presidents to two terms of office.

unified government A government in which the same party controls the presidency and both houses of Congress.

veto message A statement the president sends to Congress accompanying a refusal to sign a bill passed by both houses. It indicates the president's reasons for the veto. A two-thirds vote of both houses overrides the veto.

White House Office Personal assistants to the president with offices in the White House. These aides oversee the political and policy interests of the president and do not require Senate confirmation for appointment. They can be removed at the discretion of the president.

Theme A The Power of the President Versus Other Institutions

Instructor References

Nigel Bowles, *The White House and Capitol Hill*, New York: Oxford University Press, 1987.

Thomas E. Cronin, *The State of the Presidency*. 2nd ed. Boston: Little, Brown, 1980. Provocative, wide-ranging, and highly useful volume.

James W. Davis, *The American Presidency: A New Perspective*. New York: Harper & Row, 1987. A good overview.

George C. Edwards III, *At the Margins: Presidential Leadership of Congress*. New Haven: Yale University Press, 1989.

George C. Edwards III and Stephen Wayne, *Presidential Leadership*. New York: St. Martin's Press, 1985. Excellent work on presidents' leadership problems, the obstacles to their leadership, and the kind of presidential skills necessary to overcome those obstacles.

Louis W. Koenig, *The Chief Executive*. 5th ed. New York: Harcourt Brace Jovanovich, 1986. An updated version of a classic text.

Michael Nelson, ed., *The Presidency and the Political System*. Washington, DC: Congressional Quarterly Press, 1984. Nineteen essays that comprehensively treat the relationship between the president and the political system.

Richard E. Neustadt, *Presidential Power*. 3rd ed. New York: Wiley, 1990.

Richard M. Pious, *The American Presidency*. New York: Basic Books, 1979. Thorough, encyclopedic account of the office.

Summary

Two models of executive leadership exist in representative democracies, prime ministers and presidents. A prime minister is chosen not by the voters, but by members of Parliament. In Britain's parliamentary system, for example, the prime minister is a party leader, chosen by elected officials of the party, and selected on the basis of the ability to hold the party together inside Parliament. Once in power, the prime minister appoints other ministers (equivalent to cabinet officers) from among members of his or her party in Parliament, a fact that gives the prime minister great leverage over party members. In addition, the prime minister is assured of a great deal of loyalty from ministers because of the tradition of collective responsibility, which requires ministers publicly to support all government policies or, if in disagreement, to resign from office. Moreover, the prime minister is shielded from bearing personal blame for policy failures through the doctrine of ministerial responsibility, which obliges the minister with responsibility for a department with a failed policy to resign. Eighteen British cabinet ministers have done so since World War II. A prime minister is quite likely to have had high-level administrative experience in the national government as well as in Parliament itself (twentieth-century British prime ministers have served an average of twenty-four years in Parliament before reaching the highest office).

Presidents, on the other hand, are chosen by conventions in which party professionals are a minority; they are chosen in election years with an eye to appealing to a majority of the voters and are unlikely to have had administrative experience in Washington. They often lack a majority in one or both houses of Congress, and they select cabinet members in order to reward personal followers, recognize interest groups, or gain expertise in the cabinet.

The president's constitutionally defined powers, found mostly in *Article II*, are not impressive. The power of commander-in-chief was, at first, not considered to entail much authority; the main military force was expected to be state militias, and the president, according to Arthur Schlesinger, Jr., was thought to lack any independent offensive capability without prior congressional approval. When the navy captured a pirate vessel, for example, Thomas Jefferson ordered the ship released because the president "was unauthorized by the Constitution, without the sanction of Congress, to go beyond the line of defense." The president also possesses the power to "take care that the laws be faithfully executed." The wording seems to imply that the president is allowed to do no more than carry out the laws of Congress, but subsequent Supreme Court interpretations of this clause, notably In re Neagle (1890), have expanded the scope of presidential authority to act without a specific congressional mandate in domestic affairs. Nonetheless, the chief source of increased presidential power can be found in politics and public opinion: the American people look to the president for leadership and hold him responsible for national affairs. In an influential book, Richard Neustadt has argued that the president's success depends not on any formal power but on his ability to persuade, especially the people within the Washington establishment. From a few vague and unimpressive powers in Article II, the issue is now whether the president has grown too powerful and the presidency too "imperial."

The Framers debated the office of the presidency at great length. On the one hand, they feared the possibility of monarchical tendencies if the office was made too powerful. On the other hand, they felt that a large nation with foreign enemies required an executive with substantial powers. They were also concerned that the president should not dominate Congress and that Congress should not dominate the president. The assumption that George Washington would be the first president, coupled with the successful balancing of the interests of the small and the large states in the *Electoral College*, allowed the Framers to cede substantial powers to the presidency.

The emergence of the modern presidency is the outcome of nearly two hundred years of American history. The first presidents (from Washington to John Quincy Adams) exercised few powers and established the legitimacy of the presidency, greatly aided by the fact that the national government had little to do. Andrew Jackson, although opposed to a large and powerful federal government, believed in an independent and strong presidency and greatly extended the powers of the office. After the end of Jackson's second term (1837), Congress reasserted its power and, with the exception of occasional presidential assertions under Polk, Cleveland, and especially Lincoln, remained the dominant institution until the time of the New Deal.

Discussion Questions

1. What factors enabled Congress to dominate the American government in the nineteenth century? Was the problem a series of weak governments? For example, how many presidents between Jackson and Lincoln can the class name? Historian Henry Adams argues that the declining quality of presidents since Washington is enough to disprove the theory of evolution. If the early presidents were so great, why did Congress dominate even them?

2. The text concludes that presidential authority began to increase as a result of national crises. Why didn't presidential power increase after the nation's first three wars (the War of 1812, the Mexican War, and the Spanish-American War)? Were the wars different or was the nation different?

3. Aaron Wildavsky's "two presidencies" thesis suggests that presidents are more successful with Congress in foreign policy than in domestic policy. From 1948 to 1964, Congress passed 73.3 percent of the president's defense policy proposals, compared to 40.2 percent of his domestic proposals. Why is the president more successful in foreign policy? The difference in success rates narrowed between 1965 and 1975 (55 percent foreign policy versus 46 percent domestic policy). What explains the recent poorer performance of the president in foreign policy? The *Student Handbook* contains data on the Wildavsky's thesis in the "Applying What You've Learned" exercise.

Data and Perspectives for Analysis

A. Presidential Support in Congress

The level of presidential support in Congress varies widely, not only among presidents but also during a president's tenure. Have your students examine the chart below that compares presidential support in Congress from 1953–1991. The percentages are based on votes on which presidents took a clear position.

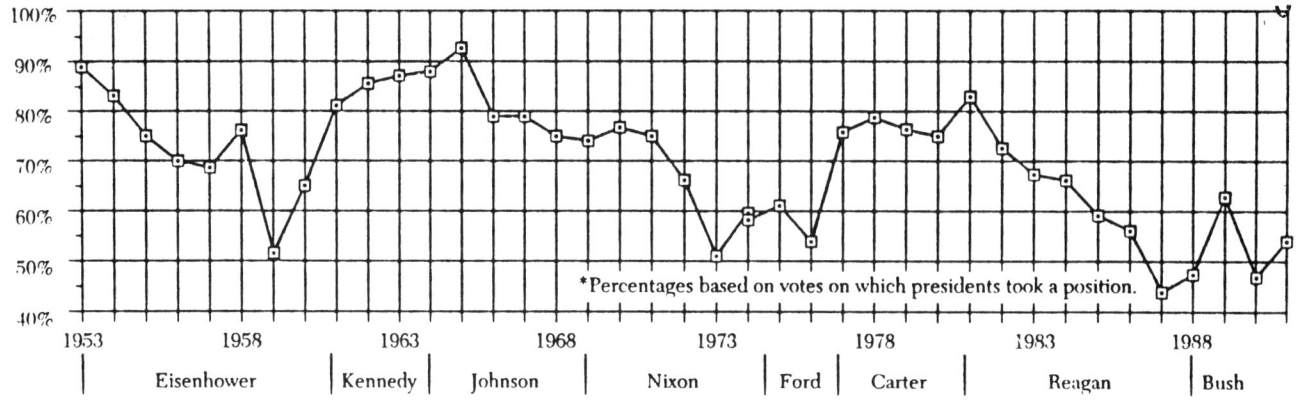

Eisenhower	Kennedy	Johnson	Nixon	Ford	Carter	Reagan	Bush
1953 89.0	1961 81.0	1964 88.0	1969 74.0	1974 58.2	1977 75.4	1981 82.4	1989 63.0.
1954 82.8	1962 85.4	1965 93.0	1970 77.0	1975 61.0	1978 78.3	1982 72.4	1990 46.8
1955 75.0	1963 87.1	1966 79.0	1971 75.0	1976 53.8	1979 76.8	1983 67.1	1991 54.0
1956 70.0		1967 79.0	1972 66.0		1980 75.1	1984 65.8	
1957 68.0		1968 75.0	1973 50.6			1985 59.9	
1958 76.0			1974 59.6			1986 56.1	
1959 52.0						1987 43.5	
1960 65.0						1988 47.4	

Source: Robert J. Spitzer, *President and Congress: Executive Hegemony at the Crossroads of American Government*. New York: McGraw-Hill, 1993, p. 80

Discussion Questions

1. Does the chart support the text's assertion that Congress is more likely to support a president whose popularity is high? Look at obvious periods of presidential popularity or unpopularity, like the Watergate era and the "honeymoon" phase.

2. Why do Republican presidents, notably Eisenhower and even Nixon at first, enjoy such high levels of success despite facing Democratic Congresses? Why was President Carter considered a poor leader given the high proportion of his legislation that passed Congress?

3. Does presidential support of a particular piece of legislation mean that the president actually agreed with the bill?

B. Presidential Greatness

Americans often discuss presidential greatness. Who was the most effective president in history? Numerous polls on this question have been conducted among American historians. The results of six polls are presented on page 203. Have the class analyze the various rankings. What factors are associated with presidential greatness—a time of national crisis, ideology (liberal or conservative), and so on?

Presidential Performance Evaluations

Schlesinger Poll (1948)	Schlesinger Poll (1962)	Maranell Accomplishment Poll (1970) Accomplishments of Administrations	U.S. Historical Society Poll (1977) Ten Greatest Presidents	Chicago Tribune Poll (1982)	Murray Poll (1982) Presidential Rank
Great	*Great*	1. Lincoln	1. Lincoln	*Ten Best Presidents*	1. Lincoln
1. Lincoln	1. Lincoln	2. F. Roosevelt	2. Washington	1. Lincoln (best)	2. F. Roosevelt
2. Washington	2. Washington	3. Washington	3. F. Roosevelt	2. Washington	3. Washington
3. F. Roosevelt	3. F. Roosevelt	4. Jefferson	4. T. Roosevelt	3. F. Roosevelt	4. Jefferson
4. Wilson	4. Wilson	5. T. Roosevelt	5. Jefferson	4. T. Roosevelt	5. T. Roosevelt
5. Jefferson	5. Jefferson	6. Truman	6. Wilson	5. Jefferson	6. Wilson
6. Jackson	*Near Great*	7. Wilson	7. Jackson	6. Wilson	7. Jackson
Near Great	6. Jackson	8. Jackson	8. Truman	7. Jackson	8. Truman
7. T. Roosevelt	7. T. Roosevelt	9. L. Johnson	9. Polk	8. Truman	9. J. Adams
8. Cleveland	8. Polk	10. Polk	10. J. Adams	9. Eisenhower	10. L. Johnson
9. J. Adams	9. Truman	11. J. Adams		10. Polk (10th best)	11. Eisenhower
10. Polk	10. J. Adams	12. Kennedy		*Ten Worst Presidents*	12. Polk
Average	10. Cleveland	13. Monroe		1. Harding (worst)	13. Kennedy
11. J. Q. Adams	*Average*	14. Cleveland		2. Nixon	14. Madison
12. Monroe	11. Madison	15. Madison		3. Buchanan	15. Monroe
13. Hayes	12. J. Q. Adams	16. Taft		4. Pierce	16. J. Q. Adams
14. Madison	13. Hayes	17. McKinley		5. Grant	17. Cleveland
15. Van Buren	14. McKinley	18. J. Q. Adams		6. Fillmore	18. McKinley
16. Taft	15. Taft	19. Hoover		7. A. Johnson	19. Taft
17. Arthur	16. Van Buren	20. Eisenhower		8. Coolidge	20. Van Buren
18. McKinley	17. Monroe	21. A. Johnson		9. Tyler	21. Hoover
19. A. Johnson	18. Hoover	22. Van Buren		10. Carter (10th worst)	22. Hayes
20. Hoover	19. B. Harrison	23. Arthur			23. Arthur
21. B. Harrison	20. Arthur	24. Hayes			24. Ford
Below Average	20. Eisenhower	25. Tyler			25. Carter
22. Tyler	21. A. Johnson	26. B. Harrison			26. B. Harrison
23. Coolidge	*Below Average*	27. Taylor			27. Taylor
24. Fillmore	22. Taylor	28. Buchanan			28. Tyler
25. Taylor	23. Tyler	29. Fillmore			29. Fillmore
26. Buchanan	24. Fillmore	30. Coolidge			30. Coolidge
27. Pierce	25. Coolidge	31. Pierce			31. Pierce
Failure	26. Pierce	32. Grant			32. A. Johnson
28. Grant	27. Buchanan	33. Harding			33. Buchanan
29. Harding	*Failure*				34. Nixon
	28. Grant				35. Grant
	29. Harding				36. Harding

Note: No polls rate either W. Harrison or Garfield because of their short tenures in office.

Source: Larry Berman, *The New American Presidency* (Boston: Little, Brown, 1987), pp. 124−125.

Additional Lecture Topics

A-1. Is the President Too Powerful?

L. Gordon Crovitz and Jeremy Rabkin, eds., *The Fettered Presidency: Legal Constraints on the Executive Branch*. Washington, DC: American Enterprise Institute, 1989.

Hugo Heclo and Lester Salamon, *The Illusion of Presidential Government*. Boulder, CO: Westview, 1981.

Edmund S. Muskie, Kenneth Rush, and Kenneth W. Thompson, *The President, the Congress and Foreign Policy*. Boston: Boston University Press, 1986. You probably will want to use lecture time to lay out both sides of the factual case and leave the normative question of whether the president ought to have more or less power for class discussion (see Abstract A).

John Spanier and Joseph Nogee, *Congress, the Presidency, and American Foreign Policy*. New York: Pergamon, 1981.

Harvey G. Ziedenstein, "The Reassertion of Congressional Power: New Curbs on the President," *Political Science Quarterly*, Fall 1978. Reprinted in Caraley and Epstein, eds., *The Making of American Foreign and Domestic Policy*.

A-2. Historical Origins of the Presidency

Louis W. Koenig, *The Chief Executive*. 5th ed. New York: Harcourt Brace Jovanovich, 1986. See Chapter 2, pp. 21–37.

David C. Kozak and Kennedth N. Ciboski, eds., *The American Presidency: A Policy Perspective from Readings and Documents*. Chicago: Nelson-Hall, 1985. See Gregor Reinhard's article, "The Origins of the Presidency," pp. 1–13.

Stanley Milkis and Michael Nelson, eds., *The American Presidency: Origins and Development, 1776–1990*. Washington, DC: Congressional Quarterly Press, 1990.

C. C. Thach, Jr., *The Creation of the Presidency, 1775–1789: A Study in Constitutional History*. Baltimore: John Hopkins University Press, 1922.

Arthur M. Schlesinger, Jr., *The Imperial Presidency*. New York: Popular Library Press, 1974. See Chapters 1 and 2 on the intentions of the Founding Fathers concerning the presidency.

Abstract For Theme A

Presidential Power—Should It Be Curbed?

The perennial question of whether the president of the United States is too powerful vis-a-vis other institutions of the American political scene is debated in George McKenna and Stanley Feingold, eds., *Taking Sides: Clashing Views on Controversial Political Issues*, 2nd ed. (Guilford, CT: Dushkin, 1981). In Reading 6, "Is the President Too Powerful?" Michael Novak ("Yes") and Theodore Sorenson ("No") argue the issue forcefully.

Novak's case is built on a need for constitutional balance and an equally important need to curb the symbolic power of the president, power largely yielded to him through television. As Novak puts it:

> Thus, television places in the president's hands enormous metaphysical powers not provided for in the Constitution—powers over reality, powers over appearances, powers over perception . . . his *presence* dominates the attention of citizens who sit in silence and only listen.
>
> If we are to reform the presidency, the heart of the matter is the president's power over reality, his symbolic power. The social reality of the United States cannot be left to definition by one man alone.

Accordingly, Novak's first suggested reform is to have *a single spokesman who can personify the Congress of the United States*. This "Opposition Spokesman" would not be a potential presidential nominee, but rather would pledge not to seek the presidency, thereby enhancing the position's political credibility.

Second, the president "should be obliged on a biweekly basis to come before leaders of the opposition for a public, hour-long accounting of his policies" (p. 112). These conferences would be in addition to normal presidential press conferences. In this way, the president would be held more closely accountable through the interrogation conducted by key members of the congressional opposition.

Third, the president's cabinet should contain a number of individuals from the opposition party. As Novak asserts, "better that the president should know in his own councils the questions troubling the opposition than face them only *ex post facto* and across Capitol Hill."

Fourth, Novak argues that the presidency should be divided into *two functions*: the head of state and the chief executive. This division would strip the presidency of being the "personification" of the nation and of the "moral stature to which his deeds did not entitle him" (p. 112). The head of state would be elected for a ten-year term (at the beginning of each decade) and would handle the ceremonial duties while setting the tone, style, and direction of the government.

By contrast, Ted Sorenson argues that the constant crises and dangers that confront America require the strongest presidency possible. To Sorenson, the president *already* has enough constitutional limitations placed on his powers. Furthermore, "by definition, inclination, and long training, Congress cannot provide executive leadership" (p. 116). Sorenson cites Congress's inability to react to the 1973 oil embargo. He goes on:

> Nor can a collective legislative body, any more than a weak and passive President, convey the sense of dedication needed to redirect our energies and restore our sense of discipline and worth.... (p. 117)

Sorenson responds to Novak's suggestion for separating the presidency by stating that "neither our traditions, our politics, nor our concepts of efficiency nearly divide the head of state and head of government functions" (p. 118). Transplanting features of the parliamentary system will not work. Thus adopting a "vote of no confidence" would have negative consequences.

> In this country, the power to bring the executive branch down with a legislative vote of "no confidence" would introduce utter confusion. Many congressmen, fearful of the cost of campaigning, would not support such a motion when merited. But many with safe seats who are about to seek reelection anyway would support it regardless of merit; and given the recently volatile nature of the electorate's emotions and pressures, Presidents might be shuffled in and out before they could rearrange the furniture in the Green Room. At the very least every President would be forced, far more than at present, to gratify the demands of a variety of special factions, cliques, and pork barrel interests. (p. 119)

In Sorenson's words, presidents (like containers) should not easily be disposable.

Questions for Discussion

1. Do any of Novak's proposals make sense in terms of presidential accountability? Why or why not?
2. Does a president gain any political power from his ceremonial duties?

Answer Guidelines

These questions are open-ended. Answers will vary. The new edition of McKenna and Feingold (1991) has an interesting debate on whether the president's power has been eroded.

| **Theme B** | The Institutionalization of the Presidency |

Summary

Since the New Deal era, the president has headed a vast bureaucracy responsible not only for implementing government policy but also for providing policy initiatives. The job became too big for any single person to manage and culminated in a report from the Brownlow Commission in 1937 bluntly declaring that "the president needs help." The result was the creation of the *White House Office* and the *Executive Office of the President*.

The White House staff was initially quite small, with presidents often personally answering the telephone and their own mail. The president did not even have a paid secretary until 1857. Rapid growth followed the 1937 recommendation. The staff numbered 51 persons in 1943 and spiraled to 583 in 1971; after this swelling of White House personnel President Carter reduced the staff to 351, a number that increased only slightly by 1990, to 386. Presidents have developed three strategies for organizing the White House Office. Under the *circular* mode, several assistants have direct access to the president. This arrangement maximizes the flow of information to the president but produces internal confusion over lines of authority. Under the *pyramid* mode, a chief of staff controls access to the president and positions are organized in a hierarchical formation. This arrangement is more orderly but frequently isolates the president from needed information. Presidents have generally preferred the pyramidal structure, with Carter and Reagan shifting to this mode to cut back on the demands on their time imposed by the circular model. According to Thomas Cronin, presidents have begun to rely more heavily on White House staff for policy proposals than cabinet departments, a fact that creates a stressful relationship within the executive branch. Under the *ad hoc* mode, the president employs task forces and informal groups.

The Executive Office (EOP), which technically includes the White House Office and Office of the Vice President, consists of agencies that perform staff services for the president but are not located in the White House itself. Fourteen separate agencies existed in the EOP in 1990. Unlike the White House Office, most of these agencies have a specific function outlined in law, and their heads must receive Senate confirmation. The two most important units in the EOP are the Office of Management and Budget and the National Security Council.

The *cabinet* consists of the heads of the federal departments. Occasionally, under Eisenhower, for example, the cabinet has come close to being a truly deliberative body. But cabinet members are heads of vast organizations that they seek to defend, explain, and enlarge. Only a tiny proportion of employees in cabinet departments (under 1 percent) can be appointed by the president. Whereas cabinet members once had strong independent political followings, they are now likely to be appointed for their administrative experience or expertise. The president is fortunate if most cabinet members turn out to agree with him on major policy questions, and there is an inevitable rivalry between the White House staff and the department heads.

Given the president's lack of constitutional powers and his inability to depend on cooperation from Congress or even support from the executive branch, he must necessarily rely on persuasion if he is to accomplish much. His persuasive powers are aimed at three audiences: (1) his fellow politicians and leaders in Washington, (2) party activists and officeholders outside Washington, and (3) "the public"—really many different publics, each with a different view or set of interests. Any statement the president makes will be carefully scrutinized (and perhaps attacked); therefore, recent presidents have had fewer and fewer impromptu discussions and press conferences and have made more and more prepared speeches. The purpose is to generate personal popularity, which will translate into congressional support; the more popular the president, the higher the proportion of his bills that Congress will pass. Any popularity the president succeeds in gaining is temporary, however. Every modern president except Eisenhower has lost popular support between his inauguration and the time he left office.

In addition to the ability to appoint people to office and to persuade the public, the president has three additional prerogatives (two of them quite controversial) with which to influence policy.

1. *The veto.* The president can exercise this constitutional power of the office by sending a *veto message* back to Congress or by doing nothing if Congress adjourns within ten days of sending the bill to the president: this is called a *pocket veto*. The president does not have the *line-item veto*; he must accept the entire bill or veto all of it. The veto is nevertheless a powerful weapon, because historically less than 4 percent of presidents' vetoes have been overridden.

2. *Executive privilege.* The president has traditionally claimed the right to keep secret communication within the executive branch, based on the principle of separation of powers (which would be compromised if the internal workings of one branch could be scrutinized by another branch) and on the president's need to obtain confidential and candid advice from advisers (who could not be frank if their communications were made public). In the Watergate tapes case (*United States* v. *Nixon*) the Supreme Court held that executive privilege did not allow the president to withhold evidence from a criminal investigation.

3. *Impoundment.* Many presidents have refused to spend money appropriated by Congress for programs they did not like. Nixon was particularly aggressive in doing this and eventually provoked Congress to pass the Budget Reform Act of 1974, which severely limited presidential impoundment. It is not clear that this matter is settled, however, because the Supreme Court has declared the legislative veto unconstitutional.

Immediately upon taking office, the president is faced with the need to present a *State of the Union* address and to formulate a program of policy changes. The president must also fill hundreds of appointive posts and submit a new budget. His campaign proposals are usually quite general (to avoid alienating any voters) and his program is expected to have something for everyone. There are essentially two ways for a president to develop a program: have a policy on almost every topic (Carter) or concentrate on only a few major initiatives or themes (Reagan). For help in formulating his program, he can draw on his aides and campaign advisers, federal bureaus and agencies, academic and other outside specialists, and interest groups. A controversial proposal may be leaked to the press, or floated as a *trial balloon* to test possible adverse public reaction. The president's ability to plan is constrained by his limited time and attention span, the likelihood of an unexpected crisis, and the fact that most federal programs can be changed only at the margin.

Almost every president since Herbert Hoover has tried to reorganize the federal bureaucracy. How the bureaucracy is organized can provoke bitter fights, because reorganization often has important implications for the way policies are implemented and for which interest groups gain or lose. The president may reorganize by submitting legislation and having it approved by Congress in the form of a regular law.

Discussion Questions

1. Why can the president not sit down with a group of able and intelligent advisers and produce an effective program to address the problems facing the nation?

2. The text describes both the character and staffing method of recent presidents. Does a president's personality have much to do with how he selects a staffing method (circular, ad hoc or pyramidal)? Why must the president rely on his staff to devise policy when the bureaucracy already exists for this purpose?

3. Presidents frequently sign legislation with which they disagree. Why doesn't the president simply veto such laws since Congress seldom manages to override a veto? Would a line-item veto give the president too much of an advantage over Congress?

Data and Perspectives for Analysis

A. The Need to Institutionalize the Presidency

The movement to institutionalize the presidency arose for many reasons. Perhaps the major reason was the president's need to acquire information untainted by the prejudice of the bureaucracy. A second reason was the necessity of the president to supervise the activities of the executive branch. Too many presidential directives had become lost in the maze of bureaucratic politics. The president had to make certain his orders were properly obeyed.

These two dilemmas are aptly illustrated in the story of the Cuban missile crisis of 1962. The U.S. government had discovered that the Soviets had constructed nuclear missile silos on the island of Cuba. President Kennedy demanded the immediate removal of the missiles. The Soviet reply caught Kennedy by surprise: these missiles would be removed only in exchange for the removal of American missiles in Turkey. The problem was that Kennedy had long before ordered the removal of the obsolete missiles in Turkey. The world was brought to the brink of nuclear war because a presidential order had been disregarded—and by the military, no less. It should be clear why the president needs a personal staff to replicate the duties of the bureaucracy. The paradox of President Kennedy's situation is described on the following page:

> The President believed that he was President and that, his wishes having been made clear, they would be followed and the missiles removed. He therefore dismissed the matter from his mind. Now he learned that the failure to follow up on this matter had permitted the same obsolete Turkish missiles to become hostages of the Soviet Union.
>
> He was angry. He obviously did not wish to order the withdrawal of the missiles from Turkey under threat from the Soviet Union. On the other hand, he did not want to involve the U.S. and mankind in a catastrophic war over missile sites in Turkey that were antiquated and useless. He pointed out to the State Department and the others that, to reasonable people, a trade of this kind might look like a very fair suggestion, that our position had become extremely vulnerable, and that is was our own fault.

Robert F. Kennedy, Thirteen Days.
New York: Signet Books, 1969, p. 95.

B. Presidential Popularity

Does a president's popularity during an election have any relationship to how he is perceived as president? Few presidential candidates receive a "highly favorable" rating that matches their popularity while in office. The data on presidential popularity are contained in the text.

Why doesn't a president seeking reelection retain his popularity during the campaign? How could President Carter have more people consider him "highly favorable" compared to Ronald Reagan and yet lose in the 1980 election?

Voters Giving "Highly Favorable" Rating to Major-Party Presidential Candidates, 1952–1980

	Percentage of Voters Giving Rating		
	Republican candidate	Democratic candidate	Total
1952	47	37	84
1956	59	33	92
1960	40	42	82
1964	16	49	65
1968	38	25	63
1972	41	21	62
1976	28	41	69
1980	23	30	53

Source: Gallup Poll, *New York Times*, October 31, 1980; in Anthony King, "How Not to Select Presidential Candidates: A View from Europe," in Robert E. DiClerico, ed., *Analyzing the Presidency* (Guilford, CT: Dushkin, 1990), p. 6.

Additional Lecture Topics

B-1. Presidential Corruption

Victor Lasky, *It Didn't Start with Watergate*. New York: Dial, 1977. Although written for a rather dubious moral purpose—to convince Americans that Watergate was really nothing to get upset about—and sometimes irresponsible, as in dealing with the case of Marilyn Monroe's death, this is a useful collection of every piece of foul play and moral laxity the author could find committed by a Democratic president.

J. Anthony Lukas, *Nightmare: The Underside of the Nixon Years*. New York: Viking Press, 1976. Lukas is hardly more balanced or insightful than Lasky, but he has produced a collection of accounts of wrongdoing at least as useful.

You will have little trouble entertaining students greatly with this kind of material. The serious questions that should be kept in mind are: Is the presidency inherently more corrupt than the institutions that rival it for power—Congress, the courts, state and local governments? Are the mechanisms for checking presidential corruption adequate? Are they more or less effective than the means of checking corruption in Congress, for example? Is presidential abuse of power more or less dangerous than similar abuses in other branches?

B-2. The Institutionalization of the Presidency

Stephen Hess, *Organizing the Presidency*. 2nd ed. Washington, DC: Brookings Institution, 1988.

Gordon R. Hoxie, "The Cabinet in the American Presidency, 1789–1984," *Presidential Studies Quarterly*, Spring 1984, pp. 209–230.

Bradley D. Nash, ed., *Organizing and Staffing the Presidency*. New York: Center for the Study of the Presidency, 1980.

Arnold Peri, *Making the Managerial Presidency, 1905–1980*. Princeton, NJ: Princeton University Press, 1986.

James P. Pfiffner, *The Strategic Presidency*. Chicago: Dorsey Press, 1988.

James P. Pfiffner, ed., *The Managerial Presidency*. Pacific Grove, CA: Brooks-Cole Publishing, 1991.

B-3. The President's Personality: How Much Does It Matter?

James David Barber, *The Presidential Character: Predicting Performance in the White House*. 3rd ed. Englewood Cliffs, NJ: Prentice-Hall, 1985.

Alexander George, "Assessing Presidential Character." *World Politics*, January 1974.

Fred Greenstein, "Eisenhower as an Activist President: A Look at New Evidence." *Political Science Quarterly*, Winter 1979–1980, pp. 575–600.

Fred I. Greenstein, "A President Is Forced to Resign: Watergate, White House Organization, and Nixon's Personality." In Allan P. Sindler, ed., *America in the Seventies*. Boston: Little, Brown, 1977.

Fred Greenstein, ed., *Leadership in the Modern Presidency*. Cambridge: Harvard University Press, 1988.

Doris Kearns, "Lyndon Johnson's Political Personality." *Political Science Quarterly*, Fall 1976.

The effect of personality on politics is a subject more of speculation than of science. But personality *is* important, and you can convey to your students both the theories about why it is and some knowledge of the tenuousness of these theories.

Abstract 1 for Theme B

President Reagan's Presidential Style

For most of his tenure in office, President Reagan enjoyed unparalleled levels of personal popularity from the American people. However, beginning in 1987, the unfolding of the Iran-Contra scandal plus a series of "kiss-and-tell" books written by ex-administration officials began to tarnish the presidential image. A *Wall Street Journal* article of May 13, 1988, p. 46, written by Gerald F. Seib and Alan Murray, entitled "Portrait of Reagan Painted by Kiss-and-Tell Books Shows a Commander Who Rarely Takes Command," started this way:

> Ronald Reagan is a president who rarely gives orders, meekly follows plans and schedules composed by others and often doesn't understand the intricacies of the issues he faces.
> ... it's the picture of President Reagan that emerges from a series of kiss-and-tell books by former top aides, the latest of which is the celebrated book by the former chief of staff, Donald Regan.
> Though each of these authors claims to be an admirer of the president, their biting firsthand accounts are far more damaging to President Reagan's image than anything that has been charged by his enemies.... The mosaic that emerges from some of the little-publicized anecdotes in those books shows a passive chief executive who often is manipulated by staff members far more ambitious and driven than he is.

Thus, former domestic adviser Martin Anderson's book revealed a president who basically responded to suggestions rather than making demands or giving instructions. Michael Deaver, former budget director, argued that Mr. Reagan did not "fully comprehend the power of his office." Former Chief of Staff Regan observed that President Reagan never questioned the schedules prepared by his staff, while viewing those schedules "as being something like a shooting script in which characters came and went, scenes were rehearsed and acted out, and the plot was advanced one day at a time."

Regan's book reinforced the idea that the president often had a "vague and impressionistic" understanding of issues.

> In a story also recounted by Mr. Regan, Mr. Stockman tells how the president frequently repeated one story to illustrate his ideas about reducing the nation's massive budget deficit. In the vehicle registration department in California, the president recalled, "they kept the records in thousands of metal filing cabinets. Except the records were twice as wide as the file drawers.... We just ordered new metal cabinets which were twice as wide, so the records would fit without folding. It saved thousands of work hours. This is the kind of thing that management can accomplish."
> Mr. Stockman writes that he would hear "the filing cabinet story many times over the next four years. It was the single lens through which the President viewed the federal budget."

Seib and Murray do point out that Reagan's detached operating style could sometimes work effectively, as was the case in the removal of Marcos from the Philippines. Finally, the White House, in response to the plethora of adverse publicity about the president's style, vigorously asserted that Mr. Reagan's management and leadership techniques had produced a highly successful presidency.

Questions for Discussion

1. Can a "passive" president be just as effective a leader as an "activist" president? Explain fully.

2. What does the *Wall Street Journal* article reveal about the importance of the president–advisers relationship?

3. Do you think it is ethical for ex-administration aides to write "kiss-and-tell" books about a president who is still in office?

Answer Guidelines

You may wish to delve more deeply into Barber's "presidential character" theories, that is, the "active-positive" versus "passive-positive" presidential types. The other questions should elect spirited discussion of an open-ended nature in the classroom. You might also pursue the accuracy of the old adage that a president "is only as good as the quality of his advisers."

Theme C	How the President Is Selected

Summary

The key problem in presidential selection is to establish the legitimacy of the presidency itself: to promote public acceptance of the office, its incumbent, and its powers, and to establish an orderly transfer of power from one incumbent to the next. Presidents are selected by the electoral college, an institution that discourages the emergence of serious third parties and focuses the campaign on large, competitive states.

No president except FDR has ever served more than two full terms. Assassination, death, and inability to be reelected have all taken a toll. Accordingly, the vice president has become president eight times as provided for in the Constitution. The Twenty-fifth Amendment, approved in 1967, provides for the vice president to take over in cases of presidential disability; it also provides for the nomination of a new vice president.

The president may leave office through death, disability, resignation, or *impeachment*. An impeachment is like an indictment: a set of charges. For the president to be removed from office he must be impeached by the House and convicted by a two-thirds vote of the Senate. Andrew Johnson was impeached in 1868 because of policy differences with Congress over Reconstruction, and he escaped conviction in the Senate by only one vote. Richard Nixon resigned when faced with impeachment for the Watergate cover-up.

Future presidential power is inextricably linked to the complexity of modern problems and the constraints posed by other governmental institutions, the media, interest groups, and the public. Rules for presidents to follow include using political influence early in the term, avoiding too many details, and delegating power to subordinates but overseeing them closely.

Discussion Questions

1. What does the "peaceful and orderly transfer of power" from one president to the next have to do with presidential legitimacy? Can a revolutionary government or a military junta ever be legitimate? How and why are we better off with a legitimate presidency?

2. The Constitution enumerates three qualifications for the presidency: a candidate must be at least thirty-five years old upon assuming office and a natural-born citizen of the United States, and must have resided in the United States for fourteen years. Barry Goldwater, who ran for the presidency in 1964, was born in Arizona before it was admitted to statehood. Could he have been disqualified from serving as president? Would a test-tube baby be eligible for the presidency since its birth is not "natural"? Herbert Hoover did not live in the United States for fourteen consecutive years before assuming office. Could he have been removed from office for that reason?

Data and Perspectives for Analysis

A. Winning in the Electoral College

Imagine that three men are running for the presidency in 1996. Candidate A (Democrat), Candidate B (Republican), and Candidate C (Independent). On election day in November, the total popular vote ends up as follows:

Candidate A	36,450,918
Candidate B	35,943,645
Candidate C	14,634,332

Candidate A has "carried" (won the greatest number of popular votes in the state) the following states:

New Jersey	Louisiana	Minnesota	Oregon
New York	Arkansas	Nevada	Texas
Massachusetts	Indiana	Virginia	Alaska
Pennsylvania	Tennessee	Illinois	Iowa
Connecticut			

Candidate B has won in the following states:

Kentucky	Alabama	Montana	Maine
California	Michigan	Idaho	Kansas
Florida	Missouri	Utah	Ohio
New Hampshire	Oklahoma	Washington	Colorado
Rhode Island	Wyoming	Maryland	Vermont
North Carolina	North Dakota	Nebraska	Delaware
New Mexico	South Dakota	Wisconsin	Georgia
District of Columbia			

Candidate C has won the following states:

South Carolina	Hawaii	Mississippi	Arizona
West Virginia			

1. Remember, there are 538 total electoral votes in the electoral college. In order to be elected, a candidate must receive a majority (270 or more) electoral votes. From the electoral college data, has candidate A, B, or C won the election? What happens if no candidate receives 270 electoral votes? How are a president and vice president then chosen (what procedures are followed, according to the U.S. Constitution)? Finally, could a few "faithless electors" change the outcome of this election—why or why not?

2. What percentage of the total popular vote did each candidate receive?

3. How many electoral votes did each candidate receive? Second, regardless of the hypothetical outcome in this election, how is it possible for a candidate to be elected president, yet still lose in the popular vote?

B. The Electoral College and Election Strategy

The Electoral College makes the actual selection of the American president. To win the presidency, a candidate must piece together a coalition of support among states that sometimes have little in common. Have students analyze the data below and devise a strategy that would enable a Democratic candidate to win.

Voting Blocks in the Electoral College, 1968–1988

States Voting Democratic since 1968					*Number of Elections*		*States Voting Republican since 1968*				
Four		*Five*		*Six*		*Six*		*Five*		*Four*	
Hawaii	4	Minnesota	10	District of Columbia	3	Alaska	3	Arkansas	6	Alabama	9
Massachusetts	12					Arizona	8	Connecticut	8	Louisiana	9
Rhode Island	4					California	54	Delaware	3	Mississippi	7
West Virginia	5					Colorado	8	Florida	25	Pennsylvania	23
Total	25					Idaho	4	Iowa	7	Texas	32
						Illinois	22	Kentucky	8	Washington	11
						Indiana	12	Maine	4	Wisconsin	11
						Kansas	6	Michigan	18	Total	102
						Montana	3	Missouri	11		
						Nebraska	5	North Carolina	14		
						Nevada	4	Ohio	21		
						New Hampshire	4	Oregon	7		
						New Jersey	15	South Carolina	8		
						New Mexico	5	Tennessee	11		
						North Dakota	3	Total	151		
						Oklahoma	8				
						South Dakota	3				
						Utah	5				
						Vermont	3				
						Virginia	13				
						Wyoming	3				
						Total	191				

Note: A majority of the electoral college, needed to elect a president, is 270 votes.

Source: Stephen J. Wayne, *The Road to the White House 1992: The Politics of Presidential Elections.* New York: St. Martin's Press, 1992, p. 193.

Additional Lecture Topics

C-1. The Electoral College: Useful Institution or Anachronism?

Martin Diamond, *The Electoral College and the American Idea of Democracy*. Washington, D.C.: American Enterprise Institute, 1977. Eminent political scientist defends the electoral college, primarily on philosophical grounds. Pamphlet length.

Neal Peirce and Lawrence Longley, *The People's President: The Electoral College in American History and the Direct Vote Alternative*. 2nd ed. New Haven: Yale University Press, 1981.

Lawrence D. Longley, "The Electoral College." *Current History*, August 1974. Cogent attack on the institution.

"The Proposal for the Direct Election of the President: Pro and Con." *Congressional Digest*, March 1979.

Task Force on Reform of the Presidential Election Process, *Winner Take All*. New York: The Twentieth Century Fund, 1979. A provocative moderate reformist proposal, which claims to retain "the best features of the existing system while avoiding the problems that direct election would have."

Richard Watson, *The Presidential Contest*. 3rd ed. Washington, DC: Congressional Quarterly Press, 1988. See pp. 60–66 for concise material on the electoral college.

C-2. The Vice Presidency—Role and Importance

James W. Davis, *The American Presidency: A New Perspective*. New York: Harper & Row, 1987. See Chapter 14.

Joel Goldstein, *The Modern American Vice-Presidency*. Princeton: Princeton University Press, 1982.

Paul C. Light, *Vice-Presidential Power*. Baltimore: Johns Hopkins University Press, 1984.

Marie D. Natoli, *American Prince, American Pauper*. Westport, CT: Greenwood, 1985.

These sources give a good overview of the vice presidency and its relationship to the executive branch and public policy.

Abstract 1 for Theme C

The Increasing Importance of the Vice Presidency

Until the last few decades, the vice presidency was seen as an insignificant job by most politicians. A plethora of political quotes attest to this fact. Thus, in 1848, Daniel Webster, when offered the vice presidential nomination, replied, "I do not propose to be buried until I am really dead." John Nance Garner, FDR's vice president, once characterized the office as not being worth a bucket of "warm spit." John Adams termed the office "insignificant" and Woodrow Wilson (as a professor) asserted "how little there is to be said about it." Such assessments, however, no longer square with the office's growing significance.

Due to the increasing threat of assassination, death, or resignation, recent presidents have tried to involve their vice presidents in the affairs of the state. Two recent publications explore this trend.

In *Presidential Leadership* by George C. Edwards and Stephen J. Wayne (St. Martin's Press: 1984, pp. 190–194) and *Presidents and Politics—The Limits of Power* by Charles Funderbunk (Belmont, Calif.: Brooks-Cole: 1982, pp. 156–160), several important points are made. Both texts assert that a vice presidential nomination can be valuable preparation for later accession to the presidency (building up party credibility, contacts, and national media exposure). Furthermore it may, in and of itself, allow the individual to "train" for the chief executive slot, provided that the vice president is given the opportunity to do so by the incumbent president. Walter Mondale, Carter's vice president, is quoted by Edwards and Wayne as follows (p. 194):

> I don't know of any other office, outside of the presidency, that informs an officer more fully . . . about the realities of federal government and the duties of the presidency or that remotely compares to that of the vice president as it is now being used.

Mondale goes on to state that he learned more about national affairs as vice president than during his twelve years in the Senate (Carter permitted Mondale to attend all cabinet meetings, to perform valuable administrative tasks, and to have meetings with him on a regular basis).

Furthermore Mondale, like George Bush in the Reagan administration, had his importance maximized because he followed certain unwritten rules as vice president. As Funderburk points out in *Presidents and Politics*, a president must trust his vice president not to upstage him or his programs. This trust may be difficult to build because of the way vice presidents are placed on the national ticket to "balance" the ticket's voter appeal politically, geographically, and often ideologically. Often the two men are rivals at the convention or incompatible personally. Once elected, a president may shunt his vice president aside as a natural outgrowth of the earlier primary campaigns. (John F. Kennedy's staff apparently did this to Lyndon Johnson, despite JFK's own attempts to involve his vice president in important domestic and international activities.) Still, a vice president who follows those "unwritten rules" may still exercise some degrees of influence. Those rules, according to Edwards and Wayne, involve never complaining to the press; never taking credit away from the president;

always supporting the president's final policy even if privately opposed to it; and sharing the dirty work, such as traveling extensively on what may often be boring ceremonial and/or political fence-mending events (p. 192).

On balance, though, the role for recent vice presidents has expanded. As Edwards and Wayne show, LBJ in 1961 had roughly twenty professional and clerical aides. Currently, the vice president has over seventy assistants, and his office in the West Wing is only a short distance from the Oval Office (formerly his office was in a separate building). Perhaps presidents are beginning to realize that the growth of the vice presidency

> has not only benefited the vice president, it has worked to the president's advantage as well. It has provided the president with additional institutional resources for the performance of his ceremonial and symbolic functions; it has provided him with additional personal resources for the exercise of his political and public-opinion roles; and it has provided the president with additional policy advice from an official who shares his national and political perspective. (Edwards and Wayne, p. 194)

Questions for Discussion

1. Imagine that a vice president openly attacked the president's policies and/or decisions. What would probably be the president's response?
2. Would it be helpful if the presidential nominee chose a vice presidential running mate after the convention was over? Why or why not?

Answer Guidelines

A vice president who openly attacked his president would probably be excluded from the inner circle of power and might even be asked to resign. Choosing a running mate after the convention would give the presidential nominee time to consider an individual compatible with his political philosophy and style. However, it could be argued that the final decision might not be any different from a preconvention decision, because the imperative of "balancing the ticket" would remain.

Abstract 2 for Theme C

"Van Buren's Jinx" and Myths About the Vice Presidency

In an article by Joel K. Goldstein entitled "Van Buren's Jinx," (*New York Times*, May 28, 1988, p. 15), the author deflates a number of "obsolete stereotypes" about the vice presidency. In order to understand fully the "Van Buren jinx"—no sitting vice president has been elected president in more than 150 years—Goldstein confronts the first myth, that, "the vice presidency is often portrayed as a sinecure, the last stop in the public careers of men of modest talents." While the statement was perhaps true in the nineteenth century, the post-New Deal period has largely undercut its validity. As Goldstein puts it:

> In fact, the Vice Presidency has attracted an impressive list of candidates during the last 40 years or so. Presidential nominees perceived as having a reasonable chance of winning have their pick of running mates. During the last 40 years, only two men—Gov. Nelson A. Rockefeller of New York in 1960 and Senator Edward M. Kennedy in 1968—have declined invitations to run on a ticket their party perceived to have reasonable hope of success.
>
> Men (and now women) of distinction openly and routinely covet the second spot. Since 1948, for example, those who sought the Vice-Presidency included Gov. (later Chief Justice) Earl Warren, Senate majority leader Lyndon B. Johnson, Hubert H. Humphrey, Senator (later Secretary of State) Edmund S. Muskie, Walter F. Mondale and Bob Dole.

The second myth equates the vice presidency with "political oblivion." Goldstein argues that the vice presidency has actually been the best springboard to occupying the White House.

> Nine Vice Presidents have become President following death or resignation of the incumbent. Four other Vice Presidents have won the Presidency. Put differently, one-third of America's Presidents

served first as Vice President. Two Vice Presidents—Richard M. Nixon in 1960 and Mr. Humphrey in 1968—narrowly lost the Presidency. Moreover, nearly every recent Vice President has become a leading Presidential contender.

The third myth sees the vice presidency as "an empty job, that its occupant attends funerals but does little else." Goldstein notes that both Walter Mondale and George Bush have certainly belied this contention and, more recently, Albert Gore even more so. While the job of vice presidency may be "awkward," it is by no means a political graveyard.

Theme D   Presidential Power and Future Reforms

Summary

Despite the effects of the Vietnam War, Watergate, and various administration scandals, the president of the United States remains the central figure in American politics. He is the only official (apart from the vice president) who is elected by the entire nation. Accordingly, he is far more likely to possess a *national* perspective, unlike members of Congress, who are elected from a much narrower geographical base. Consequently, the president has been transformed into the symbol of the nation (particularly in the media age) and the one individual whom the average American citizen sees as *the* representative of the federal government in Washington. Public expectations that the president will be able to solve in a rapid fashion the various problems afflicting the nation are, however, unrealistic, especially given the constraints on a president's power emanating from media scrutiny, congressional obduracy, bureaucratic procrastination, interest groups, and so forth. More than ever, a president must be skilled in the arts of persuasion and the communication of a vision for the nation. Even then, setbacks and a decline in popularity are inevitable.

Advocates of expanding and strengthening presidential power as a means of improving presidential performance often suggest a number of reforms. In *The American Presidency—A New Perspective* by James W. Davis (New York: Harper and Row, 1987), pp. 421–446, some of the pros and cons of selected reforms are discussed. One reform involves the *substitution of parliamentary government for the separation of powers structure*. In this plan, the voters would have some reassurance that the president could carry out his legislative program without congressional opposition. However, critics maintain that members of the president's own party could defy their chief executive and vote against the programs proposed by the White House. Davies summarizes the case against parliamentary government in the following manner:

> The merger of executive and legislative leadership does not guarantee governmental effectiveness. As Norman C. Thomas has commented: "In all probability . . . an American parliamentary system would be characterized by a multiplicity of political parties, given our social pluralism, and hence it might encourage chronic instability like that of the French Fourth Republic or the current Italian Republic." (p. 425)

Another reform involves the concept of the *plural executive*. As Davis puts it, "some reformers believe that the job of president has become too big to be entrusted to one person" (p. 426). In addition to the Novak plan (see Abstract A), Rexford Tugwell, a member of FDR's "brains trust," some years ago called for a constitutional arrangement of two vice presidents to be elected along with the president; each would handle a variety of administrative duties, thus permitting the president "to function full-time as a policy maker in the critical area of government" (p. 427). Historian Barbara Tuchman has also proposed a six-person directorate elected for six years, to encourage governmental efficiency and downplay the disastrous effects of one leader's ego. Other plural executive plans abound, but Davis points out their flaws: "competition and disputes within the executive, a splintering and confusion of responsibilities, and further growth of the executive branch" (p. 429). Davis wonders if a collective executive could reach vital decisions in times of crisis and whether accountability could be effectively assigned.

Another reform is the well-publicized *single six-year term* for the president. This proposal, which had the backing of President Carter, rests upon the assumptions that one nonrenewable six-year term would take the president out of reelection worries, allow enough time to achieve his domestic and foreign-policy goals, and liberate the chief executive from the pressures of special-interest groups and party politics.

But Davis points out the flaws in this proposal too: (a) The president would be a "lame duck" from the day of his election. (b) Clark Clifford's admonition that "the notion that a president should be above politics (is) inconsistent with our system of government. . . . Politics, in the final analysis, is an essential part of democracy. A president above politics is a president remote from the processes of government and removed from the thoughts and aspirations of his people" (p. 437). (c) The presidential selection process would be "intensified" with . . . Thomas Cronin's warning that "ideological competition would be more aggressive and perhaps more bitter at present."

A final reform which has been considered is the *repeal of the Twenty-second Amendment*. Davis favors such a move, since it would eliminate the lame-duck condition of a second-term president. To some critics, the amendment is antidemocratic, since it frustrates the public's will in choosing an effective leader for a third term (it should be noted that the amendment was a Republican-inspired idea aimed at eliminating future FDRs). Conversely, an argument can be made that eight years of presidential tenure is enough for any individual. Furthermore, the two-thirds limitation permits the infusion of fresh ideas and administrative dynamism that usually accompany a new presidential era.

Questions for Discussion

1. Do any of these proposed reforms have a chance of becoming political reality—why or why not?

2. Could the American political system adjust to a parliamentary system?

Answer Guidelines

Open-ended discussion in the classroom could generate lively arguments for and against the suggested reforms.

13

The Bureaucracy

Overview and Objectives

In this chapter the student will be introduced to what is "big" about big government: the bureaucracy. Both the distinctiveness and the size of the federal government bureaucracy will be reviewed, along with the various roles that have been assigned to it throughout its history. Significant aspects of the bureaucracy today include the extent and character of its authority, how members are recruited, and other factors that help explain the conduct of bureaucrats in office. Finally, the chapter will look at the ways in which Congress attempts to control the behavior of bureaucrats and at various "pathologies" of various large bureaucracies. After reading and reviewing the material in this chapter the student should be able to do each of the following:

1. Compare and contrast the American and British models of government bureaucracy.

2. Sketch the history of the growth of bureaucracy in this country, and the different uses to which it has been put.

3. Show how bureaucracy continues to grow today, even though the number of persons directly employed by government has not greatly increased lately.

4. Discuss the recruitment, retention, and personal characteristics of federal bureaucrats.

5. Show how the roles and missions of the agencies are affected by both internal and external factors.

6. Review congressional measures to control the bureaucracy, and evaluate their effectiveness.

7. List the "pathologies" that may affect bureaucracies, and discuss whether they are relevant to the federal government bureaucracy today.

8. Discuss why it is so difficult to reform the bureaucracy.

Chapter Outline with Keyed-in Resources

I. Distinctiveness of the American bureaucracy (THEME A: SIZE AND POWER OF THE BUREAUCRACY)
   A. Constitutional system and traditions make bureaucracy distinctive
      1. Supervision shared
      2. Federalist structure shares functions
      3. Adversary culture leads to defense of rights and law suits

A code of silence envelops many members of the British bureaucracy. The top 3,500 civil servants must take an oath of secrecy not to divulge any official information, even if the material is not classified. The oath is binding for life and enforced by a criminal sanction.

    B. Scope of bureaucracy
        1. Little public ownership of industry in the United States
        2. High degree of regulation in the United States of private industries

Surprisingly, the country in Western Europe with the highest degree of public ownership of industry is Austria. Almost two-thirds of all corporate capital belongs to the public sector, and over 25 percent of the labor force works in nationalized industries or in industries controlled by national banks.

  II. The growth of the bureaucracy
    A. The early controversies
        1. Senate consent for removal of officials is challenged by supporters of a strong president
        2. President is given sole removal power but Congress funds and investigates

President Andrew Johnson was impeached for violating the Tenure of Office Act, which forbade the president from removing any executive official who had been confirmed by the Senate without the Senate's permission. Johnson dismissed Secretary of War Edwin Stanton, a holdover from Abraham Lincoln's cabinet. The constitutionality of the Tenure of Office Act is highly dubious. Johnson, of course, was not convicted by the Senate.

    B. The appointment of officials
        1. Officials affect how laws are interpreted, tone of administration, effectiveness
        2. Use of patronage in nineteenth and early twentieth centuries to reward supporters

Patronage was often accompanied by corruption. The Grant administration went so far as to auction off certain federal jobs, with the position of Indian agent going for $12,000.

        3. Civil War a watershed in bureaucratic growth; showed weakness of federal government
    C. A service role
        1. 1861–1901: shift in role from regulation to service
        2. Reflects desire for limited government; laissez-faire beliefs; Constitution's silence
    D. A change in role
        1. Depression and World War II lead to government activism
        2. Introduction of heavy income taxes supports a large bureaucracy
  III. The federal bureaucracy today (THEME B: CONTROL OF THE BUREAUCRACY)
    A. Direct and indirect growth
        1. Modest increase in number of government employees
        2. Indirect increase through use of private contractors much greater

While the private sector performs many functions on behalf of the federal government, pay scales are not equitable. A study conducted in 1988 and given to President Reagan discovered a 25 percent disparity between federal wages and wages in the private sector.

    B. Growth in discretionary authority
        1. Delegation of undefined authority by Congress

The federal bureaucracy has responded to the delegation of authority. The number of pages in the *Federal Register*, where proposed and final bureaucratic regulations appear, exploded from 9,652 pages in 1960 to 63,553 pages in 1981.

        2. Primary areas of delegation
            a. Subsidies to groups
            b. Grant-in-aid programs
            c. Enforcement of regulations

C. Factors explaining behavior of officials (ADDITIONAL LECTURE TOPIC B-1)
  1. Recruitment and retention
     a. The competitive service: most bureaucrats compete for jobs through OPM
        (1) Appointment by merit based on written exam

On federal employment exams, certain groups are awarded additional points. Veterans, for example, receive a bonus of five points on their exam scores; disabled veterans get ten extra points.

     b. The excepted service: most are appointed by other agencies on the basis of qualifications approved by OPM
        (1) Examples: Postal Service employees, FBI agents
        (2) But the president can also appoint employees: presidential appointments, Schedule C jobs, NEA jobs
        (3) Pendleton Act (1883): transferred basis of government jobs from patronage to merit

To limit political corruption among bureaucrats, Congress enacted the Hatch Act. Under this law, federal bureaucrats cannot be candidates in partisan elections, campaign on behalf of any candidate, or hold office in a political party.

        (4) Merit system protects president from pressure and protects patronage appointees from new presidents ("blanketing in")
     c. The buddy system
        (1) Name-request job: filled by a person whom an agency has already identified for middle- and upper-level jobs
        (2) Job description may be tailored for person
        (3) Circumvents usual search process . . .
        (4) . . . But also encourages "issue networks" based on shared policy views
     d. Firing a bureaucrat

It is difficult to fire a federal employee even for extreme indiscretions. For example, a New York postal worker shot a customer in the stomach during an argument. He was dismissed but won reinstatement and $5,500 in back pay because the termination papers were filed incorrectly. When the papers had been filed correctly the employee was again dismissed—but he got to keep the $5,500.

        (1) Most bureaucrats cannot be fired
        (2) Exception: Senior Executive Service (SES)
        (3) SES managers receive cash bonuses for good performance
        (4) But very few SES members have actually been fired or even transferred

The SES is composed of about 7,100 members. To qualify, a person must serve at the highest three GS levels (or the top in the Executive Schedule). About half of the members of the SES in an agency receive bonuses of up to 20 percent of their base salary annually.

     e. The agencies' point of view
        (1) Agencies are dominated by lifetime bureaucrats who have worked for no other agency
        (2) Assures continuity and expertise . . .
        (3) . . . But also gives subordinates power over new bosses: can work behind boss's back through sabotage, delaying, etc.

Even presidents have difficulty at times in obtaining cooperation from the bureaucracy. President Kennedy once commented to an adviser, "I agree with you, but I don't know if the government will."

  2. Personal attributes
     a. Allegations of critics:
        (1) Higher civil servants are elitist
        (2) Officials are biased toward the Democrats

A 1992 study released by the Office of Personnel Management revealed the following profile of the average federal worker, excluding postal employees and political appointees. The average full-time employee is 42.4 years old, earns $33,736 a year, and has served 13.4 years; 56 percent of the work force is male and 28 percent are veterans; African-Americans hold 16.8 percent of jobs and Hispanics 5.5 percent; 36 percent have a bachelor's degree or higher.

    b. Results of survey of bureaucrats show that they
     (1) Are more liberal than the average citizen
     (2) Do not take extreme positions
    c. Correlation between type of agency and attitudes of employees: activist versus traditional
    d. Professional values of officials
  3. Do bureaucrats sabotage their political bosses?
    a. If so, such sabotage hurts conservatives more than liberals
     (1) Bureaucrats tend to be liberal
    b. But loyalty to bosses runs strong—despite power of bureaucrats to obstruct or complain
     (1) Whistleblower Protection Act (1989) created Office of Special Counsel
     (2) "Cooperation is the nature of a bureaucrat's job"
    c. Most civil servants: Highly structured roles make them relatively immune from personal attitudes
    d. Professionals such as lawyers and economists in the FTC: loosely structured roles may be much influenced by personal attitudes
     (1) Professional values help explain how power is used
  4. Culture and careers

A 1988 survey of senior officials in the federal government revealed a high degree of dissatisfaction with their work, with 57 percent saying they would not recommend a career in public service.

    a. Each agency has its own culture
    b. Jobs with an agency can be career enhancing or not
    c. Strong agency culture motivates employees
     (1) But it makes agencies resistant to change

A good example of bureaucratic resistance to change is illustrated by an incident that occurred during the Cuban Missile Crisis. Secretary of Defense Robert McNamara was concerned about how American sailors would board any Soviet ships that attempted to enter Cuba. McNamara was handed the Navy Manual, to which he responded: "I don't give a damn how John Paul Jones would do it. I want to know how you are."

  5. Constraints
    a. Biggest difference between a government agency and a business firm
     (1) Hiring, firing, pay, procedures, etc.
    b. General constraints
     (1) Administrative Procedure Act (1946)
     (2) Freedom of Information Act (1966)
     (3) National Environmental Policy Act (1969)
     (4) Privacy Act (1974)
     (5) Open Meeting Law (1976)
     (6) Assignment of single jobs to several agencies
    c. Effects of constraints
     (1) Government moves slowly
     (2) Government acts inconsistently

Conflict in the bureaucracy can reach embarrassing proportions. During the Nixon administration, war flared up between Pakistan and India. Which country did the United States support? The State Department and the Department of Defense publicly supported different sides.

                    (3) Easier to block action than take action
                    (4) Reluctant decision making by lower-ranking employees
                    (5) Red tape
            6. Why so many constraints?
                a. Constraints come from citizens: agencies' responses to demands for openness, honesty, fairness, etc.
            7. Agency allies
                a. Agencies often seek alliances with congressional committees or interest groups

Harold Seidman estimates that cabinet secretaries spend about 10 percent of their time attending to departmental business and 40 percent of their time testifying before congressional committees.

                    (1) "Iron triangle"
                b. Far less common today—politics has become too complicated
                    (1) More interest groups, more congressional subcommittees, easier access for individuals
                    (2) Far more competing forces than ever given access by courts
                c. "Issue networks": groups that regularly debate government policy on certain issues
                    (1) Contentious and partisan
                    (2) New president often recruits from networks
    IV. Congressional oversight

The need for oversight is illustrated by this story. In 1978, the GAO put Donald Duck's name on the payroll of the Department of Housing and Urban Development at a salary of $99,999—twice the salary authorized by law for any position in the department. The error was never detected, making Donald Duck not only a spurious member of the department but the highest-paid one at that.

        A. Forms of congressional supervision
            1. Creation of agency by Congress
            2. Statutory requirements of agency behavior
            3. Authorization of money, either permanent or fixed number of years
            4. Appropriation of money allows spending
        B. The Appropriations Committee and legislative committees
            1. Appropriations Committee most powerful
                a. Most expenditure recommendations are approved by House
                b. Has power to lower agency's expenditure request
                c. Has power to influence an agency's policies through "marking up" an agency's budget
                d. But becoming less powerful due to:
                    (1) Trust funds: e.g., Social Security
                    (2) Annual authorizations
                    (3) Meeting target spending limits
            2. Legislative committees are important when
                a. A law is first passed
                b. An agency is first created
                c. An agency is subject to annual authorization
            3. Informal congressional controls over agencies
                a. Individual congressmen can seek privileges for constituents
                b. Congressional committees may seek committee clearance: right to pass on certain agency decisions
                c. Committee heads may ask to be consulted
        C. The legislative veto
            1. Declared unconstitutional by Supreme Court in *Chadha* (1983)
            2. Weakens traditional legislative oversight but Congress continues creating such vetoes

D. Congressional investigations
   1. Power inferred from power to legislate
   2. Means for checking agency discretion
   3. Means for limiting presidential control
V. Bureaucratic "pathologies" (THEME C: BUREAUCRATIC "PATHOLOGIES")

According to a survey in the mid-1970s, a large difference exists between general public opinion of the bureaucracy and specific attitudes of those who have actually dealt with a government agency. While only 31 percent of the public at large felt that federal agencies did a good job, 82 percent of those having experienced the bureaucracy directly believed that they were treated fairly.

A. Red tape—complex and sometimes conflicting rules among agencies
B. Conflict—agencies work at cross-purposes
C. Duplication—two or more agencies seem to do the same thing
D. Imperialism—tendency of agencies to grow, irrespective of benefits and costs of programs
E. Waste—Spending more than is necessary to buy some product or service

VI. Reforming the Bureaucracy (THEME D: ETHICS IN PUBLIC ADMINISTRATION) (ADDITIONAL LECTURE TOPIC D-1)
A. Numerous attempts to make bureaucracy work better for less money
   1. Eleven attempts to reform this century alone
   2. National Performance Review (NPR) in 1993 designed to reinvent government
      a. Differs from previous reforms that sought to increase presidential control
      b. Emphasizes customer satisfaction by bringing citizens in contact with agencies
   3. NPR calls for innovation and quality consciousness by:
      a. less centralized management
      b. more employee initiatives
      c. customer satisfaction
B. Bureaucratic reform always difficult to accomplish
   1. Most rules and red tape due to struggle between president and Congress
   2. This struggle makes bureaucrats nervous about irritating either branch
   3. Periods of divided government worsen matters, especially in implementing policy
      a. Republican presidents seek to increase political control (executive micromanagement)
      b. Democratic congresses respond by increasing investigations and rules (legislative micromanagement)

Important Terms

Administrative Procedure Act A law passed in 1946 requiring federal agencies to give notice, solicit comments, and (sometimes) hold hearings before adopting any new rules.

*annual authorization The practice of a legislative committee setting limits on the amount an agency can spend on a yearly basis. This practice is a recent one and curtails the power of the appropriations committees.

*appropriation Money formally set aside for a specific use that originates from the House Appropriations Committee.

*authorization legislation Legislation that originates in a legislative committee stating the maximum amount of money that an agency may spend on a given program.

buddy system A job description by an agency which is tailor-made for a specific person. These appointments occur in middle- and upper-level positions in the bureaucracy.

*bureaucracy A large organization composed of appointed officers in which authority is divided among several managers.

bureaucratic culture An informal understanding among fellow employees of an agency as to how they are supposed to act.

*****committee clearance** The right of congressional committees to pass on certain agency decisions, although usually not binding.

*****competitive service** The set of civil servants appointed on the basis of a written exam administered by the Office of Personnel Management or by meeting certain selection criteria. This service comprises about two-thirds of federal bureaucrats.

conflict A bureaucratic pathology in which some agencies seem to be working at cross-purposes to other agencies.

*****discretionary authority** The ability of a bureaucracy to choose courses of action and make policies not spelled out in advance by laws.

duplication A bureaucratic pathology in which two government agencies seem to be doing the same thing.

Freedom of Information Act A law passed in 1966 giving citizens the right to inspect all government records except those containing military, intelligence, or trade secrets or material revealing private personnel actions.

imperialism A bureaucratic pathology in which agencies tend to grow without regard to the benefits their programs confer or the costs they entail.

*****iron triangle** The policy-making network composed of a government agency, a congressional committee, and an interest group. This network is less common today because of the variety of interest groups that exist and the proliferation of congressional subcommittees.

*****issue network** Members of Washington-based interest groups, congressional staffers, university faculty, experts participating in think tanks, and representatives of the mass media who regularly debate government policy on a certain subject. Such networks are replacing the "iron triangles."

*****laissez-faire** A belief in a freely competitive economy that was widely held in the late nineteenth century.

*****legislative veto** Congressional veto of an executive decision during the specified period it must lie before Congress before it can take effect. The veto is effected through a resolution of disapproval passed by either house or by both houses. These resolutions do not need the president's signature. In 1983, the Supreme Court voided such vetoes, but Congress continues to enact laws containing them.

*****name request job** A job in the federal bureaucracy that is filled by a person whom an agency has already identified.

National Environmental Policy Act A law passed in 1969 requiring agencies to issue an environmental impact statement before undertaking any major action affecting the environment.

noncareer executive assignments A form of patronage under the excepted service given to high-ranking members of the regular competitive service, or to persons brought into the civil service at a high level who are advocates of presidential programs.

Open Meeting Law A law passed in 1976 requiring agency meetings to be open to the public unless certain specified matters are being discussed.

oversight Congressional supervision of the bureaucracy.

patronage Bureaucratic appointments made on the basis of political considerations. Federal legislation significantly limits such appointments today.

Pendleton Act A law passed in 1883 which began the process of transferring federal jobs from patronage to the merit system.

Privacy Act A law passed in 1974 requiring government files about individuals to be kept confidential.

*****red tape** A bureaucratic pathology in which complex rules and procedures must be followed to get things done.

Schedule C job A form of patronage under the excepted service for a position of "confidential or policy-determining" character below the level of the cabinet and subcabinet.

Senior Executive Service A special classification for high-level civil servants created by the Civil Service Reform Act of 1978. Members of this service can be hired, fired, and transferred more easily than ordinary civil servants. They are also eligible for cash bonuses and, if removed, are guaranteed jobs elsewhere in the government. The purpose of the service is to give the president more flexibility in recruiting, assigning, and paying high-level bureaucrats with policy-making responsibility.

*spoils system Another phrase for political patronage, that is the practice of giving the fruits of a party's victory, such as jobs and contracts, to loyal members of that party.

*trust fund Money outside the regular government budget to pay for benefits like social security. These funds are beyond the control of congressional appropriations committees.

waste A bureaucratic pathology in which an agency spends more than is necessary to buy some product or service.

Whistleblower Protection Act A law passed in 1989 which created an Office of Special Counsel to investigate complaints from bureaucrats claiming they were punished after reporting to Congress about waste, fraud, or abuse in their agencies.

Theme A   Size and Power of the Bureaucracy

Instructor Reference

Anthony Downs, *Inside Bureaucracy*. Boston: Little, Brown, 1967. A classic text.

Frederick S. Lane, ed., *Current Issues in Public Administration*. 3rd ed. New York: St. Martin's Press, 1986. Excellent readings on a wide range of issues involving the bureaucracy.

Charles T. Goodsell, *The Case for Bureaucracy*. 2nd ed. Chatham, NJ: Chatham House, 1985.

Philip Heymann, *The Politics of Public Management*. New Haven: Yale University Press, 1988.

Francis E. Rourke, *Bureaucracy, Politics, and Public Policy*. Boston: Little, Brown, 1984. A good analysis of the sources of bureaucratic power.

Francis Rourke, ed., *Bureaucratic Power in National Policy Making,* 4th ed. Boston: Little, Brown, 1986.

Harold Seidman and Robert Gilmour, *Politics, Position, and Power*. 4th ed. New York: Oxford University Press, 1986.

Richard Stillman, *The American Bureaucracy*. Chicago: Nelson-Hall, 1987.

James Q. Wilson, "The Rise of the Bureaucratic State." *Public Interest*, Fall 1975.

Summary

A *bureaucracy* is a large, complex organization composed of appointed officials. Bureaucracy is an obvious feature of all modern societies, but American governmental bureaucracy is distinctive in three ways. First, political authority over the bureaucracy is shared among several institutions. Second, most federal agencies share their functions with agencies of state and local government. Finally, America's *adversary culture* means that the actions of bureaucrats are often fought in court.

The Constitution makes little mention of the bureaucracy, other than to give the president power to appoint various sorts of officials. In 1789 Congress gave the president power to remove officials without congressional assent, but the question of who (if anyone) would actually control the bureaucracy has been hotly contested throughout American history.

Throughout most of American history, *patronage* was the chief means of determining who would hold federal jobs. Congress was the dominant institution, the president usually accommodated congressional preferences in appointments, and thus appointments were made to reward local supporters of Congress members or to build up local party organizations. By the middle of the nineteenth century there were a lot of federal jobs: from 1816 to 1861 the number of federal employees increased eightfold, with the Post Office accounting for most of this increase. The Civil War and postwar period saw the creation of many additional bureaus. A strong commitment to *laissez-faire* meant that these agencies did not for the most part regulate, but rather served specialized constituencies such as farmers or veterans. The bureaucracy as we know it today is the product of the New Deal (whose programs gave broad but vaguely defined powers to agencies) and of World War II (during which the government made use of the vastly increased revenues the income tax allowed).

The Supreme Court has interceded to restrict political patronage on constitutional grounds. The first step was taken in *Elrod* v. *Burns* (1976) in which the Court noted that important First Amendment interests in the protection of free speech must be taken into consideration in patronage firings. According to the majority, the public's interest in the effective implementation of policy "can be fully satisfied by limiting patronage dismissals to policy-making positions." Four years later, in *Branti* v. *Finkel*, the Supreme Court elaborated by explaining that "the question is whether the hiring authority can demonstrate that party affiliation in an appropriate requirement for the effective performance of the public office involved." As such, the mere fact that a bureaucrat occupied a policy-making position no longer constituted the ultimate factor in a patronage firing. This line of cases was brought to conclusion with *Rutan* v. *Republican Party of Illinois* (1990), when the Court extended the *Branti* standard to "promotion, transfer, recall, and hiring decisions based on party affiliation and support." Thus patronage has reached the point of nearing political extinction.

People often think of "big government" in terms of the size of the bureaucracy, but the number of civilian federal employees has *not* been growing since World War II. What has increased is the number of *indirect* federal employees—those working for state or local governments or private firms funded by federal programs. However, the power of the bureaucracy is a function not of its size but of the degree to which appointed officials have *discretionary authority*: the ability to choose courses of action and to make policies not spelled out in advance by laws. The vast increase in expenditures channeled through the bureaucracy, as well as the vast expansion in the number of regulations issued during the past thirty years, shows that the bureaucracy has indeed become very powerful.

Discussion Questions

1. Students have a skewed perspective of the federal bureaucracy. Although it is perceived as somewhat alienated from the concerns of the American public, only 12 percent of federal bureaucrats live in the metropolitan Washington, D.C., area. Why do so few bureaucrats reside near the heart of the government? What does this fact suggest about the degree of alienation of bureaucrats?

2. Students tend to believe that the federal bureaucracy is overly large because of the number of civil servants working in social welfare agencies. However, 37 percent of civilian employees work in defense-related agencies, while many social welfare programs are administered by state and local governments. Given these facts, is it accurate to say that the federal government is not responsible for the problems of poorly managed social welfare policies?

3. The six major regulatory agencies have authority over $170 billion of commerce in the United States. Since Congress delegates authority to these agencies, and the president cannot remove the heads of regulatory agencies except for cause, who is to blame if the economy performs poorly? What can Congress do if it dislikes a rule made by a regulatory agency?

Data and Perspectives for Analysis

As the size and power of the bureaucracy have expanded, the public's confidence in it has eroded. Have your students analyze the data below and explain the change in the public's attitude toward the growth of bureaucratic power.

Statement	Percent of the Public Agreeing				
	1958	1970	1974	1980	1991
The government wastes a lot of money	43	69	74	78	75
Government is run for the benefit of a few big interests	24	50	66	70	70
You cannot trust the government to do right most of the time	23	44	62	73	70
People like me don't have any say about what the government does	31	36	40	39	34**
Public officials don't care much what people like me think	25*	47	50	52	59

* in 1960
** in 1989

Source: David H. Rosenbloom, *Public Administration: Management, Politics, and Law in the Public Sector,* 3rd ed. New York: McGraw-Hill, 1993.

Abstract for Theme A

How Bureaucracy "Really Works"

In Charles Peters's *How Washington Really Works,* rev. ed. (Reading, Mass.: Addison-Wesley, 1983), an especially intriguing chapter (Chapter 3, pp. 35–52) is devoted to "The Bureaucracy." The editor-in-chief of the *Washington Monthly* makes some telling observations about the "permanent government in Washington that consists of people whose power does not depend on election results" (p. 35). These observations follow.

1. Bureaucrats suffer from "an excess of caution" and "are looking for protection against anything that could disturb their quiet but steady progress up the career ladder" (p. 35). Accordingly, the bureaucrat's hostility to evaluation of his performance is strong, because a negative report will hinder merit salary increases.

2. A government agency's primary concern is expanding its budget while avoiding budget cuts (this results in end-of-fiscal-year spending sprees so that it will not appear that the agency was overbudgeted). When faced with a budget cut, one ploy used is the "Firemen First Principle" (p. 40) whereby an agency bureaucrat translates the cut into "bad news for members of Congress who are powerful enough to restore the amount eliminated. In other words, he (the bureaucrat) chops where it will hurt constituents the most, not the least" (p. 40). An example would be Amtrak's 1975 strategy, which involved the proposed dropping of routes through the districts or states of members of Congress who were also chairmen of key committees: Appropriations, Commerce, and so on. By endangering essential services, the clever bureaucrat can also enlist the aid of the public as well.

3. "Fat" in the federal budget relates to four "inflations" (p. 44): inflated slots, pay, job descriptions, and grades. Inflated slots are explained by Peters in the following manner:

> Suppose the country were being overrun by Albanian moths. The Department of Agriculture would ask the Civil Service Commission for authority to establish positions for, say, 200 Albanian Moth Control Officers. Because of the emergency, the authority would be granted, and Agriculture

would have 200 new slots. Suppose the Albanian moths were then brought under control. Would the slots be abolished? Certainly not. Now you understand slot inflation. (p. 44)

Payroll inflation means that "many federal employees are paid too much for the jobs they do." In the GS-13, -14, and -15 levels, Peters states there are two hundred thousand employees earning $35,000 to $55,000 per year. These employees also receive annual merit increases, making their salaries quite competitive with, if not superior to, salaries in the private sector. Inflated grades are related to payroll inflation because thousands of workers have higher salaries and rank than the level of work requires. (The Civil Service Commission in 1977 estimated that a total of $780 million was overpaid to these workers.) Finally, inflated job descriptions simply mean more money, even if the embellishment does not accurately portray the real work in a position. (Thus elevator operators turn into "vertical vehicle controllers.")

4. Supervisors who wish to fire incompetent employees face a Herculean task, because hearings and regulations may drag out the process for years. Peters reveals that the "government's rate of discharge for inefficiency in only one-seventh of 1 percent" (p. 47).

5. Despite the image of the civil service as a merit system, "the fact is that getting a government job has only the most modest relation to merit" (p. 47). Peters points out that veterans get a bonus of five points on civil service exam scores and that disabled veterans receive an additional ten. Nonveterans can employ another trick:

The trick is to get their names requested from the Civil Service Commission by the agency filling the job, and the way to do that is to know someone inside the agency. People already in the system are the first to know about a job opening, and knowing both the applicant and the job, they can tailor the job description to fit the person they want to hire. So the civil service is a patronage ring based not on politics but on friendship. Insiders call it the "buddy system" (p. 48).

6. Peters argues that, instead of abolishing the civil service, perhaps 50 percent of federal jobs, as they open up, should be filled with individuals who are eligible to be fired if they do not shape up. The capability of firing people quickly has two advantages: getting rid of undesirables and attracting to the civil service risk takers and innovators, who will be creative rather than being satisfied with career stagnation and survival at any cost.

Questions for Discussion

1. If civil servants could be fired without great difficulty, how would continuity of policy implementation and expertise be affected in the bureaucracy?

2. What procedures can you think of that would counter the effects of the four "inflations" enumerated by Peters?

3. Should the veterans' bonus be eliminated? Why or why not?

Answer Guidelines

The ability to fire civil service workers without undue harassment would run into opposition not only from traditional bureaucrats but from federal unions as well. Assuming the policy could be implemented, the real prospect of being fired might have an energizing effect on civilian bureaucrats. Conversely, it might inhibit recruitment of future employees. The four inflations could be countered somewhat by placing salary limitations or even a freeze on higher grade levels. Inflated slots might eventually require large, across-the-board reductions. Finally, the veteran's bonus is a controversial matter. Veterans have strong political ties to Congress members and bureaucrats alike, and there is a general feeling that they are entitled to the bonus as payment for their service to the nation. However, the bonus does violate the merit principle, the so-called basis of civil service dynamics.

Theme B   Control of the Bureaucracy

Instructor References

Gary Bryner, *Bureaucratic Discretion*. New York: Pergamon Press, 1987.

Barbara Craig, *"Chadha": The Story of an Epic Constitutional Struggle*. New York: Oxford University Press, 1988.

William T. Gormley, Jr., *Taming the Bureaucracy*. Princeton, NJ: Princeton University Press, 1989.

Herbert Kaufman, *Are Government Organizations Immortal?* Washington, DC: Brookings Institution, 1976.

Jack Knott and Gary Miller, *Reforming Bureaucracy: The Politics of Institutional Choice*. Englewood Cliffs, NJ: Prentice-Hall, 1987.

Kenneth J. Meier, *Politics and the Bureaucracy*. Monterey, CA: Brooks-Cole Publishing, 1987.

Dennis Riley, *Controlling the Federal Bureaucracy*. Philadelphia: Temple University Press, 1987.

Bernard Rosen, *Holding Government Bureaucracies Accountable*. 2nd ed. New York: Prager, 1989.

Bruce Smith and James Carroll, eds., *Improving the Accountability and Performance of Government*. Washington, DC: Brookings Institution, 1982.

Summary

Federal bureaucrats exercise a great deal of power, especially when operating under discretionary authority. It is therefore important to understand what influences bureaucratic conduct. In general, four factors explain the behavior of governmental officials:

1. *Recruitment and reward.* In the nineteenth century, presidents could appoint virtually every federal employee on the basis of *patronage*. This practice, sometimes called the "spoils system," was based on the belief that the winning candidate should be entitled to reward supporters. Government employment could easily function in this manner for two reasons. First, the number of federal employees was small, making a wholesale change of personnel a simple task to accomplish. From 1816 to 1851, total federal employment grew from 4,479 to a mere 25,713. And second, the jobs required little expertise or specialized knowledge, with the postal service accounting for over two-thirds of all positions. The spoils system became obsolete as the size of the federal government spiraled after the Civil War and as a higher level of professional credentials became needed to perform the more complex tasks assigned to the national bureaucracy. The impetus for change was the assassination of President Garfield by a disgruntled office seeker, Charles Guiteau. The result was the Pendleton Act in 1883, which began the process of transferring federal hiring to a *merit system*. Today, no more than 3% of federal employees are exempt from the merit system.

    Once hired, a federal bureaucrat normally serves a one-year trial period before being granted "tenure." A tenured bureaucrat is extremely difficult to fire, with the average termination process (including appeals) lasting about two years. Thus, in practice, almost no one is ever fired and executives develop informal strategies for dealing with incompetent employees. The Senior Executive Service (SES) was created in 1978 to provide presidents with a core group of neutral, professional managers in the upper grades of the bureaucracy. To ensure competence, members of the SES—who join on a voluntary basis—are subject to easier transfer and firing procedures as well as to pay increases determined by performance. The SES has not worked out as intended; almost no member of the group has been fired, and salary raises have been fairly automatic.

In spite of the merit system, hiring in federal agencies remains political, especially at the middle and upper levels. An agency can hire a particular individual on a *name-request* basis, giving rise to the *buddy system*. This practice allows the maintenance of issue networks based on shared policy views; bureaucrats in consumer-protection agencies, for example, may hire people from Naderite groups. The end-product of the recruitment and reward structure is that most bureaucrats become quite comfortable in their position and defensive about their agency, adopting an "agency" point of view.

2. *Personal attributes.* Bureaucrats at the middle and upper levels of government are not representative of the American public. They tend to be highly educated, middle-aged white males. But none of these factors explains much about the attitudes bureaucrats hold. Surveys have found top-level bureaucrats slightly more liberal than the average voter but not as liberal as members of the media. Yet even this generalization is a bit misleading. Attitudes tend to vary depending on the agency for which a bureaucrat works. Those employed by "activist" agencies (FTC, EPA) are much more liberal than those who work in "traditional" agencies (Commerce). While attitudes differ, they do not necessarily influence bureaucratic behavior. The reason is that much of bureaucratic work is governed by standardized rules and procedures. It is only where roles are loosely structured that a civil servant's attitudes come into play.

3. *The nature of the job.* Some agencies have a sense of *mission,* a clear doctrine that is shared by its members. Such agencies (the Forest Service, the FBI, and the Public Health Service) are easy to manage and have high morale but are hard to change and are resistant to political direction. To be sure, a sense of mission probably infiltrates most agencies to some degree; a survey by Kenneth Meier and Lloyd Nigro revealed that federal bureaucrats believe in the importance of their agency's work. Thus the mission of the agency may become synonymous with the public interest in the minds of many bureaucrats. An agency's mission, however, must be accomplished within an array of laws, rules, and regulations—dealing with hiring and firing, freedom of information, accounting for money spent, affirmative action, environmental impact, and administrative procedures. The most important constraint on an agency is the nature of the bureaucracy itself, which constitutes a large organization composed of agencies with overlapping and even conflicting missions. These characteristics make controlling the bureaucracy difficult, no matter which party occupies the White House.

4. *External forces.* All government bureaus must cope with seven external forces: executive branch superiors, the president's staff, congressional committees, interest groups, the media, the courts, and other rival government agencies. All federal agencies are nominally subordinate to the president. In practice, agencies that distribute benefits among significant, discrete groups, regions, or localities within the United States (such as HUD, Agriculture, and Interior) tend to be closely overseen by Congress. Others (such as State, Treasury, or Justice) are more under the control of the president. Bureaucrats, like people generally, desire *autonomy*—to be left alone, free of bureaucratic rivals and close political supervision. They may obtain autonomy through the skillful use of publicity to build public support, as did the FBI and NASA. A less risky strategy is to develop strong allies in the private sector that will provide political support in Congress. However, this limits the freedom of the agency; it must serve the interests of its clients. Thus the Maritime Administration supports high subsidies for the shipping industry, and the Department of Labor could never recommend a decrease in the minimum wage. External forces influence agency decisions in the form of the so-called "iron triangle"—the informal policy network involving an agency, an interest group, and a congressional committee. The iron triangle analogy is misleading because an agency will be faced with conflicting interest-group demands. The National Farmers Union favors high subsidies to farmers, whereas the American Farm Bureau Federation takes a free-market position. Organized labor favors strict enforcement by the Occupational Safety and Health Administration, whereas business is opposed.

Interest groups are important to agencies because they are important to Congress. Congress has a formidable array of powers to deal with the bureaucracy. First, congressional statutes establish the existence of an agency and occasionally specify in detail how agencies should behave. Lately, however, Congress has given broad discretion to agencies. Second, money must be *authorized* and then *appropriated* by Congress. The agency is thus beholden to the legislative committee that authorizes funds and to the Appropriations Committee of the House.

For many decades, Congress made increasing use of the *legislative veto* to control bureaucratic or presidential actions by vetoing a particular decision within a thirty- to ninety-day period. However, in June 1983, the Supreme Court declared the legislative veto unconstitutional (the *Chadha* case). This decision's exact effect on congressional oversight of the bureaucracy is still uncertain. Finally, congressional investigations are the most visible and dramatic form of oversight.

Discussion Questions

1. The text defines bureaucracy as "a large, complex organization composed of appointed officials." What does this mean? Can you envision a large, *simple* organization? Could such an organization accomplish anything consistently?

2. The text's definition of bureaucracy includes the phrase "appointed officials." Why do the "large, complex" organizations in our society not have elected rather than appointed officials? Would this not be more democratic? Why are more officials of the federal government not elected? Should we elect the secretary of defense or the secretary of HEW, for example? Would this make these officials more responsive to public opinion? What about an undersecretary of defense? What about every officer above captain in the military services? Would the president be more or less able to control the bureaucracy if many officials were independently elected? Would concerted, consistent action be more or less likely if many more officials were elected?

Instructor: Discuss independently elected state officials here. Are the governor and the attorney general getting along well and working together? Or, as is often the case, are they politically at odds?

3. The text lists four factors that account for the behavior of bureaucrats. Which of these are "benign" and which are "pathological"? Would you *want* the behavior of bureaucrats to be most heavily determined by (a) the manner in which they are recruited and rewarded; (b) their personal attributes, such as their socioeconomic background and their political attitudes; (c) the nature of the jobs they have; (d) responsiveness to outside forces—political superiors, legislators, interest groups, or journalists?

4. What difference does the buddy system make in federal hiring? Does this system not embody the worst of both worlds, allowing appointments neither by a publicly accountable official (such as the president) nor by merit? Are there possible advantages to the buddy system?

5. Why is it so hard to fire a federal employee? What procedures must be used? Are the procedures reasonable? Should any federal executive be expected to spend as much time and effort as is necessary to get rid of an incompetent employee?

6. The Pendleton Act has produced both beneficial and harmful effects. On the one hand, it has lessened the fear of job loss among civil servants, making the bureaucracy sometimes inert to presidential direction. It takes two years on average to fire an incompetent or insubordinate civil servant. On the other hand, bureaucrats should have some immunity to resist improper orders from politically motivated superiors. How can these twin goals of competence and political neutrality be balanced more perfectly than they are today?

7. The *Chadha* decision invalidated the legislative veto. Why does Congress continue to enact laws with such provisions? Could Congress adequately supervise the exercise of delegated authority by bureaucrats without a legislative veto?

Data and Perspectives for Analysis

Students tend to consider the federal bureaucracy as composed of clerical workers for the most part. This perception is misleading. The following table lists the functions performed by the bureaucracy as well as the skill levels of its employees. Have students investigate the pay scales for entry-level positions in the federal bureaucracy and compare these salaries with those for similar jobs in the private sector.

Full-Time Civilian White-Collar Employees of the Federal Government (by selected occupational category)

Employment Category	Number of Employees
General administrative, clerical, and office services	450,267
Engineering and architecture	166,976
Medical, dental, and public health	141,698
Accounting and budget	132,747
Business and industry	95,273
Legal and kindred	74,680
Supply	60,546
Social sciences, psychology, and welfare	56,972
Investigation	56,423
Biological sciences	54,824
Personnel management and industrial relations	50,431
Physical sciences	44,378
Transportation	41,325
Education	30,287
Information and the arts	21,708
Quality assurance	19,458
Equipment, facilities, and service	17,738
Mathematics and statistics	15,363
Library and archives	10,083
Veterinary medical science	2,728
Copyright, patent trademark	2,042

Source: U.S. Office of Personnel Management, *Federal Civilian Workforce Statistics Monthly Release, Employment Trends as of March 1986*, pp. 70–75.

Additional Lecture Topic B-1

The Carter Civil Service Reforms

Bruce Buchanan, "The Senior Executive Service: How Can We Tell If It Works?" *Public Administration Review*, May–June 1981, pp. 349–358.

Mark Huddleston, "The Carter Civil Service Reforms: Some Implications for Political Theory and Public Administration." *Political Science Quarterly*, Winter 1981–1982, pp. 607–621.

Charles H. Levine, ed., *The Unfinished Agenda for Civil Service Reform*. Washington, D.C.: Brookings Institution, 1985.

Frederick C. Mosher, *Democracy and the Public Service*. 2nd ed. New York: Oxford University Press, 1982.

Felix Nigro and Lloyd F. Nigro, *Modern Public Administration*. 6th ed. New York: Harper & Row, 1984. See Chapter 7, "Politics of Civil Service Reform" (pp. 116–136).

Abstract for Theme B

Problems in "Reforming" the Bureaucracy

Reforming the bureaucracy is not an easy task, as nearly every president has found out upon entering office. In Leonard Reed's "Bureaucrats 2, Presidents 0," (originally published in *Harper's Magazine*, November 1982, but reprinted in Bruce Stinebrickner, ed. *American*

Government—85/86 Annual Edition, Guilford, CT: Dushkin, 1985, pp. 141–144), the problems of Jimmy Carter and Ronald Reagan are delineated. Reed, a former civil servant and currently a contributing editor of the *Washington Monthly*, asserts that President Carter's 1978 historic Civil Service Reform Act accomplished far less than expected.

The media portrayed the Act as making it easier to fire bureaucratic "incompetents." Yet, in the aftermath of the Act, the number of civil servants fired actually *declined* as a percentage of the 2.5 million federal workers. Second, the claim was made that "a special counsel would . . . protect bureaucratic whistle-blowers who reported wrongdoing or waste in the bureaucracy." Yet this "special counsel" has performed poorly and has appeared more concerned with ferreting out troublemakers than with defending them. Third, Carter's Senior Executive Service corps of 6,000 was lauded by the media as a group of "highly skilled managers who may not transfer among government agencies without loss of rank, and are therefore less likely to abandon public service" (p. 141). Members of the SES corps would be giving up their secure tenured positions for the "risks and rewards of competitive life" but at the same time would be eligible for sizable bonuses if they performed effectively. If they did not measure up, they would be dismissed. However, Reed reveals that in more than three years of operation, "out of the 6,200 career members of SES, exactly one has been dropped for poor performance. Risk?" (p. 144).

Reed outlines several reasons behind the failures of reform—from federal unions that are overzealous in protecting each employee's job security and their right (gained from the 1978 reforms) "to bargain over virtually any change in working conditions" (p. 142) to the obsessive, fruitless expenditure of bureaucratic energies on "turf battles and lobbying for higher budgets—rather than in serving the broader public" (p. 144). Reed then proceeds to analyze Reagan's contributions to reform.

The Reagan contribution has been the RIF (reduction in force) approach, resulting in the dismissal of close to ten thousand federal employees. This total number was exceedingly modest, but the real problem was that RIF did a poor job of weeding out incompetents. In a RIF, "seniority is everything; competence hardly enters into the equation. Somebody whose job is eliminated may 'bump' a less senior fellow worker in the same or lower grade out of his job." This chain reaction continues, so that "for every worker eventually laid off, three or four are displaced in this process" (p. 144). The results are peculiar, to say the least: A GS-14 psychologist ends up working as a GS-3 in a mailroom. Furthermore, the psychologist (like other highly trained professionals in the bureaucracy) retains his GS-14 salary. When this is multiplied in countless cases, enormous sums of money are expended for personnel who are performing menial tasks. RIF's economic advantages soon dissipate.

Reed concludes that it is possible to enact bureaucratic reforms, but that it will require an extremely determined president who is willing to challenge the existing bureaucratic system. To Reed, it remains unclear "why the federal civil servant must be afforded extravagant protections against being erroneously fired that his counterparts in the private sector do not enjoy" (p. 144).

Questions for Discussion

1. What has happened to members of the SES corps since 1982? Have a greater number been dismissed, as originally conceived in the reform plan of 1978?

2. What has happened to the Reagan RIF tactics from 1982 to the present? Have the problems enumerated in Reed's article continued during this time?

Answer Guidelines

The answers to these questions will require the class to do some research. You may wish to assign specific research tasks to selected members of your class.

Theme C   Bureaucratic "Pathologies"

Summary

There are five major problems with bureaucracies: red tape, conflict, duplication, and imperialism, and waste.

1. *Red tape* is the existence of complex rules and procedures that must be followed to get something done. Any large organization must have some way of ensuring that one part of the organization does not operate out of step with another.

2. *Conflict* exists when some agencies work at cross-purposes with other agencies. The Agricultural Research Service tells farmers how to grow crops more efficiently, while the Agricultural Stabilization and Conservation Service pays farmers to grow fewer crops. Because Congress has 535 members and little strong leadership, it is not surprising that it passes laws that promote inconsistent or even contradictory goals.

3. *Duplication* occurs when two government agencies seem to be doing the same thing, such as when the Customs Service and the Drug Enforcement Administration both attempt to intercept illegally smuggled drugs.

4. *Imperialism* refers to the tendency of agencies to grow without regard to the benefits their programs confer or the costs they entail. Because government agencies seek vague goals and have vague mandates from Congress, it is not surprising that they often take the broadest possible view of their powers. If they do not, interest groups and judges may prod them into doing so. The decision of the Department of Transportation to require wheelchair lifts on all buses was an example of this process.

5. *Waste* occurs when an agency spends more than is necessary to buy some product or service. An example would be the much-publicized purchase of $300 hammers by the military.

One severe criticism relating to "costs" is waste. The Grace Commission reported horror stories of the government's paying enormous and outrageous sums for inexpensive items. These stories are exaggerated, because standard accounting practices are overlooked. However, waste is still a reality resulting from red tape and from the fact that bureaucrats have no personal financial incentive to help keep costs down.

It should be clear that bureaucratic problems are hard to correct. Congress cannot make the hard policy choices and set the clear priorities necessary to eliminate conflict and duplication. Government exists partly to achieve the kind of vague goals that resist clear cost-benefit analysis; eliminating red tape might make coordination more difficult. But although Americans dislike "the bureaucracy" in general, studies show that they like the appointed officials with whom they deal.

Discussion Questions

1. The text says that red tape is partly a consequence of bigness and largely a result of legal and political requirements. Is this a sufficient explanation? Is there more red tape in government than these two factors can explain? Might not bureaucrats have a tendency to be more concerned that elaborate *procedures* are followed than that certain substantive *outcomes* happen? Is there a bureaucratic mind-set that might produce this result?

Instructor: See Robert Merton on "goal displacement" in his Reader in Bureaucracy *(New York: Free Press, 1952). Might it not be safer for the bureaucracy to generate red tape than to generate results?*

2. Is bureaucratic imperialism more likely to be a problem in an agency like the Post Office or in an agency like the Office for Civil Rights? Why?

3. Explain why bureaucrats have little motivation to keep costs down. Can this situation be remedied? If so, how?

Data and Perspectives for Analysis

A. An Example

An amusing story illustrates at least three bureaucratic pathologies: red tape, conflict, and duplication.

> Soon after becoming President, Jimmy Carter was conferring in his White House hideaway office with an aide when two mice scampered across the carpet. The General Services Administration (GSA), which cares for federal buildings, was summoned, and the President resumed his grapplings with the affairs of state.
>
> But the mouse problem persisted. Days before the Latin American heads of government arrived for the signing of the Panama Canal treaties, one small gray creature crawled inside a White House wall and died. The Oval Office became scented with the odor of the deceased. The GSA was again summoned. The agency declared in its report to the President that it had killed all the mice inside the White House and that therefore the expired mouse must have come from outside the edifice. An "outside" mouse, GSA explained, was the responsibility of the Interior Department, which cares for the White House grounds.
>
> The Interior Department respectfully, but firmly, demurred. Obviously, the mouse was now "inside" since it was embedded within a White House wall. "I can't even get a damned mouse out of my office," the President complained. He summoned an official from each agency to sit before his desk to witness the odor. Soon the bureaucratic deadlock was broken and the Oval Office's normal atmosphere was restored. But the episode troubled an aide who had overseen its resolution and whose own grand notions of presidential power included the expectation that a presidential command, once given, was promptly and automatically obeyed. Ruefully he observed, "It took an interagency task force to get that mouse out of here."
>
> <div style="text-align:right">Louis W. Koenig, <i>The Chief Executive</i>, 4th ed.
(New York: Harcourt Brace Jovanovich, 1981), p. 1.</div>

B. The Quality of Bureaucratic Performance

Members of the bureaucracy are perceived negatively as being inefficient and incompetent. This stereotype is not supported by the experiences of presidential appointees who interact with and supervise federal civil servants. These people, after all, have much at stake since compliance with presidential initiatives can most easily be blocked at the implementation stage. Have your students analyze the data below to discern any trends, such as differences between Democratic and Republican administrations. Since federal civil servants tend to be more liberal than the public, shouldn't Democratic administrations benefit from greater cooperation? If not, what factors tend to mute personal values in the administrative context? Why were Reagan appointees more critical of bureaucratic competence and responsiveness? The data have many rich tangents to pursue.

Presidential Appointees Rate the Career Bureaucrats

Administration	Competence*	Responsiveness*
Johnson	92%	89%
Nixon	88%	84%
Ford	80%	82%
Carter	81%	86%
Reagan	77%	78%

* Positive ratings

Source: National Academy of Public Administration, Presidential Appointees Project, *Leadership in Jeopardy: The Fraying of the Presidential Appointments System* (Washington: NAPA, 1985). The survey was mailed to all living presidential appointees in these administrations whose address was known. The response rate was 56 percent.

Abstract 1 for Theme C

"Bureaucracies Never Die, They Don't Even Fade Away"

Bureaucratic agencies have amazing longevity, even when they are marked for extinction. This is due largely to the influence these agencies have with key sectors of Congress as well as with interest groups—what some have called the "iron triangle" relationship. Two articles in the *New York Times* illustrate this fact of bureaucratic life. In "Plans to Keep Agency from the Ax," by Robert D. Hershey (January 31, 1985, p. 10), the plight of the Small Business Administration under the Reagan administration is explored. The SBA has always been a favorite target of budget cutters, according to Hershey, but it has somehow managed to survive over the years. As Hershey puts it:

> Always it has survived, creating in the process a huge constituency for its ever-expanding programs, which are meant to promote free enterprise by aiding small companies with counseling, loan guarantees and loans, including of late low-interest disaster loans for such "nonphysical" losses as the ski operator who passes a winter without snow or the fisherman who has a bad season.
>
> This year, however, the Reagan administration has taken dead aim on the agency, proposing to wipe it out at a savings put at $1.6 billion a year.

Despite the goal of eliminating the SBA, Hershey reveals that the Reagan administration would have to face a strong alliance of SBA defenders: Congress members, interest groups, and the administrative head, James C. Sanders. Sanders began a "discreet" campaign to keep the SBA alive. Interest groups, such as accounting firms specializing in services to small businesses, the National Federation of Independent Business (representing half a million companies), the National Association of Realtors, and well over a hundred other business organizations all spoke out against abolition. Finally, on Capitol Hill, small business was "almost as popular as motherhood and as risky to even seem to oppose" (the SBA had offices in close to one hundred congressional districts). Senator Weicker of Connecticut declared the effort to abolish SBA "short-sighted" and Representative Mitchell of Maryland declared that the proposed abolition would, if implemented, inflict a death blow to "this important sector of the economy." In short, though the threat to SBA was deemed serious, Hershey asserts that the most likely outcome would be continued survival as a separate agency.

A similar article by Barbara Gamarekian, "Despite Plans for Its Demise, Agency Hangs On" (July 9, 1985, p. 12), dealt with Vista (Volunteers in Service to America), a program that was a survivor of the old "War on Poverty" agenda of the Johnson administration. During the past five years, Vista's budget had been slashed, recruitment curtailed, and its directors changed repeatedly. Once again, congressional supporters rallied to the agency's rescue. But Gamarekian also notes that 80,000 former Vista volunteers were lobbying in a strong collective effort. Unlike the SBA case, Vista was opposed more on ideological grounds. Conservatives saw the agency as too left-wing, given its work with the poor and minorities and its connection with political organization among the powerless. Supporters acknowledged that the public perception was that Vista was either dead or a credit card, but they nevertheless intended to press their drive for extension of the agency's life for another three years beyond 1986.

Questions for Discussion

1. Did both the SBA and Vista survive? If you had to pick between the two, which appeared to have the better chance and why?
2. If you were an agency head whose organization was threatened, what specific survival strategy would you follow?

Answer Guidelines

It would appear that the SBA had stronger institutional roots than Vista within the "triangle." The public also seems to have been more aware of SBA's role than of Vista's somewhat more obscure function. Obviously, a strategy designed to build coalitions of support in Congress and the public interest group cluster would be the most beneficial.

Abstract 2 for Theme C

The U.S. Postal Service: A Bureaucratic "Pathology"?

In an article in *USA Today*, September, 1985, pp. 10–15, "The U.S. Postal Service: The Last Dinosaur," James Bovard asserts that the USPS (U.S. Postal Service) "is probably the worst-managed and one of the least honest corporations in America." The USPS has failed to incorporate technical innovations to improve its delivery service, has deliberately pressured private mail-delivery systems to stop their operations, and has been wasteful, inefficient, and corrupt. Because the postal service possesses a monopoly on first-class mail, its public trust has been abused, as people are forced to confront "increasingly worse service at ever-higher prices."

Bovard shows how the USPS has repeatedly tried to prevent challenges from competent mail-delivery private companies or groups through legal intimidation:

> In 1971, a Federal district court prohibited a private firm from carrying Christmas cards in Oklahoma on the basis that the plaintiffs, a postal employees' union, suffered "significant loss of work time, overtime, employment benefits . . . and morale. . . ."
>
> In 1976, in New York, a pack of Cub Scouts tried to raise money by delivering Christmas cards. Postal Service lawyers ordered them to stop and threatened the ten-year-olds with a $76,500 fine. A *New York Times* editorial regretted that the Postal Service's carriers were not as fast as its lawyers.
>
> In 1978, the P.H. Brennan Hand Delivery Service offered same-day delivery of mail in Rochester, N.Y. for 10 cents a piece; the Postal Service could not guarantee overnight delivery even for 15 cents. The Brennan Service operated during snowstorms (when the Postal Service did not even try to deliver), never lost a letter, and never had a complaint. . . . However, the Postal Service persuaded a judge to issue a "cease and desist" order on account of the "threat to postal revenues."

Bovard argues that historically it has been private competition that has forced USPS to upgrade the quality of its service. Without that competition challenging USPS's bureaucratic monopoly, citizens might still be going to the local post office as they did in the nineteenth century, rather than having mail delivered to their homes.

Bovard reveals how the USPS has failed in creating centralized bulk-mail centers (it is far behind UPS) and electronic mail services. Thus, in Bovard's words, "postal service innovation efforts have an almost unbroken record of failure. The postal bureaucracy has repeatedly obscured costs, exaggerated benefits, and proved incapable of learning from its mistakes."

The most telling flaw of the USPS has been declining service and soaring postal rates. The USPS has lied to the citizenry regarding next-day delivery of local mail (private studies show anywhere from 20 percent to over 50 percent of local mail takes two or three days). Even the USPS admits that it takes 10 percent longer today to deliver a first-class letter than it did sixteen years ago. Also, soaring first-class postal rates relate to uncontrollable salaries for postal workers, whom Bovard views as having low productivity, poor attendance records, and few incentives to improve work habits, since they are given incredible fringe benefits and have little chance of ever being fired. Bovard even cites examples of postal employees who commit abuses of privacy by opening the mail illegally.

The author summarizes his main thesis as follows:

> No amount of tinkering will solve the postal problem. For fifteen years, postal officials have warned us that allowing competition would mean worse service at higher prices, and, for fifteen years, service has deteriorated while rates have soared. Since we're already getting the adverse side effects, we have nothing to lose by trying competition. The ideal solution is to open the floodgates to private competition. There is no excuse for nationalizing the transport of small envelopes. In 200 years, government has yet to reveal a genius for the task. As long as the mail is carried by a tenured bureaucracy with no incentive to move quickly, service will continue to be slow, expensive, and doubtful. (pp. 158–159)

Questions for Discussion (Open-ended responses are encouraged.)

1. What advantages and disadvantages could flow from ending the postal service's monopoly of mail delivery?

2. Would firing postal workers who are ineffective help postal efficiency?

Theme D   Ethics in Public Administration*

Summary

The role of ethics in the administration of public policy was not considered a relevant topic in the nineteenth century because it was assumed that politics did not enter into the management of public programs. An administrator carried out the law and had no discretion in the exercise of this duty. As Frederick Mosher points out, "A neutral, efficient civil service was viewed as not merely desirable; it was essential to democracy itself." Woodrow Wilson echoed this sentiment in 1887 by noting that the "field of administration is a field of business." The movement to incorporate ethics into public administration developed as an element of "progressive reform" to eliminate corruption in government. The foal was to substitute hiring on the basis of merit in place of political patronage. The federal government adopted this position with the enactment of the Pendleton Act in 1883 that required testing to obtain certain federal jobs. Merit was perceived as the solution to abuses in the management of public programs. Sociologist Emile Durkheim went so far as to exalt professionalism as the source of modern morality.

However, scholarly has swung against professionalism, even to the point of attacking it as contrary to the democratic spirit. The problem with professionalism is two-fold. First, it induces a tendency in bureaucrats to strive to achieve efficiency often at the expense of the public interest. In the words of George Berkley, professionalism produces "blinders" as bureaucrats attempt to do what is best rather than what the public wants. Second, professionalism contributes to divided loyalties. An administrator is caught between competing obligations: serving the public, upholding professional standards, and protecting his or her agency. In this environment, survival of the agency frequently becomes equated with the public interest in the minds of many bureaucrats. The danger to society is that administrative morality may come to resemble standard operating procedures.

It was only in the 1940s that scholars began to challenge the assumption that bureaucrats lacked discretion in the implementation of public policy. This realization came at a time when the Supreme Court began to allow Congress to delegate authority to civil servants to "fill in the details" of public programs. Neither discretion nor the policy role could be exercised by an administrator without engaging in choice. It is at this point that ethics enter the picture. How can an administrator decide correctly in light of the differing ethical standards that exist? Professional organizations in the field of public administration began to formulate codes of ethics to control bureaucratic discretion. After all, an administrator must know what is ethical in order to act ethically. The first code of ethics at the state level did not appear until 1967. In a short time, nonetheless, such codes have proliferated.

Ralph Clark Chandler analyzed numerous codes of ethics and concluded that they are designed to reflect an image of the ideal bureaucrat but fail to instruct a bureaucrat on the substance of ethics. No code can anticipate the array of gut-wrenching decisions an administrator must make in the daily management process. Codes are too ambiguous to apply in concrete situations. For this reason, John Burke has reasoned that rules of conduct are necessary but they cannot replace substantive judgment. Ethical lapses will continue to plague the management of public programs as the price of human nature. The excesses of a public administrator can be limited but never eliminated.

---

*Adapted from Brian M. Murphy, "Ethics in Local Government Administration," in Richard D. Bingham et al., *Managing Local Government: Public Administration in Practice.* Newbury Park, CA: Sage Publications, 1991, pp. 156–169.

Data and Perspectives for Analysis

What kinds of standards govern bureaucratic behavior? The code of ethics reprinted below is a good example. Have your students examine the specific criteria and discuss whether they are practical or too abstract to be relevant to concrete situations. Are any significant "standards" of behavior missing in light of recent scandals?

Code of Ethics
American Society for Public Administration

Demonstrate the highest standards of personal integrity, truthfulness, honesty and fortitude in all our public activities, in order to inspire public confidence and trust in public institutions.

Serve in such a way that we do not realize undue personal gain from the performance of our official duties.

Avoid any interest or activity which is in conflict with the conduct of our official duties.

Support, implement, and promote merit employment and programs of affirmative action to assure equal employment opportunity by our recruitment, selection, and advancement of qualified persons from all elements of society.

Eliminate all forms of illegal discrimination, fraud, and mismanagement of public funds, and support colleagues if they are in difficulty because of responsible efforts to correct such discrimination, fraud, mismanagement, or abuse.

Serve the public with respect, concern, courtesy, and responsiveness, recognizing that service to the public is beyond service to oneself.

Strive for personal professional excellence, and encourage the professional development of our associates and those seeking to enter the field of public administration.

Approach our organization and operational duties with a positive attitude, and constructively support open communication, creativity, dedication, and compassion.

Respect and protect the privileged information to which we have access in the course of official duties.

Exercise whatever discretionary authority we have under law to promote the public interest.

Accept as a personal duty the responsibility to keep up to date on emerging issues, and to administer the public's business with professional competence, fairness, impartiality, efficiency, and effectiveness.

Respect, support, study, and when necessary, work to improve federal and state constitutions and other laws which define the relationships among public agencies, employees, clients, and all citizens.

Source: Adopted by the ASPA National Council, March 27, 1985; in George J. Gordon, *Public Administration in America,* 4th ed. (New York: St. Martin's, 1992), p. 189.

Additional Lecture Topic D-1

Improving Bureaucratic Performance

Herbert Kaufman, *Are Government Organizations Immortal?* Washington, DC: Brookings Institution, 1976.

Jack Knott and Gary Miller, *Reforming Bureaucracy: The Politics of Institutional Choice.* Englewood Cliffs, N.J.: Prentice-Hall, 1987.

Dennis Riley, *Controlling the Federal Bureaucracy.* Philadelphia: Temple University Press, 1987.

Bernard Rosen, *Holding Government Bureaucracies Accountable.* New York: Praeger, 1982. Covers a variety of techniques to control bureaucracies.

Bruce Smith and James Carroll, eds., *Improving the Accountability and Performance of Government.* Washington, D.C.: Brookings Institution, 1982.

Alan F. Westin, ed., *Whistle-Blowing.* New York: McGraw Hill, 1980.

Abstract for Theme D

Bureaucracy and Democracy

An underlying question in this chapter has been whether bureaucracies are compatible with the principles of democracy. To some authorities, they clearly are not. David Nachmias and David H. Rosenbloom argue in "Democracy and the Growing Bureaucracy" (in Robert Harmel, ed., *American Government—Readings on Continuity and Change,* New York: St. Martin's Press, 1988, pp. 401–406) that there is an inherent tension between the two organizational forms when a direct comparison of their requirements is made (p. 405)

Democracy Requires	*Bureaucracy Requires*
Plurality	Unity
Equality	Hierarchy
Liberty	Command
Rotation in office	Duration in office
Openness	Secrecy
Equal access to participation in politics	Differentiated access, based on authority
Election	Appointment

Furthermore, the authors assert, "the primary difficulty integrating bureaucratic government into a democratic political framework is that control of public bureaucracies by elective and appointive political authorities is highly problematic." As implied in the chapter, career bureaucrats and elected officials do possess divergent perspectives, which emanate both from administrative styles and respective clientele groups. The bureaucratic style is oriented toward long-term survival in the political system, whereas a congressman or other public official faces the very real possibility of electoral defeat. Consequently, the gradualism and caution associated with the bureaucrat will clash with the policy impatience of the official. Furthermore, the expertise of the bureaucrat in a narrow policy area can rarely be matched by a congressman, who must be a generalist of sorts. A congressman, president, or other top political appointee must usually respond to a wide range of groups, whereas career civil servants frequently form close links to agency clients (example: Veterans' Administration and the VFW). Shared perspectives emerge from this link, and thus political policies that run counter to those perspectives will invariably be resisted, delayed, or obstructed in some manner.

A good example of this political phenomenon was President Reagan's experience with the Environmental Protection Agency (EPA) in the early 1980s. President Reagan felt that the EPA's past vigorous enforcement of antipollution laws had been counterproductive, hindering economic progress for the sake of relatively modest gains in pollution control. He named as EPA administrator Anne Gorsuch Burford, who proceeded to oversee major budgetary and staff cuts in the agency. However, environmentalists, upset over the agency's new policy direction, aligned themselves with sympathetic congressmen and EPA bureaucrats at odds with Burford's leadership. The eventual result was Burford's resignation, more congressional allocations for antipollution controls, and the appointment of William Ruckleshaus, who promptly advocated a return to vigorous enforcement of laws protecting the environment.

The EPA experience illustrates a valuable lesson in the "bureaucracy-democracy" dilemma—one cannot always assume that bureaucratic actions are hostile to the public will. Indeed, bureaucracies can possibly check abuses of power by elected officials or frustrate ill-conceived public policies set forth by new national administrations. In short, bureaucracies cannot be equated with the automatic undermining of democratic precepts, even if their organizational and operational requirements are different.

Discussion Questions

1. In what ways can bureaucracies strengthen democratic political processes?

2. Would you favor the limitation of career bureaucrats' government service to a maximum number of years? Why or why not?

14

The Judiciary

Overview and Objectives

This chapter introduces the student to the final and perhaps most unusual branch of American government: the courts. The chapter will explain how courts, particularly the Supreme Court, came to play a uniquely powerful role in forming public policy in this country, and how that role has been played to very different effects at different stages of history. Other important considerations include how justices are selected, the jurisdictions of the various courts, and the steps that a case must go through on its way to Supreme Court review. The chapter concludes with an assessment of the power courts have in politics today, the limitations on that power, and why judicial activism seems to be on the increase. After reading and reviewing the material in this chapter the student should be able to do each of the following:

1. Explain what "judicial review" is, and trace its origin in this country to *Marbury v. Madison*.

2. List and comment on the three eras of varying Supreme Court influences on national policy, from the days of slavery to the present.

3. Explain what is meant by a "dual" court system and describe the effects it has on how cases are handled and appealed.

4. List the various steps that cases go through to be appealed to the Supreme Court and explain the considerations involved at each level.

5. Discuss the dimensions of power exercised today by the Supreme Court and the opposing viewpoints on the desirability of activism by that court.

6. Develop arguments for and against an activist Supreme Court.

Chapter Outline with Keyed-in Resources

I. Introduction
   A. Only in the United States do judges play so large a role in policy-making

The policy-making potential of the federal judiciary is enormous. Woodrow Wilson once described the Supreme Court as a constitutional convention in continuous session.

   1. Judicial review: right to rule on laws and executive acts on basis of constitutionality

In theory, the power of judicial review is possessed by state courts as well. It is not unusual for a state court to declare an act of Congress in violation of the Constitution.

            a. Chief judicial weapon in system of checks and balances
        2. In Britain, Parliament is supreme
        3. In other countries, judicial review means little
            a. Exceptions: Australia, Canada, Germany, India, and a few others
    B. Debate is over how the Constitution should be interpreted
        1. Strict constructionism ("interpretivism"): judges are bound by wording of Constitution
        2. Activist ("legislative"): judges should look to underlying principles of Constitution

Judicial activism is often maligned for allowing courts to usurp the power of legislatures. Senator George Norris of Nebraska complained in 1930: "We have a legislative body, called the House of Representatives, of over four hundred men. We have another legislative body, called the Senate, of less than one hundred men. We have, in reality, another legislative body, called the Supreme Court, of nine men; and they are more powerful than all the others put together."

        3. Not a matter of liberal versus conservative

Justice Harry Blackmun clearly expressed the strict constructionist view in a dissenting opinion in *Furman v. Georgia* (1972), which voided the death penalty as then administered: "Cases such as these provide for me an excruciating agony of the spirit. I yield to no one in the depth of my distaste, antipathy, and, indeed, abhorrence, for the death penalty. . . . Were I a legislator, I would vote against the penalty. . . . I do not sit, however, as a legislator. . . . Our task here . . . is to pass on the constitutionality of legislation that has been enacted and that is challenged. This is the sole task for judges. We should not allow our personal preferences as to the wisdom of legislative or congressional action, or our distaste for such action, to guide our judicial decision." Blackmun later changed his mind on the constitutionality of the death penalty.

            a. A judge can be both conservative and activist, or liberal and strict constructionist
            b. Today: most activists tend to be liberal, most strict constructionists conservative
II. The development of the federal courts (THEME A: THE HISTORY OF THE FEDERAL JUDICIARY)
    A. Founders' view
        1. Most Founders probably expected judicial review but not playing so large a role in policy-making.
        2. Traditional view: judges find and apply existing law
        3. Activist judges would later respond that judges make law
        4. Traditional view made it easy for Founders to justify judicial review
        5. Hamilton: courts least dangerous branch
        6. But federal judiciary evolved toward judicial activism
    B. National supremacy and slavery: 1789–1861
        1. *McCulloch v. Maryland*: federal law declared supreme over state law
        2. Interstate commerce clause is placed under the authority of federal law; conflicting state law void
        3. *Dred Scott v. Sandford*: Negroes were not, and could not become, free citizens of the U.S.; a direct cause of the Civil War

In a poll conducted in the early 1980s, political scientists ranked the *Dred Scott* opinion as the worst decision ever rendered by the Supreme Court.

    C. Government and the economy: Civil War to 1936
        1. Dominant issue of the period: whether the economy could be regulated by state and federal governments
        2. Private property held to be protected by the Fourteenth Amendment
        3. States seek to protect local businesses and employees from the predatory activities of national monopolies; judicial activism

  4. The Supreme Court determines what is "reasonable" regulation
  5. The Court interprets the Fourteenth and Fifteenth amendments narrowly as applied to blacks
 D. Government and political liberty: 1936 to the present
  1. Court establishes tradition of deferring to the legislature in economic cases
  2. Court shifts attention to personal liberties and is active in defining rights
III. The structure of the federal courts (THEME B: THE STRUCTURE AND JURISDICTION OF THE FEDERAL COURTS)
 A. Two kinds of federal courts
  1. Constitutional courts
   a. Created under Article III
   b. Judges serve during good behavior
   c. Salaries not reduced while in office
   d. Examples: District Courts (94), Courts of Appeals (12)
  2. Legislative courts
   a. Created by Congress for specialized purposes
   b. Judges have fixed terms
   c. No salary protection
 B. Selecting judges
  1. Party background some effect on judicial behavior, but ideology does not determine behavior
  2. Senatorial courtesy: judges must be approved by that state's senators for district courts
  3. The "litmus test"
   a. Presidential successes in selecting compatible judges
   b. Concern this may downplay "professional qualifications"

Perhaps an extreme example of Congress's downplaying the professional qualifications of judicial nominees occurred with President Nixon's nomination of G. Harold Carswell to the Supreme Court. In defending Carswell's generally poor judicial record, Senator Roman Hruska argued: "Even if he is mediocre, there are a lot of mediocre judges and people and lawyers. They are entitled to a little representation, aren't they, and a little chance? We can't have all Brandeises, Cardozas, and Frankfurters."

   c. Greatest impact on Supreme Court
IV. The jurisdiction of the federal courts
 A. Dual court system

State courts are the real workhorses in the dual court system. In the early 1990s, state courts averaged about 90 million cases annually compared with 270,000 in federal courts.

  1. One state, one federal
  2. Federal cases listed in Article III and Eleventh Amendment of Constitution
   a. Federal-question cases: involving U.S. matters
   b. Diversity cases: involving citizens of different states

In a diversity case, the federal judge must apply the applicable *state* law to the case, not federal law.

   c. All others are left to state courts
  3. Some cases can be tried in either court
   a. Example: if both federal and state laws have been broken (dual sovereignty)
   b. Justified: each government has right to enact laws and neither can block prosecution out of sympathy for the accused
  4. State cases sometimes can be appealed to Supreme Court
  5. Exclusive federal jurisdiction over federal criminal laws, appeals from federal regulatory agencies, bankruptcy, and controversies between two states
 B. Route to the Supreme Court
  1. Most federal cases begin in district courts

    a. Most are straightforward, do not lead to new public policy
  2. Supreme Court picks the cases it wants to hear on appeal
    a. Uses writ of certiorari ("cert")

Other avenues exist for taking an appeal to the Supreme Court aside from the writ of certiorari. A "writ of certification" can be used when a U.S. Court of Appeals requests instructions from the Supreme Court on a point of law never before decided. A "writ of appeal" is available, in simple terms, when the constitutionality of a government action is in question or when a decision from a three-judge district court is appealed.

    b. Requires agreement of four justices to hear case

According to Justice Stevens, between 23 and 30 percent of the cases accepted by the Supreme Court receive the bare minimum of four votes. Only 9 percent receive a unanimous vote.

    c. Usually deals with significant federal or constitutional question
      (1) Conflicting decisions by circuit courts
      (2) State court decisions involving Constitution
    d. Only 3 to 4 percent of appeals are granted certiorari
    e. Others are left to lower courts
      (1) Results in diversity of constitutional interpretation
 V. Getting to court (THEME C: CASES BEFORE THE COURT)
  A. Deterrents

To deter the volume of appeals, the Supreme Court has begun to impose fines for "frivolous" cases that waste the judiciary's time and resources.

   1. Court rejects 95 percent of applications for certiorari
   2. Costs of appeal are high
    a. But these can be lowered by
      (1) *In forma pauperis:* plaintiff heard as pauper, with costs paid by government
      (2) Payment by interest groups who have something to gain (e.g., American Civil Liberties Union)
    b. Each party must pay its own way except for cases in which it is decided:
      (1) that losing defendant will pay (fee shifting)
      (2) Section 1983 suits
   3. Standing: guidelines

The requirement of "standing" has evolved over time. For example, in the famous *Dred Scott* decision, the court costs and lawyers' fees of Dred Scott were actually paid by his owner. In other words, the defendant paid for his opponent to sue him! Today, such an arrangement would violate the precept of standing that requires a controversy between "adversaries."

    a. Must be controversy between adversaries
    b. Personal harm must be demonstrated
    c. Being taxpayer not entitlement for suit
    d. Sovereign immunity
  B. Class-action suits
   1. Brought on behalf of all similarly situated
   2. Financial incentives to bring suit
   3. Need to notify all members of the class since 1974 to limit such suits
 VI. The Supreme Court in action (THEME D: THE SUPREME COURT IN ACTION)
  A. Oral arguments by lawyers after briefs submitted

The Supreme Court jealously guards its time during oral arguments. Two lights are placed in front of a lawyer arguing before the Supreme Court: a white light shines to inform the attorney that five minutes remain, and a red one to instruct the attorney to cease immediately. When a lawyer asked Chief Justice Hughes how much time remained in his allotment, he answered, "Fourteen seconds, Mr. Counsel."

1. Each side has half-hours, but justices can question
2. Role of solicitor general

The solicitor general may decide that the federal government won a case it should have lost. In that situation, a confession of error is filed with the Supreme Court. The Court, however, is under no obligation to accept the government's position.

    3. *Amicus curiae* briefs

The Supreme Court must give its permission to accept an *amicus* brief. The Court is generous in its consent, taking 85 percent of all requests to file such briefs.

        4. Many sources of influence on justices, e.g., law journals
    B. Conference procedures (ADDITIONAL LECTURE TOPIC D-1)
        1. Role of chief justice: speaking first, voting last
        2. Selection of opinion writer: concurring and dissenting opinions
    C. Voting patterns of the court
        1. Liberal and conservative blocs
            a. Civil liberties issues
            b. Economic issues
        2. Swing votes
        3. Blocs on the Burger/Rehnquist courts
VII. The power of the federal courts (THEME E: THE POWER OF THE FEDERAL JUDICIARY) (ADDITIONAL LECTURE TOPIC E-1)
    A. The power to make policy
        1. By interpretation

In interpreting the Constitution, the Supreme Court has wide latitude. In the words of former Chief Justice Hughes: "We are under the Constitution, but the Constitution is what the judges say it is. . . ."

        2. By extending reach of existing law
        3. By designing remedies
    B. Measures of power
        1. Number of laws declared unconstitutional (over 120)
        2. Number of prior cases overturned; not following *stare decisis*
        3. Deference to the legislative branch (political questions)
        4. Kinds of remedies imposed; judges go beyond what justice requires
        5. Basis for sweeping orders either from Constitution or interpretation of federal laws
    C. Views of judicial activism
        1. Supporters
            a. Courts should correct injustices
            b. Courts are last resort
        2. Critics
            a. Judges lack expertise
            b. Courts not accountable; judges not elected
        3. Possible reasons for activism
            a. Too many lawyers; but real cause adversary culture
            b. Easier to get standing in courts
    D. Legislation and the courts
        1. Laws and the Constitution are filled with vague language
            a. Gives courts opportunity to design remedies
            b. Can interpret them in different ways
        2. Federal government is increasingly on the defensive in court cases; laws induce litigation
        3. The attitudes of federal judges affect their decisions
VIII. Checks on judicial power
    A. Judges are not immune from politics or public opinion

The correlation between public opinion and Supreme Court decisions is a much debated topic. According to John Schmidhauser, "the public policy choices of the justices are to some extent inhibited by a sense of institutional obligation acquired after ascension to the Supreme Court." Schmidhauser found that voting decisions on the Supreme Court failed to break along sectional lines prior to the Civil War, even on issues related to slavery and to the commerce clause.

      1. Effects will vary from case to case
      2. Decisions can be ignored
         a. Examples: school prayer, school desegregation
         b. Usually if resister is not highly visible
   B. Congress and the courts
      1. Confirmation and impeachment proceedings alter composition of courts
      2. Changing the number of judges

The number of justices sitting on the Supreme Court is determined by Congress. The current number of nine justices was established in 1869. However, the membership of the Court has ranged from five to ten justices.

      3. Revising legislation declared unconstitutional
      4. Altering jurisdiction of the courts and restricting remedies
      5. Constitutional amendment

Constitutional amendments have been used in numerous instances to reverse decisions by the Supreme Court. According to Henry Abraham, six amendments have been adopted specifically to alter decisions by the Supreme Court.

   C. Public opinion and the courts

The fictional character Mr. Dooley, a creation of Finley Peter Dunne, once commented, "No matter whether th' constitution follows th' flag or not, th' supreme coort folls th' illiction returns."

      1. Defying public opinion frontally is dangerous, especially elite opinion
      2. Opinion in realigning eras may energize court
      3. Public confidence in court since 1966 has varied
      4. Change caused by changes of personnel and what government is doing
   D. Reasons for increased activism
      1. Growth of government
      2. Activist ethos of judges

Important Terms

*activism An approach to judicial review which holds that judges should discover the general principles underlying the Constitution and its often vague language, amplify those principles on the basis of some moral or economic philosophy, and apply them to cases.

*amicus curiae A Latin term meaning "friend of the court." Refers to interested groups or individuals, not directly involved in a suit, who may file legal briefs or oral arguments in support of one side.

*briefs Legal documents submitted by lawyers to courts which set forth the facts of a case, summarize any lower court decisions on the case, give the arguments for the side represented by the lawyer filing the brief, and discuss decisions in other cases that bear on the issue.

*civil law Rules defining relationships among private citizens.

*class-action suit A case brought into court by a person on behalf of not only himself or herself but all other persons in similar circumstances. The Supreme Court in 1974 tightened rules on these suits to only those authorized by Congress and those in which each ascertainable member of the class is individually notified if money damages are sought.

*concurring opinion An opinion by one or more justices who agree with the majority's conclusion but for different reasons that they wish to express.

conservative/strict constructionist bloc One of three groups of justices in the 1970s and 1980s, including Chief Justice Warren Burger, who took a consistently conservative position on issues.

*constitutional court Lower federal courts created by Congress which exercise the judicial powers delineated in Article III of the Constitution. Its judges, therefore, enjoy two constitutional protections—they serve "during good behavior" and their salaries may not be reduced while in office.

*courts of appeals The federal courts that have the authority to review decisions by federal district courts, regulatory commissions, and certain other federal courts. Such courts have no original jurisdiction; they can hear only appeals.

*criminal law A body of rules defining offenses that are considered to be offenses against society as a whole and for which conviction could result in a prison term.

*dissenting opinion The opinion of the justices on the losing side.

*district courts The lowest federal courts where federal cases begin. They are the only federal courts where trials are held.

*diversity cases Jurisdiction conferred by the Constitution on federal courts to hear cases involving citizens of different states. The matter, however, must involve more than $50,000, and even then the parties have the option of commencing the suit in state court.

dual sovereignty A doctrine holding that state and federal authorities can prosecute the same person for the same conduct.

*federal-question cases Jurisdiction conferred by the Constitution on federal courts to hear all cases "arising under the Constitution, the laws of the United States, and treaties."

*fee shifting A practice that enables plaintiffs to collect their costs from a defendant if the defendant loses. The Supreme Court has limited fee shifting to cases in which it is authorized by statute.

*in forma pauperis A petition filed with the U.S. Supreme Court by a pauper. The normal $300 filing fee is waived for such petitions.

*judicial review The right of federal courts to declare laws of Congress and acts of the executive branch void and unenforceable if they are judged to be in conflict with the Constitution.

*legislative courts Lower federal courts created by Congress for specialized purposes. These courts are staffed with people who have fixed terms of office. Members of the staffs, moreover, can be removed from office and have their salaries reduced while in office.

liberal/activist bloc One of three groups of justices in the 1970s and 1980s, led by Justice William Brennan, who took a consistently liberal position on issues. It was usually in the minority.

*litmus test A test of ideological purity used by recent presidents in selecting judges to nominate to federal courts.

Marbury v. Madison A decision of the Supreme Court written by Chief Justice John Marshall in 1803 which interpreted the Constitution as giving the Supreme Court the power to declare an act of Congress unconstitutional. This decision is the foundation of the federal judiciary's power of judicial review.

McCulloch v. Maryland A decision of the Supreme Court written by Chief Justice John Marshall in 1819 which held that the power of the federal government flows from the people and should be generously construed so that any laws "necessary and proper" to the attainment of constitutional ends are permissible, and that federal law is supreme over state law even to the point that the state may not tax an enterprise (such as a bank) created by the federal government.

*opinion of the Court An ipinion by the Supreme Court that reflects the majority's view.

*per curiam opinion A brief and unsigned opinion by the Supreme Court.

*plaintiff The party that initiates a suit in law.

*political question An issue that the Court refuses to consider because it believes the Constitution has left it entirely to another branch to decide. Its view of such issues may change over time, however.

*remedy A judicial order setting forth what must be done to correct a situation a judge believes to be wrong.

Section 1983 case A provision in the U.S. Code which allows a citizen to sue state and local government officials who have deprived the citizen of some constitutional right or withheld some benefit to which the citizen is entitled. If the citizen wins, he or she can collect money damages and lawyers' fees from the government.

senatorial courtesy The tradition by which the Senate will not confirm a district court judge if the senator who is from that state and of the president's party objects.

solicitor general The third-ranking officer in the Justice Department, who decides what cases the federal government will appeal from lower courts and personally approves every case the government presents to the Supreme Court.

*sovereign immunity A legal concept that forbids a person from suing the government without its consent. Congress has given its consent for the government to be sued in many cases involving disputes over contracts or damage done as a result of negligence.

*standing A legal concept that refers to who is entitled to bring a case. Three basic rules govern standing. First, there must be an actual controversy between real adversaries. Second, the person bringing suit must show that he or she has been harmed by the law or practice involved in the complaint. Third, merely being a taxpayer does not entitle a person to challenge the constitutionality of a governmental action.

*stare decisis An informal rule of judicial decision making in which judges try to follow precedent in deciding cases. That is, a court case today should be settled in accordance with prior decisions on similar cases.

*strict constructionism An approach to judicial review which holds that judges should confine themselves to applying those rules that are stated in or clearly implied by the language of the Constitution.

Supreme Court of the United States The highest court in the federal judiciary specifically created by the Constitution. It is composed of nine justices and has appellate jurisdiction over lower federal courts and the highest state courts. It also possesses a limited original jurisdiction.

swing bloc One of three groups of justices in the 1970s and 1980s that vacillated between liberal and conservative voting positions.

voting blocs Groups of justices on the Supreme Court who tend to take consistent positions on issues.

*writ of certiorari An order issued by the Supreme Court granting a hearing to an appeal. A vote of four justices is needed to issue the writ. Only about 3 or 4 percent of all appeals are accepted.

Theme A   The History of the Federal Judiciary

Instructor References

Vincent Blasi, *The Burger Court: The Counter-Revolution That Wasn't.* New Haven, CT: Yale University Press, 1983.

George L. Haskins and Herbert A. Johnson, *History of the Supreme Court of the United States.* New York: Macmillan, 1983.

Robert G. McCloskey, *The American Supreme Court.* Chicago: University of Chicago Press, 1960.

Summary

The power of the Supreme Court evolved slowly. In the first three years of the nation's existence, the justices did not hear any cases at all. The Supreme Court's immediate priority was to establish its institutional legitimacy. This goal was accomplished in a series of developments under the leadership of Chief Justice John Marshall: (1) defeat of the impeachment proceeding, based purely on political charges, against Justice Samuel Chase that validated the doctrine of judicial independence; (2) the issuance of a single majority opinion that enabled the Court to speak with one authoritative voice in lieu of each justice writing separately; and (3) assumption of the power of judicial review in *Marbury v. Madison* (1803), making the Supreme Court an equal partner in the governing process with Congress and the president.

Once secure in its position, the Supreme Court turned to the task of adjudication. The history of Supreme Court decision-making falls into three eras differentiated by the type of issue that dominated judicial attention during a particular period of time.

1. From 1787 to 1865, federal–state relations and slavery were the great issues. In *Martin v. Hunter's Lessee* (1816), the Court asserted its right to impose binding interpretations of federal law upon state courts. Three years later, *McCulloch v. Maryland* upheld the supremacy of the federal government in a conflict with a state over a matter not clearly assigned to federal authority by the Constitution. Although federal preeminence was written into constitutional theory, it was not until after the Civil War that the theory applied in practice. In fact, the Court played an important role in intensifying regional tensions through its decision in *Dred Scott v. Standford* (1857), in which slaves and their descendants were held not be citizens of the United States. This decision, moreover, was only the second time that a federal law was declared unconstitutional by the Supreme Court. The Court's reluctance to use judicial review attests to its still uncertain status in the early part of the nineteenth century.

2. From 1865 to 1937, the dominant issue was the relationship between government and the economy. The Court acted to support property rights and held that the due process clause of the Fourteenth Amendment protected commercial enterprises from some forms of regulation. The justices were merely reflecting the prevailing *laissez-faire* philosophy of the time. The Court, however, was not blind to the injustices of capitalism and upheld state regulations in over 80% of such cases between 1887 and 1910. As the justices attempted to balance the public interest against private property rights, their decisions became riddled with inconsistencies in distinguishing "reasonable" from "unreasonable" regulation or in separating "interstate" from "intrastate" commerce. According to Justice Holmes, the Court had lost sight of its mission by forgetting that "a Constitution is not intended to embody a particular economic theory." The necessities of the Great Depression would compel a revision in constitutional theory on economic issues.

3. From 1938 to the present, the Court has switched its focus to the protection of personal liberties. This change was partially prompted by the political pressure generated by Franklin Roosevelt's unsuccessful effort to "pack" the Supreme Court with justices favorable to his New Deal economic package. As the Court allowed the government a freer hand on economic regulation, it took up the challenges presented by social and political upheaval following World War II, such as free speech and racial integration. Only recently has the number of civil liberties cases in the Court's docket begun to shrink, perhaps as a reaction to the conservative majority appointed by Presidents Reagan and Bush.

Discussion Questions

1. What problems did the Court have in trying to limit economic regulation in the era between the Civil War and the New Deal? In attempting to limit regulation, was the Court reading its own political views into the Constitution or striving for a neutral interpretation of the document? Did the Founders believe in private property and want it protected? Was the Fourteenth Amendment intended to prevent economic regulation?

2. What was the "switch in time that saved nine"? What does it suggest about the Supreme Court and the other branches of government? Why did the Warren Court not retreat or reverse itself in the wake of adverse public reaction? How was its situation different from that of the Court during Franklin Roosevelt's administration?

3. How would one distinguish *successful* from *unsuccessful* assertions of judicial power? What is it that puts *Marbury* in one class and *Dred Scott* in another?

Data and Perspectives for Analysis

The different eras of Supreme Court history testify to the importance of the values of judges in reaching decisions. The following table demonstrates how Supreme Court decisions are affected by the personal ideologies of the justices.

Civil Liberties Claims (proportion of times favoring the claim)

Justice	1981 Term	1983 Term	1985 Term
Rehnquist	21.7%	19.7%	12.7%
Burger	23.5	36.4	21.5
O'Connor	32.9	22.5	31.6
Powell	34.1	33.3	31.6
White	45.1	36.0	30.3
Stevens	50.6	64.0	57.7
Blackmun	60.5	45.2	66.7
Marshall	79.0	82.2	88.4
Brennan	78.0	81.6	83.5

Source: Adapted from Stephen L. Wasby, *The Supreme Court in the Federal Judicial System*, 3rd ed. (Chicago: Nelson-Hall, 1988), p. 253.

Theme B The Structure and Jurisdiction of the Federal Courts

Summary

The only federal court that must exist under the Constitution is the Supreme Court; other courts can be established or abolished by Congress. Courts established by Congress include "constitutional" courts, such as the district courts and the courts of appeals, and "legislative" courts with special functions, such as the Court of Military Appeals. Judges on the constitutional courts serve for life. Presidents therefore attempt to appoint judges who share their own views, but they have had only mixed success. President Carter appointed a greater percentage of blacks and women to federal court judgeships than did President Reagan, although Reagan did appoint the first woman to the Supreme Court. Both presidents selected judges on a strongly partisan basis. However, the behavior of Supreme Court justices, even if politically similar to the president, is still difficult to predict once they are on the bench. Finally, the custom of *senatorial courtesy* gives senators a veto power over candidates from their states for lower-level appointments.

We have a dual court system—one state, one federal. Federal courts hear *federal-question* cases "arising under the Constitution, the laws of the United States, and treaties" and *di-*

versity cases involving citizens of different states. The vast majority of all cases heard by federal courts begin in the district courts. From there, there are two routes to the Supreme Court: *appeal*, which applies to about 10 percent of the Court's cases, and writs of *certiorari*, which the Supreme Court can exercise great discretion in granting, thus controlling its work load. Because the Supreme Court reviews less than 1 percent of cases from federal appeals courts, the law can often be different in different parts of the country.

In 1988, Congress acted to limit the number of cases appealed to the Supreme Court under the writ of appeal. These writs proved particularly burdensome to the Court because it was technically required to hear them. "From this perspective," according to David Barnum, "appeal cases constituted an unavoidable and time-consuming segment of the Supreme Court's decision-making responsibility." In response, Congress narrowed the Court's mandatory jurisdiction to one type of appeal—those involving cases brought from three-judge district courts in which an injunction was either granted or denied. Consequently, almost all appeals to the Supreme Court today utilize the writ of certiorari.

The distinction between a writ of certiorari and a writ of appeal is significant in relation to the creation of precedent. A denical of a writ of "cert" has no value in terms of precedent, meaning the justices are expressing no opinion on the ruling contained in the lower court's decision. However, a denial of a writ of appeal can be cited as reflecting Supreme Court agreement with the decision of the last court to rule on the case, although some justices have recently critized this interpretation. A writ of appeal from a U.S. District Court will be "summarily affirmed" rather than simply denied. As such, the 1988 legislation will relieve pressure on the Supreme Court to take cases simply to avoid condoning a decision with which it disagrees.

Data and Perspectives for Analysis

The structure of the federal judicial system is complex. The chart below maps the flow of the appellate process.

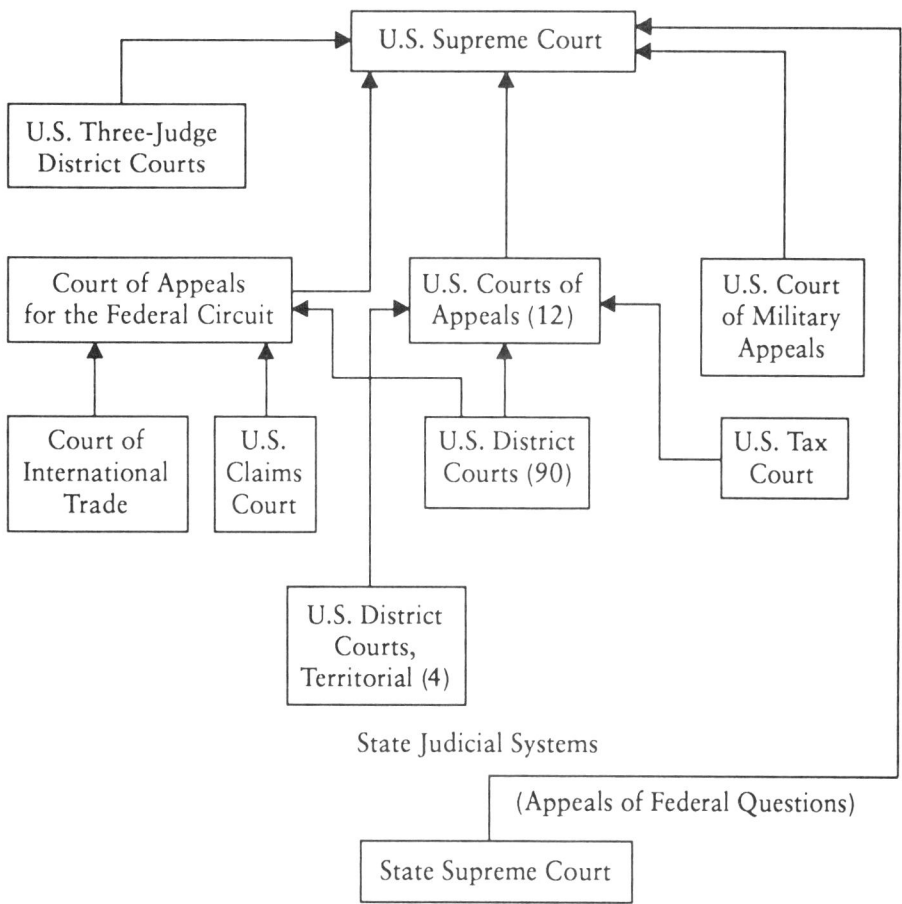

The text explains the jurisdiction of the Supreme Court, U.S. courts of appeals, and U.S. district courts. The jurisdiction of the remaining federal courts is presented below:

1. U.S. Court of International Trade: Congress has conferred original jurisdiction in three areas:

    —claims against the U.S. on import restrictions
    —actions by the U.S. to collect customs
    —review of the classification and value of goods by customs agents

2. U.S. Claims Court: Congress has conferred original jurisdiction in three areas:

    —claims against U.S. in contract
    —damages for unjust conviction or imprisonment against the United States
    —infringement of patents by the U.S. government

3. U.S. Tax Court: Congress has conferred jurisdiction to review the decisions of the Internal Revenue Service in two areas:

    —deficiencies or overpayments on income, estate, or gift taxes
    —penalties against private foundations

4. U.S. three-judge district courts: Congress has conferred original jurisdiction in three categories of cases:

    —challenges to legislative reapportionment
    —most civil rights cases
    —violations of federal campaign laws

5. U.S. Court of Military Appeals

    a. Mandatory review of court-martial convictions

    —general or flag officers
    —death sentences

    b. Discretionary review of court-martial convictions

    —sentences of more than one year's imprisonment
    —bad conduct discharges

Theme C Cases Before the Court

Summary

Though many an individual may vow to take a case "all the way to the Supreme Court," it is obvious that the chance of its being accepted and heard by the Court is slim, especially if the case does not involve, among other issues, crucial federal-state relationships, a question of constitutional interpretation, or a challenge to civil liberties. Yet when a case does work its way up through the federal court structure and is heard by the Court, the implications of its decision can be major ones indeed for American society. Also, the very act of agreeing to hear a case can be portentous.

The Court's actions in 1988 bear out the above assertions. For example, a January 13 decision held, by a 5–3 vote, that "public school officials have substantial authority to censor school newspapers and other student expression" (see *Wall Street Journal*, January 14, 1988, p. 54, for a description of the case by Stephen Wermiel). The case involved a 1983 action by a St. Louis principal who had deleted articles from the student newspaper about teenage pregnancy and divorce, deeming them inappropriate. Three student editors filed a suit in a U.S. district court, which ruled that the students' First Amendment rights had not been violated. A U.S. court of appeals reversed the lower court's ruling in 1986, arguing that the censorship was not justified. The Supreme Court's subsequent ruling suggested a continuing trend of limiting the rights of students (other Court rulings had restricted students from making "vulgar speeches" and allowed school officials to make searches of student property without a warrant). However, there were sharp dissenting opinions from Justices Brennan, Blackmun, and Marshall. The minority described the principal's action as "brutal censorship," contrary to the spirit of teaching youth an appreciation of our democratic liberties, and constituting a hindrance to the expression of unpopular ideas in the press. Conversely, the majority of the court contended "that school-sponsored newspapers and similar activities aren't intended to provide a public forum for student views, but rather are part of the curriculum and must be subject to official control to make sure the purposes of such programs are met" according to Wermiel's analysis. In short, did the Court uphold the authority of school officials or deny students basic First Amendment rights?

On May 16, 1988, the Court again touched upon an important constitutional and social issue—the right of individual privacy versus the power of the state. In *California* v. *Greenwood*, the Court, by a 6–2 vote, ruled that the police could search an individual's garbage or trash left outside his or her residence although they had no warrant or previous suspicion of criminal activity (see *New York Times*, May 17, 1988, p. 1 for a description of the case). Again, Justice Brennan dissented, arguing that no one had the right to scrutinize "our sealed trash containers to discover some detail of our personal lives." Justice White, speaking for the majority, asserted that "the police cannot reasonably be expected to avert their eyes from evidence of criminal activity that could have been observed by any member of the public." (The case originated when police found evidence of narcotics use in sealed garbage bags, resulting in Greenwood's eventual arrest.)

In June, 1988, the Court agreed to hear a crucial sex-discrimination case that had the potential to sensitize employers to "sexual stereotyping" in the workplace. In a *Wall Street Journal* article entitled "Supreme Court to Rule on Sex-Bias Case" (June 14, 1988, p. 37) Michael J. McCarthy described the case of Ann B. Hopkins. Ms. Hopkins had been denied partnership in the "big eight" accounting firm of Price Waterhouse, despite being extremely effective in her job. Price Waterhouse contended that she was an overbearing and arrogant manager, but Ms. Hopkins contended that her superiors denied her promotion because she did not "fit" the feminine image entrenched in the minds of her male colleagues. She had been told to walk, talk, and dress in a more feminine manner if she desired the promotion. Both the district and the appeals court agreed with Ms. Hopkins's contention of sex discrimination. The Supreme Court would now review her case in October, 1988. Author McCarthy contended that a victory for Ms. Hopkins "would likely extend the scope of Title VII, the portion of the Civil Rights Act of 1964 that covers sex discrimination."

Discussion Questions

1. How did the Court rule in the Hopkins case? Research the wording of the final decision and explain the judicial reasoning expressed.

2. Which side of the school newspaper and "garbage-privacy" cases would you have taken and why?

Theme D   The Supreme Court in Action

Instructor Reference

John A. Jenkins, "The Partisan: A Talk with Justice Rehnquist," *New York Times Magazine*, March 3, 1985, p. 28. Excellent inside judicial perspectives from a conservative chief justice.

H. W. Perry, Jr. *Deciding to Decide: Agenda Setting in the United States Supreme Court.* Cambridge, MA: Harvard University Press, 1991.

Rebecca Mae Salokar. *The Solicitor General: The Politics of Law.* Philadelphia: Temple University Press, 1992.

Summary

The Supreme Court hears oral arguments beginning at ten in the morning, with each attorney typically allocated a half-hour. Justices are permitted to interrupt attorneys to ask questions at any time, and the clock is not stopped no matter how long the question. Attorneys are not allowed to read but may use notes. Lights indicate how much time is left—a white one signaling five minutes and a red light notifying attorneys to stop. The proceedings are taped but are not aired on radio or television.

The justices meet in secret conference to discuss and vote on cases. No one is permitted in the room. The associate justice with the least seniority has the responsibility of running errands to obtain books or answering knocks at the door. The conference by tradition commences with a handshake. The chief justice speaks first on cases and is followed by justices in order of seniority; votes are taken in reverse sequence on the assumption that junior members may be intimidated if voting last. During the tenure of Chief Justice Burger, a pattern began in which formal votes were often not taken and the chief "interpreted" the outcome of the case. If in the majority, the chief justice assigns the writing of the opinion; if in the minority, the associate justice with the most seniority has the duty of assigning the writing of the Court's opinion. The opinion is circulated in draft form to the other justices who may suggest changes, even on the threat of changing their vote. It sometimes happens that what began as a majority opinion may lose enough support to end up as a dissenting opinion. A justice is permitted to change his or her vote until a judgment is announced in open session.

The entire Court is not required to be present to vote on a case. A quorum exists so long as six justices are participating. In a tie vote, the decision of the last court to hear the case prevails but it does not mean that the justices are expressing agreement with the ruling; the vote of each justice is not publicly revealed in such situations.

The recent trend on the Supreme Court is greater fragmentation in voting. Far fewer decisions are decided unanimously, declining from close to 90 percent in the nineteenth century to less than 30 percent today. Justices are more willing to articulate their own views and are producing a higher rate of both *concurring* and *dissenting* opinions. Concurring opinions are important in establishing whether the Court's decision is creating precedent. "Occasionally," Lawrence Baum explains, "because of disagreement about the rationale, no opinion gains the support of a majority of judges; in this situation, there is a decision but no authoritative interpretation of the legal issues in the case." In other words, some decisions of the Supreme Court bind only the parties involved in the lawsuit but not parties in future litigation even if the same legal issues and facts are presented in a case.

Additional Lecture Topic D-1

Decision Making and Voting Patterns on the Supreme Court

David W. Rohde and Harold J. Spaeth, *Supreme Court Decision-Making*. San Francisco: Freeman, 1976.

Jeffrey A. Segal and Albert D. Cover, "Ideological Values and the Votes of U.S. Supreme Court Justices," *American Political Science Review*, 83 (June 1989): 557–565.

Nina Totenberg, "Behind the Marble, Beneath the Robes." *New York Times Magazine*, March 16, 1975, pp. 60–65.

Stephen L. Wasby, *The Supreme Court in the Federal Judicial System*. 3rd ed. Chicago: Nelson-Hall, 1988.

Richard L. Williams, "Justices Run 'Nine Little Law Firms' at Supreme Court." *Smithsonian*, February 1977.

Bob Woodward and Scott Armstrong, *The Brethren*. New York: Simon & Schuster, 1979.

This lecture could not only focus on the question of "ideological factionalism" on the Court but might also review some examples of decision making, which in turn could reflect the interplay of judicial personality upon the legal issues in each case.

Data and Perspectives for Analysis

Presidents have not always been successful in their judicial nominations. Justices frequently disappoint their nominating president. Chief Justice Burger, for example, wrote the opinion requiring President Nixon to turn over his tapes in the Watergate investigation. Harry Truman once gave an amusing interview about one of his failures in office—the nomination of Justice Tom Clark to the Supreme Court:

> *Interviewer:* What do you consider the biggest mistake you made as President?
> *Truman:* Tom Clark was my biggest mistake. No question about it.
> *Interviewer:* I'm sorry sir. I'm not sure I understand.
> *Truman:* That damn fool from Texas that I first made Attorney General and then put on the Supreme Court. I don't know what got into me. He was no damn good as Attorney General, and on the Supreme Court . . . it doesn't seem possible, but he's been even worse. He hasn't made one right decision that I can think of. And so when you ask me what was my biggest mistake, that's it. Putting Tom Clark on the Supreme Court of the United States. . . .
> *Interviewer:* How do you explain the fact that he's been such a bad Justice?
> *Truman:* The main thing is . . . well, it isn't so much that he's a *bad* man. It's just that he's such a dumb son of a bitch. He's about the dumbest man I think I've ever run across. And lots of times that's the case. Being dumb's just about the worst thing there is when it comes to holding office, and that's especially true when it's on the Supreme Court of the United States.

Abstract 1 for Theme D

The Personal Side of Supreme Court Decision-Making

On January 22, 1973, the Burger Supreme Court ruled by a 7–2 vote that state laws prohibiting abortions during the first three months of a woman's pregnancy were unconstitutional (*Roe v. Wade*). This ruling flatly rejected President Nixon's position on the abortion issue, and three of the justices whom he had appointed—Burger, Powell, and Blackmun—came down on the side of the majority. That decision was the outcome of a complicated pattern of interpersonal relationships among members of the Court, intensive internal lobbying, political trade-offs, and ideological clashes.

In *The Brethren*, by Bob Woodward and Scott Armstrong (New York: Simon and Schuster, 1979), which is excerpted in Peter Woll's *Behind the Scenes in American Government*, 4th ed. (Boston: Little, Brown, 1983, pp. 276–295), the story of *Roe v. Wade* is revealed in minute detail. Woodward and Armstrong chronicle Justice Harry Blackmun's efforts under great pressure to write the majority opinion. The pressure began with the deep-seated conviction of Justice Douglas (the most liberal member of the Court) that the "broad constitutional guarantee of 'liberty' . . . included the rights of a woman to control her body" and that state laws in Georgia and Texas that restricted abortions had to be declared invalid by the Court. Douglas, however, suspected that Chief Justice Burger wanted to "stall" any decision, because he was sensitive to President Nixon's views on abortion, particularly in a presidential election year. Douglas felt his view on the matter was correct, because Burger was assigning Blackmun, a notoriously slow writer, to write the main opinion draft. However, Blackmun, despite Douglas's intimation that he was unfit for the task, nevertheless felt he was qualified because he had been a legislative counsel at the Mayo Clinic earlier in his judicial career. The lobbying now began.

> Douglas broke his usual rule and paid a visit to Blackmun. Though he would have much preferred that Brennan write the draft, he told Blackmun, "Harry, I would have assigned the opinion to you anyway." (p. 281)

Burger, as Douglas suspected, tried to slow Blackmun's progress. On top of all this, there were Blackmun's own self-doubts, as Woodward and Armstrong relate:

> Blackmun knew that his colleagues were concerned about what they perceived as his indecisiveness. But what others saw as an inability to make decisions, he felt to be a deliberate withholding of final judgment until all the facts were in, all the arguments marshalled, analyzed, documented. (p. 283)

Blackmun, through his exhaustive research, was surprised to find that abortion had become a crime in the nineteenth century in the United States largely because of the risk it entailed as a medical operation. However, modern medicine had minimized this risk. Further research convinced Blackmun that the state laws should be invalidated, but he was unable to communicate his legal reasoning clearly in his initial drafts. Even his own law clerks found his logic flawed and confusing. Subsequently Justice Byron White, an opponent of abortion, found Blackmun's opinion "juvenile" and "vague." Still, Blackmun did pick up enough support from the other justices, with the result that it appeared a majority would back a pro-abortion stance.

But Burger was still stalling. Enraged, Douglas threatened to "go public" and reveal his dissent and Burger's intransigence.

> No one in the history of the Court had published such a dissent. . . . They (the other justices) pleaded with Douglas to reconsider. His dissent would undermine the Court's credibility, the principal source of its power. Its strength derived from the public belief that the Court was trustworthy—a nonpolitical deliberative body. Did he intend to undermine all that?
>
> Douglas insisted. He would publish what he felt like publishing. And he would publish this if the request to put over (delay) the abortion decision was not withdrawn. (p. 289)

Finally, Douglas relented, agreeing not to make his dissent public. Despite delays instigated by Burger, the decision was finally announced in January, 1973. Thousands of letters followed, many protesting the Court's decision and vilifying Blackmun, the decision's main author. Few members of the public knew the internal struggles and the long travail that had preceded the abortion decision.

Discussion Guidelines

You may wish to read this abstract to the class and then elicit comments and/or questions. Questions related to the excerpt should develop as a natural outgrowth of the discussion. You could emphasize the very real political struggle that is an integral part of the Supreme Court decision-making process. As a further classroom project, a full-length review of *The Brethren* could be assigned to one or two members of the class.

Abstract 2 for Theme D

The Selection of Justice Anthony M. Kennedy

President Reagan's search in 1987 and 1988 to fill the Supreme Court seat left vacant by moderate Lewis Powell led to some difficult battles with the Senate. The president's first nominee, Robert H. Bork, was overwhelmingly rejected by the Senate after several tumultuous months of hearings. The second nominee, another conservative appeals court judge, Douglas H. Ginsburg, withdrew his name from consideration after admitting that he had used marijuana. Finally, the administration settled on a federal appeals court judge from California, Anthony M. Kennedy, who fit in with the "judicial mainstream" and whose personal life was above reproach. Kennedy was confirmed by the Senate on February 3, 1988, by a vote of 97-0. On February 18, he was sworn in as the nation's 104th Supreme Court justice.

The reasons behind Kennedy's acceptance are delineated in an article in *Time* entitled "Far More Judicious: In Round 3, Anthony Kennedy Offers Pragmatic Conservatism" (November 23, 1987, pp. 16–18) by George J. Church. The following key points were made in the article:

1. Kennedy's "pragmatic conservatism" (as opposed to the judicial dogmatism of Bork) appealed to both liberals and conservatives. As a possible swing vote on a divided court, senators perceived him to be both flexible and thoughtful regarding future judicial controversies.

2. Kennedy had made "legal history" in two cases: a 1980 decision against the legislative veto (the practice violated the separation of powers); and a 1983 dissent asserting the "good faith" doctrine of search warrants (a belief in proper execution of a warrant later found invalid). There were also some 1,400 decisions and over 400 written opinions in which Kennedy had been involved as an appellate judge.

3. Kennedy had avoided "propounding sweeping doctrines of how to interpret the Constitution." While a conservative and an advocate of judicial restraint, Kennedy was prone to consider cases "one by one." Cases involving dismissal of homosexuals from the navy, "comparable worth" pay scales for women, and freedom of the press all demonstrated this judicial demeanor.

4. Kennedy, unlike Bork, did assume that the Constitution protected one's privacy. In short, Kennedy was described as "decent instead of dogmatic, sensitive instead of strident" by Harvard Law School Professor Laurence Tribe (Tribe had led the opposition against Bork).

Questions for Discussion

1. If you had been a senator considering Kennedy, what images would be conjured up by the description of the nominee as a "pragmatic conservative"?

2. What impact did the failure to approve Bork and Ginsburg have upon the willingness of the Senate and the administration to approve Kennedy?

3. If possible, cull out some of the key votes that Kennedy has cast on the Court. What conclusions, if any, can be drawn about his judicial philosophy?

Theme E	The Power of the Federal Judiciary

Instructor References

Gary Bryner and Dennis L. Thompson, *The Constitution and the Regulation of Society*. Provo, UT: Brigham Young University, 1988.

Robert A. Carp and C. K. Rowland, *Policymaking and Politics in the Federal District Courts*. Knoxville, TN: University of Tennessee Press, 1983.

Robert A. Carp and Ronald Stidham, *The Federal Courts,* 2nd ed. Washington, DC: Congressional Quarterly Press, 1991.

Donald Horowitz, *The Courts and Social Policy*. Washington, DC: Brookings Institution, 1977.

David M. O'Brien, *Storm Center: The Supreme Court in American Politics,* 3rd ed. New York: W. W. Norton, 1993.

Jeremy Rabkin, *Judicial Compulsions*. New York: Basic Books, 1989.

Christopher Wolfe, *The Rise of Modern Judicial Review*. New York: Basic Books, 1986.

Summary

Courts play a larger role in public policy in the United States than in any other nation in the world. The Supreme Court's chief weapon in the constitutional system of checks and balances is *judicial review,* the power to declare laws of Congress and acts of the executive branch unconstitutional and therefore void. There are two competing views of how judicial review should be exercised. The *strict constructionist* or *interpretivist* view holds that judges should confine themselves to applying those rules that are stated in or clearly implied by the language of the Constitution. The *legislative* or *activist* view argues that judges should discover the general principles underlying the Constitution and amplify those principles on the basis of some moral or economic philosophy. Today judicial activists tend to be liberals, and strict constructionists tend to be conservatives, but fifty years ago just the opposite was the case.

The Founders would be surprised to find the courts so activist. They believed that judges should find and apply existing law, not make new law. Alexander Hamilton wrote in *Federalist* No. 78 that "liberty can have nothing to fear from the judiciary alone," because the courts have neither the power of the purse (which Congress has) nor the use of the military (since the president is commander-in-chief).

In order to use the courts to influence public policy, one has to get to court. To do this requires *standing,* and it requires *resources.* The average citizen has no chance of paying the high costs necessary to take a case all the way to the Supreme Court. However, there are a number of ways in which plaintiffs who are of average or even low income can have their interests represented in court. First, indigent persons can file petitions in *forma pauperis* and be heard for nothing. The *Gideon* case was an example of this. A variety of interest groups (such as the ACLU or the NAACP) will take cases that promote their purposes. State and local governments often raise important issues, and they have their own attorneys. Although the traditional practice in American courts is that parties to a lawsuit pay their own legal expenses, Congress increasingly has been passing laws that allow individuals to sue government and corporations and have their legal fees paid by the defendant. Finally, *class-action suits* allow a plaintiff to sue someone, not merely on his or her own behalf, but on behalf of all persons in similar circumstances. Some cases of this sort are not profitable to bring: The NAACP got no money for winning the *Brown* case. However, when money damages can be won on behalf of a large group of people, lawyers can reap huge rewards, so lawyers willing to take on such cases are readily found. Since 1974 the Supreme Court has restricted this practice.

The concept of *standing* is not a constitutional requirement. It was created by judicial interpretation of a provision in Article III that restricts federal courts to "cases and controversies." The problem is defining what constitutes a "case" or a "controversy." According to Chief Justice Warren, "those words limit the business of the federal courts to questions presented in an adversary context and in a form historically viewed as capable of resolution through the judicial process." Standing is the term used to embody these principles. As currently construed by the Supreme Court, it means a court will decline to hear a case unless the complaining party (plaintiff) proves that a genuine conflict exists between two adverse parties and that he or she has suffered a personal injury to a legally protected right. In other words, federal courts will not hear hypothetical issues and waste their time issuing an "advisory opinion." A conflict must be genuine, neither too early (ripe) nor too late (moot). Moreover, the injury must be a personal one, not a remote injury shared generally with many others—such as bringing suit as a taxpayer. However, since standing is largely a product of judicial invention, it is sometimes ignored when a situation warrants settlement by a court. For example, every abortion case would technically be moot because the pregnancy would long be over by the time an appeal reached the Supreme Court; the doctrine of standing has been relaxed in these appeals on the ground that the issue was "capable of repetition yet evading review."

Another traditional barrier to the citizen's right to sue is the doctrine of *sovereign immunity,* which refuses standing to citizens seeking to bring suit against the government for damages. "The doctrine of government immunity," Harold Grilliot has written, ". . . originated from the English notion that 'the king can do no wrong.' " This restriction has been eased in two ways. On the one hand, Congress has waived federal immunity from certain lawsuits, including most claims involving torts (since 1946) and contract violations (since 1855). On the other hand, federal officials are not protected by sovereign immunity for conduct that exceeds their lawful authority. In addition, the Eleventh Amendment prevents a state from being sued in federal court without its consent.

Once a case is taken by a federal court, the outcome can exert profound influence over public policy. Federal judges have at least four avenues for making policy decisions. First, a congressional statute or presidential action can be ruled unconstitutional. The Supreme Court has voided over 120 federal laws under its power of judicial review. Second, national policy can be changed whenever the Supreme Court opts to decide an issue differently. The doctrine of *stare decisis,* or the practice of following precedent, is not inflexible and can be repudiated whenever justice demands a break with prior decisions. As Justice Frankfurter eloquently put it, "Wisdom too often never comes, and so one ought not to reject it merely because it comes late." Third, the Supreme Court has become less likely to leave certain questions (such as apportionment and contraception) to other branches by declaring them *political questions* and therefore not proper subjects for judicial resolution. The result has been to place the federal judiciary in the midst of numerous controversial disputes. And fourth, judges retain a great deal of power in fashioning *remedies,* sometimes to the point of micromanaging what is needed to accomplish justice. For example, federal judge Frank Johnson, in correcting conditions at an Alabama mental health institution, went so far as to require that toilets must be "free of odor" and that each patient must have a "comfortable bed."

Those who favor judicial activism point to outcomes of which they approve and say that courts provide representation to the poor and powerless. Opponents say that courts have no special expertise in managing complex institutions and have difficulty balancing competing interests in complex cases. Further, if judges make (rather than merely interpret) law, they become unelected legislators, contrary to the intent of the Constitution.

The reasons for judicial activism are many. It is *not* the case that the courts are powerful because we have so many lawyers. America had more lawyers per capita in 1900, when the courts played a more limited role. Due to *class-action suits* and the rise of private attorneys in general, it has become easier for persons to get into court. Increasingly, Congress has passed vague laws that require bureaucratic interpretation. Laws outlaw "discrimination" or require that agencies operate "in the public interest" without defining either. Parties adversely affected by decisions under vague laws challenge them in court. Judges' attitudes affect what they do. If courts once existed solely to settle disputes, today they also exist, in the eyes of their members, to solve problems. Finally, courts have become more powerful as government in general has become more powerful.

There are checks on judicial power. A judge has no police force or army, and a person can disobey if the act is not highly visible and if he is willing to risk being charged with contempt of court. The Senate must approve judicial nominees, and Congress has the power to *impeach* federal judges. Neither of these powers amounts to much, because simple policy disagreements are not considered sufficient to warrant the exercise of either of these prerogatives. Congress can change the number of judges either on the Supreme Court or in the lower federal judiciary. Congress and the states can amend the Constitution. Congress can alter the jurisdiction of the federal courts and prevent them from hearing certain kinds of cases. All of these checks have their limits. Amending the Constitution is difficult. Attempts to change the size of the Court, like the Roosevelt *court-packing* plan, are likely to run into opposition from a public that still accords considerable prestige to the Court. The Supreme Court might rule attempts to limit the jurisdiction of the courts unconstitutional. Presidential attempts to produce a less activist Supreme Court have largely failed.

Discussion Questions

1. Why do presidents give careful thought to the personal political views of judicial candidates? Isn't legal competence more important? Shouldn't they prefer a judge who will simply "interpret" the Constitution, whatever his or her personal views?

2. What resources are required to go before the Supreme Court? Is this more or fewer resources than are required to try to gain power in elections? More or fewer resources than are required to effect policy change through lobbying? How widespread in society are these resources? Is this situation most consistent with the elitist view of American government, with the pluralist view, or with the popular democratic view?

3. What sorts of legal doctrines or principles will an activist judiciary favor? Look over the key terms in the Summary above and explain whether each is more consistent with judicial activism or with judicial restraint. Which interpretation of each term is most consistent with judicial activism (for example, broad rather than narrow remedies)? Which tend to increase and which to restrict the number of cases brought before the Court? Which require that judges be bound by the judgments of legislatures? Has the tendency been to change these doctrines in a way consistent with judicial activism or consistent with judicial reserve?

4. Is the judiciary still the "least dangerous" branch? Do judges lack the "sword of the community"? Can a school board opposed to busing simply refuse to obey a federal judge's order? What will happen to the board if it does? Do judges lack command of the "purse"? Have they no power to order the spending of tax money?

5. How do we know that the attitudes of judges powerfully affect what they do? How many cases can you think of where the Court reversed its own earlier decision? If the Constitution (or relevant law) was the same before and after the reversal, doesn't this mean that either before or after the reversal—or perhaps in both cases—judges were acting on the basis of their own beliefs rather than on the basis of the Constitution? Can you think of other reasons for a reversal?

6. What are the checks on the power of the judiciary? Are they potent and easily invoked, or weak and difficult to invoke? Can you give examples where the judiciary was checked by other branches of government? Why haven't vastly unpopular decisions, such as those on busing and school prayer, been successfully overturned?

Data and Perspectives for Analysis

The influence of the Supreme Court on national policy is clearly traced in the pace of racial integration following the *Brown* decision in 1954. Note that integration did not occur immediately. What factors contributed to the delay in integration? What could the Supreme Court have done to expedite the process? What could the Supreme Court have done if President Eisenhower had not cooperated by calling up troops to ensure the integration of public schools in Little Rock, Arkansas? Could integration have taken place without support from other branches of government? Why didn't Congress or the president act first to end segregation?

Percentages of Black Elementary and Secondary Students Going to School with Any Whites in Eleven Southern States[a]

School Year	Percentage
1954–1955	0.001%
1956–1957	0.14
1958–1959	0.13
1960–1961	0.16
1962–1963	0.45
1964–1965	2.25
1966–1967	15.9
1968–1969	32.0
1970–1971	85.6
1972–1973	91.3

[a] The states are Alabama, Arkansas, Florida, Georgia, Louisiana, Mississippi, North Carolina, South Carolina, Tennessee, Texas, and Virginia.
Source: Lawrence Baum, *The Supreme Court*, 2nd ed. Washington, DC: Congressional Quarterly Press, 1985, p. 199. Reprinted by permission of CQ Press.

Additional Lecture Topic E-1

What Is the Proper Role of the Supreme Court?

Henry J. Abraham, *The Judicial Process*. 5th ed. New York: Oxford University Press, 1986. See Chapters 8 and 9.

Lawrence Baum, *The Supreme Court*. 2nd ed. Washington, DC: Congressional Quarterly Press, 1985. An excellent overview of the Court.

Archibald Cox, *The Role of the Supreme Court in American Government*. New York: Oxford University Press, 1976.

Stephen C. Halpern and Charles M. Lamb, eds., *Supreme Court Activism and Restraint*. Lexington, MA: Heath, 1982.

Leonard W. Levy, ed. *Judicial Review and the Supreme Court*. New York: Harper & Row, 1967. See especially pieces by Levy, Thayer, Rostown, and Freund.

David M. O'Brien, *Storm Center: The Supreme Court in American Politics*. 2nd ed. New York: Norton, 1990.

Herbert Wechsler, "Toward Neutral Principles of Constitutional Law." *Harvard Law Review*, 73 (1959): 1–35.

The key questions are: (a) Are there neutral, consistent (some would say mechanical) procedures that judges can use to judge cases in a way consistent with the Constitution? (b) If so, should judges use them, rather than attempting to expand or adopt constitutional protections? (c) If no such procedures exist, is there any principled basis on which justices can "judge," or are their rulings necessarily merely expressions of their policy preferences?

Abstract for Theme E

The Supreme Court and Student Searches

On January 15, 1985, the Supreme Court, by a 6-3 ruling, asserted that public school teachers and officials were allowed to search students for incriminating evidence so long as there were "reasonable grounds" for that search. The Court's rationale is described in a *New York Times* article, "Justices Uphold Student Searches When Reasonable," by Linda Greenhouse (January 16, 1985, p. 1). This ruling was consistent with most state and federal lower-court rulings, which had confirmed the constitutionality of the "reasonable grounds" concept. However, in this particular case, which

> grew out of a New Jersey high school official's search of a . . . student's pocketbook for evidence of smoking . . . the New Jersey Supreme Court had found that reasonable grounds *did not exist for the search in question*, which turned up evidence that the student possessed and was selling marijuana. . . . New Jersey argued in its appeal that the Fourth Amendment's prohibitions against unreasonable search and seizure *do not apply to a search by school officials*. Such officials, the state asserted, are *standing in for parents* and should be as free of constitutional structures in conducting a search as a parent would be in disciplining a child at home. The National Association of Secondary School Principals and the National School Boards Association both filed briefs supporting that argument.

The Court rejected the *in loco parentis* argument of New Jersey, but it argued that the Fourth Amendment's "probable cause" was too restrictive a standard to apply in the school setting. While members of the Court admitted that the privacy of a student was important, the need for school officials to maintain discipline in the learning environment was far more important. It followed that some "easing" of search restrictions ("reasonable grounds" instead of "probable cause") was necessary.

Three justices dissented, mainly arguing that the decision in *New Jersey* v. *T.L.O.* dangerously weakened Fourth Amendment standards. Greenhouse concluded her article by stating the case's implications:

The decision left a number of important questions to be answered in future cases. Justice White noted that the Court was expressing no view on whether evidence obtained by the school authorities through an illegal search can be used in court; whether the standard announced today also applies to searches of lockers or desks; what standard would apply to searches undertaken at the behest of the police; and whether the authorities need "individualized suspicion" before searching a particular student.

Questions for Discussion

1. Could the Court's ruling in *New Jersey* v. *T.L.O.* be applied to college students on campus? Why or why not?

2. How will the Court rule on questions raised in Greenhouse's concluding paragraphs in the future? Speculate.

Answer Guidelines

Mostly an open-ended discussion. Regarding college campuses, one could theorize that the Court might find a college campus to be significantly different from a high school and thereby insist on "probable cause" as a search standard.

PART FOUR

The Politics of Public Policy

15

The Policy-Making Process

Overview and Objectives

In this chapter, we move from the study of political and governmental institutions (president, Congress, courts, etc.) to the study of the policies that all of those institutions have produced. The purpose of this chapter is to provide the student with a set of categories (majoritarian, interest group, entrepreneurial and client politics), the better to understand politics in general and the remainder of the book in particular. After reading and reviewing the material in this chapter the student should be able to do each of the following:

1. Explain how certain issues at certain times get placed on the public agenda for action.

2. Identify the terms "costs," "benefits," and "perceived" as used in this chapter.

3. Use the above terms to define the four types of politics presented in the text: majoritarian, client, interest group, and entrepreneurial, giving examples of each.

4. Review the history of business regulation in this country, using it to exemplify the above four types of politics.

5. Discuss the roles played in the process of public policy formation by people's perceptions, beliefs, interests, and values.

Chapter Outline with Keyed-in Resources

    I. Setting the agenda (THEME A: THE AGENDA-SETTING PROCESS)
       A. Most important decision affecting policy-making is deciding what belongs on the political agenda
          1. Shared beliefs determine what is legitimate
          2. Legitimacy affected by
             a. Shared political values
             b. Weight of custom and tradition
             c. Changes in way political elites think about politics
       B. The legitimate scope of government action

In *McCulloch* v. *Maryland* (1819), the Supreme Court gave Congress wide latitude in expanding the "legitimate" scope of governmental power. Chief Justice John Marshall defined the parameters of federal authority in terms of what the government was attempting to accomplish: "Let the end be legitimate, let it be within the scope of the Constitution, and all the means which are appropriate, which are plainly adapted to that end, which are not prohibited, but consistent with the letter and spirit of the Constitution, are constitutional."

          1. Always gets larger
             a. Changes in public's attitudes
             b. Impact of events
          2. May be enlarged without public demand, even when conditions improving
          3. Groups: a motivating force in adding new issues
             a. May be organized (e.g., corporations) or disorganized (urban minorities)
             b. May react to sense of "relative deprivation"—people's feeling that they are worse off than they expected to be
                (1) Black riots of the 1960s
             c. May produce an expansion of governmental agenda
                (1) New commissions and laws
             d. May change the values and beliefs of others
                (1) White response to urban riots
          4. Institutions a second force adding new issues
             a. Major institutions: courts, bureaucracy, Senate, national media
             b. Courts
                (1) Make decisions that force action by other branches: school desegregation, abortion
                (2) Change the political agenda

In separate but companion studies, Robert Dahl and Richard Funston argue that the Supreme Court is more likely to lag behind public opinion rather than set the political agenda. The reason is generational. The justices on the Supreme Court are nominated by popularly elected presidents and, for that reason, their views probably reflect prevailing public opinion at the time of their appointment. Their lengthy tenure on the Court, however, almost ensures that their attitudes will become outdated. Thus the Supreme Court is typically a tardy member of the ruling coalition.

             c. Bureaucracy
                (1) Source of political innovation: size and expertise
                (2) Thinks up problems to solve
                (3) Forms alliances with senators and their staffs
             d. Senate
                (1) More activists than ever
                (2) Source of presidential candidates with new ideas
             e. Media
                (1) Help place issues on political agenda
                (2) Publicize those issues placed there by others, e.g., safety standards proposed by Senate

5. Political agenda can change because of
   a. Changes in popular attitudes, which result in gradual revision of the agenda
   b. Critical events, spurring rapid changes in attitudes
   c. Elite attitudes and governmental actions, occasioning volatile and interdependent change

Public opinion is volatile on whether the government is engaging in too much activity. In 1978, 38 percent of Americans believed the federal government had too much power. This figure dropped to 28 percent in 1986, despite the antigovernment rhetoric of President Reagan. Thus the public's willingness to accept changes in the political agenda produced by governmental action is unstable.

II. Making a decision (THEME B: COSTS, BENEFITS, AND POLICY)
   A. Nature of issue
      1. Affects politicking
      2. Affects intensity of political conflict
   B. Costs and benefits of proposed policy a way to understand how issue affects political power
      1. Cost: any burden, monetary or nonmonetary
      2. Benefit: any satisfaction, monetary or nonmonetary
      3. Two aspects of costs and benefits important
         a. Perception affects politics
         b. People consider whether it is legitimate for a group to benefit
      4. Politics a process of settling disputes over who benefits and who ought to benefit
      5. People prefer programs that provide benefits at low cost
      6. Perceived distribution of costs and benefits shapes the kinds of political coalitions that form, but not who wins
III. Majoritarian politics: distributed benefits, distributed costs
   A. Gives benefits to large numbers
   B. Distributes costs to large numbers
   C. Initial debate in ideological or cost terms, e.g., military budgets
IV. Interest-group politics: concentrated benefits, concentrated costs
   A. Gives benefits to relatively small group
   B. Costs imposed on another small group
   C. Debate carried on by interest groups (e.g., labor unions versus businesses)
V. Client politics: concentrated benefits, distributed costs
   A. Relatively small group benefits; group has incentive to organize
   B. Costs distributed widely
   C. Most people unaware of costs, sometimes in form of pork-barrel projects
VI. Entrepreneurial politics: distributed benefits, concentrated costs
   A. Gives benefits to large numbers
   B. Costs imposed on small group
   C. Success depends on people who work on behalf of unorganized majorities but not always
   D. Legitimacy of client claims is important; superfund an example
VII. The case of business regulation (THEME C: THE CASE OF BUSINESS REGULATION)

The role of the federal government in regulating business is a much debated topic. Jerry Wurf, former president of the American Federation of State, County, and Municipal Employees, summarizes the case for regulation quite dramatically: "Regulation is the key to a civilized society."

   A. The question of wealth and power
      1. One view: economic power dominates political power
      2. Another view: political power a threat to a market economy
      3. Text cautious; weighs variables
   B. Majoritarian politics

1. Antitrust legislation in 1890s
   a. Public indignation strong but unfocused
   b. Legislation vague; no specific enforcement agency

Historian Gabriel Kolko contends that big business did not oppose the passage of antitrust legislation. Indeed, according to Kolko, many corporations and banks secretly assisted in the drafting of antitrust laws because the weak laws that were eventually passed appeased public demands for curtailing the excesses of business without hindering corporate behavior significantly.

2. Antitrust legislation in the twentieth century strengthened
   a. Presidents take initiative in encouraging enforcement
   b. Politicians, business leaders committed to firm antitrust policy
   c. Federal Trade Commission created in 1914

The regulatory process seldom reacts quickly to address public problems. Even minor matters can take a long time to correct. For example, it took the FTC thirteen years to prevent the manufacturers of Geritol from advertising their product as capable of curing "tired" blood, whatever that might be.

   d. Enforcement determined primarily by ideology and personal convictions
C. Interest-group politics
   1. Labor-management conflict
      a. 1935: labor unions seek government protection for their rights; business firms in opposition
         (1) Unions win
         (2) Wagner Act creates NLRB
      b. 1947: Taft-Hartley Act a victory for management

Although President Truman vetoed the Taft-Hartley Act, he applied the law with vigor in labor disputes. If the law had to exist, Truman believed he might as well use it.

      c. 1959: Landrum-Griffin Act another victory for management
   2. Politics of the conflict
      a. Highly publicized struggle
      b. Winners and losers determined by partisan composition of Congress
      c. Between enactment of laws, conflict continues in NLRB
   3. Similar pattern found in Occupational Safety and Health Act of 1970
      a. Reflects a labor victory
      b. Agency established
D. Client politics
   1. Agency capture likely
   2. Licensing of attorneys, barbers, etc.
      a. Restricts entry into occupation or profession
         (1) Allows members to charge higher prices
      b. People not generally opposed
         (1) Believe regulations protect them
         (2) Costs are not obvious
   3. Regulation of milk industry
      a. Prevents price competition and keeps price up
      b. Public unaware of inflated prices
   4. Tobacco regulations also benefit tobacco growers
   5. Citizens have little incentive to organize
E. Entrepreneurial politics; relies on entrepreneurs to galvanize
   1. 1906: Pure Food and Drug Act protected consumer
   2. 1960s and 1970s: large number of consumer and environmental protection statutes passed (e.g., Clean Air Act, Toxic Substance Control Act) (THEME D: THE POLICY ENTREPRENEURSHIP OF RALPH NADER)
   3. Policy entrepreneur usually associated with such measures (e.g., Ralph Nader, Edmund Muskie) (ADDITIONAL LECTURE TOPIC D-1)

a. Often assisted by crisis or scandal
b. Debate becomes moralistic and extreme
4. Risk of such programs: agency may be "captured" by the regulated industry

The capture of an agency can occur through a rotating pattern of employment. To obtain expertise, regulatory agencies must recruit from the regulated industry. Agency officials return to the private sector for employment once their terms expire. Consider the relationship between the Civil Aeronautics Board (CAB) and Texas Air (chaired by Frank Lorenzo). Lorenzo purchased financially troubled Eastern Airlines and began selling the more profitable parts of the company. This act, coupled with the absence of a new contract, led to a strike by the machinists. Neither CAB nor its parent Department of Transportation (DOT) intervened in the labor dispute. Eastern was removed from Texas Air's control by court order, only to declare bankruptcy. Why didn't CAB act? Perhaps because six former members of CAB worked for Texas Air, while three former Texas Air officers were in DOT.

  a. Newer agencies less vulnerable
   (1) Standards specific, timetables strict
   (2) Usually regulate many different industries; thus do not face unified opposition
   (3) Their existence has strengthened public-interest lobbies
   (4) Allies in the media may attack agencies with probusiness bias
   (5) Public interest groups can use courts to bring pressure on regulatory agencies

VIII. Perceptions, beliefs, interests, and values (THEME E: PERCEPTIONS, BELIEFS, INTERESTS, AND VALUES)
 A. Problem of definition
  1. Costs and benefits not completely defined in money terms
  2. Cost or benefit a matter of perception
  3. Political conflict largely a struggle to make one set of beliefs about costs and benefits prevail over another
 B. Types of arguments used
  1. "Here-and-now" argument
  2. Cost argument
 C. Role of values
  1. Values: our conceptions of what is good for our community or our country
  2. Emphasis on self-interest

Self-interest may be the central motivation in all of politics. In Harry Truman's words, the pocketbook is the most vital part of a voter's anatomy.

  3. Ideas as decisive forces
 D. Deregulation
  1. Example: airline fares, long distance telephoning, trucking
  2. A challenge to "iron triangles" and client politics
  3. Explanation: the power of ideas
   a. Idea: governmental regulation was bad
   b. Notion started with academic economists, who were powerless but persuaded politicians
   c. Politicians acted for different reasons
    (1) Had support of regulatory agencies and consumers
    (2) Industries being deregulated were unpopular
  4. Reducing subsidies
   a. Example: tobacco industry
    (1) Supported by members of Congress from tobacco-growing states
    (2) Allowed growers to borrow against unsold tobacco ... and not pay back loans

It is difficult to find an adequate agricultural substitute for farmers to grow in place of tobacco. In North Carolina, tobacco earned $906 million in 1989—eight times the amount derived from all vegetables grown in the state. An acre of sweet corn, for example, yielded about $586, compared with $3,478 for an acre of tobacco.

          (3) Public went along until smoking became issue
          (4) New system: growers pay subsidies
          (5) Widely held beliefs (against smoking) defeated narrow interests (subsidies)
5. Presidents since Ford have sought to review governmental regulation
6. Many groups oppose deregulation
   a. Dispute focuses mostly on how deregulation occurs
   b. "Process regulation" can be good or bad
7. The limits of ideas
   a. Some clients are just too powerful
      (1) Dairy farmers, agricultural supports
   b. But trend is toward weaker client politics

Important Terms

*benefit Any satisfaction, monetary or nonmonetary, that people will enjoy if a policy is adopted.

*boycott A term that refers to any concerted effort to get people to stop buying goods and services from a merchant or farmer in order to punish that person or to coerce him or her into changing policies. It has become a favorite tool of interest-group politics.

*client politics Policies from which some identifiable, though often small, group will benefit, but for which a large part of society will pay the cost. The beneficiary of the policy is the "client" of the government.

*cost Any burden, monetary or nonmonetary, that some people must bear if a policy is iadopted.

cost argument The political tactic of pointing out what people will lose if a policy is adopted rather than what they may gain.

deregulation The reduction or elimination of government controls on an economic activity.

*entrepreneurial politics Policies from which society as a whole or some large part of it benefits, but which impose substantial costs on a small but identifiable segment of society. Those who work on behalf of the unorganized or indifferent majority are called policy entrepreneurs.

here-and-now argument The political tactic of pointing out that what happens now or in the near future is more important than what happens in the distant future.

*interest-group politics Policies that gain benefits for some relatively small but identifiable group and impose costs on another small but equally identifiable group. Issues of this kind tend to be fought out by organized interest groups.

*logrolling Mutual aid among politicians through which legislators support one another's pet projects. In client politics, this tactic involves legislators' trading votes on pork-barrel projects.

*majoritarian politics Policies that aim to benefit large numbers of people at a cost large numbers of people will have to bear. Interest groups are not important in this type of politics.

*policy entrepreneurs Individuals who work on behalf of the unorganized or indifferent majority. Such people are those both in and out of government who find ways of pulling together a legislative majority on behalf of interests that are not well represented in the government.

political agenda The issues about which public policy will be made. These issues change with shifts in popular attitudes, elite interests, critical events, and governmental actions.

pork-barrel politics Projects that benefit localities as clients. Many of these projects are not worthwhile, although some are.

process regulation Sometimes called social regulation, it includes rules aimed at improving consumer or worker safety and reducing environmental damage.

relative deprivation The sense of being worse off than one thinks one ought to be. It explains why citizens can become aroused even when not living in poverty or under oppression, such as the black riots in the 1960s.

values People's conceptions of what is good for the country or for their community.

Theme A	The Agenda-setting Process

Instructor Reference

Roger W. Cobb and Charles D. Elder, *Participation in American Politics: The Dynamics of Agenda Building*, 2nd ed. Baltimore: Johns Hopkins University Press, 1983. An effective exploration of how the building of policy agendas permeates the entire political system.

John W. Kingdon, *Agendas, Alternatives, and Public Policies*. Boston: Little, Brown, 1984. An excellent overview of the policy process.

Brinton H. Milward and Wendy Laird, "Where Does Policy Come From?" in B. Guy Peters and Bert Rockman, eds., *The Discipline of Public Administration*. Chatham, NJ: Chatham House, 1991.

Guy Peters, *American Public Policy: Promise and Performance*. 2nd ed. Chatham, NJ: Chatham House, 1986. See Chapter 3 on agenda setting.

Mark Rushefsky, "Agenda Setting—Agenda Erosion: The Ebb and Flow of Policy Issues." Paper presented at the annual convention of American Political Science Association, Washington, DC, August 29–September 1, 1991.

Summary

In order to evaluate the various views on how government works outlined in Chapter 1 (the Marxist view, the pluralist view, the Weberian view, and so on), it is necessary to look at concrete cases of policy making. A wide variety of outcomes must be explained. Business corporations, for example, have been able to get some of their desired political outcomes (low tax rates on capital gains and favorable treatment of investments) but have had to accept other policies that they did not want (increased regulation in most industries and high corporate tax rates).

The most important factor affecting policy-making is what goes on the political *agenda*. At any given time, there exist beliefs about what is *legitimate* for the government to do. Over the last several years, the scope of what is considered legitimate government activity has vastly increased: Politics is now about nearly everything. There have been several reasons for this: First, whatever government now does is generally accepted as legitimate; programs, once enacted, do not again have to overcome the presumption that something is "none of government's business." Events—a war, depression, or coal mine disaster—seem to require that government do something about the problem. Sometimes the scope of government is expanded in the absence of any public demand, and even when the problem is resolving itself without government intervention. OSHA, passed in 1970, and the antipoverty programs of the 1960s are two examples. Often, interest groups promote these policies: The AFL-CIO lobbied for OSHA, and black riots in the cities gave impetus to the War on Poverty. These groups may be motivated by a sense of *relative deprivation*: Although they may not be badly off compared to other groups or to their own past situation, they are worse off than they think they ought to be.

Several institutions have a particularly important role in the agenda-setting process. The courts, by issuing far-reaching decisions, may force the hands of other political institutions. Court orders outlawing southern school segregation are a good example. The bureaucracy now often devises and advocates new government initiatives. The 1960s "Great Society," for example, was largely the product of the *professionalization of reform*. In the 1960s the Senate became an incubator for new policies and an instrument for building national constituencies for liberal causes. In the 1980s the Senate retained its initiative but became more likely to promote conservative causes. Finally, the national press determines which issues to publicize and which to ignore.

Discussion Questions

1. Who sets the agenda? Look over the following list of individuals and *rank* them, starting with the one who has the *most* ability to put an item on the public agenda and ending with the one who has the *least* power to put an issue on the agenda.

    a. The president of General Motors
    b. The president of CBS
    c. The managing editor of the CBS evening news program
    d. A. U.S. senator
    e. A poor ghetto black
    f. An average blue-collar worker
    g. An average millionaire
    h. A federal district judge
    i. A white parent who resents having a child bused
    j. Ralph Nader
    k. An aide to a U.S. senator
    l. An editor of the *New York Times*
    m. A member of the House of Representatives

Instructor: You might wish to have students do this individually with pencil and paper, and then discuss and compare rankings.

2. What *means* would each of the individuals listed have to put an item on the agenda?

3. Would any of the individuals listed have the power to keep an item *off* the agenda? If no single person has this power, might a group be able to do so?

4. Is it true, as the text says, that "many people believe that whatever the government now does it ought to do?" Can you think of counterexamples—areas of government activity that a majority oppose and demand be eliminated?

5. Why is "relative deprivation" important? What would be the political consequences of "lowered expectations?" What would be the political consequences of a rise in people's expectations faster than the government's ability to meet these demands? What would be the result of people's expectations that government do things that—regardless of its resources—it cannot do? Has any of these situations arisen? Are our expectations too high? Or can we reasonably expect government to do more to solve pressing problems than it is now doing? Discuss with regard to (a) providing health care; (b) eliminating poverty; (c) providing a sound moral climate in our communities; (d) reducing crime; and (e) reducing the use of narcotics.

6. The text considers the political agenda from the perspective of the issues that receive public attention. However, can't issues kept off the political agenda sometimes have equal political consequence? For example, the topic of gun control failed to obtain much political scrutiny for a long time despite overwhelming public support. Is the concept of a "political agenda" an accurate reflection of the policy-making process, or does it ignore critical aspects of how political decisions are formulated?

Abstract for Theme A

Creating a Policy Agenda

A policy agenda, in its simplest form, means "things to be done" by the various levels and units of government. These things or "issues" that require political action are of two distinct types of agendas: "systemic" and "institutional." As described by Charles O. Jones in *An Introduction to the Study of Public Policy* (Monterey, CA: Brooks-Cole, 1984, pp. 57–73), and by James E. Anderson, *Public Policy-Making* (New York: Praeger, 1975, pp. 59–67), the systemic agenda is the vast, general collection of issues present at the three levels of government and deemed important and "worthy" of political remedy. Conversely, the institutional agenda "is composed of those problems to which public officials give serious and active attention. An institutional agenda is an action agenda and will be more specific and concrete than a systemic agenda" (Anderson, p. 59). In short, crime is a systemic agenda item that merits discussion in the abstract, but a program of police training subsidized by congressional appropriations would call for the institutional response.

Both Anderson and Jones divide the institutional agenda into new and old (or continuing) items; the latter are such problems as Social Security reform, the budget, and defense spending. It may be difficult to get new items onto the agenda, because decision-makers commit most of their resources (time and study) to familiar problems. As Jones puts it, "under these circumstances, institutional agendas become self-perpetuating: what was on the list last year turns up again this year" (p. 58).

How, then, can a new problem gain the attention of decision-makers? Both authors point to the *crisis* that "breaks the ordinary pattern of doing business" (Jones, p. 58) or "serves to dramatize an issue and attract wide attention" (Anderson, p. 61) or trigger the response of public officials. Examples of this trigger include the launching of Sputnik in 1957 (placing space exploration on the national policy agenda) and the Arab oil embargo of 1973 (introducing energy conservation as a new agenda item). According to Jones, there are three effects of a crisis on institutional agenda: *displacement, expansion,* and *rippling.*

Displacement "refers to one major issue losing its high ranking due to new events (energy issues replacing environmental issues after the oil embargo of 1973)." Expansion "refers to the discovery of related problems (the oil embargo led to concerns about Middle-Eastern instability, national energy independence, and even urban transportation patterns)." Rippling "refers to the effect of priorities set at a higher level of government on the activities of lower levels or on the private sphere." (Example: the organization of state and local energy units after the setting of national energy priorities.) In short, a crisis may sometimes be the only hope for those who wish to rearrange a stagnant political agenda (Jones, p. 59).

Anderson asserts that a crisis can be given added urgency by the media, which can help organize the political agenda. The media become even more vital when problems exist that do not have the dramatic overtones of a true crisis but deserve attention by public officials. For a variety of reasons, decision-makers may make "nondecisions," such as keeping off both the systemic and institutional agendas those problems "that would threaten their existence or values" (Anderson, p. 64) or run counter to the prevailing "political culture." Thus, attempts by radical groups to eliminate the federal income tax conflict with widespread public acceptance of the tax system. In such cases, Jones characterizes government as taking a "let it happen" stance: total passivity toward the particular agenda demand (Jones, p. 63). This contrasts sharply with the government roles of either "encouraging" or "making it happen" by helping weaker groups to articulate demands in the most active sense or shouldering the full burden of setting priorities and defining problems.

Regardless of the government response, Jones asserts that the attention an issue receives depends on three features: its impact on significant numbers of people, acknowledgment that proposed solutions will solve a truly serious problem, and the existence of a clear and understandable remedy for that problem (p. 65). As an example, Jones cites the case of automobile safety from the 1960s. The question of unsafe cars potentially affected every driver in the United States. The increasing number of highway deaths (from 38,000 in the late 1950s to more than 54,000 in the late 1960s) attested to the gravity of the problem. Finally, the publicity given to automobile safety crusader Ralph Nader (through the publication of his book *Unsafe at Any Speed* and his struggles with General Motors) lent credence to the charges that there was a conspiracy among members of the "automobile accident industry" (doctors, engineers, and lawyers) who actually profited from highway deaths. Public clamor was intensified by the media and by investigations led by Senator Ribicoff of Connecticut. The obvious solution to poor car safety was national legislation; the National Traffic and Motor Vehicle Safety Act was passed in 1966. Ironically, the "rippling" effect of the car safety crisis soon resulted in investigations of food purity, consumer product safety, occupational safety and health, and coal-mine safety (pp. 70–72).

Anderson also cites case studies in coal mining and environmental pollution as examples of issues achieving agenda status. For over two decades the Coal Mine Safety Act of 1952 was seen by the miners themselves as a weak policy, because the act authorized the Bureau of Mines to administer its provisions (the Bureau was viewed by the miners as being a "captive" of the mine owners). Despite pleas for coal-mining reform, nothing happened for well over two decades (the nondecision process). Coal mining was concentrated in only a few areas of the country, and great numbers of Americans seemed unconcerned about the problems of the industry.

The crisis "trigger" occurred on November 20, 1968, when the Consolidated Coal Company's No. 9 mine suffered an explosion, trapping and eventually killing seventy-nine miners. The tragedy attracted national attention. Miners staged further protests and threatened to strike unless policy makers took some action. West Virginia passed a state law providing for compensation to miners who suffered black-lung disease. On the national level, under the urging of President Nixon, Congress overwhelmingly passed a mine-safety bill by lopsided margins in both houses (p. 65).

Environmental pollution has aroused increased concern as a result of changes in the political culture, because Americans generally have reached a level of affluence at which they increasingly value recreational resources and aesthetic pleasures. In addition, the large majority of educated Americans understand the dangers of pollution. Finally, pollution affects everyone, and it is a difficult issue for policy-makers to oppose (how can one favor dirty air and water?). As a consequence, "pollution control appears highly likely to remain on the policy agenda at all levels of government for years to come" (p. 66).

Questions for Discussion

1. What problems are likely to be found on the current congressional and/or presidential institutional agenda? How would the two agendas be similar? How would they be different?

2. What "crises" have dramatically changed the national policy agenda in the past two or three years?

Answer Guidelines

This abstract can serve as a focal point for discussing current public policies. You could elicit policy problems from the class, thereby compiling a profile of both presidential and congressional institutional agendas and perhaps even listing the items in order of priority. The president's most recent State of the Union address might be a good starting point for discussion. The "crises" portion of class discussion should prove interesting, because students may remember recent events particularly clearly. Library research can also be assigned if time permits.

Theme B   Costs, Benefits, and Policy

Instructor References

Clark E. Cochran et al., *American Public Policy: An Introduction*. 3rd ed. New York: St. Martin's Press, 1990. A clear introduction to the theme.

Thomas R. Dye, *Understanding Public Policy*. 6th ed. Englewood Cliffs, NJ: Prentice-Hall, 1987. Covers a wide range of policies.

Hank Jenkins-Smith, *Democratic Politics and Policy Analysis*. Pacific Grove, Calif.: Brooks/Cole, 1990.

Dennis J. Palumbo, *Public Policy in America: Government in Action*. 2nd ed. New York: Harcourt Brace College Publishers, 1994.

Stuart S. Nagel, *Public Policy: Goals, Means and Methods*. New York: St. Martin's Press, 1984. See Chapter 3 on comparing costs and benefits with "marginal rates of return."

James Q. Wilson, *Political Organizations*. New York: Basic Books, 1973. Chapter 15. An earlier version of the theory expounded here in somewhat more detail.

Summary

Once an issue gets on the agenda, examining the costs and benefits that the proposed policies generate can help us understand how the issue will be resolved. A *cost* is any burden, monetary or nonmonetary, that people must bear, or think they must bear, if the policy is adopted. A *benefit* is any satisfaction, monetary or nonmonetary, that people believe they will enjoy. It is people's *perceptions* of costs and benefits that matter; people who bear *hidden* costs will not mobilize against a policy. Furthermore, ideas about whether it is legitimate for a particular group to receive a benefit or bear a cost matter, and these ideas sometimes change over time. AFDC was once a noncontroversial program; increasingly, its beneficiaries have come to be seen as undeserving.

People prefer government programs that give them substantial benefits at low cost. Politicians thus have an incentive to impose programs with costs that are small, far off, or borne by "someone else."

In cases where both costs and benefits are widely distributed, *majoritarian politics* prevails. Social Security and national defense are examples of this sort of politics. The outcome tends to be decided by majority opinion, debates are carried on in ideological terms, and interest groups are not so important. Once this new policy is adopted and the proposed benefits become real and cost-effective, debate ends and the program usually prospers.

When both costs and benefits are narrowly concentrated, *interest-group politics* prevails. Here, highly organized groups represent both sides. The decisions of the National Labor Relations Board, the question of whether Nazi party members can march in a Jewish community, and whether the FCC should allow cable broadcasts in competition with the networks represent these kinds of issues.

When benefits are concentrated and costs are distributed, *client politics* prevails. Farm-price supports and government controls aiding the airline industry are examples. If the benefits are to go to localities, they are referred to as *pork-barrel* projects. (Combining pork-barrel projects attracts a majority coalition through the process of "logrolling.") Here those receiving the benefits tend to be well organized and vocal politically, whereas those bearing the costs are unorganized, because each individual must pay so little. In recent years, greater effort has been made to help people become more aware of these facts about client politics.

Finally, in cases where benefits are distributed and costs are concentrated, *entrepreneurial politics* prevails. Antipollution and safety requirements for automobiles and the California taxpayers' revolt, which slashed property taxes, are examples. It is remarkable that such policies ever pass, because the American political system allows so many opportunities for organized interests to block action. Yet entrepreneurial politics has increased in frequency because of the presence of many policy entrepreneurs, such as Ralph Nader, Senator McCarthy, and Howard Jarvis, who represent themselves as acting "in the public interest" and who manage to pull together a legislative majority in favor of the policy. The leadership of a policy entrepreneur is not always necessary if significant numbers of voters or legislators become angry at the high cost of a particular group benefit.

Discussion Questions

1. Why is it that costs and benefits are what people believe them to be? Would it not be better to look at who really pays and who really benefits, regardless of the perception? Are people often wrong about whether and how much a policy costs and benefits them?

2. Of the four types of politics outlined in this chapter, which are exemplified in each of the following cases?

    a. Homosexuals convince a city council to pass an ordinance outlawing discrimination against them in jobs and housing.
    b. A citywide referendum reverses the council ordinance protecting homosexuals.
    c. A presidential candidate promises to cut the size and power of the federal bureaucracy.
    d. Congress considers the military situation in Europe and decides to appropriate money to increase troop strength there.
    e. The Massachusetts congressional delegation seeks to have the F-18 fighter plane built because its jet engines are produced in that state.
    f. A civil rights group sues for a citywide desegregation program involving busing.
    g. A governor creates a commission on the status of women and appoints several members of the feminist movement to it.
    h. A campaign is mounted to have a nuclear weapons "freeze."

3. Are some of the four types of politics described in this chapter *better* than the others? Do some tend to be inherently unfair in the way they distribute power over policy making? Do some tend to produce bad outcomes? Which, and why?

4. Do some of the four types of politics tend to benefit liberals and others conservatives or do liberals and conservatives benefit equally from all four?

Data and Perspectives for Analysis

Ask all your students to watch the evening news on one of the national networks on a particular evening. Have the students list the news items that involved a film or remote presentation—eliminating brief items read by the anchor and feature material that involves no significant public issue. Have the students classify each item according to the sort of politics it exemplifies, using the text's four categories. Discuss the students' classifications in class.

Abstract for Theme B

EPA Regulatory Policy and the Cost-Benefit Equation

"EPA Plans to Curb Use of Pesticide Found in Wells" is the title of a short article that appeared in the *Wall Street Journal* (June 23, 1988, p. 16). Written by staff reporter Barbara Rosewicz, the article noted that the EPA was proposing to regulate the use of aldicarb, a very toxic chemical which had been found in a large number of wells in at least sixteen states. Aldicarb is a pesticide used on potatoes, citrus fruit, and a variety of other crops. But it can seep into the underground water supply, i.e., well water, thus causing, at least in the short run, the inhibiting of nerve impulses, "stomach aches, nausea, dizziness, disorientation, and even death." The EPA was proposing a ban on using aldicarb three hundred feet or less from wells, but it was also leaving a great measure of control to the states:

> Instead of blanket nationwide rules, the proposal incorporates a new EPA strategy that leaves much of the regulation to the states. Because the potential for ground-water contamination varies geographically, the plan calls for states to impose the toughest restrictions in areas with the worst contamination or most vulnerable ground water.
>
> The proposal provides few details on standards and leaves open the question of who should be responsible for cleaning up contaminated wells.

Rosewicz noted that the manufacturer of aldicarb (Rhone-Poulenc, Inc.) was cooperating with the EPA and helping to monitor well contamination in a number of states. Rosewicz ended the article by observing that the EPA found "19 different pesticides contaminating wells in 23 states. It hasn't identified the next pesticide it will regulate for ground-water contamination."

Questions for Discussion

1. After reviewing the synopsis of the article, decide which governmental level should pay for cleaning up the contaminated wells. Explain reasons for your analysis.

2. If you were a taxpayer in a state with a large number of contaminated wells, would you be willing to pay more in state taxes to purify underground water supplies containing aldicarb and other pesticides?

Answer Guidelines

Open-ended discussion will probably ensue in the classroom, but you may wish to point out that contaminated underground water supplies can ultimately affect all residents of a state, rural and urban alike. Also, clean, drinkable water is a goal on which everyone can agree. Some discussion might also center on whether the EPA's regulatory actions are proper or strong enough.

Theme C   The Case of Business Regulation

Instructor References

Martha Derthik and Paul Quirk, *The Politics of Deregulation*. Washington, DC: Brookings Institution, 1985.

Marshall Goodman and Margaret Wrightson, *Managing Regulatory Reform: The Reagan Strategy and Its Impact*. New York: Praeger, 1987.

Larry Greston, Cynthia Fraleigh, and Robert Schwab, *The Regulated Society*. Pacific Grove, CA: Brooks-Cole, 1988.

Michael Reagan, *Regulation: The Politics of Policy*. Boston: Little, Brown, 1987.

Leonard Weiss and Michael Klass, eds., *Regulatory Reform: What Actually Happened?* Boston: Little, Brown, 1986.

Summary

Efforts by government to regulate business illustrate the four kinds of policy-making as well as the wealth–power relationship. Some see the existence of the large corporation as a source of economic power capable of dominating political activity and thus undermining democracy. The reasons for this view are that wealth can buy influence, that politicians and businessmen often spring from similar backgrounds, and that public officials are deeply concerned about economic growth. Others fear that demagogic politicians succumb too easily to attacks against business in the competitive struggle for votes.

Majoritarian politics, where costs and benefits are distributed, has resulted in antitrust legislation such as the *Sherman Act* (a relatively weak and vague law regarding business regulation), the *Federal Trade Commission Act*, and the *Clayton Act*. It might seem that such legislation would be opposed by business, but in fact some businesses benefit from antitrust legislation because they can use it against competitors. Antitrust activity remains a strong policy commitment today, though the intensity of federal initiatives varies with different administrations and their respective political ideologies.

When both costs and benefits of a policy are narrowly concentrated, interest-group politics prevails. Because both sides are usually well organized to press their interests, issues are seldom settled; rather, there is a continuous struggle. Struggles between business and labor over the Wagner Act, the Taft-Hartley Act, and the Occupational Safety and Health Administration and conflicts among various business, labor, and geographic interests over railroad regulation (beginning in 1887) are examples. These struggles have been affected by partisan configurations in Congress and by prevailing economic conditions.

Client politics comes in to play when a proposal is made that would confer substantial benefits on a relatively small group at the expense of many other people. Sometimes the benefit is a straight subsidy, but more often it is disguised as a form of regulation. Programs designed to support the price of dairy and tobacco products or to benefit the shipping industry are key examples. (Agricultural price supports rose fivefold between 1981 and 1983.) Finally, client-oriented government regulation is *not* the result of corrupt deals between industry and regulator but rather the result of effective organization by those who benefit at the expense of those unorganized people who pay.

Entrepreneurial politics, which imposes concentrated costs on business in order to benefit consumers or the general public, has been practiced with increasing frequency in recent years. (Historically, examples include the Pure Food and Drug Act and the Securities and Exchange Commission.) In the 1960s and early 1970s, about two dozen laws in the consumer and environmental protection area were passed by Congress. Some "self-serving" or "public-spirited" policy entrepreneur must mobilize support behind such bills. Senators, who enjoy high visibility and frequently harbor presidential ambitions, often perform this function; examples include Estes Kefauver in the area of drug laws, Edmund Muskie as the chief architect of air- and water-pollution bills, and Abraham Ribicoff and Warren Magnuson in relation to the National Traffic and Motor Vehicle Safety Act of 1966. A crisis or scandal—such as the publication of Upton Sinclair's *The Jungle* or Ralph Nader's *Unsafe at Any Speed*—makes entrepreneurial politics easier. In some cases, congressional hearings alone can dramatize an issue.

Entrepreneurial politics often takes on a moralistic tone, portraying opponents as devils and attacking supporters inside government, like Edmund Muskie, for not being tough enough. It might be supposed that an agency established through entrepreneurial politics would be particularly subject to "capture" by the business groups it regulates; and indeed the FDA was at one point very favorably disposed toward the pharmaceutical industry. However, newer agencies tend to have one administrator who can be held responsible. They often have strict standards and timetables established by Congress, and they are likely to regulate many different types of industries and thus not face unified business opposition. Furthermore, the existence of these agencies strengthens the "public-interest" lobbies that initially called for their creation. The media will also attack probusiness bias in these agencies. Finally, the courts oversee regulatory agencies to an unprecedented degree.

Discussion Questions

1. *Instructor: Ask for a show of hands on the following questions.* How many of you knew, before you read the text, that the federal government propped up the price of milk? How many knew about subsidies to the maritime industry? How many know anything about ICC regulation of the interstate bus industry? The moving industry?

2. Why do those who bear the costs (higher milk prices or taxes to support the maritime industry) not oppose these sorts of policies? Would it be *rational* to oppose them? Would it be rational to *know* about them?

Instructor: See Anthony Downs, An Economic Theory of Democracy *(New York: Harper & Row, 1957), Chapter 13, on this point.*

3. Does the government agency administering economic controls have more power when the controls are the result of client politics or when they are the result of interest-group politics? Why?

4. Suppose big business *had* vigorously opposed the Sherman Antitrust Act but that it had been passed anyway. What sort of politics would have been required for this to happen?

5. Why is the Senate particularly likely to become an arena for entrepreneurial politics?

6. How does a crisis often aid the policy entrepreneur? Why must entrepreneurial politics take on a moralistic tone? What problems afflict entrepreneurial politics? Are all issues equally likely to be exploited by a policy entrepreneur? Or can some be exploited more than others? Are the most exploitable issues usually those objectively most in need of public scrutiny and action? Give examples.

7. Why are policies produced by the process of entrepreneurial politics likely to be subverted in the long run? Why does the public, having been involved in the issue, not continue to insist that the "public interest" be served? Why can the process of policy entrepreneurship not ensure the continued success of such policies?

Data and Perspectives for Analysis

A. Entrepreneurial Politics

William C. Mitchell has written about the process that the text refers to as "entrepreneurial politics."

> Occasionally we have mobilization fads—issues that capture the attention of many citizens. By group efforts they work toward solutions of some recently discovered problem.... Students across the nation discovered pollution of the environment about them. Within a few short weeks they had mobilized ... to wage a war against pollution. Slogans such as "Can Man Survive?" were soon made popular.
>
> Typically, great problems develop slowly without much public awareness. A catastrophe suddenly grasps people's attention. Leaders come to the fore to mobilize opinion and finally public action. As the issue becomes popular, its supporters demand concerted mobilization of resources. Politicians and the government join the crusade. The government drafts legislation, and opposition groups gather their own resources in defense of their rights and privileges against encroachment and diminution of income. Eventually, laws are usually passed and a millennium is prophesied. In a hasty effort to amend past errors, funds are appropriated ... bureaucracies are established; and new vested interests are created. Mobilization becomes routinized and all the old fervent followers with emotions spent settle back into accustomed ways assuming the problem is now being controlled.
>
> William C. Mitchell, *Public Choice in America*
> (Chicago: Markham, 1971), pp. 39–40.

1. Is this a fair description of the process of entrepreneurial politics? If not, what is inaccurate about it?

2. Does Mitchell take a favorable or a jaundiced view of entrepreneurial politics? How, if at all, is his view different from the text's? What *problems* with entrepreneurial politics are implied by Mitchell?

3. Does Mitchell suggest that entrepreneurial politics is futile over the long run? Is he right?

B. The Question of Regulatory Effectiveness and Deregulation

In Michael Parenti's *Democracy for the Few*, 5th ed. (New York: St. Martin's Press, 1988), charges are leveled against regulatory agencies for being generally ineffective. Deregulation is viewed in a negative light as well. Parenti asserts the following:

1. "Since its establishment in 1977, the Office of Surface Mining (OSM) has done little to regulate strip mining. At least 6,000 sites have been mined since 1977 without the legally required environmental controls, resulting in thousands of miles of landslides and polluted streams." Also, more than half of the 4,000 mine owners who were operating illegally refused payment of fines to the OSM (p. 262).

2. "Often, agencies are insufficiently staffed to handle the enormous tasks that confront them. The federal government has twenty-five inspectors to monitor the transportation of hazardous wastes over the entire country" (p. 262).

3. Reform-minded administrative agencies run into deep opposition from capitalist, corporate America. Industries can challenge the jurisdiction of agencies in court or use their influence on key members in Congress to weaken an agency's power. Parenti notes that this has happened to the FTC (p. 265).

4. "Given a desire to survive and advance, bureaucrats tend to equivocate in the face of controversial decisions, moving away from dangerous areas and toward positions favored by the strongest of the pressures working on them. With time, the reform-minded agency loses its crusading spirit and settles down to serving the needs of the industry it is supposed to regulate" (p. 266).

5. "Many career administrators eventually leave government service to accept higher-paying jobs in companies whose interests they favored while in office. This promise of a lucrative post with a private firm can exercise a considerable influence on the judgments of the ambitious public administrator" (p. 266).

6. Independent regulatory commissions "frequently become protectors of the industries they are supposed to regulate, granting monopoly privileges to big companies that cost the public billions a year." Parenti mentions that the telephone companies and media networks control the FCC, the food and drug companies handle the FDA, and energy producers direct the efforts of the FERC (p. 267).

7. "Deregulation in the public-service realm does not make business more productive or even more competitive, if anything it removes a set of competing interests—those of the public—and simply leaves business freer to pursue profits without incurring any obligation for the social effects of that pursuit" (p. 273).

8. "Business is not really committed to some abstract principle of 'free enterprise.' Regulations that enhance profits are supported and those that cut into profits are denounced as violations of 'sound business practice.' It is only in the latter case that the cry for deregulation is heard throughout America's boardrooms" (p. 274).

9. "Government agencies more vigorously pursue their enforcement efforts against small companies because—unlike the big firms—they have less influence in Congress and can less afford to defend themselves in drawn-out litigation" (p. 274).

Have students research any or all of the propositions set forth by Parenti. Research can take the form of term papers, debates, or oral presentations.

Abstract for Theme C

The Issue of Government Regulation

The question of excessive governmental regulation is debated in George McKenna and Stanley Feingold, eds., *Taking Sides: Clashing Views on Controversial Political Issues*. 2nd ed. (Guilford, CT: Dushkin, 1981). Steven Kelman ("Citizens Need Protection," pp. 130–136) and Barry Crickmer ("Regulation Is Counter-Productive," pp. 124–129) center their debates around the basic question of costs versus benefits: whether, in general, the plethora of federal regulations (and regulatory agencies) on business enterprises enhances the quality of American life or actually retards economic growth and progress. Regarding the latter, Crickmer terms federal regulation "inflationary, irritating, costly, and even farcical . . . the worst is that it isn't working" (p. 124). He proceeds to make the following points:

1. Studies show that the FDA's overly conservative rules about new drugs "were costing American consumers three or four times as much as the economic benefits they produced . . . a too-cautious approach to approval of new drugs might foreclose or delay lifesaving advances in pharmaceutical technology" (p. 125).

2. Federal automobile regulations actually raise repair costs and promote greater consumption of gasoline.

3. "Reformist-minded" members of Congress, the desire of the media to "sensationalize" alleged problems and appropriate quick fixes, and misguided "crusaders" all contribute to the enactment of unnecessary regulatory policies.

4. "Profit incentive will reduce the accident and disease rate to the lowest level consistent with an efficient allocation of resources" (p. 127). In other words, manufacturers or businessmen will take all steps necessary to improve the working environment of their employees because it makes sense to do so. They themselves will assure a steady supply of trained workers, reduce insurance costs, and help avoid possible lawsuits. Self-interest, then, not government interference, is the key to workers' safety and prosperity.

5. Regarding pollution-control efforts, "control costs" raise prices without adding to the value of the product. Those extra costs make the business less competitive in the marketplace. Also, the federal government should clean up its own act; some of its facilities (such as TVA) are terrible polluters.

6. Finally, "industrial workers must apparently be protected from all risk, regardless of cost and their willingness to accept those risks, in return for high pay and other benefits" (p. 129).

Steven Kelman offers the following rejoinders to Crickmer:

1. In the most fundamental sense, government regulation is essential if injustices promoted by private, greedy individuals are to be either curbed or eliminated. "In any society, one of the basic tasks of government is to decide which acts of individuals are so harmful to others that they cannot be freely permitted" (p. 131).

2. There are many beneficial effects of regulation—clean water, consumer protection, reduction of accidents in the workplace, reduction in deaths due to occupational diseases, purer air (EPA standards), saving of childrens' lives (childproof containers on household poisons), fewer highway deaths (car safety regulations), and so on.

3. Regulations are not a major cause of inflation, nor are their costs excessive. Critics of regulation overlook direct savings that flow from those same regulations. As an example, "the actual monetary cost of pollution-abatement measures . . . is the cost to firms of capital equipment, energy and maintenance *minus* the savings in medical bills, damaged crops, premature corrosion of property . . ." (p. 134).

4. Further, those who dislike regulation costs overlook "widespread benefits that do not have a direct monetary value . . . the air smells better for 5 million people; 100,000 people get to see mountains in the distance which they would not have seen had the air not been as clean . . . there is no way of objectively determining whether these nonmonetary benefits justify the new monetary costs" (p. 134).

5. Simple cost-benefit calculations pale beside the ideals of justice, fairness, and human dignity—ideals that regulation promotes.

6. Studies show that in many areas, such as the environment, regulatory legislation creates more jobs than it costs.

7. Regulation *can* at times be excessive and even unjustified (for example, retrofitting older urban subway systems for a relatively small number of handicapped people), but "the thrust of the current movement against social regulation in the United States is a wish by the strong to regain prerogatives. . . . This assault on the concept of regulation must be resisted if we are to continue to be a decent people living in a decent society" (p. 136).

Questions for Discussion

1. Which arguments seem most compelling, and why?

2. Can consumers count on having their welfare looked after by businesspeople and manufacturers without government coercion? Why or why not?

Answer Guidelines

The responses will naturally vary among students. You may wish to discuss with the class the influence of the Reagan philosophy on the issue of regulation since 1981.

Theme D	The Policy Entrepreneurship of Ralph Nader

Summary

Ralph Nader is probably the most eminent consumer rights advocate in America. His career began in the 1960s when he accused General Motors of manufacturing automobiles which were "unsafe at any speed." After General Motors hired detectives to investigate his private life, Nader promptly sued the corporate giant. He won the court judgment and used the settlement to create a consumer empire of public-interest research, lobbying, and litigating organizations: the Center for the Study of Responsive Law; a Health Research Group; the Tax Reform Research Group; and Public Interest Research Groups (PIRGs), located in a number of states and on college campuses across the country. In addition, his Congress Watch analyzes congressional actions on consumer and environmental issues. Nader's interest in protecting the public has run the gamut from automobile safety to antismoking regulations to nuclear power plants to congressional reforms (not an exhaustive list!).

An insight into Nader's philosophy was provided by Thomas Whiteside's thoughtful *New Yorker* article of October 15, 1973, exploring Nader's basic belief that "new styles of violence" were being directed at the American people, for which existing laws provided few remedies. Nader revealed the following to Whiteside:

> Air pollution alone is a devastating form of violence. It takes far more lives and maims far more victims each year than street crime, and destroys more property each year than all the bank robbers' hauls a thousand times over. According to government figures, bank robbers have gotten away with more than twenty million dollars a year in recent years—their biggest ever—but the cost of air pollution alone in one recent year ran to more than sixteen billion dollars.

Nader went on to explain the importance of the law vis-à-vis business.

> The law has to be made to develop definitions of violence that correspond to the conditions we face. In terms of the violence it is currently committing, industry is largely beyond the law. . . . The law has developed to punish certain positive acts, not certain kinds of inaction. As matters stand, institutions are structured in such a way that corporations can achieve their economic objectives by inaction—for example, by reducing their costs through *not* taking steps to reduce the pollution they create. When you couple this deficiency of the law with the new style of violence that doesn't provoke an image of a criminal act, such as a common street crime, you have a combination of the power to devastate increasingly large sections of humanity and a decreasing degree of personal accountability. That is a prescription for social suicide. The president of a chemical company knows that no matter what his company does *he* won't go to jail, as long as he *personally* does not act, or instruct his subordinates to act, in violation of the law.

Whiteside notes how dedicated Nader is to alerting the American people to these new forms of violence, his ability to use the congressional process effectively, and his appeal to the media (at least during the 1970s). However, Nader's successes of the late 1960s and early 1970s did meet resistance. Lewis F. Powell, Jr., before he became a member of the U.S. Supreme Court, charged that Nader was assaulting the free-enterprise system and that corporate power was the target of his hatred. Powell urged that business galvanize its political resources in an aggressive way against the Naders of the world, for "there should not be the slightest hesitation to press vigorously in all political arenas for support of the enterprise system. Nor should there be reluctance to penalize politically those who oppose it."

Nader's crusading antibusiness approach was not especially welcome during the Reagan era of deregulation, and his popularity with the public dimmed somewhat. However, his successful sponsorship of past legislation in the areas of highway safety, federal meat inspection standards, environmental protection (EPA), freedom of information, OSHA, and air bags must not be taken for granted. Despite criticism from the media and in Congress, which saw Nader as frequently unwilling to compromise on consumer policies, Nader's consumer groups initiated investigations into the nuclear power industry, the Educational Testing Service, the postal service, and the insurance industry. Nader continued to target the giant corporations as well, arguing that the Reagan administration was a tool of General Motors, Exxon, and Du Pont. Finally, Nader continued to organize citizens' groups at the local level, for example, Citizen Utility Boards (to monitor public utility rates) and Buyers Up (to lower home heating fuel costs through citizen-small business cooperative arrangements). In short, Nader remained true to his self-concept of a citizen who wished to achieve justice in society.

Discussion Questions

1. Have students review some of Nader's legislative accomplishments. How have those accomplishments affected their daily lives?
2. Some of Nader's supporters have argued that Nader does not wish to "destroy" the capitalist economic system but only to reform it along morally correct standards. Does this objective appear to be the core of Nader's approach?

Additional Lecture Topic D-1

Ralph Nader and Entrepreneurial Politics

"U.S. Holds Carcinogenic Data from Workers, Nader Charges." *Chemical Marketing Reporter*, February 1985, p. 15.

Chris F. Best, "Ralph Nader and the Lloyd's Conspiracy." *Risk Management*, March 1986, p. 16.

John C. Boland, "Nader Crusade: The Anti-Business Lobby Is Alive and Kicking." *Barron's*, October 12, 1981, pp. 11, 16–26.

"Environment: A Fading Ralph Nader Rewrites His Strategy." *Business Week*, April 9, 1979 (Industrial Edition), p. 72.

S. Piontek, "Nader Sees a 'Consumer Revolution' Responding to the Dominance of a Few Financial Giants." *National Underwriter—Life and Health Insurance*, August 6, 1983, pp. 4, 8.

Arthur Snow and Burton A. Weisbrod, "Consumer Interest Litigation: A Case Study of *Nader v. Allegheny Airlines*." *Journal of Consumer Affairs*, 16 (Summer 1982): 1–22.

Theme E   Perceptions, Beliefs, Interests, and Values

Summary

Perceptions, beliefs, interests, and values are all related to the struggle to have one's own cost-benefit definition prevail over an adversary's. Complicating the policy process is the fact that most programs are intricate packages of costs and benefits and that the total package is perceived differently by different sectors of the polity. Sometimes costs are hidden: FDA regulation is seen as a guarantee of safe drugs, but the fact that it keeps useful drugs off the market for long periods is not generally known. People generally discount the future, so *present* costs and benefits are particularly important in political struggles. If consumers think they will pay for the expense of a policy, they are likely to oppose it. People may prefer to consider what happens in the near future rather than in the distant future (the "here-and-now" argument). Also, according to the cost argument, citizens react more to what they believe they will lose than to what they think they will gain from a proposed policy.

Important to the policy process is the passage of time. Perceptions change and so do elite attitudes, interests, beliefs, and values. Thus, when important elites adopted a procompetition outlook in the 1970s and 1980s, deregulation of many industries followed.

Airline deregulation is a case in point. The Civil Aeronautics Board (CAB) was originally created to help the infant civil aviation industry in the 1930s. This was a classic case of client politics, because the major airlines benefited from restricted competition and higher air fares. In 1978, however, Congress voted to end airline regulation, thus converting client politics into entrepreneurial politics. The perceptions and values of key individuals within and outside government had changed. Economists argued that airline regulation was too costly for consumers. In Congress, deregulation hearings led by Senator Kennedy accelerated the policy process. The media amplified the issue as well. Even the CAB chairman and his staff apparently favored deregulation. Thus the Airline Deregulation Act was passed in 1978, and dissolution of the CAB was planned for 1984.

The 1980s continued the era of deregulation, as the business community both favored and opposed the trend (fear of competition). Presidents Ford, Carter, and Reagan contributed to the trend as well. Deregulation remained controversial because rules governing social regulation (rather than economic regulation) were being changed. But on balance, the changing attitudes of key political elites have made it far easier for entrepreneurial politics to prosper.

Discussion Questions

1. Why is the fact that people "discount the future" important in understanding regulatory policy? Does this fact tend to produce more or less rational policies?

2. Why are there often hidden costs to regulatory policies? Are these costs really "hidden," or does some lack of foresight or bias in the information process prevent them from being taken into account when regulations are drafted?

3. How and why does the issue of airline deregulation represent a shift from client politics to entrepreneurial politics?

Data and Perspectives for Analysis

Interest and Ideology and the Farm Bill

In March 1975 Congress voted on a bill proposing to increase federal farm-price supports on a wide variety of agricultural products. The bill would substantially increase the income of farmers, as well as cause a rise in the prices that consumers have to pay for farm products. The table on the following page shows the percentage of Congress members in each of six categories who voted *for* the farm bill.

	Percentage of All Employed in Agriculture in Congressional District in 1970		
Congressional Member's Ideology[a]	Less Than 0.25%	Between 0.25% and 1%	Over 1%
Conservative	37%	71%	89%
	(98)	(70)	(29)
Liberal	60%	88%	78%
	(171)	(26)	(23)

[a]Liberals are those members of Congress with *Congressional Quarterly* conservative coalition support scores below 50; conservatives, those with scores above 49. See the *Congressional Quarterly Almanac* for 1975. For the vote on this bill see *Weekly Report*, March 22, 1975, p. 622.

1. What factors seem to have determined how a member of Congress voted on the farm bill? Which was most important?
2. Why would liberals be more likely to favor the farm bill if they had few farm constituents?
3. How does the effect of having farm constituents differ for liberals and conservatives? Can you suggest an explanation?
4. Was this bill an example of pure client politics or was some other factor important?

Additional Lecture Topics

E-1. Federal Regulation of Health and Safety: An Evaluation

Nina Cornell et al., "Safety Regulation." In Henry Owen and Charles Schultz, eds., *Setting National Priorities: The Next Ten Years*. Washington, DC: Brookings Institution, 1976.

Steven Kelman, "Regulation by the Numbers." *Public Interest*, Summer 1974.

Robert Crandall, "Curbing the Costs of Social Regulation." *Brookings Bulletin*, Winter 1979.

Albert L. Nichols and Richard Zeckhauser, "Government Comes to the Workplace: An Assessment of OSHA." *Public Interest*, Fall 1977.

Joseph A. Page and Mary-Win O'Brien, *Bitter Wages*. New York: Grossman, 1973. See especially Chapters 8–10 and the introduction by Ralph Nader.

Alan Stone, *Regulation and Its Alternatives*. Washington, DC: Congressional Quarterly Press, 1982.

John Mendeloff, *Regulating Safety: An Economic and Political Analysis of Occupational Safety and Health Policy*. Boston: MIT Press, 1980.

James Crawford, "The Dismantling of OSHA." *The Nation*, September 12, 1981. A good follow-up to the Nichols and Zeckhauser article.

Nathan Glazer, *The Limits of Social Policy*. Cambridge, MA: Harvard University Press, 1988.

Michael Reagan, *Curing the Crisis: Options for America's Healthcare*. Boulder, CO: Westview Press, 1992.

For current issues, see the periodical *Regulation*, an extremely useful, heavily antiregulation publication of the American Enterprise Institute. On the proregulation side, see the *Progressive* and the *Nation*.

E-2. Alternatives to the Present Regulatory Scheme

Stephen Chapman, "The Homely Sister." *New Republic*, February 3, 1979. Argues for deregulation of buses.

William T. Gromley, ed., *Privatization and Its Alternatives*. Madison, WI: University of Wisconsin Press, 1991.

Edward J. Mitchell, ed., *The Deregulation of Natural Gas*. Washington, DC: American Enterprise Institute, 1983.

Thomas Gale Moore, *Trucking Regulation: Lessons from Europe*. Washington, DC: American Enterprise Institute, 1976. There is a great deal of variation in the way European nations regulate their trucking industries. Moore argues, with the help of a lot of data, that countries with less regulation have better service at lower prices. Look particularly at Chapters 6 and 7.

Roger Noll and Bruce M. Owen, eds., *The Political Economy of Deregulation: Interest Groups in the Regulatory Process*. Washington, DC: American Enterprise Institute, 1983.

Michael Pertshuk, *Revolt Against Regulations*. Berkeley, CA: University of California Press, 1982.

Lester Salamon, ed., *Beyond Privatization: The Tools of Government*. Washington, DC: Urban Institute, 1989.

Charles Schultz, *The Public Use of Private Interest*. Washington, DC: Brookings Institution, 1977. (A shorter version appeared in *Harper's*, May 1977.) Schultz argues for the use of taxes and incentives instead of intrusive regulation as a means of serving the public purpose.

Fred L. Smith, "Why Not Abolish Anti-Trust?" *Regulation*, January/February 1983, pp. 23–28.

Susan J. Tolchin and Martin Tolchin, *Dismantling America: The Rush to Deregulate*. Boston: Houghton Mifflin, 1983.

Abstract for Theme E

The Effects of Ten Years of Airline Deregulation

The benefits and demerits of airline deregulation a decade after its implementation formed the basis of Nathaniel C. Nash's *New York Times* article (March 20, 1988, p. E5), entitled "Assessing the Effects of Airline Deregulation." Nash presented data from the Council of Economic Advisers, the Brookings Institution, the FTC, GAO, FAA, NTSB, and the Air Transport Association. The data illustrated that (a) passengers were now "flying for less . . . on more discount fares"; (b) more people were passengers (173.1 million in 1971 versus 450 million in 1987); (c) the number of total accidents involving commercially scheduled airlines had declined (68 during the 1965–1975 time period, 32 during the 1976–1986 period); and (d) both the percentage of Americans who had flown in a commercial plane and the percentage of seats filled had increased substantially (49 percent in 1971 versus 72 percent in 1987; 48.5 percent in 1971 versus 62.6 percent in 1987, respectively). But conversely, the "skies remained crowded," with airline delays of fifteen minutes or more staying at a high level; also, accident rates for small planes had not declined appreciably.

Nash noted the negative side of deregulation thus:

> Talk of gridlocked runways producing untold numbers of delayed flights and tales of frustrated travelers elbowing each other out of the way at ever more crowded airports have led to lament in some quarters for the days when the federal government designated the price of tickets and the routes commercial carriers could fly, and businessmen and the affluent were the principal jet travelers.

On the positive side, Nash notes that a number of economists believe that "lower fares and additional flights brought by deregulation are worth more than $12 billion (in savings) to consumers." Nash quotes the Council of Economic Advisers' 1988 Report to the president that "discount prices for flights over 2,500 miles have dropped by 35 percent in real terms. He also cites the Brookings Institution's argument that "both business and pleasure travelers have benefited from deregulation" and the opinions of other experts that airlines provide service to 150 small communities as a result of deregulation. Finally, congested airports are affected by more than deregulation: "the five year economic expansion has been a primary engine stimulating the record levels of air travel . . . and a lack of airport capacity and management problems are to blame for much of the congestion."

Questions for Discussion

1. Despite the apparent advantages of deregulation, can other negative points be considered? Have students research the issue further.

2. Are the apparent savings in air fares experienced by consumers common to other industries that have been deregulated? Have students cite some examples from their own research on the question.

16

Economic Policy

Overview and Objectives

The purpose of this chapter is to introduce the student to an area of public policy that affects everyone in one way or another: economic policy. The chapter will cover both the divided attitudes that voters have toward a "good" economy and the competing theories that economists offer on how to obtain a good economy. The various agencies that participate in formulating government economic policy will be reviewed, along with the many stages of producing and implementing the annual federal budget. Finally the controversial areas of government spending and tax reform will be discussed. After reading and reviewing the material in this chapter the student should be able to do each of the following:

1. Show how voters have contradictory attitudes regarding their own and others' economic benefits.//
2. List and briefly explain the four competing economic theories discussed in the chapter.
3. Assess the nature and impact of "Reaganomics."
4. List the four major federal government agencies involved in setting economic policy, and explain the role of each.
5. Analyze federal fiscal policy in terms of the text's four categories of politics.
6. Trace the history of federal government budgeting practices up to the present day.
7. Comment on the prospects and the desirability of lowering federal spending and reforming the income tax.

Chapter Outline with Keyed-in Resources

I. Economic health (THEME A: POLITICS AND ECONOMICS)
  A. How voters think; economic well-being majoritarian politics
    1. Voters influenced by their immediate economic situation

There is a good reason for voters to be concerned about their economic situation since it profoundly affects their personal lives. According to M. Harvey Brenner, a 1 percent increase in unemployment is statistically correlated with a 4.1 percent rise in the suicide rate.

    2. Voters worry about nation as a whole as well as their own situations
    3. Voting behavior and economic conditions correlated at national level but not individual level
       a. People understand what government can and cannot be held accountable for

        b. People see economic conditions having indirect effects on them even when they are doing well
    B. What politicians try to do
        1. Elected officials tempted to take short-term view of the economy
        2. Government uses money to influence elections but government will not always do whatever is necessary
            a. Government does not know how to produce desirable outcomes
            b. Attempting to cure one economic problem often occurs at cost to another

The inadequacy of economic predictions was underscored by Robert Heilbroner, former president of the American Economic Association, who lamented about "a growing awareness of intellectual incompetence" on the part of professional economists.

        3. Ideology plays large role in determining policy
            a. Democrats tend to want to reduce unemployment
            b. Republicans tend to want to reduce inflation
II. Economic theories and political needs
    A. Monetarism—asserts that inflation occurs when there is too much money chasing too few goods (Milton Friedman)
        1. Advocates increase in money supply about equal to economic growth
    B. Keynesianism—government should create right level of demand

Keynes was frustrated in trying to persuade Franklin Roosevelt to adopt his economic theories. "I'm afraid your president," Keynes complained, "knows little about economics." Keynes was probably correct. FDR was lost in the swirl of data: "He [Keynes] must be a mathematician rather than a political economist." But Keynes prevailed; even the conservative Richard Nixon once remarked, "We are all Keynesians."

        1. Assumes that health of economy depends on what fraction of their incomes people save or spend
        2. When demand is too low, government should spend more than it collects in taxes by creating public works programs
        3. When demand is too high, government should increase taxes
    C. Planning—free market too undependable to ensure economic efficiency; therefore government should control it (John Kenneth Galbraith)
        1. Wage-price controls
        2. Industrial policy—government directs investments toward particular industries
    D. Supply-side tax cuts—need for less government interference and lower taxes (Arthur Laffer)
        1. Lower taxes would create incentives for investment
        2. Greater productivity would produce more tax revenue
    E. Ideology and theory (THEME B: "REAGANOMICS" AND THE DEFICIT) (ADDITIONAL LECTURE TOPIC B-1)
        1. People embrace an economic theory partly because of their political beliefs
    F. "Reaganomics"
        1. Combination of monetarism, supply-side tax cuts, and domestic budget cutting
        2. Goals not consistent
            a. Reduction in size of federal government
            b. Increase in military strength
        3. Effects
            a. Rate of growth of spending slowed (but not spending itself)
            b. Military spending increased
            c. Money supply controlled
            d. Federal taxes decreased
            e. Large deficits incurred, dramatically increasing size of national debt

The large deficits were, of course, not anticipated by Reagan. His 1982 budget projected a deficit for that year of $24.1 billion; the actual result was a deficit of $110.6 billion, off by 358.8 percent.

           f. Unemployment decreased
    III. The machinery of economic policy making
         A. Fragmented policy making; not under president's full control

The Employment Act of 1946 requires the president to prepare an annual economic report to be submitted to Congress, with the federal government assuming responsibility for promoting maximum employment, productivity, and purchasing power. It was this law, according to James Davis, that "made the president overseer of the economy."

            1. Council of Economic Advisers—members chosen are sympathetic to president's view of economics and are experts
               a. Forecasts economic trends
               b. Prepares annual economic report for president
            2. Office of Management and Budget

OMB has lost much of its original goal of fulfilling a nonpolitical role. In a warning by Charles Dawes, first head of the then-Bureau of the Budget, the agency "will cease to be useful in the hands of the president" if it "ever becomes obsessed with the idea that it has any work except to save money and improve efficiency in routine business."

               a. Prepares estimates of federal government agencies; negotiates department budgets
               b. Ensures that agencies' legislative proposals are compatible with president's program
            3. Secretary of the Treasury—reflects point of view of financial community
               a. Provides estimates of government's revenues
               b. Recommends tax changes; represents nation with bankers and other nations
            4. The Fed (Federal Reserve Board)
               a. Independent of both president and Congress
               b. Regulates supply and price of money
            5. Congress most important in economic policy-making
               a. Approves taxes and expenditures
               b. Consents to wage and price controls
               c. Can alter Fed policy by threatening to reduce its powers
         B. Effects of interest-group claims
            1. Usually majoritarian: economic health good for all
            2. Sometimes interest group: protectionism in 1980s
    IV. Spending money
         A. Conflict between majoritarian and client or interest-group politics
         B. Sources of conflict reflected in inconsistencies in public opinion
         C. Politicians have incentive to make two kinds of appeals
            1. Keep spending down and cut deficit
            2. Support favorite programs of voters
    V. The budget (THEME C: THE BUDGET PROCESS)
         A. Earlier practices
            1. Merely adding expenditures before 1921
            2. No unified presidential budget until 1930s
            3. Separate committee reactions after that
         B. Congressional Budget Act of 1974: procedures
            1. President submits budget
            2. House and Senate budget committees analyze budget
            3. Budget resolution in May proposes budget ceilings
            4. Congress tries to get members to appropriate funds
            5. Congress adopts second budget resolution that "reconciles" budget ceiling with total individual appropriations bills
            6. Weakness: May resolution frequently ignored
            7. Failures of process after 1981
            8. Passage of Gramm-Rudman Balanced Budget Act (1985)

a. Called for
   (1) A target cap on the deficit each year, leading to a balanced budget
   (2) A spending plan within those targets
   (3) If a lack of agreement on a spending plan exists, automatic across-the board percentage budget cuts (a "sequester")
b. Very unpopular . . . but necessary
9. "Read my lips—no new taxes": Bush in 1990
   a. Produced a sequester of close to $100 million
   b. Result was
      (1) Increased taxes
      (2) Cut in defense spending
      (3) New budget procedures
   c. But total spending went up almost 5 percent
10. 1993 budget bill mirrors 1990 budget
    a. Caps appropriations in specific areas
    b. Caps discretionary spending
    c. Peace dividend not enough even to cover costs of inflation
C. Difficulties in reducing spending
   1. Interest-group pressure to increase funds for programs
   2. Much of budget is expenditures representing past commitments that cannot be altered (e.g., contracts, Social Security benefits, national debts): "uncontrollable"
   3. Performance of economy unpredictable
VI. Levying taxes
   A. Tax policy reflects blend of majoritarian and client politics
      1. "What is a 'fair' tax law?" (majoritarian)
         a. Tax burden is kept low
            (1) Americans do pay less than citizens of most other industrialized nations

In 1989, the top marginal rate in Sweden was 72 percent when personal income reaches $46,000. Like the United States, Sweden simplified its tax structure by specifying two brackets, 31 percent and 51 percent.

         b. Requires everyone to pay something
            (1) Americans do cheat less than others
      2. "How much is in it for me?" (client)
         a. Requires the better-off to pay more
            (1) Progressiveness is a matter of dispute: hard to calculate
            (2) Many loopholes: example of client politics
      3. Client politics (special interests) makes tax reform difficult
         a. But Tax Reform Act passed (1986)
   B. The rise of the income tax
      1. Most revenue derived from tariffs until 1913 and ratification of Sixteenth Amendment

In 1932, the average income tax paid by an American was $15 annually. This amount jumped to $4,300 by 1990.

      2. Taxes then varied with war (high), peace (low)
         a. High rates offset by many loopholes: compromise
         b. Constituencies organized around loopholes
      3. Tax bills before 1986 dealt more with deductions than with rates
      4. 1986: low rates with smaller deductions
   C. The politics of tax reform
      1. Majoritarian politics resurfaced in demand for fairness

The demand for fairness was lodged on behalf of the American public. However, the tax structure for businesses was just as inequitable. A report by the Joint Committee on Taxation in Congress in 1985 gave numerous examples of loopholes and exemptions producing disparate effect. According to the report, the real tax rate paid by companies varied by industry: 35.6 percent for soap manufacturers, 26.3 percent for computer companies, 9.9 percent for insurance companies, and 3.5 percent for auto manufacturers.

    2. Several kinds of entrepreneurs involved
        a. Professional economists opposing inefficiencies
        b. Supply-side ideologists
        c. Publicists exposing "tax cheats"
    3. Success requires support of key politicians
    4. Tax politics once again majoritarian, as in 1913
    5. Left unanswered: elimination of budget deficits

Important Terms

*budget A document that announces how much the government will collect in taxes and spend in revenues and how those expenditures will be allocated among various programs.

*budget deficit A situation in which the government spends more than it takes in, thus pumping more money into the economy.

*budget resolution A total budget ceiling and a ceiling for each of several spending areas submitted by the Budget Committees in the House and Senate to their respective chambers. These resolutions must be adopted in May to serve as targets to guide the work of each legislative committee as it decides what should be spent in its area.

*budget surplus A situation in which the government takes in more money than it spends, thus draining money out of the economy.

Congressional Budget Act of 1974 The law that altered the procedure by which Congress enacts the national budget. Budget committees were created in both houses, which then submit to each house a resolution proposing a total budget ceiling and a ceiling for each of several spending areas. Once these resolutions are adopted, individual appropriations are decided. Congress then adopts a second resolution reconciling the budget ceiling with individual appropriations bills.

Council of Economic Advisers A group of three professional economists created in 1946 to give the president impartial expert advice on the economy. It is responsible for forecasting economic trends, analyzing economic issues, and helping prepare the economic report the president submits each year to Congress. Since the president selects the CEA's membership, its recommendations usually reflect the ideological preferences of the president.

*economic planning A somewhat socialistic economic theory that holds that the government should plan at least a part of a country's economic activity by controlling wages and prices or through industrial policy to make the economy operate both effectively and fairly.

Federal Reserve Board A federal agency created in 1913 composed of seven "governors" who control the Federal Reserve System. The "Fed" is independent of both the president and Congress. Its most important function is to regulate the supply of money and therefore its value.

*fiscal policy An attempt to use taxes and expenditures to affect the economy.

*fiscal year October 1 to September 30, the period of time for which federal government appropriations are made and federal books are kept.

Gramm-Rudman Balanced Budget Act A law passed in 1985 which proposed cutting the budget until there was no longer a deficit. The deficit was to be reduced by a specified amount each year between 1986 and 1991. If a spending plan could not be agreed on within those targets, an automatic across-the-board percentage cut in federal programs would occur, except for exempted programs. The procedure was abandoned in 1990.

*industrial policy A form of governmental planning which became popular with academics in the 1980s and which maintains that the failure of smokestack industries to revive through market forces requires the government to direct investments. As a result, either these industries would recover or new industries would take their place.

*Keynesianism A liberal economic theory developed by English economist John Maynard Keynes, who believed that economic health depends on the proportions of income which are saved and spent. The government's task is to create the right level of demand. When demand is too low, the government should pump money into the economy through spending on its programs. When demand is too great, the government should take money out of the economy by increasing taxes or cutting spending.

loophole politics A form of client politics involving deductions, exemptions, and exclusions by which people shelter some of their income from taxation. Client groups were getting a subsidy from the federal government equal to the amount of a tax break.

marginal rate The percentage of the last dollar a person earns that must be paid out in taxes.

*monetarism A conservative economic theory that holds that inflation occurs when too much money is chasing too few goods. Since the federal government has the power to create money, it should ensure a steady, predictable increase in the money supply at a rate about equal to the growth in the economy's productivity; beyond that, it should leave matters alone and let the free market operate.

*monetary policy An attempt to use the amount of money and bank deposits and the price of money (interest rate) to affect the economy.

Office of Management and Budget Created as the Bureau of the Budget in 1921 and made part of the executive office in 1939, its chief functions are to prepare estimates of the amount that will be spent by federal agencies, to negotiate with other departments on the size of their budgets, and to make sure legislative proposals of departments are in accord with the president's programs.

*peace dividend Following the collapse of the Soviet Union, the expected sums of money freed up by cuts in post-Cold War defense spending that could be transferred to domestic spending.

*price and wage controls The means of economic planning which reflect the belief that the government should intervene in inflationary times by regulating the maximum prices that can be charged and the wages that can be paid. Such controls would be imposed only on the largest industries.

*Reaganomics The economic program instituted by President Ronald Reagan in 1981 which combined the theories of monetarism, supply-side tax cuts, and domestic budget cutting. The goal was to reduce the size of the federal government, to stimulate economic growth, and to increase American military strength.

secretary of the treasury Head of the Department of the Treasury nominated for office by the president. The secretary provides estimates of the revenue the government can expect from existing taxes and the projected revenues from changes in tax laws. The secretary also represents the United States in its dealings with the top bankers and finance ministers of other nations.

*sequester A provision of the Gramm-Rudman Balanced Budget Act that requires an automatic, across-the-board percentage cut in federal programs—except for certain exempt programs—if the Congress and president cannot agree on a spending plan within a specified target set for that year by the law.

Sixteenth Amendment A constitutional amendment ratified in 1913 which authorized Congress to levy an income tax. The amendment was necessary because of a Supreme Court decision in 1895 which voided Congress's effort to impose such a tax.

*supply-side economics A conservative economic theory that maintains that sharp tax cuts increase the incentive for people to work, save, and invest. The greater productivity of the economy stimulated by these increased investments would produce more revenue for the government despite the tax cut.

tariff A tax on goods imported into a country.

tax expenditures A term used by policy entrepreneurs denouncing tax loopholes as subsidies to groups that had not been made as appropriations through the normal annual congressional process.

Tax Reform Act of 1986 A law that effected a major change in tax policy resulting from the resurfacing of majoritarian politics that demanded fairness. Instead of high rates with big deductions, the law substituted low rates with much smaller deductions. More than a dozen tax brackets were replaced by two tax brackets.

uncontrollable spending Budget outlays that are already committed and cannot be altered for either legal or political reasons. This spending includes contracts, payments to individuals guaranteed by law, and interest on the national debt. About three-fourths of governmental expenditures fall into this category.

Theme A   Politics and Economics

Instructor References

Martin Anderson, "Is Supply-Side Economics Dead?" *American Spectator*, November 1983, p. 10.

Claude E. Barfield and William A. Schambra, *The Politics of Industrial Policy*. Washington, DC: American Enterprise Institute, 1986.

Milton Friedman, *There's No Such Thing as a Free Lunch*. LaSalle, IL: Open Court, 1975. See Chapter 2.

John K. Galbraith, *The New Industrial State*. Boston: Houghton Mifflin, 1978.

George Gilder, *Wealth and Poverty*. New York: Basic Books, 1981. The economic "bible" for supply-siders.

Peter A. Hall, ed., *The Political Power of Economic Ideas*. Princeton, NJ: Princeton University Press, 1990.

Donald F. Kettl, *Government by Proxy: (Mis?)Managing Federal Progams*. Washington, DC: Congressional Quarterly Press, 1987.

Robert Lekadman, "A Keynes for All Seasons." *New Republic*, June 20, 1983, pp. 21–25.

Carl Lieberman, *Making Economic Policy*. New York: Prentice-Hall, 1991.

Denise E. Markovich and Ronald E. Pynn, *American Political Economy*. Pacific Grove, CA: Brooks-Cole, 1988.

Edward Nell, *Prosperity and Public Spending*. Boston: Unwin Hyman, 1988.

Paul Samuelson and W. Nordhaus, *Economics*. 13th ed. Part 2. New York: McGraw Hill, 1989.

Lester C. Thurow, *The Zero-Sum Society*. New York: Simon & Schuster, 1981.

Summary

The state of the national economy is an extremely important issue for public officials and voters alike. Because elected officials realize the widespread impact of economic policies, they will try to take steps to improve the economy and hence to attract votes (at least in the short run). One school of thought holds that voters are primarily influenced by perceptions of their own improving or worsening economic status. The other school of thought believes that voters are concerned about the state of the nation and whether the party in power is pursuing wise economic policies. Empirical evidence seems to support both theories in part. However, in the 1984 presidential election, the defeat of Walter Mondale appeared to violate the first hypothesis. Conversely, voters may be more influenced by the condition of the economy as a whole than by their personal financial situation when they vote in presidential elections, and they hold the president responsible for that condition. Gerald Ford in 1976, Jimmy Carter in 1980, and George Bush in 1992 lost large majorities of the voters who said they were worse off financially than they had been a year before the election.

Thus a central fact about the federal government's role in the economy is presidential accountability to the voters. But unfortunately, the president and his economic advisers often cannot control the economy's progress, because external variables (such as world trade conditions or an oil embargo) and the proliferation of economically influential federal agencies can frustrate the proposed fiscal game plan. Furthermore, economic forces are so unpredictable and volatile (a specific policy can easily backfire) that the search for economic prosperity begins to resemble a game of Russian roulette. Accordingly, partisan ideological preferences for a specific economic theory usually shape policy directions on such matters as unemployment, inflation, and reduction of the federal debt.

Four major theories on the management of the economy are discussed in the text.

1. *Monetarism.* Monetarists such as Milton Friedman hold that inflation is the result of too much money chasing too few goods. This occurs when government prints too much money. When government tries to stop inflation by decreasing the money supply, unemployment increases. Rather than adopting these start-and-stop policies, it would be better if government allowed the money supply to increase steadily and consistently at a rate about equal to the growth in the productivity of the economy.

2. *Keynesianism.* For Keynesians, the market will not automatically operate at a full-employment, low-inflation level. When people spend too little, unemployment results, and government should pump more money into the economy by running a deficit (that is, by spending more than it takes in). When demand is too great, government should run a surplus. Thus an activist government fiscal policy is necessary.

3. *Planning* (wage and price controls, industrial policy). Economists such as John Kenneth Galbraith feel that large institutions in the economy (corporations and labor unions) have the ability to escape competitive pressures and raise prices, whatever the money supply or level of consumer demand. Thus the government must control wages and prices. But with the curbing of inflation in the 1980s and the voluntary lowering of wages and prices, a different type of planning by government was considered. *Industrial policy* reflected the federal government's desire to direct investment to "sick" but vital smokestack industries—steel and auto—in imitation of the Japanese model.

4. *Supply-side tax cuts.* This relatively new theory, propounded by people such as Arthur Laffer and Paul Craig Roberts, holds that high taxes create inflation and economic stagnation by removing people's incentive to work. Thus cutting tax *rates* will encourage work and investment and even bring in more tax revenue as economic activity expands. This theory forms the core of "Reaganomics."

Clearly, economic forecasting and implementation are an inexact science. Still, economists do provide important data to government and remind the public that "there's no such thing as a free lunch." The fact that the federal government spends one-fourth of the GNP and collects substantial income taxes *is* significant. So it follows that presidents must have economic policies that can reconcile the self-regarding and other-regarding perspectives of the voters.

Data and Perspectives for Analysis

The Economy as a Key Predictor of the 1988 Election

Prior to the national nominating conventions of 1988, the media began to speculate on the outcome of the Bush-Dukakis presidential race. Dukakis at this time was leading in the polls, although Bush had narrowed the gap somewhat. But an article in the *Atlanta Journal and Constitution* (July 3, 1988, p. 3E) by Alan I. Abramowitz, "Bush-Dukakis Race: A Photo Finish?", discussed the merits of a computer model that, when applied retroactively, had successfully predicted the outcome of every presidential election since World War II. The model's "average error" in predicting the popular vote for president had been under one percentage point, far less than the Gallup poll's sampling error of some three points or more. Abramowitz explained how the computer model worked:

> The computer model is based on the assumption that the overriding factor in the election is whether voters want to continue the policies of the incumbent president and his policy.... The computer model uses three pieces of data to evaluate the sentiment of the electorate: the popularity of the incumbent president, the condition of the economy, and the timing of the election. These factors can be measured at the time of the election and statistically combined to form a prediction of the popular vote for president.

In short, a strong economy and a popular incumbent are crucial factors, according to this model. Thus Nixon lost in 1960 because while Eisenhower was immensely popular, the economy grew by only 0.7 percent in that election year. Conversely, the economy grew by 3.6 percent in 1968, but Humphrey had to contend with a highly unpopular Lyndon Johnson.

Regarding the 1988 election, Reagan's approval rating was 51 percent in March, 1988, and the economy had grown during the first quarter of the year at an annual rate of 3.8 percent. The forecast for the entire year's economic growth rate was pegged at about 3.5 percent. Based on these data, the computer model predicted a virtual dead heat for the November election—Bush 50.2 percent, Dukakis 49.8 percent.

Research Assignment

Have students research the overall economic growth rate for the 1988 election year and also chart President Reagan's personal approval rating during the same time period. Did the eventual outcome of the 1988 presidential election correlate with these two variables or not? Be sure to ask students whether they uncovered any event from May to November that might have communicated to the voters that the economy was either doing exceptionally well or on the downturn.

Theme B   "Reaganomics" and the Deficit

Summary

"Reaganomics" was a combination of monetarism, supply-side tax cuts, and domestic budget-cutting. President Reagan's economic goals, though not entirely consistent or harmonious simultaneously, included reducing the size of the federal government, increasing military strength, and stimulating overall economic growth. The actual results involved the slowing of the federal government's spending rate (aggregate spending was not reduced), the curbing of inflation, the lowering of income taxes by about 23 percent over three years, and, unfortunately, the creating of huge national deficits.

It was the issue of the deficit that haunted the Reagan administration for much of its second term in office. Critics argued that the following real economic dangers to the country emanated from the deficit: (a) a financial burden on future generations; (b) competition between individual and business borrowers for the same dollars, driving up the cost of these dollars as well as interest rates (foreign investment and fiscal surpluses by state and local governments may have forestalled this development only temporarily); (c) economic havoc on a greater scale than the 1981–1982 debacle following the inevitable recession every four or five years (the business cycle); (d) the likelihood of a new wave of inflation once the federal government printed "new money" not based on economic growth but on an artificial need to fill the "savings pool."

Leonard Silk's plea for a realistic budget plan to curb the deficit (*New York Times*, July 1, 1988, p. 26) reflects the above views. Silk notes that international problems for the U.S. also flow from the federal deficit:

> The connection between a nation's internal and external deficits is clear: If a nation invests more than it saves and consumes more than it produces—as the United States has been doing—the excess must be covered by an inflow of foreign capital. The greater the internal budget deficit, the lower the rate of national savings and the greater the dependence on foreign capital.
>
> The persistent United States budget and trade deficits have lessened the ability of the nation to control its economy and hampered its leadership of the non-Communist world. Among American politicians and economists alike, there is now a consensus that to remedy the nation's external weakness, the structural budget deficit must be reduced, and if possible eliminated, in the next four or five years.

Silk points out the lack of a political consensus on how to reduce the deficit. Neither Bush nor Dukakis would openly admit that taxes would be raised during their administration. Furthermore, the persistence of budget deficits would increase interest payments on the federal debt. In short, there seemed to be no solution in sight.

The underlying factor in balancing the budget was the strength of special-interest groups who collectively endorsed the "deficit-elimination" concept in theory, but who individually preferred cuts in government spending to be made in areas of low concern or taxes to be raised in a way that would have minimal impact upon their own group's welfare. To put it another way, constituencies existed for virtually every item of the domestic budget, but a constituency expressly devoted to the elimination of the deficit was virtually nonexistent. An equally important factor was the Democratic-Republican squabbling over the "cause" of the deficit. Democrats blamed Reagan's steep tax cut in 1981, which permanently reduced government revenues, coupled with his expensive national defense modernization and buildup program. Republicans linked the cause of the deficit to the failure of a Democratically controlled Congress to reduce the cost of wasteful and unnecessary domestic welfare programs.

The political dilemma and a possible solution for the deficit are summed up nicely by two observers of the Reagan era:

> As long as the President resists any increase in personal income taxes, cuts in defense, or changes in social security policy, and as long as Congress maintains entitlements and preserves safety nets, scant progress on deficit reduction will be made. But there is no need for this deadlock to be permanent. It is not impossible to imagine a President and Congress, operating in a changed political climate, mixing tax increases and military "build-downs" with gradual reductions in entitlements. Such a strategy seems especially feasible, given a President with a fresh mandate and a Congress that is more centrally directed than before. Indeed, deficit reduction may be one of the first issues addressed once the stalemate of the Reagan years is broken. (See Paul E. Peterson and Mark Rom, "Lower Taxes, More Spending, and Budget Deficits" in Charles O. Jones, ed. The *Reagan Legacy*, p. 238.)

Questions for Discussion

1. What steps to reduce the federal deficit (if any) have been taken by the Bush administration that took office in 1989? What about the Clinton administration?

2. Have students research the arguments of economists that the deficit is not as dangerous as some people claim. Have them report their research findings to the class for appropriate evaluation and discussion.

Lecture Topic B-1

The Politics of "Reaganomics"

Fred I. Greenstein, ed., *The Reagan Presidency: An Early Assessment*. Baltimore: Johns Hopkins University Press, 1983.

Thomas J. Hailstones, *A Guide to Supply-Side Economics*. Richmond, VA: Dame, 1982.

Douglas Hibbs, *American Political Economy*. Cambridge: Harvard University Press, 1987.

Charles O. Jones, ed., *The Reagan Legacy: Promise and Performance*. Chatham, NJ: Chatham House, 1988. See Chapter 7.

B. B. Kymlicka and Jean V. Matthews, eds., *The Reagan Revolution?* Chicago: The Dorsey Press, 1988. See Part IV.

Arthur Laffer and Jan Seymour, *The Economics of the Tax Revolt*. New York: Harcourt Brace Jovanovich, 1979.

David C. Stockman, *The Triumph of Politics*. New York: Avon, 1986.

Charles F. Stone and Isabel V. Sawhill, *Economic Policy in the Reagan Years*. Washington DC: Urban Institute Press, 1984.

Lester C. Thurow, *The Zero-Sum Solution*. New York: Simon & Schuster, 1985.

Abstract for Theme B

Comparing Economic Performance in the 1970s and 1980s

John E. Schwarz in *America's Hidden Success: A Reassessment of Public Policy from Kennedy to Reagan*, rev. ed. (New York: W. W. Norton, 1988, pp. 166–175) compares the "record" of the 1980s with that of the 1970s. His assessment is hardly flattering to Reaganomics. His basic argument is summarized in the following passage:

> Rather than quickening, the pace of economic growth during the Reagan era slowed noticeably when compared with the 1970s.... From 1980 through 1986 the GNP (2.5 percent average growth per year), industrial production (3.0 percent average growth per year), and per capita disposable income (1.8 percent average growth per year) all rose at real rates below those of the 1970s. From 1970 through 1980 the GNP grew on a yearly average of 3.2 percent, industrial production climbed by 3.8 percent, and per capita income grew on average by 2.0 percent a year.

Schwarz is similarly not complimentary to Reaganomics even in areas of apparent success. He attributes the decline in inflation to "the elimination of the international energy price increases" and the rise in investment to "a surge of demand-side growth" rather than "enhanced productivity, as supply-siders had predicted."

On balance, therefore, Schwarz considers the nation's experiment with Reaganomics a hopeless failure with no redeeming qualities. He concludes by quoting David Stockman, director of the Office of Management and Budget under President Reagan (p. 185): "With the benefit of hindsight, they [historians] will know the immense damage to the nation's balance sheet and living standards that resulted from these ... years of fiscal profligacy. By then, the secret of Reagan's fabulous free lunch will be beyond dispute." After reading Schwarz, one wonders: Where are you Jimmy Carter?

Theme C The Budget Process

Instructor References

John B. Gilmour, *Reconcilable Differences? Congress, the Budget Process, and the Deficit*. Berkeley: University of California Press, 1990.

Dennis S. Ippolito, *Uncertain Legacies: Federal Budget Policy from Roosevelt through Reagan.* Charlottesville: University of Virginia Press, 1991.

Dennis S. Ippolito, "The Budget Process and Budget Policy: Resolving the Mismatch," in Frederick S. Lane, ed., *Current Issues in Public Administration*. 5th ed. New York: St. Martin's Press, 1994, pp. 297–305.

Donald Kettl, *Deficit Politics: Public Budgeting in Its Institutional and Historical Context.* New York: Macmillan, 1992.

Howard E. Schuman, *Politics and the Budget: The Struggle Between the President and Congress*. 3rd ed. Englewood Cliffs, NJ: Prentice-Hall, 1992.

Aaron Wildavsky, *The New Politics of the Budgetary Process.* Boston: Little, Brown, 1988.

Summary

The budgetary process invariably involves choices: which specific areas should be funded, which ones should be cut, who stands to benefit from the shape of the budget, and possibly whose "loophole" will be closed. These "political facts of life" cannot be ignored, so budgetary policy must be constructed through the collective (and frequently opposing) viewpoints of a number of federal institutions and individuals.

In the executive branch, the *Troika* consists of:

1. *The Council of Economic Advisers,* which generally represents the promarket views of professional economists. Both Republican and Democratic administrations, however, appoint ideologically sympathetic economists.

2. *The Office of Management and Budget,* which has the responsibility of preparing a federal budget in accordance with the president's program. It tries to be both a nonpartisan analyst of spending and budget patterns and (especially under Stockman) an activist trying to impose the president's wishes on the bureaucracy.

3. *The secretary of the treasury,* who is generally expected to represent the bankers' point of view.

The *Federal Reserve System*, which regulates the nation's money supply and interest rates, is theoretically independent of both the president and Congress, because its members serve fourteen-year terms. Actually the president has *some* influence over "the Fed," though high interest rates caused by its policies hurt Jimmy Carter's reelection prospects in 1980.

Then, of course, there is Congress, which must approve all taxes and almost all expenditures. Until 1974 the annual *budget* of the United States was pretty much the sum of what the committees in a decentralized Congress wanted to spend. The *Congressional Budget Act* of 1974 attempted to impose some centralization on the process. Now *budget committees* in each house produce a May *budget resolution* that, when adopted, imposes ceilings on overall spending and on spending in each area (such as health and defense). These ceilings are supposed to guide legislative committees in drawing up specific appropriations bills. Of course, there is nothing to prevent Congress from ignoring its May budget resolution; however, the process has imposed some discipline on the institution. President Reagan used the process in 1981 to get Congress to vote about $36 billion in spending cuts in fiscal 1982. It was necessary to his strategy to get Congress to vote for a total package of cuts *before* it could vote on any individual cut.

In recent years, congressional-presidential agreement on a budget resolution has become more difficult to obtain. The 1985 budget dilemma was a good example, as Congress debated further budget cuts proposed by President Reagan amidst an intense array of partisan and public pressures. These budget problems accelerated the call by the states for a constitutional convention to consider a balanced-budget amendment. Cutting spending is necessarily a difficult matter, because about three-fourths of all federal outlays are *relatively uncontrollable*. (Despite initial Reagan cuts of $3.5 billion, total federal spending continued to climb, albeit at a slower growth rate—9 percent as opposed to an earlier 13 percent.) Many of these uncontrollable expenditures could in fact be controlled if Congress were willing to reduce benefits to individuals, but this is politically risky (the House in 1985, for example, refused to tamper with Social Security benefits).

Cutting taxes, by contrast, would seem to be politically very popular. However, people object less to income taxes, which are withheld from paychecks and never seen, than to local property taxes. Further, Americans are more concerned about balancing the budget than about cutting taxes. Finally, tax cuts exacerbate the chronic series of deficits that the federal government has run over the last quarter-century (only the years 1960 and 1969 have seen surpluses). Thus when Reagan attempted to implement the supply-side economic theory in 1981, he found it quite difficult to round up the votes in Congress. He was able to do so only by adding a large number of "sweeteners" for special interest groups to his basic three-year, 27 percent, across-the-board cut. Over the long run, the most important provision of this tax bill was the *indexing* of tax brackets, beginning in 1985. This eliminated automatic *de facto* tax increases caused by *bracket creep* and explicitly forced Congress to raise taxes if it wished to raise more revenue. In 1985 Congress members balked at more tax increases. Instead they focused attention on President Reagan's tax reform package. The hope was that eliminating loopholes, together with cutting the tax rates, would balance out in terms of revenue (revenue-neutral). However, the attempt to close loopholes in the prevailing tax structure soon encountered intense interest group resistance. The result was that the tax package passed in 1986 reflected a number of compromises, despite its reform orientation.

Discussion Questions

1. Does the president have the necessary tools to "manage the economy"? Is there any justification for such a decentralized system?

2. Why are the majority of federal expenditures considered "uncontrollable"? Are there any that Congress really could not cut if it wanted to? For example, could Congress not cut (or at least fail to increase) Social Security payments?

3. Why is it difficult to coordinate federal spending policies and federal tax policies?

4. Why is the government not a neutral, efficient instrument for controlling the economy? Which of the following is the chief problem?

    The incompetence, rigidity, or lack of coordination of the federal bureaucracy
    Lack of knowledge or ability on the part of the president or Congress
    The activities of interest groups outside the government
    The attitudes and opinions of the American public at large

5. How do politicians manipulate monetary and fiscal policy for political purposes? Is this a new development? Is this a process of "buying votes"? If so, how is it morally different from passing out cash in front of a polling place? If people want more money rather than less, is it not *democratic* for politicians to try to give it to them?

6. To what extent does the public have a say—through things like elections—in economic policy? Does the public demand particular economic policies? If not, how does the public have an effect?

    Instructor: Discuss here the difference between prospective *policy voting and* retrospective *evaluation. This distinction will be very important in foreign policy also.*

7. How would economic policy making change if the public were *better informed* about economics and politics? Which of the following would change?

    The difficulty of closing tax loopholes
    The uncontrollability of most of the federal budget
    Social Security increases in election years
    The fact that taxes consume over one-fourth of our GNP
    The fact that unemployment is low in election years
    Government's desire to stimulate economic growth
    The fact that the president's advisers differ greatly in their perspectives on economic policy

8. Consider the foregoing list. Which of the facts listed are the result of *biases* in the making of economic policy, and which are the result of democracy's functioning reasonably well? Are the biases you detect the result of (a) inadequacies in our governmental institutions; (b) the workings of the interest-group process; (c) lack of information or logic on the part of the voters; or (d) selfishness on the part of politicians who wish to remain in power?

Instructor: Students need to be made aware that alternative (d) begs the important questions. Why does self-interest on the part of politicians lead to poor policy?

9. If politicians can manipulate the economy so as to gain reelection, has meaningful democracy disappeared? Will it have disappeared if politicians become *more effective* in manipulating the economy? Or would that make the system more democratic?

Data and Perspectives for Analysis

Do Presidents Manipulate the Economy?

The performance of the economy is a reliable predictor of the victor in presidential elections. Since 1832, incumbent presidents or their parties lost 67 percent of the time in election years that coincided with a recession (but only 24 percent of the time when the economy was not in recession). Clearly, presidents have an incentive to ensure the health of the economy in election years. Presidents have numerous tools to influence the economy to their advantage. However, an immediate jolt to the economy is usually purchased at the expense of negative long-term consequences.

Consider the following studies:

> Michael Berry from the University of Virginia found that stocks rise in presidential election years and fall the year after inauguration.
>
> Fred Alvine of Georgia Tech University discovered that investments in stocks average a 15 percent return in the year before a presidential election, 3.6 percent the year following an election, and minus 15.2 percent in the second year of a president's term.
>
> Edward Tufte of Yale University found that real disposable income increased in fifteen election years since 1946 and declined in only six.
>
> Stocks have risen in every presidential election year since 1960, with the exception of 1984.

Questions for Discussion

1. What tools does the president possess to manipulate the economy? Why would a president not want to manipulate the economy during an election year?

2. Could Congress prevent a president from the opposing party from manipulating the economy? How? If so, why didn't Congress stop President Reagan from doing so in 1984?

Abstract for Theme C

"Cures" for the Federal Deficit: The Balanced-Budget Amendment and the "Liquidation" of U.S. Assets

Huge, seemingly unending annual deficits became the key economic issue affecting the Reagan administration's second term in office. In 1985 Congress and the president struggled to find a political formula that would result in only a modest reduction in the deficit. Perhaps other methods to solve the deficit problem should be considered—hence the renewed argument for a constitutional amendment requiring a balanced budget, as well as the more novel suggestion that the federal government sell its lands and other assets to "pay off" that deficit.

The balanced-budget amendment had been gathering momentum for some years. By the mid-1980s, well over thirty states were calling for a constitutional convention to consider such an amendment. The pros and cons of the amendment had been argued in an August 30, 1982, debate in *U.S. News and World Report* between Republican Governor Robert List of Nevada, and Democratic Governor William A. O'Neill of Connecticut (pp. 63–64). Governor List, who favors the balanced-budget amendment, made the following points:

1. Congress will not or cannot balance the budget because of special interests. Thus an amendment stating that Congress would require a three-fifths vote (instead of the current majority) to authorize deficit spending would increase accountability and limit the possibility of budget imbalances in the future.

2. Polls show that the public overwhelmingly backs the balanced-budget amendment as a way of controlling federal spending.

3. Although the amendment might result in decreases of federal subsidies to the states, proper fiscal management could overcome this problem.

4. Individuals in Congress who oppose the amendment "generally are those who like to go home and take credit for all the expenditures in their district or state and blame the deficits on all the other members of Congress. That just isn't going to work anymore."

Governor O'Neill made the following counterarguments:

1. The amendment would unduly restrict flexibility in spending: "Flexibility is also required when the country is in difficult economic straits, as it is at present with unemployment at its highest level in more than 40 years."

2. The amendment would worsen the fiscal condition of the states, because they "would be given the burden of carrying out programs that the federal government should be responsible for." For example, the problems of the poor concern all levels of government, not just the states or cities.

3. There is already a federal law mandating that Congress balance the budget. If Congress ignores this statute, why would it not simply ignore an amendment?

4. The amendment makes a basic change in the democratic process, because two-fifths of either house could block additional spending. That is, this amendment "substitutes minority for majority rule."

5. The amendment will eventually lead to additional unemployment across the country, because the contraction of federal spending is "permanent."

6. The public would not support this amendment if they realized the specific economic consequences attached to it, such as cuts in Social Security, education grants, welfare, and the like.

Another approach to "curing" the deficit was propounded by Laurence W. Beilenson and Robert W. Poole, Jr., in a *Wall Street Journal* column of July 15, 1985, entitled "Time to Think Again About Liquidating U.S. Assets" (p. 35). The authors argue that advocates of the balanced-budget amendment "have an obligation to show *how* the budget can be balanced without large tax increases." Their method is to sell off U.S. assets, an approach with historical precedent (from 1817 to 1835, federal revenues from land sales, tariffs, and other charges went into a sinking fund to repay the national debt). The authors go on to argue that

> every dollar raised by selling government assets should go into a sinking fund, and we should pass a rigid balanced-budget amendment. Such an amendment sounds like pie in the sky today, but would be quite credible if accompanied by liquidation of the national debt and budget cutting.
>   The U.S. government owns sufficient assets to pay off most or all of the $1.5 trillion national debt.

Thus the "replacement costs" of government buildings, gold reserves (revalued), and the conversion of all government securities from par to market values *plus* millions of acres of public lands (including federal oil and gas rights—onshore and offshore) would, collectively, virtually wipe out the debt. (Oil and gas rights alone totaled $800 billion in 1981.) To satisfy environmental trade-offs, sales of land to private parties would include "a right of reversion to the original owner in case defined misuse occurs."

The authors also cite Senator Moynihan's proposal of March, 1985, involving the government's sale of its entire $280 billion loan portfolio to private investors, which would contribute at least $150 billion toward retiring the debt. The authors conclude that deficits remain a "menace to our economic health. We can grow our way out of our fiscal morass, but not without some pruning first."

Questions for Discussion

1. Should a balanced-budget amendment become part of the Constitution? Why or why not?

2. Does Beilenson and Poole's proposal make sense? Why or why not? Why does the federal government not proceed to sell off its assets?

Answer Guidelines

Opinions in class will vary, but you can shape the discussion by pointing out the economic consequences (or lack of them) of restricted federal spending. You can also raise the question of whether deficits can be "lived with," provided that their increase is moderate. Conversely, deficits do squeeze out private individuals and businesspeople seeking credit. Interest rates could soar, which in turn could choke off car and home sales and inhibit those investments that produce additional jobs. Regarding the "asset-selling" proposal, it is clear that a variety of interest groups would oppose this plan, particularly environmental groups who regard private ownership of former public lands as tantamount to exploitation of precious natural resources.

17

Social Welfare

Overview and Objectives

This chapter covers over fifty years of the political history of efforts to establish, maintain, expand, or cut those major programs that give or claim to give government help to individuals in need. After reading and reviewing the material in this chapter the student should be able to do each of the following:

1. Describe the goals of the American social welfare system, and contrast its programs with those of the British in terms of centralization.

2. Describe the major elements of the American system, including the Social Security Act of 1935, the Economic Opportunity Act of 1964, and the Medicare Act of 1965. Why did these acts pass, whereas the Family Assistance Plan of 1969 failed? What generalizations can be made about welfare politics?

3. Explain why some welfare policies can be considered majoritarian politics and others client politics. Give examples and indicate the political consequences of each.

4. Analyze and comment on the promise and the performance of the Reagan administration in cutting welfare programs while maintaining the "safety net" intact.

5. Discuss the many politics of health care reform.

Chapter Outline with Keyed-in Resources

I. Overview of welfare politics in the United States (THEME A: AMERICAN WELFARE IN COMPARATIVE PERSPECTIVE)
   A. Who deserves to benefit?
      1. Insistence it be only those who cannot help themselves
      2. Slow, steady change in deserving/undeserving line
      3. Alternative view: fair share of national income; government redistributes money
      4. Preference to give services, not money, to help deserving poor
   B. Late arrival of welfare policy
      1. Behind twenty-two European nations
      2. Contrast with Britain in 1908
   C. Influence of federalism
      1. Federal involvement "illegal" until 1930s
      2. Experiments by state governments
         a. Argued against federal involvement since states already providing welfare
         b. Lobbied for federal involvement to help states

II. The four laws in brief (THEME B: WELFARE POLITICS AS MAJORITARIAN POLITICS)
   A. Social Security Act of 1935

The first Social Security recipient was Ida Fuller in 1940, who initially received monthly checks for $22.34. She died in 1975 at age one hundred, having collected $20,944.42 in total payments on a contribution to the system of $22.

      1. Great Depression of 1929—local relief overwhelmed
      2. Elections of 1932—Democrats, FDR swept in
         a. Legal, political roadblocks—was direct welfare unconstitutional?
         b. Fear of more radical movements
            (1) Long's "Share Our Wealth"
            (2) Sinclair's "End Poverty in California"
            (3) Townsend's old-age program
      3. Cabinet Committee's two-part plan
         a. "Insurance" for unemployed and elderly

Today, over 90 percent of the working population participates in the Social Security program, with about 15 percent of the public receiving benefits.

         b. "Assistance" for dependent children, blind, aged
         c. Federally funded, state-administered program under means test
   B. Economic Opportunity Act of 1964
      1. War on Poverty at a time of prosperity
      2. Pockets of poverty found (Michael Harrington)
      3. Proposals acquire urgency
         a. March on Washington, August 1963
         b. Kennedy assassination, November 1963
      4. Service provided, not money, through Economic Opportunity Act
         a. Job Corps
         b. Literacy programs
         c. Neighborhood Youth Corps
         d. Work-study program
         e. Community Action Program
      5. Resulted in complex and controversial organizations based in neighborhoods
   C. Medicare Act of 1965
      1. Medical benefits omitted in 1935: controversial but done to ensure passage
      2. Opponents
         a. AMA
         b. House Ways and Means Committee under Wilbur Mills
      3. 1964 elections: Democrats' big majority altered Ways and Means
      4. Objections anticipated in plan
         a. Application only to aged, not to everybody
         b. Only hospital, not doctors', bills covered

Medicare is composed of two programs for the elderly. Part A provides hospital insurance. Part B is a voluntary supplement, in which 98 percent elect to enroll, for medical insurance covering doctors' bills.

      5. Broadened by Ways and Means to include Medicaid for poor; pay doctors' bills for elderly

Only 45 percent of the eligible poor are currently receiving Medicaid benefits. Participation rates vary widely by state, ranging from 20 percent to 90 percent depending on the state.

   D. Family Assistance Plan of 1969
      1. Growth of AFDC and doubling of costs from 1964 to 1969
      2. Criticisms
         a. Subsidizing the able-bodied
         b. Benefits too low

AFDC payments for a family of three range from $114 a month in Alabama to $533 a month in California.

        c. Harm to families by encouraging them to break up
        d. Demeaning tests for eligibility
    3. Nixon proposed bold departure in FAP
        a. Guaranteed minimum income for family with children
        b. Work requirement or job training
        c. Earned income offset but discounted
        d. Benefit ceiling
    4. House passage due to support of Wilbur Mills since reduces welfare cheating
    5. Senate defeat
        a. Conservative Russell Long chaired Finance Committee
        b. Liberals unsatisfied, suspicious; conservatives feared cost
    6. Programs *and* idea dead
        a. McGovern in 1972 offered a version but withdrawn
        b. Carter after 1976; but earned-income tax credit enacted in 1975
III. Two kinds of welfare programs
    A. Majoritarian politics: almost everybody pays and benefits
        1. Social Security Act, Medicare Act are examples
    B. Client politics: everybody pays, relatively few people benefit
        1. AFDC program, CAP program of War on Poverty are examples
    C. Majoritarian politics
        1. Programs with widely distributed benefits and costs
            a. Beneficiaries must believe they will come out ahead
            b. Political elites must believe in legitimacy of program
        2. Social Security and Medicare looked like "free lunch"
            a. Benefits and taxes were initially small
            b. Many players, few beneficiaries

Eli Ginzberg estimates that fifty workers were contributing to Social Security for each recipient in 1945; the ratio had slipped to three to one by 1980 and could reach two to one by 2035.

        c. Medicare costs were underestimated
    3. Debate over legitimacy: Social Security (1935)
        a. Constitution did not authorize federal welfare (conservatives)
        b. But benefits were not really a federal expenditure (liberals)
    4. Good politics unless cost to voters exceeds benefits
    5. Three things changed politics of Social Security and Medicare
        a. Tax increases necessary to pay for retirement benefits
        b. Older people began to live longer
        c. Cost of health care shot up
    D. Client politics
        1. Programs pass if cost to public not perceived as great and client considered deserving
        2. AFDC became controversial once perception changed to no longer helping deserving poor but unmarried black women
            a. American values believe welfare encourages husbands to avoid responsibilities and poor women to have babies
            b. Americans prefer service strategy to income strategy
                (1) Charles Murray: high welfare benefits made some young people go on welfare rather than seek jobs
                (2) No direct evidence supports Murray
            c. Preference for "giving people a hand rather than a handout" explains passage of War on Poverty in 1964
    E. The many politics of health-care reform (THEME C: THE POLITICS OF HEALTH CARE POLICY)

1. President Clinton announced new health care policy in 1993
2. Many presidents endorsed health plans without success
3. Not till Medicare Act of 1965 did federal government begin a big role in health care, but only for elderly
4. New issue emerged over rising cost of health care
   a. Nixon urged HMOs
   b. Carter proposed a cap on hospital payments by insurance
   c. Reagan changed law to allow Medicare to reimburse a fixed amount

In 1960, medical spending accounted for 6.2 percent of the GNP. That figure had risen to 11.1 percent of the GNP by 1988.

5. Clinton concerned not only by cost but number of people not covered
   a. Task Force on National Health Care formed under Hillary Rodham Clinton
   b. Plan proposes placing entire economy under federal regulation

F. Majoritarian versus client politics
   1. Clinton wanted health plan seen as majoritarian issue
   2. But Americans happy with current health insurance
   3. Clinton's alternative was to make health care client politics
      a. Needed client to have either allies in Congress or be seen as deserving
      b. Public unlikely to help marginal members of society
   4. Clinton's strategy shifted to making health care majoritarian issue by getting public fearful of losing their insurance
   5. Hillary Clinton injected entrepreneurial politics by attacking drug manufacturers and insurance companies
   6. Rival plans emerged
      a. Single-payer plan
      b. Voluntary plan for employers
      c. Clinton began calling his plan "managed competition" as a compromise to rival plans
   7. Questions of average citizen
      a. Would people have to pay higher taxes for benefits they already had?
      b. Would people retain the right to choose their own doctor?
      c. Would the U.S. continue to be in the forefront of developing new drugs and methods of treatment?
      d. If all employers were required to provide health insurance mostly at their own expense, would they cut back on the number of people they hire?
      e. Should there be one national or several state plans?

IV. Toward a new welfare politics (ADDITIONAL LECTURE TOPIC B-1)
   A. Majoritarian welfare programs: Who will pay? How much?
   B. Client-oriented welfare programs: Who should benefit? How should they be served?

Poverty has increasingly become a gender issue. In 1960, only 26 percent of families in poverty were headed by women; by 1988, about half of poor families were headed by women.

   C. Costs
      1. Problem: "indexing" of Social Security payments to inflation
         a. Made increases automatic
      2. Bipartisan commission raised taxes, age at which people become eligible
      3. Medicare was tougher
         a. Politically impossible to raise taxes or cut benefits
         b. Approach: price controls in 1983
            (1) Regulations and restrictions on what doctors and hospitals can charge
            (2) Flat fee for each treatment
            (3) Some hospitals cut services in response
         c. Medicare Catastrophic Coverage Act of 1988
            (1) Designed to protect elderly against costs of catastrophic illness

                (2) Costs to be paid by more affluent elderly
                (3) Beneficiaries revolted, and act was repealed

The political clout of the elderly should not be ignored; 17 percent of voters in national elections are sixty-five or over.

            4. Any universal health plan would present more cost problems than Medicare
                a. Clinton proposes to recover costs by more efficient, streamlined system
        D. Legitimacy
            1. Question: how can perceived legitimacy of poor people be increased?

In 1939, Franklin Roosevelt framed the legitimacy of welfare in terms of national character: "The test of our progress is not whether we add more to the abundance of those who already have much; it is whether we do enough for those who have too little."

            2. Family Support Act of 1988
                a. Requires states to collect child-support payments from deserting fathers
                b. Requires states to train welfare mothers
                c. Passed Congress by wide margins
            3. Head Start
                a. Provides preschool education to poor children
                b. Popular with conservatives and liberals
                    (1) Targets poor families
                    (2) Provides services rather than money
                    (3) Helps children
        E. The "family issue"
            1. Attempt by Democrats to co-opt Republicans
            2. Emphasis on strengthening family ties

The average length of time a two-parent family stays in poverty is only 4.6 years.

            3. Examples: minimum wage, government-supported day care, parental leave from work
            4. Problem: debate over morality
                a. What values should be encouraged?
        F. The homeless
            1. Disagreement over number of homeless
            2. Adopted policy satisfies neither liberals nor conservatives
            3. Federal government supports state and local programs
        G. Immigrants
            1. 90 percent of all immigrants in six states
            2. Studies indicate impact of immigration on wages or unemployment of less-skilled workers is nil
            3. But public perceives immigration as harming American workers
            4. Economic effects of immigrants is mixed
                a. Decline in earnings of low-skilled workers
                b. Immigrants pay more in taxes than received in government services

Important Terms

Aid to Families with Dependent Children A component of the original Social Security Act which provides financial assistance to families with children. Depending on state requirements, either one or two parents can be present in families in which the breadwinner is unemployed.

*assistance program Part of the plan that emerged from Franklin Roosevelt's Cabinet Committee on Economic Security that called for aid to the blind, dependent children, and the aged.

client politics A type of policy-making in which relatively few people benefit, but everybody pays, such as AFDC.

***earned-income tax credit** A little-noticed provision of the tax law of 1975 which entitled poor families with children to receive money from the government if their total income fell below a certain level. The program is a form of "negative income tax" in which an annual income is guaranteed.

Economic Opportunity Act of 1964 The law instituting the key program of Lyndon Johnson's War on Poverty. Its major provisions included creation of the Job Corps, literacy programs, the Neighborhood Youth Corps, work-study subsidies for college students, and the Community Action Program.

Family Assistance Plan of 1969 A welfare program proposed by President Nixon at the urging of his urban affairs adviser, Daniel Patrick Moynihan, under which every family with children would receive a guaranteed minimum income, all able-bodied recipients would be required either to work or to enter a job training program, and any money earned by recipients would offset their benefits but at a rate less than dollar-for-dollar. The plan was never enacted.

Family Support Act of 1988 A welfare program intended to address the major criticisms of AFDC. It requires states to establish the paternity of children born out of wedlock and to collect child-support payments from fathers who have deserted their families by withholding child support from the absent parent's paycheck. All states are required to enroll parents receiving AFDC benefits in job training and job placement programs.

Head Start A federally funded program that provides preschool education to children from poor families.

***income strategy** The rationale behind the type of welfare program disliked by the American public which involves giving people direct financial assistance rather than services.

***insurance program** Part of the plan that emerged from Franklin Roosevelt's Cabinet Committee on Economic Security that called for insurance for the unemployed and elderly to which workers would contribute and from which they would benefit when unemployed or upon retirement.

majoritarian politics A type of policy-making in which almost everybody benefits and almost everybody pays, such as Social Security.

***means test** An eligibility requirement for participation in a welfare program in which aid is conditioned on proving need.

Medicare Act of 1965 One of the federal government's major welfare programs, focusing on health care. It is composed of two parts. First, the Medicare program covers the hospital expenses and doctors' bills of the aged. The second component, called Medicaid, covers medical assistance for the poor.

Medicare Catastrophic Coverage Act of 1988 A welfare program in which the federal government paid the annual hospital bills for catastrophic illnesses of the elderly. The cost of this additional coverage was paid largely by the elderly themselves. Opposition by the elderly culminated in the act's repeal in 1989.

***service strategy** The rationale behind the type of welfare program favored by the American public which helps poor people through job training or government jobs rather than by giving them direct financial assistance.

Social Security Act of 1935 The first major welfare program enacted by the federal government during the administration of Franklin Roosevelt in response to the Great Depression. It called for two kinds of programs: (1) an insurance program for the unemployed and elderly, and (2) an assistance program for the blind, dependent children, and the aged.

Theme A   American Welfare in Comparative Perspective

Instructor References

Henry J. Aaron and William B. Schwartz, *The Painful Prescription*. Washington, DC: Brookings Institute, 1984.

Lawrence Jacobs, *The Health of Nations: Public Opinion and the Making of American and British Health Policy*. New York: Cornell University Press, 1993.

Charles Lockhart, *Gaining Ground: Tailoring Social Programs to American Values*. Berkeley: University of California Press, 1989.

Summary

Like every modern nation, the United States has scores of programs that are intended to help needy people. However, we think about welfare differently than other nations do. Americans are concerned with who *deserves* to be helped, and of course this raises the problem of distinguishing between the *deserving* and the *undeserving* poor. Other nations are more likely to attempt to *redistribute* income on the basis of some notion of "fair shares." Americans wish to promote self-reliance and are uneasy about just giving people money. We therefore prefer to provide services, rather than income, to the poor.

The welfare state (at least at the national level) came late to the United States. In Britain, with power concentrated in the hands of a prime minister and a liberal majority in parliament, new welfare programs were implemented in the early twentieth century. Thus in 1906 a national system of old-age pensions was set up, and five years later a nationwide scheme of health and unemployment insurance was established. During this time the progressive movement in the United States was concerned with good-government issues, not the welfare state. Furthermore, the American system of federalism meant that the right of the federal government to institute welfare programs was a matter of controversy. Many state governments had welfare programs before the 1930s. The existence of these programs created a lobby for federal programs and also required much federal policy to operate through state bureaucracies.

Of course, the comparison between *when* welfare programs were inaugurated ignores differences in the services provided. It was not until after World War II that Britain initiated a broad range of government services, most notably with the creation of the National Health Service in 1948. Thus the British not only acted earlier but more expansively in the area of social welfare programs. Yet British values had to undergo a massive change to reach this point. According to Chiam Waxman, the English retained the belief that poverty was a sign of a person's moral faults well into the nineteenth century, even maintaining workhouses for the poor. The debate on health care in the United States may be signaling that America is moving slowly but confidently down the same path. The question is whether American values will ever tolerate the same level of government control as in Britain.

Discussion Questions

1. The United States provides a less generous welfare system than most Western European nations. As a result, the United States lags behind many European nations in life expectancy and infant mortality. What factors account for this difference in welfare generosity? Do these factors indicate that the United States should expand its welfare system?

2. Does the United States derive any benefits from not having the broad welfare coverage of European nations? Have the class consider the other side of the coin. In 1968, 5.5 percent of the Dutch work force was considered at least partially disabled, a figure that reached 16 percent by 1989. Only 50 percent of adults worked by 1990. In Sweden, workers are absent on sick leave an average of 30.7 days a year, compared with 7.8 days for U.S. workers.

Theme B   Welfare Politics as Majoritarian Politics

Instructor References

W. Andrew Achenbaum, *Social Security: Visions and Revisions*. Cambridge: Cambridge University Press, 1986.

Fay Lomax Cook and Edith J. Barrett, *Support for the American Welfare State: The Views of Congress and the Public*. New York: Columbia University Press, 1992.

Karen Davis and Diane Rowland, *Medicare Policy: New Directions for Health and Long-Term Care*. Baltimore: Johns Hopkins University Press, 1986.

Paul Light, *Artful Work: The Politics of Social Security Reform*. New York: Random House, 1985.

Michael Sherraden, *Assets and the Poor: A New American Welfare Policy*. Armonk: M. E. Sharpe, Inc., 1991

Summary

The text examines four welfare programs: the Social Security Act of 1935, the Economic Opportunity Act (or War on Poverty) of 1964, the Medicare Act of 1965, and the Family Assistance Plan (proposed in 1969 but not adopted). Social Security and Medicare account for two-thirds of all federal welfare expenditures.

The Social Security Act was passed during the Great Depression, which had overloaded and bankrupted state, local, and private relief efforts. Roosevelt was under fire from various radical social movements, but he had been given an overwhelming congressional majority by the elections of 1932. He got speedy approval of a program, put together by a cabinet committee, that drew on European experience and the ideas of scholars and social workers.

The War on Poverty was proposed in 1964, during a time of prosperity. However, various writers and scholars had exposed "pockets of poverty" amid affluence. The civil-rights movement drew attention to the poor economic condition of blacks. The assassination of President Kennedy in Dallas generated sympathy for Kennedy's proposals, some of which Johnson adopted. Whereas the Social Security Act distributed money and was relatively simple to administer, the Economic Opportunity Act tried to provide services to allow the poor to help themselves. How to provide these services was poorly understood, and their implementation therefore gave rise to an immense bureaucracy of hundreds of complicated organizations. The most controversial of these were neighborhood organizations founded under the Community Action Program. These often attacked established agencies and politicians, who turned to Congress for help in reining in the local CAPs.

The idea of having the government pay the medical bills of Americans was very much in the minds of those who initiated Social Security in the 1930s, but because the idea was so controversial, it was not included in the Social Security legislation. Opponents of the idea controlled the key House Ways and Means Committee in Congress and were able to block action until after the 1964 election. The Democratic landslide in that election added many Democrats to the House, and the leadership saw to it that pro-Medicare Democrats were appointed to Ways and Means. The bill, which provided for payment of hospital and doctors' bills for both the poor and the aged, passed both houses with ease.

The idea of a *negative income tax* had been advocated by economists for many years when the Nixon administration proposed its *Family Assistance Plan* in 1969. It had the political advantage of replacing the unpopular and rapidly growing *AFDC* program. The plan would have been a very bold step, using straightforward income redistribution to replace the traditional American practice of helping people only with certain narrowly defined needs. Initially, it got support from both conservatives (who thought it would reduce fraud and increase work incentive) and liberals (who thought it fairer and more generous than the existing program). Unfortunately no "reform" of welfare can simultaneously keep costs down, benefits high, and work incentives strong. Thus, although the FAP passed the House, neither liberals nor conservatives in the Senate were satisfied with it, and the measure died.

These four examples suggest five generalizations about welfare policy making:

1. The initiative in welfare policy making rests with the president, not with interest groups or Congress.

2. Debate tends to be carried out in ideological terms, with conflicting ideas about the proper role of government in the forefront. The Economic Opportunity Act was a rare exception, because the idea of providing service to help the needy help themselves is consistent with traditional American thinking.

3. Congressional voting on welfare policies follows party lines very closely. However, southern Democrats often vote with Republicans against welfare measures. Therefore, extraordinary Democratic majorities (such as existed in 1935 and 1965) are needed to pass these programs.

4. Public opinion supported Social Security and Medicare but was, at best, divided over FAP. The War on Poverty was so complex that it is difficult to make any clear statement about public opinion in regard to it. The FAP was controversial, because Americans prefer *insurance* (that is, contributory programs) to *relief*, and they prefer job creation to cash payment.

5. Interest groups played some role in the politics of some of the welfare bills, but this was usually an expression of the ideology of the group rather than of the interests of its members.

Both the 1935 old-age pension system and Medicare are examples of majoritarian politics. The initial debate concerned whether it was *legitimate* for government to provide these things; this having been decided, it quickly became good politics to increase the level of benefits. However, growing benefits and an increase in the number of old people drawing these benefits have made it more difficult to pay for these programs. The Social Security tax (on both worker and employer) was 2 percent in 1937 but had grown to 10.4 percent by 1983. Limiting benefits to the needy (a means test) is politically difficult, because Social Security was sold to the American people as an insurance program, and vast numbers of Americans are convinced that they deserve benefits. Congress has yet to come to grips with this issue. Fiscal crises continue to plague the Social Security system. Only an emergency 1983 "rescue bill," passed during the Reagan administration's first term, preserved the system for the time being. Key provisions of the bill included (a) a delay in cost-of-living adjustments by six months each year; (b) an increase in payroll taxes for employer and employee; (c) a tax on half of the retirement benefits for the elderly whose incomes exceeded $25,000 a year; (d) a requirement that new federal employees join the Social Security system; (e) an increase in taxes on self-employed persons; (f) a gradual increase in the retirement age from 65 to 67.

Other programs, especially AFDC and the Community Action Program, are examples of client politics. AFDC was not controversial at first, but as costs rose radically in the 1960s and as the public perception of the nature of the beneficiaries changed, it became good politics to attack "welfare." Thus the 1970s and 1980s saw an endless series of regulations and investigations into the "welfare mess."

Social Security's public image as an "insurance" program renders it virtually untouchable politically. AFDC, however, can be cut if entrepreneurial critics convince Congress that the money for AFDC is being wasted on undeserving people and that the social "safety net" would not thereby violated. Between 1980 and 1983, the Reagan administration directed a 5 percent cut in money spent on means-tested programs. Welfare mothers experienced real cuts, but other low-income people probably did not. Whether the "safety net" is still largely intact or torn completely asunder remains a question.

Discussion Questions

1. What were the economic and political circumstances in the country in 1964 when Congress passed the Economic Opportunity Act? How were *ideas* rather than *circumstances* predominant in getting the issue of poverty onto the agenda?

2. How did the Economic Opportunity Act propose to help the poor? Was this a good strategy from the standpoint of securing public support? Was this a good strategy from the standpoint of actually helping the poor?

3. What has been the role of public opinion in the political battles over welfare policies? What do Americans believe about the role of government in social welfare policies? How are these beliefs "equivocal"?

4. Why does Congress now feel "trapped" by the Social Security program? How could one claim that Social Security was actually the result of client politics in its early years but has become more a majoritarian issue as tax rates have increased? How did the 1983 Social Security legislation attempt to salvage the fiscal integrity of the program?

5. In 1989, the poverty line for a single person was calculated at $5,980 by the Department of Agriculture. This figure amounts to about $2.75 per day for food. Is this rate reasonable for survival? Is providing food stamps to the poor an example of majoritarian or client politics?

Additional Lecture Topic B-1

Majoritarian Politics Versus Client Politics in Social Welfare

Sheldon Danziger and Daniel Weinberg, eds., *Fighting Poverty: What Works and What Doesn't*. Cambridge: Harvard University Press, 1986.

Michael Parenti, *Democracy for the Few*. 5th ed. New York: St. Martin's Press, 1988. Chapter 7.

These readings are heavily weighed toward the view that welfare politics is client politics and as such, they serve to balance the text's emphasis on majoritarian politics. *Note:* For a real-life portrait of families on welfare, see Barbara Aarsteinsen's "Families on Welfare Say They Choose Between Paying Bills or Surviving," *New York Times*, March 26, 1985, p. 16.

Data and Perspectives for Analysis

A. Social Security and Presidential Voting

The American public has a difficult time dealing with poverty. They are uncertain whether the government should assist the poor or whether the poor are responsible for themselves. When confronted with this issue, the vast majority of the public have no idea what the proper role of the government should be. Is the value of self-reliance losing support in the nation, or are people simply reluctant to be cold-hearted? Have your students examine the data below to ascertain whether the text's conclusions on the topic are valid.

Question: "Some people think that the government in Washington should do everything possible to improve the standard of living of all poor Americans; they are at Point 1. Other people think it is not the government's responsibility, and that each person should take care of himself; they are at Point 5. Where would you place yourself on this scale, or haven't you made up your mind on this?"

	Government should improve living standard		Agree with both answers	People should take care of themselves	
	1	2	3	4	5
Percent Response	18%	12%	46%	13%	11%

Source: National Opinion Research Center, General Social Survey, Spring, 1987.

B. Public Opinion on Social Programs

In 1981, during President Reagan's campaign to cut taxes and federal spending, Louis Harris asked a national sample of Americans the following question about a wide variety of government programs:

> A major first effort of the Reagan Administration will be to cut back on federal spending. One way they plan to do this is by restricting eligibility for certain benefits the federal government now supports and by reducing the amounts of future increases in these benefits. For each of the following benefits tell me if you think federal spending should be cut by 50 percent, 25 percent, 10 percent, or hardly at all?
>
> Now let me ask you about major federal grant programs. Do you favor cutting federal spending on (*read: each item*) by 50 percent, 25 percent, 10 percent, or hardly at all?

Support of Cuts in Specific Federal Benefits and Grant Programs

Program	Favor Cut	Oppose Cut	Not Sure
Highway grants	72%	23%	5%
Welfare payment grants	72	24	4
Subsidized housing	66	28	6
Community development programs	67	29	4
CETA and other job programs	62	31	7
General revenue sharing	61	30	9
Unemployment compensation	59	38	3
Federal civilian retirement	59	35	6
Sewage treatment projects	54	41	5
Food stamps	54	41	5
Military retirement	51	45	4
Mass public transportation	46	50	4
Grants for Medicaid	39	57	4
School lunch and other child nutrition programs	35	63	2
Aid to elementary and secondary schools	34	63	3
Veterans' benefits	31	66	3
Social Security	20	77	3
Medicare for the elderly	15	83	2

Source: The Harris Survey, February 19, 1981.

1. Is the question biased? Does it tend to encourage the respondent to favor cuts or oppose them? If there is a bias, can we make comparisons *across* programs, even if the bias overstates the public's willingness to cut spending?

2. Look over the list of programs and try to judge what sort of people benefit from each. Put a *P* beside programs that mostly benefit poor people. Put a *G* beside programs that benefit the middle class and the poor about equally. Put an *M* beside programs that benefit mostly middle-class and wealthy people but *not* poor people.

3. What sort of programs are most popular—*redistributive* programs, which provide income or in-kind benefits to poor people, or *distributive* programs, which disperse benefits widely?

Instructor: Considerable discussion should be devoted to the distributive impact of various programs. Many are controversial. The view of many policy analysts, for example, is that community development programs mostly provide windfalls for certain business interests and that federal aid to education mostly benefits middle-class bureaucrats. If you feel these programs accomplish their stated objectives, you might code them with a P. Regardless, the public's preference for programs that benefit the middle class should be obvious. Compare, head-to-head, welfare versus Social Security, Medicaid versus Medicare, and food stamps versus veterans' benefits.

4. Are the *most expensive* programs, those that have contributed most to budget growth and increasing deficits, among the *most* popular programs or among the *least* popular? What does this suggest about the possibility of balancing the budget and halting the increase in federal spending?

C. Social Policy and the Graying of America

The need to devise new sets of social-welfare policies, particularly in the category of health care for the elderly, gained greater prominence in the 1988 election year (see Milt Freudenheim's "The Elderly and the Politics of Health Care," *New York Times*, May 22, 1988, p. E5). Elected officials noted that the 28 million members of the American Association of Retired Persons (aged fifty and over) accounted for nearly 25 percent of all registered voters in the nation. The elderly's chief congressional spokesman, the late Representative Claude Pepper (D, Fla.), was successful in having Medicare expanded to cover the costs of catastrophic illnesses. Other prospective legislation loomed on the horizon, involving coverage for nursing-home expenses. However, as in all public policies, questions began to emerge regarding the national economic priorities, generational fairness, and the allocation of responsibilities between the family and government.

Since the costs of these new programs would run into billions of dollars, the question of which group in society should bear the economic burdens was an important one. The economic figures were startling:

> Nursing home care cost the country about $42 billion last year, of which the taxpayers paid about $20 billion. In 30 years . . . the present arrangement would cost $120 billion, of which $65 billion would be public money. If Medicare is expanded to cover nursing home and home care for the most severely disabled, the cost to the Treasury would rise from $95 billion to $122 billion.

Complicating the picture was the essential question of "fairness":

> 30 percent of the Federal budget already goes to programs for the elderly, who make up only 12 percent of the population. Social Security taxes cut into the food and housing budgets of young workers, and benefits older people who often have homes, substantial savings and other assets.
> Growing awareness of such disparities is producing the beginnings of a political backlash among some younger Americans.

A final issue was whether families should assume more of the burden in caring for elderly parents and grandparents, rather than relying on new government programs. But certain facts remained clear—by 2010, according to CBO and the Senate Special Committee on Aging data, 13.8 percent of the U.S. population would be sixty-five or older (up from 11.3 percent in 1980), and there would be an increase of nearly 2.3 percent in those over seventy-five. Society would have to bear the brunt of this demographic change, but how would the burden be distributed?

1. Knowing the above facts, what specific type of social-welfare policy for the elderly would you devise if you were making national policy on the issue?

2. Are the young responsible for caring for the elderly no matter what the cost? Debate the issue in class.

3. Should more emphasis be placed on comprehensive private health insurance policies rather than federal intervention in the health area? Give reasons for your opinion.

Abstract 1 for Theme B

The Merits and Demerits of Social-Welfare Policies

In the post-World War II era, the most frenetic period of social-welfare policies began with Lyndon Johnson's "Great Society" programs. As David E. Rosenbaum pointed out in a *New York Times* article of April 17, 1985, entitled "20 Years Later, the Great Society Flourishes," American life in general has been dramatically affected in a number of ways because of these social-welfare laws passed in 1965. Thus in 1965, "half of all Americans over 65 had no medical insurance, and a third of the aged lived in poverty" whereas in 1985 "nearly every elderly person is covered by health insurance, and the aged are no poorer than Americans as a whole" (p. 1). The legislative milestones of the Great Society were many, including Medicare, Medicaid, federal aid to local public schools, loans for college students, the Voting Rights Act, rent supplements for poor people, training programs for health professionals, and development assistance for Appalachia. Even an official in the Reagan administration, who had charged the Great Society with being extravagant and failing the nation's poor, admitted that "much of the social safety net was accomplished during the Great Society, and whatever gets trimmed, the safety net will remain intact."

From the Reagan administration's perspective, it was especially ironic that spending on Great Society social welfare programs increased dramatically under the Ford and Nixon administrations. The relaxation of welfare eligibility rules, the widespread use of food stamps, the indexing of Social Security retirement benefits to inflation rate increases, and the easing of eligibility standards for disability cases raised federal spending levels considerably. Nevertheless, the era of "Reaganomics" sought a curb on some of these programs. But which specific programs could be cut without endangering the so-called safety net?

Medical care plans did not appear to be an especially promising area for budget cuts. In Robert Pear's article, "Medical Care Plans Created in the 60s Keep Wide Support" (*New York Times*, May 20, 1985, p. 1 ff), it was revealed that the Medicare and Medicaid health benefits to the elderly and the poor "retained the strongest bipartisan support"; Congress even authorized "a modest expansion of benefits" in an era of fiscal austerity. One reason for this support was the tremendous impact the programs had made on national health care, serving some "50 million people at a price of $93 billion" in the current year. The cost of the health programs, while increasing at a rate "three times as fast as overall federal spending since 1967," was justified by the programs' apparent contribution to lengthening life expectancy for the elderly (by two years), their broadening of health insurance for these over 65 (today 98 percent of the nation's 28 million elderly are covered by Medicare), and their contribution to a drop in the infant mortality rate. Finally, proposed reductions in Medicare and Medicaid by the Reagan administration were opposed by the American Medical Association, whose members had a vested financial interest in seeing the programs continue.

Unlike medical care, the social-welfare issues of poverty and hunger seemed to many critics of the Reagan administration to have dropped through the safety net. To those critics, budget cuts had created a widespread poverty problem, particularly among children. In another *New York Times* article by Robert Pear, "Increase Found in Child Poverty in Study by U.S." (May 23, 1985, p. 1), it was shown that "39.2 percent of all poor people are children . . . and the child poverty rate for 1983 was at the highest level since the mid-1960s." Cuts in the AFDC program had contributed to these figures. The corollary problem of hunger in America was also attributed to cuts in nutrition and income programs that left 35.3 million Americans with incomes below the federal poverty line (see "Doctors Find Hunger Is Epidemic in U.S.," *New York Times*, February 27, 1985, p. 88). A report by the Physician Task Force on Hunger revealed that "up to 20 million citizens may be hungry at least some period of time each month." Accordingly, doctors urged Congress to increase welfare and food benefits, restore free lunches in the schools, expand nutrition programs, and offer more meals for the elderly. However, it appeared unlikely that the Reagan administration would restore a significant amount of the $12.2 billion cut from food stamps and child nutrition programs during the 1982−1985 time period.

Questions for Discussion

1. How could a policy-maker rationalize the existence of widespread hunger in the United States?

2. Why are social welfare programs so difficult to eliminate or cut sharply once they have been in existence for a few years even though the general public is dissatisfied with them?

Answer Guidelines

Assuming a policy-maker was inclined to contemporary social Darwinism, he or she might assert that those who fail to eat adequately are themselves to blame for being ignorant or indifferent to nutritional needs. Conversely, one could argue that it is virtually impossible for a poor person to sustain an adequate diet. In terms of the second question, social welfare programs build up a strong clientele once they prove successful.

Abstract 2 for Theme B

The American Distribution of Income

Should it be a policy of the U.S. government to equalize income for all Americans, or at least to reduce the rich-poor gap? In "A Growing Gap Between Rich and Poor (*New York Times*, May 1, 1988, p. F3), Frank Levy presents the argument that "America's level of income inequality has been increasing steadily since 1979." While George Bush might wish to address this serious problem, the presence of large budget and trade deficits might "tempt him to leave the inequality problem alone." The specific nature of the inequality problem is delineated by Levy:

> The Census Bureau sampled 60,000 homes and reported that in 1986 average family income, including Social Security, reached $34, 294. . . . But this slow gain in average income largely reflected the gains of the top earners. Among the wealthiest one-fifth of families, the Census Bureau says that average income grew from $70,260 to $76,300—in 1986 dollars. Among the poorest one-fifth of families, average income fell from $8,761 to $8,033. This has resulted in growing inequality—$9.50 in income added at the top for every $1 lost at the bottom.

Levy also notes that education levels contributed to this gap, with college graduates increasing their earning power at the expense of high school graduates. Also, a single woman headed one American family in six; and these families, which had an average income of $13,500, were unable to compete with two-income couples.

Levy suggests that Congress should provide greater tax relief for low-income families. He also advocates keeping children in school longer, lowering the rate of teenage pregnancies, and encouraging the states as well as the federal government to come up with answers to the inequality problem. Future presidents should also commit themselves to pursuing such a multifaceted program.

Questions for Discussion

1. What dangers exist for American democracy (potentially) if the income distribution gap continues to grow larger over the next two or three decades?

2. How can increased economic growth possibly help to narrow the gap between rich and poor, or at least prevent it from becoming worse? Why didn't that happen in the 1980s, when the gap widened despite economic growth?

3. Would you favor direct-income subsidies to poor families from the federal government as a means of closing the gap? Why or why not?

4. Some observers of American society argue that there will always be a sizable gap between rich and poor. Therefore, the federal government should simply adopt a policy of "benign neglect." Do you agree or disagree? Why? Isn't the threat of poverty an incentive to work?

Theme C   The Politics of Health Care Policy

Instructor References

James Morone, ed., *National Health Reform*. Durham, NC: Duke University Press, 1994.

Howard M. Leichter, "The States and Health Care Policy: Taking the Lead," in Howard M. Leichter, ed., *Health Policy Reform in America*. Armonk, NY: M. E. Sharpe, 1992.

Michael Reagan, *Curing the Crisis: Options for America's Healthcare*. Boulder, CO: Westview Press, 1992.

Cindy Toth-Jajich and Burns Roper, "Americans' Views on Health Care: A Study in Contradictions," *Health Affairs* (Winter 1990): 149–157.

Summary

The politics of health care policy exhibits the importance of how an issue is defined. President Clinton encountered this dilemma in attempting to formulate a health reform policy that provides universal coverage while also containing costs. The program, prepared by the Task Force on National Health Care headed by Hillary Rodham Clinton, proposed placing one-seventh of the economy under federal regulation by requiring every employer to provide health insurance. To sell the program to the public, President Clinton sought to identify his reform package with majoritarian politics in which everyone would benefit. This strategy ran into a roadblock: most Americans were happy with their health insurance. Clinton could not rally support by approaching health care as a variety of client politics since many of the uninsured (the client group) were not considered sufficiently deserving of such assistance but rather were perceived as marginal members of society.

As with Social Security, majoritarian politics makes the most sense for convincing the public to embrace health care reform because it has the advantage of appealing to the widest base of potential support. President Clinton achieved this goal simply by redefining the terms of the debate. Instead of focusing on the necessity for revising the health care system, Clinton transformed the issue into one of personal security by making people contemplate what would happen to them if they lost their insurance. This possibility was a serious concern for many Americans in light of the uncertain economy. Yet success is not guaranteed merely by framing an issue as a majoritarian policy. President Clinton still confronted a difficult battle, even within his own party, over health care reform because the politics of majoritarian policy cuts both ways. If everyone not only benefits but also *pays* for the program, the President has to persuade the public that the costs do not exceed the benefits. It is not surprising, therefore, that the programs offered in competition to the president's take aim at the cost factor. President Clinton has the politics he wants but that is only the first step in the policy-making process.

Data and Perspectives for Analysis

A. Attitudes on Health Care

Any health care program that denies Americans the opportunity to select their own doctor is probably doomed to failure. The reason is that Americans trust their own doctor but not those of other people. What is remarkable is that public opinion has remained relatively stable despite all the attention on health care reform in recent years. There are clear parameters on the type of health care reform that the American public is willing to tolerate. Have your students examine the data below and discuss the kind of health care system that can be legitimately attempted in the United States.

Table 1

Personal Satisfaction with Health Care Received from Your Doctor

Year	Satisfied	Dissatisfied
1978	84%	15%
1982	88%	12%
1986	87%	12%
1990	88%	10%
1993	89%	8%

Table 2

Public Concern with Health Care Experiences of Others

Issue	1982	1987	1993
Doctors are too interested in making money	60%	56%	69%
Most doctors spend enough time with their patients	46%	36%	31%
People are beginning to lose fath in doctors	62%	NA	70%

Source: Adapted from Lawrence R. Jacobs and Robert Y. Shapiro, "Questioning the Conventional Wisdom on Public Opinion Toward Health Reform," *PS: Political Science & Politics* (June 1994): p. 209.

B. Local Governments and the AIDs Crisis

The AIDs crisis is probably the most explosive health care issue today. Public attitudes have been widely explored, but little is known about how government officials react to people with the disease. Should the public expect more understanding from officials charged with carrying out the law? Have your students examine the data and discuss the implications for public policy. The survey pertains to city managers and mayors.

Question	Disagree	Neutral/ Undecided	Agree
Discrimination in the workplace against HIV/AIDs-infected employees should be prohibited	21.4%	17.0%	61.6%
HIV/AIDs-infected workers should be discharged	76.5%	14.4%	9.0%
The City should not hire HIV/AIDs infected people, regardless of their ability to perform on the job	52.1%	20.1%	27.8%
The City has a right to collect information about a worker's health condition	11.6%	7.8%	80.6%

Source: Adapted from James D. Slack, *AIDs and the Public Work Force: Local Government Preparedness in Managing the Epidemic.* Tuscaloosa, AL: University of Alabama Press, 1991, p. 74.

Abstract 1 for Theme C

Should health care be rationed to save money for people who can be saved rather than spending it on hopeless cases? Dennis J. Palumbo (*Public Policy in America: Government in Action,* 2nd ed., New York: Harcourt Brace, 1994, pp. 175–177) provides an argument against the movement toward rationing. The issue, according to Palumbo, is easily framed: "When we consider that those over sixty-five years old comprise about 12 percent of the population but consume about a third of all health care expenditures, it is no wonder that some begin to question where the limited amount of money should be spent." Palumbo criticizes supporters of rationing for "placing concerns about collective well-being over individual rights." But that is not the real problem. Palumbo is most disturbed about "who shall decide which groups, or which types of health care will be supported." The danger is that vulnerable groups like the severely retarded or chronic schizophrenics will be the victims who are denied needed care.

The debate should not be about rationing, Palumbo argues, but about limiting the total amount spent on health care. Rationing will inevitably lead to exclusion, especially of the poor. Palumbo illustrates his point by examining Oregon's rationing system.

> In Oregon, the state first figures out how much money it can spend on health care for the poor and then decides what services will be bought. A commission made up of doctors, social workers, and health care advocates lists the total number of health services that might be provided. These are priced and ranked by a mix of social values and actuarial statistics. The total number of people below the poverty line who fall into certain categories received a standard package of doctor and hospital care and medication, which determines where the line is drawn regarding which illnesses will be treated and which not. In 1991, the line was drawn at swelling and esophagus. All conditions below that line would not be treated. . . . The plan has been criticized as making the poor accept rationing, whereas others do not. However, it also is defended on the grounds that it increases access to health services for groups that previously had little or none.

The reality is that rationing already exists for most Americans in the form of "managed care" systems, the dominant form of health care today which determine what treatments are covered and how long hospital stays can last. Yet Palumbo cautions against this trend for a simple reason: "there is no systematic method of making rationing decisions and there is some doubt that one can be developed."

18

Civil Liberties

Overview and Objectives

This chapter surveys quite a number of pressure points that have developed in the American political system regarding the liberties of individuals and the government's involvement in protecting or restricting those liberties. Included among these pressure points are national security, federal versus state enforcement of rights, First Amendment freedoms, and criminal law. After reading and reviewing the material in this chapter the student should be able to do each of the following:

1. Discuss the relationship of the Bill of Rights to the concept of democratic rule of the majority, and give examples of tension between majority rule and minority rights. Explain how the politics of civil liberties may at times become a mass issue, and offer several examples.

2. Describe the conflicts that have arisen between those who claim First Amendment rights and those who are in favor of sedition laws that might restrict freedom of speech. Explain how the Supreme Court attempts to balance competing interests. Describe the various "tests" that the Court has applied.

3. Explain how the structure of the federal system affects the application of the Bill of Rights. How has the Supreme Court used the Fourteenth Amendment to expand coverage in the federal system? Discuss changing conceptions of the due-process clause of the Fourteenth Amendment.

4. List the categories under which the Supreme Court may classify "speech." Explain the distinction between "protected" and "unprotected" speech and name the various forms of expression that are not protected under the First Amendment. Describe the test used by the Court to decide the circumstances under which freedom of expression may be qualified.

5. State what the Supreme Court decided in *Miranda* v. *Arizona,* and explain why that case illustrates how the Court operates in most such due-process cases.

6. Analyze why the resolution of civil liberties issues involves "politics" as well as "law." Discuss the political factors that influence the Supreme Court when it decides fundamental civil liberties issues.

Chapter Outline with Keyed-in Resources

I. The politics of civil liberties
   A. The objectives of the Framers

1. Limited federal powers
2. Constitution: a list of "do's," not "do nots"
3. Bill of Rights: specific "do nots"
   a. Not intended to affect states

A major justification used by the Supreme Court for not applying the Bill of Rights to the states is the wording of the First Amendment, which is addressed to Congress. Hence, the Court concluded, the Bill of Rights was never intended to curtail the behavior of state governments (*Barron v. Baltimore*, 1833).

      b. A limitation on popular rule
II. Politics, culture, and civil liberties (THEME A: THE POLITICS OF CIVIL LIBERTIES)
  A. Liberties become a major issue for three reasons
  B. Rights in conflict: Bill of Rights contains competing rights
    1. *Sheppard* case (free press versus fair trial)

The famous criminal attorney F. Lee Bailey was an unknown novice when he represented Dr. Sheppard, who was charged with murdering his wife. This case established Bailey's career.

    2. *New York Times* and Pentagon Papers (common defense versus free press)
    3. Kunz anti-Jewish speeches (free speech versus public order)
    4. Struggles over rights same pattern as interest-group politics
  C. Policy entrepreneurs—most successful during crises; especially war, by arousing people
    1. Sedition Act of 1789, during French Revolution
    2. Espionage and Sedition Acts of World War I
    3. Smith Act of World War II
    4. Internal Security Act of 1950, Korean War
    5. Communist Control Act of 1954—McCarthy era
    6. 1968 law on inciting riots—ghetto riots, Vietnam
  D. Cultural conflicts
    1. Original settlement by white European Protestants produced Americanism
    2. Waves of immigration brought new cultures, conflicts
      a. Jews offended by creches at Christmas
      b. English-speakers prefer monolingual schools
    3. Differences even within given cultural tradition
III. Interpreting and applying the First Amendment (THEME B: FIRST AMENDMENT RIGHTS)
  A. Speech and national security (ADDITIONAL LECTURE TOPIC B-1)
    1. Original Blackstone view: no prior press censorship
    2. Sedition Act of 1789 followed Blackstone view
    3. By 1917–1919, Congress defines limits of expression
      a. Treason, insurrection, forcible resistance
      b. Upheld in *Schenck* via test of "clear and present danger"
      c. Author Holmes dissents, saying test not met
    4. Fourteenth Amendment "due process" originally not applied to states

The Supreme Court initially hesitated to use the due process clause of the Fourteenth Amendment to "incorporate" the Bill of Rights against state governments because the Fifth Amendment also includes a due process provision. If the Fourteenth Amendment was meant to apply the Bill of Rights to the states, the Court reasoned that a second due process clause would not have been added to the amendment since one already existed.

      a. *Gitlow* elicits "fundamental personal rights"
    5. Supreme Court moves toward more free expression after WWI
      a. But Communists convicted under Smith Act under "gravity of evil"
      b. By 1957: test of "calculated to incite"

In 1957, the Supreme Court made an important distinction between advocacy of a belief versus advocacy of an action. The First Amendment provides complete protection to the advocacy of beliefs. Only when a person advocates an illegal action does the First Amendment not protect speech.

    c. By 1969 (*Brandenburg*): "imminent" unlawful act
    d. 1977: American Nazi march in Skokie, Illinois, held lawful
    e. "Hate" speech permissible but not "hate crime"
  B. What is speech?
    1. Some forms of speech not fully protected; four kinds
    2. Libel: written statement defaming another by false statement

Contrary to popular belief, most libel suits are unsuccessful. A study by the law school at Stanford University discovered that only 10 percent of libel suits succeed if reversals by appellate courts are taken into account.

    a. Oral statement: "slander"
    b. Variable jury awards
    c. "Actual malice" needed for public figures

The Supreme Court permits each state to establish libel standards for private persons. Most states use "negligence" in place of the "actual malice" standard for public figures. Negligence means that a person had "doubts" about the truth of a statement that defamed another.

    3. Obscenity
      a. Twelve years of decisions; no lasting definition
      b. 1973 definition: patently offensive by community standards of average person
      c. Balancing competing claims remains problem
      d. Localities decide whether to tolerate pornography but must comply with strict rules
      e. Protection extended: nude dancing only marginally protected
      f. Indianapolis statute: pornography degrading but court disagreed
      g. Zoning ordinances upheld
    4. Symbolic speech
      a. Acts that convey a political message: e.g., flag burning, draft card burning
      b. Not generally protected
      c. Exception is flag burning: restriction of free speech
 IV. Who is a person?
  A. Corporations, etc. usually have same rights as individuals
    1. Boston bank, anti-abortion group, California utility
    2. More restrictions on commercial speech
      a. Regulation must be narrowly tailored and serve public interest
      b. Yet ads have some constitutional protection
    3. Young people may have fewer rights
      a. Hazelwood: school newspaper can be restricted
 V. Church and state (ADDITIONAL LECTURE TOPIC B-2)

The free exercise and establishment clauses occasionally conflict with one another, when obeying one clause requires transgressing the other. For example, students who oppose exposure to "worldly" things pose a problem in public schools. Exempting the students from activities such as watching a video would award preference to a religion, a practice forbidden by the establishment clause, whereas forcing the students to view the video contravenes the free exercise clause. What to do? The Supreme Court typically favors the free exercise clause in such conflicts—in this case, exempting the students.

  A. The free exercise clause
    1. Relatively clear meaning: no state interference similar to speech
      a. Law may not impose special burdens on religion
      b. But no religious exemptions from laws binding all

Some free exercise decisions, however, do exempt people from legal liability when disobeying laws of general application. In *Wisconsin* v. *Yoder*, the Supreme Court allowed parents of the Amish faith not to comply with a state compulsory education statute requiring children to attend school until age 16.

        c. Some cases difficult to settle
           (1) Conscientious objection to war, military service
           (2) Refusal to work Saturdays; unemployment compensation
           (3) Refusal to send children to school beyond eighth grade
    B. The establishment clause
        1. Jefferson's view: "wall of separation"
        2. Congress at the time: simply "no national religion"
        3. Ambiguous phrasing of First Amendment

The ambiguity of the establishment clause largely stems from one word: "respecting." The clause does not simply forbid the government from establishing a state religion. Rather, it forbids the government from passing any law "respecting" an establishment of religion. The word "respecting" suggests that any law concerning religion falls within the scope of the establishment clause.

        4. Supreme Court interpretation: "wall of separation"
           a. 1947 New Jersey case
           b. Later struck: school prayer, "creationism," in-school released time, benediction at graduation
           c. But allowed: some kinds of aid to parochial schools
           d. Three-part test for constitutional aid

The three-part test used for determining violations of the establishment clause is a subject of controversy. The Supreme Court has on several occasions declared that these tests are not the exclusive means for interpreting the establishment clause. Yet the Court has not agreed on any alternative. Nonetheless, the days of the tripartite test are surely numbered.

           (1) Secular purpose
           (2) Neither advances nor inhibits religion
           (3) No excessive government entanglement
           e. Recent departures: Nativity scenes, etc.
  VI. Crime and due process
    A. The exclusionary rule (THEME C: SEARCHES AND SEIZURES)
        1. Most nations punish police misconduct apart from the criminal trial
        2. United States punishes it by excluding improperly obtained evidence
        3. Supreme Court rulings
           a. 1949: declined to use exclusionary rule
           b. 1961: changed, adopted it in *Mapp* case

Evidence obtained in violation of the exclusionary rule is not automatically barred from trial. While such evidence cannot be used to convict, it can enter the trial to impeach the credibility of the defendant if he or she takes the stand.

    B. Search and seizure
        1. When can "reasonable" searches of individuals be made?
           a. With a properly obtained search warrant with probable cause
           b. Incident to an arrest
        2. *What* can police search incident to an arrest?
           a. The individual being arrested
           b. Things in plain view

The "plain view" doctrine requires that evidence be found "inadvertently." If police believe contraband exists, a warrant should be obtained. The police must simply stumble across evidence for the plain view doctrine to apply. But in 1990 the Court removed this restriction.

           c. Things under the immediate control of the individual

3. What of an arrest while driving?
    a. Answer changes almost yearly
    b. Court attempts to protect a "reasonable expectation of privacy"
    c. Privacy in body and home but not from government supervisor
4. Testing for drugs and AIDS
    a. Mandatory AIDS testing called for, not yet in place
    b. Government drug testing now in courts but private testing OK
    c. Supreme Court: some testing is permissible
        (1) Law enforcement and railroad employees
        (2) Random sobriety checks on drivers
        (3) Key: concern for public safety or national security
C. Confessions and self-incrimination
    1. Constitutional ban originally against torture, etc.
    2. Extension of rights in 1960s
        a. *Escobedo*
        b. *Miranda* case—"Miranda rules" to prove voluntary confession

Miranda warnings must be given if two conditions are satisfied. First, a person must be detained. Neither a formal arrest nor custody is required. A person is "detained" if unable to "come and go" as he or she pleases. Second, a person must be questioned. Statements made without police questioning are admissible in court despite the absence of Miranda warnings.

D. Relaxing the exclusionary rule
    1. Positions taken on the rule
        a. *Any* evidence should be admissible
        b. Rule had become too technical to work
        c. Rule a vital safeguard
    2. Supreme Court moves to adopt second position

Important Terms

*clear-and-present-danger test A legal interpretation that reconciled two views of the First Amendment right of free speech, the first that Congress could not pass any law to restrict speech and the second that it could punish harms caused by speech. Congress could only punish speech that created a "clear and present danger" of bringing about the actions that Congress is authorized to prevent.

Communist Control Act A federal law enacted in 1954 which declared the Communist party to be part of a conspiracy to overthrow the government.

*due process clause of the Fourteenth Amendment A constitutional amendment ratified in 1868 that has been used by the Supreme Court to prevent state governments from infringing "fundamental personal rights," such as freedom of speech.

Espionage Act and Sedition Act Federal laws enacted in 1917 and 1918 which made it a crime to utter false statements that would interfere with the military, to use the mails to advocate treason or resistance to laws, or to express any disloyalty intending to incite resistance to the war effort.

*establishment clause One of two First Amendment clauses dealing with religion. It forbids government involvement in religion, even on a nonpreferential basis. It is designed to erect a wall of separation between church and state.

*exclusionary rule A rule of criminal procedure which holds that evidence gathered in violation of the Constitution cannot be used in trial.

*freedom of expression One of two parts of the First Amendment protecting freedom of speech, of the press, and of assembly, and the right to petition the government.

*freedom of religion One of two parts of the First Amendment protecting the free exercise of religion and the prohibition against an establishment of religion.

*free exercise clause One of two First Amendment clauses dealing with religion. It forbids Congress from prohibiting individuals' practice of religion. In general, the Supreme Court allows people to practice their religion so long as they do not cause serious harm to others.

*good-faith exception A modification of the exclusionary rule allowing evidence in a trial even though it was obtained without following proper legal procedures if the police believed a defective warrant was valid when executed.

hate crime The imposition of a tougher sentence against a person convicted of hurting someone whose behavior was motivated by racial or ethnic hate.

Internal Security Act A federal law enacted in 1950 which required members of the Communist party to register with the government.

*libel A form of speech not given automatic constitutional protection, consisting of any written statement defaming the character of another person with a falsehood. Public figures must also prove "actual malice" exists.

*McCarthyism An allegation against a person who unfairly impugns the motives, attacks the patriotism, or violates the rights of individuals. The term originated from the unsubstantiated charges by Senator Joseph McCarthy in 1950 against people working for various government agencies in claiming they were communists.

Miranda warnings Informing a person taken into custody of the right to remain silent, the right to have a lawyer present during questioning, and the right to consult a lawyer without charge if unable to afford one. The requirement that the Miranda warning be delivered to detainees is a protection derived from the Fifth Amendment's right not to incriminate oneself. Police failure to give the warning makes any confession presumed to be involuntary.

obscenity A form of speech not given automatic constitutional protection, defined as a work that, taken as a whole, appeals to the prurient interest as judged by community standards, that depicts sexual activity in a patently offensive manner, and that lacks literary, artistic, political, or scientific value.

*prior restraint Government censorship of the press in which a newspaper is told in advance what it can publish.

*probable cause A condition that must be satisfied before a judge can issue a search warrant. It requires that a judge must be persuaded by the police that good reason exists to believe that a crime has been committed and that the evidence bearing on that crime will be found at a certain location.

public figure A person of public stature, such as a celebrity or elected official, who must prove "actual malice" to win a libel suit.

*search warrant An order from a judge authorizing the search of a place. The warrant must describe what is to be searched and seized and is issued only after a judge is convinced by police that probable cause exists to believe that a crime has been committed and that evidence bearing on the crime will be found at a certain location.

Sedition Act A federal law enacted in 1798 which made it a crime to express anything false, scandalous, and malicious about officers of the federal government or to excite hatred against the government itself.

Smith Act A federal law enacted in 1940 which made it illegal to advocate the overthrow of the government by force or violence.

*symbolic speech A form of speech not given automatic constitutional protection, involving an illegal act meant to convey a political message.

*wall-of-separation principle An interpretation of the establishment clause embraced by the Supreme Court that allows no government involvement with religion, even on a nonpreferential basis.

Theme A The Politics of Civil Liberties

Instructor References

Henry J. Abraham, *Freedom and the Courts: Civil Rights and Civil Liberties in the U.S.* 5th ed. New York: Oxford University Press, 1988. An excellent overview of the entire topic.

Robert Bork, *The Tempting of America: The Political Seduction of the Law.* New York: Free Press, 1990.

John Brigham, *Civil Liberties and American Democracy*. Washington, DC: Congressional Quarterly Press, 1984. A good analysis of Americans' fundamental liberties and how the Supreme Court guarantees those liberties.

Herbert M. Levine and Jean Edward Smith, *Civil Liberties and Civil Rights Debated*. Englewood Cliffs, NJ: Prentice-Hall, 1988.

James Morton Smith, *Freedom's Fetters: The Alien and Sedition Laws and American Civil Liberties*. Ithaca, NY: Cornell University Press, 1956. Good historical treatment of the evolution of civil liberties.

David O'Brien, *Storm Center: The Supreme Court in American Politics*. New York: Norton, 1990.

Summary

Generally, we would not think that the rights of small minorities would need special protection. They ought to be protected by the same process of "client politics" that protects the subsidies of milk producers and shipping interests. But sometimes conflicts over civil liberties arise between small groups, for example, when Nazi party members wish to march in a heavily Jewish suburb. Sometimes the government itself is one of these groups, as in the Pentagon Papers case. This, of course, is interest-group politics. But civil liberties may also become an issue demanding political action when a political entrepreneur can dramatize a real or imagined threat posed by some minority to commonly held values. This situation has happened only a few times in American history: with the *Sedition Act* of the late eighteenth century; the *Smith Act* of 1940, which was used against communists in the 1950s; and the era of urban riots and Vietnam in the late 1960s.

In each of these cases, either war or the threat of war provided the emotional energy for the issue. In each case, the situation arose suddenly and disappeared just as suddenly within a few years. In most cases, the restrictions imposed on free expression have been fewer in each succeeding crisis. The Supreme Court, which has defined the limits of free expression throughout the twentieth century, has functioned as a delayed-action brake, first accepting efforts to limit expression and then, after the crisis has died down, overruling them. The result has been increasing protection afforded to political expression. For example, the Espionage Act was used to prosecute several radical speakers and pamphleteers during the 1920s. The Court generally upheld these prosecutions but developed the "clear and present danger" test. In the 1950s, the Court first upheld the prosecution of Communists under this test, but then went to great pains to distinguish between philosophical belief (which could not be punished) and advocacy (which could). By 1969, in the case of Clarence Brandenburg, even advocacy of an illegal act was held to be protected unless it was likely to incite imminent lawless action.

The general tendency of the Supreme Court has been to expand the protections of the Bill of Rights. This process began slowly. In *Barron v. Baltimore* (1833), the Court ruled that the Bill of Rights did not apply to the states: "These Amendments contain no expression indicating an intention to apply them to State governments. This Court cannot so apply them." This situation was not to change until the adoption of the Fourteenth Amendment in 1868, which forbade states to "deprive any person of life, liberty, or property, without due process of law." The Supreme Court would later use the word *liberty* in the due process clause to "incorporate" provisions of the Bill Rights and apply them to state governments. But the Court, even today, has not incorporated every provision of the Bill of Rights. Instead, it adopted a practice in *Palko* v. *Connecticut* (1937) called "selective incorporation," through which only those provisions involving principles of justice "so rooted in the traditions and conscience of our people as to be ranked fundamental" are applied to the states. Once a federal right is incorporated, however, state laws are held to the same standards as federal laws in relation to that right. This does not mean that state courts have no role to play in the area of basic liberties. The federal Bill of Rights establishes the minimum level of individual rights that states must observe. They can always give additional freedoms to their citizens. As the Court itself commented, its rulings "do not affect the State's power to impose higher standards . . . than the Federal Constitution if it chooses to do so." Thus the Georgia Supreme Court held in 1992 that nude dancing is a form of protected speech under the state's constitution, despite the U.S. Supreme Court's ruling to the contrary with respect to the First Amendment.

Discussion Questions

1. What, if anything, was *wrong* with the Sedition Act? Should the government not have the right to punish false statements made against it? Did the act provide substantial protection for the defendant? Pay close attention to the exact wording of the act and to how it was actually enforced.

2. What did the Espionage Act of 1917 and the Sedition Act of 1918 attempt to outlaw? Were they *broader* or *narrower* in their prohibitions than the Sedition Act of 1798? Is it *reasonable* for a government to attempt to outlaw the things proscribed in the 1917–1918 legislation? How were these acts enforced—in a way consistent with the language of the acts or in some other way? Why do you suppose the acts of 1917 and 1918 were not repealed after the end of the war?

3. What did the Smith Act of 1940 attempt to outlaw? Was it broader or narrower in its prohibitions than the Espionage and Sedition Acts? Discuss particularly the "membership clause" in this context.

4. Is a major "backlash" against civil liberties, which might involve legislation such as the Smith Act or the Espionage and Sedition Acts, possible in the United States today? Would the Supreme Court stand in the way of such a backlash? Would public opinion be receptive to such legislation? If you think that such a backlash is possible, what might bring it about?

Data and Perspectives for Analysis

It is sometimes surprising for students to learn that the entire Bill of Rights does not apply to state governments. In other words, some provisions of the Bill of Rights can be violated by the states. This is a consequence of the doctrine of "selective incorporation." On the following page is a list of the rights that have and have not been incorporated.

Provision	Case Incorporating Right
First Amendment	
Free exercise	*Cantwell* v. *Connecticut* (1940)
Establishment of religion	*Everson* v. *Board of Education* (1947)
Free speech	*Gitlow* v. *New York* (1925)
Free press	*Near* v. *Minnesota* (1931)
Assembly	*DeJonge* v. *Oregon* (1937)
Petition	*Hague* v. *CIO* (1937)
Second Amendment	
Bear arms	Not Incorporated
Third Amendment	
Quartering soldiers	Not Incorporated
Fourth Amendment	
Search and seizure	*Wolf* v. *Colorado* (1949)
Fifth Amendment	
Double jeopardy	*Benton* v. *Maryland* (1969)
Self-incrimination	*Malloy* v. *Hogan* (1964)
Just compensation	*Chicago, Burlington & Q.RR* v. *Chicago* (1897)
Grand jury	Not Incorporated
Sixth Amendment	
Speedy trial	*Klopfer* v. *North Carolina* (1967)
Public trial	In re *Oliver* (1948)
Impartial trial	*Parker* v. *Gladden* (1966)
Notice	*Cole* v. *Arkansas* (1947)
Confrontation	*Pointer* v. *Texas* (1965)
Compulsory process	*Washington* v. *Texas* (1967)
Counsel	*Gideon* v. *Wainwright* (1963)
Seventh Amendment	
Civil jury	Not Incorporated
Eighth Amendment	
Cruel & unusual punishment	*Robinson* v. *California* (1962)
Excessive fines & bails	Not Incorporated

Adapted from: Lee Epstein and Thomas Walker, *Constitutional Law for a Changing America: Rights, Liberties, and Justice.* Washington, DC: Congressional Quarterly, 1992, p. 32.

Theme B   First Amendment Rights

Summary

In the 1960s, the Supreme Court began broadening the way in which constitutional rights are interpreted. In the area of free expression, the First Amendment now guarantees virtually any form of communication, although several exceptions exist. First, *libel*—false statements that harm a person's reputation—remains unprotected, but it has been made more difficult to prove in certain situations. Public figures must prove "actual malice," an extremely high burden in which a defamed person must establish that a statement was uttered either in the knowledge that it was false or with reckless disregard. In 1991, the Court went so far as to exclude fabricated quotations from the definition of libel so long as the misquote did not "materially change" the meaning of what was actually said. *Obscenity* is the second form of speech not protected under the First Amendment. The problem is that it is not entirely clear what constitutes pornography for constitutional purposes. The absence of a precise definition of obscenity has led to anomalies, such as the rap group 2-Live Crew being acquitted of pornography in Broward County, Florida, despite the conviction of a record store owner for selling albums in the same county that contained the same songs. The Court's current *Miller* test of obscenity hardly articulates a satisfactory standard for banning a particular kind of speech.

The third variety of speech rendered at least partially unprotected under the First Amendment is called *symbolic speech*. Expression of this kind typically involves some type of behavior designed to communicate an idea. Speech expressed through conduct is frequently referred to as "speech plus," the plus being the conduct. Activities considered symbolic speech include demonstrating and marching, pouring blood on army recruiting records, and wearing a black armband as a protest. Such speech is not wholly without constitutional safeguard, but it is entitled to a lesser degree of protection. In the words of Justice Goldburg, "We emphatically reject the notion . . . that the First and Fourteenth Amendments afford the same kind of freedom to those who would communicate ideas by conduct . . . as these amendments afford to those who communicate ideas by pure speech" (*Cox v. Louisiana (I)*, 1965). Thomas Tedford summarizes the Supreme Court's position in determining whether behavior is considered "symbolic speech" in the following way: (a) the speaker must have an intent to convey a message; (b) the audience must be likely to understand the message; and (c) the speech must make a contribution to the body of knowledge. The Court has allowed the government more latitude in regulating the conduct associated with symbolic speech than the expressive component itself. Thus the government can punish the burning of a draft card as a form of protest, since its goal in making the regulation is not to suppress the idea being communicated but to defend the national security. On the other hand, the government cannot forbid the burning of the American flag as a form of protest since the behavior does not threaten a breach of peace, making the suppression of an idea as the only purpose behind the law.

The fourth type of expression lacking complete constitutional protection is *commercial speech*. At first, the Supreme Court placed commercial speech entirely outside the First Amendment (*Valentine v. Chrestensen*, 1942) but eventually provided it limited coverage: "Advertising," according to Justice Harry Blackmun in *Bigelow v. Virginia* (1975), is "not stripped of all First Amendment protection" so long as it is truthful and of value to the public. It is only when advertising is either deceptive or involves an illegal or harmful product that commercial speech is subject to total suppression.

The religion clauses of the First Amendment are caught in a similar web of confusion. The free exercise clause was initially treated, in the words of Leo Pfeffer, as a "stepchild" of the free speech clause. Until the 1960s, cases raising free exercise claims were typically decided on the basis of principles of free speech. In *Sherbert v. Verner* (1963), the Court gave the free exercise clause an independent identity and required the government to provide a "compelling interest" to justify any burden on the practice of religion. The confusion enters through the manner in which this tough standard was implemented, with the Court almost always deciding against the free exercise claim. In 1990, a fatal blow to *Sherbert* was rendered in *Employment Division v. Smith*, in which the "compelling interest" test was held inappropriate to criminal conduct. People can no longer rely on the free exercise clause to exempt their behavior from a law of "general applicability" that is not designed as an attack on a particular religion. The Religious Freedom Restoration Act returned to the *Sherbert* standard, displacing *Smith*.

Many of the same problems haunt the establishment clause, which, in the words of Thomas Jefferson, is intended to erect a "wall of separation" between church and state. It is generally agreed that the clause forbids the creation of an official religion and restricts the government from becoming involved in church matters, even on a nonpreferential basis. Beyond that, the meaning of the establishment clause remains elusive. The Court in *Lemon v. Kurtzman* (1971) articulated a three-part test to determine violations of the establishment clause: (1) government policy must have a "primary purpose" that is secular; (2) a government policy must have a "primary effect" that neither advances nor inhibits religion; and (3) a government policy must not result in an excessive entanglement between church and state. These tests have produced an unparalleled amount of uncertainty, to the point where some courts have openly refused to abide by the *Lemon* standards, while others have distorted their meaning to reach a desired conclusion. Thus the ambiguity of both religion clauses awaits further judicial clarification.

Discussion Questions

1. Another area of speech not given automatic constitutional protection is "fighting words": words that would provoke a reasonable person to fight. But what if the words are true (unlike libel)? Should the First Amendment permit the punishment of truth? Could blowing cigarette smoke in someone's face constitute a form of symbolic speech? Should fighting words be protected as a form of speech?

2. Why did Justice Black say that the right to privacy was an "ambiguous concept" that could expand or shrink to fit the views of the judges using it? Consider each of the following hypothetical laws. Which could be considered a violation of the right of privacy and which could not?

    a. A law outlawing prostitution
    b. A law enforcing the concept of common-law marriage by requiring couples who live together to accept the same financial and other responsibilities as officially married couples
    c. A law requiring gun registration
    d. A law outlawing child abuse
    e. A law setting a minimum wage for maids and cleaners
    f. A law requiring each household to have certain sorts of fire alarms and fire extinguishers
    g. A law allowing the arrest of drunken drivers, even if they are not observed driving recklessly or causing an accident
    h. A law making the use of marijuana a crime
    i. A law making the use of saccharin a crime
    j. A law outlawing homosexual acts between consenting adults

3. What is the Supreme Court's current definition of obscenity? Is this definition clear? Could it guide a publisher who wished to publish a certain book but who wondered whether it was "obscene"? If "pornography" cannot be clearly defined, what does this suggest about who will be prosecuted for selling it, and why?

4. The free exercise clause protects religious behavior. But what is a valid "religion"? Are the Moonies protected in the exercise of their beliefs? What about members of a Satanic group? How can courts distinguish fraudulent religious claims from legitimate ones? For example, Oral Roberts said Jesus Christ appeared to him as a nine-hundred foot figure with the request that people contribute money to Roberts in order to cure cancer; is this a fraud or not?

Data and Perspectives for Analysis

A. Search Warrant Requirements

The principal justification for the suppression of pornography is that exposure to such material leads to sexually deviant behavior, rape in particular. In a 1985 opinion poll, 73 percent of the public agreed with the statement that pornography leads to rape. Yet most research tends to challenge the validity of this correlation (e.g., President's National Committee on Obscenity and Pornography, 1970).

The Supreme Court is not ignorant of the tenuous connection between pornography and rape. To quote Chief Justice Burger in *Paris Adult Theatre* v. *Slaton* (1973): Even though "there is no conclusive proof of a connection between antisocial behavior and obscene material, the legislature of Georgia could quite reasonably determine that such a connection does exist." Is this argument persuasive? Doesn't the argument amount to the following reasoning: since no proof exists that green mice are on the moon, the government could conclude that such mice are present on the moon? This argument had been earlier rejected by Justice Marshal in *Stanley* v. *Georgia* (1969): " . . . the State may no more prohibit mere possession of [obscenity] on the ground that it may lead to antisocial conduct than it may prohibit possession of chemistry books on the ground that they may lead to the manufacture of homemade spirits." Is Marshall more convincing?

Consider the facts:

- 82 percent of rapes are preplanned, not spontaneous acts of sexual passion (Herman, p. 42)
- 85 percent of rapes are not by a stranger but by an acquaintance (*ibid*)
- Most rapists have normal psychological profiles and lifestyles except for a high sense of inferiority that tends to manifest itself in aggression (Amir, p. 314)
- Rapes are frequently accompanied by ridicule and humiliation of the victim (Brownmiller, p. 195)

Do these facts suggest that rape is a product of sexual lust triggered by pornography? Most research takes a contrary position, calling rape a crime of violence. Check the following resources.

Susan Brownmiller. *Against Our Will: Men, Women, and Rape.* New York: Simon & Schuster, 1975.

Dianne Herman. "The Rape Culture." In *Seeing Ourselves,* edited by John and Nijole Benokraitis. Englewood Cliffs, NJ: Prentice-Hall, 1989.

Gary LaFree. *Rape and Criminal Justice: The Social Construction of Sexual Assault.* Belmont, CA: Wadsworth, 1989.

Menachem Amir. *Patterns in Forcible Rape.* Chicago: University of Chicago Press, 1971.

Additional Lecture Topics

B-1. First Amendment Rights

Lee C. Bollinger, *Images of a Free Press.* Chicago: University of Chicago Press, 1991.

Andrea L. Bonnicksen, *Civil Rights and Liberties.* Palo Alto, CA: Mayfield, 1982. See Chapters 2–4 on the First Amendment.

Robert F. Cushman, *Leading Constitutional Decisions.* 17th ed. Englewood Cliffs, NJ: Prentice-Hall, 1987. See Chapter 6 for discussion of eight seminal cases affecting First Amendment rights.

David M. O'Brien, *The Public's Right to Know: The Supreme Court and the First Amendment.* New York: Praeger, 1982.

Richard Polenberg, *Fighting Faiths.* New York: Knopf, 1987.

B-2. Church-State Separation

Robert S. Alley, ed., *The Supreme Court on Church and State.* New York: Oxford University Press, 1988. Up-to-date coverage of the main cases relating to the establishment and free exercise clauses.

Derek Davis, *Original Intent: Chief Justice Rehnquist and the Course of American Church/State Relations.* Buffalo: Prometheus Books, 1991.

Robert Booth Fowler, *Religion and Politics in America.* Metuchen, NJ: Scarecrow Press, 1985. Good overview of the subject.

Leonard Levy, *The Establishment Clause: Religion and the First Amendment.* New York: Macmillan, 1986.

Richard Morgan, *The Supreme Court and Religion.* New York: Free Press, 1975. Emphasizes the sources of conflict inherent in church-state relations.

Frank Sorauf, *Wall of Separation.* Princeton: Princeton University Press, 1976. An extensive analysis of the political-legal context of church-state lawsuits.

Paul J. Weber and Dennis A. Gilbert, *Private Churches and Public Money*. New York: Greenwood Press, 1981. This political dilemma is delineated fully.

Abstract 1 for Theme B

The Continuing Question of Church-State Separation

A recent case dealt with the issue of school prayer and, more specifically, an Alabama "moment-of-silence" law. The case of *Wallace v. Jaffree* "High Court Upsets Alabama Statute on School Prayer" (*New York Times*, June 5, 1985, p. 1, by Linda Greenhouse) evolved when an Alabama state law permitting public school students to have a one-minute period of silent meditation or prayer was challenged by Ishmael Jaffree, an agnostic, who objected to these "religious observances" for his children in the Mobile, Alabama, schools. An Alabama Federal District Court judge had upheld the law on the basis that the Constitution did not prevent the states from establishing an official religion (Justice Stevens, who would write the majority opinion, termed the judge's opinion "remarkable").

By a 6–3 vote, the Supreme Court overturned the Alabama law. Justice Stevens explained the Court's rationale by asserting that the Alabama law had violated the establishment clause through its deliberate attempt to "foster religious activity" in the classroom. In other words, the Alabama legislature "intended to characterize prayer as a favored practice. Such an endorsement is not consistent with the established principle that the government must pursue a course of complete neutrality toward religion." The Alabama law provided that the moment of silence could be used for meditation or *voluntary prayer*. And the legislator who had introduced the law admitted that his intention was to return prayer to the classroom.

However, the *Jaffree* ruling did not necessarily mean that "moment-of-silence" laws in twenty-five other states were all unconstitutional as well. The Court suggested that, if these laws could be identified "with the broader purpose of enabling students to choose, *without any pressure from the state*, how to use their moment of silence," then they might very well be consistent with the First Amendment. As Justice Stevens asserted, "the legislative intent to return prayer to the public schools is, of course, quite different from merely protecting every student's right to engage in voluntary prayer during an appropriate moment of silence during the school day." In a separate, concurring opinion, Justice O'Connor argued that "moment-of-silence laws in many states should pass Establishment Clause scrutiny because they do not favor the child who chooses to pray during a moment of silence over the child who chooses to meditate or reflect. It is difficult to discern a serious threat to religious liberty from a room of silent, thoughtful school children." In short, the constitutional validity of other "moment-of-silence" laws would probably be considered on a case-by-case basis.

Questions for Discussion

1. How would the three-part test disqualify the Alabama law?
2. Why does the issue of school prayer continue to be such a controversial civil liberties question?

Answer Guidelines

The Alabama law violated the "secular purpose" condition of the three-part test by being explicitly oriented toward the promotion of prayer in the public schools. Religious instruction is an integral part of America's historical heritage. To many Americans, public schools should reflect important societal and historical values—among these, religious teachings.

Abstract 2 for Theme B

Does the First Amendment Protect Pornography?

The controversy over whether pornographic materials are protected by the freedom-of-speech provision of the First Amendment to the Constitution has raged for decades. Neither a number of Supreme Court rulings nor two presidential commissions (reports were submitted in 1970 and 1986) have irrevocably resolved this issue. Hendrick Hertzberg and James C. Dobson (a member of the Meese Commission) debate the question in *Taking Sides: Clashing Views on Controversial Political Issues*, 7th ed., edited by George McKenna and Stanley Feingold (Guilford, CT: Dushkin, 1991). Hertzberg's charge of a stacked commission and fears of suppressing freedom of speech originally appeared in the *New Republic*, July 14, 1986 (pp. 246–252 in McKenna and Feingold's text). His main points were the following:

1. The Reagan-appointed Meese Commission was biased, unprofessional, underfinanced, and skewed to hear witnesses who were actually "coached" by the commission's staff to affirm the "porno-victim" thesis.

2. The Meese Commission's conclusion was that "pornography is 'harmful,' and that therefore the police powers of the state should be mobilized to suppress it" (p. 249).

3. The Commission's report "is bound to play an important part in a decentralized but wider effort to constrict personal liberty and freedom of expression." Local, self-appointed censors will be encouraged by the Meese Report (p. 250). However, the attacks made by these local groups will not cover hard-core pornography but rather men's magazines or books that treat sex in a realistic manner. (Hertzberg cites the pressure placed on 7-Eleven convenience stores to remove *Playboy* and *Penthouse* from store shelves. Government intimidation did succeed in having the chain comply.)

4. Hertzberg writes that "once it is established that indirect government pressure on magazine distributors is okay, there is no guarantee that such pressure won't be applied to publications that the reigning ideologues don't like for political reasons" (p. 251).

5. To Hertzberg, "the Meese Commission has simply failed to demonstrate that pornography constitutes a meaningful threat to the public interest" (p. 251).

Conversely, James C. Dobson, a member of the Meese Commission, argues that pornography is harmful to society (McKenna and Feingold, pp. 253–258). He argues as follows:

1. The Commission was not a biased group of conservatives, but rather a diverse assembly, which took the task of finding solutions to the pornography problem seriously. Witnesses on both sides of the pornography question were invited to testify before the commission.

2. One key recommendation was that "government should begin enforcing the obscenity laws that are already on the books . . ." (p. 254).

3. The Commission argued that the eradication of explicit material that was violent in nature was necessary to protect society. Extreme forms of pornography, especially those that demeaned or humiliated women (and went far beyond so-called normal sexuality) should be abolished as well. The same prohibition should also apply to child pornography.

4. The various "harms" that pornography produces include the perpetuation of the "rape myth" concerning women (women are falsely depicted as wanting to be assaulted), the addictiveness to pornographic materials to which some men fall prey, the effect of lewd materials on impressionable youngsters and teenagers (resulting in higher incidences of unwed pregnancy and unwanted abortions), the fact that organized crime profits immensely from the distribution of pornographic materials ($7 billion a year), the attachment of sex-related crimes to "outlets for obscenity," the dangerous impact upon public health, and the ultimate effect upon the sanctity of society and family life.

Questions for Discussion (Open-ended replies are desirable.)

1. In your opinion, is there a link between the availability of pornography and unacceptable social behavior in the United States? What are some reasons for your opinion?

2. Research the impact of the Meese Commission's findings upon public opinion. How did the Meese Commission differ in its findings from the 1970 presidential commission, which was appointed by Lyndon Johnson and made its report during the Nixon Administration?

Theme C   Searches and Seizures

Summary

Many controversial civil liberties cases occur in the area of criminal procedure, especially the Fourth Amendment's guarantee against "unreasonable searches and seizures." The wording is important. The Fourth Amendment does not forbid all searches by the government but only those that are *un*reasonable. Thus a "reasonable" search is permitted. What makes a search reasonable? A warrant. To obtain a warrant, a police officer must appear before a judge and establish "probable cause." This means that the officer must present enough evidence to convince a "reasonable" person that an illegal good is located at a particular place. If convinced, the judge will issue the warrant.

The warrant must be "reasonably specific." That is, it must clearly indicate the location to be searched and the item sought. Warrants can be executed in the absense of the occupant. However, officers do not always require a warrant to conduct a search. The text outlines the major exceptions to the warrant requirement, but the Supreme Court has recognized at least six exceptions: (1) searches conducted after an arrest; (2) plain view searches; (3) consent searches; (4) vehicle searches; (5) stop-and-frisk searches; and (6) searches pursuant to exigent circumstances.

When a person is arrested, the officer has the right to search the suspect's body for safety purposes since the criminal could either possess a weapon or destroy evidence. Aside from the body itself, the Supreme Court allows the officer to search any area within the person's "immediate control." In addition, the police can make an "inventory search" of articles in the possession of the person, including his or her car and items in the car (*Colorado v. Bertine,* 1987) if impounding the vehicle.

The second exception to the warrant requirement is known as "plain view" searches. Under this doctrine, an officer is permitted to seize evidence so long as two conditions are met. First, the officer must have the legal right to be at the location. Thus an officer in a person's home under a warrant has the right to seize any other evidence discovered during the search. Second, the police must have "probable cause" that the items observed are evidence of a crime or are contraband (*Arizona v. Hicks,* 1987). It is important to note that the plain view doctrine applies only to vision, on the assumption that no other sense has a similar degree of reliability.

The third exception to the warrant requirement occurs when a person voluntarily agrees to a search. While the police cannot coerce or trick a person into providing consent (such as lying about the possession of a warrant), an officer is under no obligation to inform the individual of the right to refuse the search. Once consent is given, nonetheless, the search can be terminated at any time and the officer must leave the premises.

The fourth exception to the warrant requirement involves searches of mobile vehicles (*Carroll v. U.S.,* 1925) because, unlike a house, they can escape with evidence before an officer can obtain a warrant. This exception applies to all vehicles, like boats, automobiles, and planes. Two factors must be satisfied to conduct such searches without a warrant. First, the officer must have probable cause to believe illegal evidence or contraband is contained in the vehicle *before* making the search. And second, the officer must have probable cause that the vehicle was about to be moved and that no opportunity existed to acquire a warrant (*Albert v. State,* 1980). The scope of the search is defined by the object being sought; the police may inspect any place the evidence could "reasonably" be located (*United States v. Ross,* 1982). Consider the following example. A sheriff in Florida decided to combat the use of Interstate 95 for the transportation of drugs by posting a sign stating that a drug search of vehicles would occur immediately ahead. Any car which made a U-turn after the sign would be stopped for probable cause of drug procession. Is this acceptable? Yes, since the U-turn created a reasonable belief of drug possession and the vehicle was moving. Nonetheless, the sign was removed after national media attention made it ineffective.

The fifth exception to the warrant requirement is known as "stop and frisk" and applies only in circumstances where reason exists to believe public safety is imperiled. The "stop and frisk" exception requires the following conditions to be met: (1) the officer must have "reasonable suspicion" that a crime is about to be committed; (2) the officer may pat down the outer clothing of the suspect in seeking a weapon; and (3) the officer may invade the suspect's clothing only upon feeling something that "reasonably" could be a weapon. If the officer finds criminal evidence that might justify an arrest, the officer may make a full search. This is true even though the mere possession of a weapon is not a crime.

The sixth—and final—exception to the warrant requirement involves exigent (emergency) circumstances. These are situations in which police do not have the time to secure a warrant before evidence is destroyed, a criminal is about to escape, or preservation of life or serious injury are at stake. A common exigent circumstance entails "hot pursuit." When a crime has been committed, the police may pursue a suspect immediately upon the commission of a crime without a warrant in hand. However, the pursuit must be "continuous and uninterrupted" in which the police are following an unbroken chain of evidence. The scope of the search is limited to places where the suspect or weapons might reasonably be found.

What if the police make an unreasonable search and seizure, violating one of the exceptions? The "exclusionary rule" forbids such evidence from being used against the suspect in obtaining a conviction (*Mapp* v. *Ohio*, 1961). The goal of the rule is to deter police from conducting illegal searches, knowing that they face no penalty for violating the law. Critics of the exclusionary rule argue that society should not be punished simply because the police erred. Most countries, in contrast, permit illegally seized evidence to be used in court, but allows criminals to sue police officers in a civil suit for transgressing their rights.

The Supreme Court has diluted the exclusionary rule in two ways. First, unconstitutionally obtained evidence can be used to impeach a defendant's testimony and will merely be excluded as evidence demonstrating guilt (*New York* v. *Harris*, 1971). Second, if an officer secures a warrant and believes it valid in "good faith," the evidence will be allowed in court even if the warrant is later found defective (*Massachusetts* v. *Sheppard*, 1984). The Fourth Amendment, despite some erosion from the standards imposed by the Warren Court, remains a vibrant constitutional safeguard.

Data and Perspectives for Analysis

Search Warrant Requirements

In May 1985, the Supreme Court was confronted with the case of *California* v. *Carney*, involving the constitutional question of whether a search warrant was needed for a motor home. The *New York Times* (May 14, 1985, p. 13) described the salient facts of the case as follows:

> The decision concerned a motor home that was parked, with its curtains drawn, in a downtown San Diego parking lot. After receiving evidence that the vehicle was being used to distribute narcotics, the police watched it for more than an hour. They then entered and searched it without a warrant and found marijuana in several places in the kitchen area.
> The California Supreme Court overturned the owner's conviction, ruling that for purposes of a search warrant the vehicle should have been treated like a home. The state then appealed to the United States Supreme Court.

If you have the time, you may wish to select nine students at random to debate this case in class. To help get the discussion started, distribute the following guidelines:

1. Was the motor home in this case in the same class a a fixed, residential home, in view of the fact that it was actually a "mini-motor home" that was not parked at a fixed location or connected to utility lines? Despite the fact that the motor home could be driven away, it did have bunk beds, a kitchen, and other furnishings.

2. Should the state court have applied the so-called automobile exception to the Fourth Amendment's search warrant requirement? This exception was first created in 1925, based on the rationale that "the inherent mobility of an automobile, plus the 'diminished expectation of privacy' that people have in their cars compared to their houses, combine to make it impractical to require the police to obtain a warrant as long as probable cause exists to believe the law is being violated."

3. Did the police have "probable cause" in this case to search the motor home?

Note: In the *New York Times* article by Linda Greenhouse, the Supreme Court actually ruled, in a 6–3 decision written by Chief Justice Burger, that the motor home, though it possessed some of the characteristics of a home, more nearly resembled a car and could therefore be searched without a warrant. Justices Stevens, Brennan, and Marshall dissented, Stevens asserting that the automobile exception should apply only to mobile homes actually "traveling on the public streets." "Although . . . not . . . a castle," it was still the "functional equivalent of a hotel room, a vacation and retirement home, or a hunting and fishing cabin" and therefore should have required a search warrant. It should be interesting to see if your simulated Supreme Court arrives at a similar decision.

19

Civil Rights

Overview and Objectives

This chapter focuses on the two most intense and protracted struggles for civil rights in recent times: that of blacks and that of women. After reading and reviewing the material in this chapter the student should be able to do each of the following:

1. Contrast the experience of economic interest groups with that of black groups in obtaining satisfaction of their interests from the government. Indicate why in most circumstances the black movement involved interest-group rather than client politics. Describe the strategies used by black leaders to overcome their political weaknesses, and explain why the civil rights movement has become more conventional in its strategy in recent years.

2. Summarize the legal struggles of blacks to secure rights under the Fourteenth Amendment, and indicate how the Court construed that amendment in the civil rights cases and in *Plessy* v. *Ferguson*. Discuss the NAACP strategy of litigation, and indicate why it was suited to the political circumstances. Summarize the rulings in *Brown* v. *Board of Education* and compare them with those in *Plessy* v. *Ferguson*.

3. Discuss the rationale used by the Supreme Court in ordering busing to achieve desegregation. Explain the apparent inconsistency between *Brown* and *Charlotte-Mecklenburg*. Indicate why these decisions are not really inconsistent, and explain why the courts chose busing as an equitable remedy to deal with *de jure* segregation.

4. Trace the campaign launched by blacks for a set of civil rights laws. Explain why nonviolent techniques were used. Discuss the conflict between the agenda-setting and the coalition-building aspects of the movement. Demonstrate how civil rights advocates could overcome sources of resistance in Congress.

5. Describe the differences between the black movement and the women's movement. Indicate the various standards used by the courts in interpreting the Fourteenth Amendment, and explain how these standards differ depending on whether blacks or women are involved.

6. Explain why ratification of the Equal Rights Amendment proved impossible, despite strong congressional and popular support.

7. Explain the important role women play in the American economy.

Chapter Outline with Keyed-in Resources

    I. Introduction
       A. Civil rights issue
          1. Group is denied access to facilities, opportunities, or services available to other groups
             a. Usually along ethnic or racial lines
          2. Issue is whether differences in treatment are "reasonable"
             a. Some differences are: e.g., progressive taxes
             b. Some are not: e.g., classification by race subject to "strict scrutiny"

The Supreme Court has upheld racial discrimination on the part of the federal government. In a series of cases, the Court accepted the government's argument that the crisis of World War II created a "compelling interest" justifying the relocation of American citizens of Japanese ancestry to detention centers. However, Congress recently authorized payment of $20,000 per detainee in compensation as a form of apology.

    II. The black predicament (THEME A: CIVIL RIGHTS—CLIENT, INTEREST-GROUP, OR MAJORITARIAN POLITICS?)
       A. Perceived costs of granting black rights not widely shared
          1. Concentrated in small, easily organized populations
          2. Interest group politics versus lower-income whites
          3. Blacks at disadvantage in interest-group politics since not able to vote in many areas
       B. Majoritarian politics worked against blacks
          1. Lynchings shocked whites, but little was done
          2. General public opinion was opposed to black rights
          3. Those sympathetic to granting black rights opposed the means
       C. Progress depended on
          1. Finding more white allies or

Blacks found American Jews to be sympathetic allies in the struggle for civil rights. This alliance has become strained in recent years over the issue of affirmative action. Jews consider the use of goals a dangerous legal precedent since quotas were employed in the past to limit the number of Jews allowed in certain programs.

          2. Shifting policy-making arenas
       D. Civil rights movement did both
          1. Broadened base by publicizing grievances
          2. Moved legal struggle from Congress to the courts
   III. The campaign in the courts (THEME B: CIVIL RIGHTS AND THE COURTS)
       A. Ambiguities in the Fourteenth Amendment
          1. Broad interpretation: Constitution colorblind
          2. Narrow interpretation: equal legal rights
          3. Supreme Court adopted narrow view in *Plessy* case
       B. "Separate but equal"

When the case of *Plessy v. Ferguson* was brought to the Supreme Court in 1896, Louisiana classified a person as legally "Negro" if he or she possessed one sixty-fourth black blood. Thus Mr. Plessy, although only one-eighth black, fell easily within the legal definition of "Negro."

          1. NAACP campaign objectives in education through courts
             a. Obviously unequal schools
             b. Not so obviously unequal schools
             c. Separate schools inherently unequal
       C. Can separate schools be equal?
          1. Step 1: obvious inequalities
             a. Lloyd Gaines

        b. Ada Lois Sipuel
    2. Step 2: deciding that a separation creates inequality in less obvious cases
        a. Heman Sweatt
        b. George McLaurin
    3. Step 3: making separation inherently unequal
        a. 1950 strategy to go for integration
    4. *Brown* v. *Board of Education* (1954)

The Supreme Court in the *Brown* decision relied primarily on the psychological experiments of Dr. Kenneth Clark to establish that separation of the races produces a sense of inferiority in young black children. Dr. Clark's experiments, initially conducted in the late 1940s, were replicated in the mid-1980s. Surprisingly, the results were much the same, leading the researchers to conclude that little has changed despite the successes of the civil rights movement.

        a. Implementation
            (1) Class-action suit
            (2) All-deliberate speed
        b. Collapse of resistance in 1970s
    5. The rationale
        a. Detriment to pupils by creating sense of inferiority
        b. Social science used because intent of Fourteenth Amendment unclear and need for unanimous decision
    6. Desegregation versus integration
        a. Ambiguities of *Brown*

It was not until 1969 that the Supreme Court held that school desegregation with "all deliberate speed" was over. Schools had to be integrated from that point. Thus the end of segregation in public schools should be dated 1969, not 1954.

            (1) Unrestricted choice or integrated schools?
            (2) *De jure* or *de facto* segregation?
        b. 1968 rejection of "freedom of choice" plan settles matter: actual mixing
        c. *Charlotte-Mecklenburg*, 1971
            (1) Proof of intent to discriminate
            (2) One-race school creates presumption of intent
            (3) Remedies can include quotas, busing, redrawn lines
            (4) Every school not required to reflect system racial composition
        d. Some extensions to intercity busing
        e. Busing remains controversial (ADDITIONAL LECTURE TOPIC B-1)

Today 61 percent of students ride buses to public schools. However, only 4 percent of students are bused under a court-ordered program. "White flight" has emptied cities of white students eligible to be bused for integration purposes.

            (1) Some presidents oppose but still implement it
            (2) Congress torn in two directions
        f. 1992 decision allows busing to end if segregation caused by shifting housing patterns
 IV. The campaign in Congress (THEME C: LEGISLATIVE ACTION ON CIVIL RIGHTS)
    A. Mobilization of opinion by dramatic event to get on agenda
        1. Sit-ins and freedom rides
        2. Martin Luther King, Jr.
        3. From nonviolence to "long, hot summers"
    B. Mixed results
        1. Agenda-setting success
        2. Coalition-building setbacks since methods seen as lawbreaking
    C. Legislative politics
        1. Opponents' defensive positions
            a. Senate Judiciary Committee controlled by southern Democrats

            b. House Rules Committee controlled by Howard Smith
            c. Senate filibuster threat
            d. President Kennedy reluctant
        2. Four developments broke deadlock
            a. Public opinion change
            b. Violent white reactions of segregationists media focus
            c. Kennedy assassination
            d. 1964 Democratic landslide
        3. Five bills pass, 1957–1968
            a. 1957, 1960, 1965: voting rights laws
            b. 1968: housing discrimination law
        4. 1964 civil rights bill: the high point—employment, accommodations
            a. Broad in scope, strong enforcement mechanisms
            b. Johnson moves after Kennedy assassinated
            c. Discharge petition, cloture invoked
        5. Effects since 1964
            a. Dramatic rise in black voting
            b. Mood of Congress shifted: pro–civil rights
                (1) 1988 overturn of Reagan veto of antidesegration law
V. Women and equal rights (THEME D: WOMEN AND EQUAL RIGHTS)
    A. Supreme Court's reasonableness standard
        1. Less stringent than racial "suspect classification": reasonableness test

In *Craig* v. *Boren* (1976), the Supreme Court articulated a new standard to be employed in the area of sexual discrimination. In place of the reasonableness standard used in earlier cases, the Court now requires the government to demonstrate an "important interest" in justifying policies that discriminate on the basis of sex.

        2. Gender-based differences prohibited by courts
            a. Age of adulthood
            b. Drinking age
            c. Arbitrary employee height-weight requirements
            d. Mandatory pregnancy leaves
            e. Little League exclusion
            f. Jaycees exclusion
            g. Unequal retirement benefits
        3. Gender-based differences allowed by courts
            a. All-boy/All-girl schools
            b. Widows' property tax exemption
            c. Delayed promotions in navy
            d. Statutory rape
    B. The draft
        1. *Rostker* v. *Goldberg* (1981): Congress may register only men for the draft
        2. Secretary of defense in 1993 allows women in air and sea combat
    C. The ERA
        1. Prompt ratification appeared likely in 1972
        2. In trouble by 1974–1975
        3. Stalled by 1978 at 35 states of 38 needed
        4. Dead by 1982, despite congressional extension
        5. Reasons for defeat
            a. Draft issue: women in combat
            b. Workplace protection eroded
    D. Abortion (ADDITIONAL LECTURE TOPIC D-1)
        1. Decided by states until 1973
        2. 1973: *Roe* v. *Wade*
            a. Struck down Texas ban on abortion
            b. Woman's freedom to choose protected by Fourteenth Amendment ("right to privacy")

In *Roe* v. *Wade*, the Supreme Court held that a fetus is not a "person" under the Constitution and therefore has no rights. The Court reached this conclusion after surveying each instance where the word "person" appears in the Constitution. For example, a person eligible for the presidency must be thirty-five years old, a natural-born citizen, and a resident of the United States for at least fourteen years. Thus, according to the Court, the word "person" is used in a "postnatal" sense, referring to someone who has already been born.

> (1) First trimester: no regulations
> (2) Second trimester: no ban but regulations to protect health
> (3) Third trimester: abortion ban
> c. Critics claimed life begins at conception
> (1) Fetus entitled to equal protection
> (2) Supporters said no one can say when life begins
> (3) "Pro-life" versus "pro-choice"
> d. Hyde amendment (1976): no federal funds for abortion

The Hyde amendment has taken several forms over the years. In some versions, Medicaid funds can be used for abortions when pregnancy results from rape or incest as well as in situations in which the mother's life is in danger from pregnancy. The Supreme Court indicated that no constitutional obstacles would prevent Congress from forbidding Medicaid funds even when the life of the mother is in peril. *Roe* does not require the government to facilitate abortions.

> e. Gag order imposed under Bush, removed under Clinton
> 3. 1973–1989: Supreme Court withstood attacks on *Roe* v. *Wade*
> 4. 1989: Court upheld Missouri law restricting abortions

The Missouri case has fueled speculation that the Supreme Court is preparing the ground for reversing *Roe* v. *Wade*. The preamble to the Missouri law declares that human life begins at conception, a position clearly at odds with *Roe*, which held that a fetus is not a person. The Supreme Court refrained from voiding this section of the law on the ground that a preamble has no legal force, making it unnecessary to rule on its constitutionality. Is the Court tipping its hand? New personnel on the Court seems to have strengthened the likelihood *Roe* will survive.

> 5. *Casey* decision does not overturn *Roe* but permits more restrictions: 24-hour wait, parental consent, pamphlets
> VI. Women and the economy
>   A. After ERA defeat, a split in women's movement grew
>   1. Press for equal rights as ultimate objective, or . . .
>   2. . . . Make economic status top priority over legal status

The gap in pay between men and women actually widens as corporate positions increase in importance. One survey conducted in 1989 discovered that female vice presidents in Fortune 500 companies earn an astounding 42 percent less than male vice presidents.

>   3. Urgency of second position arose from new economic circumstances
>   4. These circumstances led to new objectives: women's-economic-equity issues
>   a. Government-funded day care
>   b. Enforcement of child support from divorced spouse
>   c. Pregnancy leave
>   d. Comparable worth
>   (1) Pay by ranking of job's intrinsic difficulty
>   (2) Utilized in several places now; problematic
> VII. Affirmative action
>   A. Equality of results (THEME E: AFFIRMATIVE ACTION)
>   1. Racism and sexism overcome only by taking them into account in designing remedies
>   2. Equal rights not enough; people need benefits
>   3. Affirmative action should be used in hiring

B. Equality of opportunities
      1. Reverse discrimination to use race or sex as preferential treatment
      2. Laws should be colorblind and sex-neutral
      3. Government should only eliminate barriers
   C. Targets or quotas?
      1. Issue fought out in courts

The issue of affirmative action should diminish in controversy in the last part of this decade. By the year 2000, a recent government study estimates, only 15 percent of the new entrants in the job market will be white men—too few to make affirmative action a divisive factor in employment.

         a. No clear direction in Court decisions
         b. Court is deeply divided
            (1) Affected by conservative Reagan appointees
         c. Law is complex and confusing
            (1) *Bakke*: numerical minority quotas not permissible
            (2) But Court ruled otherwise in later cases
      2. Emerging standards for quotas and preference systems
         a. Must be "compelling" justification
         b. Must correct an actual pattern of discrimination
         c. Must involve actual practices that discriminate
         d. Federal quotas will be given deference
         e. Voluntary preference systems will be easier to justify

Voluntary affirmative action programs can be instituted by companies in the private sector on a temporary basis only. A deadline for the program's expiration must be clearly specified.

         f. Not likely to apply to persons who get laid off
      3. Congressional efforts to defend affirmative action not yet successful
      4. "Compensatory action" (helping minorities catch up) versus "preferential treatment" (giving minorities preference, applying quotas)
         a. Public supports former but not latter
         b. In line with American political culture
            (1) Support for individualism
            (2) Support for needy

Important Terms

*affirmative action Programs attempting to compensate for past discrimination by giving preference to minorities and women in areas like hiring and promotion. The Supreme Court has announced a complex set of standards governing this field. In general, quotas or preference systems instituted by government employers must be supported by proof of past discrimination and have a "compelling" justification. Such preference systems, however, cannot extend to layoffs, only hiring and promotion.

aliens Any person who is not a U.S. citizen.

Brown v. Board of Education A Supreme Court decision in 1954 which overruled the doctrine of "separate but equal" by forbidding segregation in public education. The Court held that segregation produces a detrimental "feeling of inferiority" in black children.

*civil rights A legal requirement that all government classifications must be reasonable.

Civil Rights Act of 1964 A federal law banning discrimination in public accommodations and employment. It also authorized the attorney general to bring suit to force the integration of public schools on behalf of citizens.

*comparable worth A doctrine requiring salaries to be determined by the "worth" of a job, not by the pay it commands in the market. Each job is ranked by an expert in terms of its difficulty, with points assigned based on the skill, training, and responsibility of the job. This form of "economic equity" has been adopted by the states of Minnesota and Washington.

*compensatory action A position favored by a majority of Americans that supports helping disadvantaged people catch up, usually by giving them extra education, training, or services.

*de facto segregation A form of segregation which exists "in fact." Such segregation occurs through housing patterns and informal social pressures, not through law.

*de jure segregation Segregation produced by law. This form of segregation was outlawed by the *Brown* decision in 1954.

Equal Rights Amendment A constitutional amendment proposed by Congress to the states for ratification in 1972 which would have required that rights could not be abridged or denied on account of gender. The amendment failed to be ratified by the necessary three-fourths of the states, falling short by three states even after Congress extended the ratification period. Recent efforts to revive the amendment have not been successful.

*equality of opportunity A goal opposed to that of affirmative action holding that people should compete in the marketplace equally and be judged by their worth; the Constitution and application of laws should be color-blind and sex-neutral; and preferential treatment on the basis of either race or sex is reverse discrimination.

equality of results The goal favored by most civil rights and feminist organizations, who advocate affirmative action as a realistic necessity since the burdens of racism and sexism can be overcome only by taking race and sex into account in designing remedies. People cannot compete on an equal footing unless the government intervenes to bring everyone to a comparable starting position.

Fourteenth Amendment A constitutional amendment ratified in 1868 that forbids states from (1) denying the "privileges and immunities" of citizenship, (2) depriving any person of due process of law, or (3) denying any person equal protection of the laws.

Hyde amendment A congressional restriction barring the use of Medicaid funds to pay for abortions except when the life of the mother is at stake. The Supreme Court upheld this restriction in 1980.

*Jim Crow A phrase from a song by Thomas Rice that came to be a slang expression for blacks and was later applied to laws and practices that segregated blacks from whites.

National Organization for the Advancement of Colored People An organization formed in 1909 to further the civil rights of blacks. Its major emphasis has been the litigation of cases in courts. The organization has achieved notable successes, most significantly in overturning the doctrine of "separate but equal."

*nonviolent civil disobedience A tactic employed in the early demonstrations of the civil rights movement in the 1950s and 1960s that involved peaceful violation of the law.

Plessy v. Ferguson A Supreme Court decision in 1896 that upheld the separate but equal doctrine, by which different races could be assigned to separate facilities so long as the facilities were of equal condition. The doctrine was overturned in 1954.

preferential treatment A position opposed by a majority of Americans that supports giving minorities preference in hiring, promotions, college admissions, and contracts.

*reverse discrimination A position advocated by those favoring an equality of opportunity that opposes giving preferential treatment to blacks and women on the ground that the Constitution should be color-blind and sex-neutral.

Roe v. Wade A Supreme Court decision in 1973 that holds that the due process clause of the Fifth Amendment implies a right of privacy, allowing women to choose whether to have an abortion within certain guidelines. In the first three months of pregnancy, the decision belongs solely to the woman; in the fourth through the six months, states can enact laws protecting the mother's health but cannot forbid abortions; abortions can be forbidden beginning in the seventh month of pregnancy.

Rostker v. Goldberg A Supreme Court decision in 1981 allowing Congress to require men to register for the military draft but not women.

*separate-but-equal doctrine A doctrine approved by the Supreme Court in *Plessy* v. *Ferguson* that allowed states under the Fourteenth Amendment to provide separate facilities for blacks and whites so long as the quality of the facilities were similar. The doctrine was overturned in *Brown* v. *Board of Education* in 1954.

*strict scrutiny The standard by which the Supreme Court judges classifications based on race. To be accepted, such a classification must be closely related to a "compelling" public purpose.

*suspect classifications A judicial policy that regards treating people on the basis of their race or ethnicity as unreasonable and subjects such classifications to strict scrutiny.

Swann v. Charlotte-Mecklenburg A Supreme Court decision in 1971 dealing with the constitutionality of court-ordered busing to integrate public school systems. The Court held that busing is a permissible option for integration if certain conditions are met, notably that the school system has engaged in racial discrimination in the past.

white flight Whites' moving out of cities to suburbs to avoid mandatory busing or other integration measures imposed on school systems.

women's-economic-equity issues New interests, largely economic in nature, of women's organizations pressed upon Congress in the 1980s. These interests included government-funded day care, child-support enforcement, pregnancy leave, and comparable worth.

Theme A	Civil Rights—Client, Interest-Group, or Majoritarian Politics?

Instructor Reference

Norman Amaker, ed., *Civil Rights and the Reagan Administration*. Washington, DC: Urban Institute, 1988.

Charles W. Eagles, ed., *The Civil Rights Movement in America*. Jackson: University Press of Mississippi, 1986.

Summary

All laws and policies treat different classes of people differently. Tax laws, for example, require higher-income people to pay taxes at a higher rate than lower-income people. Increasingly, however, the courts have said that race and ethnicity are *suspect classifications* and that laws that make such distinctions will be subjected to especially strict scrutiny.

We must ask why racial and ethnic minorities require any special protection, given that client politics generally makes government highly solicitous of the interests of cohesive minority groups. First, racial politics has often been interest-group politics. Certain groups (for example, southern white workers or officeholders) have been keenly aware of being in competition with blacks for certain valued things. Second, to the extent that racial politics was majoritarian politics, blacks were disadvantaged by antiblack attitudes among a majority of citizens, North and South. In 1942 a national poll showed that only 30 percent of whites thought that black and white children should attend the same schools. Polls done in the 1960s showed that even citizens who favored racial integration harbored skeptical or negative attitudes toward the civil rights movement.

The civil rights movement was able to prosper politically by changing strategies. By publicizing its grievances, the movement acquired more white supporters and developed into a viable political force in Congress. This change is reflected in public attitudes. In 1972, for example, only 52 percent of whites in the South would vote for a qualified black candidate running for the presidency, but that number rose to 72 percent by 1989. While the civil rights movement has achieved legitimacy in the white community, prejudice itself has not ceased influencing policy attitudes. In a 1991 survey, 78 percent of whites believed blacks are more likely to prefer living on welfare; 62 percent thought blacks less likely to be hard working; 56 percent viewed blacks as more prone to violence; and 53 percent considered blacks less intelligent. Thus the transformation of civil rights into majoritarian politics has been more successful at the abstract level. As a result, suspicion lingers within the civil rights coalition, with 25 percent of blacks in 1988 feeling that most whites want to "keep blacks down."

Civil rights became "good politics" as witnessed by the behavior of former segregationist Senator Strom Thurmond who added an African-American to his staff and began voting in favor of numerous civil rights measures. Yet the movement would have achieved only limited success if it had depended entirely on majoritarian and interest-group politics in Congress since these activities require the continual mobilization of supporters and resources. For this reason, the civil rights movement had a second element in its strategy that sought to shift the policy-making arena away from Congress to the courts since it was clearly easier to sustain impartial persuasion over a long period than to lobby politicians. This "double-headed" strategy, by attacking the policy-making process on two fronts, was able to gain different types of benefits from each arena.

Discussion Questions

1. Why are some laws that treat people differently legitimate and others a denial of civil rights? Consider the following list of persons and ways in which the government might treat them differently from other people. Is each distinction *arbitrary*, is it *unreasonable*, or is it related to a *legitimate* public policy?

   - Homosexuals—for the regulation of sexual practices
   - Women—in deciding who should be drafted
   - Rich people—in deciding how much people should pay in taxes
   - Hispanics—in deciding the language of instruction in primary schools
   - Businesspeople—in deciding whether federal health and safety inspectors can search premises without a search warrant
   - Women and men—in deciding how much each should have to pay for life insurance policies
   - Property owners—for purposes of voting on property taxes
   - Blacks—in deciding who should be the principal of a ghetto school

2. In the foregoing cases, is there some *objective* way of determining which distinctions are arbitrary or unreasonable? Or is this decision mainly a function of one's political ideology? Is there any one of these distinctions for which no reasonable argument could be made, and which could in no way relate to a legitimate public policy? Note that even the first would be endorsed by some black power or black separatist spokespersons, on the basis that black pride and self-assertion can best be developed separate from whites. Does this mean that "civil rights" is not a solid analytical category but rather a rhetorical symbol?

3. The Department of Justice counted 99 acts of racial violence in 1980. That number jumped to 276 acts in 1987. At the same time, the federal government brought fewer cases involving civil rights violations for litigation in the courts; 280 cases were filed in 1980, versus 28 in 1988. Has the issue of civil rights become dominated by client, interest-group, or majoritarian politics? Explain.

4. Civil rights cannot become an issue of majoritarian politics without the support of whites. Public opinion has shifted in that direction. In 1967, 76 percent of whites felt blacks were treated the same as whites. This figure dropped to 64 percent in 1987, showing greater white awareness of discrimination. Why was less accomplished in civil rights in the 1980s despite white awareness, especially since the economy was generally healthy? What does this fact reveal about the relationship of majoritarian politics to civil rights?

5. What prevented black gains in those arenas where majoritarian politics prevailed?

Data and Perspectives for Analysis

The aim of the civil rights movement is to elevate the condition of minority populations in the United States politically, socially, and economically. The movement has achieved most success in the context of political rights where legal barriers have been erased to enable full participation in the political process. The same cannot be said for social and economic equality, where the gains of minority groups have lagged. A good example that cuts across both categories (social and economic) is to examine employment status, since a person's job correlates with both social position and financial holdings.

The data below compare the occupations held by women and blacks in 1980 and 1990. The differences between the two groups are revealing of the changes in American society.

Profession	*Percent Women* 1980	1990	*Percent Black* 1980	1990
Doctors	9.2%	18.1%	5.7%	8.0%
Lawyers	13.0%	21.6%	4.3%	6.3%
Executives	31.6%	42.7%	8.4%	12.4%
Engineers	6.5%	10.9%	4.6%	6.5%
Real estate sales	48.2%	51.4%	4.6%	6.2%
Teachers (K–12)	77.8%	81.2%	24.3%	21.8%
Secretaries	98.8%	98.9%	9.1%	12.3%
Computer programmer	37.9%	34.2%	8.3%	11.7%
Police	8.9%	12.1%	15.6%	22.1%
Registered nurses	95.3%	94.5%	17.4%	18.6%
Maids/Janitors	40.4%	47.3%	60.7%	55.6%
Cashiers	83.2%	82.5%	21.7%	33.8%

Source: 1990 Census (reported in *Atlanta Journal-Constitution*, August 16, 1992, A4).

Questions for Discussion

1. Why have women done better in achieving upward professional mobility than have African-Americans? Is a different type of politics involved? Are women really a "minority" since they constitute over half of the nation's population?

2. Has the civil rights movement succeeded in the economic arena? Why has it been more difficult to promote equality in the economy than in politics? Does economic policy utilize a different kind of politics than political issues like voting rights?

Theme B Civil Rights and the Courts

Instructor References

Harry S. Ashmore, *Hearts and Minds: The Anatomy of Racism from Roosevelt to Reagan.* New York: McGraw-Hill, 1982.

Richard Kluger, *Simple Justice*. New York: Knopf, 1976. Good history of events that led up to *Brown v. Board of Education*.

David L. Korp, *Just Schools: The Idea of Racial Equality in Education*. Berkeley: University of California Press, 1982. An overview of the struggle for integration in American schools.

Donald G. Nieman, *Promises to Keep: African-Americans and the Constitutional Order, 1776 to the Present*. New York: Oxford University Press, 1991.

Howard Schuman et al., *Radical Attitudes in America*. Cambridge: Harvard University Press, 1985.

J. Harvie Wilkinson III, *From "Brown" to "Bakke": The Supreme Court and School Integration; 1954–1978*. New York: Oxford University Press, 1979.

C. Vann Woodward, *The Strange Career of Jim Crow*. New York: Oxford University Press, 1957. Classic treatise on southern segregation.

Summary

Given that blacks lacked the vote in many areas of the nation and, further, were outnumbered by whites who opposed racial integration, it was natural that the first victories of the civil rights movement came in the courts. This campaign was based on the *equal protection* clause of the Fourteenth Amendment, which says that a state cannot "deny to any person within its jurisdiction the equal protection of the laws." The members of Congress who drafted and passed this amendment were rather vague about exactly what it meant (although they apparently did not think it meant that integrated schools were required). The Supreme Court, in *Plessy v. Ferguson*, upheld racial segregation with the *separate-but-equal* doctrine.

The *NAACP*, founded in 1909, began a long, concerted campaign to coax the Court to move gradually toward requiring integration. The first phase, during the years 1935 through 1950, involved getting the Court actually to require that separate black schools be equal. Phase II, in the famous *Brown* case, involved persuading the Court to overturn the separate-but-equal doctrine. In *Brown*, the Court held that separate is inherently unequal, because segregation "has a detrimental effect upon the colored children" by generating "a feeling of inferiority as to their status in the community," which may "affect their hearts and minds in a way unlikely ever to be undone." Phase III required overcoming massive resistance in the South. In 1964, ten years after *Brown*, only about 2 percent of the black pupils in the eleven states of the Old Confederacy were attending schools with whites. However, persistence on the part of the federal courts and a softening of southern attitudes (helped by an increase in black voting) produced an end to effective resistance. By 1970 the dual system was a thing of the past.

Phase IV involved the continuing and highly controversial process of creating racial balance, as opposed to mere nondiscrimination. This has produced the highly controversial policy of busing and has brought the issue to the North, where most segregation is *de facto* (the result of residential segregation) as opposed to the *de jure* (legally enforced) segregation in the South. That courts called for busing may seem paradoxical, because busing requires that state and local governments must use race as the determinant of school assignment, whereas the *Brown* decision held, in effect, that they could *not* use race in such a way. For the Court, racial balance is not, in itself, a constitutionally required outcome, but rather a *remedy* for past discrimination. Thus the Court has required busing to achieve a "unitary school system" and eliminate "all vestiges of state-imposed segregation." Also, as a practical matter, the presence or absence of discrimination is difficult to ascertain, whereas the percentages of blacks and whites in schools (or in other places) is easily observed. Judges and administrators naturally tend, therefore, toward percentage quotas.

The judicial effort at imposing integration on the country has reached the point of legal fatigue. In two decisions coming in successive years, the Supreme Court would condone a method by which school systems could gracefully exit from busing. The first case, *Board of Education of Oklahoma City v. Dowell* (1991), involved an attempt to reintroduce neighborhood schools for kindergarten through fourth grade to relieve the travel burden on young children, a change that left the basic student profile in 15 of 58 elementary schools as single race. The Court upheld the plan, ruling that federal supervision of local schools was always designed as a temporary measure. At some point, according to Chief Justice William Rehnquist, democratic process at the local level must be restored. A desegregation decree could be dissolved after a "reasonable period," despite never attaining the goal of complete integration, if everything "practicable" was done to eliminate past discrimination.

The term "practicable" failed to provide sufficient guidance to lower courts. When exactly does busing cease to function as a "practicable" solution? The Supreme Court outlined a more workable standard in *Freeman* v. *Pitts* (1992). DeKalb County, Georgia, suffered from a school system with massive skews in racial balance at individual institutions. Fifty percent of the system's black students were attending public schools with 90 percent or more minority enrollment while, within the same district, 25 percent of white students were attending schools with 90 percent or more white enrollment. The school system sought to exonerate itself of discriminatory intent by blaming the segregation on demographic factors. The county's minority population had increased from 27 percent in 1980 to 42 percent in 1990 and averaged a 9 percent annual loss in white student enrollment during the decade.

The Supreme Court unanimously concluded that the existing segregation was not caused by the school system. Although DeKalb County had maintained a dual school system in the past, the county had made a "good faith" effort to compensate for this discrimination by complying with previous court decrees. "Once racial imbalance due to the *de jure* violation has been remedied," Justice Anthony Kennedy wrote, "the school district is under no duty to remedy an imbalance that is caused by demographic factors." A school system in current compliance with the law cannot logically be required to correct anything.

The significance of the *Freeman* decision is that the Supreme Court articulated a standard for suspending busing that most school systems are probably capable of realizing. Unless a school board has been derelict for the past twenty years, most—but not all—should have made a "good faith" effort to reform by now, especially since noncompliance would have been punished by a federal court injunction long ago.

It would seem that the controversy over busing to achieve racial integration is legally exhausted. Nonetheless, public classrooms in the United States have not been changed much. According to a study by the Harvard Project on School Desegregation, the number of black children in 1992 attending majority black institutions was the highest since 1968, 67 percent compared to 77 percent. The Supreme Court may have silenced the controversy but not the problem.

Discussion Questions

1. What exactly did the Fourteenth Amendment guarantee to black people? Did Congress intend it to abolish segregation? If not, why might it give the courts "ample opportunity" to attack segregation? Is this not like saying that the Thirteenth Amendment (outlawing "involuntary servitude") could be used to overrule the draft or that the First Amendment (freedom of speech) could be used to overturn laws against perjury? Is there a difference? If not, *should* the Court rule the draft unconstitutional? Or *may* it rule the draft unconstitutional if it believes it to be bad policy?

2. In failing to use the Fourteenth Amendment to attack segregation, was the Court merely interpreting the amendment as reasonably as it could, or was it straining logic in order to allow segregation? Consider the civil rights cases in relation to the text of the amendment. Consider also the Richmond County case.

3. Why didn't the *Brown* decision abolish racial discrimination in private schools? In 1976, the Supreme Court held that private schools could be prevented from discriminating in admissions, based on a post–Civil War law forbidding discrimination in contracts. How does this statute apply to admissions policies in private schools? What if a private school opposes integration on religious grounds?

4. What was the Court's argument in overruling *Plessy*? Suppose it could be proved that segregation did *not* have a detrimental effect on black children? Would this require that the Court—in the interests of logical consistency—rule differently in *Brown*?

Instructor: See the Data and Perspectives for Analysis section that follows.

5. Private clubs, facilities not generally open to the public, could continue to discriminate despite passage of the Civil Rights Act in 1964. Why? Can Congress do anything about this problem?

6. How has the Court moved from (a) interpreting the Fourteenth Amendment to mean that blacks cannot be relegated to particular schools because of their race to (b) requiring that a particular racial balance must exist in schools? Why was it important that the first busing cases to come to the Court were from southern states that had practiced *de jure* segregation? How was the difficulty in measuring the absence of discrimination important?

7. Suppose you favor busing. Is there any reasonable basis for saying that the Constitution requires busing? Did the people who wrote the Fourteenth Amendment *intend* it to require busing and racial balance? Is there anything in the *language* of the Fourteenth Amendment that could reasonably be said to require more than that the government treat blacks in a "colorblind" way? Would you want the Court to require busing even if you thought it had *bad* results? Is the key matter not then the question of whether busing is good or bad *policy*? If so, is asking the courts to decide this question not also asking them to legislate?

8. Suppose you oppose busing. On what basis can you claim that the Court has no *right* to impose busing? Should it adhere to the *intentions* of those who wrote the Fourteenth Amendment? If it did, would *Brown* not have been impossible? Is there anything in the language of the Fourteenth Amendment that is inconsistent with segregation in equal facilities?

Data and Perspectives for Analysis

A. The Changing Patterns of School Integration

The patterns of school integration which have evolved since the historic decision of *Brown* contain some interesting components. As Edward B. Fiske points out in "School Integration Patterns Change" (*New York Times*, June 13, 1988, p. 8), research studies show that "whites who move out of large urban school districts are replaced not by blacks but by a mixture of blacks, Hispanics, and Asian-Americans, many of whom are isolated from each other." In short, a multiracial, urban educational environment has emerged for school administrators. Furthermore, despite the original vision of a fully integrated educational system in America, Fiske quotes a National School Boards Association study indicating "no significant progress on the desegregation of black students in urban districts since the mid-1970s," with some school areas even displaying "severe increases in racial isolation." (These areas include Tampa, Charlotte, and Las Vegas, where schools were slightly *more* segregated than they were in the early 1970s. An even greater degree of segregation existed in the school districts of Atlanta and Detroit.)

Furthermore, the study reported that

> only 3 percent of white students now attend school in central city school districts and . . . such schools "have become almost irrelevant to the nation's white population." By contrast . . . "the largest central city districts remain vitally important to blacks and Hispanics."

The multiracial character of the inner-city school was demonstrated in New York City, where a typical student population was 61 percent black, 28 percent Hispanic, 7 percent white, and 4 percent Asian (from the perspective of a black student who is in attendance). Racial antagonisms that ensued from this mixture handicapped the proper use of school time and facilities. Finally, schools that were primarily oriented to help blacks found their faculties and resources unsuited to teaching Hispanics and other students who were unable to speak English.

Questions for Discussion (Open-ended)

1. If you were a school administrator in an urban district with a multiracial student body, how would you promote a school environment conducive to learning?

2. Do you believe inner-city schools to be equal in quality to schools in suburban areas that may have a more homogeneous student population?

3. Do you think that the degree of segregation in urban schools will decrease over the next two to three decades? Cite reasons for your opinion.

B. Integration and Black Self-Concepts

The decision in *Brown* v. *Board of Education* seemed to be heavily based on the effects of segregated schooling on the self-concepts of black children. Segregation, it was argued, harmed the self-concept of black students, and a famous "footnote 11" cited psychologists' studies to back this assertion. A recent review of the literature by Edgar G. Epps concludes as follows:

> Despite the fact that research results are conflicting in some areas and inadequate in others, a few generalizations can be drawn. First, low occupational and educational aspirations do not seem to be a major problem of black students. (It is) not entirely clear whether desegregation depresses black students' aspirations. . . .
>
> In the area of self-esteem, similar conclusions seem justified. First, there is no reason to believe that blacks suffer from low self-esteem. In fact, it appears that blacks have higher overall self-esteem than whites. . . . At best, all that can be said is that there is little evidence that desegregation seriously impairs black self-esteem; nor can it be said that desegregation, in itself, enhances self-esteem.
>
> In other areas such as sense of control over one's environment, anxiety, and motivation, there is even less evidence, and broad generalizations seem even less warranted. . . . All one can say is that the evidence seems to point in the negative direction for anxiety and in the positive direction for motivation.
>
> "The Impact of School Desegregation on Aspirations, Self-Concepts and Other Aspects, of Personality," *Law and Contemporary Problems*, Spring 1975, pp. 312–313.

1. How does Epps's view of the effects of segregation on black students compare with the one the Court accepted in 1954?

2. If we assume that Epps is correct and that the Court was wrong in 1954, does this mean that the Court ought to reverse *Brown*? Why is it quite unlikely that the Court will reverse *Brown*?

3. If the Court should not reverse *Brown*, what line of logic could it use to outlaw segregation? Should it have used another line of logic in 1954?

Additional Lecture Topic B-1

The Busing Controversy

Judith Bentley, *Busing: The Continuing Controversy*. New York: Watts, 1982.

Paul R. Dimond, *Beyond Busing: Inside the Challenge to Urban Segregation*. Ann Arbor: University of Michigan Press, 1985.

Douglas S. Gatlin, Michael W. Giles and Everett F. Cataldo, "Policy Support within a Target Group: The Case of School Desegregation," *American Political Science Review,* 72 (1978): 985–995.

Donald Philip Green and Jonathan A. Cowden, "Who Protests: Self-Interest and White Opposition to Busing," *Journal of Politics,* 54 (May 1992): 471–496.

Anthony J. Lukas, *Common Ground: A Turbulent Decade in the Lives of Three American Families*. New York: Random House, 1986.

Richard A. Pride and J. David Woodward, *The Burden of Busing: The Politics of Desegregation in Nashville, Tennessee.* Knoxville: University of Tennessee Press, 1985.

Bernard Schwartz, *Swann's Way: The School Busing Case and the Supreme Court.* New York: Oxford University Press, 1986.

Abstract for Theme B

"Pro" and "Con" Views on Busing

The practice of court-ordered busing as a means of achieving integration in the public schools remains a highly controversial one in American politics nearly fifteen years after its inception. Public opinion continues to be divided on the issue. Thus, in the spring of 1983, a NORC poll revealed that 79 percent of whites were opposed to the practice and that 43 percent of blacks also expressed negative views. Many black parents are unwilling to support busing programs that do not take their children to schools that are markedly superior to those in their own neighborhoods or that have a significantly better racial balance. Nevertheless, the Supreme Court has upheld the validity of busing wherever and whenever segregated school districts were the result of deliberate educational administrative decisions.

In Herbert M. Levine's *Point-Counterpoint*, 2nd ed. (Glenview, IL: Scott, Foresman, 1983), David J. Armor and William L. Taylor debate the need for enforced busing. Armor (pp. 135–143) makes the following points *against the use of school busing*:

1. Busing is "the most unpopular, least successful, and most harmful national policy since Prohibition" (p. 135). There are three basic reasons for this: extensive public opposition and white flight (the latter creating racial isolation in many cities); the failure of desegregation to produce its promised social and educational benefits; and busing's fundamental inequity—"by rejecting a neighborhood school policy on the grounds of housing segregation, the courts deprive parents of their traditional right to choose schools close to home" (p. 136).

2. Busing in Los Angeles during 1978 to 1980 provoked an enormous "white flight" of students. Most of the "minority receiver schools" remained segregated "as an astonishing 60 percent of the 20,000 bused white students never showed . . . " (p. 137). Even after the courts decided to cluster four or five white schools with a single minority school, white enrollments averaged between 30 and 40 percent. In all, "between 1976 (the year before the first court order) and 1980, Los Angeles white enrollment declined from 219,000 (37 percent) to 125,000 (24 percent)." White flight is not confined to Los Angeles; the same phenomenon occurred in the public schools of Boston, Denver, Dayton, and Columbus, Ohio, as well (p. 138). The beneficiaries of this exodus have been the private schools.

3. A number of educational studies refute the traditional contention that desegregation clearly and unequivocally benefits black students. New achievement gains are statistically insignificant or modest. Also, some studies show that desegregation has negative effects on race relations (p. 140).

4. Finally, the assumption by the courts "that housing segregation has been influenced significantly by school segregation" is incorrect. So is the legal thesis that "but for school segregation, housing segregation would be nonexistent or considerably reduced" (p. 141).

Taylor, a civil rights activist and lawyer, argues for busing as follows:

1. The courts have intervened with court busing only "when acts of intentional racial discrimination have been proven" (p. 130). Otherwise, they have moved cautiously or even refrained from ordering busing.

2. Busing has led to educational gains and has been supported by the communities involved. School achievement scores of minority students in such communities as Sacramento, Fort Worth, Nashville, and Louisville "increased significantly" after desegregation through busing (p. 132). Studies that showed a decline in achievement were "methodologically flawed." Studies prove that desegregation plans requiring "substantial busing" (metropolitan or countywide programs) were the most successful in raising achievement scores for black children.

3. Regarding the issue of white flight, "while school desegregation may have a one- or two-year impact, declines in the enrollments of central city schools stem far more from the continuing suburbanization of whites, a movement of more than thirty years' standing, than from desegregation orders" (p. 133).

4. Regarding public opinion, one poll reveals "that most people in communities that have undergone segregation react favorably to the experience after the plans have been in effect for three years" (p. 133). Evidence also suggests that busing-created desegregation on a metropolitan basis actually leads to residential integration more than to white flight (p. 133). Racine, Wisconsin; Wichita, Kansas; and Charlotte-Mecklenburg, North Carolina, are examples.

5. Because desegregated schools widen the horizons of both black and white schoolchildren, a greater number of blacks go on to first-rate colleges and universities and become part of mainstream America. In short, desegregation through busing is sound educational policy for all Americans.

Discussion Questions/Answer Guidelines

Open-ended discussion is probably best for this abstract. You may wish to draw on your students' own experiences with busing and contrast those experiences with the arguments presented above.

Theme C   Legislative Action on Civil Rights

Summary

To get new civil rights laws from Congress required a more difficult, decentralized, and uncertain strategy than that used in the courts. To get civil rights on the national political agenda required dramatizing the problems of blacks in ways that shocked the conscience of those whites who were not racists but who were ordinarily indifferent to black problems. Beginning in the late 1950s, sit-in demonstrations at segregated lunch counters, "freedom rides" to attempt to integrate public transportation, and protest marches began to proliferate, under no central leadership. Black riots from 1964 to 1968 alienated many whites but increased the bargaining power of black leaders opposed to violence. But most important, protest demonstrations precipitated violent reactions from southern authorities and individuals. In 1963 in Birmingham, Alabama, authorities used police dogs and high-pressure hoses to repel marchers. In 1964 in Neshoba County, Mississippi, three workers in a voter registration drive were murdered by Ku Klux Klansmen. In 1965 in Selma, Alabama, two civil rights workers were killed, and police clubbed demonstrators.

These incidents created a national coalition for new civil rights legislation. Opponents of such legislation held three important defensive positions in Congress: (a) the Senate Judiciary Committee; (b) the House Rules Committee, and (c) the filibuster in the Senate. Between 1957 and 1968 five major pieces of civil-rights legislation passed Congress. Those of 1957 and 1960 were rather mild. The far-reaching 1964 *Civil Rights Bill* was passed on the basis of momentum generated by violent incidents in the South and by the assassination of President Kennedy in Dallas. The House Rules Committee reported the bill out under the threat of a discharge petition, and cloture was used to break a filibuster in the Senate.

Because of the massive Democratic majorities in Congress following the 1964 election, the 1965 act passed much more easily. It made it easier for blacks to register and vote, and it succeeded in greatly increasing black participation in southern elections.

Discussion Question

1. What dramatic incidents aided the civil rights movement? Could southern political leaders have prevented the progress of the movement? Compare the reactions of officials in Albany, Georgia, and in Birmingham, Alabama. To what extent did the civil rights movement aim to provoke an extreme reaction? Did it succeed?

Abstract for Theme C

Jesse Jackson's 1988 Presidential Campaign

The 1988 presidential race saw the emergence of Jesse Jackson as a serious contender for the presidential nomination. Acquiring some seven million votes in the various presidential primaries and caucuses, Mr. Jackson demonstrated convincingly that a black leader could attract the support of white voters as well. As described by staff reporter Joe Davidson of the *Wall Street Journal* ("For Jackson, the Challenge Now Is to Transform a Campaign into a Lasting Political Movement," June 20, 1988, p. 42), Jackson's failure to secure the presidential nomination of his party did not tarnish some genuine political accomplishments:

> He has succeeded in creating a movement across racial lines—a movement of society's have-nots—and giving that movement a driving focus for its political aspirations....
>
> ... Mr. Jackson's defenders say ... that he has fundamentally changed the perception of how far a black can go in America. "Jackson's legacy is that he had made it possible to conceptualize a black in the presidency and therefore in any other major executive position in the country," says Roger Wilkins of the Institute for Policy Studies and an adviser to the Jackson campaign. "Jackson has made the unthinkable thinkable."
>
> But Mr. Jackson has also managed to begin the process of growing beyond a race-based candidate, some observers say. While he won only about 12 percent of the white vote in the Democratic primaries ... he still did far better than in 1984, and clearly struck a chord with many whites.
>
> Once thought of only as a "black leader," Mr. Jackson now has ... "evolved past being a symbol of black America, by being a symbol of progressive change in domestic policy and our foreign policy."

Davidson quotes other observers to the effect that Jackson had become a symbol of modern race relations and, while following the agenda of Martin Luther King, had generated far greater white support than the legendary civil-rights leader had obtained in his lifetime. Finally, Davidson notes that Jackson's ambitions went far beyond the 1988 campaign, for his ultimate aim was to strengthen the influence of his constituency by building a lasting, multiracial national political movement that would extend into the next decade or even longer. In short, would Jackson's presidential campaigns institutionalize the concept of a black American as president to a growing number of Americans, so that an electoral victory would someday become a political reality?

Questions for Discussion

1. Do students envision a black leader as president in the near future? Why or why not?

2. Have students research the key themes of Jackson's 1988 campaign. How did some of these themes appeal to white voters?

3. Recent black politicians, like David Dinkens and Douglas Wilder, have adopted moderate positions on most issues and have even favored fiscal conservatism. Which position—the liberal stance of Jackson or the more moderate one of Wilder—is best aimed at improving the condition of black citizens? Explain.

Theme D Women and Equal Rights

Instructor References

Mary Berry, *Why ERA Failed*. Bloomington: Indiana University Press, 1986.

Zillah R. Eisenstein, *Feminism and Sexual Equality*. New York: Monthly Review Press, 1984.

Cynthia Harrison, *On Account of Sex: The Politics of Women's Issues, 1945–1968*. Berkeley: University of California Press, 1988.

Laura Crites and Winifred Hepperle, *Women, the Courts, and Equality*. Beverly Hills, CA: Sage, 1987.

Sylvia Ann Hewitt, *A Lesser Life: The Myth of Women's Liberation in America*. New York: Morrow, 1986.

Ethel Klein, *Gender Politics*. Cambridge: Harvard University Press, 1984.

Susan Gluck Mezey, *In Pursuit of Equality: Women, Public Policy and the Federal Courts*. New York: St. Martin's Press, 1992.

Barbara Deckard Sinclair, *The Women's Movement*. New York: Harper & Row, 1983.

Gilbert Y. Steiner, *Constitutional Inequality: The Political Fortunes of the Equal Rights Amendment*. Washington, DC: Brookings Institution, 1985.

Dorothy McBride Stetson, *Women's Rights in the U.S.A.: Policy Debates and Gender Roles*. Pacific Grove, CA: Brooks-Cole, 1991.

Summary

The movement to expand the rights of women has paralleled the black movement in many ways. However, laws treating women differently have traditionally claimed to protect them. Feminists reject the claim that women differ from men in ways that justify differences in legal status, and Congress has passed laws requiring equal pay for equal work and prohibiting discrimination in employment and in educational programs. The Supreme Court, too, has moved far in the feminist direction by requiring, in 1971, that any law that classifies people on the basis of sex "must be reasonable, not arbitrary, and must rest on some ground of difference having a fair and substantial relation to the object of the legislation, so that all persons similarly circumstanced shall be treated alike." This test is less rigorous than that applied to racial classifications that are "inherently suspect." Thus the Court has overturned some laws that treat the sexes differently and has upheld others (most notably the all-male draft legislation). The Court held in the 1981 case of *Rostker* v. *Goldberg* that Congress may draft men but not women without violating due process. In addition, Congress has barred the use of federal funds for abortions, but the Court has also broadened the right to abortions by ruling that a woman does not need to have the permission of her husband or parents prior to the operation.

The passage of the *Equal Rights Amendment* seemed for a time to be a foregone conclusion. It sailed through Congress in 1972 and was approved by twenty-two state legislatures within a year. Then it ran into trouble, as strong opposition mobilized. Even extending the period of time allowed for ratification to June 1982 failed to achieve the necessary thirty-eight states for ratification. Not only were many women opposed to the amendment, but some of the concrete consequences (for example, some interpreted it as requiring the drafting of women) seemed less appealing than the actual language of the amendment. Exactly what the consequences would be was uncertain. The ERA symbolized conflict over a broad range of cultural values in the United States. It is possible, however, that the Court will simply interpret the equal protection clause of the Fourteenth Amendment in a way that will achieve most of what the ERA intended.

Abstract 1 for Theme D

Women's Rights and the Issue of Comparable Worth

With defeat of the ERA, the premier women's issue of the 1980s became that of "pay equity," or the more general concept of "comparable worth." According to Carol Lawson's article "NOW Focuses on Pay Equity for Women" (*New York Times*, April 29, 1985, p. 15), the New York State chapter of NOW asserted that "comparable worth" between men and women in the workplace was essential because

> 50 million working women earn an average of 60 cents for every dollar that men earn . . . by the year 2000 women's wages would be 74 percent of those for men (estimate by the Rand Corporation). . . . The effect of the comparable worth concept would be to raise the status of women's work, which has traditionally been undervalued and underpaid, to the status of men's work. . . .
>
> The concept of pay equity calls for employers to assess the intrinsic value of different jobs by measuring the knowledge, skills, and effort required by employees, their responsibilities, and their working conditions. Thus, it enables employers to compare, say, what a secretary does with what a truck driver does. If the two jobs end up at about the same place on a numerical scale, proponents of comparable worth contend, they should command the same salary.

NOW members were buoyed by previous court, city, and state decisions that in the past had supported the comparable-worth concept: the 1983 federal court decision ordering the state of Washington to pay more than $800 million to thousands of female employees (the women were paid about 20 percent less than males who held equivalent jobs); the move by Colorado Springs, Colorado, to implement pay equity for municipal employees; and the state of Minnesota's allocation of $26 million for needed salary adjustments.

"Comparable worth" has its critics, however. Ironically, earlier in the month of April, 1985, the United States Commission on Civil Rights rejected the doctrine by a 5-2 vote. A more elaborate repudiation can be found in an earlier *New Republic* article written by Charles Krauthammer (July 30, 1984, pp. 16–18) entitled "From Bad to Worth." Krauthammer rejects the central NOW notion that women's wages are depressed due to a past legacy of discrimination—the "crowding" of women into fields such as nursing, teaching, and secretarial work. This sexual stereotyping has kept women in, but it has also kept men out, "thus artificially excluding potential wage competition from half the population" and thus protecting these women's jobs from a major pool of competition. He also rejects the claim that the job market is inherently discriminatory toward women and holds that any attempt to prove by an arbitrary numerical scale that, for example, nurses are paid less than they deserve is absurd. And how can one equate the knowledge and skills related to a job with the working conditions that are an integral part of that job?

> But does ten points in knowledge and skills make up for ten points in hazardous working conditions? Who is to say that a secretary's two years of college are equal in worth to—and not half or double the worth of—the trucker's risk of getting killed on the highways?

Krauthammer also rejects the argument that people with identical qualifications, training, and experience should automatically be paid the same, because this argument foolishly overlooks the fact that the "actual" work performed by the individual is the key to salary differentials.

Krauthammer concludes that the logical implications of comparable worth would eventually affect everyone, because it is the rare individual who feels that he or she is overpaid. Any search for the "just wage" is as elusive as the search for the "just price" in a capitalist system. If women in different occupations feel they are underpaid, they should organize and collectively bargain with their employers for higher wages and better working conditions. In short, to Krauthammer "comparable worth" is an irrational attempt to substitute a law for the inevitable dynamics of the marketplace.

Questions for Discussion

1. What are some of the societal and economic problems raised by the issue of comparable worth?
2. If comparable worth is not the answer to closing the salary gap between men and women, what *is* the solution? Or is there none?

Answer Guidelines

This issue should lead to a lively, open-ended discussion among members of the class. You may wish to stage a brief, formal debate between the proponents and opponents of comparable worth, perhaps after the debaters can research the issue more carefully.

Abstract 2 for Theme D

The Pros and Cons of Abortion

The controversy over whether abortion should be outlawed continues to divide the American public more than fifteen years after the Supreme Court ruling in *Roe v. Wade*. Prolife adherents assert that millions of lives have been snuffed out since the decision and that abortion treats the sanctity of human life immorally and with contempt. Proabortion groups stress the freedom of choice that a woman should have vis-a-vis her reproductive life. They also deny the prolifers' contention that human life (and the related idea of a legal "person") begins at conception.

The outlines of this debate are found in George McKenna and Stanley Feingold, eds., *Taking Sides: Clashing Views on Controversial Political Issues*, 7th ed. (Guilford, CT: Dushkin, 1991), in articles by President Ronald Reagan and Professor Beverly W. Harrison (pp. 262–272). President Reagan argues that (a) abortion is "not a right granted by the Constitution"; (b) abortion concerns every individual, since the death of an unborn child "diminishes the value of all human life"; (c) the public would roundly condemn the practice of abortion once they became fully aroused over and informed about the practice; (d) the unborn child is a "person" who can feel pain and who can be treated by modern medicine while still in the womb; (e) unwed mothers should be persuaded to have their children and then be helped by society to rear them; and (f) a newborn's physical or mental handicaps do not justify extinction. In short, to President Reagan, the "sanctity of life" prevails over the "quality of life."

Professor Harrison's excerpt, entitled "Our Right to Choose," stresses that (a) women have rights to bodily self-control and procreative choice; (b) abortion involves a *conflict between rights* (the unborn and the mother) rather than sole emphasis upon the rights of the fetus; (c) a fetus is not a "person" since it lacks consciousness, reasoning, self-motivated activity, the capacity to communicate, and the presence of self-concepts/self-awareness; (d) "the physical and emotional well-being of the pregnant woman, as a valuable existent person, still outweighs the incremental value of the fetus her life sustains" (p. 271); and (e) abortions will continue to be practiced, whether or not they are legal.

These two viewpoints on the practice of abortion leave little ground for political or ethical compromises. This may be one reason why the issue is one of the most intense in American society and why the political arena remains a forum for proposed constitutional amendments banning abortion or stressing the "rights" of the unborn.

Proposed Classroom Activity

Have students form two teams to debate the issue of legalized abortion. It would be helpful if the students on the teams were given time out of class to prepare the necessary materials, both pro and con, for the class debate. Let the remainder of the class serve as a collective "judge" to determine which side presented its case more persuasively.

Additional Lecture Topic D-1

The Abortion Issue

Paige C. Cunningham and Edward R. Grant, eds., *Abortion and the Constitution: Reversing Roe v. Wade Through the Courts*. Washington, DC: Georgetown University Press, 1987.

Nanette J. Davis, *From Crime to Choice: The Transformation of Abortion in America*. New York: Greenwood Press, 1985.

Marilyn Falik, *Ideology and Abortion Policy Politics*. New York: Praeger, 1983.

Stephen M. Krason, *Abortion: Politics, Morality and the Constitution*. New York: University Press of America, 1984.

Barbara Milbauer and Bert N. Obrentz, *The Law Giveth: Legal Aspects of the Abortion Controversy*. New York: McGraw-Hill, 1983.

Rosaline Petchesky, *Abortion and Women's Choice*. New York: Longman, 1984.

Hyman Rodman et al., *The Abortion Question*. New York: Columbia University Press, 1987.

Eva R. Rubin, *Abortion, Politics and the Courts: Roe v. Wade and Its Aftermath*. New York: Greenwood Press, 1982.

Laurence Tribe, *Abortion: The Clash of Absolutes*. New York: W. W. Norton, 1990.

Theme E Affirmative Action

Summary

In the 1970s, the attention of the civil rights movement shifted from passage of legislation to its implementation. The unresolved question was whether "civil rights" required merely the absence of discrimination or whether it required that steps be taken to ensure equality. The public clearly wants the government to provide simply *equality of opportunity* rather than attempt to achieve *equality of results*. The Supreme Court has straddled the issue of affirmative action, a policy designed to compensate for past discrimination by giving preference to minorities in hiring and promotion. Affirmative action has been attacked for numerous reasons. First, it is accused of amounting to "reverse discrimination," causing whites to suffer for the benefit of minorities; discrimination, the argument submits, is always wrong. Second, detractors of affirmative action contend that the persons paying the cost of past wrongs are themselves innocent victims. Young white males are not responsible for discrimination by their fathers, yet they are the ones being hurt by affirmative action, while at the same time minority members who never experienced the discrimination of the past are the ones being rewarded.

Defenders of affirmative action rejoin that racial discrimination still exists. Despite affirmative action, the median income of black families fell 4 percent compared with that of white families in the 1980s. Evidence of explicit discrimination is not difficult to find. The Fair Employment Council of Greater Washington has been using "testers" to document instances of discrimination. A tester is a minority member with similar qualifications to a white candidate seeking the same job. In 1992, the Council found that 22.4 percent of Hispanic job applicants encountered discrimination when matched against slightly less qualified white applicants. Second, all things are not equal; 40 percent of African-American children are living in poverty and begin life at a disadvantage. In the words of President Johnson, "You do not take a person who, for years, has been hobbled by chains and liberate him, bring him up to the starting line of a race and then say, 'You are free to compete with all the others,' and still justly believe that you have been completely fair."

While strong arguments exist on both sides, the American public is one sided in its opposition to affirmative action. A 1991 *Newsweek* survey revealed that 72 percent of whites and 42 percent of blacks disapproved giving preference to minorities in hiring, even when the minority applicant and the white job applicant are equally qualified.

The success of affirmative action has yielded mixed results. Since 1970, the number of African-Americans and women in management positions has increased four times. From 1983 to 1990 alone, the number of women executives and managers rose from 32.4 percent to 40 percent. However, the phenomenon known as the "glass ceiling" has prevented both women and blacks from reaching the top levels of management. Promotions tend to cease in the middle executive ranks. One the positive side, Rosabeth Moss Kanter discovered that Fortune 500 companies with affirmative action programs had "significantly higher" long-term profitability and growth because such programs translated into higher worker productivity.

The Supreme Court has decided a series of cases dealing with affirmative action. The decisions reflect deep division in the Court, making for many inconsistencies. The key factor seems to be whether a particular job or program had a history of past discrimination. With respect to government programs, quotas cannot be created without a showing of past discrimination; private companies, on the other hand, cannot use quotas but may use flexible goals even without evidence of past discrimination. In addition, neither public nor private programs can use affirmative action criteria in layoffs, only in hiring and promotion. This simple summary disguises the many fine distinctions the Court has drawn in its decisions. The book is far from closed on affirmative action.

Discussion Questions

1. Racial discrimination is *not* forbidden by the Fourteenth Amendment if the government has a "compelling interest." Such an interest was found to justify the confinement of over 112,000 persons of Japanese ancestry during World War II. Was the government's action correct given the wartime emergency? Consider the following facts: 99.3 percent of the Japanese were American citizens, 36 percent were under age nineteen, none was accused of disloyalty, 70,000 were native-born Americans. The government defended its action as a way to prevent sabotage. As General DeWitt wrote to President Roosevelt: "The very fact that no sabotage has taken place to date is a disturbing and confirming indication that such action will be taken." Is this argument sufficient to demonstrate a "compelling interest"?

2. Busing seldom occurs in the United States for purposes of integration. In 1984, 61 percent of students rode buses to school but only 4 percent did so to achieve school integration. The reason is the phenomenon known as "white flight"—white city-dwellers moving to the suburban areas. To illustrate, Atlanta city schools are 91.7 percent black, while the immediate suburbs are almost entirely white (Gwinnett County, 2.7 percent black; Fayette County, 4 percent black; Douglas County, 7 percent black). Should suburban schools be forced to bus with city schools? Does it matter that suburbanites do not pay taxes to support city schools? If busing into suburban areas is forbidden, how can poor black children receive a quality education and escape poverty? Wouldn't it be less expensive in the long run to pay for busing than for welfare?

3. Studies have shown blacks to be falling farther behind whites in income despite affirmative action programs. Does this mean that such programs are not working, or that the need for the programs remains?

Data and Perspectives for Analysis

Affirmative action programs are controversial. On the one hand, opponents claim that such programs constitute "reverse" discrimination—whites are harmed rather than blacks. All forms of discrimination are wrong. On the other hand, supporters of affirmative action programs respond that the effects of past discrimination must be remedied. Blacks (and women) remain at a disadvantage as reflected in income differentials between the races (and sexes).

Examine the case of *Regents of the University of California v. Bakke* (1978). Allen Bakke, a thirty-two-year-old white male, applied for admission to the medical school at the University of California at Davis. The school annually admitted 100 students, 84 regular admission and 16 special admission. Enrollment requirements were relaxed in the special-admission program. However, only members of specific "disadvantaged" groups were eligible for special-admission consideration. Bakke was rejected in two attempts at enrollment.

Acceptance decisions are largely a product of two factors, undergraduate Grade Point Average (GPA) and performance on the Medical College Admissions Test (MCAT). The profile of the 1973 class on these criteria are listed below:

	GPA	Verbal	MCAT Scores Quantitative	General
Bakke	3.44	96	94	72
Regular	3.51	81	76	69
Special	2.62	46	24	33

Allen Bakke was denied admission. Given the above data, how does your class feel about the fairness of the school's decision? While 12% of the population is black, only 2% of the nation's doctors are black. Does this inequity change the opinion of the class? Why aren't more doctors black if not because of discrimination?

20

Foreign Policy

Overview and Objectives

This chapter presents a survey of selected topics in United States foreign policy (or rather "policies"), focusing on the political processes involved in arriving at those policies. After reading and reviewing the material in this chapter the student should be able to do each of the following:

1. List the constitutional powers of the president and compare them with the authority of Congress in foreign affairs. Indicate why it is naive to read the Constitution literally in order to determine which institution has the major responsibility to conduct foreign policy. Explain why the president has a larger role than the Framers intended.

2. Compare the president's powers with those of a prime minister in a parliamentary system.

3. Explain why checks on the powers of the national government in foreign affairs are primarily political rather than constitutional.

4. Give reasons for the volatility of public opinion on foreign affairs. Explain the advantages that the president obtains when he acts resolutely in crises. Describe the problems that the president may face, using public opinion on the Vietnam War as an example.

5. Explain the worldview concept and describe the containment strategy of Mr. X. Summarize essential elements of the Munich-Pearl Harbor and post-Vietnam worldviews. Discuss the revisionist argument that it is the material interests of elites, rather than their principles, that explain American foreign policy. Indicate the possible objections to this view.

6. Discuss post-cold war policy and the growing role of the United Nations.

Chapter Outline with Keyed-in Resources

I. Kinds of foreign policy (THEME A: FOREIGN POLICY AS MAJORITARIAN POLITICS)
   A. Majoritarian politics
      1. Perceived to confer widespread benefits, impose widespread costs
      2. Examples
         a. War
         b. Military alliances
         c. Nuclear test ban or strategic arms limitation treaties
         d. Response to Berlin blockade by Soviets

The Berlin blockade posed a major problem in providing sufficient supplies to feed the population. The daily airlift brought 12,940.9 tons of cargo on 1,398 flights. A plane was landing in West Berlin every 61.8 seconds! The blockade lasted 238 days.

        e. Cuban missile crisis

A recent conference brought together the American and Soviet crisis-managers who participated in the 1962 episode. At this conference the Americans learned for the first time that some of the missile silos had been completely assembled. The purpose of the American naval quarantine of Cuba was to prevent the final components from reaching the island to make the missiles operational.

        f. Covert CIA operations
        g. Diplomatic recognition of People's Republic of China
    B. Interest-group politics
      1. Identifiable groups pitted against one another for costs, benefits
      2. Examples
        a. Cyprus policy: Greeks versus Turks
        b. Tariffs: Japanese versus steel
    C. Client politics
      1. Benefits to identifiable group, without apparent costs to any distinct group
      2. Example: policy toward Israel (transformation to interest group politics?)

The state of Israel has to lobby effectively since the country is so dependent on American aid. Direct contributions by the United States total about $3 billion annually, accounting for 10 percent of Israel's GNP.

    D. Who has power?
      1. Majoritarian politics: president dominates, public opinion supports but not guides
      2. Interest group or client politics: larger congressional role
      3. Entrepreneurial politics: Congress the central political arena
II. The constitutional and legal context
    A. Constitution creates "invitation to struggle"
      1. President commander in chief but Congress appropriates money
      2. President appoints ambassadors but Senate confirms
      3. President negotiates treaties but Senate ratifies
      4. But Americans think president in charge and history confirms
    B. Presidential box score
      1. Presidents relatively strong in foreign affairs
        a. More success in Congress on foreign than on domestic affairs
        b. Unilateral commitments of troops upheld but stronger than Framers intended
          (1) 1801: Jefferson sends navy to Barbary

While Jefferson did take action against the Barbary pirates, his interpretation of presidential power was narrow. Jefferson forced the navy to relinquish a captured pirate vessel because the president "was unauthorized by the Constitution, without the sanction of Congress, to go beyond the line of defense."

          (2) 1845: Polk sends troops to Mexico
          (3) 1861: Lincoln blockades southern ports

President Lincoln did not think a declaration of war was necessary to justify his actions, even though a blockade is an act of war, because the Southern states were in rebellion; they were not a sovereign nation according to Lincoln.

          (4) 1940: FDR sends destroyers to Britain
          (5) 1950: Truman sends troops to Korea
          (6) 1960s: Kennedy, Johnson send forces to Vietnam
          (7) 1983: Reagan sends troops to Grenada

                        (8) 1989: Bush orders invasion of Panama
                        (9) 1990: Bush sends forces into Kuwait
            2. Presidents comparatively weak in foreign affairs
                a. Other heads of state find U.S. presidents unable to act

The president may be somewhat constrained in foreign affairs, but the power of commander in chief provides much greater authority in the area of war-making. In the words of Harry Truman, the war powers of the American president would make even Ghengis Khan "green with envy."

                        (1) Wilson, FDR unable to ally with Britain before World War I, World War II
                        (2) Wilson unable to lead United States into League of Nations
                        (3) Reagan criticized on commitments to El Salvador, Lebanon
                        (4) Congressional debate on Bush's waging of Gulf War
        C. Evaluating the power of the president
            1. Depends on one's agreement/disagreement with policies
            2. Supreme Court gives federal government wide powers
                a. Reluctant to intervene in Congress-president disputes
                        (1) Nixon's enlarging of Vietnam War
                        (2) Lincoln's illegal measures during Civil War

The Supreme Court did void President Lincoln's violations of constitutional power but waited until after the Civil War was concluded to do so. In *Ex Parte Milligan* (1866), the Court held that "no doctrine involving more pernicious consequences, was ever invented by the wit of men than that the [Constitution's] provisions can be suspended during any of the great exigencies of government."

                        (3) Carter's handling of Iranian assets
                        (4) FDR's "relocation" of 100,000 Japanese Americans
        D. Checks on presidential power: political rather than constitutional
            1. Congress: control of purse strings (ADDITIONAL LECTURE TOPIC A-1)
            2. Limitations on the president's ability to give military or economic aid to other countries
                a. Arms sales to Turkey
                b. Blockage of intervention in Angola
                c. Legislative veto (previously) on large sales of arms
            3. The War Powers Act of 1973
                a. Provisions

The War Powers Act requires consultation prior to the use of military force: "The President, in every possible instance, shall consult with Congress before introducing United States Armed Forces into hostilities." No president has found it "possible" to comply with this requirement, even when President Carter took four months to plan the failed rescue attempt of American hostages in Iran.

                        (1) Only sixty-day commitment of troops without declaration of war
                        (2) All commitments reported within forty-eight hours
                        (3) Legislative veto (previously) to bring troops home
                b. Observance (no president has acknowledged constitutionality)
                        (1) Ford: *Mayaguez* incident
                        (2) Carter: attempted hostage rescue in Iran
                        (3) Reagan: troops to Lebanon, Grenada
                c. Supreme Court action
                        (1) Struck the legislative veto
                        (2) Other provisos to be tested
                d. Impact of act doubtful even if upheld
                        (1) Brief conflicts not likely to be affected; Congress does not challenge successful operation
                        (2) Even extended hostilities continue: Vietnam, Lebanon

4. Intelligence oversight
    a. Only two committees today—not the previous eight
    b. No authority to disapprove covert action
    c. But "covert" actions less secret after congressional debate
    d. Congress sometimes blocks covert action: Boland Amendment
III. The machinery of foreign policy
    A. Consequences of major power status
        1. President more involved in foreign affairs

President Kennedy once quipped that domestic policy can defeat a president at reelection whereas foreign policy can only destroy the nation.

        2. More agencies shape foreign policy
    B. Numerous agencies not really coordinated by anyone
    C. Secretary of state unable to coordinate
        1. Job too big for one person
        2. Most agencies owe no political or bureaucratic loyalty
    D. National Security Council created to coordinate

Since Henry Kissinger's tenure, Congress has required by law that the national security adviser be confirmed by the Senate.

        1. Chaired by president and includes vice president, secretaries of state and defense, director of CIA, chair of Joint Chiefs
        2. National security adviser heads staff
        3. Goal of staff is balanced view
        4. Grown in influence since JFK but downgraded by Reagan
        5. NSC rivals secretary of state
    E. Consequences of multicentered decision-making machinery
        1. "It's never over" due to rivalries within and between branches
        2. Agency positions influenced by agency interests
IV. Foreign policy and public opinion
    A. Outlines of foreign policy shaped by public and elite opinion
        1. Before World War II, public opposed United States involvement
        2. World War II shifted popular opinion because:
            a. Universally popular war
            b. War successful
            c. U.S. emerged world's dominant power
        3. Support for active involvement persisted until Vietnam
            a. Yet support for internationalism highly general
            b. Public opinion now mushy and volatile
    B. Backing the president
        1. Public's tendency to support president in crises
            a. Strong support to rally round the flag
            b. Boost in popularity immediately after crisis, except arms for hostages swap
        2. Yet presidents shun risky international ventures
            a. Support deteriorates if crisis not quickly resolved
            b. Support deteriorates if stalemate
        3. Lesson: fight popular crusade or short and victorious wars
    C. Mass versus elite opinion
        1. Mass opinion (ADDITIONAL LECTURE TOPIC A-2)
            a. Generally less well informed (Central America)

The lack of foreign affairs knowledge is demonstrated by a poll taken in 1985 which revealed that only 60 percent of the public knew that the United States had supported South Vietnam during the Vietnam War.

            b. Generally supportive of president, etc. (1968 Democratic Convention)
            c. Apt to judge undertakings by their success
            d. Conservative, less internationalist

     2. Elite opinion
        a. Better informed
        b. More volatile (Vietnam, Cambodia)
        c. Protest on moral, philosophical grounds
        d. More liberal and internationalist
 V. Cleavages among foreign policy elites (THEME B: THE FOREIGN POLICY ELITE)
    A. Foreign policy elite divided
    B. How a worldview shapes foreign policy
       1. Definition of worldview: comprehensive mental picture of world issues facing United States and ways of responding
       2. Example: article by "Mr. X" on containment of USSR (ADDITIONAL LECTURE TOPIC B-1)

George Kennan has noted on numerous occasions that the containment policy was misinterpreted. He alleges that he was not proposing military containment of the Soviet Union, only political.

       3. Not unanimously accepted, but consistent with public's mood, events, and experience
    C. Three worldviews
       1. Isolationism paradigm
          a. Opposes getting involved in European wars
          b. Adopted after World War I since war accomplished little
       2. Appeasement (containment) paradigm
          a. Reaction to appeasement of Hitler in Munich
          b. Pearl Harbor ended isolationism in U.S.
          c. Post-war policy to resist Soviet expansionism
       3. Vietnam (disengagement) paradigm
          a. Reaction to military defeat and political disaster of Vietnam
          b. Crisis interpreted in three ways
             (1) Correct worldview but did not try hard enough
             (2) Correct worldview but applied in wrong place
             (3) Worldview itself wrong
          c. Critics believed worldview wrong and new one needed based on new isolationism
    D. View of elites about Vietnam affects foreign policy views today
       1. Elites with disengagement view in Carter administration

Contrary to popular belief, the military buildup actually commenced under President Carter, with an annual budget increase for defense averaging 3 percent. Carter's last budget proposed a 4.7 percent increase in the military allocation. The military budget increased 26 percent from 1981 to 1986.

       2. Replaced during Reagan administration
       3. Elites active in think tanks and universities when out of power
       4. Elites in Clinton administration opposed Vietnam
 VI. The beginning of a new era
    A. 1989: fundamental shift in U.S.-Soviet relations
       1. Soviet empire was crumbling
          a. Gorbachev needed to rebuild economy
          b. Could not afford to repress freedom movements
          c. Outcome was breakup of Eastern bloc
          d. Withdrew troops from Afghanistan
          e. Cut military spending
    B. Antiappeasement view welcomed fall but wary
       1. USSR is still dangerous with changes for economic reasons

On April 1, 1991, the Warsaw Pact—the Soviet-led military alliance—formally disbanded.

       2. Policy positions

            a. Maintain U.S. military strength
            b. Do not give economic aid to USSR until more democratic
            c. Be wary of new arms control agreements
        C. Disengagement
            1. Elites are more optimistic
                a. Changes are fundamental and irreversible
                b. Europe is safe
                    (1) No longer need for troops
                    (2) Ballistic arsenal can be cut
            2. Aid to Gorbachev to prevent dangerous leaders coming to power
        D. Rival positions by 1991 coup
            1. Yeltsin replaces Gorbachev
            2. USSR abolished and CIS formed
            3. Fragmented USSR alters world politics
        E. America's role in the new era (THEME C: A NEW WORLD ORDER?)
            1. Threats remain
                a. More coups in Russia
                b. Fighting within and among the remnants of Soviet empire
                c. Ancient antagonisms in explosive regions like Middle East
                d. Spread of nuclear weapons
            2. Elite opinion will influence foreign policy
                a. Disagreement whether U.S. should be world's policeman or cut back on armed forces
                b. Split corresponds to differences between liberals and conservatives
        F. Growing role of the United Nations
            1. UN has history of settling conflicts but U.S. and USSR rarely provided forces
            2. Since USSR collapse, UN no longer dominated by cold war conflict
                a. Kuwait effort controlled by U.S. but not opposed by Russia
                b. UN peacekeeping missions more numerous
            3. Some American leaders welcome U.S. military cooperation with UN
            4. Other leaders oppose U.S. forces being directed by an international organization
            5. Liberals favor UN cooperation, conservatives oppose

Important Terms

antiappeasement The worldview adopted by American elite opinion after the failure of the effort to avoid conflict with Adolf Hitler by granting ever-greater territorial concessions. This view, which supports the containment of aggressive world powers, was the policy followed by the United States to prevent expansion of the Soviet sphere of influence after World War II through a network of defensive alliances in Europe and Asia. Its adherents welcome the collapse of the iron curtain but remain wary of Soviet military power.

cold war A term that refers to the nonmilitary struggle between the United States (and its allies) and the Soviet Union (and its allies). A cold war is distinguished from a hot or shooting war.

containment The policy proposed by George Kennan which advocated that the United States prevent Soviet expansion through counterforce and subsequently became the basis of the anti-appeasement worldview.

disengagement view The worldview adopted by American elite opinion as a result of the U.S. military defeat in Vietnam. Its advocates support "new isolationism" in which the United States would avoid extending its military commitments overseas as the world's police force.

*domino theory An analogy used by President Eisenhower to justify giving aid to South Vietnam to prevent it, and thus its southeast Asian neighbors, from being taken over by communists.

intelligence oversight The requirement that the CIA notify the House and Senate intelligence committees of all intelligence activities, including covert actions. However, the committees do not have authority to disapprove such actions.

*iron curtain A phrase used by Winston Churchill to refer to the political barrier, maintained by the Soviet Union, to free travel and communication between Eastern and Western Europe.

*isolationism The worldview adopted by American elite opinion after World War I which held that the United States should avoid alliances with other countries.

National Security Council A committee created by statute to coordinate the foreign policy establishment. The council is chaired by the president, and its membership includes the vice president and the secretaries of defense and state. By custom, the director of the CIA and the chairman of the Joint Chiefs of Staff also serve. The staff is headed by the national security adviser. The council's purpose is to present the president with a balanced account of the views of the major government agencies on national security issues.

rallying round the flag The tendency for a president's level of public approval to increase after a foreign crisis, whether force is used or not. A high level of support, however, exists only during the early stages of an international crisis; it deteriorates if the crisis is protracted.

spook speak Jargon used by the Central Intelligence Agency and other intelligence organizations to refer to their activities and procedures.

*Third World Originally a French term referring to nations neutral in the cold war between the United States and the Soviet Union, the phrase now refers to almost any underdeveloped nation in Africa, Asia, Latin America, or the Middle East.

two presidencies The thesis of presidential power formulated by Aaron Wildavsky which concludes that the president is weak and closely checked by Congress in domestic affairs but is quite powerful in foreign affairs.

Vietnam view *See* disengagement view.

War Powers Act A law passed in 1973 which aimed to restrict the president's ability to use military force. Its key provision is that the president must remove troops within sixty days of their introduction into a hostile situation unless Congress declares war or authorizes an extension of the commitment. No president has acknowledged the constitutionality of the act, and certain provisions involving legislative vetoes may in fact be void.

*worldviews A comprehensive picture of the critical problems facing the United States in the world and of the appropriate and inappropriate ways of responding to these problems.

Theme A   Foreign Policy as Majoritarian Politics

Instructor References

Cecil V. Crabb, Jr., *American Diplomacy and the Pragmatic Tradition.* Baton Rouge, LA: Louisiana State University Press, 1989.

James E. Dougherty and Robert L. Pfaltzgraff, Jr., *American Foreign Policy: FDR to Reagan.* New York: Harper & Row, 1986.

Louis Henkin, *Constitutionalism, Democracy, and Foreign Affairs.* New York: Columbia University Press, 1990.

Roy Macridis, ed., *Foreign Policy in World Politics.* Englewood Cliffs, NJ: Prentice-Hall, 1985. See Chapter 4, "America's Foreign Policy," by Robert J. Art, pp. 114–169.

Jerel A. Rosati, *The Politics of United States Foreign Policy*. Fort Worth, Texas: Holt, Rinehart and Winston, 1993.

John Spanier and Eric M. Uslaner, *American Foreign Policy Making and the Democratic Dilemmas*. 2nd ed. New York: Holt, Rinehart & Winston 1985. See Chapters 2 and 3 on presidential and congressional roles in foreign policy.

John Spanier, *American Foreign Policy Since World War II*. 11th ed. Washington, DC: Congressional Quarterly Press, 1988.

Summary

The relationship between democracy and foreign policy must be viewed as problematical. For Tocqueville, democracies could not apply the firmness of purpose, efficiency of execution, secrecy, and patience that effective foreign policy requires. During the Vietnam War era, on the other hand, it was often charged that too much secrecy and firmness of purpose (without regard to popular wishes) were the problem. This chapter is chiefly concerned with foreign policy insofar as it displays the characteristics of majoritarian politics. The "grand issues" of war, peace, and global diplomacy are the subject of this sort of politics. Of course, interest-group politics may affect foreign policy, as in the Greek-Turkish conflict over Cyprus, or in tariff battles in which the users of imports (as well as those who want to keep them out) are well organized. Client politics may play a role, too—providing aid to corporations doing business abroad and historical American support for Israel are two examples. (More recently, Arab Americans and energy interests have mobilized on the other side of this last issue, and it more nearly resembles interest-group politics). If an issue is majoritarian in nature, the president usually dominates. If interest group or client politics is involved, Congress plays a much larger role.

The Constitution offers the president and Congress an "invitation to struggle" in the conduct of foreign affairs. The president is commander in chief of the armed forces, appoints ambassadors, and negotiates treaties. But the Senate must approve those treaties and ambassadorial appointments. Congress must appropriate money to fund military (or other) ventures abroad, and it must declare war. This enumeration of powers suggests that the president and Congress are evenly matched; in fact, the president is far more powerful. He often sends troops abroad without formal congressional assent (five of this nation's eleven major wars have not been formally declared), and he is much more successful in gaining congressional approval of foreign policy proposals than of domestic policy proposals. Aaron Wildavsky has concluded that there are *two presidencies*, a weak domestic one and a strong foreign one. Note, however, that even in foreign affairs the U.S. president is weaker than chief executives in other democracies.

The Supreme Court has fairly consistently held that the conduct of foreign policy is a *political question* to be decided between the president and Congress. It not only has held that the federal government holds powers never mentioned in the Constitution, but has also upheld extreme cases of violations of civil liberties when defended on the grounds of internal security during wartime (for example, the relocation of Japanese-Americans during World War II).

Congress does have some ability to check the president, however. Its control of the purse strings is probably its most important weapon. Congress imposed three kinds of restrictions on the president after the end of the Vietnam War: (1) It limited military or economic aid to other countries (Turkey and Angola are examples); (2) It enacted the War Powers Resolution, which required congressional approval of any commitment of American troops in hostile situations abroad for over sixty days. However, in the *Chadha* case, the Supreme Court struck down a portion of the act that authorized legislative vetoes to control arms sales abroad. Even if the rest of the law is sustained by the courts in the future, its practical political significance is questionable, because Congress is not likely to challenge the president in either a brief military operation such as the one in Grenada or in a protracted conflict such as the Vietnam War. Also, President Reagan's commitment of U.S. Marines into Lebanon revealed congressional flexibility in that an eighteen-month period was authorized rather than the original sixty days; (3) It created intelligence oversight committees in both houses in order to control the CIA's activities, including covert operations.

Before World War II, public opinion was isolationist, opposing foreign involvements. That war seems to have been a great watershed. Since that time Americans have become much more internationalist, although considerable "mushiness" marks their responses to public opinion polls. In times of crisis, Americans rally to the support of the president. They tend to endorse the president's actions. Before Nixon sent troops into Cambodia only 7 percent of Americans supported such a move; afterward, 50 percent said they approved. Approval of the president also tends to increase after a foreign policy crisis. Even a great fiasco such as the Bay of Pigs has this effect. However, if the crisis is not resolved and a protracted and costly stalemate seems to ensue, support deteriorates. The Vietnam and Korean wars were examples of this phenomenon. We tend to think of the Korean War as having been less unpopular than the war in Vietnam; however, it was *elite* opinion, not public opinion, that was particularly opposed to Vietnam. Mass opinion is largely uninformed about world affairs (Central America) and tends to support the president. Elite opinion is generally knowledgeable and far more critical of presidential actions in foreign policy. Mass opinion supports war policies so long as they appear to be successful. Elite opinion is more volatile and moralistic. Thus elites became more upset over U.S. policy in Vietnam when policy accentuated the *offensive*, while the average citizen dislikes U.S. *defensive* actions. Also, mass opinion more strongly opposed antiwar protests than college-educated elites. Mass-elite cleavages are even more pronounced when attitudes of actual foreign policy makers and average citizens are compared, the former being more liberal and internationalist in outlook.

Discussion Questions

1. Why did Tocqueville believe that democracies have great trouble conducting foreign affairs effectively? What claims are made by those who believe the exact *opposite*—that policies are made badly when elites have too much discretion and are made better when they are aired democratically?

2. What about foreign policy issues today? Can you think of any cases in which our policy was harmed by open debate? Can you think of any cases in which our policy was harmed by being made in secret and where open debate would have produced a better policy? What about (a) the Panama Canal treaty; (b) peace negotiations in the Middle East; (c) the recognition of Communist China? (*Instructor: Add more recent examples.*) How much of the policy-making in each of these circumstances was done in secret? Was there a good reason for secrecy, or was secrecy used as a means of "putting something over" on somebody?

3. If the Constitution does not make the president clearly dominant in foreign affairs, how has he managed to exert so much power? Could Congress be dominant if it wanted to? Does Congress fail to exercise power (a) for policy reasons (unified leadership is needed and Congress knows that it cannot provide it); (b) for institutional reasons (the president has access to better information than Congress does); or (c) for political reasons (Congress members do not profit politically from tackling foreign policy issues)?

4. On what basis have most people judged whether the president's powers are too extensive or too limited? Does the same go for domestic affairs? Why is it shortsighted to judge the presidency on the basis of the ideology of its incumbent?

5. What role has the Supreme Court played in foreign policy? How does this compare to the role it has played in civil rights or in business regulation? Why has the Court been so much more restrained in foreign policy? Can what the Constitution *says* explain the Court's position? For example, you can make a reasonable case that the Fourteenth Amendment prevents much government regulation of the economy (as a conservative Court asserted before 1937) and a reasonable case that amendment outlaws segregation (as the Warren Court claimed in 1954). Can you not also make a case that the Vietnam War was unconstitutional?

6. Does the fact that public opinion follows presidential initiatives mean that policies cannot reasonably be said to be democratic? Does this not mean that the president can do what he wants to do and then count on public support?

7. How are foreign affairs more politically profitable for the president than domestic affairs? Does this suggest that the president will allot too much attention to foreign affairs relative to domestic affairs? Does this suggest that the president is at a disadvantage in dealing with foreign leaders who need not worry about public opinion in their nations?

8. Why does the president or Congress not ask the Supreme Court to rule on the overall constitutionality of the entire War Powers Act?

9. Why can the American public not support a long drawn-out conflict overseas?

10. Congress enacted the War Powers Act to curtail presidential power in the area of warmaking. Can't the president still invade any country he wants to without prior congressional approval? Doesn't the War Powers Act make legal what was once probably not so—the ability of the president to start a war on his own? How does the War Powers Act apply to nuclear war?

Data and Perspectives for Analysis

A. Troop Commitments and the War Powers Act

The War Powers Act has been controversial since its enactment in 1973. President Nixon vetoed the resolution only to be overridden by Congress. Every president since Nixon has complained that the act imposes unconstitutional restraints on the president's role as commander in chief. Has the act constituted an impediment to presidential authority?

Consider the instances in which American forces were introduced into hostile environments from 1974 to 1986 and the manner in which presidents complied with the War Powers Act. What conclusions can be drawn from the table below? Does the party of the president (Democratic or Republican) make a difference? What is different about the times presidents reported to Congress under the act?

U.S. Troop Commitments, 1974–1986

Deployment	War Powers Application
Cyprus evacuation (1974)	No Report
Cambodian resupply (1974)	No Report
Cambodian reconnaissance (1974)	No Report
Danang sealift (1975)	Report/Sec. 4(a)(2)
Cambodian evacuation (1975)	Report/Sec. 4(a)(2)
Vietnam evacuation (1975)	Report/Sec. 4
Mayaguez incident (1975)	Report/Sec. 4(a)(1)
Lebanon evacuation (1976)	No Report
Korean reenforcement (1976)	No Report
Zaire airlift (1978)	No Report
Iranian rescue mission (1980)	Report/No section specified
Advisers in El Salvador (1981)	No Report
Sinai multinational force (1982)	Report/Sec. 4(a)(2)
Lebanon—PLO evacuation (1982)	Report/No section specified
Lebanon—U.S. evacuation (1982)	Report/No section specified
Chad reconnaissance (1983)	Report/Sec. 4
Lebanon peacekeeping force (1983)	Report/Sec. 4
AWACs to Chad (1983)	Report/Sec. 4
Grenada invasion (1983)	Report/Sec. 4(a)(1)
Gulf of Sidra (1986)	Report/No statute cited
Libyan retaliation (1986)	Report/No statute cited

Source: Daniel Paul Franklin, "War Powers in the Modern Context," *Congress and the Presidency* (Spring 1987): 80.

B. Public Opinion and World War

Majoritarian politics involves costs and benefits that are shared by the nation as a whole. Perhaps the most prominent such issue is the decision whether the nation should go to war. The post-cold war era has changed the foundation on which world politics operated since the conclusion of World War II. One might suspect that the world has issued a collective sigh of relief as the prospect of nuclear war subsides. That is not the case, at least in the United States. What is surprising, however, is the degree of regional variation in how Americans view the likelihood of a future world conflagration.

A survey by the *Atlanta Journal-Constitution* and the University of North Carolina in 1994 posed the following question: "Do you think there will be another world war at some point, or not?" The results reveal an interesting national dynamic at work. While 49 percent of southerners responded affirmatively, only 36 percent of nonsoutherners considered a future world war likely. What accounts for the divergence in levels of pessimism?

Jill Vejnoska (*Atlanta Constitution*, June 8, 1994: A3) queried experts in southern history and culture for an explanation. She discovered that religion plays an important role in one's outlook toward global conflict.

> Those who identified themselves as Baptists or Methodists were much more likely (55 percent) to think there would be another world war than 'other Protestants' or Jews (both 42.8 percent). Even more significant, perhaps, respondents who said they believed the Bible was 'scientifically, historically and literally true' were much more likely to believe another world war was on the way.

Vejnoska interprets these results to signify that southerners are prone to accept the Biblical conclusion that Armageddon is inevitably on its way.

Aside from religion, Vejnoska also identified another factor behind the greater pessimism of southerners—their higher rate of military service. About half of career military personnel in the United States live in the South. Vejnoska quotes Walter Edgar, director of the University of South Carolina's Institute for Southern Studies, who contends that southerners "may be thinking about or familiar with various flashpoints around the world that may erupt."

Since war is a majoritarian policy, the nation will not react uniformly if global tensions begin to escalate. Southerners are almost resigned to this fate while nonsoutherners are more likely to interpret events as less menacing.

Additional Lecture Topics

A-1. Congressional-Presidential Struggles over Foreign Policy

Seyom Brown, *On the Front Burner—Issues in U.S. Foreign Policy*. Boston: Little, Brown, 1984. See Chapter 2 on problems of policy control faced by executive, pp. 15–43.

Duncan Clark, "Why State Can't Lead," *Foreign Policy* (Spring 1987): 128–142.

James Dull, *The Politics of American Foreign Policy*. Englewood Cliffs, NJ: Prentice-Hall, 1985. See Chapter 7 on congressional powers and roles in foreign policy, pp. 88–106.

Frederick H. Hartmann and Robert L. Wendzel, *To Preserve the Republic*. New York: Macmillan, 1985. See Chapter 6 on general presidential-congressional relationships and the reasons behind the growth of congressional assertiveness.

Glenn P. Hastedt, *American Foreign Policy*. Englewood Cliffs, NJ: Prentice-Hall, 1988.

Barbara Kellerman and Ryan J. Barilleaux, *The President as World Leader*. New York: St. Martin's Press, 1991.

Thomas E. Mann, "Making Foreign Policy: President and Congress," in Thomas E. Mann, ed., *A Question of Balance: The President, The Congress and Foreign Policy*. Washington, DC: Brookings Institute, 1990, 1–34.

A-2. Public Opinion and Foreign Policy

Cecil V. Crabb, *American Foreign Policy in the Nuclear Age*. 5th ed. New York: Harper & Row, 1988. See Chapter 8, "The Public Context of Foreign Policy."

Roger Hilsman, *The Politics of Policymaking in Defense and Foreign Affairs*. Englewood Cliffs, NJ: Prentice-Hall, 1987. See Chapters 11–13 on the media, public opinion, and the electorate.

Ole R. Holsti and James N. Rosenau, *American Leadership in World Affairs: Vietnam and the Breakdown of Consensus*. Boston: Allen and Unwin, 1984. The war's effect on Americans' traditional support of the post-1945 consensus.

Ralph P. Levering, *The Public and American Foreign Policy: 1918–1978*. New York: Morrow, 1978. Good historical survey illustrating the public's shift from isolationism to interventionism.

John E. Mueller, *War, Presidents, and Public Opinion*. New York: Wiley, 1973. Explores how the "coalition of minorities" influences presidential popularity over time, especially as a war drags on without prospects of victory.

Eugene R. Wittkopf, *Faces of Internationalism: Public Opinion and American Foreign Policy*. Durham, NC: Duke University Press, 1990.

Abstract for Theme A

A Further Look at the War Powers Act

In John Spanier and Eric M. Uslaner's *American Foreign Policy Making and the Democratic Dilemmas* (op. cit.), the foreign policy implications of the War Powers Act are scrutinized more closely (pp. 68–75). First, the authors point out the most important provisions of the resolution:

   a. The resolution states that the president, shall, in every possible instance, consult with Congress *before* using U.S. Armed Forces.

   b. Even when the president uses his emergency powers, the War Powers Act requires that he immediately make a full report to Congress and obtain congressional authority to continue the action after sixty days, with an extension of thirty additional days if troops are in danger. If he fails to receive legislative concurrence, he must terminate the action at that time.

   c. Even before this sixty-day deadline, Congress can terminate the action through a concurrent resolution, which would not be subject to a presidential veto (p. 68).

From the authors' viewpoint, the War Powers Act altered the Constitution "from reading that war cannot be waged without the consent of Congress to [reading that] the president can wage war until Congress stops him" (p. 69).

However, the historical record shows that Congress, for the most part, has been reluctant to precipitate a true confrontation with the president over implementing the act. When the U.S. merchant ship *Mayaguez* was seized by the Cambodians in 1975, President Ford informed Congress that military forces were rescuing the ship and the crew, but he did not consult them *prior* to sending the rescue force. Likewise, President Carter did not consult Congress about the ill-fated 1980 attempt to rescue American hostages held in Iran. Finally, U.S. support of covert action in Central America, though it raised the war powers issue, did not end in the act's implementation.

Perhaps the most crucial test of the War Powers Act was President Reagan's dispatch of U.S. Marines to Lebanon in 1982–1983 as part of an international peacekeeping force. Congress charged that the marines were involved in a combat situation, but President Reagan denied this. The result was an eighteen-month compromise instead of the normal sixty days for the marines' tenure, though the president removed the marines much earlier after a tragic bombing of their barracks.

In the 1983 Grenada invasion, President Reagan sent a force of marines onto the tiny island both to save American lives and to thwart Cuban control. As Spanier and Uslaner explain it, the

> president sent Congress a letter informing its leaders of the invasion . . . but he did not invoke the resolution. Again, Reagan insisted that the law could not tie his hands as commander in chief. Democrats, particularly in the Senate, were especially critical of the president's action. Both houses of Congress insisted on invoking the War Powers Act forcing the president to remove the troops within 60 days unless Congress approved an extension. (p. 72)

Spanier and Uslaner conclude that "the limits of presidential discretion in the use of force" remain cloudy and that "perhaps only a major large-scale intervention abroad by U.S. forces will resolve the issue" (p. 73). Still, some basic problems remain regarding the War Powers Act. First, what happens if the president and Congress differ as to what constitutes a national emergency or crisis? The act wrongly assumed that a crisis will always be crystal clear to both branches, which was not the case in Grenada. Second, from a practical viewpoint, can any presidential administration consult Congress in advance of an important military operation? The potential adversary would be forewarned and American fighting men endangered. Finally, can Congress really be a participant in crisis decision making? The authors cite President Ford's position during the *Mayaguez* incident, which was complicated by difficulty in communicating with key legislators (who were out of town), the pressures of time, the reluctance of Congress members to accept a preliminary consensus, and the strong likelihood of leaks (pp. 73–74). The authors also assert that Congress might not want to be informed:

> Paradoxically, however, one might question how many congressmen really want to know what the president is planning. It is one thing to blame him for failure afterwards and suggest that had he consulted with Congress this failure could have been avoided; it is another matter to also be held accountable for disaster. Perhaps it is for this reason that not too many voices were raised in protest about the lack of consultation after the failure of the mission to rescue the hostages in Iran. (p. 74)

In a final observation, the authors note the effect of the *Chadha* decision on the constitutionality of the War Powers Act. In their view, the requirement of presidential consultation with Congress when American troops are sent overseas is not affected. But what Congress may not be able to do after the *Chadha* case "is to force withdrawal of troops engaged in hostilities" (p. 75). As a rejoinder, "the Congress has not admitted defeat on the war powers issue, claiming that the Supreme Court decision on the immigration bill may not cover all aspects of the legislative veto" (p. 75).

Questions for Discussion

1. Imagine you are a justice on the Supreme Court. Using the *Chadha* decision and the historical record, give your individual ruling on the constitutionality of the War Powers Act.

2. Is Congress capable of being a joint decision-maker in times of international crisis? Why or why not?

Answer Guidelines

Question 1 is wide open for discussion. Regarding Question 2, it seems highly unlikely that Congress could act quickly enough in a crisis to be an effective partner of the president. Given the extraordinary demands made on policy makers in a crisis, it would be hard for a collective ensemble of 535 men and women to duplicate the information-gathering capabilities and administrative efficiency available to the president and his immediate coterie of advisers.

Theme B The Foreign Policy Elite

Instructor Reference

David Halberstam, *The Best and the Brightest*. New York: Random House, 1969. A fascinating study of the foreign policy elite that constructed the Vietnam worldview from 1961 to 1968.

Summary

Public opinion provides support for presidential initiatives in foreign policy but no *specific* direction. In foreign policy, more than in other policy areas, elite *worldviews* determine policy. A worldview is a more or less comprehensive picture of the critical problems facing the United States in the world and of the appropriate ways of responding. Elite worldviews are typically the result of learning the "lessons" of some foreign policy disaster. Prevailing worldviews can change rapidly, as the era of American "imperialism" (1898–1900) and the Klingberg Cycle attest. However, from the end of World War II until 1976 the dominant worldview was based on the lessons of *Munich and Pearl Harbor*. Munich taught a generation that it is futile to compromise with aggression and to attempt "appeasement." Pearl Harbor discredited the view that America could successfully remain aloof from foreign entanglements. Thus the strategy of *containment* required that any Soviet attempt at expansion be met with counterforce.

Failure of America's Vietnam policy (which was an application of the lessons of Munich and Pearl Harbor) impressed on a new generation of foreign policy experts a very different view. The *Vietnam worldview* inclined toward minimizing, rather than maximizing, American interventions abroad; less military spending; more emphasis on negotiation with the Soviet Union; and a more favorable view of the Third World. The elite holding the Vietnam worldview came to power with Jimmy Carter in 1976. The Soviet invasion of Afghanistan provoked Carter to take a tougher stand toward the Soviet Union, and the Iranian hostage crisis made Americans more willing to be assertive with foreign nations. When Ronald Reagan took office in 1981, he brought with him advisers and cabinet secretaries committed to a military buildup, a tougher line toward Russia, and the restoration of the Munich-Pearl Harbor worldview. In the 1984 election, the Democratic party (particularly Gary Hart) attacked Reagan's policy for neglecting the social factors (in Central America) that encourage communism and also for relying excessively on force. The Pearl Harbor-Vietnam cleavage in foreign policy views parallels the cleavage between the Republican and the Democratic parties' leadership in America's role in the world.

Discussion Questions

1. Do foreign policy elites tend to learn the lessons of history and benefit from previous mistakes?

2. Generalize how the prevailing worldviews of the foreign policy elites of the Democratic party differ from those of the Republican party. Does a worldview exist today with the collapse of communism?

Additional Lecture Topic B-1

The Cold War: Origins and Conclusion

1. Origins

Dean Acheson, *Present at the Creation*. New York: Norton, 1969. A classic memoir on the events that contributed to the outbreak of the cold war.

David Carlton and Herbert M. Levine, eds., *The Cold War Debated*. New York: McGraw-Hill, 1988. See Chapter 1 on the Yalta Conference and Chapter 6 on alleged U.S. responsibility for the cold war.

James V. Compton, ed., *America and the Origins of the Cold War*. Boston: Houghton Mifflin, 1972. A superb collection of articles dealing with the years 1943–1947. Strong on examples of historical revisionism.

Herbert Feis, *From Trust to Terror—The Onset of the Cold War, 1945–1950*. New York: Norton Press, 1970. One of the best histories of this crucial five-year period.

Charles Gati, ed., *Caging the Bear: Containment and the Cold War*. Indianapolis and New York: Bobbs-Merrill, 1974. Incisive material on the many aspects and implications of Kennan's original containment thesis.

Walter LaFeber, *America, Russia, and the Cold War 1949–1990*. New York: McGraw Hill, 1991.

2. Conclusion

David Calleo, *Beyond American Hegemony: The Future of the Western Alliance*. New York: Basic Books, 1987.

Bogadan Demitch, *The End of the Cold War*. Minneapolis: University of Minnesota Press, 1990.

William Hyland, *The Cold War Is Over*. New York: Times Books, 1990.

Edward Hamilton, ed., *America's Global Interests: A New Agenda*. New York: Norton, 1989.

Abstract 1 for Theme B

The "Lessons" and Effects of the Vietnam War

What was the long-range impact of the Vietnam War on American society and foreign policy? Ten years after the end of the war, the *New York Times* devoted a number of articles to exploring that impact. Adam Clymer's "What Americans Think Now" (*New York Times Magazine*, March 31, 1985, p. 34) revealed a number of significant poll findings about the public attitudes of the post-Vietnam generation.

1. The Vietnam War's "lessons" about placing restraints on American military power seemed to be losing strength. "When asked if United States troops should be used in a list of crises, support was higher in 1985 in every case." Now 54 percent favored using troops to save Western Europe from invasion, compared to 40 percent in 1976. Even more interesting was that eighteen- to twenty-nine-year-olds, those who would probably do the actual fighting, favored saving Europe by a 55 percent to 37 percent margin. Even support for using troops in El Salvador to stop communism had increased (measured against a 1983 poll); 47 percent supported their use and 43 percent opposed it (compared to a June, 1983, *New York Times* poll that showed 32 percent in favor and 57 percent opposed).

2. The legacy of distrust toward the government and the military created by Vietnam "was wearing away." However, the picture in this area was still mixed. Whereas 59 percent of college-educated youths felt that Washington could be trusted to do the right thing "all or most of the time," only 45 percent of the rest of the population agreed with that assessment. (This was still higher than the 35 percent in 1974 who trusted government but much lower than the 76 percent who did so in 1964, prior to Vietnam.) Still, the sense of alienation was strong in the Vietnam generation, now in their thirties, among whom 61 percent agreed that "the government is pretty much run by a few big interests."

3. Faith in the military had grown since 1975, with 68 percent expressing confidence in the armed forces, as opposed to only 58 percent in 1975.

4. However, the Vietnam War remained distinctly unpopular. Only 19 percent of the public stated that the United States was right in getting involved in Vietnam, and 73 percent said that the nation "should have stayed out." Clymer concludes his analysis of public attitudes as follows:

> The Vietnam experience is deeply contradictory. For example, many people say the war was immoral but still believe it taught us that we must sometimes back unwholesome governments because Communist regimes are worse. One indisputable lesson is how little many in the United States know, or are willing to remember, of the searing Vietnam War. In the latest poll, just three Americans in five could say the United States sided with South Vietnam.

Allan E. Goodman and Seth P. Tillman's "10 Years Later, Lessons of the Vietnam War" (*New York Times*, March 24, 1985, p. E-23) is more concerned with the historical effects on America's conduct of foreign policy and its domestic political system. The authors' basic contention is that history has not fully vindicated either the opponents or the proponents of the war. For example, the domino theory has "proved to be largely but not entirely false. Most of Southeast Asia did not fall under Communist rule, but all three of the countries of Indochina did." The "doves" miscalculated when they presumed Hanoi's rule would be benign (Hanoi imposed a Stalinist-like rule over the united Vietnam), and the "hawks" overestimated the injury that America's reputation would suffer from its defeat in Southeast Asia.

Goodman and Tillman point out that the end of American involvement in Vietnam actually had some neutral or conservative effects.

> The Soviet Union has profited only marginally and China not at all from the spread of Communism in Indochina. The United States has suffered no setbacks in the third world directly attributable to Vietnam. Our European allies and Japan were relieved. . . . The opening to China and the normalization of relations became possible only when it was clear that the United States would soon be out of Indochina, and the most significant period of *detente* with the Soviet Union began as the war came to a close.

Perhaps it was the *domestic* consequences of Vietnam that were the most striking. The authors contend that Vietnam divided the American people, destroyed the Johnson presidency, divided and demoralized the Democratic party (the party is still feeling the effects of that division today), and "undermined trust between Congress and the executive. . . . For reasons largely attributable to Vietnam, Congress has become a suspicious, meddlesome, and frequently disruptive partner in American foreign policy." Thus, to the authors, the Reagan administration represented "a return to pride and patriotism . . . a 'conservative restoration' marked by militancy in foreign policy and a decline of social concern at home."

So the fundamental lessons of Vietnam remain: (a) the issue of when to intervene and when not to and for how long; (b) the need not to label every possible intervention as being analogous to Vietnam; and (c) the clear verdict "that no foreign venture can succeed without solid domestic foundations—moral and cultural no less than political and economic. . . . "

Questions for Discussion

1. If the United States were forced into a combat that became protracted, would current public acceptance of military intervention change substantially? Why or why not?
2. How could American foreign policy elites create a supportive consensus before and during a future military intervention, thus avoiding another Vietnam?

Answer Guidelines

The obvious key to both of these queries is the length of the involvement as well as the prospects for victory. Quick, successful interventions prevent public and congressional criticism from building. Regarding the construction of a supportive consensus, it would seem to be an imperative that the president enunciate foreign policy goals that are unambiguous and can be directly linked to the security of the United States. It follows that future American commitments overseas will have to be quite selective in order to avoid the cry of "no more Vietnams."

Theme C A New World Order?

Summary

The breakup of the Soviet Union seems to have confused the direction of American foreign policy rather than to have helped clarify it. The neat bipolar world of the cold war has yielded to a multiplicity of "hot spots." The United States has not yet defined the role it should play in what President George Bush called the "new world order." Should the nation extinguish the fires of national turmoil, or should the country disengage from the world by cutting back on its armed forces and intervening only when its own security is at stake? The problem is that the foreign policy elite is divided over America's responsibility in resolving global conflicts. Vietnam still haunts the memories of the elite establishment whenever the issue of intervention is raised.

Liberals, who largely share the disengagement worldview, endorse greater cooperation with the peacekeeping efforts of the United Nations. Such cooperation, they believe, would enable the United States to reduce its military apparatus (freeing money for domestic activities), minimize the direct level of American involvement in world conflicts, and furnish legitimacy to the use of military force when needed. Conservatives, who generally embrace the antiappeasement worldview, are more cautious about withdrawing from the world in a unilateral fashion. They point to numerous threats that warrant continued vigilance on the part of the United States: the proliferation of nuclear weapons, instability in Russia, and regional antagonisms. Antiappeasement elites resist relinquishing control of American troops to the direction of the United Nations, since to do so would amount to an abandonment of national independence.

Given the division in elite opinion, it is not surprising that American foreign policy has been characterized recently by uncertainty and fluctuation. This pattern of decision-making is reflected in the behavior of both post-cold war administrations. President Bush, according to Terry Deibel writing in *Foreign Policy*, exhibited a "mixture of competence and drift" that Charles Kegley interpreted as indicating Bush would rather retain the containment worldview than formulate a new vision. As in domestic policy, the Bush presidency sought to "stay the course" in foreign affairs despite confronting a set of changed priorities. President Clinton has not fared much better in managing the altered context of the world environment. He was immediately thrown into a host of crises involving an array of widely scattered countries: Somalia, Bosnia, Rwanda, Haiti, North Korea. He reacted more in line with the disengagement worldview that Republican Senator John McCain described in the following manner in 1994: "The Administration appears to use threats to relieve itself of the need to take further action in dealing with a difficult problem." Clinton seems to eschew intervention unless under the cover of a United Nations mandate.

The sudden demise of the Soviet Union has paralyzed United States foreign policy, with the national elite refusing to surrender worldviews conceived when global politics operated under different rules. The country's elite is surely in need of what President Bush labeled the "vision thing" to produce some degree of consensus and to give consistency to American foreign policy in a new world order.

Discussion Questions

1. Two worldviews for American policy divide the national elite: disengagement and antiappeasement. Which of these worldviews is more consistent with the current reality of global politics? Should the United States always await the approval of the United Nations before intervening in a world crisis? Didn't this policy contribute to the situation in Bosnia? But if the United States had acted in opposition to other world powers, what would have been the consequences?

2. President Bush spoke of a "new world order" but failed to explain the nature of this order. Should the U.S. assist in the rebuilding of Russia? When should the U.S. get involved in a conflict that does not threaten its own national security, such as in Bosnia? Can American deaths be justified where the nation is not in danger?

3. The worldviews of the national elite have been formed to correspond to a global situation that no longer exists. Does a third alternative exist?

21

Military Policy

Overview and Objectives

This chapter explores the structures for making military policy and particularly the vexing question of defense expenditures. After reading and reviewing the material in the chapter the student should be able to do each of the following:

1. Explain why the 1947 and 1949 Defense Reorganization Acts prevented the merger of services in the Defense Department. Review the present structure of the department, and explain how it contributes to interservice rivalries. Explain why presidents find it difficult to use the Joint Chiefs of Staff to control defense policy making. Discuss the reforms adopted in 1986.

2. Analyze the key allocative decisions about the defense budget. Indicate factors that make the decisions on the budget incremental. Explain how the congressional role in deciding on weapons systems has changed in recent years.

3. Explain how the condition of the defense industry makes necessary a "follow-up" system in the distribution of contracts. Indicate the extent to which "client" defense politics affects U.S. industry, and compare the performance of defense contractors with that of similar nondefense companies.

4. Explain why the cost overrun problem is due primarily to bureaucratic rather than political factors, and describe proposed reforms of the system.

Chapter Outline with Keyed-in Resources

I. Introduction
   A. Inconsistent image of American military
      1. *Top Gun* versus *Dr. Strangelove*
      2. Majoritarian politics versus "gigantic boondoggle"
   B. Majoritarian view
      1. Everyone is protected, every taxpayer pays
      2. Size and purpose of military reflects
         a. International situation
         b. Public opinion
   C. Client politics view: "boondoggle"
      1. Only beneficiaries are "fat cats"—generals, defense contractors, etc.

Defense contractors do indeed find military work lucrative. A study by the Navy Department in 1986 discovered that the profits generated from military contracts provide many companies with most of their total annual profit even when they account for only a fraction of a company's business. For example, sales to the Department of Defense account for 42 percent of Boeing's business but 94 percent of its profits; the same is true of McDonnell-Douglas, with defense sales representing 69 percent of its business and 98 percent of its profits.

           a. But everyone pays
- 2. Military budget reflects lobbying skills of Pentagon
- 3. Peace is frustrated by military-industrial complex

II. The structure of defense decision making (THEME A: HOW ARE MILITARY SPENDING DECISIONS MADE?)
- A. National Security Act of 1947
  1. Department of Defense
     a. Secretary of Defense (civilian), as are secretaries of army, navy, air force
     b. Joint Chiefs of Staff (military)
  2. Reasons for separate uniformed services
     a. Fear that unified military will become too powerful
     b. Desire of services to preserve their autonomy
     c. Interservice rivalries intended by Congress to receive maximum information
- B. 1986 defense-reorganization plan
  1. Joint Chiefs of Staff
     a. Composed of uniformed head of each service, with the chair and vice chair appointed by president and confirmed by Senate
     b. Chair since 1986 principal military adviser to president
  2. Joint Staff
     a. Officers from each service assisting JCS
     b. Since 1986 serves chair; promoted at same rate
  3. Unified commands
     a. Eight unified commands and two specified commands
     b. Since 1986 more power to command's CINC
  4. The services
     a. Each service headed by civilian secretary responsible for purchasing and public affairs
     b. Senior military officer oversees discipline and training

The position of secretary of the navy has a good track record for promoting political aspirations. Both Theodore and Franklin Roosevelt held the post early in their political careers. However, perhaps the magic of the job works only for Roosevelts.

    5. The chain of command
       a. Chair of JCS does not have combat command
       b. Uncertainty whether 1986 changes will work

III. The defense budget
- A. Total spending (ADDITIONAL LECTURE TOPIC A-1)

Expenditures on a weapons system seem to follow the "bow-wave"—spending levels begin low during the development phase, increase when production is initiated, and decline as production slows. The Department of Defense budgets accordingly.

1. Small peacetime military until 1950
   a. Not disarm after Korea due to Soviet threat
   b. Military system designed to repel Soviet invasion of Europe and small-scale invasions
2. Changes in spending reflect public opinion
   a. Military spending rides rollercoaster
   b. Greater change in defense outlays than other parts of budget
3. Demise of U.S.S.R. produced debate
   a. Liberals: sharp defense cuts; U.S. not serve as world's police
   b. Conservatives: some cuts but retain well-funded military since world still dangerous

4. Desert Storm postponed debate and focused it on "smart weapons" and whether to cooperate in U.N. efforts
5. Bush started defense cuts; Clinton ordered bottom-up review, which concluded:
   a. Threat now regional wars
   b. Military should be capable of fighting two regional wars at once
   c. Cut number of new weapons but continue purchasing some subs and planes to keep production lines operating

B. Allocating defense dollars
  1. Majoritarian politics shapes total spending; interest-group politics shapes allocation among services
  2. Support for each service
     a. Joint Chiefs tend to allocate to each service about equally

The navy, Hedrick Smith reports, is by reputation the most adept at competing for money. Its share of the defense budget amounts to about one-third, compared with 24 percent for the army.

     b. Congressional committees reinforce their tendency
     c. Key allocative decisions become incremental ones
     d. Weapons systems take one-third
  3. Congressional influence
     a. Variation over the years
        (1) Detailed decisions before World War II
        (2) Retreat from activism during World War II
        (3) Assertive again, but promilitary after World War II
        (4) 1970s and 1980s: close scrutiny of new weapons
           (a) philosophical debate on SDI, MAD (ADDITIONAL LECTURE TOPIC A-2)

A major political (and legal) hurdle for the SDI program is whether it violates the Antiballistic Missile Treaty of 1972, which bans development of any space-based antimissile weapons system.

     b. Congress follows a two-step process on new measures
        (1) Ideological debate on merits of proposal
        (2) Pursuit of constituency interest if approved

IV. What do we get for our money?
  A. Personnel
    1. From draft to all-volunteer force in 1973
    2. Volunteer force: depends on sufficient candidates
       a. "Baby bust" generation of 1990s
       b. More women in military
       c. Ban lifted against women on combat ships in 1993 but Congress consulted if ground combat involved
       d. "Don't ask, don't tell" compromise adopted by Clinton on homosexuals in military
  B. Big-ticket hardware
    1. Main reasons for cost overruns

Cost overruns are quite common. Lawrence Korb learned of forty-seven weapons that were produced at double the initial estimate. The C-5A transport, for example, was projected to cost $23 million a plane; it ended up costing $60 million a plane.

       a. Unpredictability of cost of new items
       b. Contractor incentives to underestimate at first
       c. Military chiefs want best weapons money can buy
       d. "Sole sourcing" of weapons without competitive bids
       e. Holding down budget by "stretching out" production
    2. Latter four factors can be controlled; first cannot

- C. Small-ticket items
    1. Seemingly outrageous prices come from allocation of overhead, small run of items produced
    2. Others result from "gold-plating" phenomenon
- D. Readiness

Franklin Spinney contends that high-tech weaponry is partly to blame for decaying readiness. The rising costs of these weapons required the Pentagon to purchase in smaller quantities, forcing prices higher.

    1. This area the favorite for short-term budget cutting
        a. Other cuts would hurt constituents, etc.
        b. Cuts here show up quickly in money saved
- V. Congress versus the executive (THEME B: INSTITUTIONAL CONFLICT AND MILITARY POLICY)
    - A. Defense policy an invitation to struggle
        1. Passive role by Congress during World War II
        2. Micromanagement by Congress since Vietnam
    - B. Increased congressional scrutiny due to:
        1. Changes in executive branch, where a large military attracted interest
        2. Constituent service in form of pet projects

Important Terms

armed services committees Committees in the House and Senate which, since World War II, oversee the entire military service.

*cost overruns A situation that applies to the purchase of big-ticket military hardware in which actual costs greatly exceed estimated costs.

equal-allocation formula A method of accounting once employed by the Pentagon in which overhead is arbitrarily allocated equally to each part in the manufacturing of an item. This system has been replaced.

*gold plating The tendency of the military to ask for everything at once in procuring a new weapon.

Joint Chiefs of Staff A committee consisting of the uniformed heads of each military service, plus a chairman and a (nonvoting) vice chairman appointed by the president. Since 1986, the chairman has been designated the president's principal military adviser in an effort to give him more influence over the Joint Chiefs.

Joint Staff The staff providing assistance to the Joint Chiefs, consisting of several hundred officers from each of the four services who draw up plans for various military contingencies. Since 1986, the chairman of the Joint Chiefs exercises control over the staff. The secretary of defense ensures that officers assigned to this staff are promoted at the same rate as officers whose careers are spent entirely with their own service.

*micromanagement Congressional participation in shaping detailed decisions involving military matters. This behavior emerged as a consequence of the war in Vietnam.

*military-industrial complex The supposedly unified political bloc consisting of the Defense Department and the industries that build military weapons.

Military Reform Caucus An important congressional caucus that emerged in the 1980s which combined a majoritarian politics theory of the goals of national defense and a client politics theory of the methods used to achieve these goals. The caucus included both liberal and conservative members of Congress.

mutual assured destruction (MAD) A strategy whereby the two superpower nations, the United States and the Soviet Union, deterred the use of nuclear weapons through the threat of massive retaliation if the other power used its nuclear weapons first.

National Security Act A statute passed in 1947 which created the Department of Defense, headed by a civilian secretary of defense. The secretaries of the army, the air force, and the navy as well as the chairman of the Joint Chiefs of Staff are under the authority of the secretary of defense.

service Any one of the three branches of the American military—army, navy (including Marine Corps), and air force. Each is headed by a civilian secretary responsible for purchasing, auditing, congressional relations, and public affairs. A military chief oversees the discipline and training of the uniformed forces in that branch and represents his or her service on the Joint Chiefs of Staff.

sole sourcing The purchasing of weapons without competition that takes away the manufacturer's incentive to control costs.

Strategic Defense Initiative (SDI) A controversial weapons system, popularly called Star Wars, proposed by President Reagan. The program envisions building a system that would intercept enemy missiles before they could reach the United States.

Unified Commands The organizations to which most combat forces of the United States are assigned. Eight such commands exist: five control forces assigned to specific geographical areas, and three handle specialized forces (space, transportation, and special operations).

Theme A	How Are Military Spending Decisions Made?

Instructor References

Joseph G. Bock, *The White House Staff and the National Security Assistant: Friendship and Friction at the Water's Edge.* New York: Greenwood Press, 1987.

James Clotfelter, *The Military in American Politics.* New York: Harper & Row, 1973.

Edward N. Luttwak, *The Pentagon and the Art of War.* New York: Touchstone, 1985.

Richard Smoke, *National Security and the Nuclear Dilemma.* 2nd ed. New York: Random House, 1987.

Gregg Walker, David A. Bella, and Steven J. Sprecher, *The Military-Industrial Complex: Eisenhower's Warning Three Decades Later.* New York: Peter Lang Publishing, 1991.

Bob Woodward, *The Commanders.* New York: Simon and Schuster, 1991.

Summary

The conventional view of national defense policy making is that it is an example of majoritarian politics, with benefits and costs widely distributed. The rival theory of the *military-industrial complex* holds that spending for national defense is the result of client politics. Money is spent to benefit military officers and/or corporations and/or members of Congress with concentrations of military spending in their districts.

In evaluating these theories, it is important to remember that the *National Security Act of 1947* set up a structure to ensure civilian control of the military. The four armed forces are separate entities, each with the right to communicate directly with Congress. This results in bureaucratic infighting among the services, but it is not merely infighting. The process ensures that the maximum amount of information will get to Congress, which must referee the conflicts. The total level of military spending is heavily determined by the president. Truman decided that the military could get no more than one-third of the federal budget; Eisenhower decided on 10 percent of the GNP as a maximum. Kennedy let defense spending rise, but his secretary of defense, Robert McNamara, made the decisions about how the money would be spent. Defense spending has simply not steadily increased. In 1980 it amounted to $70.7 billion (in 1972 dollars), whereas in 1955 it had been $75.8 billion (in 1972 dollars).

Changing the allocation of defense spending *among* the military services is more difficult than changing the total level of spending. Each service fights to prevent its share of the pie from being cut, and each has important political allies among interest groups and in Congress. Thus each major service receives roughly a third of the defense budget, and any changes are incremental. The key decisions surround the purchase of major new weapons systems, and these decisions produce an intense political debate involving the Pentagon, the White House, Congress, and various interest groups. Congress is an important part of that debate, but its role has changed over the years. Before World War II, Congress made exceedingly detailed decisions about military matters. During the war, it retreated somewhat. After the war until the late 1960s, Congress pushed for larger military programs than the president favored. In the late 1960s, as a result of Vietnam, Congress took a more critical stance toward the military. After 1977, Congress again seemed more receptive to defense spending. Congress was now in step with public opinion, which also desired higher levels of defense spending. Both President Carter and President Reagan contributed to the defense buildup. However, the increases in military spending raised the traditional issue of "guns versus butter," the argument being that money spent on defense sacrifices social welfare programs. However, there is no firm evidence that this tradeoff actually operates.

The decisions of individual members of Congress on defense spending seem to be independent of the interests of their district, discrediting the "pork barrel" explanation of the military budget. Rather, ideology seems to be the determining factor. Certain decisions affecting localities, such as the closing of a military base, do mobilize members of Congress to defend their district interest, thus reflecting client politics.

One might expect large corporations to push for more defense spending. However, most corporations do little defense work: one study showed that about three-fourths of the largest one hundred companies receive less than 5 percent of their sales from military contracts. Furthermore, defense contracting is not particularly profitable. Several studies have shown that firms carrying out a great deal of defense contracts are less profitable than similar ones with few or none. Defense Department officials do worry about the health of defense contractors, however. As one large contract nears an end, and effort is usually made to direct another to the same company: the *follow-up imperative.*

Cost overruns are common in military procurement. The reason is not particularly sinister: Most weapons must be invented before they can be built and cannot be purchased "off the shelf." It is difficult to predict what the weapon will cost because it does not yet exist. The problem is exacerbated by the insistence of military officers on the best technology possible and by the tendency of defense contractors to submit unrealistically low bids on the assumption that they will afterward be reimbursed for cost overruns. One partial solution, adopted in the 1970s, is the "fly before you buy" procedure by which the government commissions the production of prototypes of competing models (for example, airplanes) and buys in quantity only after seeing their actual performance.

Discussion Questions

1. Military spending has consumed a decreasing percentage of the gross national product. Does this prove that the military budget is not excessively large? Is this fact consistent with the existence of a military-industrial complex? Is it consistent with the domination of American politics by the military-industrial complex? Is it consistent with the domination of American politics by large corporations?

2. Much recent discussion has been devoted to the "peace dividend"—the money the United States will save in military spending with the end of the cold war. The question is whether this money should be channeled into social programs. Who will make the ultimate decision on this question? Many experts contend that the United States will not experience any savings from the peace dividend. Why?

3. Should the United States purchase weapons manufactured by other countries if these weapons prove superior and cheaper? Each branch of the military purchases its own weapons systems, which leads to problems. For example, because the army and navy had incompatible communications systems, during the Grenada invasion a soldier was forced to use his AT&T calling card to call the Navy Department in order to direct offshore naval fire. Should the services be required to purchase the same merchandise when feasible? What reasons exist for not doing so?

4. What does it mean to say that decisions about the allocation of the military budget are incremental? Why can we not engage in rational planning and substantial reallocations of resources? Is defense any different from other policy areas in this regard?

5. How does Congress differ from the president as a maker of defense policy? To which branch would we look for rational planning? For representation of various and diverse interests? For representation of public opinion? For technical expertise in evaluating weapons systems?

6. The text says that military officers "naturally" want the best new weapons that modern technology can devise. How do they differ from the average driver, who would prefer to drive a Rolls-Royce but may have to settle for a Volkswagen? Military officers do not, for the most part, actually use the weapons they buy (leaving that to lower-ranking officers and enlisted persons) so why would they have a bias toward overcomplex and expensive (as opposed to simple and cost-effective) weapons?

7. What are the advantages of the "fly before you buy" procedure? Who might be expected to favor, and who to oppose, this practice? Why?

Data and Perspectives for Analysis

A. Public Opinion and Defense Spending (Gallup poll)

"There is much discussion as to the amount of money the government in Washington should spend for national defense and military purposes. How do you feel about this: Do you think we are spending too little, too much, or about the right amount?"

	Too Much	About Right	Too Little
1960	18%	45%	21%
1969	52	31	8
1971	49	31	11
1973 (February)	42	40	8
1973 (September)	46	30	13
1974	44	32	12
1976	36	32	22
1977	23	40	27
1979	21	33	34
1981	15	22	51
1983	45	31	14
1985 (January)	46	36	11
1987	44	36	14

1. What changes do you see in public attitudes toward military spending in the early 1970s, the mid-1970s, and the early 1980s?

2. Are changes in the level of military spending consistent with these attitudes?

3. What happened to the level of military spending in the late 1970s and through the 1980s?

4. Are these data consistent with democratic control of the level of military spending? Do they *prove* that military spending is responsive to public opinion? What other hypotheses can explain the fact that military spending dropped after 1968 and began to rise after 1976?

5. Complete the poll data through the *most recent* year possible. Have attitudes changed appreciably since 1987?

B. Pentagon Procurement Fraud, 1988

In June 1988, federal investigators seized documents across the country in what was revealed to be a two-year secret investigation of fraud and bribery in the Pentagon's process of procuring military weapons and hardware. By early July, some of the preliminary findings were apparent, as outlined by reporter David E. Rosenbaum in an article entitled "Pentagon Fraud Inquiry: What Is Known to Date" (*New York Times*, July 7, 1988, pp. 1 and 12). Rosenbaum reported the following key points:

1. The investigation was keying on the relationship between Defense Department procurement officials, defense contractors, and consultants who worked as intermediaries between the Pentagon and the contractors. Under suspicion were some of the largest defense corporations in the nation.

2. There were three types of illegal activity:

   Consultants working for one company obtained from Defense Department employees confidential information on the terms of bids submitted by other companies competing for the same contract; ... officials changed specifications for contracts to make them more favorable to a particular company, and ... companies supposedly competing for the same contract acted in collusion.

   In some instances, it is suspected that Pentagon officials were bribed, In other cases, they are suspected of rigging the bidding because they were promised jobs outside the Government or simply did it as a favor to a consultant or company (p. 12).

3. Charges of bribery, conspiracy, theft of government property, and violations of conflict-of-interest laws were among the crimes under investigation. Indictments were not expected until the end of 1988.

4. In one example of the skulduggery, the McDonnell-Douglas Corporation, the nation's largest military contractor, was illegally provided with government information from a consultant with contacts in the Pentagon; this "gave the company a large edge over its competitors in bidding for government contracts" (p. 12). Apparently, the material involved data on the F-16 (built by the rival General Dynamics Corporation), future navy plans to develop the F-18 with the French, and a secret project to develop the navy's next generation of fighter aircraft. This kind of information would allow McDonnell-Douglas to benefit at the expense of its rivals, since inside information, illegally obtained through payoffs, would increase the chances of its being awarded the government contract, worth billions of dollars.

5. The charges of corruption had their origins in the Reagan administration's desire to replace "sole-source contracting" (military contracts awarded without competition) with "competitive bidding." As it turned out, competition did save money, but it also heightened the value of "inside information" for defense firms.

Research Assignment

Assign students the task of tracing the outcome of the defense procurement scandal. Have them report on the money involved, the lessons for the Defense Department, and subsequent reforms, if any, of the procurement process.

Additional Lecture Topics

A-1. Defense Spending

Kenneth Adelman and Norman Augustine, *The Defense Revolution: Strategy for the Brave New World*. San Francisco: ICS Press, 1990. A discussion of how the U.S. buys weapons.

Thomas L. Brewer, *American Foreign Policy: A Contemporary Introduction*. 2nd ed. Englewood Cliffs, NJ: Prentice-Hall, 1986. See Chapter 8 on trends in military expenditures.

"Defense and the Federal Deficit." In *Great Decisions—1987*. New York: Foreign Policy Association, pp. 15–24. An examination of what defense spending "buys," the impact of defense upon the deficit, and the components of the defense procurement process.

James Fallows, *National Defense*. New York: Random House, 1981. A short paperback exploring the idea that more defense money does not necessarily make the nation more secure.

A. Ernest Fitzgerald, *The Pentagonists: An Insider's View of Waste, Mismanagement, and Fraud in Defense Spending*. Boston: Houghton Mifflin, 1989.

William H. Gregory, *The Defense Procurement Mess*. Lexington, MA: Lexington Books, 1989.

William Kaufman, *Glasnost, Perestroika, and U.S. Defense Spending*. Washington, DC: Brookings Institution, 1990.

Charles W. Kegley and Eugene R. Wittkopf, *American Foreign Policy: Patterns and Progress*. New York: St. Martin's Press. See pp. 268–276 for a concise summary of defense spending's salience for foreign-policy elites.

Tim Weiner, *Blank Check: The Pentagon's Black Budget*. New York: Warner Books, 1990.

A-2. The Case For and Against Star Wars

Robert M. Bowman, *Star Wars—A Defense Expert's Case Against the Strategic Defense Initiative*. New York: St. Martin's Press, 1986.

Sidney D. Drell et al., *The Reagan Strategic Defense Initiative: A Technical, Political, and Arms Control Assessment*. Cambridge, MA: Ballinger, 1985. Very strong on ABM Treaty and linkages to SDI.

Robert M. Lawrence, *Strategic Defense Initiative: Bibliography and Research Guide*. Boulder, CO: Westview Press, 1987. Good introductory essays on SDI's background.

Keith P. Payne, *Strategic Defense: "Star Wars" in Perspective*. Lanham, MD: Hamilton Press, 1986. A case is made for SDI and prospects for successful arms control agreements.

Senator Larry Pressler, *Star Wars—The Strategic Defense Initiative Debates in Congress*. New York: Praeger, 1986.

John Tirman, ed., *The Fallacy of Star Wars*. New York: Random House, 1984. Based on studies conducted by the Union of Concerned Scientists.

Abstract 1 for Theme A

Star Wars and Military Spending

In his television address of March 23, 1983, President Reagan proposed the Strategic Defense Initiative, an open-ended research program designed to develop a space-based defense system against ballistic missiles. This effort, dubbed "Star Wars" by the media, would probably not be finished before the end of the century, according to the president, and would employ lasers, particle-beam weapons, and other varieties of space technology.

The president's Star Wars proposal generated both intense criticism and heartfelt support. By the middle of 1985, the arguments pro and con had coalesced into clearly identifiable propositions. Typical of the opposition were speeches on the Senate floor, by Senator

William Proxmire (D-Wis.), summarized in the *Congressional Digest* of March 1985 (p. 77ff). As the ranking minority member of the Senate Committee on Appropriations, Proxmire was particularly concerned about the enormous cost of developing Star Wars—a "wasted" allocation of $24 billion (if not more) over the next five years. The money would be "wasted" because, according to Proxmire, the system would never work. Even if by some miracle the system could be put into operation, the dangers of nuclear war would be increased, not lessened, because the side that fell behind in the development of such a defensive system would be tempted to launch a nuclear strike before the adversary could fully deploy its Star Wars system. Proxmire summarizes his views in the following paragraph:

> So what is wrong with Star Wars? What is wrong is that there is no real prospect that a defensive antimissile system would work. None. None. It will not work. Why not? Because whatever dynamic progress we can expect from a defense against missiles, we can surely anticipate an equally potent and opposite reaction from offensive missiles. (p. 83)

In short, the Soviets could take some relatively cheap countermeasures to defeat the U.S. space-defense system.

These countermeasures could include building more nuclear warheads to overcome the defense (saturation), employing low-flying cruise missiles from Soviet submarines and surface ships that a laser-based space system could not touch, mounting "precursor attacks" (detonating nuclear weapons in space to blind, cripple, or destroy the defensive armada or attacking the relatively delicate ground stations in the United States that would relay battle data to and from the defensive weapons), and even spinning missile boosters at several revolutions per minute, thus reducing the laser dwell-time on any part of the rocket area.

Advocates of Star Wars defended the cost of the system, even tacitly accepting final cost estimates anywhere from several hundred billion to a trillion dollars (all research and deployment costs). Protection against nuclear devastation is a worthwhile goal, they said, regardless of cost. (See Ben Bova's "If Star Wars Works," *New York Times*, February 12, 1985, p. 27.) Soviet defensive countermeasures could be overcome by new space technologies and, assuming that both superpowers developed similar defenses, could free the world from the scourge of nuclear war.

In the final analysis, it was apparent that Congress would permit funding for initial research costs. Whether a complete Star Wars system would ever be built and deployed remained an open question for opponents and proponents alike.

Questions for Discussion

1. What appears to be the current prevailing view about the feasibility of Star Wars technology? Has this view changed appreciably since 1983?
2. Would a mutual deployment of Star Wars systems by both superpowers (in roughly the same time period) help prevent nuclear war? Why or why not?
3. Is Star Wars needed now since the demise of the Soviet Union? If so, why?
4. Is the nuclear threat today more one of a small device smuggled into the country than a nuclear missile launch?

Abstract 2 for Theme A

Spending Defense Dollars on a "Muscle-Bound" Navy

Whether a weapons system justifies its costs is an age-old question in the realm of defense spending, particularly in the modern era of federal deficits. This question formed the basis of a *New York Times Magazine* article of April 24, 1988, by defense authority Charles R. Morris, entitled "Our Muscle-Bound Navy" (pp. 98, 102, and 104). Morris questions whether the navy's continued emphasis upon the aircraft carrier, with its tremendous cost, is justified by the minimal offensive capabilities that it offers. Morris makes the following assertions in the article:

1. A modern carrier group actually has little offensive striking power. Of the ninety or so planes on a carrier, only thirty-eight to forty are attack planes. All the rest, along with support ships, are there to defend the carrier. The entire battle group costs some $18 billion and needs $1 billion annually to operate (p. 98).

2. The navy's "maritime strategy," which envisions carrier-based bombers attacking Soviet military bases and airfields supporting the Soviet fleet, is based upon assumptions that "range from the risky to the wildly implausible" (p. 102). Carrier fleets would be attacked by Soviet backfire bombers and would be extremely vulnerable to antiship missiles like the French-made Exocet (now in the arsenals of eighteen nations). Furthermore, the Soviets have far more sophisticated missiles than the Exocet; these missiles are much harder to see on radar screens, possess complex electronic countermeasures, and can be launched as far away as three hundred miles. "Soviet naval tactics call for attacking with whole clouds of missiles launched from both airborne and seaborne platforms, at a variety of angles, altitudes, and distances" (p. 102).

3. A carrier's defensive system could not withstand a determined barrage attack. The F-14 outside defensive perimeter would be breached and close-in defensive weapons like the Phalanx could be penetrated "by waves of small, fast, high explosive, and relatively inexpensive projectiles" (p. 102).

4. The issue "is not whether the United States needs carriers; the issue is whether the military investment dollar should be so disproportionately devoted to them—why wouldn't a dozen carriers, or even fewer, be more than enough?" (p. 104).

5. The navy's carrier role could be replaced in part by B-52s and B-1Bs, which could engage Soviet backfires or missile ships in an effective fashion. Furthermore, smaller fighters could be designed with "vertical/short takeoff and landing" capabilities that would fly from smaller carrier decks. Smaller ships would permit a more diverse set of deployment opportunities "in a wider range of military situations" (p. 104).

6. If the current naval procurement program is left untouched (building more carriers), America's military investments will be "distorted" and strained to the limit. Finally, new orders for ships may not have to be canceled. Rather, simply retire the oldest carriers over the next ten years or so, instead of refitting them at enormous cost. In short, the next administration should rethink the Reagan administration's naval procurement strategies.

Project for Class Discussion

Invite a naval officer (active or retired) to comment on the issue of aircraft carriers and cost-effectiveness. The officer's remarks should provoke lively class discussion.

Theme B   Institutional Conflict and Military Policy

Instructor References

Thomas E. Mann, ed., *A Question of Balance: The President, the Congress, and Foreign Policy*. Washington, DC: Brookings Institution, 1990.

Arthur M. Schlesinger, Jr., *The Imperial Presidency*. Boston: Houghton Mifflin, 1989.

George Szamuely, "The Imperial Congress," *Commentary* (September 1987): 27–32.

Summary

Federal law ensures that the military is under civilian control as a means to preserve democratic government. The president, vice president, and secretary of defense (as well as the secretaries of the army, navy, and air force) cannot be current members of the armed services.

The command structure alone, however, was not considered sufficient protection against military intervention in the political process. Federal law took the additional step of promoting interservice rivalry to hinder military coordination except at the highest levels of civilian authority. The absence of cooperation produced consequences that compromised national security and created inefficiency, such as duplicate weapon systems that could not interface. In 1986, Congress reorganized the command structure to provide more harmony in national defense decision-making by making the chair of the Joint Chiefs of Staff the president's principal military adviser, requiring the Joint Staff to assist each service, and giving more power to the commanders in chief of the unified commands.

These actions were taken at the same time Congress was in the process of reasserting its authority in managing the military. Decisions on the procurement of weapon systems and the closing of military bases were subjected to intense congressional scrutiny. The military budget was amenable to such probing due to its size and the opportunity for members of Congress to perform constituency service by bringing home jobs in the form of defense contracts. Congressional subcommittees involved in matters pertaining to the armed services proliferated and, with this development, the opportunities for the executive branch and Congress to collide in military policy expanded as well. Thus while military decision making was streamlined, the Defense Department became bogged down in other areas that made its daily operation and long-term planning more cumbersome.

It is not surprising that career military officers chafe when caught in the institutional war between the president and Congress. Jerel Rosati explains how the military interprets this situation.

> Given the nature of the American Constitution, the military perspective is that the civilian leadership, symbolized by the president and the Congress, decide when and where to go to war; but once the decision has been made, it is time for the politicians and civilians to stand aside and let the military do what it does best: fight wars. Some within the military also have concluded, therefore, that the services should control the administrative and operational process during times of peace as well as war, since peace is a time in which to prepare for war.

The role of Congress in what some consider "micromanaging" the military is a subject of debate. One the one hand, it enhances institutional conflict but, on the other hand, it is within congressional power under the Constitution. Efficiency and democracy are often at odds.

22

Environmental Policy

Overview and Objectives

Environmental policy, like economic and welfare policy, reflects the nature of the American political system. Unlike economic or welfare issues, however, environmental issues lend themselves to entrepreneurial politics, which requires mobilizing the media, dramatizing the issue, and convincing members of Congress that their political reputations will suffer if they do not cast the right vote. It is politics in which an unorganized public benefits at the expense of a well-organized groups, such as a manufacturer. After reading and reviewing the material in this chapter the student should be able to do each of the following:

1. List three reasons why environmental policy tends to be so controversial, providing examples of each.

2. Describe the role of (a) the American political system and (b) local politics in shaping environmental policy. Contrast these with environmental policy making in England.

3. Distinguish among the following styles of politics in terms of who benefits and who pays: entrepreneurial, majoritarian, interest group, and client.

4. Describe the role of entrepreneurial politics in the government's efforts to reduce air and water pollution from stationary sources, such as factories.

5. Outline the major provisions of the following legislative acts: the Clean Air Act of 1970; the Water Quality Improvement Act of 1970; the revised Clean Air Act of 1990; and the National Environmental Policy Act of 1969.

6. Describe the role of majoritarian politics in the government's efforts to reduce automobile emissions. Explain why majoritarian politics has worked in some cases and not others.

7. Describe the role of interest-group politics in the government's efforts to resolve the acid rain controversy. List proposed alternative solutions and outline the terms of the compromise reached by Congress and the Bush administration.

8. Describe the role of client politics in the government's efforts to regulate the use of agricultural pesticides and timber cutting in U.S. forests.

9. Give three reasons why it is so difficult to develop a sane environmental policy in this country. Provide examples of how the EPA is dealing with these problems.

10. Discuss the results of environmental protection measures that have been taken since 1970.

Chapter Outline with Keyed-in Resources

    I. Introduction
       A. Environmental policy: why is it so controversial?
          1. Creates both winners and losers
             a. Losers may be interest groups or average citizens
             b. Losers may not want to pay costs
                 (1) Example: auto emissions control
          2. Shrouded in scientific uncertainty
             a. Example: greenhouse effect

The EPA estimates that the greenhouse effect will increase the world's temperature by two degrees centigrade by 2040 and five degrees centigrade by 2100. "Two degrees is significant," the report concluded, "in comparison with the temperature changes that produced ice ages."

          3. Takes the form of entrepreneurial politics
             a. Encourages emotional appeals: "good guys" versus "bad guys"
             b. May lead to distorted priorities

The clash of priorities is illustrated in the use of pesticides. Farmers contend that pesticides keep food prices down, but studies have linked them with numerous health risks. Dioxin, now a banned chemical, has been discovered in the tissue of 99 percent of Americans. How is it passed on? A 1986 study revealed that breast-fed infants consume eighteen times more of the chemical in a single year than the government estimates is safe for a lifetime. If breast milk were sold in the marketplace, it would not pass government health standards. Dioxin is so toxic that one drop in ten thousand gallons of water is considered a dangerous concentration.

                 (1) Example: cancer versus water pollution
   II. The American context (THEME A: THE POLITICS OF ENVIRONMENTAL PROTECTION)
      A. Environmental policy is shaped by unique features of American politics
          1. More adversarial than in Europe
             a. Rules are often uniform nationally (e.g., auto emissions)
             b. But many regulators and rules, strict deadlines, and expensive technologies required
             c. Often government (pro-) versus business (anti-)
             d. Example: Clean Air Act
                 (1) Took thirteen years to revise in Congress
             e. In England, rules are flexible and regional

A comparison of the American with the British situation in environmental matters should be balanced with a comparison in another direction. A good example was reported by Associated Press in 1989. In the Ukraine, an industrial worker discarded a cigarette in a river, producing an instant conflagration, which resulted in the worker's suffering second-degree burns. And don't forget the Cuyahoga River fire in Cleveland, Ohio, in the early 1960s, which burned down a bridge. Environmental improvement has occurred here.

                 (1) Compliance is voluntary
                 (2) Government and business cooperate
                 (3) Yet policies are effective
          2. Depends heavily on states
             a. Standards are left to states, subject to federal control
             b. Local politics decides allocations
             c. Federalism reinforces adversarial politics; separation of powers provides multiple points of access
      B. Types of politics (ADDITIONAL LECTURE TOPIC A-1)
          1. Entrepreneurial politics
             a. Most people benefit, few firms pay costs

            b. Example: factories and other stationary sources
         2. Majoritarian
            a. Most people benefit, most people pay
            b. Example: air pollution from automobiles
         3. Interest group
            a. Some groups benefit, other groups pay
            b. Example: acid rain controversy

In 1985, the Office of Technological Assessment calculated that acid rain has decreased agricultural production in the United States by 6 to 7 percent.

         4. Client
            a. Most people pay, some groups benefit
            b. Example: pesticide control

In 1987, the EPA estimated the potential cancer risk from contamination of food by pesticides. The highest cancer risk was posed by tomatoes, accounting for 15 percent of the total cancer risk from pesticides. The other most dangerous food products (in rank order) are beef (11 percent), potatoes (9 percent), oranges (6.4 percent), lettuce (5.8 percent), and apples (5.5 percent). This is surely information to share.

   III. Entrepreneurial politics: pollution from factories
      A. Gave rise to environmental movement in 1960s
         1. Santa Barbara oil spill, Earth Day, an aroused public
         2. Led to formation of EPA and passage of Clean Air Act

The importance of the environment was highlighted when President Bush proposed elevating the EPA to the Department of Environmental Affairs in 1990.

      B. Resulted in tough new pollution standards for factories and power plants
         1. Congressional efforts led by Muskie
         2. Spurred on by Ralph Nader
         3. Produced Clean Air Act of 1970
         4. Produced Water Quality Improvement Act of 1970
            a. Passed over Nixon's veto
            b. Goal was to eliminate all pollutant discharges into waters
            c. Required oil companies to use best technology available
            d. Implemented by EPA
            e. Citizens had right to sue EPA
         5. Public sentiment stifled industry lobbies
      C. *Exxon Valdez* spill
         1. Renewed public outcry in early 1990s
         2. Improvements must be made "regardless of costs" according to public

Public opinion reflects contradictory positions on the environment. While Americans support environmental improvement "regardless of costs," 71 percent oppose paying $200 in additional taxes each year to increase federal spending to reduce air pollution (Gallup, 1989). Clearly, public concern over the environment depends on how the issue is phrased.

            a. But costs fall on average citizens
            b. Example: costs of reducing automobile pollution
   IV. Majoritarian politics: pollution from automobiles (THEME B: TRANSPORTATION AND THE ENVIRONMENT)
      A. Clean Air Act imposed tough restrictions
         1. Public demanded improvements
         2. 1975: 90 percent reduction of hydrocarbons and carbon monoxide
         3. 1976: 90 percent reduction in nitrogen oxides
         4. Required catalytic converters
      B. Emergence of majoritarian politics in auto pollution
         1. States were required to restrict public use of cars

In 1989, the South Coast Air Quality Management District adopted a program to eliminate gas-burning vehicles from the Los Angeles area within two decades. The program will be implemented in stages. City officials must convert their vehicles to "clean fuels" (like methyl) by 1991, rental cars and taxis by 1993, and all other vehicles by 2009. Existing vehicles will not be banned, but tough emission standards will force them from the streets.

        a. If auto emissions controls were insufficient—L.A., Denver, New York, etc., then car pools, gas rationing, parking bans
        b. Efforts failed: opposition too great
        c. Congress and EPA backed down, postponing deadlines
    2. Consumers, auto industry, and unions objected
        a. Loss of horsepower
        b. Loss of competitiveness
        c. Loss of jobs
    3. Clean Air Act was weakened in 1977 but revived 1990 with tougher standards
  C. Public will support tough laws
    1. If costs are hidden (e.g., catalytic converters)
    2. But not if they have to change habits (e.g., car pools)
  D. Majoritarian politics when people believe costs are low
    1. National Environmental Policy Act of 1969 (NEPA)

Recall that majoritarian politics usually involves a high degree of presidential leadership. The NEPA contained a provision placing the responsibility for forming environmental policy on the president's shoulders. The law created the Council on Environmental Quality to advise the president and required the president to submit an annual environmental quality report to Congress.

        a. Requires "environmental impact statement" (EIS)
        b. Does not require specific action
        c. Passed Congress with overwhelming support
        d. But encouraged numerous lawsuits that block or delay projects
        e. Popular support remains strong
          (1) Costs appear low, benefits high
  E. Majoritarian politics when people believe the costs are high
    1. Increased gasoline taxes
        a. Would discourage driving, save fuel, reduce smog
        b. Most would pay, most would benefit
        c. But costs come long before benefits
        d. And benefits may not be obvious
    2. Easier to raise gas tax if benefits are concrete
        a. Highways, bridges, etc.
V. Interest group politics: acid rain (THEME C: ENVIRONMENTAL POLICY WITHOUT PUBLIC INTEREST)

The role of interest groups can be subtly disguised. Remember the text's chapter on interest groups and its conclusion that the most important resource available to interest groups is a monopoly on information. This conclusion is relevant to the discussion of environmental protection. Consultants hired by the EPA in 1983 discovered that 30 percent of EPA reports on pesticides were written by officials from chemical companies. In fact, 20 percent of these studies were copied verbatim from pesticide company reports.

  A. Source of acid rain
    1. Burning of high-sulfur coal in midwestern factories
    2. Winds carry sulfuric acid eastward
    3. Rains bring acid to earth
  B. Effects of acid rain
    1. Acidification of lakes
    2. Destruction of forests
    3. Long-term and some short-term effects are unclear

  C. Regional battle
    1. East versus Midwest, Canada versus the United States
    2. Midwestern businesses deny blame and costs
  D. Solutions and compromise (ADDITIONAL LECTURE TOPIC C-1)

Note that the debate on acid rain has avoided discussion of nuclear power as an alternative fuel source to coal. Public opposition seems to preclude nuclear energy; no order for a new nuclear power plant has been placed in the United States since 1978. The same is not true everywhere. France, for example, provides about 75 percent of its electricity from nuclear power.

    1. Burn low-sulfur coal one alternative
      a. Effective but expensive
      b. Low-sulfur coal comes from West, high-sulfur is local
    2. Install smokestack scrubbers a second alternative
      a. Costly, not always effective, and leave sludge
      b. But allow use of cheap high-sulfur coal
    3. Congress voted for scrubbers for all new plants
      a. Including those that burned low-sulfur coal
      b. Even if plant was next to low-sulfur coal mine
    4. Political advantages
      a. Protected jobs of high-sulfur coal miners
        (1) Powerful allies in Congress
      b. Environmentalists preferred scrubbers
        (1) "Definitive" solution to problem
      c. Scrubber manufacturers preferred scrubbers
      d. Eastern governors preferred scrubbers
        (1) Made their plants more competitive
    5. Practical disadvantages
      a. Failed to allow for plants that burn low-sulfur coal
        (1) Why spend money on scrubbers?
      b. Scrubbers didn't work well
      c. Failed to address problem of existing plants

What is the largest source of acid rain? Electric utilities, according to the American Council for an Energy-Efficient Economy. Electric utilities are responsible for 65 percent of sulfur dioxide emissions.

    6. Stalemate for thirteen years
    7. Two-step regulation proposed by Bush
      a. Before 1995: some plants could choose their approach
        (1) Fixed reduction, but plants decide how to do
      b. After 1995: sharper reductions for many more plants
        (1) Requiring some use of scrubbers
      c. Sulfur dioxide allowances could be bought and sold
      d. Financial compensation for coal miners who lose jobs
    8. Became part of Clean Air Act of 1990

The technological demands of the Clean Air Act of 1990 will be costly. The Bush administration estimated that the law would cost about $22 billion by the year 2005.

  E. Other example: zoning regulations
    1. Residents versus developers
  F. New interest groups
    1. More fervent and committed than before

One of the more radical new environmental groups is called Earth First! (the exclamation point is part of the group's name). The group practices a form of environmental sabotage called "monkey wrenching." The tactic involves destroying logging equipment (by cutting hydraulic hoses or by pouring Drano into radiators) and "spiking" trees with nails to damage the blades of saws (an "S" is spray-painted on such trees as a warning). The group has cost the lumber industry about $25 million in damage. Although no membership rolls are kept, Earth First! has about 15,000 members—and no formal leaders.

    2. Able to block change in policies
    3. Examples
      a. Environmental protection industry
      b. Environmental Defense Fund
      c. Labor unions
    4. Momentum remains with policymakers
 VI. Client politics: agricultural pesticides
  A. Issue: control of use and runoff of pesticides
    1. Farmers have mostly resisted policy entrepreneurs, with DDT an exception
  B. EPA efforts to evaluate safety of all pesticides
    1. Given mandate by Congress in 1972
    2. Program has not succeeded
      a. Too many pesticides to evaluate
        (1) Many have only long-term effects needing extended study
        (2) Expensive and time-consuming to evaluate
      b. Benefits of pesticides may outweigh harm
    3. Political complications
      a. Farmers are well represented in Congress
      b. Subsidies encourage overproduction

Pesticide use has not increased crop yields. In 1945, corn in the United States was grown by rotation, without pesticides. Only 3.5 percent of the crop was lost to insects in that year. Corn is now the crop for which the largest amount of pesticides is used, but 12 percent of the crop is lost to insects each year. Do pesticides even work?

        (1) Overproduction encourages overuse of pesticides
      c. Damage is hard to see and dramatize
    4. EPA budget is small
    5. Few pesticides have been removed from market
      a. Only those receiving heavy media coverage like DDT in 1972
    6. Client politics has won out
  C. Environmentalists versus loggers
    1. Issue: "clear-cutting" of forests
    2. Congress has supported loggers
      a. Forest Service forced to sell lumber at below-market prices
      b. Subsidizes industry
    3. Spotted owl: getting the media involved—i.e., entrepreneurial politics
 VII. The environmental uncertainties (THEME D: THE FUTURE ENVIRONMENT)

The uncertainties of the environmental problem should not deter action. In 1978, the Council on Environmental Quality concluded that "most researchers agree that 70 to 90 percent of all cancers are caused by environmental influences and are hence theoretically preventable."

  A. Why is a sane environmental policy so difficult to formulate and effect?
    1. Many environmental problems are not clear-cut
    2. Goals are often unclear
      a. Public opinion can shift
    3. Means of achieving goals ("command and control strategy") are complicated by:
      a. Local circumstances
      b. Technological problems
      c. Economic costs
  B. Examples of EPA and politics
    1. What is the problem?
      a. EPA not left alone to define problem

                    b. Scandals and congressional demands can shift priorities

Congressional supervision of environmental policy has produced numerous scandals. In 1980, the Superfund program was created to clean up hazardous toxic waste sites. A budget of $16 billion was allocated over a five-year period, and a list of 850 priority dumping locations was compiled by the EPA. In 1983, Congress discovered that only six of the sites had been cleaned, and in two of these, the cleanup amounted to relocating leaking disposal drums. Less than 20 percent of the fund had been used. Opposition by the Reagan administration to the program negated its implementation.

    2. What are our goals?
       a. Many are completely unrealistic
       b. Forced to ask for extensions and revisions
    3. How do we achieve our goals?
       a. Rules have been replaced by incentives
          (1) Offsets
          (2) Bubbles
          (3) Pollution allowances
       b. Complaints about command and control strategy are now coming from environmental groups and government
          (1) Clinton administration is reexamining old approaches
          (2) People are learning from experience

VIII. The results
   A. Environment has improved since 1970 in some aspects
      1. Less air pollution
      2. Maybe less water pollution but harder to judge
      3. Hazardous wastes remain a problem

Important Terms

*acid rain Rain, snow, or dust particles containing sulfuric (or nitric) acid which fall onto land. One source is from burning fuel, especially coal with a high-sulfur content. The problem is most critical in the midwestern and Great Lakes region, where steel mills and power plants emit sulfuric fumes carried eastward by prevailing winds. Acid rain is blamed for turning many lakes in the eastern United States and Canada acidic as well as for killing forests.

*bubbles An incentive devised by the Environmental Protection Agency to replace some rules and referring to the total amount of air pollution which can come from a given factory. A company is free to decide which specific sources of pollution within the factory must be reduced and how to meet the standard.

Clean Air Act A federal statute passed in 1970 which imposed tough restrictions on the amount of pollutants emitted by automobile tail pipes. A second provision required states to develop land use and transportation rules to help attain air quality standards. The revision of the act in 1990 set new, tougher auto emission control standards but pushed the compliance deadline back to 1995. In addition, the 1990 law requires power plants to reduce their emissions of sulfur in two phases, with power plants nationwide contributing to the cost.

*command and control strategy An approach to achieving environmental goals which relies on issuing rules and enforcing them in court. It falsely assumes that rule-makers and rule-enforcers know how to achieve the greatest environmental gain at the least cost.

Earth Day A national event in 1970 which signified the birth of the environmental movement and has since been observed annually. It generated much publicity and applied pressure on Congress.

*environmental impact statement A document that the National Environmental Policy Act requires federal agencies to prepare evaluating the consequences of any proposed activity that will "significantly" affect the quality of the human environment.

Environmental Protection Agency The federal agency responsible for administering pollution and environmental programs.

National Environmental Policy Act A federal statute enacted in 1969 which requires federal agencies to prepare environmental impact settlements before undertaking activities that will "significantly" affect the quality of the human environment. The law requires only a statement rather than some specific action. Opponents of government-sponsored projects have used this law to block or delay many projects.

*offsets An incentive devised by the Environmental Protection Agency to replace some rules. If a company wants to open a new plant in an area with polluted air, it can do so if the pollution it generates is offset by a reduction in pollution from another source in that area. To get that reduction, the new company may buy an existing company and close it down.

*pollution allowances An incentive devised by the Environmental Protection Agency to replace some rules. If a company reduces its polluting emissions by more than the law requires, it can either use these reductions to cover a future plant expansion or sell them to another company as an offset.

scrubber A complicated and expensive device that removes sulfurous fumes from gas before it leaves a smokestack. This technology is one means of addressing the problem of acid rain. Congress enacted legislation in 1977 requiring these devices to be installed in all new coal-burning plants.

Water Quality Improvement Act A federal statute passed in 1970 which made oil companies liable for up to $14 million in clean-up costs for oil spills. A bill passed in 1972 enacted even tougher new standards and deadlines for reducing water pollution.

Theme A	The Politics of Environmental Protection

Summary

In the 1988 election, George Bush said he wanted to be remembered as the "environmental president." Public concern over the condition of the environment has escalated in recent years. The United States could afford to avoid the issue longer than many nations since its vast territory accommodated population growth and the problems of industrialization were confined. The initial recognition of a problem was signaled by the creation of the first national park in 1872.

The federal government has typically been the pacesetter in environmental policy by establishing uniform national standards with strict compliance deadlines, resulting in an adversarial relationship between the government and the chief polluters—businesses. Congress allows the implementation of its policies to be determined at the local level, and federalism thus reinforces the adversarial nature of environmental politics as states and cities fight over standards. The mechanics of environmental policy-making, however, vary with the type of politics involved: entrepreneurial (factory pollution), majoritarian (automobile pollution), interest group (acid rain), or client (use of pesticides in farming).

Discussion Questions

1. The text does not, of course, discuss each major environmental issue. What type of politics (client, majoritarian, etc.) is involved in the disposal of toxic wastes? nuclear power?

2. Why didn't Congress or the president invite businesses to assist in devising environmental regulations, as occurred in England? How could the participation of business leaders in England result in a greater degree of improvement in water quality, compared with the United States, where businesses were excluded?

3. Wouldn't cities and states be reluctant to impose strict pollution standards to avoid the loss of industry? What's wrong with the idea of Congress creating a national pollution standard that is equally applied in all areas of the country? If the standards developed by Congress are so tough, why has the environment become such a major political issue—did the policies fail, or are the problems new?

Data and Perspectives for Analysis

It has become commonplace to demean regulatory efforts by the government. Environmental policy is particularly open to such criticism since the government has set the pace in the area. Perhaps environmental policy should not be the plaything of politicians. Is the criticism justified? This question can only be answered by determining how successful government policies have been in reducing pollution.

The table below presents data on the amount of air pollutant emissions that existed in 1970 (the year the Clean Air Act was passed) and in 1987. Keep in mind that the number of automobiles and electric utilities has increased in this period.

Air Pollutant Emissions, by Pollutant and Source (1970–1987)
(in millions of metric tons, except lead, in thousands of metric tons)

	Source					
	Road Vehicles		Electric Utilities		Industrial Processes	
Pollutant	1970	1987	1970	1987	1970	1987
Carbon monoxide	64.2	33.4	0.2	0.3	9.0	4.7
Sulfur oxides	0.3	0.5	15.8	13.5	6.4	3.1
Particulates	0.9	1.1	—	0.5	10.5	2.5
Lead	156.0	2.8	0.3	0.1	23.9	2.0

Source: *Statistical Abstract of the United States, 1990.* (Washington, DC: U.S. Government Printing Office, 1989).

Abstract for Theme A

The quality of the environment to a large degree rests with state governments, who have the responsibility for implementing national standards. Is this a wise decision on the part of Congress? Clark Cochran et al., in *American Public Policy: An Introduction*, 3rd ed. (New York: St. Martin's Press, 1990), pp. 129–130, provide a critical assessment of the role of state governments in environmental policy.

> The issue of state responsibility for environmental enforcement remains unresolved. Early regulatory efforts concentrated authority in the hands of state government, with limited success. There is evidence that a reduction of the federal government and transfer of responsibility for environmental policy to the states will result in a general weakening of standards.
>
> One reason is that the governing coalitions within state governments have a relatively narrow political base. In other words, compared with the national level, the proportion of the population concerned with political events at the state level is relatively small. Public-opinion polls indicate that less than 30 percent of the electorate regularly follows state government actively. Consequently, it is relatively easy for a special-interest groups to gain considerable power in state government.
>
> State governments also face severe staffing problems. Job vacancies reach levels as high as 20 percent in the regulatory agencies of some states, and the turnover of trained, qualified personnel is also a problem. Limited fiscal resources is a source of this problem.
>
> A third problem emerges when federal agencies, primarily the EPA, fail to issue regulations in a timely manner. The result is a negative impact on state enforcement procedures. Inconsistency, confusion, and delay thus follow as states operate without federal leadership.

A fourth problem grows from a perception that federal regulations fail to appreciate states' unique needs, producing inflexible program requirements. The inflexibility is viewed by the states as a barrier to state initiative, as states are faced with implementing rigid programs that may not meet their needs.

A fifth problem stems from the perception that federal EPA officials may not be interested in establishing a meaningful communications linkage with the states. A lack of responsiveness by the EPA builds perceptions at the state level that the "feds" do not understand and do not care about the problems and issues faced by state officials.

A sixth problem is conflicting interests among the states themselves. Not all states are threatened to the same degree by the same environmental pollutants. Acid rain is unevenly distributed across the nation and is not an issue in certain areas of the country. States vary with respect to their economic base. Strict environmental policies have differing levels of economic impact across the nation. Given the differences among the states, dissatisfaction with environmental policies adopted at the federal level will be manifested at the state level, and interstate conflict may lead to policy deadlocks in Congress and the EPA.

These six problems relate to the issue of dividing leadership responsibility between the federal government and the fifty states. Leadership requires the expenditure of financial resources. It was the policy of the Reagan administration to reduce the degree of leadership and financial responsibility of the federal government, but the states have not been overly eager to assume the leadership role in enforcement policy.

Questions for Discussion

1. Is the preservation of federalism purchased at a price in the area of environmental policy?

2. Are the criticisms of Cochran et al. unjust to the states? For example, aren't the states in a better position to know their major environmental problems than the national government?

3. Would the states be better able to handle environmental problems involving majoritarian politics than interest group politics?

Additional Lecture Topics

A-1. The Environmental Movement and Public Policy

William R. Burch and Donald R. Deluca, *Measuring the Social Impact of Natural Resource Policy*. Albuquerque: University of New Mexico Press, 1984.

Michael E. Burns, *Low-Level Radiation Waste Regulation: Science, Politics, and Fear*. Chelsa, MI: Lewis Publishers, 1988.

Samuel Hays, *Beauty, Health and Permanence: Environmental Politics in the United States, 1955–1985*. Cambridge: Cambridge University Press, 1989. A good overview of the changes in public policy on the environment.

James Lester and Ann O'M. Bowman, eds., *The Politics of Hazardous Waste Management*. Durham, NC: Duke University Press, 1983. A comprehensive collection of essays on a complex problem.

Pietro Nivola, *The Politics of Energy Conservation*. Washington, DC: Brookings Institute, 1986.

Walter Rosenbaum, *Environmental Politics and Policy*. 2nd ed. Washington, DC: Congressional Quarterly Press, 1990. Summarizes trends in both policy and implementation.

Theme B   Transportation and the Environment

Summary

Much of environmental policy is connected to the nation's transportation system, especially to the use of automobiles. A host of environmental problems can be associated with cars in some way: (1) the greenhouse effect (cars and light trucks emit 20 percent of fossil fuel carbon dioxide); (2) ozone depletion (cars produce 27 percent of hydrocarbons); and (3) smog (cars generate 34 percent of nitrogen oxide). These issues will be difficult to solve anytime soon. At present, 147.5 million vehicles are operating in the United States, and the number of cars in use is increasing two times faster than the rate of population growth. A crisis is also looming from the perspective of land availability; the amount of land nationwide devoted to parking lots is equivalent to the size of the state of Georgia.

If anything the situation will worsen, for two reasons. First, Americans are driving more; the number of miles driven annually swelled 20 percent from 1980 to 1987, and transportation accounts for a growing proportion of the nation's oil consumption, up from 55.9 percent in 1980 to 62.9 percent in 1989. The second factor contributing to the persistence of automobile pollution is the country's transportation policy. In February 1991, President Bush proposed a $105 billion transportation program that focuses on upgrading highways and limiting funds for mass transit. The future, in other words, is committed to the automobile.

Automobile pollution is an issue of majoritarian politics because everyone benefits from clean air, while car owners will be required to finance any policy to address the problem. The political dilemma is getting the public to support tough laws. From past experience, the public will tolerate antipollution policies when costs are hidden (e.g., installation of catalytic converters) but will resist policies demanding a change in driving habits (e.g., car pools). When costs are high, public support can be rallied by linking a tax increase to a concrete project, such as a bridge or highway. As with any majoritarian policy, the role of the president is crucial in the adoption of a proposal.

Discussion Questions

1. Could a policy to build mass transit systems in metropolitan areas be effected by majoritarian politics, since the benefits may not be widely distributed due to the number of cars already in operation? Is mass transit doomed because most beneficiaries would be poor?

2. In a 1991 survey by Golin/Harris Communications, 64 percent of respondents favored mandatory jail terms for decision makers in organizations who fail to comply with environmental regulations. Should mandatory jail terms be imposed against auto manufacturers who produce cars that exceed federal emission standards? Is air pollution somehow less serious than toxic waste pollution?

3. According to Senator Howard Metzenbaum, the amount of oil lost in the *Exxon Valdez* spill is equivalent to the additional oil consumed daily due to the increased speed limit (65 mph) on rural highways. Moreover, this increase in oil consumption is contributing to a quicker depletion of the ozone layer. Do these two environmental concerns warrant lowering the maximum speed to 55 mph on all highways? If not, what justifies retaining the policy?

4. Do you agree with President Bush's proposed transportation policy? Why did the president propose highway improvement over mass transit?

Data and Perspective for Analysis

Public opinion on the environment reveals some interesting insights into the priorities among various segments of society. A good class exercise challenging students to evaluate their own values is having them explain the reasons behind the public's beliefs on environmental problems. Why do people believe as they do? To a large degree, perceptions of the urgency of the environmental crisis depend on how a problem affects an individual's life. Present the data in the following tables to class.

Table 1
Are you a strong environmentalist?

Characteristic	Strong Environmentalist	Nonenvironmentalist
Sex		
Male	42%	21%
Female	40	20
Ethnic background		
White	42	18
Nonwhite	30	34
Education		
College graduate	43	19
High school graduate	41	19
Not high school graduate	38	27
Region		
East	44	20
Midwest	42	20
South	36	23
West	43	16
Age		
18–29 years	31	28
30–49 years	39	18
50 years and over	49	17
Household income		
$50,000 and over	38	19
$30,000–$49,999	43	14
$15,000–$29,999	42	22
Under $15,000	42	22
Political Party		
Republicans	38	20
Democratic	43	19
Independent	41	22

Table 2
Are you worried about this problem a great deal?

Problem	Worried a Great Deal	Not Worried at All
Pollution of rivers, lakes	72%	3%
Contamination of soil and water by toxic waste	69	3
Air pollution	63	4
Ocean and beach pollution	60	5
Loss of natural habitat for wildlife	58	5
Contamination of soil and water by radioactivity	54	7
Damage to earth's ozone layer	51	8
Acid rain	41	11
Greenhouse effect	35	12

Source: George Gallup, Jr., *The Gallup Poll: Public Opinion*, pp. 121–123. Copyright 1990 by Scholarly Resources, Inc. Reprinted by permission of Scholarly Resources, Inc.

Abstract for Theme B

More Environmental Damage from Cars

Most environmental criticism of the automobile is related to pollution from exhaust emissions. However, car air conditioners have come under attack too. Why? "Car air conditioners," writes Meg Dennison, "are the largest source of the country's contribution to ozone depletion." In response, Vermont in 1989 enacted the nation's first law to ban car air conditioners that use a chemical linked to destruction of the ozone layer. Dennison (in "Vermont Moves to Save the Ozone Layer," *Philadelphia Inquirer*, May 12, 1989) discusses this "landmark legislation":

> Starting with the 1993 model year, the legislation would ban the sale or registration of cars equipped with air conditioners that use chlorofluorocarbons, or CFCs, for coolant. Car air conditioners were singled out partly because they use CFC-12, considered the type of CFC most damaging to the ozone layer. Home refrigerators use a different type of CFC.

Ozone damage has been connected to increases in skin cancer, eye disease, and plant destruction. But cars are not the only source of CFC-12. Aerosol spray cans, certain noisemakers, and photographic cleaning equipment use CFCs as well. The Vermont law applies to most of these products too.

At present, auto manufacturers have developed no alternatives to CFC-12, although research programs are under way to find a substitute.

Questions for Discussion

1. Is the Vermont law fair? Suppose a person moved into the state with a car using CFC-12 as an air conditioning coolant. Would the person be forced to sell the vehicle?

2. The benefits of the law are not concrete and the costs are high. How could a majoritarian policy of this kind be enacted into law?

Theme C   Environmental Policy Without Public Interest

Summary

The politics of acid rain often loses sight of the public interest because any governmental response to the problem of acid rain necessarily involves interest-group politics. As a result, debate on the issue is less about what is the "best" policy than what is at stake politically. The problem is too low in visibility to attract much attention. In 1989, only 41 percent of respondents in the Gallup poll cited in Table 2 were much worried by acid rain—fewer than were concerned about the loss of tropical rain forests. A regional basis exists in attitudes toward environmental pollutants. With respect to air pollution, respondents to a Gallup poll in 1988 who lived in eastern states expressed a higher level of concern (58 percent) than respondents in the Midwest (46 percent), South (45 percent), and West (50 percent). What accounts for this regional disparity? One factor may be that the consequences of acid rain are concentrated on the eastern seaboard.

This lack of public anxiety over acid rain allows the battle to be waged in terms of interest group priorities. After all, the costs of a policy dealing with acid rain will be borne by midwestern businesses and labor unions in industries that burn high-sulfur coal, mainly electric utilities and steel mills. The investment in new technology is fought by industries already in decline; unions fear loss of jobs to defray the expense of installing devices like scrubbers, which reduce sulfur emissions. Coal miners were also distressed about job security.

The Clean Air Act of 1990 reflects the compromises necessary to appease powerful interest groups. Eastern interests won the law's provision that scrubbers be installed in all coal-burning plants by the year 2000, while midwestern interests received provision for financial compensation for jobs lost in complying with the law as well as the nationwide dispersion of the cost of installing scrubbers. In the end, everyone got something but no one got everything. Was anyone really concerned with how the public made out on the deal?

Discussion Questions

1. Does any group dominate the controversy over acid rain? Why isn't acid rain classified as "entrepreneurial politics," in which benefits are widely distributed but costs are imposed on a small group?

2. In interest-group politics, political parties usually do not play a decisive role because of internal divisions. Is this true in the issue of acid rain? For example, shouldn't Republicans favor the claims of midwestern states (pro-business) and Democrats the claims of eastern states (pro-environment)?

3. Since the scientific evidence about acid rain is still ambiguous, does the Clean Air Act of 1990 go too far by requiring companies to invest in expensive technology (i.e., scrubbers)? The phenomenon of acid rain is hardly a concern outside eastern states, so what other evidence does the government need to act? Is it fair to make plants nationwide contribute to the cost of installing scrubbers when many have done nothing to contribute to the problem?

Data and Perspectives for Analysis

The scientific evidence about the causes of acid rain may still be uncertain, but the problem cannot be ignored. Public apathy is a major factor accounting for the lax government response to the issue. Students should be aware of how quickly healthy lakes and forests are disappearing, no matter what the cause. Some alarming data from pre-unification West Germany are presented below. What could account for such a sudden change? If industry has been spewing sulfur into the atmosphere for a long time, why did the forest damage occur over the span of a single year?

Changes in Forest Damage in West Germany, 1982–1983

Species	Portion of Forest Affected	
	1982	1983
Spruce	9%	41%
Fir	60	76
Pine	5	43
Beech	4	26
Oak	4	15
Others	4	17
Total	8	34

Source: Sandra Postel, "Acid Rain Is a Global Threat," in *The Environmental Crisis: Opposing Viewpoints* (St. Paul, MN: Greenhaven Press, 1986), p. 237. From Der Bundesminister Für Ernährung, Landwirtschaft und Forsten, "Neuartige Waldschäden un der Bundesrepublik Deutschland," Bonn, Germany, 1983.

Additional Lecture Topic

C-1. The Acid Rain Controversy

John Carroll, *Environmental Diplomacy*. Ann Arbor: University of Michigan Press, 1984. The foreign policy dimension, focusing on the United States and Canada.

Diane S. Gilleland and James H. Swisher, eds., *Acid Rain Control: The Costs of Compliance*. Carbondale, IL: Southern Illinois University Press, 1984.

Jon Luoma, *Troubled Skies, Troubled Waters: The Story of Acid Rain*. New York: Viking Press, 1984. Less scholarly but good for lecture material.

Office of Technology Assessment, *Acid Rain and Transported Air Pollutants*. Washington, DC: U.S. Government Printing Office, 1984.

James Ragens and Robert Rycroft, *The Acid Rain Controversy*. Pittsburgh: University of Pittsburgh Press, 1986. The scholarly viewpoint is well presented.

Theme D The Future Environment

Instructor Reference

Peter Borelli, ed., *Crossroads: Environmental Priorities for the Future.* Washington, DC: Island Press, 1988.

Lester Milbrath, *Envisioning a Sustainable Society: Learning Our Way Out.* Albany: State University of New York Press, 1989.

Robert Paehlke, *Environmentalism and the Future of Progressive Politics.* New Haven: Yale University Press, 1989.

Norman Vig and Michael Kraft, eds., *Environmental Policy in the 1990s.* Washington, DC: Congressional Quarterly Press, 1990.

Summary

It is difficult to predict the future of environmental politics. Evidence indicates that many current environmental problems are intensifying while new problems are continually emerging. Science has been unable to develop workable solutions to most forms of pollution. Such uncertainty precludes the formulation of a coherent public policy. As a result, this is an area where politics will necessarily lag behind technology. Science must define a direction.

But citizens do not have to stand idle while the condition of the environment deteriorates. Certain steps can be taken that yield immediate environmental improvement: recycling, car pooling, using mass transit, cutting home water use. Some action can be accomplished by way of legislation; four states, for example, require inspection of automobile emission systems, and another twenty-nine have county or city programs. Other action can be taken by private enterprise; one city in Japan has a twelve-story parking garage—for bicycles! In other words, scientific uncertainty does not forestall responsible public behavior.

Data and Perspectives for Analysis

An environmental awareness now exists in the United States. The future depends on this awareness enduring. Have Americans altered their behavior in response to the environmental crisis? The answer appears to be in the affirmative. Present the data below to your class. Inquire what steps students have taken to deal with environmental pollution. Will they continue to behave responsibly, or is environmentalism a fad?

Which of the following things, if any, have you or other household members done in recent years to improve the quality of the environment?[a]

Voluntarily recycled newspapers, glass, aluminum, motor oil, other items	78%
Cut household's use of energy by improving insulation or changing heating or air conditioning system	76
Replaced "gas-guzzling" automobile with more fuel-efficient one	66
Cut household's use of water	65
Contributed to environmental, conservation, or wildlife preservation group	49
Cut down on use of car by car pooling or taking public transportation	42
Boycotted a company's products because of its record on environment	29
Did volunteer work for environmental, conservation, or wildlife preservation group	16
None of the above	2

[a]Multiple responses were given.

Source: George Gallup, Jr., *The Gallup Poll: Public Opinion*, p. 123. Copyright 1990 by Scholarly Resources, Inc. Reprinted by permission of Scholarly Resources, Inc.

Abstract for Theme D

The Future from an International Perspective

The world is changing. The causes of international friction are changing as well. Tension between countries is increasingly rooted in environmental terms rather than in military ones. Former president Jimmy Carter (in "World Needs New Thinking," *Atlanta Constitution,* July 9, 1991) presents an astute analysis of future international conflict.

> As nations today evaluate their security interests, their frames of reference must shift profoundly. . . . New power centers, chiefly based on economic strength, are ascending. Conflict is rooted increasingly in racial, ethnic, religious, nationalistic and self-determination causes quite independent of ideological politics.
>
> At the outset of the Persian Gulf war, the Carter Center had identified 112 ongoing conflicts in the world. . . . Many of these conflicts illustrate that threats to domestic tranquillity are much more likely to come from drug trafficking, secessionists, religious extremists, explosive urban-population growth, hopelessly declining living standards or deprivation of life-sustaining resources, such as water or energy, than from invading armies.
>
> What is common to these threats is that they can attack a people's quality of life as surely and as fatally as any military aggression. . . . "Security" must be redefined for the '90s and beyond, taking into account that the safety of a nation's citizenry . . . can be jeopardized as much by a neighboring country's smokestacks or diversion of water of supplies as by its war machines.
>
> Security politics must be re-grounded with respect to realities like global interdependence, the imperative of sustainable development, the ominous appearance of environmental threats that are global in nature and conflicts over vital natural resources. . . .
>
> It is likely that the North-South, or rich nation-poor nation, gap will replace the struggle between East and West as the engine of violence and conflict for the future.
>
> Environmental deterioration and resource depletion in the developing world exacerbate the situation. What rich nations and their citizens consider inconveniences or burdens readily shifted to others easily become matters of life and death to the poor.
>
> The political rivalries and tensions that already exist among leadership groups and that, in the extreme, cause violence, are intensified drastically when people believe that their very survival is at stake—when there is no fuel wood to cook daily meals, when there is no drinking water, when the land is no longer farmable, when exploding populations overwhelm available resources, to say nothing of health, education, housing and other social infrastructures. . . . In the future, transfer of appropriate technology to developing countries will furnish more security than military advisers. . . . Environmental defense spending will buy more security than military spending. . . .
>
> Nations of the world are preparing now for the U.N.-sponsored Earth Summit to be held next June in Brazil. It will address the environmental security of the planet, in the context of assuring lives of quality for all. Many nations of the South already understand this new security agenda; it springs from their daily struggles to survive.
>
> It is not so clear that the prosperous North has embraced this new agenda. We Americans, for our part, are doing little to exhibit leadership. Instead, our policies continue the course of wasteful energy consumption, undermine international family-planning assistance and impede most international efforts to rectify global environmental problems.
>
> While there are opportunities before us daily that should be seized to incorporate a new definition of security into our national policies and behavior, the Earth Summit will take the measure of American leadership in this arena.

Questions for Discussion

1. President Carter paints a bleak picture of the environmental future. He argues that the environment could lead to the next series of wars in the world. Is he an alarmist? Did the war with Iraq prove that American military strength is still the world's best protection?

2. Are Americans as apathetic about the environment as President Carter alleges? Don't opinion surveys indicate that most Americans are taking some steps to improve the environment? Would Americans make the necessary sacrifices to help developing countries improve their environment? If not, will the North-South conflict prophesied by President Carter occur?

Research Assignment

Have students research the Earth Summit held in 1992. What were the issues under discussion? What was the position of the United States on these issues?

PART FIVE

The Nature of American Democracy

23

Who Governs?

Overview and Objectives

This chapter is largely a recapitulation of previous ones, for the purpose of reviewing the four types of politics already discussed (majoritarian, interest group, client, and entrepreneurial) and of examining the validity of the several theories of power in American government (Marxist, elitist, bureaucratic, and pluralist). After reading and reviewing the material in this chapter the student should be able to do each of the following:

1. Provide definitions and examples of the four different types of policy outputs of government. The student will find it helpful to review Chapters 15–22 on policy-making and the corresponding sections of the *Student Handbook*.

2. Explain the function of public opinion in the four types of policy outputs and indicate under what circumstances the public is most influential and least influential.

3. Describe the Marxist, elitist, bureaucratic, and pluralist theories. Indicate the utilities and shortcomings of each theory as described by the text. Again, the student will find it helpful to review the chapters on policy-making and the corresponding sections of the *Student Handbook*.

Chapter Outline with Keyed-in Resources

I. Introduction
   A. Chapter question: who governs?
      1. Who governs affects distribution of political power
      2. Policies adopted by government determines who governs
   B. Classification of policies has two advantages
      1. Looks at comprehensive list of policies rather than generalizing
      2. Focuses on how policies affect people in terms of costs and benefits

II. Four kinds of politics (THEME A: DISTRIBUTION OF COSTS AND BENEFITS—A REVIEW)
   A. Majoritarian politics
      1. Public opinion
         a. Usually a discernible public opinion exists since issues highly visible
            (1) Sometimes specific
            (2) Sometimes general
            (3) Sometimes contradictory
         b. Long-term disregard of public opinion is dangerous for politicians

Some politicians do not feel overly constrained by public opinion. Theodore Roosevelt is an example of this rare breed of politician: "People used to say of me that I . . . divined what the people were going to think. I did not 'divine' . . . I simply made up my mind what they ought to think, and then did my best to get them to think it."

         c. President and advisers play key role in development
      2. Ideological debate
         a. Often precipitated by proposals of new programs
         b. Examples
            (1) Family Assistance Plan
            (2) Keynesian economics
            (3) Supply-side economics
      3. Worldview
         a. Debate outcomes often institutionalize new worldviews
            (1) When public opinion loose (foreign policy), worldview of elites significant
            (2) When public opinion tight (macroeconomics), freedom of elected officials narrow
         b. Crises may provide decisive leverage to alter worldview
            (1) Depression

A crisis situation makes the public willing to follow a leader who promises change and action. When Franklin Roosevelt was elected president during the Great Depression, Will Rogers commented: "The whole country is with him just so he does something. If he burned down the Capitol we would cheer and say 'Well, we at least got a fire started anyhow.'"

            (2) Pearl Harbor
         c. Other forces can alter worldview
            (1) Education
            (2) Mass media
            (3) Changing perceptions—welfare legislation
      4. Political parties
         a. Relatively important role when new policies are adopted
         b. But bipartisan support *after* new policies succeed

Social Security is an example of a majoritarian policy that has acquired bipartisan support. Paul Light quotes an aide of President Reagan's as saying: "We have to realize that social security is as American as Mom and apple pie. It might not be the best retirement program, but it's the one the people know."

   B. Interest-group politics

1. Changing cleavages in society source of proposals
   a. Sources of interest-group policy proposals found in new
      (1) Technologies
      (2) Markets
      (3) Regions
      (4) Organizations
   b. Dominant group sometimes able to block another from organizing

Organizing efforts to gain support for gay rights confront resistance from a majority of the public. In a survey taken in 1991, 38 percent of respondents in suburban Atlanta said they would be "not likely" or "not very likely" to vote for a qualified person they agreed with on the issues if they knew that person was homosexual; 41 percent said Atlanta's gay community had a negative effect on the city, compared with 22 percent responding that the influence was positive.

      (1) Unions
      (2) Blacks
2. Political parties
   a. Usually not decisive because of internal division caused by crosscutting pressure
   b. Exception: labor-management issues
3. Continuing struggle
   a. Moves into bureaucracy, courts, later legislative sessions
   b. Agencies less vulnerable to "capture" than are those of client politics
   c. Public opinion and presidential leadership usually weak
   d. Mass media rarely play an important role
C. Client politics
   1. Visibility
      a. Typically low visibility
      b. Subject to change
         (1) Importation of foreign oil

The level of oil importation has lost much of its salience to the American public with OPEC overproduction causing a flooding of the market in the 1980s and early 1990s. Yet American dependence on imported oil has increased after the oil shortages of the 1970s. In the 1950s, the United States imported only about 10 percent of the oil it consumed; that figure reached 38 percent by 1986. The nation has become increasingly vulnerable to oil blackmail while at the same time the issue has become less visible.

         (2) Cost of electricity
      c. Noneconomic groups can also lose out: extremists take advantage
   2. Political parties
      a. Usually only a slight role—pork-barrel packaging

The pork barrel may be a small element of client politics, but it is an important one. Even the president can do little about it. President Carter in his 1978 budget proposed cutting 19 water projects and placing 320 other projects under review. Congressional opposition forced Carter to remove 307 of the projects designated for review and restore three of the canceled projects.

      b. Problem of client group: getting on the agenda at all
      c. Conducive to political corruption
   3. Identifying the clients
      a. Sometimes sponsorship by vicarious representatives
      b. Economic Opportunity Act: professionals and bureaucrats
   4. Serving the clients
      a. Creation of client-serving government agencies
         (1) CAB
         (2) FCC
         (3) VA

    b. Low-visibility client politics less common now: more opponents and court intervention
    c. Agency proliferation creates some offsetting forces
        (1) Antitrust Division of Justice Department
  D. Entrepreneurial politics
    1. Compelling symbols
        a. Needed because appeal to self-interest is too slight
        b. Public's perception of dangers and values hinges on such manipulation; symbols change each generation
            (1) Atheists, Communists
            (2) Coal mining, nuclear power dangers
        c. Sometimes no compelling symbol found: gun control

It appears that the gun control lobby may have found the compelling symbol needed to combat the National Rifle Association: James Brady, President Reagan's former press secretary who was injured in John Hinckley's assassination attempt. Brady has become a difficult figure to ignore in his lobbying efforts.

    2. Promotion by the media
        a. Great importance of reporters, editors; often tacit alliance with entrepreneur
        b. Political parties less significant
    3. Capture of the agencies
        a. These agencies most susceptible to capture; group an incentive to weaken
        b. Example: FDA, by pharmaceutical industry
    4. The Courts
        a. Play an important role
        b. Initial deference to popular mood by courts
        c. Later develop balancing tests
III. Competing theories of political power (THEME B: POWER IN AMERICAN SOCIETY)
  A. Marxist theory
    1. Definition: ownership of means of production determines political outcomes
    2. Frequently cited aspects
        a. Foreign policy—but political, not corporate, factors dominate
        b. Defense policy—but political, not corporate, factors dominate

Corporate considerations have occasionally intervened in foreign policy. When Secretary of State James Baker was asked to justify America's military response to Iraq's invasion of Kuwait, he responded with one word: jobs.

    3. Economic determinists will point to client relationships in economic policy
        a. Maritime, dairy subsidies
        b. Farm-price supports
        c. Oil-import quotas
        d. Tax treatment of preferred groups
    4. Other examples of client politics noneconomic, making determination an incomplete explanation
        a. Ethnic groups
        b. Racial groups
        c. Women's groups

The women's movement is an example of a noneconomic crusade that has shifted to the economic arena. The fight over "comparable worth" signals a change in focus for the movement.

    5. Client politics limited by public and elite opinion
        a. Airline deregulation
        b. Banking deregulation
        c. Windfall profits tax
    6. Marxist rejoinder

        a. Control of political agenda crucial—but agenda much more open since 1930s by collapse of legitimacy barrier
        b. Distribution of political resources crucial—but redistribution now more accessible
            (1) Party nominations decayed
            (2) Primary elections became decisive
            (3) Mass media replaced partisan, elite media
            (4) Race and gender barriers to voting were torn down
            (5) Issue organizations grew easier to form
    B. Elitist theory (ADDITIONAL LECTURE TOPIC B-1)
        1. Definition: single elite with common background makes all policy, influenced only weakly by popular opinion

Thomas Dye's study of the institutional elite in the United States discovered a remarkable similarity in background characteristics among this discrete group. Take education: "Elites are notably 'Ivy League': 54 percent of corporate leaders and 42 percent of governmental leaders are alumni of just twelve well-known private universities."

        2. Client politics a partial confirmation of elite theory
        3. But an ambiguity persists
            a. Elite may be beneficiary of policies, or . . .
            b. . . . Elite because of social characteristics, irrespective of policy interests
        4. Client politics also shows how costs/benefits influence affected groups' ability to shape policy
            a. Client politics is illustration, not confirmation, of elite theory
            b. Activist federal judiciary an example: power from professional background
        5. Foreign policy an especially interesting case
            a. Elite power not from partisan politics but from group membership
            b. Yet that group less socially distinctive now than formerly
        6. Most popular version today: career politicians in Congress make decisions without regard to public opinion
            a. But these elites are popularly elected unlike elites of the past
    C. Bureaucratic theory
        1. Definition: government by large organizations made up of appointed career officials
        2. Bureaucracy most powerful where laws are least precise

The Supreme Court has given constitutional imprimatur to the increased power of federal bureaucrats. In the 1930s, the Court allowed Congress to delegate authority to bureaucrats using vague standards.

            a. Weapons procurement
            b. Civil rights law enforcement
            c. Foreign policy
            d. Regulation of business
        3. Bureaucratic discretion is
            a. Sometimes inevitable because of subject matter
            b. At other times avoidable, when Congress unable to make tough decision
        4. Recent tendency in Congress: reduction of bureaucratic discretion
            a. Environmental legislation and drug laws
            b. Exact standards increase social cost
        5. Another avenue of increasing bureaucratic power: source of the agenda
            a. Economic Opportunity Act (1964)
            b. Medicare Act (1965)
        6. Power of bureaucracy not dependent on kinds of politics but clarity of congressional laws
    D. Pluralist theory

Proponents of pluralism support the validity of their theory over alternative explanations of political power by examining actual decision-making situations. Pluralists fault competing theories for failing to go beyond the realm of abstract theory. In the words of Nelson Polsby, "How can one tell, after all, whether or not an actor is powerful unless some sequence of events, competently observed, attests to his power?"

1. Definition: policies come from conflict, bargaining among affected groups
   a. Obviously an accurate description of interest-group politics
   b. But it overestimates extent of group formation, activity
2. In client politics, little incentive for affected groups to organize
3. In majoritarian politics, interest groups play marginal role
4. Rise of entrepreneurial politics makes pluralism more applicable
   a. Greater variety of groups represented today than in 1950s
5. Pluralism still an inadequate explanation
   a. No clear explanation of entrepreneurial politics
   b. No full accounting of role of judiciary

Important Terms

bureaucratic theory The political theory that the influence of government bureaucracies has become so great that elected officials and their key advisers are almost powerless to affect policy. This theory overestimates the power of the bureaucracy. The bureaucracy is powerful when the law confers wide discretion and less so when the task is specified by law in exact language. Thus it is the clarity and consistency of congressional laws which determine bureaucratic power.

client politics Political activity in which the benefits of a policy are concentrated on a small, easily organized group while the costs are widely distributed among the public at large. These factors make the policy low in visibility and limit the role played by political parties. Such policies have become less common as more organized interests act on behalf of the public and as courts intervene more often in public policy disputes.

elite theory The political theory that one elite makes public policy, whatever the nature of the issue. Client politics does not confirm the theory but only illustrates how the distribution of the costs and benefits of a public policy differentially influence the abilities of the affected groups to shape that policy.

entrepreneurial politics Political activity in which the benefits of a policy are widely distributed but the costs are concentrated on a small group. The public is usually indifferent to such policies and must be mobilized through skilled leadership and the media. Emotional appeals using compelling symbols are frequently employed for this purpose. Government agencies created as a result of the policy are vulnerable to capture, with courts likely to intervene.

interest-group politics Political activity in which the costs of a policy are concentrated on a small group while the benefits are concentrated on a different but equally small group. Such policy proposals are generated by changing economic and social cleavages in society which force interests to organize. Political parties are usually divided and play no role in the resolution of the matter. The dispute over the policy will persist even after its passage or defeat, but in the bureaucratic or judicial arenas. Neither the president nor public opinion is a significant factor.

legitimacy barrier A shared public belief that limits access to the political agenda, depending on whether an issue is considered an appropriate subject for government action. This barrier has collapsed as politics has become involved in nearly everything.

majoritarian politics Political activity in which the costs and benefits of a proposed course of action are widely distributed. The president and his advisers play the dominant role, with debate focused in ideological terms. The outcome of the debate is often the institutionalization of a new worldview. The ideological nature of the policy diminishes once the policy is adopted and proves popular.

Marxist theory The political theory that the economic structure of a society shapes its politics and determines political outcomes. The theory explains client politics only when a government advantage involves an economic client. But as client politics becomes concerned with noneconomic matters, the theory falls short as an explanation and fails to account for the boundaries imposed by public and elite opinion.

pluralist theory The political theory that policies are made by conflict and bargaining among organizations that represent affected groups. The theory overestimates the extent to which interest groups form and are active. With the rise of entrepreneurial politics, the theory has become more applicable to American government. Yet it remains incomplete by failing to take into account either client or majoritarian politics and by failing to offer a clear explanation of entrepreneurial politics.

Theme A   Distribution of Costs and Benefits—A Review

Summary

Majoritarian politics, in which both costs and benefits are widely distributed, is seen in the 1935 Social Security Act, in the 1890 Sherman Antitrust Act, in the general foreign policy posture of the United States, and in the general features of macroeconomic policy. On such issues, there is a discernible public opinion that affects election outcomes. The president and his principal advisers play a leading, if not dominant, role in the development of policy. Debate is carried out in ideological terms, and the outcome of such debates is often the institutionalization of a new worldview, as when interventionists won out over isolationists with the onset of World War II. Parties tend to be important in the adoption of majoritarian policies, and a lopsided partisan majority in Congress is often necessary to pass them.

Interest-group politics, in which both costs and benefits are concentrated, is seen in a series of bills regulating labor-management relations (the National Labor Relations Act, the Taft-Hartley Act), in the tension among the military services over the allocation of the defense budget, and in the conflict between blacks and whites in local communities with segregated schools. Changing economic and social cleavages generate interest-group conflict, as when a variety of economic changes and rivalries set off the debate over the Commerce Act of 1887. Usually all relevant interests are organized, though sometimes one group blocks the organizing efforts of its rival: business succeeded in blocking union organization in many cases until the 1930s, and segregationist whites impeded black organization until the civil rights movement. In both these cases, popular attitudes were hostile to the unorganized groups, and their organization required a strategy for enlisting popular support. Only a few interest-group conflicts correspond to party lines (labor-management issues are the best example). The passage of a bill does not end interest-group conflict; it is carried on in the courts or in the bureaucracy, generally out of public view.

Client politics, in which benefits are concentrated and costs distributed, are seen in merchant marine and dairy subsidies, flood-control projects, and "loopholes" in tax laws. Client politics is low-visibility politics. In rare cases when client politics achieves widespread visibility, client benefits are often taken away (as was the case with restrictions on oil importation in the early 1970s). Political parties play only a small role in client politics, and if a sponsor for a proposal can be found, it usually passes by a lopsided majority in Congress. Client politics tends to create client-serving agencies (such as the Civil Aeronautics Board or the Veterans' Administration). Client-oriented policies are easier to challenge now, because small groups claiming to represent diffuse interests (they may or may not actually do so) can more easily get courts to intervene and can raise money through direct mail.

Entrepreneurial politics, in which costs are concentrated and benefits are diffuse, can be found in regulation of the drug industry, attacks on political radicals by people such as Senator Joseph McCarthy, and the activities of Ralph Nader and Howard Jarvis (the California antitax crusader). Policy entrepreneurs must depend on emotional appeals, because they are unable to mobilize self-interest. A compelling symbol (such as "clean air" or a "communist conspiracy") is necessary, and the media must publicize the issue.

Discussion Questions

1. The text rejects the notion that our government handles all issues in the same way. What evidence does it offer to disprove (a) the Marxist view; (b) the pluralist view; and (c) the "Weberian" view? Can we reasonably conclude that none of the three is adequate?

2. Of the four kinds of politics outlined in Chapter 15, are some *better* than others? Do some produce better results than others? Are some fairer? Why?

    Instructor: This question is repeated from Chapter 15. It is worth raising twice, to determine whether the students' initial reactions are confirmed by the chapters on policymaking.

3. Are some of the four types of politics becoming more prevalent? Are some becoming less prevalent? Which ones, and why?

4. Your answers to Questions 1 and 2 should allow you to generalize about whether American politics functions better than, or not so well as, it used to. Which changes in American politics have had positive effects, and which ones have had negative effects? Consider, for example: (a) the fact that entrepreneurial politics is more prevalent; (b) the fact that government has many more policies; (c) the growth and proliferation of interest groups; (d) the decline of the parties; and (e) the increase in judicial activism.

Data and Perspectives for Analysis

Social Security is the classic example of majoritarian politics because both the costs and benefits of the program are widely distributed. Yet the program is experiencing difficulties maintaining an equitable distribution of costs to benefits. In particular, the aging of the nation is resulting in fewer people working to support each beneficiary. The ratio of cost to benefit is becoming skewed. What does this mean in terms of Social Security's maintaining its status as a majoritarian policy? Could Social Security transform itself into entrepreneurial politics in the future if population trends continue? What would such a change mean to Social Security recipients?

Consider the two tables presented on the following page. Table 1 illustrates how the cost-benefit ratio is changing. Table 2 shows the generational gap in attitudes toward Social Security: the program is not held in high esteem by those bearing the cost of supporting the beneficiaries. Perhaps the politics of Social Security could be in the process of changing.

Table 1 Social Security (OASDI) Covered Workers and Beneficiaries, 1945–2065

Year	Covered Workers[a] (thousands)	Beneficiaries[b] OASI	DI	Total	Covered Workers per OASDI Beneficiary	Beneficiaries per 100 Covered Workers
1945	46,930	1,106	—	1,106	42.4	2
1950	48,280	2,930	—	2,930	16.5	6
1955	65,200	7,563	—	7,563	8.6	12
1960	72,530	13,740	522	14,262	5.1	20
1965	80,680	18,509	1,648	20,157	4.0	25
1970	93,090	22,618	2,568	25,186	3.7	27
1975	100,200	26,998	4,125	31,123	3.2	31
1980	112,980	30,385	4,734	35,119	3.2	31
1985	121,300	32,776	3,874	36,650	3.3[c]	30[c]
1986	124,500	33,349	3,972	37,321	3.3[c]	30[c]
1987	127,917	33,917	4,034	37,952	3.4[c]	30[c]
1990	132,396	35,581	4,203	39,784	3.3	30
1995	139,177	37,815	4,608	42,422	3.3	30
2000	144,261	39,251	5,285	44,536	3.2	31
2005	148,453	40,801	6,032	46,832	3.2	32
2010	151,428	43,943	6,880	50,824	3.0	34
2015	152,614	49,654	7,351	57,005	2.7	37
2020	152,286	56,765	7,589	64,354	2.4	42
2025	151,648	63,320	7,970	71,290	2.1	47
2030	151,494	68,323	7,914	76,236	2.0	50
2035	151,830	71,078	7,799	78,877	1.9	52
2040	152,017	71,688	7,833	79,521	1.9	52
2045	151,895	72,033	8,091	80,124	1.9	53
2050	151,614	72,895	8,218	81,113	1.9	53
2055	151,478	73,982	8,211	82,193	1.8	54
2060	151,566	74,773	8,152	82,925	1.8	55
2065	151,668	75,232	8,177	83,409	1.8	55

Note: "OASI" indicates Old-Age and Survivors' Insurance; "DI" indicates Disability Insurance. Projections (1990–2065) are the so-called Alternative II-B projections. See Source for further reference.
[a] Workers who pay OASDI taxes at some time during the year.
[b] Beneficiaries with monthly benefits in current-payment status as of June 30.
[c] Preliminary.
Source: Harold Stanley and Richard Niemi, *Vital Statistics on American Politics*. 2nd ed. (Washington, DC: Congressional Quarterly Press, 1990), p. 356. Reprinted by permission of CQ Press.

Table 2 Confidence in Social Security, by Age Group, 1982

How much confidence do you have that the Social Security system will have the funds to provide retirement benefits to you or your spouse upon retirement?

Confidence	New Arrivals 18–24	Now Working 25–34	Middle-Aged 35–49	Nearly Retired 50–64	Retired 65+
Complete	3%	3%	5%	13%	21%
A great deal	11	8	10	22	34
Only a little	45	44	44	41	29
No confidence	38	45	39	21	7

Source: NBC News/Associated Press poll, November 1982. Total interviews equaled 1,583.

Theme B Power in American Society

Summary

Marxist theory, or more accurately, economic determinism, is most consistent with the vast array of client-serving policies. However, many racial, ethnic, and gender groups (as opposed to economically defined groups) have also gotten privileged treatment via the Office for Civil Rights, the Equal Employment Opportunity Commission, and the Civil Rights Commission. Public and (especially) elite opinion also matters. Economic determinism can explain the fact that the CAB for many years protected the interests of the major airlines, but it cannot explain how deregulation occurred. A Marxist might rejoin that the principal influence of corporate power is in keeping threatening policies off the political agenda. With the vast increase in the number of governmental policies in the 1930s and 1960s, this argument carries little weight. Politics is now about nearly everything.

Elitist theory is most consistent with the power of the courts and with the way foreign policy is made. Because almost all governmental decisions are made by a few people, one could say that almost all politics is elitist. But elitist theory asserts that it is always the *same* elite that makes policy, that it acts in concert (or at least has a common background), and that it is not substantially influenced by public opinion.

Bureaucratic theory is applicable when the bureaucracy gains broad discretionary authority, as in the cases of weapons procurement by the military, the enforcement of civil rights laws, and the regulation of business. In other cases (Social Security or veterans' benefits) the law specifies precisely how benefits must be distributed. In some recent cases (clean air and water laws), Congress has tried to limit bureaucratic discretion by specifying exact standards. Increasingly, the bureaucracy has gained influence by becoming the source of the agenda of politics: government grows by generating demands upon itself.

Pluralist theory is obviously an accurate description of interest-group politics; however, it overestimates the extent to which interest groups form and are active. Thus it cannot explain client politics very well, nor is it of much use in the few but important cases in which majoritarian politics prevails. Nor can the vastly increased role of the courts be fitted into pluralist theory, because the judiciary is not easily described as a group with interests. However, the pluralist theory presents a more accurate picture of American politics now than it did in the 1950s when, ironically, it was most popular with political scientists.

Discussion Questions

1. Does the demise of communism in the world mean the end of Marxist political theory? Since none of the countries were really Marxist except in name, is it fair to say that Marxism has not been refuted?

2. Does the change of the Veterans' Administration from an independent agency to a cabinet-level department mean it is no longer involved in client politics? Is it less subject to capture?

3. How are policies made in the United States if none of the political theories examined in the text is correct? If this question can never be answered, why should political power be studied since all answers will be flawed?

4. Are there any elites that have disproportionate influence in American politics? Is there only one such elite, or are there many that sometimes act at cross-purposes? Are there any elites that have broad power across all policy areas? Or do elites tend to have their influence limited to a narrow area?

Additional Lecture Topic B-1

Elitism in American Politics

Peter Bachrach, *The Theory of Democratic Elitism: A Critique*. Boston: Little, Brown, 1967. A good review of classic elitist literature.

G. William Domhoff, *The Higher Circles*. New York: Random House, 1970. An older but still valuable treatment on the "upper class as governing class."

G. William Domhoff, *Who Rules America Now?* Englewood Cliffs, NJ: Prentice-Hall, 1983.

Thomas R. Dye, *Who's Running America—The Bush Era*. 5th ed. Englewood Cliffs, NJ: Prentice-Hall, 1990. A comprehensive survey of institutional elites in America.

Thomas R. Dye and L. Harmon Zeigler, *The Irony of Democracy*. 7th ed. Monterey, Calif.: Brooks-Cole, 1987. Democracy rests on elite commitment to preserving freedom, not on the masses.

Gwen Moore, "Women in Elite Positions," *Sociological Forum* (December 1988): 566–585.

C. Wright Mills, *The Power Elite*. New York: Oxford University Press, 1956.

Leonard and Mark Silk, *The American Establishment*. New York: Basic Books, 1980.

Suggested Student Reading

See Chapter 1 of Dye and Zeigler, pp. 19–20. A capsule portrait of the similar class and occupational backgrounds of key officials in administrations from Truman to Reagan.

Abstract 1 for Theme B

"Elite" Versus "Pluralistic" Government in the United States

The debate over whether America is ruled by a "power elite" that is not accountable to the public versus the pluralistic contention that multiple groups compete for power (ensuring no permanent domination of policy or political resources) is considered by Michael Parenti and Andrew M. Greeley in McKenna and Feingold's *Taking Sides: Clashing Ideas on Controversial Political Issues*. 7th ed. (Guilford, CT: Dushkin, 1991, pp. 24–36). Parenti rejects the notion of pluralist democracy in the United States, contending that public policies benefit the dominant economic sectors of society: corporations and other wealthy private interests. Greeley asserts that power is so diffuse in American society that the lack of power concentration becomes the chief obstacle to social reform.

In an excerpt from his *Democracy for the Few* (New York: St. Martin's Press, 1980) Parenti makes the following major points:

1. The pluralists' contention that (a) power is shared among a variety of population sectors and (b) no one group "enjoys permanent defeat" is invalid (p. 24). American government serves *first* "those who control the wealth of society . . . and . . . corporate business occupies a particularly strategic position" (p. 26). Because business controls the economy of the nation, and because the economy is such a vital "political" issue, the linkage between the two "worlds" becomes inevitable.

2. The pluralist argument that the business community is far from monolithic in its agreement on all issues is correct. However, conflicts that do emerge are the "conflicts of haves versus haves and they seldom include the interests of the unorganized public" (p. 26). Also, there is ample evidence of "collusion" between business and governmental elites.

3. "The diffusion of power does not necessarily mean the democratization of power" (p. 27). In this sense, power-sharing is confined to propertied interests that are in turn becoming less competitive and more concentrated and collusive in economic ownership and political power.

4. It is true that nonelites do have victories, but these victories are "cosmetic," because the realities of power in a capitalist system will not permit true reform. "Those who have the interest in fundamental change have not the power, while those who have the power have not the interest" (p. 28). Accordingly, the officeholders' prime duty is not to fight for social change but to prosper by staying in office. The way they stay in office is to respond first to those who control the resources of society and not the unorganized public. In short, the overriding goal of the political system is to support state capitalism by ensuring both profits and prosperity. Investment incentives may not be tampered with or eliminated by major redistributions in income and taxation.

Greeley defends the pluralist viewpoint as follows:

1. Some basic facts of elitism exist—some people are more powerful than others, certain groups can have decisive power on specific issues, some very critical decisions are made by a "handful of men," and well-organized pressure groups influence society out of all proportion to their size (the NRA on gun control, for example).

2. There cannot be a power elite, or "establishment," simply because there is no overwhelming concentration of power in the political system. In other words,

   since power is widely distributed among a vast number of governmental, bureaucratic, business, labor, social, civic, educational, and religious groups, change on a matter that large segments of the population deem important can only occur when the opinions of all these groups are listened to and at least in some fashion respected (p. 33).

3. Intensive bargaining and coalition formation are indispensable ingredients of the American political system. This does slow the system's ability to solve problems, but it is preferable to replacing the process with an undemocratic, all-powerful elite. The solution is that coalitions must be formed more rapidly if critical problems are to be resolved.

Discussion/Answer Guidelines

You should use the abstract to promote general, wide-ranging discussion from the perspective of the entire course.

Abstract 2 for Theme B

How "Elites" Should Treat the "Masses"

In *The Irony of Democracy*, (op. cit.), Dye and Zeigler admit that elites cannot always be trusted to preserve democratic values, even when those elites are democratically elected. As the authors phrase it, "*all* elites are capable of repressive measures when they feel threatened by mass unrest" (p. 446). Still, elites should follow guidelines so that potential repression is avoided. The following assertions represent those key principles as outlined by Dye and Zeigler (pp. 447–450):

1. *Preserve fundamental constitutional principles designed to modify mass influence in government.* These concepts include republicanism, federalism, separation of powers, checks and balances, and judicial review. In other words, "these arrangements, which make it difficult for majority preferences to become public policy, must be strengthened . . . if we are to avoid the evils of 'an unjust and interested majority' that will 'outnumber and oppress the rest'" (p. 447).

2. *Avoid crises that directly threaten mass security and well-being.* Discontinuities in economic conditions will heighten mass insecurity and make the public "vulnerable to the appeals of counterelites." In addition, levels of personal security must be assured, otherwise the masses may ignore traditional democratic values in their quest for personal safety (p. 447).

3. *Maintain legitimacy and authority.* Elites should avoid demagoguery and antiintellectual or prejudicial appeals, which will "inspire mass fears or hatreds." Elites must also be willing to employ force against terrorist actions of all kinds (p. 448).

4. *Develop community and group identifications among the masses and center mass attention upon community problems.* The weakening of family, group, or community affiliations within the masses can lead to atomization of the individual and hence serious disruption of society (p. 448).

5. *Allow the elite system to remain open to segments of the masses that are upwardly mobile.* The masses can accept inequalities if they believe that they have the opportunity to rise within the system of power, as opposed to being stuck in a "caste system" that prevents advancement. Such openness also has the effect of siphoning off revolutionary leaders from the masses and promoting the "circulation of elites" (pp. 448–449).

6. *Do not allow elites to trigger unrealistic mass expectations about the improvement of serious social and economic problems;* if they do, revolutionary rhetoric and actual instability can be the result (p. 449).

7. *Avoid exaggerating social problems;* doing so might create a belief among the masses that "society" is responsible for their problems (p. 449).

8. *Set common national goals that can unify the masses and stabilize society.* Otherwise, "if the masses feel that society is directionless, that their lives have no particular meaning or purpose, then they are susceptible to counterelites who offer to fill the void in their lives" (p. 449).

Class Discussion Guidelines

Students should be reminded that Dye and Zeigler consider the masses to be far less democratic in their ideals and attitudes than elites. Yet, are the elite guidelines listed by the authors considered by some students antidemocratic? If so, why? Do most students think the guidelines are realistic or not? See if they can think of examples from American political life that either support or contradict Dye and Zeigler's approach.

24

To What Ends?

Overview and Objectives

The purpose of this chapter is to review the objectives of U.S. government. Many of these objectives are inconsistent, because people want different things and elected representatives are reluctant to disappoint voters. As a result, the U.S. government has developed into a large and activist government. The factors associated with this development are discussed in this chapter. After reading and reviewing the materials in this chapter the student should be able to do each of the following:

1. Identify the key factors associated with the growth of government.

2. Describe the restraints on the growth of government.

3. Discuss the consequences of activist government.

4. Assess the influence of the political structure and of ideas on the process of serving some goals rather than others.

5. Explain how the political system has changed and evaluate proposals for reforming it.

Chapter Outline with Keyed-in Resources

I. Introduction
   A. Activities of American government have expanded greatly
   B. Until twentieth century
      1. Few people cared about national politics
      2. Governors and mayors were more visible than presidents

An excellent example illustrating the initial lack of regard in which national offices were held is John Jay's decision to step down as the country's first chief justice of the U.S. Supreme Court to become governor of New York. That would never happen today.

      3. Federal government was small and predictable
      4. Republicans favored
         a. High tariffs
         b. Tight money
         c. Punishment of South
      5. Democrats favored
         a. Lower tariffs

Democrats supported lower tariffs in order to aid farmers in selling their goods overseas. If the United States adopted high tariffs, other countries would retaliate with higher tariffs against American goods, and in 1850 about two-thirds of the labor force was employed in agriculture. Republicans, in contrast, favored higher tariffs to protect domestic industry since a high tariff increased the cost of imported goods and made them less competitive. This position accounts for the strong Republican base in New England where three-fourths of all workers in manufacturing nationwide were concentrated in 1850.

          b. Loose money
          c. Accommodation with South
    C. Today government reaches almost all activities
       1. No single public policy philosophy
       2. Many goals and interests
       3. Many contradictions
II. Competing interests
    A. Conflicting interests of the people
       1. Policies will seek to serve people's interests (ADDITIONAL LECTURE TOPIC A-1)
       2. Policies will be inconsistent
    B. A popular majority is a coalition of people who want different things from government
       1. Majorities form and re-form as policies are demanded
       2. Politicians win elections by promising to do things for various coalitions

The public does not place much trust in the promises of politicians. In a Gallup poll in 1989, only 16 percent of the public said that members of Congress had a "very high" degree of honesty—finishing even below lawyers, at 18 percent.

III. Restraints on growth of government (THEME A: THE GROWTH OF GOVERNMENT)
    A. For first 150 years government grew slowly

In 1913, total government spending amounted to $33 a person. By 1936, with New Deal programs well under way, the figure had risen sharply to $130 a person.

       1. Supreme Court defined government authority narrowly
       2. Popular opinion supported a limited governmental role
       3. Political system was designed to limit government
    B. System limiting government makes it difficult to abolish programs
IV. Consequences of activist government
    A. Need to assess costs and benefits of programs
    B. General political consequences of enlarged scope of activity
       1. Bureaucratization of all organizations
       2. Rise of competing policies
       3. Less control by the electorate through decline of parties and turnout
       4. Greater risk of government failure and decline in public confidence
V. The influence of structure
    A. Parliamentary model if adopted here would do the following:
       1. Executive would have fewer legislative restraints
       2. More bureaucratic centralization

Not all parliamentary systems possess a high level of bureaucratic centralization. For example, only 10 percent of public employees in Germany work for the national government. About a third work for local governments and a half for state governments. The degree of bureaucratic centralization also depends on the constitutional division of governmental power.

       3. Less citizen participation to challenge block policies
       4. Higher taxes and more secrecy
    B. U.S. model
       1. More local authority
       2. Greater citizen participation

VI. The influence of ideas (THEME B: THE IDEA OF "AMERICAN DECLINE")
  A. Preoccupation with rights
    1. Assumption that affected groups have a right to participate in policy formation
    2. Willingness to resort to courts
  B. Effects of rights on government functions
    1. Harder to make government decisions
    2. More "red tape"
  C. Elite opinion influences what rights given priority
    1. Favors freedom of expression over management of property
    2. Mass opinion less committed to freedom of expression
  D. Freedom versus equality an enduring tension
    1. Advantages of freedom are remote
    2. Advantages of equality are obvious

The power of ideas should not be underestimated. Ideas influence behavior. For example, American political culture supports a capitalist economic system. Only 36 percent of Americans support a governmental role in reducing income inequality, compared with 81 percent of the Italian public.

  E. Fragmentation of political system increases role of ideas
    1. Widespread enthusiasm for an idea can lead to rapid adoption of new programs
    2. Competing ideas make change difficult and today thousands of special interests
  F. Fundamental challenge: to restore confidence in the legitimacy of government itself
VII. Should the system be changed?
  A. System has changed: Old System versus New System
  B. Two critics of current system: federal government too weak or too strong
  C. Reducing the barriers to action
    1. Separation of powers precludes effective national leadership
    2. Increase in presidential authority needed to increase accountability

The public perceives a certain weakness in the presidency compared to the other branches. In a 1990 survey, 31 percent believed the Supreme Court was more powerful than the president, with only 21 percent taking the contrary position.

    3. President must be in charge of bureaucracy instead of Congress
    4. Proposals for reducing separation of powers
      a. Presidential appointment of members of Congress to cabinet
      b. Permit president to dissolve Congress
      c. Special election for a "failing" president
      d. "Team" president and congressional representatives in each district
      e. Single six-year term for president
      f. Increase term of House members from two years to four years
    5. Reforms would combine old and new systems
    6. Defenders of system respond to criticisms
      a. British parliamentary system has not worked better than U.S. system
      b. Congressional cabinet officers no guarantee of better legislative success

At present, the Constitution contains what is known as the "incompatibility clause" (Article I, Section 6), preventing members of Congress from serving in the executive branch. It reads: "No Senator or Representative shall, during the Time for which he was elected, be appointed to any civil office under the Authority of the United States, which shall be created, or the Emoluments whereof shall have been encreased during such time."

      c. Special elections are expensive and confusing for voters
      d. District "team" would be destabilizing
      e. Six-year term would reduce presidential accountability
      f. System's problems mainly the result of ineffective leaders
  D. Reducing the barriers
    1. Government does too much, not too little and has grown helter-skelter

2. No politician has incentive "to do less for anybody"
   3. Must avoid pushing "add button" repeatedly through either a balanced budget amendment or limit on taxes

The "adding button" mentality has led to the movement for a balanced budget amendment to the Constitution. To put the issue in perspective, how much would *each* American citizen have to pay to retire the existing federal deficit? According to CBS news, about $16,200 (calculated in February 1993, with the amount increasing daily).

   4. Big government hard to manage
   5. Allow president line-item veto
   6. Narrow authority of federal courts
   7. Opponents respond
      a. Government spends nonbudget money
      b. President could use line-item veto to spend more
      c. Curtailing courts is an attack on citizen rights
   E. Term limits
      1. Unclear if term limits would make system more or less democratic
      2. Proposal: House members six terms and senators two terms
      3. Possibility that courts might not uphold term limits as constitutional
      4. Effect uncertain, either create citizen-legislators or make dependent on staff and interest groups
      5. Unlikely for term limits to succeed since doubtful Congress would propose such an amendment
   F. Who is right?
      1. Two-hundred year old Constitution is not necessarily outdated
      2. Compare performance of U.S. government to other nations

Important Terms

line-item veto A proposal to enable the president to disapprove a particular part of a bill and approve its other provisions. Although most state governors possess this power, the president is required to accept or reject bills in their entirety.

New System The policy-making system that took form during the 1930s in the United States and has lasted to the current time. It is characterized by a large agenda, the end of debate over the legitimacy of government action, the diffusion of power in Congress, and the multiplication of interest groups.

Old System The policy-making system that existed in the United States from the founding of the nation to the 1930s. It has a small agenda, was dominated by centralized leadership, debated the legitimacy of the federal government to take action on new issues, and focused on domestic affairs.

term limits A proposal to limit members of the House to six terms and senators to two terms. The constitutionality of the proposal is unclear.

Theme A   The Growth of Government

Summary

The most striking change in American government in recent times has been the expansion in the scope of its activities. For most of the history of the Republic, government has been very limited. The prevailing interpretation of the Constitution limited the federal government, and popular opinion, so far as we can judge it, supported a restricted definition of federal authority. Finally, the separation of powers and other checks and balances made it difficult to enact policies. (Now, the same system makes it difficult to revise or eliminate old programs.)

The rise of activist government has had several consequences. First, as government gets bigger, its members must devote more time to managing existing programs and less time to debating new ideas. The result is an increasing bureaucratization of government and less likelihood of reducing the size of government. Despite the Reagan administration's efforts to shrink the federal role, big government remains a fixture in American political life. Second, it is probably true that the more government does, the more it will appear to be acting in inconsistent, uncoordinated, and cumbersome ways. For example, government has some policies (highway construction and mortgage insurance) that make it easy for people to move out of cities and other policies (grants for neighborhood development) that encourage people to stay. This situation arises not out of perversity or stupidity, but rather because government is responsive to different groups that want different things. Politicians get elected by promising things to groups, and promises tend to become programs. Third, an activist government is less under the control of electoral activity than a passive one. The people for whom one votes can do little to alter the ongoing programs of government; thus we should not be surprised that electoral turnout is down and that interest-group activity is up. Interest groups can have an effect on low-visibility programs beyond the reach of elected officials. Finally, the more government tries to do, the more it will be held responsible and the greater the risk of failure. Thus it is no surprise to find a steep decline in public confidence in government since the early 1960s.

Both the structure of government and the ideas held in a political system matter. If the United States had a centralized, parliamentary regime based on the European model, many policies would have been adopted more quickly. However, individuals and groups would find it harder to protect their interests by blocking policies that would harm them. In the realm of ideas, Americans are particularly prone to define relationships in terms of *rights*. Elaborate procedures protect individuals from the arbitrary exercise of power and make it more difficult to make governmental decisions or to manage large institutions. The question of what rights need to be protected is a matter on which opinions change. Increasingly, Americans value equality over liberty (as Tocqueville foresaw), and among elites, there is considerable support for equality of results as opposed to equality of opportunity. All of this is important because, as the political system has become more fragmented (with the decline of parties, proliferation of interest groups, and decentralization of Congress), it has come more under the sway of ideas.

The negative features ascribed to an activist government fail to explain why the policies adopted by the American political system almost mirror those of European parliamentary systems. The reason is that the hurdles imposed by separation of powers are relaxed during the times of national crisis. To be sure, public confidence tends to rise when the government presents a new political agenda to address the country's needs. In the midst of stagflation in 1978, 38 percent of Americans believed the federal government had too much power; this figure dropped to 28 percent by 1986 despite the antigovernment rhetoric of President Reagan. The country seemed to be moving again, and the people were willing to trust the government with power. An activist government is capable of producing change only when it remains active, not mired under its own weight.

Discussion Questions

1. What changes will an activist government cause in private institutions? Can you observe this in your own university? How many people on this campus are hired mainly to deal with the government?

2. If parliamentary systems are able to adopt policies more quickly, is the U.S. political structure less advanced than those of European countries? Does this feature at least partially explain why the United States is falling behind Japan in many areas?

3. If Americans prefer equality over liberty, why do they resist affirmative action programs? Why was the Equal Rights Amendment defeated? If liberty is not as important as once was the case, are the rights of free speech and free press in danger? Could this be the reason that rights like abortion are under attack?

4. Do ideas really have *autonomous* influence, or are some of the ideas that the text mentions merely symbols for the interests of groups? That is, do some groups have an advantage because Americans really believe in certain ideas (such as broad political participation)? Or are ideas propounded because certain groups (middle-class political activists) have an interest in them? How many changes in American politics in recent years can be explained by the changing power of various *groups* and how many by the power of ideas?

Additional Lecture Topic A-1

A Critique of the Past, Present, and Future Role of Government

Charles Bullock, James Anderson, and David W. Brady, *Public Policy in the 80s*. Monterey, CA: Brooks-Cole, 1983. A review of contemporary and future problems and possible policy solutions is this work's main thrust.

Roger A. Freeman, *The Wayward Welfare State*. Stanford, CA: Hoover Institution Press, 1983. A conservative's criticism of welfare trends and government intervention is delineated.

John K. Galbraith, *Economics and Public Purpose*. New York: New American Library, 1973. Though somewhat dated, this work remains a clear rationale for greater governmental intervention.

Burke Marshall, ed., *A Workable Government?* New York: Norton, 1987. Analyzes the Constitution and the political system from a "200 years perspective."

Dennis Palumbo, *Public Policy in America—Government in Action*. 2nd ed. Orlando, FL: Harcourt Brace Jovanovich, 1994. Covers a wide number of policy issues.

John E. Schwarz, *America's Hidden Success: A Reassessment of Public Policy from Kennedy to Reagan*. Rev. ed. New York: Norton, 1988. An effective analysis of programs created and implemented in the 1960s, 1970s, and 1980s. The author argues that government policies can be beneficial.

Abstract 1 for Theme A

"Copernican Politics" and the Future "Ends" of Government

Critics of American government note that its expansion does not necessarily mean a concomitant growth in the number of "intelligent" solutions to the problems of the present or the future. Indeed, bureaucratic proliferation retards innovation in policy and may very well obscure consideration of proper "policy questions." To Colorado Governor Richard D. Lamm, government leaders must ask "heretical questions" as a way of rethinking future political goals. Just as Copernicus revolutionized history by asking whether the earth revolved around the sun instead of accepting the orthodox belief that the sun revolved around the earth, so must public officials attack our now invalid but "once essential dogmas" involving the policy agenda.

In "Copernican Politics—It's Time to Ask Heretical Questions," originally published in *The Futurist* of October 1983 and reprinted in *American Government 85/86* (Guilford, CT: Dushkin Press, 1985, pp. 242–246), Governor Lamm asks the following "heretical questions."

1. *Is our political system equal to the problems of the twenty-first century?* In this question, Lamm asks whether anyone can really run the country, because each presidency of the past four has become "paralyzed." Politicians of both parties are captured by special interests, and public expectations (built up by excessive campaign and political rhetoric) are rarely satisfied. Does either political party have the answers to contemporary problems?

2. *Are we entering the world of the static economic pie?* American economic growth rates have declined appreciably, and the "good old days of 5 percent economic growth" are gone (p. 243). International competition from Japan and Germany has clearly hurt American industry. Thus "in 1965, American industrial companies, with sales of over $1 billion, represented 70 percent of all such companies in the world. By 1980, the American share had fallen to 40 percent" (p. 243). Similarly, the American share of global GNP had dropped from 30 percent to 20 percent between 1970 and 1980. If Americans are condemned to live in a no-growth or slow-growth economy for the foreseeable future, our political institutions will have to make decisions allocating resources more prudently and efficiently.

3. *Can society afford what medical technology can invent?* The astounding cost of medical treatment, including heart transplants and other organ-transplant techniques, is growing far faster than the inflation rate. How will these costs be contained, especially in view of the fact that "medical science can invent more technology than society can clearly pay for"? (p. 243)

4. *Does increased spending on health care bring increased health?* To Lamm, our spending on the health care system really supports a system of "illness care," a system that "plays a small role in our national health" (p. 244). It would be better to invest our money in "health promotion, education, and motivation," thereby increasing life expectancy by some eleven years (p. 244).

5. *Can we continue to be so generous to the elderly?* Lamm estimates that by the year 2000, 17 percent of the population will be over sixty-five (compared to 11 percent today). Thus pensions and the medical costs of the elderly will take a quantum leap in the future. The "question must change from 'Have we done enough?' to 'Have we done too much for the elderly?'" (p. 244).

6. *Are energy shortages a matter of inadequate supply—or excessive demand?* The propensity of America to overcome shortages through increases in production overlooks the central cause of the energy crisis: excessive demand. Energy production has increased, but only marginally, so "America's energy dependence has eased not because we have produced more but because we are consuming less." In short, energy frugality is a national habit that must be encouraged by elected officials at all levels of government (pp. 244–245).

7. *Can we protect our resource supplies or must we reduce our demands?* America is still vulnerable to an oil embargo. A total cutoff of Middle Eastern oil would, according to Lamm, cause a 10–25 percent drop in America's GNP (equivalent to the decline in the Great Depression). Not only is America vulnerable to an oil stoppage, but the nation's economy is increasingly dependent "upon a number of imported minerals vitally necessary for the production of strategic equipment such as oil refineries, power stations, and computers." This vulnerability can be reduced by "innovation, recycling, and reuse." In short, Lamm urges that we "dramatically restructure our society to use less" (p. 245).

8. *Can the "nation of immigrants" continue its traditional immigration policies?* Lamm asserts that America's unemployment and resource problems, among others, will force us to reexamine our current "demographic insanity to continue to accept twice as many immigrants as the rest of the world combined." The United States must recognize that it cannot be "the home of last resort to all the displaced people in the world." Lamm goes on to argue that our country "is no longer a frontier; our humanity can no longer be boundless." Adding millions of new immigrants would compound our existing "multiple economic problems" as well as "diminish our standard of living significantly" (pp. 245–246).

9. *Can democracy survive lowered expectations?* Our democracy must face the ultimate "Copernican question" of whether the American people can adjust to an age of restricted material advancement, assuming that geopolitical conditions turn against us. Would the social cohesion of the nation and the legitimacy of our governmental structure both disappear as a result? (p. 246).

10. *When will we face up to our hard choices?* Lamm stresses that "the future will not be an extension of the recent past." American leaders must plan for the long term while simultaneously avoiding counterproductive short-term solutions. Lamm summarizes his case in the following manner:

> We should adopt only those life-styles, industries, processes, and institutions that, when pursued over the long term, do not lead to disasters, but rather to a future that can be sustained by the resources of this planet.
> This path will be difficult and may be impossible ... especially in a society such as the United States that has no tradition of doing with less, no tradition of the English stiff upper lip. We drift along, vainly hoping we will not have to make hard choices, hoping that some Keynesian on the left or supply-sider on the right will rescue us. But it's not happening.
> We forget the Hegel aphorism: "Freedom is the recognition of necessity." We forget to ask the hard, heretical questions of our time (p. 246).

Questions for Discussion

1. What possible solutions or answers can be devised by political leaders vis-a-vis each of the ten questions posed by Lamm?
2. Can Americans adjust to an era of scarcity? Why or why not? How could government help or hinder that adjustment?

Answer Guidelines

Copy possible policy solutions on the blackboard so that the entire class can assess their utility and political feasibility. A classroom poll could be taken to ascertain attitudes toward the question of "adjusting to national scarcity."

Abstract 2 for Theme A

The Influence of Governmental Structure on Political Problem-Solving

While some political analysts may hunger for the United States to adopt a parliamentary system and a unitary governmental structure, the advantages of policy experimentation and innovation embedded in federalism were readily apparent in the Reagan era. In a *Wall Street Journal* article entitled "States Enlarge Roles as Congress Is Unable to Solve Problems" (June 28, 1988, pp. 1 and 16), staff reporter David Wessel reveals how pragmatic state governors were able to solve problems that Congress could not. Where Washington's problem-solving power was frustrated by ideological disputes, budget deficits, and a plethora of competing interest groups, governors were finding voters willing to pay higher taxes if new or better public services were provided. Wessel describes the following profiles in policy experimentation at the state level:

> Michigan earmarks 5 percent of its state pension funds for local venture-capital investments. At a time when Washington can't make tough choices posed by medical technology, Oregon explicitly refused to pay for organ transplants for a few poor children in order to free funds to provide basic care for many. Arkansas, in a program based on an Israeli model, gives low-income parents daily homework assignments to do with their preschool children to help them prepare for kindergarten. (p. 1)

Apparently, Americans feel more comfortable with state than federal activism. In addition, Americans feel that state governments waste less of their tax money than the federal government (14 percent of those surveyed picked the state level as being the most wasteful, but two-thirds chose the federal level).

Wessel points out that state creativity and vision were not always highly regarded. In 1957, President Eisenhower had dubbed the states as "powerless satellites of the national government," and in 1962 columnist James Reston considered the states overwhelmed with insoluble problems. Ironically, it was the Reagan administration's focus on political decentralization and its cuts in aid that forced the states to confront their problems. Political talent gravitated to the states, state constitutions were changed to allow governors longer terms in office, and ensuing campaigns by those executives convinced voters to pay more for education, transportation, health care, and the environment. Voters, apparently trusting state officials, were mobilized perhaps most effectively in the state of Arkansas under the aegis of Governor Clinton. Despite a state per-capita income ranking forty-seventh in the nation, an archaic constitution, and a generally depressed economy, Governor Clinton convinced the public to improve the state's educational system through a 1 percent sales tax increase, thus subsidizing higher teacher's salaries, better student testing, and teacher competency tests as well. The Arkansas effort—from conception to legislative output—took nine months, a minuscule time when compared with the arduous labors of congressional legislation. In short, state governments were becoming the political laboratories of the 1980s and of the 1990s as well.

Questions for Discussion (Open-ended replies are desirable.)

1. Can students in the class think of any innovative or experimental public policies implemented recently by their respective states? Place examples on the board.

2. Carry out a class survey. Do students seem to regard the states as politically more effective than the federal government? Why or why not?

Abstract 3 for Theme A

The Costs of Activism

While Americans have often feared the encroachment of the federal government on privacy, civil liberties, and freedom in general, they have also not been averse to receiving "benefits" from that same federal government. The adage that Americans are "theoretical conservatives, operational liberals" has some truth to it. The Reagan administration was elected on the theme that government was the "villain," but by the late 1980s, the plethora of national problems—the deficit, the homeless, drug abuse, educational standards, AIDS, health care, the plight of the elderly, among others—had seemingly shifted the perception of the electorate to the pole of federal activism once more.

Perhaps no candidate sensed the potential of this shift more than the Reverend Jesse Jackson during the 1988 presidential primaries. The Jackson agenda for social change was indeed costly, but it had definite appeal. In the first of two *Wall Street Journal* articles of April 8, 1988 (p. 42), staff reporter Joe Davidson described Jackson's philosophical approach to government:

> Without apology, he tells crowds he wants an activist role for the federal government—and increased taxes to pay for it.... Mr Jackson is forthright in prompting a style of governance that would take a much more active interest in protecting and providing for citizens than the Reagan Administration thinks is correct. His code of conduct for business, for example, would require companies that move from a community to share the costs of extended health benefits, retraining and placement for laid-off workers....
>
> At a United Auto Workers rally in Kenosha, Wis., Mr. Jackson drew cheers when he said the federal government could certainly help displaced auto workers since it had aided Chrysler Corp. In rural and urban communities alike, he gets enthusiastic reaction when he says, "If we can save Chrysler, Penn Central Railroad and Continental Bank, we can save the family farm."

Jackson went on to call for raising the minimum wage, comparable worth in the job market, and cutting Defense Department budget increases so that some $60 billion could be saved for social programs. In short, Jackson called for an expansion of the nation's government to reverse the Reagan formula of taking from the have-nots and giving it to the haves.

In the second article, Alan Murray delineated the complex finances of the Jackson programs. The Jackson platform called for a

> long list of new government programs, including national health insurance, a doubling of the education budget, and a variety of other economic, social, environmental, and energy programs.... The total cost could easily run to $100 billion or more.
>
> And that isn't all. The Rev. Jackson's campaign literature also suggests he has plans for a vast expansion of government regulation of the economy. He would not only roll back the "deregulation" trend that began under President Jimmy Carter but also impose an array of new regulations on corporations. Among other things, he says he would "elaborate a code of conduct for American business."

Murray cites some poll evidence to show that while Americans had moved back to a greater acceptance of federal activism, the "halcyon days of the New Deal" had not been resurrected. Conversely, Jackson supporters argued that there were urgent national needs requiring federal action, and that the public would back these policies, especially when considered on an individual basis.

How was Jackson going to fund all of these new programs? As itemized by Murray: (a) $20 billion would be raised by increasing the personal income tax rate to 38.5 percent on top incomes; (b) another $20 billion would come from raising the corporate tax rate; (c) defense cuts would equal $60 billion (as mentioned previously); (d) $10 billion would be raised through a tax to discourage mergers and speculation; (e) additional closings of tax loopholes would net another $10 billion. The grand total available for deficit reduction and new programs would thus be $120 billion.

Controversy remained over whether the above newly generated revenues would cover all of Jackson's agenda. His proposals included universal health care, doubling the nation's education budget, the formation of a domestic World Bank (to revitalize neighborhoods and low-income housing), a comprehensive national child care policy, adult education and literacy, family counseling, school dropout prevention, increased food stamps and nutritional education, the rebuilding and insulating of homes to make them energy efficient, AIDS treatment, a "Marshall Plan" development plan for the Third World, and the elimination of toxic waste dumps. Despite Jackson's inability to secure the presidential nomination in 1988, some of his policy ideas struck a chord of tentative approval in key segments of the American electorate. Depending on the composition and philosophical tone of the new administration, the Jackson agenda could be considered further, but probably in less grandiose form.

Questions for Discussion

1. Which element of the Jackson program of "social activism" appeals most to you and why? Which component makes the least sense to you and why?

2. Did any of Jackson's proposals receive major attention during the presidential campaign between the Democratic and Republican nominees? If so, which ones? If not, why not?

Theme B   The Idea of "American Decline"

Summary

The basic question of where the American political system is heading in the future has been recently addressed by a number of like-minded historians, political scientists, and economists. Their "school of thought" has a central theme—that the United States is facing a period of relative decline both domestically and internationally. Peter Schmeisser summarizes this school's intellectual impact in a *New York Times Magazine* article entitled "Taking Stock—Is America in Decline?" (April 17, 1988, pp. 24ff.). Schmeisser delineates the thinking of three noted "philosophers of decline"—Paul Kennedy (*The Rise and Fall of the Great*

Powers), David P. Calleo (*Beyond American Hegemony*), and Walter Russell Mead (*Mortal Splendor*)—in the following description:

> The United States, like other great powers before it, rose to a position of global dominance largely through economic and technological achievements. Reaching its zenith just after World War II, the United States devoted increasingly large proportions of wealth to the military in an effort to maintain (and even raise) the post-1945 high-water mark of hegemony. In the four decades since the war, say the philosophers of decline, America has failed to strike the proper balance between these overseas commitments and the demands of a maturing domestic economy. Left uncorrected, this imbalance, which Kennedy terms "imperial overstretch," will continue to erode the economic foundations that are the true base of our global power. (p. 24)

America's international decline has been hastened by rising economic centers of competition (notably the EEC and Japan). Lack of private savings, the shift from manufacturing to service industries, emphasis on short-term paper profits at the expense of investment in infrastructures, and a deteriorating educational system "all contributed to the shrinkage of the economic base *relative* to those of other nations. The Japanese and German boats were rising faster; America's boat, while clearly not sinking, rose more slowly" (p. 66).

Domestic decline has been a result of poor leadership, the power of entrenched interest groups to distort the national economic interest, the excesses of federal spending, and the "fiscal myopia of the Reagan years" (p. 66). Both Kennedy and Mead are highly critical of the budget and trade deficits, trillion-dollar defense budgets and decreasing rates of private investments.

Schmeisser observes that there are political leaders who have responded positively to the "decline" thesis by calling on government to help workers and management adjust to shifts in the post-World War II global economy. However, there are also dissenters, who argue that the Reagan years strengthened America at home and abroad. Other critics of the thesis accept the ideas of relative decline and overstretch, but dispute the aura of inevitability that their proponents seem to suggest. However, Paul Kennedy is skeptical of the will of the nation's leaders to arrest historical trends:

> Kennedy steers clear of giving odds on America's chances of averting decline.... But he does see vulnerabilities that will be difficult—if not impossible—to correct. As the current budget deadlock illustrates, ours is a system riddled with interest groups and resistance to change. Kennedy says he cannot imagine any "comprehensive proposal"—for increasing taxes, diverting capital toward savings and making massive investments in education—surviving long on Capitol Hill. He questions whether *any* of the Presidential aspirants are capable of orchestrating the necessary changes. Observes Kennedy, "anybody advocating American *perestroika* is going to have a hell of a fight on his hands" (p. 96).

Data and Perspectives for Analysis

A. A Rejoinder to the Decline Hypothesis

Samuel Huntington ("The U.S.—Decline or Renewal?" *Foreign Affairs*, Winter 1988/89, pp. 76–96) has attempted to rebut allegations that the United States is in a state of decline. According to Huntington, three core propositions are offered by proponents of the decline hypothesis:

> First, the United States is declining economically compared to other market economy countries, most notably Japan but also Europe and the newly industrializing countries.... Second, economic power is the central element of a nation's strength, and hence a decline in economic power eventually affects other dimensions of national power. Third, the relative economic decline of the United States is caused primarily by its spending too much for military purposes, which in turn is the result ... of "imperial overstretch," of attempting to maintain commitments abroad that the country can no longer afford. (pp. 76–77)

Huntington believes these allegations are exaggerated. He presents the following arguments as refutation:

1. "Overall, the United States accounts for 22 to 25 percent of the major forms of global economic activity and has done so fairly consistently for twenty years or more" (p. 82).

2. "Between 1965 and 1980 the United States ranked fifteenth out of 19 industrialized market economies in terms of economic growth; between 1980 and 1986 the United States ranked third out of 19" (p. 82).

3. "The burden of empire usually becomes onerous when [defense spending] amounts to ten percent or more of the society's product. Defense, however, takes only six to seven percent of American GNP" (p. 86).

4. "In contrast to other countries, the United States ranks extraordinarily high in almost all the major sources of national power: population size and education, natural resources, economic development, social cohesion, political stability, military strength, ideological appeal, diplomatic alliances, technological achievement. . . . At present, no country can mount a multidimensional challenge to the United States" (p. 91).

5. "Given the openness of its politics and the competitiveness of its economy, the United States is unlikely to decline so long as its public is periodically convinced that it is about to decline" (p. 96).

B. Reforming Government

The text introduces several proposed reforms of the American government. One proposal that has attracted consistent public support is extending the president's tenure to a single, six-year term.

James W. Davis has outlined the arguments both for and against the six-year nonrenewable term. Supporters have four arguments: (1) the president could devote all his attention to the job rather than waste time seeking reelection, (2) four years is too short for a president to accomplish his goals, (3) the president would be liberated from the pressures of special-interest groups, and (4) the president would not be tempted to make decisions on the basis of political expediency.

Opponents of the proposal have several replies: (1) a president would be a lame duck upon election, (2) reelection keeps the office of president democratic by forcing accountability, (3) a president limited to six years will not be able to accomplish much more with the additional two years, and (4) the election process will become more bitter.

The following table reveals that popular support for the six-year term concept has not changed much over time.

Six-Year Presidential Term

	Yes, Favor	No, Oppose	No Opinion
1983 (Feb.)	31%	61%	8%
1981 (Jan.)[a]	30	63	7
1979	30	62	8
1973	28	64	8
1971	20	73	7
1969	18	75	7
1945[b]	25	68	7
1943[c]	29	59	12
1938	21	67	12
1936	26	74	—*

*"Don't know" figures, which were allocated between favor and oppose, are not available.
Question variations:
[a]"Would you favor changing the term of the president of the United States to one six-year term with no reelection?"
[b]"Would you favor changing the term of office of the president of the United States in the future to one six-year term with no reelection?"
[c]"Would you favor changing the term of office of the president hereafter to one six-year term with no reelection?"
Source: Gallup Report No. 209, February 1983, 12.
Source: James W. Davis, *The American Presidency: A New Perspective*. New York: Harper & Row, 1987, pp. 434–438.

PART SIX

State and Local Government

25

State and Local Government

Overview and Objectives

The purpose of this chapter is to introduce the student to some of the enormous variety of governmental arrangements, political philosophies, and policy preferences that are to be found within the United States at the level of state and local politics. After reading and reviewing the material in this chapter the student should be able to do each of the following:

1. Explain the differences between the "Jacksonian" and the "progressive" approaches to government, and show how these manifest themselves in state and local politics.

2. State why the Tenth Amendment to the Constitution has come to mean very little.

3. Differentiate between the standing of the states and of lower levels of government in the U.S. Constitution.

4. Compare and contrast state governors, legislatures, and political parties with their opposite numbers in the federal government.

5. Show how reformed and unreformed city governments differ from one another, and explain the resulting differences in policy outcomes.

6. Differentiate among the different structures used for smaller local governments.

7. Discuss the severe tax problems that states and cities face today, and analyze the historical and political sources of those problems.

8. Explain how state and local politics become federal politics, using crime control as an example.

Chapter Outline with Keyed-in Resources

I. Introduction
   A. Variations within U.S. state and local governments
      1. Few versus many directly elected officials
      2. Slight versus great power of legislative leaders
      3. Division versus fusion of powers
      4. Appointed versus elected officials
      5. Provision for direct votes on public allowed versus no such provision

Fourteen states go to the extreme of requiring voters to consider on a regular basis whether a new constitution should be drafted. The issue is automatically brought to the voters every twenty years in eight states, every ten years in four states, every sixteen years in one state, and every nine years in one state.

      6. Brief versus extensive constitutions
II. State constitutions and political philosophy (THEME A: THE POLITICAL EVOLUTION OF STATE GOVERNMENTS)
   A. Antifederalist opposition to government prevails in many state and local governments
      1. Antifederalist principles: numerous elected officials, short terms, weak executive
      2. Deep suspicion of executive power during American Revolution produced revised state constitutions
         a. Authority in legislature
         b. Legislature picked governor
         c. Few states allowed the veto
         d. Vote restricted to property owners
   B. The Jacksonian era
      1. Mood of newly enfranchised voters was antigovernment
      2. Executive power increased only to offset legislative power
      3. Result: the radical decentralization of political authority
      4. State and local governments, unlike national, had much work to do
      5. Political parties made decentralized government function
   C. The progressive response
      1. Problem with decentralized, party government: corruption and inefficiency
      2. Progressives proposed a series of responses
         a. Nonpartisan elections
         b. Fewer state officials
         c. Appointed, professional city managers
         d. Smaller legislatures, councils

Currently, state senates range in size from a high of sixty-seven members in Minnesota to a low of twenty members in both Alaska and Nevada.

         e. Direct popular vote on public issues
         f. Elimination of patronage

The first organization created to eliminate patronage was the Civil Service Reform Association in New York in 1880. By 1900, eighty-five civil service commissions were operating in cities with authority for hiring public employees. Thus the movement quickly succeeded.

3. Progressives won in some states in early 1900s
4. Jacksonian model versus progressive model
5. Progressive sentiment on rise again in early 1960s, early 1970s
6. This conflict has given rise to an amazing variety of governmental forms
7. Progressives more successful at state level
   a. Need for greater efficiency and lower costs
   b. City issues require greater participation and more representation of ethnic and racial groups
III. The legal basis of state and local government (THEME B: THE LEGAL CONTEXT OF STATE AND LOCAL GOVERNMENT)
   A. The constitutional framework of state government
      1. Tenth Amendment
         a. Appeared to reaffirm special place of states
         b. But Supreme Court has rendered it virtually meaningless
         c. Hence very few *exclusive* state powers
      2. But basic police powers belong mostly to states

The police powers allow states to regulate public morals. Hence, Nevada is the only state to permit prostitution. Under state law, prostitution is permissible in any city or county with a population under 250,000 if the community desires to legalize the practice. Thirty-six houses of prostitution are currently licensed with the state.

   B. The constitutional framework of state government
      1. State constitutions similar to federal in setting out governmental frameworks
      2. But unlike it in specifying far more details
      3. Detail is due to citizen mistrust of state government and ease of amending

Nineteen states have constitutions that have been amended over a hundred times. In addition, 230 state constitutional conventions have been held in American history—but only one national constitutional convention.

      4. Specific measures indicating mistrust
         a. Initiative: put legislative items on ballot

Oregon was the first state to adopt the initiative in 1902.

         b. Referendum: let voters reject a measure adopted by legislature
         c. Recall: remove selected official from office
      5. These measures would have been unthinkable to the Founders
   C. The constitutional basis of local government
      1. Local governments exist only at the pleasure of the states
      2. Two types of city charter
         a. Special act: applies to a named city
         b. General act: to all cities within a category
      3. Dillon's rule: interpret charters restrictively
      4. City officials usually favor home rule charter in which city has any power not specifically prohibited
      5. But many city interests are more comfortable without it
      6. Types of local governments other than cities
         a. Counties
         b. Towns, townships are subdivision of county, mostly in East and Midwest
         c. Special districts perform government function
IV. The structure of state government (THEME C: STATE AND LOCAL GOVERNMENT STRUCTURES) (ADDITIONAL LECTURE TOPIC C-1)
   A. Governors
      1. Key difference: progressive versus Jacksonian philosophy
      2. But there is more complexity and variety too
      3. Governorships range from very strong to very weak, with strong in populous, urban states
      4. Typical governorship

        a. Four-year term; can serve two terms

Forty-six states now allot their governors a four-year term, whereas in 1960 only nineteen states did. The trend is clearly toward longer terms.

        b. Not run as team with lieutenant governor
        c. Extensive powers in legislation, including line-item veto
        d. Great variety in powers of appointment
        e. Variety arises from progressive versus Jacksonian orientation of state
    5. More dynamic individuals have recently become governors

Many governors enter office with no prior political experience. In one study, 10.2 percent of state governors had never previously held political office.

    6. Democrats control most governorships
        a. State elections less influenced by overall economy
        b. They reflect traditional party allegiances
        c. They are no longer held on presidential election dates
  B. State legislatures (ADDITIONAL LECTURE TOPIC C-2)
    1. Elections and electoral districts
        a. Many legislators elected from multimember districts (about one-third)

According to Thomas Dye, one-third of the members of lower houses in state legislatures and one-sixth of state senates are elected from multimember districts.

        b. This gives the dominant party a big advantage
        c. Power of political parties in elections varies greatly
    2. The determinants of legislative elections
        a. In the South, Democrats dominate due to party loyalty
        b. Elsewhere, same forces at work as in national elections
        c. National economy influences state legislative elections
        d. Once elected, incumbent is safe if choosing to run again; Democrats dominate
    3. Apportionment
        a. *Reynolds* v. *Sims* (1964): one person, one vote
        b. Dramatic changes since then increasing racial and urban interests
    4. Professional versus amateur legislators

The background characteristics of state legislators vary greatly. In New York, Texas, and Virginia, 40 percent of legislators are lawyers, whereas only 2 percent are lawyers in Delaware and New Hampshire. Which states are more corrupt?

        a. Great interstate variety in size of districts
        b. Professionalized legislature: meets most of year, well paid, main job, sizable staff
        c. Republicans more likely to prefer amateur legislature
    5. Party organization
        a. Party leaders in legislatures can be quite powerful compared to Congress
        b. But there is much variation across states
        c. Bases of power include appointments and patronage
        d. Urbanized, industrialized states tend to have more party-line votes
    6. Committees
        a. Generally less than in Congress
        b. Higher turnover, less seniority
  C. State courts
    1. Trial courts
        a. Minor offenses: municipal courts, justices of peace, etc.
        b. Broader jurisdiction: superior, county, common pleas courts, etc.
    2. Appeals courts
        a. State equivalent of U.S. Supreme Court
        b. Usually called state supreme court

		c. Power to declare state laws unconstitutional
		d. Can also declare federal laws unconstitutional
			(1) Usually reviewed by U.S. Supreme Court
	3. Choosing the judges
		a. Partisan election

The tenure of judges is relatively safe in reelection contests. In a study over a twenty-year period, judges on major trial courts in Ohio were opposed only 27 percent of the time, 26 percent of the time in Michigan, and 7 percent of the time in California.

		b. Nonpartisan election
		c. Appointment by governor
		d. Appointment by legislature
		e. Missouri Plan (appointment followed by retention/nonretention election)

Judges appointed under the Missouri Plan are almost assured of election when running on their own in the state of Missouri itself. From 1940 to 1970, only one judge was defeated in 179 elections. None has been defeated since that time.

		f. Disagreement over whether particular process of selection produces different results
	D. Political culture
		1. Every state has its own distinctive style
V. The structure of local government (ADDITIONAL LECTURE TOPIC C-3)
	A. Reformed versus unreformed city structures

In a study by Robert Lineberry and Edmund Fowler, reformed cities both taxed less and spent less than unreformed cities.

	1. Reformed ones follow progressive ideas; unreformed ones, Jacksonian qualities
	2. Reformed cities more likely in newer areas of country
	3. Many favor reformed/unreformed mixture for larger cities: strong mayor and district elections
	4. Racial consequences of elections further complicate these differences
	B. Mayor-council plan: elected mayor and council
		1. Weak mayor system: shares power with city council
		2. Strong mayor system: directly elected
	C. Council-manager plan: elected council, hired manager, middle-sized cities
	D. Commission plan: elected commissioners with separate responsibilities
	E. Metropolitan government plan: to govern large cities better
		1. Annexation: add surrounding suburbs to city
		2. Consolidation: of city and county governments
		3. Contracted services: from city to counties for services
		4. Metropolitan government: govern entire area, with some local autonomy
		5. Special districts: to manage specific services
		6. Councils of governments: voluntary cooperation
VI. Politics and policies (THEME D: POLITICS AND POLICIES)

U.S. mayors surveyed in 1978 listed their worst problems as refuse and solid waste.

	A. Policy-making in states differs from federal government
		1. States find it harder to live within their means
			a. Balanced budget required in thirty states
			b. More difficult to borrow money
		2. Cities and states compete to attract business, residents, and tourists
			a. Good business climate requires low taxes, simple regulations, and cost control
			b. Federal government does not worry much about maintaining a good business climate
	B. States with Jacksonian government find it easier to maintain a good business climate

        1. Weak governments have harder time raising taxes and imposing regulations
        2. More common in South with limited government tradition
        3. Progressive states emphasize redistributing income and regulating business
        4. Progressive tendency in reformed cities: fluoridation and professional police
    C. Politics and representation
        1. Progressive states and reformed cities differ in how people are represented
        2. At-large, nonpartisan elections hinder minorities in winning office
        3. But unreformed cities make it harder for minorities to get favorable policies even though they are more likely to come to power in them
        4. Party machines no longer of much value to minorities
VII. Taxes and tax revolts
    A. Taxing and spending dominate state and city politics because:
        1. Services provided directly to citizens
        2. Taxes more visible than federal income tax
        3. Taxes do not often reflect how much people earn
    B. City and state politicians face demand for more services and lower taxes
        1. Compromise sought but sometimes voters' anger at tax bill leads to "tax revolt"
        2. Revolt more likely where property taxes rise higher than income
        3. Proposition 13 an example
    C. States have responded by economizing, cutting services
        1. Or raised new revenues through lotteries
    D. State laws complicate tax issues
        1. Unlawful for rich communities to spend much more money on education than poor communities
            a. Paid for by property taxes
            b. Poor communities have less property tax revenue
        2. Alternative is statewide taxes
            a. But states face budget deficits
VIII. The States in American politics and federal politics in the states
    A. Distinctive features of American political system
        1. Decisions of state and local government important
        2. Diversity in the way decisions are made
        3. Struggle between state and federal governments
    B. The case of crime control
        1. Crime not on federal agenda before late 1960s
            a. National government believed not to have constitutional power in crime control
            b. Assumption local matters handled locally
        2. Expansion of federal role
            a. Power to regulate interstate commerce broadly interpreted
            b. Growing crime rate
        3. Crime on national agenda, e.g., Brady Bill

According to the Federal Bureau of Investigation, handguns were used in 55.6 percent of the murders committed in 1992. The accuracy of handguns remains suspect, with the victim missed in four out of five nonfatal handgun crimes between 1987 and 1992.

        4. Problems with enlarged federal role
            a. Money and people to fight crime exist at the local level
            b. No one knows how to cut crime rate
        5. Reasons effective crime control impossible to achieve
            a. Moral values cannot be created by law
            b. Lack of jobs in impoverished areas
            c. Success of drug dealers an incentive
            d. Gangs provide safety and income
    C. The changing face of crime-control policy
        1. Federal government has tried three strategies
            a. Provide money and assistance to local law enforcement

b. Make state crimes into federal crimes
   c. Regulate activities contributing to crime
2. In 1960s and 1970s emphasized money and assistance strategy (LEAA, NIJ, BJS) but crime went up
3. Reagan and Bush shifted to other two strategies
4. States now want more federal involvement in enforcing laws, unlike previously
5. But law enforcement remains local matter

Important Terms

*amateur legislature A term used to describe a state legislature that does not meet most of the year, whose members are not well paid and who do not regard being a legislator as their main job, and lacks a sizable staff.

*annexation A method of attempting to govern a metropolitan area as a whole by having the central city acquire the surrounding suburbs. This system works best when suburban and central-city residents are about the same in race, social class, and political interest.

*city-county consolidation A method of attempting to govern a metropolitan area as a whole by merging city and county government into one.

commission plan A form of city government in which power is in the hands of an elected commission rather than a single head of the executive branch. Each commissioner takes responsibility for some part of city administration. This plan is not popular because it makes management more complex and leadership divided.

*council-manager plan A form of city government in which the people vote for city council members, who then appoint a professional city manager to take charge of most or all of the city's administration. Most elections are nonpartisan and at large and the civil service is strong. This form of government is most common in midsize cities.

councils of governments A conference of mayors and city managers in a metropolitan area which aims to work out agreements to deal with problems on a voluntary basis.

county The largest territorial governmental unit between a state and a city or town. Every state but two has such a form of government, with most counties administered by an elected board of county supervisors or commissioners.

*Dillon's rule A legal principle holding that municipal charters must be interpreted narrowly. A city can exercise only those powers specifically given to it or powers either necessarily implied by these stated powers or essential to the accomplishment of governmental tasks. Any doubts about what the city can do under its charter are to be resolved against the city.

*general-act charter A charter issued by a state that applies to a number of cities that fall within a certain classification, usually based on population.

governor The elected chief executive of a state government. The typical governor is elected for a four-year term (forty-six states) and is limited to two terms of office (twenty-four states). Most have the authority to prepare the state budget, veto legislation, take command of the state's National Guard, and grant pardons or clemency to persons convicted of crimes.

*home-rule charter A municipal charter that does not observe Dillon's rule and allows a city government to do anything not prohibited by the charter or by state law. This form of charter is now in effect in many large cities.

*initiative A method for voters to place legislative measures, even constitutional amendments, directly on the ballot by getting enough signatures on a petition. Twenty-one state constitutions allow this method of legislation.

*Jacksonian model The view that most officials in state and local governments should be elected to ensure their accountability to voters, that average citizens should retain authority over experts, and that specific neighborhoods should be represented on city councils. The model has been more successfully implemented at the local level than at the state.

malapportionment The drawing of district lines to give an advantage in representation in the state legislature to some parts of a state, usually rural ones, at the expense of other parts, usually urban and suburban ones. The U.S. Supreme Court ended this practice in 1964.

*mayor-council plan The most common form of city government in the United States in which authority is vested in an elected mayor and council. The system varies in the degree to which a mayor has power over the administration of a city.

*metropolitan government plan A form of governing large metropolitan areas to deal with problems that are not restricted within city boundaries. One method of metropolitan government is annexation of surrounding suburbs by the central city. A second method is consolidation of city and county governments into one. A third is creation of a metropolitan government for the entire area, but leaving autonomy to local governments. The fourth and most common method is to create special districts to manage specific services.

Missouri Plan A system of selecting judges which is used in sixteen states. Governors appoint judges from lists of candidates produced by screening committees of citizens and lawyers. When judges complete their first term of office, their names are placed on the ballot without opposition. If approved by a majority of voters, they remain in office.

*municipal corporation The legal classification of a city, meaning that city has been chartered by the state to exercise certain defined powers and provide certain specific services. The charter can either apply to a certain named city (specific-act charter) or to a number of cities that fall within a certain classification (general-act charter).

*patronage The use of money, jobs, and contracts by party leaders to control the behavior of officeholders.

*police power A generally recognized state power to promote public health, safety, and morals by laws and regulations.

*professional legislature A term used to describe a state legislature that tends to meet during most of the year, whose members are well paid, and possess a sizable staff, and who regard being a legislator as their main job.

*progressive model The view that few officials in state and local governments should be elected, that power should be concentrated more in executive than in legislative hands, that governmental actions should be based on technical expertise, and that city council members should be elected from the city at large rather than from small districts. The model has been more successfully implemented at the state level than at the local.

*Progressive movement A movement by upper middle-class citizens beginning after the Civil War to limit the power of political parties and machine rule. The goal was to purify politics and make government more efficient.

Proposition 13 A measure adopted by the voters of California in 1978 as part of a tax revolt. Property taxes were limited to 1 percent of the market value of the land or house. Property assessments could not go up by more than 2 percent a year, and new taxes would require a two-thirds vote of the legislature. Passage of the measure touched off tax revolts in other states.

*recall A procedure that enables voters to remove an elected official from office. If enough signatures are gathered on a petition, the official must go before the voters, who can vote to leave the person in office, remove the person from office, or remove the person and replace him or her with someone else. Fifteen states permit this procedure.

*referendum A procedure that enables voters to reject a measure adopted by the state legislature. Thirty-seven states allow for this procedure, sometimes with the state constitution specifying that certain kinds of legislation must be subject to such a vote.

*reformed city A form of city government structured on the progressive model. Elections are nonpartisan; the city council is elected at large; executive powers are in the hands of an appointed city manager; and the civil service is strong.

*representative town meeting A modification of the town meeting system as towns grew into cities. It reduced the number of persons who attended the meeting to one or two hundred by having voters elect town meeting representatives.

Reynolds v. Sims A decision by the U.S. Supreme Court in 1964 which required the populations of districts represented in the houses of state legislatures to be substantially equal. The rule to be followed is "one person, one vote."

*special-act charter A charter issued by a state that applies to a certain named city and lists what that city can and cannot do.

special district A form of local government with specific responsibility for a single function, like handling sewage treatment. Over 28,000 such districts exist in the nation, and they are continually increasing in number.

*strong-mayor system A type of mayor council system in which a mayor is directly elected and has substantial authority over the administrative branch of government and important budgetary powers.

*tax revolt A citizen-initiated movement to limit or reduce taxes, with Proposition 13 in California in 1978 the most prominent example.

Tenth Amendment The provision in the Bill of Rights which gives all powers not constitutionally delegated to the national government to the states or the people, unless the power is specifically prohibited. The amendment no longer means much since the Supreme Court has refused to restrict the exercise of federal powers just because such powers intrude on powers reserved to the states.

*town meeting An annual gathering of all citizens eligible to vote who pass on proposals and choose officials to handle matters between these meetings.

township A division of a county government commonly found in eastern and midwestern states. Most have no separate government.

*unreformed city A form of city government structured on the Jacksonian model. Elections are partisan; city councils are elected from districts; executive power is in the hands of a mayor; and the civil service is weak.

*weak-mayor system A type of mayor-council system in which a mayor does not have much power over the administration of the system and does not have much influence in the city council. Such mayors are often chosen by the city council from among its members.

Theme A The Political Evolution of State Governments

Summary

State constitutions in the post-Revolutionary War era contained provisions for a relatively weak governor but a strong state legislature, which in many cases appointed the governor. The Jacksonian era decentralized political authority, strengthening the governor's office only to the extent of checking overzealous state legislators. Consequently, instead of a federal system of checks and balances, state and local liberties were to be preserved by the proliferation of large numbers of legally independent elected officials. Because of the many problems confronting state and local governments, political parties were formed as a means of increasing governmental problem-solving. Unfortunately, the benefits of party government were linked to partisan corruption as well.

The politicians of the Progressive era (post-Civil War to the early twentieth century), desirous of "purifying politics" and increasing governmental efficiency, proposed a number of reforms: nonpartisan elections; increased gubernatorial power; "professional" city managers; the diminution of "connections" between state legislators and local interests; the initiative-referendum-recall procedures; and the abolition of patronage in favor of "merit" hiring. The modern *progressive model* of government involves relatively few elected officials, a strong governor, a reliance on experts, and "at-large" elected city council members. Conversely, the *Jacksonian model* prefers numerous publicly accountable elected officials, prime authority for the average citizen, the representation of specific neighborhoods on city councils, and frequent intervention by legislators on behalf of the citizen. The modern progressive school has had most success at the state level, whereas the Jacksonian conceptual framework, better adapted to providing representation for minorities, has achieved greater effectiveness in local government.

Discussion Questions

1. Why have progressives had greater acceptance of their reforms at the state rather than the local level?

2. Assess the political pros and cons of the Jacksonian model of government vis-a-vis the progressive model, especially in terms of efficiency, representation, and overall effectiveness.

Theme B	The Legal Context of State and Local Government

Summary

The Tenth Amendment, which "reserves" powers to the states, has had limited contemporary significance since the Supreme Court generally refused to restrict the exercise of federal powers. However, the states do possess powers which are not prohibited by the Constitution. The states' *police powers*, that is, those powers which "promote health, safety, and morals," are especially significant.

State powers are managed through the individual state's constitution, which can usually be amended easily and which typically entails a plethora of specifics on all sorts of activities. The array of details can be traced to the nineteenth-century distrust of state government. Yet, some twenty-one state constitutions do provide for direct citizen political participation through the *initiative*, and a significant number of other states allow the *referendum* and the *recall*.

While the existence of the states is guaranteed by the U.S. Constitution, local forms of government do not enjoy similar legal assurances—they exist at the behest of the states. The bulk of American citizens live in cities, which are, in the legal sense, *municipal corporations* chartered by the state via a *special-act* or *general-act* charter. *Dillon's rule* provides that a charter's application be interpreted very narrowly. Consequently, city officials usually prefer a *home-rule charter*, which permits a broad, virtually unrestricted use of local political powers. Finally, other local government forms include *counties, towns or townships*, and *special districts*.

Discussion Questions

1. How does "home rule" obviate "Dillon's rule"?

2. Why are cities considered "municipal corporations"?

3. Define the various forms of local government in America.

Abstract for Theme B

David C. Saffell (*State and Local Government: Politics and Public Policy*. 5th ed. New York: McGraw-Hill, 1993, p. 29) outlines the four methods of amending state constitutions. The first is *legislative proposal* in which "a two-thirds or three-fifths vote of the legislature is required as the first step in approving an amendment. . . . Following legislative approval, the amendment is typically placed on the ballot, where a majority vote is needed for ratification." This method is available in all states and is responsible for the initiation of about 90 percent of all proposed amendments, with 75 percent approved by the voters.

The second method of changing a state constitution is by *constitutional initiative.* "It allows proponents of reform to have suggestions for limited change placed on the ballot. . . . Proponents must first get signatures on an initiative proposal. . . . As a final step, there is a referendum vote, in which most states require a majority vote on the amendment to be approved." Only seventeen states permit this option. Proposition 13, the controversial tax revolt in California in 1978, is a classic example of the initiative.

A *constitutional commission* is the third method of changing a state constitution. As the name implies, a commission is created to study the current constitution and to make recommendations for revision. "Members are usually appointed by the governor, legislative leaders, and the chief justice of the highest court in the state." Nine states had such commissions operating in the 1980s.

A *constitutional convention* is the final method of changing a constitution. "Delegates to most conventions are elected on a nonpartisan basis. . . . After action by the convention delegates, voters are asked to approve their proposals in a referendum." Five states convened conventions in the 1980s.

Theme C   State and Local Government Structures

Instructor References

Thad L. Beyle, ed., *State Government: CQ's Guide to Current Issues and Activities* 1990–1991. Washington, DC: Congressional Quarterly Press, 1990.

Virginia Gray, Herbert Jacob, and Robert B. Albritton, eds., *Politics in the American States,* 5th ed. Glenview IL: Scott, Foresman/Little, Brown, 1990.

Gerald L. Houseman, *State and Local Government: The New Battleground.* Englewood Cliffs, NJ: Prentice-Hall, 1986.

Alan Rosenthal, *Governors and Legislatures: Contending Powers.* Washington, DC: Congressional Quarterly Press, 1990.

Summary

The structures of state government correlate, if somewhat imperfectly, with the progressive and Jacksonian models (note that the tendency has been for state governments to move in the progressive direction).

State Governors

A natural division has been between the "strong" versus the "weak" chief executive. Urban, heavily populated states tend to have strong governors, whereas rural, southern states are likely to have weak executives. Typically, the nation's governors operate as follows:

1. They serve one or two four-year terms.

2. They run for office separately from the lieutenant governor, although the "team" concept is growing in popularity.

3. Unlike the U.S. president, they have a *line-item* veto (in forty-three states).

4. They have varying power to appoint officials.

5. They are, increasingly, new and energetic individuals.

6. Most of them belong to the Democratic party, due to traditional party allegiances and the off-year election process.

State Legislatures

The following represent key points about state legislatures:

1. A third of all state legislators are chosen from multimember districts, thus giving the dominant state party an advantage.

2. Traditionally, legislatures have been controlled by the Democrats, but more GOP governors are being elected.

3. The state of the national economy does influence the outcome of state legislative elections. Incumbent state legislators have impressive rates of reelection success, but turnover is still higher than in the federal Congress.

4. Reapportionment decisions in the 1960s eventually led to a more equitable division of representation between urban and rural political interests in state legislatures across the nation.

5. The salary and "professionalism" of state legislators varies. Thus, California pays legislators $37,000 a year; New Hampshire pays them only $100.

6. Party leaders in state legislatures usually exert a great deal of power, derived from their ability to select committee chairmen and the dispensing of political patronage. Also, urban, industrialized states tend to have more party-line votes than rural states.

State Courts

The key points regarding state courts are as follows:

1. There are two kinds of trial courts—minor or municipal courts and trial courts. At the top of the state judicial system is the state supreme court or its equivalent; this has the power to declare acts of state government unconstitutional.

2. There are *five* methods for picking state judges: partisan elections; nonpartisan elections; appointment by the governor; appointment by the state legislature; and the *Missouri Plan*, whereby the judge is initially appointed but then must be confirmed or rejected by the voters at the end of the first term. Regardless of the particular method of selection, it appears that the courtroom decisions of elected judges do not differ appreciably from those of appointed judges.

Local Government

Cities can be divided into *unreformed* (Jacksonian) and *reformed* (progressive) forms. The former type of city is characterized by partisan elections, a city council elected from districts, a weak civil service, and the concentration of executive power in the mayor's office. The latter type of city has nonpartisan elections, "at-large" city council elections, executive power concentrated in the hands of a city manager, and a strong civil service. A mixture of the two forms may produce the best system of city governance. Also, the racial connotations of at-large elections have led to rulings in the federal courts requiring district elections.

The *mayor-council* form of city government is the most common and is typical of either very small or very large cities. The *weak* and *strong mayor* systems relate to the degree of authority over the budget and the extent of administrative discretion allocated to the mayor.

In the *council-manager system* an elected city council appoints a city manager to supervise the city's administrative departments or agencies. Middle-size cities generally follow this system.

The *commission plan* has no single executive; each commissioner handles a department within the city's administrative infrastructure. A few large cities have this form of government.

Metropolitan governance is a complex and demanding process. *Annexation, consolidation* (the joining of city and county governments), and the creation of a *metropolitan government* (leaving a degree of autonomy to the local government) are three ways of managing metropolitan problems. Because all three methods have drawbacks, the most common structural remedy is the formation of *special districts* or authorities to handle specific services, such as water, sewage, transit, and so on. These special districts have efficient taxing and borrowing powers, but they can also be resistant to the public's will. Finally, COGs, or *councils of governments*, are another attempt to reduce conflicts and promote cooperation among local governments.

Discussion Questions

1. Which kind of governor—strong or weak—characterizes your home state?
2. What is the primary method of selecting state court judges in your home state?
3. What are some of the pros and cons of the Missouri Plan?
4. What appear to be some of the discrimination aspects of at-large elections?
5. Why does the Commission form of local government appear to be the least popular?

Data and Perspectives for Analysis

A. Methods of Judicial Selection

States utilize an array of methods to select judges. Each method accomplishes a different goal, including: preserving judicial independence, increasing accountability, and assuring professional standards. The goals, while laudable, are seldom achieved in practice since each method carries negative consequences. Replicate the table below and distribute it to your students.

Initial Judicial Selection in the States: Appellate and Major Trial Courts

Partisan Election	Appointment by Legislature	Gubernatorial Appointment	Nonpartisan Election	Merit Plan
Alabama	Connecticut	Delaware	Arizona	Alaska
Arkansas	Rhode Island	Hawaii	California	Arizona
Illinois	South Carolina	Maine	Florida	California
Indiana	Virginia	Massachusetts	Georgia	Colorado
Mississippi		New Hampshire	Idaho	Connecticut
Missouri		New Jersey	Kentucky	Florida
New Mexico		New York	Louisiana	Hawaii
New York		Rhode Island	Michigan	Indiana
North Carolina		Vermont	Minnesota	Iowa
Pennsylvania			Montana	Kansas
Tennessee			Nevada	Maryland
Texas			North Dakota	Missouri
West Virginia			Ohio	Nebraska
			Oklahoma	Oklahoma
			Oregon	South Dakota
			South Dakota	Tennessee
			Washington	Utah
			Wisconsin	Vermont
				Wyoming

Source: *The Book of the States 1990–91*, Lexington, KY: Council of State Governments, 1990, pp. 210–212.

Questions for Discussion

1. Do any regional patterns exist in the methods for selecting judges, such as among southern states or western states? If so, what accounts for the preference of a particular system on a regional basis?

2. What goals are being accomplished by each method of selection? What are the negative effects of each selection method?

3. If judges are so important, can your students name the members of the state's supreme court?

B. State Legislatures

College instructors of courses in American government frequently know much about the national government but not much about their own state government. To fill this gap, the following table is presented to assist in answering basic questions about any state government.

State	Official Name	Number and Terms				Standing Committees			Regular Sessions
		Senate		House					
		Number	Term	Number	Term	Senate	House	Joint	
Alabama	Legislature	35	4	105	4	22	23	—	Annual
Alaska	Legislature	20	4	40	2	9	9	2	Annual
Arizona	Legislature	30	2	60	2	11	16	1	Annual
Arkansas	General Assembly	35	4	100	2	10	10	4	Odd
California	Legislature	40	4	80	2	22	30	2	Odd/Even
Colorado	General Assembly	35	4	65	2	11	12	—	Annual
Connecticut	General Assembly	36	2	151	2	—	—	20	Annual
Delaware	General Assembly	21	4	41	2	18	14	2	Annual
Florida	Legislature	40	4	120	2	16	23	1	Annual
Georgia	General Assembly	56	2	180	2	24	28	—	Annual
Hawaii	Legislature	25	4	51	2	16	19	—	Annual
Idaho	Legislature	42	2	84	2	10	14	—	Annual
Illinois	General Assembly	59	4[a]	118	2	18	25	—	Annual
Indiana	General Assembly	50	4	100	2	18	25	—	Annual
Iowa	General Assembly	50	4	100	2	15	15	1	Annual
Kansas	Legislature	40	4	125	2	18	21	5	Annual
Kentucky	General Assembly	38	4	100	2	15	15	—	Even
Louisiana	Legislature	39	4	105	4	15	15	—	Annual
Maine	Legislature	35	2	151	2	—	—	19	Even/Odd
Maryland	General Assembly	47	4	141	4	6	7	8	Annual
Massachusetts	General Court	40	2	160	2	6	7	21	Annual
Michigan	Legislature	38	4	110	2	15	30	—	Annual
Minnesota	Legislature	67	4	134	2	16	18	—	Odd
Mississippi	Legislature	52	4	122	4	28	30	6	Annual
Missouri	General Assembly	34	4	163	2	22	54	5	Annual
Montana	Legislature	50	4[b]	100	2	17	14	—	Odd
Nebraska	Legislature	49	4	—	—	14	—	—	Annual
Nevada	Legislature	21	4	42	2	9	13	—	Odd
New Hampshire	General Court	24	2	400	2	17	23	4	Annual
New Jersey	Legislature	40	4[c]	80	2	14	19	3	Annual
New Mexico	Legislature	42	4	70	2	8	16	—	Annual
New York	Legislature	61	2	150	2	31	35	11	Annual
North Carolina	General Assembly	50	2	120	2	29	58	—	Odd
North Dakota	Legislature Assembly	53	4	106	2	20	19	1	Odd
Ohio	General Assembly	33	4	99	2	12	26	—	Annual
Oklahoma	Legislature	48	4	101	2	18	30	3	Annual
Oregon	Legislature Assembly	30	4	60	2	11	13	4	Odd
Pennsylvania	General Assembly	50	4	203	2	21	24	—	Annual

443

State	Official Name	Number and Terms				Standing Committees			Regular Sessions
		Senate		House					
		Number	Term	Number	Term	Senate	House	Joint	
Rhode Island	General Assembly	50	2	100	2	6	7	8	Annual
South Carolina	General Assembly	46	4	124	2	15	11	—	Annual
South Dakota	Legislature	35	2	70	2	11	11	2	Annual
Tennessee	General Assembly	33	4	99	2	12	12	1	Odd
Texas	Legislature	31	4	150	2	11	34	—	Odd
Utah	Legislature	29	4	75	2	10	10	10	Annual
Vermont	General Assembly	30	2	150	2	12	15	4	Odd
Virginia	General Assembly	40	4	100	2	11	20	—	Annual
Washington	Legislature	49	4	98	2	12	16	—	Annual
West Virginia	Legislature	34	4	100	2	15	13	2	Annual
Wisconsin	Legislature	33	4	99	2	11	26	7	Annual
Wyoming	Legislature	30	4	64	2	11	12	1	Annual

[a] All senators ran for election in 1972 and all will run every ten years thereafter. Senate districts are divided into thirds. One group elects senators for terms of four years, four years, and two years; the second group for terms of four years, two years, and four years; the third group for terms of two years, four years, and four years.

[b] After each decennial reapportionment, lots will be drawn for half the senators to serve an initial two-year term. Subsequent elections will be for four-year terms.

[c] Senate terms beginning in January of second year following the U.S. decennial census are for two years only.

Additional Lecture Topics

C-1. Governors and State Court Systems

Lois G. Forer, *Money and Justice: Who Owns the Courts?* New York: Norton, 1987.

Robert L. Morlan and David Martin, *Capitol, Courthouse, and City Hall.* 7th ed. New York: Longman, 1988.

Richard Neely, *Why Courts Don't Work.* New York: McGraw-Hill, 1983.

Coleman B. Ransone, *The American Governorship.* Boston: Greenwood Press, 1982.

Larry Sabato, *Goodbye to Good-Time Charlie: The American Governor Transformed.* 2nd ed. Washington, DC: Congressional Quarterly Press, 1983.

C-2. State Legislatures

Dennis Dersang and James Gosling, *Politics, Policy, and Management in the American States.* New York: Longman, 1989.

Marilyn Gitell, ed., *State Politics and the New Federalism.* New York: Longman, 1986.

William J. Keefe and Morris S. Ogul, *The American Legislative Process: Congress and the States.* Englewood Cliffs, NJ: Prentice-Hall, 1985.

David B. Magelby, *Direct Legislation: Voting on Ballot Propositions in the United States.* Washington, DC: Johns Hopkins University Press, 1987.

C-3. Governing Communities

J. Richard Aronson and John L. Hilley, *Financing State and Local Governments.* 4th ed. Washington, DC: Brookings Institution, 1986.

Richard Bingham et al., *Managing Local Government: Public Administration in Practice.* Newbury Park, CA: Sage Publications, 1991.

Howard P. Chudacoff and Judith Smith, *The Evolution of American Urban Society.* Englewood Cliffs, NJ: Prentice-Hall, 1988.

Virginia Gray and Peter Eisinger, *American States and Cities*. New York: HarperCollins, 1991.

John J. Harrington, *Politics and Policy in States and Communities*. 4th ed. New York: HarperCollins, 1991.

Denis R. Judd, *The Politics of American Cities: Private Power and Public Policy*. 2nd ed. Boston: Little, Brown, 1984.

David C. Nice, *Federalism: The Politics of Intergovernmental Relations*. New York: St. Martin's Press, 1987.

Bernard H. Ross, Myron A. Levine, and Murray S. Stedman, *Urban Politics: Power in Metropolitan America*. 4th ed. Itaska, IL: F. E. Peacock, 1991.

David C. Saffell, *State and Local Government: Politics and Public Policies*. 5th ed. New York: McGraw-Hill, 1993.

Abstract for Theme C

Recent Political Relations Between Legislatures and Governors

Lucinda S. Simon writes about the increasing conflicts between governors and state legislatures in an article entitled "Legislatures and Governors: The Wrestling Match" (*Journal of State Government*, Spring 1986, pp. 1–6). Simon, a state legislative consultant, notes that "conflict is the chief manifestation of a new calculus of political and institutional power in state government today." Increasingly, "the conflicts are intense, acrimonious, and, at times, fought along the constitutional boundaries of our tripartite system of government" (p. 106). What has increased these tensions? Simon points to the role of very difficult policy choices, the confusion of traditional party lines and loyalties, and cross-party coalitions in state legislatures.

However, Simon argues that the most important cause of the legislative-executive wars has been

> the developing institutional strength and assertiveness on the part of the legislature. Legislatures have been transformed, first by reapportionment, then by an era of capacity building, and finally by the consequent belief that they are truly the co-equal first branch of government.
>
> Dating from *Baker v. Carr* . . . the one-person, one-vote edicts brought a legislative membership and a public constituency eager to create a modern legislative branch.
>
> . . . the fact remains that legislatures are meeting longer, spending more time reviewing the day-to-day operations of the executive branch, and asserting their prerogatives over policy—all to the frustration of many governors who yearn for a return to the part-time legislature.
>
> Legislatures also have equipped themselves with resources to put them on an equal footing with the executive branch and to break the dependence on external information sources. Full-time professional staffs have developed and are providing legislators, legislative committees, and party caucuses with information, expertise, and ideas. (p. 107)

Simon also shows how legislative staffs and sophisticated computer capabilities have given legislators greater independence in the area of the state budget. State legislatures now have the authority to control the appropriation of federal funds and to administer federal block grants. Also, legislative budget staffs spend more time overseeing state agency spending. Simon notes that a number of additional "strong legislative controls over the state budget" exist today:

> Eight states require the governor to get legislative sign-off before cutting budgets to deal with a revenue shortfall. Most often, the requirement necessitates a special session or close consultation with legislative leaders and committees.
>
> Eighteen states limit the amounts by which the executive branch can, without consulting the legislature, reduce agency budgets in response to a revenue shortfall. Ten states allow across-the-board reductions, while nine place ceilings on executive branch cutbacks.
>
> Nineteen states have "rainy day" funds, setting aside funds to be spent in the event of an unanticipated revenue shortfall. . . .

> Forty states limit the executive's authority to transfer funds between programs within a department and almost all states require legislature approval of transfers between departments.
>
> Twenty-five states require the executive branch to seek the legislature's advice or approval before spending interim federal receipts. . . .
>
> In at least ten states, emergency funds may only be spent where such an expenditure is approved by the legislature. (p. 108)

The aforementioned legislative oversight function has also been expanded; many states have program evaluation and performance audit staffs checking on the operation and fiscal integrity of state agencies. A new wrinkle is the imposition of legislative mandates upon administrative actions for specific projects (the plans for a new prison must be submitted to the legislature by the executive branch before construction begins, for example).

Simon cautions that legislatures should not be considered the dominant actors in the states, since governors can use the veto and the media to balance the power equation. Governors personify a singularity of purpose and leadership that cannot be matched by the inherently diffuse nature of a state legislature. Yet tensions between the executive and legislative branches will continue, and political conflicts will have to be mediated in a positive fashion through mutual respect, trust, and flexibility.

Research Assignment

Discuss in class the nature of executive-legislative relationships in your particular state. Ask students to evaluate, after proper research, whether the state's politics represent generally mutual accommodation or frequent, severe conflicts between the state legislature and governor. Students should try to develop explanations for the states' current particular type of political system. Finally, do some of the budget controls itemized in the Simon abstract exist in your state? If so, which ones?

Theme D Politics and Policies

Government style, whether Jacksonian or progressive, unreformed or reformed, apparently impacts upon policy attitudes, formulation, and implementation. Progressive, reformed states and cities usually employ "experts" who are sensitive to national opinion. These states and cities may well develop reputations as "trendsetters." Conversely, Jacksonian, or unreformed, states and cities magnify the political power of elected officials, who in turn are more aware of local opinion pressures. However, exceptions abound, indicating that citizens' desires and willingness to pay for reforms (depending on their income) are also important variables in the shaping of policies.

Paying for policies requires city and state governments to consider taxation and/or public borrowing, fiscal methods that both contain potential political and economic liabilities. State and local governments find it more difficult than the federal government to raise money for three reasons: (a) psychologically, property and sales taxes are more salient than the "painless" federal income tax; (b) property tax increases are unlikely to be uniform; and (c) city and state taxes are feared to discourage outside business investment. In short, tax policy is the single most important issue, especially when one notes past citizen tax revolts (Proposition 13). Consequently, the response of state and local governments to tax revolts (and to declining federal aid) has included administrative "belt-tightening," reduction of services, "privatization" of some public services, and state-run lotteries. (In 1985, lottery sales exceeded $10 billion and the states retained about 40 percent of all proceeds.)

Discussion Questions

1. What "fiscal dilemmas" have been experienced by state and local governments in your home state? Have there been any "tax revolts"?

2. Are state lotteries a good fund-raising idea? Why or why not?

Data and Perspectives for Analysis

Role-Playing to Solve a Problem in City Government

Some headlines from the River City *Riparian*:

CITY TO BUILD NEW TENNIS CENTER—SITE NOT ANNOUNCED

CONSULTANT: TENNIS CENTER SHOULD GO WHERE THE PLAYERS ARE

WE NEED THAT REC COMPLEX: B.A.D.D.

GOOD GOVERNMENT LEAGUE: "DO WHAT'S RIGHT FOR ALL OF THE CITY"

"WHY NOT A GOLF COURSE ALSO?" ASKS W.I.M.P.

The River City Recreation Department has been given the approval to build a new tennis center, a state-of-the-art complex which will be the best in the state. It will not only be used for local recreation but will also make the city a candidate for international tennis tournaments. Two alternative sites are under consideration: one adjacent to an affluent housing area on the western outskirts of (but still within) the city, the other in a downtown redevelopment area of cleared slum land (adjacent to an existing slum).

The city council has called a public hearing to air views on the alternatives. Representatives of various groups will testify. Assign students to play the representatives and to prepare a short (one- or two-minute) synopsis of their role's position. Each student playing the simulation should think about the following: What would our basic position be? Why? What would we have to gain or lose by either location? What is our general attitude and orientation toward the council and the hearing: Is the decision going to be made here tonight? Will they listen to me? Can I influence the decision in some other way?

The Roles to Be Played

The mayor: A Democrat with strong ties to the business community
Councilperson Lee Snopes: Representing a black district (and the slum site)
Councilperson Chris Northington: Representing the affluent north and west sides
Councilperson Bob DuPress: Representing the blue-collar east and southside
Buffy and Skip Lacoste: Co-presidents of the tennis club
Josephine McEnroe: Consultant, Athletic Site and Situational Analysts, hired by tennis club
Hilda Kallikak: Head of the recreation department for the past fifteen years
Justus Johnson: Head of the Black Alliance for Downtown Development (B.A.D.D.)
George Quiche: Head of the Westside Improvement Metropolitan Partnership (W.I.M.P.)
H. Chadwick Peabody: Head of the River City Good Government League
Ernestine Profitt: Governmental affairs director of the River City Chamber of Commerce
Scoop Thurston: City editor of the River City Riparian (who will summarize the events in a closing news story)

Instructor: This role-playing scenario will probably take at least two class periods to complete. You may wish to assign to nonplaying students the task of recording the interactions among the players, so that the class can review the outcome at a later time.

Abstract for Theme D

The Ultimate Impact of Proposition 13 on California

Proposition 13 symbolized the beginning of taxpayer revolts across the nation. However, in the state of California, the long-term impact of Proposition 13 has been serious. In "California Screamin'" (*New Republic*, June 23, 1986, pp. 14–16), Peter Schrag, associate editor of the *Sacramento Bee*, makes the following points:

1. The cutting of taxes, the caps placed on public spending, and the aborting of key public services have turned California from a progressive leader among the states into a merely average performer in terms of public education and social service systems. In 1986 California stood only twenty-sixth in the nation in educational spending per enrolled child. In addition, it ranked eighteenth in per-capita spending on health and hospitals and was nearly last in amounts allocated for highway construction and repair. Finally, despite an increase of 20 percent in the state's population, the state budget was equivalent, in constant dollars, to the 1980–1981 budget.

2. California's once wonderful education system has crumbled, the norm today being an inferior junior college conglomerate, high dropout rates (they climbed dramatically once Proposition 13's passage forced the elimination of summer school course offerings), and overcrowding.

3. The reason behind the education decline is California's demographic shift to an older population of retirees and aging taxpayers unable to pay their exorbitant tax bills. Proposition 13 built upon this shift and simultaneously weakened the position of young voters with children who had educational needs. The stigma attached to tax increases has kept its hold on California governors and state legislatures alike, while new legal ceilings on expenditures further reinforce the Proposition 13 mentality.

4. California citizens are unlikely to become concerned once again with the need for community service and an improved educational system. Schrag concludes with the following remarks:

> But something important is nonetheless being lost, and that loss is deeply regrettable, not only for California but for the country whose future California once was. . . . It has all become less crazy, maybe even more mature. But in settling for average or just better than average, the state denies both itself and the country the sense of greater possibilities it so long represented.

Class Activity

Have students research additional articles on the effects of Proposition 13 on California's economic and social life. Do these articles confirm the thesis of deterioration that Schrag emphasizes in his analysis? Discuss the research findings in class.